Martin Manley's

BASKETBALL HEAVEN

1988-89

FACTS Publishing Company

Topeka, Kansas

Copyright August, 1988 by FACTS Publishing Co.

All rights reserved. No part of this book may be reproduced or transmitted in any form or by any means, electronic or mechanical, including photocopying, recording or by any information storage and retrieval system, without permission in writing from the publisher.

FACTS Publishing Company
P.O. Box 47025
1324 S. Kansas
Topeka, KS 66647

Manufactured in the United States of America

ISBN: 0-944877-01-X

Second Edition: October 1988

10 9 8 7 6 5 4 3 2 1

Martin Manley's Basketball Heaven is published annually by FACTS Publishing Company. The first edition was printed in October 1987 and may be purchased by sending $11.95 to the above address or by calling 1-913-233-2287 (Mastercard or Visa). Ask for the 1987-88 edition.

Among the thousands of items in last season's book are statistical breakdowns on years 1950-1980, 14 pages of trivia, 10 pages of late-game statistical strategies, analysis of all-time top rookies, top teams by unusual categories, Bird vs Johnson and many more.

ACKNOWLEDGEMENTS

I'm glad to have the opportunity to offer my appreciation to a number of individuals who made this book possible.

First and foremost is the NBA office which helped me with both support and information. Alex Sachare and others were instrumental in providing me with encouragement. Additionally, David Stern's leadership has created the utlimate sport - without which I would have nothing to write about.

Also high on my list are Wayne Patterson (Basketball Hall of Fame), David DuPree (USA Today), Frank Layden (Utah Jazz), Marc Hoffman (Inside Sports), Bill James (Baseball Abstract) and Pat Lafferty (Portland Trail Blazers). Each of these people provided me with some unique form of assistance.

Once again, I am indebted to my publisher who labored page by page over my additions and subtractions, all the while trying to meet dozens of requirements. Finally, thanks to Virginia Pruitt who read and edited each and every page. I am proud to author this book.

- "Hold it! Stop the game! Do you realize if we go into overtime it will tie the team O.T. record for odd numbered years?" -

INTRODUCTION

BASKETBALL:

After I wrote last year's book, I received many opportunities to talk on sports shows throughout the country. I was amazed how often I was asked something to the effect of "How does a person growing up in Kansas become so addicted to basketball?" Although some native Kansans might be offended by this query, I think it's a fair question since, admittedly, Kansas in the 1980's is not North Carolina, Indiana, Brooklyn, or Boston.

However, I grew up in the 1950's & 60's as a KU Jayhawk fan. I used to drag around a transistor radio with me whenever they played. I kept the team's stats; yelled when they won & cried when they lost. In those days, KU still had won more college games than Kentucky or, for that matter, anyone else. KU had a history of great players including Bill Bridges, Clyde Lovelette, and, of course, Wilt Chamberlain. Even at that time, with JoJo White & Dave Robisch, KU insured that basketball would remain big in Kansas - college basketball that is.

Of course, it's also true that Kansas State had some great teams in those days. In fact, the rivalry substantially heightened everyone's interest in the sport. But it wasn't just basketball, it was sports in general that Kansans loved. Kansas had a long history of great track athletes including Billy Mills, Glenn Cunningham & Jim Ryan - legends all of them. The state also had some of the best football players ever. Among them were John Hadl, Gayle Sayers, and John Riggins. Boy, have times changed on the gridiron.

Kansas produced some great basketball coaches too. How about Adolph Rupp, Dean Smith, Ralph Miller, Gene Keady, and Eddie Sutton. All went on to coach great teams. Kansas & Kansas State have had their share of famous coaches as well, including the immortal Phog Allen and the recently retired Jack Hartman. Oh, and don't forget KU's first coach, the inventor of the game - Dr. James Naismith.

That's the atmosphere I and my friends grew up in. At the time, Kansas was inferior to no other state or area in sports and certainly not in basketball. Times have changed, not withstanding last year's miracle NCAA Championship. We may not belong on a pedestal, but we do still have our share of glory. Here in Topeka, Washburn University won the men's NAIA National Basketball Championship a couple of years ago; we have a local CBA team; and we host the National AAU Tournament. Topeka sits right between KU and K-State - the proud alumnus of Danny Manning and Mitch Richmond - a couple of lottery picks in this year's NBA draft. So basketball is still king.

A valid question might be "How then did I develop such an interest in the NBA?" That question is harder to answer. It wasn't as though I lived in Kansas City and watched the Kings regularly. Even if I did, the Kings didn't arrive until 1972 and besides, they weren't exactly world beaters. My interest in the NBA developed from watching my college heroes get older and wanting to continue to see them. It developed because of CBS and WTBS and increased network coverage. It developed because the NBA game is, as I argue, the ultimate entertainment for the sports fan in our time and will only become more so in the years ahead. But most of all, it developed a few years ago when I bought a satellite dish. The rules are changing in sportsviewing. Now anyone, anywhere in the country can watch, as I do, up to 3 or 4 games a day and parts of many others. Since Bird/Johnson, the popularity of the NBA has grown and continues to grow at incredible rates. I happen to be one of those who fell in love with it along the way.

STATISTICS:

As I said earlier, I regularly kept the stats at sporting events or when I watched games on television, although at the time such record-keeping was unusual. The trick, I discovered, was to figure out how to convert what I call "raw" stats into the more entertaining and enlightening "creative" stats.

I have felt for a long time that raw statistics are becoming less and less meaningful as a way of understanding the intricacies of the game. Because of this conviction, I have tried to develop a whole series of creative statistics which I hope will disclose the many nuances implicit in the maze of numbers. I hope I can show where a player or team's strengths are in unusual ways. I don't want to be thought of as just a number *cruncher*, but rather a number *creator* - that is, one who creates a measurement or rating which otherwise would not have existed, one who discovers an important, previously concealed, bit of information that otherwise could not have been appreciated.

In baseball, raw stats are much more widely accepted. It is all more impressive the work of Bill James and others, that statistical measurement systems could have been developed in such a raw statistical sport. Baseball has such a long pre-computer history that its tradition of raw stats as the norm has become firmly rooted. That is why it is common for a baseball player to be judged by how many accumulated credits he racked up - # of homers, # of RBI's, # of runs, etc.

Basketball is different, at least in part, because it is a more recent sport. Whereas baseball is over a hundred years old, basketball's development professionally never really occurred until after World War II. When the standards and traditions were being developed for basketball, it was just natural that the statistical measurements be more contemporary. Consequently, although almost no one can tell you off the top of his or her head how many points Wilt Chamberlain scored in 1962, most serious fans know his scoring average was 50 ppg. The opposite is true in baseball. Everyone knows Roger Maris hit 61 home runs in 1961 - but quick, tell me how many homers per-game he hit. Home runs is a "raw" statistic. Points-per-game is technically a creative statistic. The definition of a "creative" statistic is that it is the product of more than one raw statistic. Points *and* games are raw, but points-*per*-game is creative.

A simple illustration of how inadequate a raw basketball statistic is, is Kareem Abdul-Jabbar's register. His raw numbers tell us that he had 1383 rebounds and 338 blocks in 1976. Does that mean anything to anyone? Oh sure, we know that 1000+ rebounds is excellent, but it used to be commonplace. 338 blocks tells us even less. On the other hand, if you look at his register in this book (page 307), you will see that 1976 was the only year that he ranked first in rebounding (48 minute basis) or first in blocked shots (also 48 minute basis). Suddenly, we know his inside play in 1976 was very special - not only with respect to the league, but with respect to his other years. How could we have determined that from 1383 & 338?

Every segment of society continues to mature statistically. Baseball originally had hits and at-bats. These are two raw stats. When combined by taking the player's hits and dividing it by his at-bats, one obtains the player's batting average. This is a creative statistic. However, the process is so common and basic that even a player's batting average is virtually a raw statistic in that part of the definition for a creative statistic is that it offers something new, unique, enlightening, or mysterious. Batting average fails to meet this criterion.

Therefore, baseball has developed a need to accomodate the inquiring mind of the fan who wants more detail, more situation, or more exposure in a stat. Game winning RBI, inherited runners, slugging pct, and others have begun to supercede the traditional runs, hits, and errors. As society becomes more and more "statistically educated", the movement in this direction will only intensify. In fact, we no longer accept standard forms of measurement. 9.2 in the hundred yard dash is now 9.97 in the 100 meters. 94 degrees temperature is now a 103.5 heat index. Our mortgages are no longer at 6%, but rather 8.85% APR, etc. etc.

Basketball is no exception. I've tried my best to help the process. The most important is the development of Production Rating which covers all facets of the game, but MVP rating, Position Dominance, and many others will shed light on unique angles the raw stats miss.

My most memorable example of how I feel compelled to take raw events or numbers and convert them to something of interest or irony happened in the fall of 1987. The event was a hole in one. "OK, that's neat", you're saying. "Now get on with the book." First, indulge me. If you understand the mental processes that took over when I hit it, you will understand me and perhaps understand the nature of creative statistics, or at least the warped minds of us who attempt to uncover them.

Although, I worked out a number system far beyond what I will go into, the facts are that the numbers 13, 1, 13 were significant. It was the 13th day of the month that I hit a hole in 1 on hole #13. My initials, MAM, are the 13th, 1st, and 13th letters in the alphabet. Since the distance of the shot was 127 yards, I looked up page 127 in last year's book which I had just finished and saw much to my amazement that the 13th best-ever rated jersey number was worn by the #1 statistical player ever (Chamberlain). His jersey number? 13, of course (look it up). Believe me, it goes on. I came up with coincidences about harmonic convergence, the 10 year anniversary of Elvis' death, my own birthday, the cart #, the club I used, the ball, the time of day, etc. It's all quite fascinating to me and could warrant several pages of discussion, but on the chance that you're all not like me, I won't proceed. Suffice it to say that this is an example of my mind at work. Still, when I reread my research, I am left with the thought that it had to happen. You know, destiny. Oh well, enough of that.

SUGGESTIONS:

The NBA offices have done an absolutely magnificent job in recent years, however, I would like them to consider keeping a few more obscure stats. These are numbers that would become very meaningful and commonplace. The first could be called a game-winning basket. A couple NBA teams keep a stat similar to this, but I would like to see it kept by the league. It could be defined as a player who makes a basket in the last 60 seconds of a game to give his team the lead for good. Of course, the sister stat could be called game-winning free throw.

Speaking of free throws, I would like to see separate stats kept for free throw % inside 1 or 2 minutes to play with the score at +/- 3 points. I think this would tell us who performs in the clutch and who chokes.

Another statistic which is kept by Harvey Pollack - the famous stat man for the 76ers - is one which I would love to see for all teams. It is called plus/minus and, in effect, takes all the points a team scores when a player is in the game and subtracts the points the team's opponents score. Since no two players play exactly the same minutes at the same time, this statistic should show in very precise terms how valuable any particular player is.

Finally, for the sake of accuracy, I would like to see four miscellaneous stats changed. First, I believe a steal should be awarded to a player who draws an offensive foul since a change in possession takes place. Secondly, no FGA should be charged to a player on a desperation shot either at the end of a quarter or as the shot clock runs down. If he makes a bizarre shot, so be it. It could be considered a free attempt - the same as when a player is fouled in the act of shooting. If it goes in, he is charged with a FGA. If it misses, however, he is not. The third miscellaneous stat I would like to see changed would be to award an assist on a play where one would have been awarded had the shooter hit his shot instead of being fouled. Though the trend of (assists < rebounds) is coming closer to (assists = rebounds), I think this is a fair way to help it happen. And it is something that I feel should happen. As it is, the power game benefits too much statistically. The last stat that should be changed is field goal percentage. At present, the NBA does not have a separate award for the 2-point FG% king. They do for the 3-pt% leader and the combined 2-pt% and 3-pt% leader, but not for 2-pt% only. I think they should dump the combined version and have only a 3-pt% leader, 2-pt% leader, and FT% leader. When you think about it, a 6 foot turnaround is not much more different from a free throw than it is from a 3 pointer.

Statistics and basketball have always been my most enjoyable past times. One without the other is OK, or perhaps even more than OK, but put them together and... well, for me anyway, it's a marriage made in heaven. Enjoy the book.

CONTENTS

INTRODUCTION		v
CONTENTS		viii
A MIRACLE SEASON		x

CHAPTER 1   **Points vs Production**   1

    Production Rating..3
    Top Playoff Performances 6
    MVP = PD + WR...6
    Defining Greatness...8
    6 Year MVP Rating 10
    10 Year MVP Rating...11
    6 Year Position Dominance 12
    10 Year Position Dominance 13

CHAPTER 2   **Fancy Formulas**   15

    "Perfect Production Rating" 16
    Defining Possession 18
    Fishing Buddies 21
    Predictive Formulas..23
    Shooting Formulas 28
    Shooting Efficiency 32

CHAPTER 3   **Team by Team Analysis**   37

    Introduction 38
    Atlanta Hawks..40
    Boston Celtics...48
    Charlotte Hornets 56
    Chicago Bulls 58
    Cleveland Cavaliers 66
    Dallas Mavericks 74
    Denver Nuggets 82
    Detroit Pistons..90
    Golden State Warriors 98
    Houston Rockets 106
    Indiana Pacers..114
    Los Angeles Clippers 122
    Los Angeles Lakers 130
    Miami Heat...138
    Milwaukee Bucks 140
    New Jersey Nets 148
    New York Knicks..156
    Philadelphia 76ers...164
    Phoenix Suns..172
    Portland Trail Blazers.......................................180
    Sacramento Kings 188
    San Antonio Spurs..196
    Seattle Supersonics 204
    Utah Jazz...212
    Washington Bullets...220

CONTENTS

CHAPTER 4	**Players' Positions**	**229**
	Position Averages 230	
	Position Value 232	
	Comparisons 233	
	Centers 235	
	Power Frowards 236	
	Small Forwards 237	
	Off Guards 238	
	Point Guards 239	
	6th Men 240	
	Rookies 241	
CHAPTER 5	**Discussion and Debate**	**243**
	Opinions 244	
	Salaries 245	
	Home Court Advantage 246	
	Schedule 249	
	Luck 250	
	3-pointers 252	
	Parity 253	
	One Dimensional Players 255	
CHAPTER 6	**The Trends**	**259**
	Offensive Trends 260	
	Miscellaneous Trends 262	
	Position Leaders 264	
	Category Leaders 266	
	Miscellaneous Leaders 268	
CHAPTER 7	**Seasonal Summaries**	**271**
	Introduction 272	
	1988 274	
	1987 277	
	1986 280	
	1985 283	
	1984 286	
	1983 289	
	1982 292	
	1981 295	
	1980 298	
CHAPTER 8	**Career Capsules**	**303**
	Introduction 304	
	Present Players 307	
	Former Players 322	

KU CHAMPIONSHIP RUN

At one point during the 1987-88 campaign, the Kansas Jayhawks were 12-8 and struggling. The preseason #1 team in the country was 1-4 in the Big 8 and had experienced a decade's worth of bad luck.

Before the season began, one of the top front line recruits, Joe Young, became a PROP-48 victim. Next, it was part-time starting forward as a freshman, Keith Harris, who spent his entire sophomore season in Larry Brown's doghouse and played sparingly. Then starting center Marvin Branch fell victim to academic woes and missed the rest of the year. Next, starting forward Archie Marshall suffered a career ending injury. Later on, part-time starting point guard Otis Livingston and back-up center Mike Massucci were kicked off the team and quit respectively because of personal problems.

Despite these incredible setbacks, and the lesser late-season injuries to starters Kevin Pritchard and Chris Piper, as well as the constant distracting rumors about Larry Brown leaving, the team began to turn it around. Ironically, the change became visible when KU lost to Kansas State at Allen Field House in Lawrence. The loss broke KU's 55 game home-court winning streak which was the NCAA's longest at the time.

If ever there would have been a reason to give up, that would have been the time. The Jayhawks had just lost 3 consecutive games in which they held double-digit second half leads. But the doomsayers apparently forgot the one constant - Danny Manning.

Manning, a senior, had vowed to show the world that he could be a leader as well as a great player; that he could perform in the big games; that he could take charge down the stretch. When Marshall was injured, Danny committed the rest of the season to his teammate and friend. The wins started coming in. The Hawks won 9 of their next 12 games to squeak into the NCAA Tournament. The 3 late season losses were to Kansas State, Duke, and Oklahoma.

When the pairings were announced, Larry Brown had been hoping for a Friday first round game instead of Thursday. The reason was because Pritchard was hurt and he wanted him to get one more day of rest. He got it. When KU saw where they were going to play games 1 and 2, they had to be happy with that too. Of all the 16 sub-regional locations, they managed to get into the one closest to home - Lincoln, Nebraska - on a court they played on every year.

After they upset 18th ranked Xavier in the first round, the Jayhawks luck continued. The next opponent was to be the #3 seeded N.C. State Wolfpack - who would have had incentive to beat Kansas. (Not only had KU stolen Danny Manning from underneath Valvano's nose, but KU had defeated N.C. State the last 3 years.) As fortune would have it however, the Hawks never had to face them as N.C. State was upset. As a result, KU played a Murray State team who had spent themselves on their emotional upset. KU won.

At the regional, KU's first opponent was to be the #2 seeded Pittsburgh Panthers of the powerful Big East. However, a funny thing happened along the way. They were upset too, by Vanderbilt. Consequently, KU got to play another team who had spent themselves on their emotional upset. Once again, KU won.

The next game was certain to be the Jayhawks last. They were to play the #1 seeded Purdue Boilermakers for a birth in the Final Four. Surprise, surprise, Purdue lost as well. More importantly, they lost to Kansas State. Now KU had incentive to knock off the higher seeded Wildcats and to revenge one of those 3 late season losses. Kansas State had spent themselves on their emotional upset of Purdue and KU won.

Remarkably, Kansas was in the Final Four. Even more fortunate was the fact that it was the 50th anniversary of the Final Four and the NCAA takes up residence in Kansas City. Since KU plays several games each year in Kemper Arena, just 30 miles from Lawrence, it's like a home away from home.

Their semifinal opponent was to be the #1 team in the country, Temple (as in 32-1 Temple). But, ...you guessed it, Temple was upset by a familiar foe to KU - Duke. Once again the Hawks had incentive to knock off the heavily favored Blue Devils - not only because KU had lost to Duke in the Final Four two years earlier, but because Duke was one of those 3 teams who had beaten KU in the last half of the season. Duke apparently spent themselves on their emotional upset of Temple. KU won.

Going into the championship game, Kansas was, presumably, to play the odds on favorite to win it all- Arizona. The Wildcats had already won 35 games - more than any other team, but they lost the semifinal game to KU's Big 8 rival, Oklahoma.

The Big 8 had not had a team in the championship game in 30 years. Now they had two. The Jayhawks entered the title match as huge 8 point underdogs. The odds against winning were going at 4-1. KU had already lost twice to Oklahoma last year, both times by 8 points. But, Oklahoma was the 3rd team to have beaten KU in the late season, and the club had already revenged Kansas State & Duke. Only Oklahoma was left. The Jayhawks had their final incentive. The 35-3 Sooners had spent themselves on their big win vs. Arizona...

The game was a masterpiece - 50-50 at halftime - an NCAA record for points in a half. As the clock wound down, Danny Manning had his greatest opportunity to shake the "disappears in late game situations" label. He proceeded to hit 4 straight free throws in the last 14 seconds to give KU an insurmountable 4 point lead. Symbolically, as Oklahoma's final shot careemed off the glass, it was Danny Manning who captured it. It was his 18th rebound - a career high. His 31 points and 5 steals were merely the exclamation point to his being voted the tournament MVP.

Never before had a team with 11 losses won the championship; never before had one player so carried a team so far against so much. For a team to have had the worst luck in the world for the first half of the season, they amazingly had the best luck in the world during the tournament. But as Manning so profoundly put it after the nets were cut, "What's luck? I think luck is when preparation meets opportunity." Manning's last words to the press after the game were "People said that we couldn't do it, that we were finished. but we're the national champions, we're number 1. What do you think of us now?"

Pete Maravich of the New Orleans Jazz
- Averaged 44.2 ppg during his career at LSU
- Basketball Hall of Fame -

CHAPTER 1

POINTS VS PRODUCTION

PETE MARAVICH

Every once in awhile a story comes along that is stranger than fiction. This is one such story.

Pistol Pete Maravich was born in the summer of 1947 (June 22 to be exact). It should have been a sign to the world of the life he was destined to lead. Maravich was born in a little town in Pennsylvania. Just across the state, exactly 2 months earlier (April 22), the Philadelphia Warriors won the very first NBA championship. The star for Philly was a player named Joe Fulks. Fulks was the overwhelming scoring leader that year in the league. Exactly 30 years later, Maravich would win the NBA's same honor - also by a wide margin.

The summer of his 40th birthday, Maravich was inducted into the Hall of Fame. Enshrined the same day was Rick Barry. Eight months later, to the day (Jan. 5, 1988) - Maravich died. Coincidentally, Barry was in Atlanta to do WTBS' NBA game-of-the-week. Atlanta was the team that had drafted Maravich and was Pete's team for his first four years in the league.

After he died, Maravich was honored at the NBA's All-Star Game (Feb. 7, 1988). As a symbolic gesture, another former Louisiana collegiate star, Karl Malone, wore Pete's #7. It was Malone's first All-Star appearance. Both he and Maravich were All-Stars with the Jazz. As Utah's only representative in the game, Malone proudly added another chapter to the lucky number. He scored 22 points (team high) and grabbed 10 rebounds (game high). It was 18 years before to the day that Pistol Pete scored the most points ever by a division 1 player vs a division 1 school (Feb 7, 1970 - 69 points).

Back in 1974, during his 4th year in the NBA, Maravich had been quoted as saying "I don't want to play ten years in the NBA and die of a heart attack at age 40." Ironically, and tragically, that is exactly what he did. His final words came only seconds before his death. "I'm really feeling good!", he said. Then he turned and walked out of the lives and into the memories of a generation of basketball fans. Goodbye Pete. We'll all miss you.

POINTS VS PRODUCTION

The basketball fan has always been somewhat enamored with points. After all, points are the ultimate measurement. The more a team gets - the more likely it is to win. If a team gets outrebounded, out hustled, shoots a worse FG%, etc., but outscores its opponents - then it played the ultimate game. They won. Still, it seems somewhat incomplete, to put it mildly, for a team or player's totals to show only a tally of points. I for one want to know more - much more. How many assists or steals did he get? How many FGA's did he take? How many times did he go to the line?

The obvious result of this curiosity is the box score. The potential problem with the "box score" and the reason I did not use it as the name of my book (I considered many options before I wrote Basketball Heaven 87/88) was because most statistics are, by nature, dry. The box score is the ultimate representation of a dry statistic because it contains only *raw* numbers as opposed to *creative* numbers. What happens most often is that a casual sports fan, anyway, will glance at the box score primarily interested in points. In some cases, perhaps, he or she may not even be aware of what is good or bad about many of the other stats. It has become my ultimate goal to have included in box scores (to the right of points) a player's Production Rating (PR) for the game.

I first introduced Production Rating last year. Although there are various other composite formulas, I firmly believe PR is superior. In last year's book I evaluated Production Rating in great detail vs. Schick, Tendex, and Efficiency according to 3 criteria - aesthetics, accuracy, and simplicity. Production Rating proved better in 8 of the 9 categories with a tie in the other one.

Before I go on, I should say that no statistical ranking can measure a clutch player's abilities in the closing seconds of a game. Nor can it measure a player's abilities to psych up his teammates or psych out his opponents. It can't measure flash, charisma, or intensity, ingredients which all go into the process of winning. Still, those categories which are statistically measurable constitute at least 90% of winning and losing.

Production Rating is very simple and very meaningful. It is a composite statistic which incorporates various positive and negative values a player accumulates during a game. Interestingly, it follows very closely the parameters of scoring. 30+ per game is *super* star, while 25-30 is *all* star. 20-25 is *very* good, while 15-20 is *kinda* good. 10-15 is a *role* player, while below 10 is a *bench* player.

The problem with points as the primary indicator of value is, of course, because it is an oversimplified measurement. For example, who is better, Dale Ellis (25.8 ppg) or Magic Johnson (19.6 ppg)? We all know the answer to that question. Ellis is, obviously, good, but he's no Magic. Therefore, if Seattle were to play Los Angeles, it would be inadequate to look at Ellis scoring 26 points while Magic scored 20 and make any determination about who had the better game. In fact, in this fictional, but average battle, Magic had 7 more assists, 2 more rebounds, 1 more steal, and 3 less missed FG's. That changes the immediate impression given by the box score. A quick glance doesn't do justice to the difference in quality of play between the participants. Without going into the specifics of Ellis vs Johnson, the reality is that, on an average, Magic Johnson would have scored 20 points, yet accomplished a Production Rating of 28. Dale Ellis would have scored 26 points, but managed a Production Rating of *only* 21.

The advantage of Production Rating is that it condenses the good and bad into one statistic. That's a great advantage when glancing at an otherwise dull box score. The fact that it also manages to fit nicely into our preconceived ideas of what is star (28) vs good (21) is just that much better. I will explain momentarily what Production Rating is all about, but first take a look at the players whose scoring least approximates their total Production Rating on a game by game basis.

GROUP A - Production Minus Points						GROUP B - Points Minus Production				
Player	**Team**	**PR**	**PPG**	**Margin**		**Player**	**Team**	**PPG**	**PR**	**Margin**
Stockton	Utah	26.54	14.68	**11.86**		D. Wilkins	Atla	30.73	24.27	**6.46**
McMillan	Seat	16.71	7.61	**9.10**		J. Malone	Wash	20.51	15.24	**5.27**
Oakley	Chic	20.54	12.37	**8.17**		Ellis	Seat	25.84	20.55	**5.29**
Johnson	LALa	27.71	19.56	**8.15**		Teagle	GoSt	12.64	7.87	**4.77**
Porter	Port	22.87	14.90	**7.97**		Dailey	LACl	13.45	9.21	**4.24**
Donaldson	Dall	14.98	7.05	**7.93**		Woodson	LACl	17.98	13.80	**4.18**
Eaton	Utah	14.27	6.96	**7.31**		Aguirre	Dall	25.09	21.13	**3.96**
Jackson	NYor	20.68	13.59	**7.09**		R. Williams	LACl	10.43	6.71	**3.72**
Lever	Denv	25.94	18.85	**7.09**		Vandeweghe	Port	20.19	16.51	**3.68**
Cage	LACl	21.24	14.53	**6.71**		G. Wilkins	NYor	17.43	13.86	**3.57**
AVERAGE		21.15	13.01	**8.14**		**AVERAGE**		19.43	14.92	**4.51**

The purpose of these lists is to show those players who are better than their scoring indicates. You will notice that I took the average of both groups. GROUP B is better by scoring, while GROUP A is better by production. It's a foregone conclusion for the knowledgable fan, but really, which group is better? Here is a graphic example of how PR can be used to simply and quickly identify the most productive players. (I have avoided saying the "best" players because no adequate definition for "best" exists to the *best* of my knowledge. I will deal with who are the "most valuable" players later in the chapter. That process will include production and team strength). Lastly, I have shown the ten players whose scoring and production are nearly equivalent.

Player	**Team**	**PR**	**PPG**	**(PR - PPG)**
Bobby Hansen	Utah	9.68	9.59	+.09
Byron Scott	LALa	21.73	21.65	+.08
Michael Jordan	Chic	35.05	34.98	+.07
Jerry Reynolds	Milw	8.03	8.03	.00
Fred Roberts	Bost	6.08	6.08	.00
Larry Drew	LACl	10.31	10.34	-.03
Karl Malone	Utah	27.63	27.66	-.03
Chris Mullin	GoSt	20.17	20.22	-.05
Phil Hubbard	Clev	8.31	8.41	-.10
Jon Sundvold	Sant	8.00	8.10	-.10

Production Rating

In many ways basketball is a complex sport, mostly because it requires so many instantaneous decisions by so many people for long, uninterrupted periods - not so much because of statistics or strategy. Baseball is also very complex because of the infinite number of possibilities which exist between pitches. Baseball has often been called "the thinking man's game" - so many opportunites to create strategy. Since this book is about statistics, and baseball is more "statistical" than basketball, an obvious question might be "Why write on basketball?" The reason is simple. I enjoy baseball, but I love basketball - the action, the images, the poetry, the athleticism, the majesty, (stop me!). Baseball is conducive to a composite index, but even so, it seems somewhat insufficient considering that, with the designated hitter rule, not all players play both offense and defense. Even in the National League, where the DH does not exist, the pitcher is in such a unique position, that his measurements cannot reasonably be compared to the rest of his teammates. Football is very similar in terms of the difficulty in developing one rating for all players. No player plays offense *and* defense. What about special teams? How do you statistically measure an offensive lineman's contributions? It's tough.

In this respect, basketball has a big advantage over the other two. The NBA has statistical categories which cover most every phase of the game, both offense *and* defense. More importantly, every player has the opportunity to equally participate in every statistical category. Because of this unique phenomenon, I developed a rating system which is both comprehensive and uncomplicated, and is based on what is most important - a player's total floor performance - that is his production.

(PTS + REB + AST + BLK + STL) - (T.O. + MISSED FG + MISSED FT) = CREDITS

CREDITS FOR SEASON / GAMES = CREDITS PER GAME = PRODUCTION RATING

An example would be Michael Jordan during 1988. On the positive side he scored 2868 points, collected 449 rebounds, dealt out 485 assists, blocked 131 shots, and stole the ball 259 times. On the negative side, he missed 929 field goals, 137 free throws and committed 252 turnovers. By applying the formula, he earned 2874 CREDITS. Since he played in 82 games, he had a Production Rating of 35.05. This means he earned 35.05 CREDITS per game. As you might expect, Michael was the most productive player in the league in 1988.

As I mentioned earlier, I wanted a formula which, when applied, yielded a result which had aesthetic meaning (30 is All-NBA, 25 is All-Star, 20 is good, etc.). Other formulas which end up with numbers that don't fit into preexisting categories in our thinking just cannot be expected to catch on with the general public. Who is going to remember that 850 is the best or that a .74983 led the league? But tell me that Michael Jordan ended the season with 35.05 credits-per-game, and I'll know that you're telling me that he was probably the league's most productive player. Just as if you were to tell me that he scored 34.98 points per game. I would assume by this that he was probably the league's top scorer too. (Isn't it interesting how close his PR is to his PPG?)

The second thing I wanted to accomplish with PR was to create something that could be calculated easily on a game-by-game basis. Five positive and three negative numbers are easy to add and subtract. Whereas I can figure up a player's PR using the above formula in seconds just by looking at the box score, it is, nonetheless, an inconvenience.

The third priority when creating this ultimate formula was to make sure that it covered the four major aspects of the game - shooting, rebounding, passing, and defense. As I hope to show, Production Rating not only accomplishes these 3 goals, but is based on a very fundamental premise.

My theory begins with that premise. It is both interesting and coincidental. In very general terms, each team's possession yields approximately 1 point (100 possessions = 100 points). This is not technically correct, but it is very close and certainly it is close enough for this discussion. (In the next chapter, I look at the definition of possession while attempting to reach the perfect 100 points = 100 possessions = 100 credits.) This 100=100=100 could be proven valid if I were able to identify each CREDIT with either a point or a possession.

The first step was to look at the statistical categories authorized by the NBA: games, minutes, 3-point FGA & FGM, 2-point FGA & FGM, FTA & FTM, offensive and defensive rebounds, assists, fouls, disqualifications, steals, turnovers, blocked shots, points, and scoring average. By analysis, I was able to eliminate various categories as too cumbersome, too insignificant, too irrelevant or combinations of all three. Here is a breakdown of each statistical category and arguments for or against each category being included in the formula - Production Rating.

The first statistic I want to look at is fouls. I decided to ignore fouls since it is very difficult to determine the value or lack of value a foul represents. If your team has a one point lead and your opponent has the ball 75 feet from the basket with only two seconds left, obviously to foul would be costly. Rarely, however, are fouls so clearly a negative statistic. Many fouls are considered "smart" fouls - for example forcing out-of-bounds plays, sending a poor free throw shooter to the line, or preventing a breakaway layup. Moreover, many fouls do not have any real penalty associated with them at all since they occur prior to the penalty situation. It's important to clarify one point, however. An offensive foul *is* a negative credit, but it is already listed as a turnover on the stat sheets because there was a change of possession. Since it is a negative statistic, it would be a mistake to deduct it again as a foul. Therefore, fouls can be, and I believe should be, ignored in the formula. (See page 17 for the statistical arguments behind the negativity of fouls.)

Disqualifications are a negative statistic, but the inability to play and contribute in other statistical categories already penalizes the player. Therefore, DQ's need not be considered. Scoring average is merely a reflection of points and games, both of which are already being considered in credits-per-game. Finally, minutes-played is used only in qualifying the player. This leaves thirteen categories which can be reduced to nine by simply combining some shooting groups.

I then tried to apply the remaining statistical categories to this principle of 1 point = 1 possession = 1 CREDIT. Here, in a nutshell, is how I justify taking points, missed field goals, missed free throws, total rebounds, assists, steals, turnovers, and blocked shots and turning them into a consistent, meaningful number. Five (5) positive categories minus three (3) negative categories equals total credits. This statistic is then divided by the number of games played and the ultimate evaluation is by CREDITS/games or Production Rating.

The fundamental premise here is that 1 point = 1 rebound = 1 assist = 1 steal = 1 blocked shot. On the negative side, 1 missed field goal = 1 missed free throw = 1 turnover. By relating each category or CREDIT to the concept of 1 point = 1 possession = 1 CREDIT, it can be shown to be a valid theory.

To begin with, a turnover is easy. It is a loss of a possession and thus a loss of a point. As a result, a turnover is 1 negative CREDIT. A steal is just the opposite. It is the gaining of a possession and thus the gaining of a point. As a result, a steal is 1 positive CREDIT. A rebound always represents the gaining of a possession - even an offensive rebound. The reason is that the alternative is to let your opponent get a defensive rebound and thus lose a possession. Consequently, a rebound equals 1 positive CREDIT.

This still leaves 2-point FG's, 3-point FG's, free throws, assists, blocked shots, and points. Let's look at blocked shots first. A percentage of the time a blocked shot will result in a change of possession, but many times it will not. So how can one justify making it equal to a steal or rebound? I think it can be done this way. As I said earlier, certain qualities are not measurable. One of those is intimidation. How much worse do one's opponents shoot because of a particular defensive player? Probably the only measurable statistic which incorporates this intangible facet of the game is blocked shots. As a result, just like a steal and a rebound, a blocked shot is 1 positive CREDIT - partly because of a change of possession, partly because of intimidation and defense, partly because most shots which are blocked are close to the basket and probably would have gone in, and partly because it takes time off the 24 second clock which might prevent a team from scoring on its possession.

Next we examine assists. An assist does not affect possession in any way. It is not a point either. So how can it be a CREDIT? It's not easy to explain, but here goes. Leadership, ball control, and passing comprise the largest group of intangible facets. Each of these three areas are at least partially measurable by assists. The assist leader on a team is usually the player who brings the ball up court, dribbles against pressure, risks the most turnovers, sets up scoring opportunities, calls plays, and controls tempo. Even though the assist cannot be explained in terms of possessions or points, it seems well worth a CREDIT to me.

That leaves only scoring. As I said, a point is roughly equal to a possession which is roughly equal to a CREDIT. However, what about missed shots? Every missed 2 or 3-point FGA as well as most missed FTAs are a loss of possession for the following reason. Again, the team may retain possession with an offensive rebound, but that means the possession was, in effect, lost and then regained. If the missed shot was not a negative CREDIT, the offensive rebound could not be a positive one. The only questionable area here is the missed first free throw of two attempts. There is no loss of possession, but there is an implied loss of a point or at least nearly a point since most free throws are made. A free throw is, as it says, free. To miss it is to lose something already, in effect, given to you. Finally, there is no chance to regain possession to compensate for it.

As a result of this interesting phenomenon that 1 possession = 1 point = 1 CREDIT, it is possible to measure a player's performance by taking all facets of the game into consideration. To repeat, the formula then says simply:

(PTS + REB + AST + BLK + STL) - (T.O. + missedFG + missedFT) = CREDITS

CREDITS for season/games played = CREDITS per game = Production Rating

TOP PLAYOFF PERFORMANCES

		PTS +	AST +	REB +	STL +	BLK +	FG-FGA +	FT-FTA -	TO =	CR
1.	Olajuwon	+41	+2	+26	+3	+4	15-27 (-12)	11-14 (-3)	-3 =	58
2.	Olajuwon	+40	+3	+15	+2	+1	16-24 (-8)	8-8 (-0)	-1 =	52
3.	Worthy	+36	+10	+16	+2	+0	15-22 (-7)	6-10 (-4)	-5 =	48
4.	Jordan	+55	+3	+6	+4	+1	24-45 (-21)	7-7 (-0)	-1 =	47
5.	Jordan	+44	+4	+5	+4	+2	18-25 (-7)	8-9 (-1)	-4 =	47
6.	Lever	+30	+8	+11	+3	+2	12-17 (-5)	5-6 (-1)	-1 =	47
7.	Floyd	+42	+9	+3	+1	+0	16-22 (-6)	9-10 (-1)	-2 =	46
8.	E. Johnson	+28	+10	+8	+2	+0	8-11 (-3)	10-10 (-0)	-1 =	44
9.	Olajuwon	+34	+2	+14	+1	+3	12-20 (-8)	10-11 (-1)	-3 =	42
10.	Aguirre	+34	+7	+7	+1	+2	14-20 (-6)	6-7 (-1)	-2 =	42

MVP (Most Valuable Player)
PD (Position Dominance)
WR (Winning Ratio)
MVP = PD + WR

As you remember from earlier in the chapter, Michael Jordan was the most productive player in the NBA - but was he the most valuable? I realized early on that there must be a statistical way to evaluate who had the most valid claim to MVP. The formula I came up with has served that purpose very well. Despite the subtleties of the mind, biases, early voting, etc., my statistical MVP has been the same one voted MVP roughly half of the time since the award was first presented in 1956. More impressively, with only a few exceptions, the league's MVP was always in the top 3 of my statistical list.

As widespread coast to coast exposure becomes more and more commonplace, I would expect my formula and the voters to be in closer and closer agreement. There will always be one distinction, however. Part of my MVP formula is based on playoff performance, while the league's is not. Most of the value of the MVP formula is not so much for a given season anyway. I primarily use it to help determine the greatest players ever. (See discussion of greatness beginning on page 8).

Let's use an example. By doing so the strengths of the formula should become clear. To begin with, we will look only at Position Dominance (PD). Later we will look at Winning Ratio (WR). As I have said previously, CREDITS = points + rebounds + assists + blocked shots + steals - missed FG - missed FT - turnovers. Adding and subtracting these eight categories for a given year for a given player equals so many CREDITS. By dividing the credits by games-played, a player has a Production Rating. Last year Michael Jordan amassed 2868 CREDITS. He played in 82 games, so he had a Production Rating of 35.05 credits-per-game. It would be nice to compare straight across the board this 35.05 with the Production Ratings of Paul Arizin or Rick Barry or Bob McAdoo. The problem is that during each era, Production Ratings fluctuate due to rules, tradition, and coaching. Therefore, to be fair, Michael Jordan's 35.05 can only be compared to that of other players in 1987-88. Even then, it can only be compared to other off guards, since there has been a consistent variance in Production Rating from one position to another over the years.

Now, if Michael Jordan's 1987-88 Production Rating of 35.05 can only be compared to other off guards in 1987-88, how should this be done? I finally chose to create a statistic which all off guards in 1987-88 could be evaluated against. The statistic is called Comparative Index (CI). The same index can be applied to centers in 1959, small forwards in 1976, etc. Obviously, the CI will be different in each case, but it's still the same formula. After ranking all the off guards by Production Rating, I chose four - the first, second, fifth and median.

COMPARATIVE INDEX (CI) = (1st + 2nd + 5th + median)/4

Michael Jordan was first at 35.05, Clyde Drexler was second at 27.94, Byron Scott fifth at 21.73, and Sidney Moncrief was the median off guard at 12.45. With slight deviations due to rounding...

CI = (35.05 + 27.94 + 21.73 + 12.45) / 4 = 24.30

The Comparative Index (CI) for all off guards for 1987-88 was 24.30. To find out how productive any particular off guard was last year with respect to any other player at any other time in history, one need only to divide that guard's Production Rating by the CI. For Michael Jordan it would be 35.05/24.30 = 1.442

Position Dominance (PD) = Production Rating/CI = 1.442

The nice thing about PD is that it can be applied to any player in any year at any position and will impartially show how that player performed with respect to his peers and with respect to any player in any year in NBA history. Again, the MVP formula is equal to PD which we have just looked at plus Winning Ratio (WR).

No matter how good or productive a player is, he will not be considered particularly valuable if his team loses. Value is more than just production. It has to be reflected in team success as well. The most valuable players make other players around them better and thus their teams will win most of the time. Of the top-20 all time greatest players, every one of them has a career Winning Ratio (WR) of over 50%. This means they won more games than they lost. They were not only top producers, but winners as well.

$$WR = \frac{(\text{Regular season wins} + 3 \text{ times postseason wins})}{(\text{Regular season games played} + 3 \text{ times postseason games played})}$$

As you can see, I made each playoff game 3 times as valuable as a regular season game, whether it was a win or a loss. Much of what determines value comes from how a player does in the playoffs. To continue with Jordan...

WR = [50 + 3(4)] / [82 + 3(10)] = .554

A winning ratio of .554 is respectable though not exceptionally high, as it represents a 50-32 regular season record and 4-6 in the playoffs. The highest 10-year average WR in history was earned by Sam Jones at .706. Now we can complete the formula for Michael Jordan.

MVP = PD + WR
1.996 = 1.442 + .554

An MVP rating of 1.996 is extremely high. Jordan would become one of the greatest players ever if he could do that over a ten year period. Wilt Chamberlain has the highest 10-year average of 2.068.

Greatness

Whenever a discussion of the greatest or most valuable players in any sport comes up, controversy is sure to follow. The problem is one of definition. Unfortunately, it has never been settled whether "most valuable" means most indispensable or most productive. For that matter, it has never been settled whether the player deemed indispensable or productive could play for just any team or whether he must play for a winning or even a championship team. "Greatness" confuses the issue further. Simply put, that element is the different eras that players perform in. Each era has different rules, more or fewer opposing teams, etc. The question becomes obvious. Could Jesse Owens be greater than Carl Lewis? Could Jim Brown be greater than Eric Dickerson? In fact, could any player of yesteryear be greater than the top players today? After all, today's players are bigger, stronger, and faster. Presumably, they have better training techniques, better coaching, and better travel arrangements. How then can Bob Cousy be "greater" than Isiah Thomas? How can Bob Pettit be "greater" than Buck Williams?

Greatness, it seems to me, must be measured in terms of four basic categories: dominance, winning, statistics, and endurance. I have created a formula which encompasses the subtleties of each of these categories, and as a result, claims to determine the greatest professional basketball players of all time.

The MVP rating has taken into consideration the era a player played in, other players at his position, his production, and the regular season and post-season team records. The only major category left is endurance. I decided that in order to be considered for the greatest all-time players, a player must qualify (see page 272 for qualification requirements) for at least six years. Obviously, more players will qualify for six years than ten or fifteen years. I am of the opinion that a player should qualify at least ten years to be considered truly great; however, George Mikan only qualified eight years. Consequently, I have included two lists - the top-100 6-year and the top-100 10-year ratings. I have left it up to the reader to determine which requirement he or she feels should be met.

(By the way, Mikan is a classic case of a player who couldn't begin to play with today's athletes - kind of like Greg Dreiling. However, he was the most dominant big man ever in that dominance is defined as how well a player did against like opponents in his era. Here is a guy who was voted as the best basketball player for the first half of the century. He only played healthy 8 years in the NBA & NBL, but won 7 championships and was effectively the "MVP" 7 years.)

It's reasonable to ask how a player who endures fifteen years benefits over a player who plays for ten years. I could, of course, have a list which allowed only fifteen-year qualifiers. However, that list would be meaningless since Russell, Robertson, Cousy, Chamberlain, etc. would not be on it. In fact, only a few players qualified sixteen years or more. Therefore, I decided that whether it be the six-year list or ten-year list, it would be based on the best six years or the best ten years of a player's career. This way a player qualifying fifteen years has an advantage over a player qualifying only ten or six. That is because his best years are the only ones considered. Since a fifteen-year player has more years to choose from, endurance becomes a major factor in appraising greatness.

In summation, (MVP = PD + WR) for any given year makes a statement about a player's ability to dominate by Production Rating. It also makes a statement about his team's winning percentage, both during the season and in the playoffs. "Greatness" then averages a player's best six years or ten years of MVP ratings, depending on whether you think a player should have to qualify at least ten years or not.

As I said earlier, every player in the top-20 all-time greatest players by Position Dominance (PD) only, has a career winning Ratio (WR) of over 50%. This is not an accident. What it says is that the most productive players are good enough to win - regardless of their teammates. On an average, the more productive an individual player is, the more wins - although exceptions exist. On the other hand, a player who ranked below #50 probably did not *lead* his team to success, but rather *participated* in it. For these players it would seem to be more valid to ignore WR and look only at Position Dominance (PD). Therefore, I have included two more lists - the top-100 six-year and the top-100 ten-year Position Dominance ratings. The only difference between the top-100 PD ratings and the top-100 MVP ratings is that Winning Ratio (WR) is not shown in the PD ratings. Again, remember the basic formula, MVP = PD + WR.

Finally, you as a reader have two choices to make. 1) Should a player be called the greatest ever if he only qualifies six years or should he have to qualify for at least ten? 2) Should a player's team's winning percentages be a determining factor in assessing how great a player is?

On the next four pages you will see the four lists which I previously discussed. Before you turn to them, I would like to make a few last points. Just as there are lists for 6-year and 10-year qualifiers, there are also 7-year, 8-year, 9-year, etc. Obviously, six and ten are arbitrary numbers. As a rule, there are no major differences from one list to the next one a year later except that a player who failed to qualify enough years might be on the first list and not on the second. In some cases two players will exchange positions from one list to another. An example of this would be Jerry Lucas and Jerry West. On both six-year lists Lucas is ranked higher than West. On both 10-year lists West ranks ahead of Lucas. What this means is that Lucas' "greatness" was more intensely packed into a fewer number of years, while West's "greatness" was more diffused.

Secondly, you will see that only 97 players have qualified ten years or more. It might be a bit much to say Tom Hawkins (#97) is "greater" than George Mikan who failed to make the ten-year list because he only qualified eight years (Mikan ranks #4 in six-year ratings). Therefore, it would be more appropriate to look at six-year ratings when evaluating Mikan. No doubt the average fan will look up his favorite player and choose that list which ranks the player the highest. Thus the reason for the four lists.

Although many players have qualified for six years and not ten, few of the greatest players fit that mold. George Mikan (#4) is the most obvious exception. There are a few others who played in the 1950's who qualified less than ten years. Neil Johnston (#26) and Tom Gola (#32) are two examples. And, of course, there are present players who have not yet qualified ten years. Magic Johnson (#2) and Larry Bird (#5) would be the most conspicuous cases. Although there are two top-50 six-year MVP players who began their career after 1960 and who failed to qualify at least ten years (Billy Cunningham (#29) qualified nine years, while David Thompson (#41) qualified only seven years), they are, nevertheless, the exception and not the rule.

It should be clear by now that I enjoy ratings. In the chapters ahead you will see many more. Nevertheless, I can appreciate the fact that statistics are no substitution for watching a player night in and night out to determine his value. The reality, however, is that 99% of the readers of this book never saw Mikan or Johnston or Arizin play. Probably less than 50% of the readers saw Russell or Cousy or Baylor. Even those who were fortunate enough to do so, probably only saw them occasionally. What I have tried to do is to take the names that most basketball fans have somewhere in the back of their heads and enable them to place the player in history. Maybe the player is ranked a little too high or a little too low by some other standard, but at least the majority of NBA fans who are forty years old or less and who failed to see most of these players play, will now have the opportunity to identify them by their quality. If a young reader can see that an Elgin Baylor ranks comparably with a Julius Erving, or a Wilt Chamberlain ranks with a Kareem Abdul-Jabbar, or that a Bob Cousy ranks favorably with a Magic Johnson, he or she can imagine how great those players were. At the very least, any fan will have a better appreciation for the history of the game as well as those players who made it great.

6-YEAR MVP RATING

1. Wilt Chamberlain..............2.149
2. Earvin Johnson.................2.090
3. Oscar Robertson................2.080
4. George Mikan....................2.078
5. Larry Bird........................2.046
6. Kareem Abdul-Jabbar........2.018
7. Bill Russell.......................1.955
8. Bob Cousy........................1.923
9. Julius Erving....................1.889
10. Dolph Schayes.................1.875
11. Elgin Baylor....................1.863
12. Jerry Lucas.....................1.845
13. Moses Malone.................1.832
14. Bob Pettit.......................1.822
15. Jerry West......................1.819
16. George Gervin.................1.811
17. Kevin McHale..................1.740
18. Elvin Hayes....................1.738
19. Sidney Moncrief..............1.732
20. Rick Barry......................1.728
21. George McGinnis.............1.727
22. Walt Frazier....................1.718
23. Robert Parish..................1.700
24. Harry Gallatin.................1.695
25. John Havlicek.................1.688
26. Neil Johnston..................1.664
27. Bill Sharman...................1.646
28. Alex English...................1.636
29. Billy Cunningham............1.631
30. Isiah Thomas..................1.629
31. Bob McAdoo....................1.625
32. Tom Gola........................1.623
33. Spencer Haywood............1.617
34. Vern Mikkelsen...............1.617
35. Larry Kenon...................1.617
36. Artis Gilmore..................1.614
37. Dave Cowens..................1.612
38. Marques Johnson............1.610
39. Nate Archibald................1.605
40. Andy Phillip...................1.601
41. David Thompson.............1.598
42. Maurice Cheeks...............1.594
43. Norm Nixon....................1.587
44. Adrian Dantley...............1.582
45. Bobby Jones...................1.577
46. Paul Arizin.....................1.576
47. Bob Dandridge................1.572
48. Bill Laimbeer..................1.564
49. Arnold Risen..................1.563
50. Bob Davies.....................1.563
51. Paul Westphal................1.563
52. Bob Lanier.....................1.561
53. Dan Issel.......................1.554
54. Ed Macauley...................1.554
55. Gus Williams..................1.543
56. Jim Pollard....................1.543
57. Paul Silas......................1.541
58. Dennis Johnson..............1.540
59. Maurice Lucas................1.538
60. Truck Robinson..............1.538
61. Walter Davis..................1.535
62. Pete Maravich................1.533
63. Jack Sikma....................1.528
64. Jo Jo White....................1.527
65. Jamaal Wilkes................1.524
66. Bobby Wanzer................1.515
67. Happy Hairston..............1.509
68. Gail Goodrich.................1.505
69. Willis Reed....................1.504
70. Nate Thurmond..............1.502
71. Dan Roundfield..............1.501
72. Connie Hawkins.............1.499
73. Joe Fulks.......................1.496
74. Wes Unseld...................1.493
75. Hal Greer......................1.491
76. Cedric Maxwell..............1.485
77. Terry Cummings............1.482
78. Dick McGuire................1.476
79. Rudy Tomjanovich..........1.476
80. Randy Smith..................1.473
81. Bailey Howell................1.471
82. Bill Bridges....................1.470
83. Jack Coleman................1.467
84. Larry Nance..................1.467
85. Carl Braun....................1.463
86. Clyde Lovellette.............1.461
87. Sam Jones.....................1.460
88. Dave DeBusschere..........1.457
89. Cliff Hagan....................1.456
90. Earl Monroe...................1.453
91. Chet Walker..................1.450
92. Max Zaslofsky...............1.450
93. Len Wilkens..................1.449
94. Ray Williams.................1.447
95. Kiki Vandeweghe...........1.445
96. Tom Heinsohn...............1.440
97. World Free....................1.438
98. Billy Knight...................1.433
99. Mel Daniels...................1.429
100. Zelmo Beatty...............1.426

10-YEAR MVP RATINGS

1. Wilt Chamberlain 2.068
2. Oscar Robertson 1.997
3. Kareem Abdul-Jabbar 1.963
4. Bill Russell 1.881
5. Bob Cousy 1.845
6. Julius Erving 1.819
7. Jerry West 1.776
8. Dolph Schayes 1.775
9. Bob Pettit 1.764
10. Elgin Baylor 1.760
11. Moses Malone 1.726
12. George Gervin 1.706
13. Jerry Lucas 1.678
14. Rick Barry 1.657
15. Elvin Hayes 1.651
16. Walt Frazier 1.644
17. John Havlicek 1.602
18. Robert Parish 1.571
19. Artis Gilmore 1.565
20. Bill Sharman 1.546
21. George McGinnis 1.542
22. Alex English 1.521
23. Adrian Dantley 1.503
24. Dan Issel 1.501
25. Dave Cowens 1.496
26. Harry Gallatin 1.492
27. Bob Dandridge 1.490
28. Maurice Cheeks 1.489
29. Bob Lanier 1.474
30. Bobby Jones 1.472
31. Dennis Johnson 1.469
32. Paul Arizin 1.459
33. Jamaal Wilkes 1.458
34. Jack Sikma 1.457
35. Arnold Risen 1.448
36. Spencer Haywood 1.445
37. Bob McAdoo 1.432
38. Sam Jones 1.430
39. Wes Unseld 1.427
40. Vern Mikkelsen 1.422
41. Maurice Lucas 1.418
42. Hal Greer 1.414
43. Andy Phillip 1.414
44. Paul Silas 1.409
45. Nate Archibald 1.408
46. Chet Walker 1.404
47. Gus Williams 1.397
48. Bailey Howell 1.390
49. Gail Goodrich 1.385
50. Carl Braun 1.381

51. Nate Thurmond 1.381
52. Len Wilkens 1.374
53. Dan Roundfield 1.372
54. Bill Bridges 1.366
55. Dave DeBusschere 1.361
56. Earl Monroe 1.354
57. World Free 1.346
58. Walt Bellamy 1.341
59. Dave Bing 1.333
60. Dick McGuire 1.333
61. Jo Jo White 1.322
62. Calvin Murphy 1.321
63. Zelmo Beatty 1.302
64. Cliff Hagan 1.296
65. Ron Boone 1.291
66. Richie Guerin 1.289
67. Lou Hudson 1.286
68. Alvan Adams 1.282
69. Larry Foust 1.282
70. Freddy Brown 1.279
71. Randy Smith 1.278
72. Billy Knight 1.273
73. Slater Martin 1.273
74. Reggie Theus 1.267
75. John Kerr 1.264
76. Louie Dampier 1.244
77. Mickey Johnson 1.228
78. Jack Twyman 1.206
79. Guy Rodgers 1.203
80. Dick Van Arsdale 1.191
81. Sam Lacey 1.165
82. Tom Sanders 1.153
83. Billy Paultz 1.147
84. Bob Boozer 1.146
85. Mike Gale 1.146
86. Dick Barnett 1.145
87. Caldwell Jones 1.140
88. Dick Snyder 1.109
89. Mark Olberding 1.102
90. Chris Ford 1.100
91. Wayne Rollins 1.100
92. John Johnson 1.098
93. Joe Caldwell 1.089
94. Tom Meschery 1.055
95. Tom Van Arsdale .... .971
96. Leroy Ellis .... .957
97. Tom Hawkins .... .939

NOTE: No other players qualified as many as ten years.

6-YEAR POSITION DOMINANCE

1. Oscar Robertson 1.562
2. Wilt Chamberlain 1.546
3. George Mikan 1.385
4. Earvin Johnson 1.370
5. Kareem Abdul-Jabbar 1.349
6. Bob Cousy 1.347
7. Larry Bird 1.340
8. Jerry Lucas 1.323
9. Dolph Schayes 1.297
10. Elgin Baylor 1.291
11. Bob Pettit 1.278
12. George Gervin 1.253
13. Bill Russell 1.247
14. Neil Johnston 1.225
15. Julius Erving 1.218
16. Moses Malone 1.214
17. Jerry West 1.212
18. Elvin Hayes 1.192
19. George McGinnis 1.179
20. Adrian Dantley 1.170
21. Rick Barry 1.159
22. Walt Frazier 1.152
23. Spencer Haywood 1.142
24. Bob McAdoo 1.140
25. Harry Gallatin 1.133
26. Alex English 1.119
27. Billy Cunningham 1.118
28. Sidney Moncrief 1.111
29. Pete Maravich 1.101
30. Nate Archibald 1.086
31. Andy Phillip 1.080
32. John Havlicek 1.079
33. Tom Gola 1.079
34. Paul Arizin 1.066
35. Isiah Thomas 1.066
36. Bill Sharman 1.065
37. Bob Lanier 1.061
38. David Thompson 1.057
39. Artis Gilmore 1.047
40. Larry Kenon 1.046
41. Marques Johnson 1.042
42. Richie Guerin 1.039
43. Kevin McHale 1.035
44. Ed Macauley 1.027
45. Sidney Wicks 1.027
46. Dan Roundfield 1.023
47. Walt Bellamy 1.021
48. Jack Sikma 1.016
49. Randy Smith 1.007
50. Rudy Tomjanovich 1.007
51. Paul Westphal 1.006
52. Joe Fulks 1.004
53. Billy Knight 1.003
54. Truck Robinson 1.003
55. Bill Laimbeer 1.001
56. Larry Nance .... .995
57. Nate Thurmond .... .989
58. Bernard King .... .988
59. Robert Parish .... .986
60. Bailey Howell .... .982
61. Dave Cowens .... .981
62. World Free .... .979
63. Len Wilkens .... .979
64. Terry Cummings .... .978
65. Norm Nixon .... .978
66. Reggie Theus .... .978
67. Maurice Lucas .... .975
68. Gail Goodrich .... .970
69. Willis Reed .... .970
70. Gus Williams .... .966
71. Walter Davis .... .966
72. Vern Mikkelsen .... .965
73. Arnold Risen .... .965
74. Clyde Lovellette .... .960
75. Dan Issel .... .958
76. John Drew .... .957
77. Gus Johnson .... .957
78. Bobby Jones .... .955
79. Earl Monroe .... .954
80. Bill Bridges .... .949
81. Buck Williams .... .948
82. Bob Dandridge .... .947
83. Wes Unseld .... .945
84. Lou Hudson .... .944
85. Connie Hawkins .... .944
86. Kiki Vandeweghe .... .944
87. Ray Williams .... .943
88. Calvin Murphy .... .942
89. Bobby Wanzer .... .939
90. Larry Foust .... .936
91. Bob Davies .... .928
92. Happy Hairston .... .925
93. Dave Bing .... .924
94. Dick McGuire .... .924
95. Carl Braun .... .922
96. Maurice Cheeks .... .915
97. Mike Newlin .... .912
98. Freddy Brown .... .905
99. Cliff Hagan .... .905
100. Max Zaslofsky .... .904

10-YEAR POSITION DOMINANCE

1. Wilt Chamberlain 1.479
2. Oscar Robertson 1.469
3. Kareem Abdul-Jabbar 1.320
4. Bob Cousy 1.249
5. Bob Pettit 1.236
6. Elgin Baylor 1.210
7. Dolph Schayes 1.199
8. Bill Russell 1.180
9. Jerry West 1.178
10. Julius Erving 1.161
11. George Gervin 1.161
12. Moses Malone 1.157
13. Jerry Lucas 1.156
14. Elvin Hayes 1.129
15. Rick Barry 1.096
16. Walt Frazier 1.081
17. Adrian Dantley 1.049
18. Alex English 1.027
19. Artis Gilmore 1.015
20. George McGinnis 1.002
21. John Havlicek .... .988
22. Bob Lanier .... .986
23. Harry Gallatin .... .957
24. Spencer Haywood .... .955
25. Bob McAdoo .... .953
26. Jack Sikma .... .944
27. Robert Parish .... .939
28. Paul Arizin .... .936
29. Walt Bellamy .... .932
30. Bill Sharman .... .928
31. Dan Issel .... .927
32. Dave Cowens .... .907
33. Bailey Howell .... .906
34. Maurice Lucas .... .904
35. Len Wilkens .... .902
36. Nate Thurmond .... .898
37. Dan Roundfield .... .894
38. Bob Dandridge .... .892
39. Nate Archibald .... .889
40. World Free .... .886
41. Reggie Theus .... .881
42. Gail Goodrich .... .880
43. Wes Unseld .... .879
44. Andy Phillip .... .878
45. Arnold Risen .... .877
46. Vern Mikkelsen .... .868
47. Randy Smith .... .867
48. Maurice Cheeks .... .862
49. Richie Guerin .... .861
50. Carl Braun .... .857

51. Calvin Murphy .... .857
52. Dave Bing .... .854
53. Bill Bridges .... .849
54. Billy Knight .... .849
55. Hal Greer .... .848
56. Dave DeBusschere .... .839
57. Gus Williams .... .838
58. Earl Monroe .... .836
59. Dick McGuire .... .831
60. Bobby Jones .... .826
61. Jamaal Wilkes .... .826
62. Lou Hudson .... .824
63. Larry Foust .... .819
64. Dennis Johnson .... .814
65. Chet Walker .... .807
66. Paul Silas .... .794
67. Mickey Johnson .... .779
68. Freddy Brown .... .771
69. Jack Twyman .... .766
70. Alvan Adams .... .761
71. Jo Jo White .... .760
72. Ron Boone .... .758
73. Cliff Hagan .... .755
74. Dick Van Arsdale .... .745
75. John Kerr .... .743
76. Guy Rodgers .... .731
77. Sam Jones .... .725
78. Zelmo Beatty .... .718
79. Sam Lacey .... .711
80. Bob Boozer .... .688
81. Slater Martin .... .683
82. Louie Dampier .... .663
83. John Johnson .... .655
84. Dick Snyder .... .649
85. Tom Meschery .... .628
86. Caldwell Jones .... .622
87. Billy Paultz .... .615
88. Dick Barnett .... .610
89. Tom Van Arsdale .... .604
90. Mark Olberding .... .599
91. Joe Caldwell .... .584
92. Wayne Rollins .... .578
93. Mike Gale .... .553
94. Chris Ford .... .551
95. Leroy Ellis .... .539
96. Tom Sanders .... .502
97. Tom Hawkins .... .399

NOTE: No other players qualified as many as ten years.

Kareem Abdul-Jabbar of the Los Angeles Lakers
- Probably best known for the "Sky Hook" - his own invention
- Basketball Hall of Fame -

CHAPTER 2

FANCY FORMULAS

KAREEM'S STREAK

On October 18, 1977 - the first game of the season, the Lakers' Kareem Abdul-Jabbar matched up against Milwaukee's new center Kent Benson. Benson was, and is, only Milwaukee's second #1 pick in the draft. The other was, of course, Jabbar. Early in the game, as the two battled for supremacy, Kareem punched the rookie. In doing so, he injured his hand. Jabbar was sidelined the longest period of his career (nearly 2 months) and fined a league record $5000.00.

His first game back was December 4, 1977. As if to prove his superiority, Jabbar began a streak which may never be matched. For 787 consecutive games he scored in double figures. As the two teams squared off again last year, Kareem entered the game 35-35 against his former team. This time, just as in 1977, Jabbar lost the game. This time, just as in 1977, he lost something else too. His double digit scoring streak came to a halt as he finished with only 7 points. Coincidentally, the streak ended December 4, 1987 - exactly 10 years to the day from when it began.

IN SEARCH OF...
THE "PERFECT" PRODUCTION RATING

As you know from reading chapter 1, my Production Rating formula is derived from adding (points + rebounds + assists + blocks + steals - turnovers - missed FG's - missed FT's) divided by games played. Michael Jordan had the highest Production Rating in the NBA last year, at 35.05. This is very similar to his scoring average (34.98). What this means is that his production was at a similar level as his scoring. Some players are more productive, while some are obviously less productive than their scoring. Listed below are the top-12 production leaders and the top-12 scorers. As you can see, production follows the scoring parameters pretty closely. 30+ is great, 25-30 is all-star or better, etc.

PRODUCTION	Col.1	Col.2	SCORING
Michael Jordan	35.05	34.98	Michael Jordan
Larry Bird	34.01	30.73	Dominique Wilkins
Charles Barkley	32.51	29.93	Larry Bird
Akeem Olajuwon	28.10	28.30	Charles Barkley
Clyde Drexler	27.94	27.66	Karl Malone
Magic Johnson	27.71	26.98	Clyde Drexler
Karl Malone	27.63	25.84	Dale Ellis
John Stockton	26.54	25.09	Mark Aguirre
Kevin McHale	26.28	25.00	Alex English
Fat Lever	24.51	22.85	Akeem Olajuwon
Larry Nance	24.51	22.59	Kevin McHale
Dominique Wilkins	24.27	21.40	Xavier McDaniel

However, Production Rating does not produce a case where exactly every point scored ends up as a CREDIT (Production Rating's version of a point). As it is, all the CREDITS in a season add up to slightly more than all the points (approximately 13% more). Ideally, it would be nice to have them completely equal or within 1-2%. Despite this desire to have the "perfect" Production Rating formula - none exists. Production Rating (PR) measures production extremely well. The fact that it does not precisely follow the same parameters as scoring is less than perfect, but the fact that it is even close at all is coincidental and fantastic. Everyone knows 30+ is great. Therefore PR is already capable of being understood just by looking at the rating.

Still, I would love to figure a reasonable way to make PR exactly equal to scoring so that the sum of column 1 would be equal (or very close) to the sum of column 2. Of course, it could be done by adding multipliers to the items in the formula. For example, I could take assists times .8 and blocks times .9 and subtract DQ's etc, but I reject all that because it loses simplicity. One of the big advantages to PR is that it can be calculated in seconds at the end of a game. Simplicity is essential if PR is to become accepted and commonly used. It may be fractionally less accurate to use my formula as opposed to saying points + reb + .8234 ast + .9004 blocks + steals - turnovers - .9371 missed FG's - .8118 missed FT's, but I guess I don't care. I have rarely, if ever, seen it make any real difference. Perhaps a player ranks 85th instead of 87th or 15th at his position as opposed to 16th. So what? I consider the higher priority to be a formula that is accurate, simple, and aesthetically pleasing. I cannot see how to improve on what I have. Even so, let's try.

As it is, the average NBA team racks up 122.09 CREDITS per game, yet averages only 108.16 points per game. The only way to get them to equal each other would be to apply more negatives to CREDITS. What about fouls?

FANCY FORMULAS 17

I have been asked several times why fouls are not a negative CREDIT. I will explain in detail why, but first let's look what would happen if fouls were subtracted. That same average team registers 24.11 fouls. If we subtract fouls, it now means that this team averages 97.98 CREDITS. Clearly, 97.98 is no more equal to 108.16 than 122.09 is equal to 108.16. Therefore, fouls are not the answer, or are they?

The NBA keeps a stat called team rebounds. These are rebounds which cannot be ascribed to any particular player. There are approximately 20% more rebounds (team) than those accumulated by the players. Already, we will have a problem reconciling something. If we include team rebounds in our attempt to create the perfect PR formula, which would theoretically make 108.16 CREDITS-per-game (CPG) = 108.16 points-per-game (PPG), then how can column 1 = column 2 using the same formula? The reason it can't is because there are more CREDITS for the team (team rebounds) then there are by adding up the CREDITS of all the players. Just for the heck of it, let's say we're only interested for now in creating the "perfect" formula for the team and not the players.

If we add team rebounds (roughly 8.68 per-game) we now have 130.77 CREDITS-per-game (122.09 + 8.68), but still only 108.16 ppg. Team rebounds just made the difference greater. However, if we now subtract fouls (-24.11) it starts to get pretty close. CREDITS-per-game would, at this point, equal 106.66 (130.77 - 24.11) whereas scoring is 108.16. The ratio of CPG to PPG is 106.66 / 108.16 = .986 - not far from the "perfect" 1.00.

That same ratio has gradually moved from .955 to .986 since the NBA began keeping turnovers in 1978. I predict it will continue to climb as 3-point shots increase. The reason is because, as teams hit better and better 2-pt and 3-pt percentages, CREDITS will increase while fouls will decrease. That means the numerator of the relationship CPG/PPG rises and, thus, so does the ratio. Fouls should decrease because of an increase in 3-pt shooting and recent rule changes (breakaway foul). Hence, the action is moving away from the congested lane. Despite the potential 1 point = 1 CREDIT argument, based on this discussion - I reject it categorically.

First of all, it still isn't perfect - although by the year 2,000, given the present trend, it should be extremely close. Secondly, even if it were perfect for the team, it would not be perfect for the players. The sum of the parts would not be as great as the whole because of team rebounds. But thirdly, I just cannot accept fouls as a negative credit for many reasons. In order to do so would mean that a foul was as bad as a turnover or a missed shot which always cause a change of possession. The only fouls that cause a change of possession are offensive fouls which are already a negative credit since an offensive foul is a turnover. Certainly it can't be deducted twice. My point, then, is that including fouls in Production Rating would be bad unless offensive fouls could be distinguished from defensive fouls. Unfortunately, no published statistics that I have ever seen make the distinction. That means they don't exist. Even if they did, however, it still wouldn't be acceptable.

I estimate that of the 24 fouls, only 3 are offensive. Of the 21 defensive fouls, 11 are two-shot fouls while 5 are tacked onto a made field goal. This would mean 27 FTA's per game (the amount the average team shoots less technicals). It also means 5 fouls (21-11-5 = 5) have no penalty associated with them at all. These fouls occur prior to the penalty situation in a quarter. Therefore we must eliminate 5 more fouls from consideration as negative. That makes 9 non-negative fouls [3 offensive (remember, already deducted as turnovers) and 5 non-penalty]. Of the 16 remaining fouls, 11 cause two FT attempts and 5 allow for 1 FT attempt. What we have to look at here is what is being lost vs gained with each foul.

Let's look at the five 1-shot attempts. I am not willing to accept that a foul, when attached to a made FG, is totally bad. Yes, that foul was somewhat bad, but other similar fouls may go uncalled while resulting in a missed FG by the opponent. When that happens, and it often does, how is the defender rewarded statistically? Still let's assume all five fouls in which a player gets a bucket are unique and bad. The question is... "How bad are they?" The average FT shooter in the NBA is at 76.6%. Therefore, this foul costs .766 points.

18 BASKETBALL HEAVEN 1989

Since there is the possibility of an offensive rebound it could be worse. Normally an offensive rebound occurs 32.80% of the time, but an offensive rebound on a free throw attempt is lower - approximately 25%. Since each possession yields roughly 1 point - the one shot foul cost the fouling team .766 points plus .25 possessions for each missed FT. Therefore, a foul in the act of shooting will normally cost the offending team .825 points (.766 + .059). The value .059 is derived from taking the .234 missed FT's times .25 offensive rebound capability.

A two shot foul actually costs less than the one shot foul on a made FG. It causes the loss of 1.532 points (.766 X 2) plus .059 possessions, but it gains a full possession once the free throws are shot. Thus a two shot foul costs the offending team .591 points (1.532 + .059 -1).

Therefore, the 24 fouls committed by a team during a game cost approximately 10.331 [(5 X .766) + (11 X .591)] points. I would be in favor of subtracting this 10.331 points, but from which player? How do you subtract .591 points on each shooting foul? Even if the stats were kept by the various breakdowns (and they are not), this violates the simplicity rule. Additionally, it ignores the real fact that many fouls are considered "smart" fouls since they force out-of-bounds plays, send a poor free throw shooter to the line, or prevent a breakaway layup. Add to that the fact that many fouls are committed just to stop the clock near the end of the game. The "fouler" was just trying to improve his team's chances of winning. It would be wrong to penalize him for that. It might be reasonable to say that a few points per game are actually lost because of fouls - but very few! Most assuredly, no where near 24 points. If fouls were deducted from the formula, they would have to be proven to cost 24 points. I estimate that 24 fouls is actually worth a loss of around 5 points (excluding offensive fouls which are already deducted as a turnover.) To deduct 5/24 of a point for each foul would be ridiculous. Besides, the point is that, even if I were to do so, I would only come slightly closer to the "perfect" Production Rating where points/CREDITS = 1.00. However, as I said before, I would have assassinated the simplicity rule.

DEFINING POSSESSION

A simple definition for possession is "I know one when I see one." Obviously, if a team has control they have possession. Right? If they lose control - they lose possession and the other team has it. The amount of time a team has a possession would seem to be irrelevent. As long as they have it, they have it. When they don't, they don't. Though that seems absurdly apparent, there is some debate as to what should be called a possession.

As you know from reading chapter 1, I justify the make-up of Production Rating based on the theory that all of the positive and negative values (CREDITS) which go into the formula are, in effect, equal to the gaining or losing of either a point or a possession - and that a point equals a possession, and surprise, surprise, a possession equals a point.

Now, those who debate whether a possession technically equals a point don't argue that it is at least close. In fact, nearly everyone agrees that it's close enough for Production Rating to be considered valid. But, as you might guess, if it were to be proven that a possession actually equalled .8 points, then it could be argued that the technical Production Rating formula should be adjusted so that turnovers and steals, which are based on the changing of possession, would be of different weight than a point. The problem with that argument is that even if a possession equalled as a much as .99 points, the formula would have to be adjusted. Since I believe anything within 10% is close enough to maintain accuracy, I reject the fractions as too complicated to calculate. I should say from the outset that I agree with those who say 1 possession is not exactly equal to one point - but it is close. In fact, quite close. There are two ways to determine possessions. The first is the one I subscribe to which says:

POSSESSION I = FGA's + T.O's + .4 FTA's

I'll explain. As we know, there are only a few ways to "lose possession". It seems reasonable to say that if a team lost x number of possessions then they must have had x number of possessions to lose in the first place. I'll discuss later whether every possession must be lost every time a team has it. For now, suffice it to say that a change in possession takes place when a shot is taken and missed, but rebounded by your team. There is a loss of possession (missed FG) and the regaining of a possession (offensive rebound). Therefore, two distinct possessions exist here. A possession is also lost when a team commits a turnover (offensive fouls are turnovers). Finally, possession is lost on approximately 40% of FTA's. Why? First of all, a FTA after a field goal is made (3 point play) is not relevant since I've already said a possession is lost after every FGA. If a FTA, whether made or missed, is stuck onto a FGA it doesn't matter. I am "estimating" that 20% or 1/5 of all FTA's are at the tail end of a made field goal. Of the 80% remaining, clearly half of those FTA's do not affect possession (the first FTA). Since the second FTA is the only FT which affects possession, whether the second FT is made or missed is, again, not relevant since a missed FT with an offensive rebound is, as I said before, losing, then regaining, possession. That is my definition of possession. However, another definition is as follows...

POSSESSION II = FGA's - OFFENSIVE REBOUNDS + T.O.'s + .4 FTA's

As you can see the only difference is that those who hold this definition include the deduction of all offensive rebounds. The argument is that when a team comes down the court, it has a possession. It doesn't give it up until the other team has it. And it doesn't get another one until it takes it back. This is simple and sounds great. The obvious underlying point being made here is that when a team shoots a FG and misses, but rebounds and shoots again and hits, that team scored on their only possession. The offensive rebound then does not change possession, therefore, it must be deducted from the formula.

I argue for my definition because of two primary factors. The first is simple. The shot clock is reset every time a field goal is taken, whether made or missed. Well, not every time. There is the occasional "air ball". But the vast majority of the time an offensive rebound occurs, the shot clock is reset. This is the official NBA definition of a possession. That's what the 24 second clock defines - the amount of time a team can *possess* the ball without giving it up via a shot or turnover or free throws.

The second argument for my definition is that when I created Production Rating, I held the view that every positive CREDIT was of "equal" value (points, rebounds, assists, blocks and steals). Production Rating is based on the premise of 1 CREDIT = 1 point = 1 possession. Since I justify an offensive rebound in the formula only because it is the gaining of a possession, I would then have to remove it from the formula if I were to agree that it did not gain a possession.

That is, plainly, unacceptable, as an offensive rebound is surely as valuable (though not more so) as a defensive rebound. In both cases, the ball is loose and will be controlled by either your team or the opposing team. That difference is a possession. Either you have it or your opponent has it. Whether it was offensive or defensive, the same is true. Oh sure, some offensive rebounds seem more valuable. Let's say there are 5 seconds left with the score tied and your team shoots and misses. You rebound it and stick it back in for the win. That rebound looks pretty good, but the made FG must be viewed independently from the rebound. What about when your team leads by one and your opponents shoot with 5 seconds left and miss. You rebound - denying them another opportunity - thus clinching the victory. Was that any less valuable than the previous example of your offensive rebound? I don't think so. Despite these unique or rare examples at the end of a game, the fact is that every rebound, whether offensive or defensive, results in the net difference of 1 possession. Either you have it or your opponent has it. It's that simple.

Therefore, since all rebounds are equal, I cannot justify removing offensive rebounds from Production Rating. Yet that is precisely what I would have to do if I were to say that an offensive rebound did not gain a possession. Possession II states clearly that the offensive rebound does not secure a possession, because possession was not lost until the other team had it. I say it was lost at the moment the shot was taken.

The primary argument for Possession II as the best definition for a possession is as follows. It has to do with something called floor percent. For example, a lot of people wish to know what percent of the time a team scores when it brings the ball up the court. Therefore, they say the team scored on x percent of their possessions. I've got a solution. Why not just call it "floor percentage" and leave possessions out of it. If a team brings a ball up the court and shoots 3 times and misses each, but gets the rebound and makes shot #4, then they were 1 for 1 and their floor percent was a perfect 100. Why drag possessions into it? The problem is that this feat is commonly referred to as their having been successful on that possession (singular). In fact, many reporters count possessions as trips up the floor - ignoring offensive rebounds. That is predicated on the problem of confusing possessions with floor percent. as well as not recognizing a phenomenon which I call "possession limbo".

If you think about it, the emotional problem those who subscribe to Possession II have with mine (Possession I) is that they cannot see how I can say my team had multiple possessions at the same end of the floor when the other team never had even one. You see, if I say all missed FGA's are a possession lost, then who were they lost to when my team gets the offensive rebound? Its a good question, but I have an answer.

The answer is possession limbo. My point is that every time a possession is lost (a missed FG, a turnover, a 2 shot foul), the possession goes into a temporary suspension. It doesn't always leave that holding place by going to the other team. An offensive rebound is a perfect example of a time when possession left purgatory and went to heaven (assuming my team has the ball). If the rebound is defensive the possession left purgatory and went to hell (the other guy).

Someone might say, "That's ridiculous. You only made up that argument to justify your position!" Well, not so, limbo breath. It happens naturally at other times in the game. What about when a technical FT is shot. Here is a case where a FTA was taken, yet possession was retained, whether made or missed. How about when a team has the ball, but gets tied up? They then go on to win the tip. The possession was in a temporary holding place there, but reverted to the original team. Probably the best example is at the end of a quarter when a team takes the last shot as the buzzer sounds. Whether it goes in or not doesn't affect possession since time has expired. Half the time that same team gets a new possession to start the next quarter. My point is that it is fallacous to assume that a possession can only be lost once the other team has it and that the only way to get a "new" possession is after the other team has lost it. I argue that every possession begins from a limbonic position even though the majority of the time the new possessor is not the same as the old one.

Perhaps an argument for either formula could carry more weight if it were true that one or the other came close to the 1 point = 1 possession premise I have accepted. However, by applying the NBA stats this year to both, it is easy to see that each is, for the most part, equally off. My formula is again...

POSSESSION I = (FGA's + T.O.'s + .4 FTA's)

In 1987-88 this would reap 7193 + 1372 + .4(2388) = 9520. Since there were 8869 points scored, this means my possession to point ratio is 1.073. As you can see this is 7.3% off of the "perfect" 1 point equals 1 possession. The other formula was...

POSSESSION II = (FGA's - OFF. REB's + T.O.'s + .4 FTA's)

In 1987-88 this formula would read 7193 - 1167 + 1372 + .4(2388) = 8353. Again, there were 8869 points scored so the possession to point ratio for Possession II is .942. Though slightly closer, it is still 5.8% away from being perfect.

Since both are close to 1 point = 1 possession, yet both are 6 to 7 percent off, the previous arguments for POSSESSION I hold the most weight as far as I'm concerned.

FISHING BUDDIES

Players:
Last year I introduced a very simple formula called Fishing Buddy Rating. Although it was intended as a tongue-in-cheek look at who gets the most calls from the officials, I decided it could also be used to prove or disapprove some existing theories in the NBA.

I have heard dozens of statements made by NBA people that the stars "get the calls" while the little guy pays the price. There certainly may be some truth to this, but I've watched hundreds, even thousands, of games, and feel like this claim is questionable. At least I've always felt that even if it were true, the difference is minimal. With VCRs, instant replays, stop action, etc., I have been unable to "see" proof of this.

Therefore, I decided that there might a way to determine "get the calls" validity by looking at certain stats. The two obvious ones were free throw attempts and fouls. It seemed reasonable that those players whose ratios of FTA's/fouls were the highest would be the most likely candidates for the ultimate "get the calls" players.

As a lark, I called this formula (FTA/Foul) Fishing Buddy Rating - implying that some players spend their off-time out having fun with the whistle blowers. Of course, that's not true and I have never questioned any official's integrity, but Fishing Buddy Rating (FBR) has a nice ring to it nonetheless. Shown below are the top-20 players during 1987/88 by FBR...

1.	Moses Malone	Wash	4.306	11.	Quintin Dailey	LACl	2.445
2.	Dominique Wilkins	Atla	4.043	12.	Michael Cage	LACl	2.443
3.	Adrian Dantley	Detr	3.972	13.	Kevin McHale	Bost	2.425
4.	Charles Barkley	Phil	3.421	14.	Maurice Cheeks	Phil	2.371
5.	Rolando Blackman	Dall	3.384	15.	Clyde Drexler	Port	2.348
6.	Magic Johnson	LALa	3.327	16.	Johnny Dawkins	Sant	2.326
7.	Michael Jordan	Chic	3.185	17.	Otis Thorpe	Sacr	2.307
8.	Larry Bird	Bost	2.885	18.	Mark Aguirre	Dall	2.260
9.	Karl Malone	Utah	2.666	19.	Brad Daugherty	Clev	2.247
10.	Kiki Vandeweghe	Port	2.662	20.	John Battle	Atla	2.238

It is easy to look at this list and say, "That proves the stars get the calls at both ends of the court." I disagree. Other than being interesting, it proves nothing. If a player is a star, he is a star for reasons that have very little, if anything, to do with the officiating. Common sense says that a player who excels at shooting, or rebounding, or passing, or whatever, should also excel at drawing fouls and making clean defensive plays. The facts are that the best players saturate the top lists of all categories. Logically, FBR should be no different than any other category in this respect.

If it is true then that FBR for a given year is cute, but meaningless, then what purpose does it serve? Well, in my attempt to prove or disprove "get the calls", I decided to look at how a player's FBR changed from the year in which he had his best Production Rating with that of the following year. I surmised that this would be enlightening. After all, if a player didn't quite play as well the following year, and of course, in these cases, he never did, then why should his FBR be as good or better? My point is that if a player's points and rebounds and assists, etc. are not as good as the previous year's then why shouldn't the player's ability to draw fouls and play precise defense also decline proportionately? And if it didn't, wouldn't it be because the officials perceived the player differently? Perhaps arguments could be made that these two categories are independent from the rest of a player's game, but at least for now, I am proceeding on the premise that a decline in a player's production categories should, in the main, yield a decline in his FBR as well.

What I found was interesting. In the 1980's, 29 of the best player's have had their most productive year ever. Obviously then, in all 29 cases, the player's Production Rating declined the following year. Logically, one would assume then that very few of these players would have as good a Fishing Buddy Rating in year 2 as in year 1. After all, if the other areas of expertise peaked the year before, why shouldn't FBR?

Well, as it turns out, 21 of the 29 times the player's FBR actually *improved* despite a *decrease* in production. Now *that* represents evidence that once a player reaches the highest levels in the NBA, he is then accorded more leeway by the officials in following years. Though the margins were small, the trend is unmistakable. The odds of 21/29 FBR's improving by chance, while at the same time 29/29 PR's were on the decline, are astronomical to say the least.

When I went back to previous decades, the trend was somewhat reversed. Shown below is the number of great players I researched. I also show how many of them improved their FBR the following year despite a decline in production, and the percentage of the time that happened.

Decade	# of players researched	# of players improved FBR in year 2	% of players improved FBR in year 2
1950's	5	2	.400
1960's	14	7	.500
1970's	13	4	.235
1980's	29	21	.724

Perhaps there are many reasons for the change in the 80's. It is always possible that communication is so improved that every official knows every word written about how great the greatest players are, or are supposed to be. He may also know that the world is watching every great move the player makes - never looking for fault, but rather for a chance to be amazed. Perhaps the officials subconciously choose to help create this mystique because it is what the fans want. Maybe the officials are more intimidated by bigger crowds, player's million dollar salaries, or the fear that the players have gotten too quick for the eye to see. Thus, the call should be "safe". I confess I don't know the reason why the results are what they are. They only indicate that the phenomenon exists.

Despite this research, it is really nearly insignificant. What it means is that the greatest players might get as many as 19 fewer fouls and 15 more free throws during the course of the season. Clearly, over an 82 game period, this is pretty small potatoes.

Teams:

I thought it would be equally interesting to look at the best teams in the NBA for the same reason. Just as with players, I have heard that certain teams "get the calls".

I decided to follow a similar line of reasoning in my attempt to discover if this was true. What I did was to calculate the FBR for a team in the year it won the championship - then calculate the club's FBR for the following year.

In the 19 years since 1969, (the end of Boston's dynasty and the last repeat champion prior to L.A. in 1988) 10 times the team's Fishing Buddy Rating was better the year they won the championship; 8 times it was better the following year; and 1 time there was no real difference. This indicates no substantial bias toward those teams on top.

FANCY FORMULAS

I suppose one could argue that there should have been very few instances out of 19 where the FBR was better in year 2. As it was there were 8. Maybe so, but the fact that it wasn't anything like the top players in the '80s makes it at least *seem* insignificant.

As I said earlier, I've watched so many NBA games that I could never count them. Yet, I have rarely thought an official's call cost one team the game. You could argue that half of all 1 or 2 point games are ultimately decided by the officials because odds of all "missed" calls being exactly the same for both teams are very slim. That's true, but what good is it to assume that huge numbers of games are won or lost by the officials. They're human and there's no way around it. Thank goodness for an 82 game schedule. Bad fortune on calls may make a difference to whether a team ends with 51 or 52 or 53 wins, but it is unlikely that they will ever vary much more than +/- 2 victories. In the scheme of things, scheduling, coaching, players, chemistry, fans, injuries and a host of other factors have vastly more effect on the number of wins in a season than the officiating.

PREDICTIVE FORMULAS

OLIVER

Bill James was, of course, one of the pioneers - if not *the* pioneer of the principles of sabermetrics. His interpretations of statistical information have become famous among sports fans - especially in the baseball world. One phenomenon that he discovered was that there a clear and dependable relationship between the number of runs a team scores, the number of runs they allow, and the number of games they will win.

This seems evident on the surface. Clearly, if a team is outscored over the course of a season 2 to 1, they will, on an average, lose a proportionately larger number of games than they would have lost had they done the scoring by a 2-1 ratio. The question is not so much, "Is it true that this relationship exists?" but rather, "What is the relationship?" James discovered that if you score three runs for every two scored by your opponent, you'll win nine games for each four that he wins. You can see that he is just squaring the totals. If you score four to his three, you'll win sixteen games to his nine, etc. This is interesting, but how does it apply to basketball?

A fellow by the name of Dean Oliver came up with a formula for basketball which said...

$$\frac{(\text{pts scored})^x}{[(\text{pts scored})^x + (\text{pts allowed})^x]} = \text{WINNING PERCENT}$$

... where $x = 17$ or something similar to it. I decided to run it through my computer for each team in the NBA since Dallas came into the league (in 1980/81). What I did was to calculate every team's winning percentage (wins/82) and subtract their winning percent (as defined by Oliver's formula). I then took the absolute value of that number and added it for all 184 teams (8 seasons @ 23 teams).

What I was attempting to find was the exponent which worked the best. That is, what should x be equal to in order to compare most closely with what a team's real winning percent was (wins/82)? As it turns out, 16.1 is the best exponent for this formula - at least in the 1980's. At some future date, I may research the NBA since its inception to determine how close to 16.1 "x" was during the 50's, 60's, and 70's.

As I expected, the best exponent varied for different types of teams. As a team approached being very good, the exponent rose to around 18 or 19. When a team verged on mediocrity (41 wins, 41 losses) the best exponent was much lower. Nevertheless, it shot up sharply from

41 wins so that the average (16.1) is not too far from both ends. If that doesn't make sense - it's OK because it's not necessary to understand in order to appreciate Oliver's formula. For now let's just go with an exponent of 16.1 and call it adequate for all types of teams - good, bad or average.

The question should come up at this point if it hasn't already - "Why do I (or you) want to know?" Well, if you're interested in predicting how well a team will do in a future year, this is a potentially valuable tool.

By using the formula, it effectively comes within +/- 2.375 wins (on an average) of stating what a team's actual wins were. For example, in 1981 New Jersey won 24 games. By plugging in the points-scored and points-allowed and using the 16.1 exponent, New Jersey had a calculated winning percentage of .2926683. In reality, however, they won 24 of 58 games for a true winning percentage of .2926829. This is a very slight difference of .0000146. Oliver's formula then says that New Jersey should have won 23.9988 games. I'd say that's pretty close to 24 wins. Just so you don't get the idea it always works this well consider the 1986 Seattle Supersonics. For the season, they were outscored by only 8 points despite a 31-51 record. The formula says they should have won 49.62% of the time or 40.69 games. That means they "underwon" 9.69 wins (40.69 - 31). This example represents the farthest any team was from what the formula says they should have been.

As I stated before the average deviation is +/- 2.375 wins in any given year. Sometimes a team underwon and sometimes they overwon. Shown below are the 23 teams. Column 1 lists the average wins per year they actually registered above or below what the formula says they would have won. Column 2 shows how many years each team overwon vs underwon the last eight years.

	Col. 1	Col. 2		Col. 1	Col. 2
Philadelphia	+2.79	6-2	Atlanta	-.03	3-5
Boston	+2.60	6-2	Sacramento	-.33	2-6
Golden State	+2.00	6-2	Chicago	-.84	2-5-1
LA Lakers	+1.79	8-0	Detroit	-.92	3-5
Denver	+1.24	5-3	Phoenix	-1.09	2-6
Washington	+1.23	4-4	New York	-1.42	3-5
LA Clippers	+.78	3-5	Dallas	-1.45	2-6
Houston	+.65	5-3	Indiana	-1.47	1-7
Utah	+.62	6-2	Seattle	-1.80	2-6
San Antonio	+.27	4-4	Portland	-2.34	1-7
New Jersey	+.24	4-3-1	Milwaukee	-2.86	0-8
Cleveland	+.23	4-4			

What is interesting is that Philadelphia (6-2), Boston (6-2) and the LA Lakers (8-0) - the teams with the best regular season records in this period - usually overwon. Why? I think there is a logical explanation. Oliver's formula simply says that if you win at a comparable rate as the rate at which you outscore your opponents, then your differential will be zero. Since the 76ers, Celtics, and Lakers average overwinning 1-3 wins per year, it means they probably won a lot of close games. The better teams generally do. They win a lot of games by 8-12 points that they could conceivably have won by 20 had they left their starters in in the 4th quarter. Consequently, they score enough to win, but not necessarily what they are capable of. Thus their scoring differential is behind their wins. Why then are Portland and Milwaukee last? The only possible explanation is that they won a higher percentage of blowouts (perhaps substituting less late in the game) and lost a higher percentage of close games. In fact, the two have combined for a 61-81 regular season record in 2-pt games or less since 1981. That is remarkably bad for two teams with such good overall records in the same period.

PREDICTIVE 1

Now how can Oliver's formula be used to predict the next year's record? Well, when you think about it, it makes sense that if a team overwon 5-7 games in a year - meaning that they weren't nearly as good as their record indicates - then they probably will come back to earth the following year. Additionally, they could easily have a false sense of security. That leads to arrogance and complacency - two of the very factors which prevent teams from repeating as champions.

I decided to take a look at the teams who overwon the most in any given season since 1981. Shown below are the 17 teams who overwon at least 4 games more than Oliver's formula says they should have won in a given year. You might notice that there is a wide range of quality represented, from the Celtics to the Clippers. This is evidence that the formula is not skewed badly to one particular group. Shown in the second column is the number of actual wins (either more or less) the team registered in the following year. As you can see, there is a clear and unmistakable pattern apparent. As a team overwins (wins more games than their play justified) they tend to lose a lot of ground the following year.

	Year 1	Overwins In Year 1	Change In Actual Wins In Year 2
LA Clippers	1986	8.9	-20
Golden State	**1987**	**7.8**	**-22**
Boston	1983	6.6	+6
Seattle	1985	6.2	0
Philadelphia	1986	6.0	-9
Golden State	1984	5.9	-15
Philadelphia	1985	5.2	- 4
Washington	**1987**	**5.2**	**- 4**
Houston	1982	5.1	-32
Atlanta	1983	5.1	- 3
Sacramento	1986	5.0	- 8
Philadelphia	**1987**	**4.6**	**- 9**
Utah	1982	4.5	- 3
Denver	1985	4.3	- 5
Philadelphia	1984	4.3	+6
New York	1982	4.0	-17
Boston	1982	4.0	- 7

Assuming one looks only at the teams who overwon 4 or more games in a year, it should be possible to reasonably predict a team's performance in the following year. I played around with various formulas, but finally settled on the one below...

Year 2 projected wins = (year 1 actual wins) + [(year 1 overwins)^2/-4)]

I probably don't need to point out that this is only an approximation, but had it been used coming into this season, it would have predicted the following.

	'87 actual wins	'87 overwins	'88 predicted wins using above formula	1988 actual wins
Golden State	42	7.76	26.95	20
Philadelphia	45	4.60	39.71	36
Washington	42	5.21	35.21	38

These are the only teams who would have qualified for this predictive formula from 1987 to 1988. All three were winning teams, yet this formula predicted they would all lose ground substantially (they all did). The formula specifically said that they would go from averaging 43 wins each to averaging less than 34 wins. You could have gotten pretty good odds against that happening. As it turns out, they averaged 31.

It's certainly not flawless, as the records of the 1983 Boston Celtics and the 1984 Philadelphia 76ers reflect in the previous chart on the last page; however, it is a good, reliable tool. By this standard of measurement, the Los Angeles Lakers should win approximately five less games next year. That means they should only win 57 in 1988-89. The Lakers are the only team which fits the criterion for this formula as they overwon 4.45 games last season.

PREDICTIVE 2

Finally, I should say that the teams who underwon drastically in a particular year did not then improve their record as dramatically as teams who overwon deteriorated. Even so, there is a correlation which says if a team wins substantially less games than their play throughout the season indicated they should have, they will improve their wins the following year. Looking backwards at the teams who improved the most from year 1 to year 2 since 1981, the following list shows that in all but three cases, the team underwon the previous year.

	Year 1	Change In Actual Wins In Year 2	Underwins In Year 1
New Jersey	1981	+20	0
Houston	1984	+19	-3.1
Detroit	1981	+18	-1.2
Denver	**1988**	**+17**	**-1.6**
Atlanta	1985	+16	-2.6
Utah	1983	+15	+1.1
Indiana	1986	+15	-4.8
Denver	1984	+14	-.1
New York	**1988**	**+14**	**+1.0**
Dallas	1981	+13	-2.8
Golden State	1986	+12	-1.3
Detroit	1983	+12	-2.8
Cleveland	**1988**	**+11**	**-1.5**
Dallas	1986	+11	-.2
Atlanta	1981	+11	-.6

Clearly, a correlation exists between underwins in year 1 and actual wins in year 2. However, the relationship is less defined than its counterpart (overwins in year 1). The best I can come up with is a simple formula which says...

Year 3 projected wins = (year 2 actual wins) - [(year 1 underwins) * .5]

Up to this point I have needed to use Oliver's formula to establish overwins or underwins. Once I had those I could then plug them into PREDICTIVE 1 and PREDICTIVE 2 to speculate on a team's future performance. However, in PREDICTIVE 3 and PREDICTIVE 4 I do not plan to deal with *over*wins or *under*wins but only *actual* wins.

PREDICTIVE 3

The premise of this formula is simple: To the degree that a team loses an abnormally higher number of games from year 1 to year 2, they will regain a fairly large number of wins in year 3. Shown on the next page is a chart of all teams since 1980 who lost 10 or more games from year 1 to year 2 as well as what happened in year 3.

	Year 1	Actual wins Year 2 minus Year 1	Actual wins Year 3 minus Year 2
Houston	1982	-32	+15
New York	1984	-23	-1
Seattle	1980	-22	+18
LA Clippers	1986	-20	+5
Atlanta	1980	-19	+11
LA Clippers	1981	-19	+8
Denver	1979	-17	+7
New York	1981	-17	+11
San Antonio	1983	-16	+4
Washington	1979	-15	0
New Jersey	1986	-15	-5
Indiana	1982	-15	+6
Golden State	1982	-15	+7
Golden State	1984	-15	+8
Golden State	1979	-14	+15
Cleveland	1981	-13	+8
Philadelphia	1983	-13	+6
Phoenix	1983	-12	-5
Phoenix	1981	-11	+7
Seattle	1984	-11	0
New Jersey	1980	-10	+20
Sacramento	1981	-10	+15
Denver	1986	-10	+17

As you can see, 18 of the 23 times a team lost big in year 2 they rebounded in year 3. Twice there was no change, and 3 times the team continued to lose. On an average a team rebounded to win back half of what they lost. Specifically, the average team listed above won 15.83 less games in year 2, and then 7.70 more wins in year 3. Technically, an appropriate formula might say...

Projected wins in year 3 = [(year 2 wins minus year 1 wins)/-2] + year 2 wins

As you may have noticed, I used -2 instead of -2.06 which would technically be more accurate. Even so, it's only an approximation and only valid for the teams who drop the most in a given year.

In case you are wondering whether there is a difference between the teams who dropped 20 or more from the rest of the pack - there really isn't any. Also, if you wondered whether the quality of the teams above yielded different results - they really don't. The formula tends to be equally applicable to all teams who lose 10 or more games from year 1 to year 2, whether good or bad, and regardless of whether the team dropped 10 games, 15 games or 20 games.

Only the Golden State Warriors lost 10+ games from 1986 to 1987. In actuality, they lost 22 games, from 42 wins to 20 wins. By using the formula, they should rebound to win 31.5 games in 1988. It will be interesting to see if they do. It will really be interesting to see how they win that .5 game.

PREDICTIVE 4

The premise of this principle is as simple as *PREDICTIVE 3*: To the degree that a team wins an abnormally higher number of games from year 1 to year 2, they will regress somewhat in year 3. Listed on the following page are the top teams who improved the most since 1980 and what they did the following year.

Since 1980	Year 1	Chg in actual wins in year 2	Chg in actual wins in year 3
New Jersey	1981	+20	+5
Houston	1984	+19	+3
Detroit	1981	+18	-2
Atlanta	1985	+16	+7
Golden State	1980	+15	+6
Utah	1983	+15	-4
Indiana	1986	+15	-3
Chicago	1980	+15	-11
Denver	1984	+14	-5
Dallas	1981	+13	+10
Detroit	1983	+12	-3
Golden State	1986	+12	-22
New York	1980	+11	-17
San Antonio	1980	+11	-4
Dallas	1986	+11	-2
Chicago	1984	+11	-8
Milwaukee	1980	+11	-5

Twelve teams decreased, while 5 increased. On an average each team lost 3 more games than the year before. This is hardly conclusive, especially since 4 of the top 5 teams actually *gained* again in year 3. Still, the formula for teams who make the largest gains in year 2 would read:

Year 3 projected wins = (year 2 actual wins) - 3

One point should be made, however: six times a team has gained 11 or more wins from year 1 to year 2 without adding a major member of the team - either a coach or player. When I say major, I mean MAJOR - Lever, Person, Jordan, Olajuwon, or a new head coach. Of the 6 times that happened, only once (Atlanta 1987) did the team gain again in year 3. On an average, each of these teams lost roughly 6 games more in year 3 vs year 2.

SHOOTING FORMULAS

I have always been intrigued with shooting percentages. FG% and FT% are two very early creative statistics in the NBA. As you may remember from reading my introduction to this book, I discuss the definition of a creative statistic. Just to refresh your memory, a creative statistic is the product of more than one raw statistic, and a raw statistic is merely the sum of two or more numbers. Field-goals-made is a raw number - as is field-goal-attempts. Therefore, field goal percentage (FG/FGA) is a creative statistic. The interesting thing about FG% and FT% is that from the very beginning the NBA accepted these two creative stats. That is mildly surprising because they were not so willing to accept others which today are obvious. It wasn't until 1970 that the scoring champion was no longer the person who had accumulated the most points (raw), but rather the individual who had the highest scoring average (points/games - creative). That same year (1970) the assist winner and rebound winner became the one who had the most per-game, not the highest aggregate. Of course, I go another step and say the assist winner is the person who has the most assists per minutes-played.

What happened in 1970? I think the simple answer is intellectual maturity. Creative numbers were becoming less and less intimidating and more and more enlightening. No doubt it will continue to happen - and needs to. The NBA still has not removed 3-pt FG percentages from "FG%". This is ridiculous. Charles Barkley was the 2-pt FG% king last year at 63.0%, but he only ended up third because his high-risk 3-pt FG's were not removed. When you realize that FT% is related to only FT's and 3-pt FG% is related to only 3-pt FG's, why shouldn't 2-pt FG% be the same? Of course, it should be - and I'll bet everything I own it will be someday. Consequently, I keep 3 percentages. However, in various places throughout the book I use FG% the same way as the NBA does to avoid confusion. Even so, I mention, whenever appropriate, the top 2-pt FG% shooters.

As you know by now, I have devised a fourth formula which incorporates all three into one. What I wished to do was make up a formula which was relatively simple yet treated each shot fairly. That is why I arrived at...

MANLEY I = (Points + 1/3 Free Throws Made)/ Shots Attempted

...where shots-attempted equals the sum of all field goal attempts + free throw attempts. By using this formula, the top 10 in this composite shooting index were...

MANLEY I

		SHT	2Pt%	3Pt%	FT%
1.	Stockton	1.161	.594	.358	.840
2.	McHale	1.161	.604	0-0	.797
3.	Ainge	1.138	.534	.415	.878
4.	Bird	1.136	.546	.414	.916
5.	Parish	1.130	.590	0-1	.734
6.	Barkley	1.120	.630	.280	.751
7.	Scott	1.108	.554	.346	.858
8.	Mahorn	1.106	.574	.500	.756
9.	Price	1.103	.510	.486	.877
10.	Schayes	1.095	.542	0-2	.836

I thought it would be revealing to put out to the side the player's other percentages. In the case of 3-pointers, I showed both the raw numbers as well. The reason is because it is meaningless to say one player shot 10% while one shot 0%, if the one who shot 10% was 10 of 100 while the other was 0/0 or even 0/1 or 0/2. You see what I mean. I'm sure this list looks OK to most of you. We can all see that each of these players belongs way up there. But is this the best list that could exist? Actually, I believe the answer is yes and no.

If you look closely at MANLEY I you will realize that what the formula is saying is that if a player shoots his 3-pt FG's at 33.33% and his 2-pt field goals at 50% and his free throws at 75% then he will rate a 1.000. Half the players in the NBA are above 1.000 and half are below it. The reason is because 33.33% for 3-pt FG% is average or at least "ideal average"; 50% for 2-pt FG% is also average or at least "ideal average"; and 75% for FT's is average. The three numbers are actually 31.09%, 48.61% and 76.10%; however, a formula that used all these numbers would be much more complicated in its construction. Even so, the formula which is technically better than MANLEY I is...

MANLEY II = [1/x (3-pt FGM) + 1/y (2-pt FGM) + 1/z (FTM)] / Shots Attempted

...where shots attempted equals the sum of all field goal attempts + free throw attempts and where...

X = league 3 pt FG%
Y = league 2 pt FG%
Z = league FT%

30 BASKETBALL HEAVEN 1989

My thanks to Warren Johnson for his suggestion of MANLEY II. Perhaps it is difficult to see why the numerator of MANLEY II is very similar to MANLEY I, but it is. The differences are very minute. The problem with MANLEY I is that it is always the same even though the three different percentages might fluctuate. Since the argument for its usage is that each of the components are based on what the league averages are, then technically the league averages should be used - not just 33.33%, 50% and 75%. Even so, I use MANLEY I exclusively in this book. Why? First of all take a look at the chart below.

	MANLEY I				**MANLEY II**	
1.	Stockton	1.161		1.	Stockton	1.173
2.	McHale	1.161		2.	McHale	1.170
3.	Ainge	1.138		3.	Ainge	1.167
4.	Bird	1.136		4.	Bird	1.153
5.	Parish	1.130		5.	Parish	1.143
6.	Barkley	1.120		6.	Barkley	1.127
7.	Scott	1.108		7.	Scott	1.125
8.	Mahorn	1.106		8.	Hodges	1.124
9.	Price	1.103		9.	Price	1.122
10.	Schayes	1.095		10.	Mahorn	1.115

As you can see, it makes almost no difference in a player's rank. Theoretically it could, but it rarely does. The other reason why I prefer Manley I is the simplicity issue again. Just as my Production Formula so closely resembles some very complicated process which fractionalized each component, Manley I resembles Manley II. The simplicity variable changes very little, yet it makes the evaluation of shooting easy to calculate.

POLLACK I

Many years ago, Harvey Pollack, the famous stat man for the Philadelphia 76ers, developed a very simple shooting formula that was, at the time, nearly perfect...

$$POLLACK\ I = Points\ /\ (2FGA + FTA)$$

Since the 3 pointer did not exist, what this formula did was pretty good - of course there wasn't much to do. Unfortunately, this formula, even before the three pointer, was slightly skewed towards FT shooting. Consider the following example:

	2-pt FG	2-pt FGA	FT	FTA	FT%
Player A	30	60	11	16	(69%)
Player B	30	60	3	4	(75%)

Player A's rating is .522, yet player B (.508) appears to be the better shooter. After all, he's 6% better from the line. The problem with Pollack I is that the more FG's taken compared to FT's taken hurts the player. Perhaps you could argue "If you can get all your points from the line you're better off than getting them from the field". No one can deny that a legitimate element of shooting is intelligent shot selection - not just the percentage that go in. The problem with relying too heavily on that issue with respect to validating Pollack I is that free throws are usually not so much the result of a calculated effort on the part of the shooter, but rather fortune or luck. Of course, we all realize that Adrian Dantley, Charles Barkley, etc are going to go to the free throw line a lot regardless of luck. Clearly, in their case, it is a question of ability, talent and a concious decision to create a foul by taking it to the hole. So, although it is easier to envision mental decisions as part of the field goal process, it is also true for free throws as well - just not as great. That means it is valid to discuss this with respct to Pollack I and that this formula may be totally valid given the rather obscure and difficult to measure ability to draw fouls. Therefore, Pollack I is basically OK with me.

FANCY FORMULAS 31

MANLEY I		MANLEY II		POLLACK I	
1. Stockton	1.161	1. Stockton	1.173	1. Barkley	.644
2. McHale	1.161	2. McHale	1.170	2. McHale	.641
3. Ainge	1.138	3. Ainge	1.167	3. Stockton	.632
4. Bird	1.136	4. Bird	1.153	4. Schayes	.619
5. Parish	1.130	5. Parish	1.143	5. Cartwright	.617
6. Barkley	1.120	6. Barkley	1.127	6. Parish	.609
7. Scott	1.108	7. Scott	1.125	7. Mahorn	.608
8. Mahorn	1.106	8. Hodges	1.124	8. Donaldson	.602
9. Price	1.103	9. Price	1.122	9. Dantley	.601
10. Schayes	1.095	10. Mahorn	1.115	10. Bird	.599

Still, consider the following example. Let's say two players had exactly the same number of 2-pt FG's and 2-pt FGA's. Also they had the same number of FT's and FTA's. The only differences were in the 3-pt shooting categories.

	3-pt FG/FGA	2-pt FG/FGA	FT/FTA
Player A	34/100	30/60	12/16
Player B	0/1	30/60	12/16

As you can see, technically player A is a better shooter than player B, if for no other reason than player A exceeded the league average in 3 pt shooting - whether it is 33.33% or 31.09% as I discussed earlier. Player B shot worse than the league average. Even so, Pollack I shows player A at a rating (Pollack's term "percent of potential") of .518 while player B has a rating of .522. How can player B be ahead of player A? Because the more 3 point FG's player A takes, the bigger the percentage he must make to compare favorably with player B. If player A had taken 1000 3-pt FGA's, he would have had to hit 345 to achieve the same .518, not the 340 you or I would have assumed.

As I say, this is a very small difference and Pollack I is simple to calculate so I like it alright. What is really strange to me and others who have seen it is why Pollack made a change in Pollack I. I understand what his intentions were, but it fails miserably...

POLLACK II = PTS/[2(2-pt FGA) + 3(3-pt FGA) + FTA]

It sort of makes sense when you first look at it. Before the 3 pointer, Pollack I said...

[2(2-pt FGM) + 1(FTM)] / [2(2-pt FGA) + 1 (FTA)]

Of course this is exactly the same as Pollack I stated earlier. The numerator of this version is just equal to points while the denominator is just written differently. However, as you look

MANLEY I		MANLEY II		POLLACK I		POLLACK II	
1. Stockton	1.161	1. Stockton	1.173	1. Barkley	.644	1. McHale	.641
2. McHale	1.161	2. McHale	1.170	2. McHale	.641	2. Schayes	.619
3. Ainge	1.138	3. Ainge	1.167	3. Stockton	.632	3. Cartwright	.617
4. Bird	1.136	4. Bird	1.153	4. Schayes	.619	4. Barkley	.616
5. Parish	1.130	5. Parish	1.143	5. Cartwright	.617	5. Stockton	.610
6. Barkley	1.120	6. Barkley	1.127	6. Parish	.609	6. Parish	.609
7. Scott	1.108	7. Scott	1.125	7. Mahorn	.608	7. Mahorn	.607
8. Mahorn	1.106	8. Hodges	1.124	8. Donaldson	.602	8. Donaldson	.602
9. Price	1.103	9. Price	1.122	9. Dantley	.601	9. Dantley	.600
10. Schayes	1.095	10. Mahorn	1.115	10. Bird	.599	10. Salley	.598

at the previous formula, doesn't it seem logical to just add 3(3-pt FGM) to the numerator and 3(3-pt FGA) to the denominator? If you do - you get Pollack II. It's no surprise that he came up with it. Despite the natural progression, Pollack II is very, very wrong. Take a look at the list at the bottom of the previous page.

Just because it doesn't mirror the others does not automatically justify its rejection. However, look at Pollack II's top-20 only. Do you notice anything? There are no 3-point shooters. Why? The flaw is that any 3-point shooter is going to be seriously penalized every time he takes one (unless he hits an unbelievably high percentage). Whereas Pollack II gives 3 times the credit for every made 3-pointer, he is also giving 3 times the fault for every missed 3-pointer - and most 3-pointers are missed. A missed 3-pointer is bad, but not worse than any other missed shot. He is giving 3 times the credit for it going in, but his "penalty" should be the fact that one makes a lower percentage - not 3 times the fault if it misses, which it usually does. A classic case of the flaw is the following example.

POLLACK II	3-pt FG%	2-pt FG%	FT%
Adrian Dantley (#9)*	0.0%	51.6%	86.0%
Danny Ainge (#100)	41.5%	53.4%	87.8%

* Rankings are based on meeting certain qualification requirements.

How can Adrian Dantley be ahead of Danny Ainge? He's behind in every shooting category. Ainge ranks very high in each of these 3 categories and is #3 in MANLEY I, #3 in MANLEY II, and #16 in POLLACK I. The reason Dantley is ahead is because he only shot two 3-point field goals - making none. Thus he wasn't penalized very much. Danny Ainge set an all time record by hitting 148 3-pointers. He even shot an excellent 41.5% from downtown. In the next section, you will see that Ainge was the most productive 3-point shooter in the NBA. Yet, in POLLACK II he was penalized for his great shooting. And when I say penalized, I mean penalized! How can Ainge rank #100? Clearly that doesn't make sense. Consequently, POLLACK II is so flawed that it should not be further analyzed.

SHOOTING EFFICIENCY

Another major aspect of shooting is how efficient players are. It's one thing to say that player A shot 2-pointers at a 60% rate and player B shot 2-pointers at a 55% rate, thus player A is a superior 2-point shooter. Fine, I can live with that. But what if player A was 6 out of 10 and player B was 55 out of 100. Who was the most efficient? I plan to show that player B was more efficient. Does this mean I would rather have player B (all other things being equal)? I can't say because I don't know why player A didn't shoot more often. I'm only concerned with who was most efficient and that was player B. Why?

Let's suppose that the average 2-point FG% in the NBA is 50%. The question is which player made more points for his team than he should have? The simple formula is...

2-point efficiency points = (2-pt FGM times 1/z) - 2-pt FGA

...where z = the league 2-pt field goal percentage. In this hypothetical case, player A would score +10 2-pt efficiency points [(55 X 2) - 100] while player B would score +2 2-pt efficiency points [(6 X 2) - 10]. The point here is that, in a way, it is reasonable to say player B is a "better" 2-pt field goal shooter than player A despite a lower percentage. Let's face it, a player may have a better percentage, but not shoot as often as he should. Consequently, he is less valuable as a shooter.

Of course, the other side of not shooting enough is shooting too much. One player may have a lower percentage than another, but not shoot as often. As a result, he doesn't hurt his team as much, so he is a "better" shooter despite a lower percentage.

Let me give you one final example. This is a real case scenario involving 3-pt shooters. Craig Hodges led the NBA with a .491 percentage (86/175). Danny Ainge was 6th with a .415 percentage (148/357). Even though Hodge's percent is substantially superior to Ainge's, both are very good. The question is, "Who was the more efficient shooter?" Maybe a better way of putting it is, "Who made their team more points than should have been expected based on the number of shots taken (possessions risked)?" By asking it that way it really does come down to a question of efficiency. After all, every team wants the most out of each possession. If you normally expect one point per possession, then to the degree that a player improves on that by his shooting, he was a benefit to the team.

Craig Hodges was +97.59 on 3-pt efficiency points, while Ainge was +112.10. This is based on a league average of 31.55% from 3-point land. It simply means Ainge was more efficient. In fact, he made his team nearly 15 more points over the course of the season than did Hodges. He knew that his 3-point shooting was an advantage and, although he didn't have as big an advantage as Hodges, he more than made up for it by making substantially greater use of what advantage he had (twice as many 3-point attempts).

I don't think it is right or fair, however, to say Ainge was a *better* 3-point shooter than Hodges. I let that phrase go unchallenged a few paragraphs back, but now we're talking about real people, not player A and player B. Besides *better* implies that Ainge is smarter and realizes he should shoot more. It ignores the possibility that Hodges' team may not play him as much or may not allow him as free a rein. Additionally, it doesn't deal with whether Ainge may be more open from 3 point country because Boston has the "greatest front line in the history of the NBA". All of these reasons prohibit saying Ainge is a *better* 3-point shooter than Hodges, but they have nothing to do with whether Ainge is a more *efficient* 3-point shooter than Hodges, only that he was. The reasons are another subject.

Shown below and on the next page are 8 lists. Each list shows either the top or bottom players at each of the 3 shooting categories (3-pt, 2-pt, and FT). The final two lists are the top and bottom players who have scored the most total positive or negative efficiency points.

The moral of this story is those at the top have done the best job of combining a *good* shooting percentage in a category with a *high* quantity of attempts while those at the bottom have done the worst job, combining a *poor* shooting percentage in a category with a *high* quantity of attempts. If nothing else can be said in all this, it is that Michael Jordan (7/53) should quit shooting so many 3-pointers, Joe Barry Carroll (.436) should quit shooting so many 2-pointers, and Dennis Rodman should avoid the foul line like the plague. Oh, and Mark Eaton... just don't pass him the ball.

2-PT FG EFFICIENCY POINTS

	TOP 10			BOTTOM 10	
1.	Barkley	+320	1.	Carroll	-102
2.	Jordan	+221	2.	A. King	-95
3.	McHale	+211	3.	Gminski	-94
4.	Bird	+162	4.	H. Williams	-92
5.	Ewing	+158	5.	R. Williams	-85
6.	Stockton	+153	6.	Wingate	-81
7.	Scott	+153	7.	Eaton	-80
8.	Parish	+153	8.	V. Johnson	-78
9.	Berry	+141	9.	Dailey	-78
10.	B. Williams	+117	10.	Bogues	-78

3-PT EFFICIENCY POINTS

	TOP 10			BOTTOM 10	
1.	Ainge	+112	1.	Jordan	-31
2.	Hodges	+98	2.	Floyd	-28
3.	Ellis	+80	3.	Leavell	-28
4.	Price	+80	4.	Jackson	-25
5.	Bird	+74	5.	J.S. Williams	-22
6.	M. Adams	+62	6.	Woodson	-21
7.	G. Henderson	+56	7.	Ea. Johnson	-21
8.	Tucker	+52	8.	Lever	-19
9.	Long	+31	9.	Barkley	-18
10.	Tripucka	+24	10.	Ed. Johnson	-18

FT EFFICIENCY POINTS

	TOP 10			BOTTOM 10	
1.	Bird	+68	1.	Rodman	-66
2.	Jordan	+64	2.	Berry	-53
3.	Gminski	+55	3.	G. Anderson	-53
4.	Sikma	+54	4.	K. Malone	-52
5.	Dantley	+54	5.	B. Williams	-51
6.	J. Malone	+44	6.	West	-48
7.	Ea. Johnson	+42	7.	S. Johnson	-45
8.	Blackman	+41	8.	Norman	-43
9.	D. Wilkins	+39	9.	T. Cummings	-41
10.	Woodson	+35	10.	Olajuwon	-39

TOTAL SHOOTING EFFICIENCY

	TOP 20			BOTTOM 20	
1.	Bird	+304	1.	Eaton	-107
2.	Barkley	+288	2.	V. Johnson	-105
3.	Jordan	+254	3.	R. Williams	-105
4.	McHale	+225	4.	Carroll	-104
5.	Scott	+200	5.	H. Williams	-103
6.	Ainge	+188	6.	Wingate	-91
7.	Stockton	+186	7.	A. King	-91
8.	Ellis	+160	8.	Hopson	-88
9.	Parish	+144	9.	Bogues	-83
10.	Price	+141	10.	Jackson	-82
11.	Ewing	+131	11.	Dailey	-81
12.	Worthy	+108	12.	Frank	-80
13.	Porter	+105	13.	S. Green	-79
14.	Mullin	+103	14.	Sampson	-71
15.	Schayes	+102	15.	Cage	-69
16.	Higgens	+99	16.	G. Wilkins	-69
17.	Dantley	+97	17.	Robinson	-68
18.	M. Adams	+93	18.	Floyd	-67
19.	Drexler	+91	19.	Valentine	-64
20.	Berry	+88	20.	J. Edwards	-63

Harvey Catchings of the Philadelphia 76ers
- In 11 years in the NBA his highest average was 4.7 ppg (1979)
- Basketball Hall of Fame -

CHAPTER 3

TEAM BY TEAM ANALYSIS

NEW JERSEY VS PHILADELPHIA

On March 23, 1979, the New Jersey Nets and Philadelphia 76ers replayed the last 17 minutes of a game played nearly 5 months earlier. The Nets had protested the first game because of a rule violation by the officials. During that game, 3 technical fouls were whistled against both the Nets' coach (Kevin Loughery) and their star player (Bernard King). Since the rules state only 2 technicals can be called against any one player or coach, the game was rescheduled. The 76ers led at the point of protest 84-81 and went on to win the game 123-117.

Ironically, four players helped both sides win the game. In the span between the two games, each team traded two players to the other. Eric Money and Al Skinner went from New Jersey to Philadelphia while the 76ers traded Ralph Simpson and Harvey Catchings to the Nets. All four players were listed twice in the box scores - as though they had played against themselves. Not surprisingly, this is the only time in NBA history that this has happened.

38 BASKETBALL HEAVEN 1989

TEAM BY TEAM ANALYSIS

On the following 188 pages you will find an analysis of each of the 25 teams in the NBA. Each team has eight pages dedicated to it (except for the two expansion teams, which have two). Each of the eight pages lists specific information which is consistent from team to team.

It was my intention when developing this chapter to provide the most comprehensive analysis of each team in the NBA as possible. I have provided a short history of the franchise, various overviews of the previous year, and a look into the future. Moreover, I've attempted to create and provide as much unique statistical information regarding each of these areas as I could.

Page 1: The first of the four pages recounts a brief history of the team. I try to mention several highlights, while assessing various categories for comparison purposes. I've also put together an "All-Time" team for each of the 23 franchises. This is based on a player's total accumulated credits (CRD) (see chapter 1 for definition of CREDITS). Each of a player's credits are added up for every year he played with that club. This total is shown as CRD. Wilt Chamberlain is on the All-Time teams for three separate franchises (Warriors #1, 76ers #7, and Lakers #8). Bill Russell has the highest CRD for one team (Celtics, 30,533).

You may notice a discrepancy between certain player's spans and their years (Yrs) with the team. An example would be Mickey Johnson with the Chicago Bulls. He was with the team five years, but I only show four years. The reason is because he only played thirty-eight games his first year and failed to qualify. A second example is Rick Barry with the Warriors. Barry played with the club for thirteen years, but is only credited for eight years with the team. The reason is that, after beginning with the Warriors, Barry sat out one year and spent four more in the ABA. He then resumed his NBA career with the club.

I also picked the All-Time Coach for each franchise. The statistical information associated with the individual, just as with a player's CDR rating, is only his numbers with *that* team, not those accumulated over his entire career.

Page 2: This was a difficult page to do because, with only a few exceptions (most notably Indiana - the ultimate mediocre team), there were many more highlights last year than I could cram into one page. When appropriate, I tried to include what I could in the team overview.

Page 3: On this page I try to show the subtleties of which players most influenced their team's winning and losing and how they did it. Some of the abbreviations may not be apparent. They are listed below.

SCR	= Scoring	DNP	= Did not play	SF	= Small Forward
REB	= Rebounds	PG	= Point Guard	PF	= Power Forward
AST	= Assist	OG	= Off Guard	C	= Center

In the first section I show the record by the team when a player led in each category. Since there may be more than one leader in a game, a particular vertical column will usually add up to more than 41. (I break each column down by both home and away - 41 games each.) Additionally, I chose only to analyze the top-10 players on the team because I believe that fringe players rarely ever offer anything interesting to look at statistically. In the extreme case that they did, I tried to refer to them in the overview section for the team.

Page 4: On the fourth page, I have given both the raw numbers from last year and the rankings for each player based on those numbers. About the only thing that might need clarification on this page is to explain the column headings and to make sure the reader understands that the shaded-in areas represent a player's rank. The second group shows his rank by all players who qualified (see pages 272 for qualification requirements). The 3rd group shows his rank by players at his position only. The abbreviations are listed on the following page.

MIN	= Minutes	TO	= Turnovers
PF	= Personal Fouls	G	= Games Played
DQ	= Disqualifications	GS	= Games Started
HI	= High Scoring Game Of The Year	PPG	= Points Per Game
PR	= Production Rating (see page 3 for explanation)		
SC	= Scoring Rank (per game basis)		
SH	= Shooting Rank (see page 28 for discussion)		
RB	= Above - Total Rebounds	Below - Rankings (48 min basis)	
AS	= Above - Total Assists	Below - Rankings (48 min basis)	
BL	= Above - Total Blocks	Below - Rankings (48 min basis)	
ST	= Above - Total Steals	Below - Rankings (48 min basis)	

Page 5: On the fifth page is a weekly power rating chart for each team as well as the value and rank of 32 categories. There are a couple of interesting things about the chart which separates it from other attempts at showing a team's running strength. First of all, I converted the power rating to a scale of 0 wins to 82 wins. The formula to do this is very complicated and certainly not linear. The last thing of interest is that on any given week, the rating represents the level of play the team had been exhibiting for approximately the previous three weeks. This allows the chart to more graphically show hot and cold stretches. A true power rating would fluctuate very little past mid season. More often than not it would reach an equilibrium and appear more as a general trend up or down.

The 32 categories are mostly self-explanatory, however, I should explain that, under attendance, the notation K means thousand. Also key-man-games missed represent my determination of who is a critical player. The league keeps man-games missed due to injury. There are two problems with this. The first is, despite rumors to the contrary, all men are not created equal. If Magic Johnson misses 10 games, but Brad Lohaus misses 20 - which team was hurt the worst? The other problem is that I don't distinguish as to why a player missed a game. Whether due to a family problem, or an injury or something else, the point is, he's not playing. Probably, the only other thing I need to mention on this page are the last four categories - rebounding, assists, FG%, & FT%. These records are the times a particular team did better than their opponents vs those times they were not as good.

Page 6: Column headings for the roster

J#	= Jersey Number
R#	= Round number in the draft the player was selected
D#	= Player's actual draft selection number
HT	= Height
WT	= Weight
Atla	= Number of years with his club (in this case Atlanta)
NBA	= Number of years played in NBA or ABA

Pages 7 & 8: Although I call these pages over*views*, they really represent re*views* of 1987/88 and pre*views* of 1988/89. However you look at it, I offer my *views* on strengths and weaknesses, good moves and bad. Mostly, I try to bring together the important statistical information on the proceeding pages. I hope the overviews are interesting to read. Here is the ultimate place in the book where the fun and excitement of creative statistics can be seen. I will have achieved that goal only if I create emotion - laughter, anticipation, controversy, anger, or fascination. Lastly, I resort to the traditional predictions. But even there, I vary from the mainstream by giving a best case and worst case scenario.

Atlanta Hawks .... History

The Atlanta Hawks - originally called the Buffalo Bisons - began as a franchise in 1947. From Buffalo, the club moved to Davenport, Milwaukee, and St. Louis before arriving in Atlanta in 1968.

The club's coaches have been less secure during the past 41 years than the city of Atlanta in 1864. Twenty-three generals have led their troops into battle - more than for any other franchise. Twenty-two have surrendered to superior forces. Mike Fratello is the latest to take command.

The franchise boasts five Hall-Of-Famers who have, at one time or another, coached the team. This record exceeds that of any other club as well. Interestingly, the three with winning records [Slater Martin (5-3), Andy Phillip (6-4), and Bob Pettit (4-2)] were interim coaches and, although known as great players, were not known for their coaching. The other two were among the greatest coaches ever. Both Red Auerbach and Red Holzman had records that ended in the "red". Auerbach was 28-29 while Holzman was 83-120 for the club. Ironically, it was each coach's only losing stint in their NBA coaching career.

Probably the greatest coach ever for Atlanta was Richie Guerin. Guerin guided the team from 1964-1972 and took it to the playoffs every year.

The Hawks have advanced beyond the regular season 29 times despite having a winning record in only 19 seasons. Though a fairly large number, the 29 post-season trips have yielded only 4 NBA finals appearances. All four times the club was located in St. Louis and the opponent was Boston. The Celtics won three of the four, but the one championship the franchise brought home was unique and special for both teams.

In 1958, St. Louis battled Boston to a hard-fought 6-game championship series. The Blackhawks, as they were called at the time, were attempting to pay back the Celtics for the previous year's loss in the finals. That series had gone to seven games, with Boston winning the 7th game by two points in double overtime. The next year, St. Louis won the clinching game 110-109 as Bob Pettit scored an (at the time) NBA playoff high 50 points. The loss was significant for Boston's center, Bill Russell, and coach Red Auerbach. Russell, who was injured during this series, lost his only championship in his *first* 10 years while the loss was Auerbach's only non-championship of his *last* ten years.

Quiz: What team originally drafted Dominique Wilkins?

ALL TIME HAWKS' TEAM

Player	Span	Yrs	CRD
Bob Pettit	1955-65	11	24,638
Bill Bridges	1963-71	9	15,366
Lou Hudson	1967-77	11	13,870
Cliff Hagan	1957-66	10	13,558
Wayne Rollins	1978-88	11	11,540
John Drew	1975-82	8	11,084
Dominique Wilkins	1983-88	6	10,443
Dan Roundfield	1979-84	6	9,598
Lenny Wilkens	1961-68	8	9,442
Eddie Johnson Jr.	1978-85	8	8,864

ALL TIME HAWKS' COACH

Richie Guerin	8 Years
26-34 Playoffs	8 Playoffs
327-291 Reg. Season	0 Championships

HISTORICAL PROFILE

Category	Data
Hawks' Coach	Mike Fratello
Years coached Atlanta	5
# of franchise years	42
# of coaches	23
# of winning seasons	19
# of playoff years	29
# of runner's up	3
# of championships	1
Regular season win %	49.8
Playoffs win %	45.9

**Answer:
Utah Jazz**

Atlanta Hawks .... 1987-88 Highlights

Hawks 108-98 Bulls   Tue.   December 29, 1987

The win, coupled with Detroit's loss, gave the Hawks their first exclusive ownership of 1st place in the Central Division since they were 2-0 in early November. The win was also Atlanta's 13th in 15 games, while Chicago was losing their 5th in a row. Michael Jordan outscored Dominique Wilkins 39-26 as the last two scoring champions continued their personal battle. Ironically, the leading scorer between the two has been on the losing side six straight times. Mike Fratello won his 200th NBA game and Doc Rivers registered his 1st career triple double and the first by a Hawk since 1983.

Hawks 81-71 Pistons   Tue.   January 5, 1988

The battle between the Midwest Division's two powerhouses became the league's toughest defensive struggle of the year. That was no surprise for Atlanta, winner of 11 of 12 games and leading the NBA in defense, but it was a shock for Detroit. Ironically, the Pistons were 2nd in the NBA in offensive scoring at the time (116 ppg) and had just come off a 151-142 game vs Denver (2nd highest scoring game of 87/88). What made the victory more impressive was the fact that the 71 points represented a franchise low scoring total for Detroit.

Hawks 106-94 Bulls   Tue.   January 19, 1988

The game was significant for several reasons. Dominique Wilkins outscored Michael Jordan 41-38, but it was Wilkins' 24 first quarter points which were most notable as they represented an Omni record. Randy Wittman and Doc Rivers both had double digit assists which represents the only time the Hawks accomplished that feat last season. For Wittman, his 12 assists set a career record, while Rivers' 10 assists helped him register his 2nd triple-double of the year - ironically, both vs Chicago.

Hawks 118-111 Nets   Sun.   January 24, 1988

The victory was especially important to Hawks' coach Mike Fratello. By winning, the Hawks' record went to 29-11, 1/2 game better than the Boston Celtics 28-11. That meant Fratello would replace K.C. Jones as the coach of the East All-Stars, a position Jones had held four straight years. The loss increased New Jersey's winless road record to 0-16.

Hawks 112-110 76ers   Tue.   February 9, 1988

The two point margin mirrored the number by which Dominique Wilkins outscored Charles Barkley (49-47). Despite the high scoring matchup, both players led their team in rebounding as well. Barkley had 15, Wilkins 12. The deeper irony was that this was the first game after the All-Star break and these two players were less than thrilled with the weekend. Wilkins lost the slam-dunk championship on controversial voting in the final round, while Barkley played only 14 minutes and proclaimed he would not be back again except as a starter. Obviously, both had something to prove.

Hawks 120-106 Mavericks   Tue.   March 29, 1988

The Atlanta Hawks knocked off the Midwest division-leading Dallas Mavericks on the strength of a 40 point performance by Dominique Wilkins and 17 assists by Doc Rivers. The most interesting notes were those applied to Dallas. The Hawks became the first team to sweep the season series against Dallas. They also ended two Mav's streaks, both the NBA's longest. No player had scored 40+ points vs Dallas since 1986 and 2) Dallas' mild mannered coach, John MacLeod, who was ejected during the game, had not prematurely hit the showers in nearly 9 years.

Atlanta Hawks . . . . Influence on Winning

TEAM RECORD BY

PLAYER	GAMES	SCR Leader HOME	SCR Leader ROAD	REB Leader HOME	REB Leader ROAD	AST Leader HOME	AST Leader ROAD
Dominique Wilkins	78	24-11	15-16	5-2	5-2	1-0	0-1
Glenn Rivers	80	1-0	2-3	0-1	2-0	24-7	16-17
Cliff Levingston	82	---	0-1	7-2	2-4	---	0-1
Kevin Willis	75	2-0	2-2	13-4	7-6	---	---
Wayne Rollins	76	---	---	8-1	3-6	---	---
Randy Wittman	82	3-0	1-0	---	---	1-0	1-1
Jon Koncak	49	---	---	4-1	4-3	---	---
Antoine Carr	80	---	---	3-0	0-1	---	---
John Battle	67	1-0	---	---	---	1-1	0-1
Spud Webb	82	---	---	---	---	3-4	2-1

TEAM RECORD BY SCORING *

PLAYER	PLAY	DNP	0-9	10-19	20-29	30-39	40+
Dominique Wilkins	48-30	2-2	0-2	7-4	11-10	19-10	11-4
Glenn Rivers	49-31	1-1	10-6	34-18	4-7	1-0	---
Cliff Levingston	50-32	---	21-20	27-10	2-2	---	---
Kevin Willis	44-31	6-1	17-14	22-12	5-5	---	---
Wayne Rollins	47-29	3-3	42-26	4-3	1-0	---	---
Randy Wittman	50-32	---	16-20	33-12	1-0	---	---
Jon Koncak	32-17	18-15	25-17	6-0	1-0	---	---
Antoine Carr	48-32	2-0	27-20	20-10	1-2	---	---
John Battle	43-24	7-8	23-9	15-14	5-1	---	---
Spud Webb	50-32	---	44-24	6-8	---	---	---

TEAM RECORD BY STARTING POSITION *

PLAYER	GAMES	STARTS	PG	OG	SF	PF	C
Dominique Wilkins	78	76	---	---	47-29	---	---
Glenn Rivers	80	80	49-31	---	---	---	---
Cliff Levingston	82	32	---	---	3-3	17-8	1-0
Kevin Willis	75	55	---	---	---	32-23	---
Wayne Rollins	76	59	---	---	---	---	37-22
Randy Wittman	82	82	---	50-32	---	---	---
Jon Koncak	49	22	---	---	---	---	12-10
Antoine Carr	80	2	---	---	---	1-1	---
John Battle	67	1	0-1	---	---	---	---
Spud Webb	82	1	1-0	---	---	---	---

* For further definition of each category and column heading see pages 38 & 39.

Atlanta Hawks . . . . 1987-88 Statistics

RAW NUMBERS *

PLAYER	2pt%	3pt%	FT%	MIN	PF	DQ	HI	TO	RB	AS	BL	ST
Dominique Wilkins	.476	.295	.826	**2948**	162	0	**51**	218	502	224	47	103
Glenn Rivers	.460	.273	.758	2502	272	3	37	210	366	**747**	41	**140**
Cliff Levingston	**.557**	**.500**	.772	2135	**287**	5	29	94	504	71	84	52
Kevin Willis	.520	0-2	.649	2091	240	2	27	138	**547**	28	41	68
Wayne Rollins	.512	0-0	**.875**	1765	229	2	20	51	459	20	**132**	31
Randy Wittman	.478	0-0	.798	2412	117	0	20	82	170	302	18	50
Jon Koncak	.488	0-2	.610	1073	161	1	25	53	333	19	56	36
Antoine Carr	.546	.250	.780	1483	272	7	24	116	289	103	83	38
John Battle	.458	.390	.750	1227	84	0	27	75	113	158	5	31
Spud Webb	.496	.053	.817	1347	125	0	14	131	146	337	12	63

OVERALL RANKINGS *

PLAYER	G	GS	PPG	PR	RANK	SC	SH	RB	AS	BL	ST
Dominique Wilkins	78	76	**30.73**	24.27	12	2	87	84	91	81	64
Glenn Rivers	80	80	14.17	**20.36**	30	64	131	92	3	78	19
Cliff Levingston	**82**	32	9.99	**13.78**	90	109	14	47	151	28	118
Kevin Willis	75	55	11.61	**13.33**	96	94	82	24	158	64	75
Wayne Rollins	76	59	4.42	**10.39**	125	157	28	25	159	7	143
Randy Wittman	**82**	**82**	10.04	**10.39**	126	108	109	152	49	115	132
Jon Koncak	49	22	5.69	**10.45**	DNQ						
Antoine Carr	80	2	8.81	**10.32**	DNQ						
John Battle	67	1	10.64	**8.40**	DNQ						
Spud Webb	82	1	5.98	**8.32**	DNQ						

POSITION RANKINGS *

PLAYER	POSITION	RANK	SC	SH	RB	AS	BL	ST
Dominique Wilkins	Small Forward (SF)	3	1	19	21	20	21	12
Glenn Rivers	Point Guard (PG)	5	9	27	3	3	2	10
Cliff Levingston	Power Forward (PF)	19	23	4	23	33	9	23
Kevin Willis	Power Forward (PF)	21	18	19	11	35	22	9
Wayne Rollins	Center (C)	26	26	6	13	26	6	17
Randy Wittman	Off Guard (OG)	22	22	21	31	15	20	32
Jon Koncak	Center (C)	DNQ						
Antoine Carr	Power Forward (PF)	DNQ						
John Battle	Off Guard (OG)	DNQ						
Spud Webb	Point Guard (PG)	DNQ						

*For further definition of each category and column heading see pages 38 & 39.

44 BASKETBALL HEAVEN 1989

Atlanta Hawks ....Team Info

WEEKLY POWER RATING

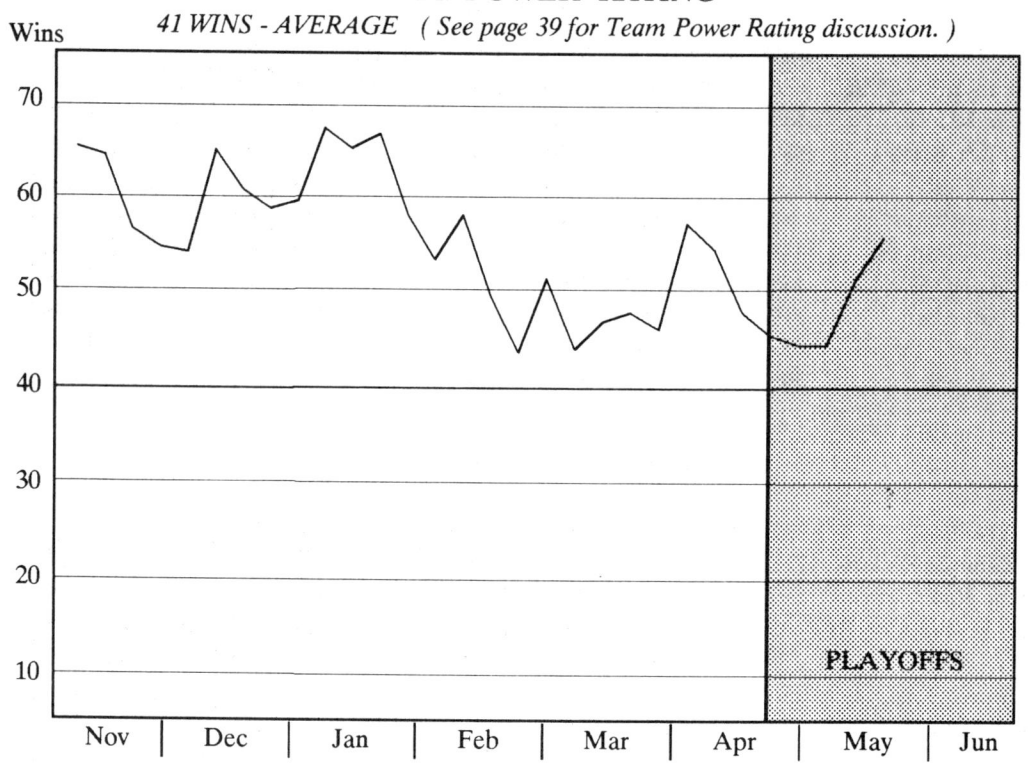

41 WINS - AVERAGE (See page 39 for Team Power Rating discussion.)

Wins axis: 10–70, Months: Nov, Dec, Jan, Feb, Mar, Apr, May, Jun (May–Jun shaded as PLAYOFFS)

Miscellaneous Categories	Data	Rank
Attendance	583K	8
Key-Man Games Missed	69	11
Season Record	50-32	7
- Home	30-11	11
- Road	20-21	3
Eastern Conference	35-23	6
Western Conference	15-9	8
Overtime Record	3-1	3
Record 5 Pts. or Less	11-12	14
Record 10 Pts. or More	27-15	9
Games Won By Bench	7	5
Games Won By Starters	2	19
Winning Streak	7	7
Losing Streak	4	4
Home Winning Streak	15	2
Road Winning Streak	3	9
Home Losing Streak	3	14
Road Losing Streak	4	1

Performance Categories	Data	Rank
Offensive Scoring (per game)	107.9	13
Defensive Scoring (per game)	104.3	4
Scoring Margin (per game)	3.6	8
Defensive FG%	.471	6
Offensive 2-point%	.492	10
Offensive 3-point%	.301	14
Offensive Free Throw %	.767	12
Offensive Rebs (Off REB/Opp Def REB)		5
Defensive Rebs (Def REB/Opp Off REB)		13
Offensive Assists (AST/FGMade)		13
Offensive Blocks (BLK/Opp FGAttempted)		2
Offensive Steals (STL/Game)		19
Turnover Margin (Off T.O. - Def T.O.)		4
Finesse (BLK + STL) / PF		13
Rebounding Record	41-39-2	11
Assists Record	46-36-0	9
Field Goal Pct. Record	49-32-1	5
Free Throw Pct. Record	40-42-0	13

Atlanta Hawks .... Miscellaneous

ADMINISTRATIVE INFORMATION

Team Offices: 100 Techwood Drive, NW
Atlanta, Georgia
30303

Telephone: (404) 681-3600
Head Coach: Mike Fratello
Home Arena: The Omni
Capacity: 16,572

1988-89 ROSTER*

J#	VETERANS	COLLEGE	POS	R#	D#	HT	WT	Atla	NBA
12	John Battle	Rutgers	G	4	84	6-2	175	3	3
35	Antoine Carr	Wichita State	F	1	8	6-9	235	4	4
32	Jon Koncak	SMU	C	1	5	7-0	260	3	3
53	Cliff Levingston	Wichita State	F	1	9	6-8	220	4	6
	Moses Malone	None	C	3	22	6-10	255	0	14
25	Glenn Rivers	Marquette	G	2	31	6-4	185	5	5
24	Reggie Theus	UNLV	G	1	9	6-7	205	0	10
4	Spud Webb	N. Carolina State	G	4	87	5-7	135	3	3
21	Dominique Wilkins	Georgia	F	1	3	6-8	200	6	6
42	Kevin Willis	Michigan State	F-C	1	11	7-0	235	4	4
8	Chris Washburn	N. Carolina State	C	1	3	6-11	255	1	2
1	Leon Wood	Fullerton State	G	1	10	6-3	183	1	4

ROOKIES	COLLEGE	POS	R#	D#	HT
Anthony Taylor	Oregon	G	2	44	6-4
Jorge Gonzalez	Argentina Nat. Team	C	3	54	7-6
Darryl Middleton	Baylor	F	3	68	6-9

* For further definition of category and column headings, see pages 38 & 39.

Atlanta Hawks .... Overview

The Hawks were a disappointment in 1987-88 to be sure. But how disappointing were they? Of the 14 preseason publications, 7 picked them to be first in their division, 7 second, and none third. As it turned out, the club tied for second and third. Though 50 wins is a pretty solid year, it is 7 wins worse than the previous year. Only Milwaukee and Phoenix (-8), Philly (-9), and Golden State (-22) were worse. Actually, I consider Atlanta to have had the third most disappointing year in the NBA, behind Indiana (#1) and Golden State (#2). The reason is simple.

Any team which drops 7 games with essentially the same players - most of whom had not reached their prime - and has lost fewer key-man games (see page 44) than the year before, has to be considered a disappointment. I felt confident that the Hawks would be unbeatable in the division and would challenge Boston in the conference. In fact, it seemed reasonable that by playoff time Atlanta's youth would defeat Boston's age. But, as we know, it didn't work out that way.

Why? Well, first of all, it's obvious that the Hawks had problems at the guard position. On the surface any team with Doc Rivers (#5 at point guard) and Randy Wittman can't be too bad - especially with two outstanding players coming off the bench (Webb and Battle). Depth was no problem on the team. As a matter of fact, depth is probably Atlanta's strongest suit. Many have argued the Hawks are the deepest team in the league. Still, the guard situation is problematic, primarily at Off-Guard. As long as opponents can double-team Dominique Wilkins, the Hawks are in trouble. Unfortunately, they were able to do it all too often last season. The reason? Randy Wittman was unable to consistently pop the perimeter jumper as he had done in the past. During 1987-88, Wittman shot .478 - the lowest of his 5 year career. Had he shot only his previous NBA average (.517), he would have scored roughly 60 points more than he did. That might have mattered a lot in some of the club's closer games. Help was needed in this area since the Hawks were only 14-14 in games decided by 6 points or less. Probably the most telling sign of how critical the #2 guard spot was to the Hawk's success was the statistic that showed the club's record when Wittman scored in double figures (34-12) vs when he did not (16-20). See what I mean?

It's no surprise that the team went shopping during the off-season. Impressively, they came up with one of the league's top off-guards - Reggie Theus. Theus ranked #8 at his position last year with Sacramento, but #5 in scoring and #4 in assists. The scoring average (21.56 PPG) should be great news for Wilkins as it is over twice Wittman's average. His passing ability should help out as well. Atlanta ranked relatively poor in assists (#13) and at times became a team with four little indians watching one big chief. It's true that Theus is going into his tenth year while Wittman is entering his 6th, but it was still a good trade for Atlanta since Theus' 1988 scoring was the second best of his career.

As if Theus wasn't enough, the Hawks snared one of the all-time great centers in the game - Moses Malone. After playing out his contract with Washington, Malone put himself up for bid. Atlanta responded with a lucrative 3 year offer. For ten consecutive years, Moses has ranked at least 4th among the league's top centers. In fact from 1981-1985 he was number 1. Granted, he can't have much left when his 3 year hitch is up, but with all of the other weapons the team has Atlanta good as any team in the NBA.

Dominique Wilkins remains the real key to the club's record. When he scored 30+ points, the team was 30-14. That's good, but the year before, the Hawks were 31-2 by the same standard. Again, the slippage is due mostly to the guard's lack of outside shooting. It's certainly not due to an off year in shooting by Dominique. His last three seasons have produced nearly identi-

Atlanta Hawks .... Overview

cal field goal percentages - .468, .463, .464. These percentages are not great, but considering the defenses mustered against him, they're not that bad either. Truthfully, though, Wilkins *is* rather one-dimensional. He is not a Bird or Magic or Jordan. He is good (#3 small forward), but other than scoring (#2 overall), he ranks #64 or worse in each of the other five performance categories. On the other hand, his worst rank of the six categories is #91 (assists). That's good because only six other NBA players ranked #91 or better according to all six standards. So, maybe he's more versatile than one-dimensional or maybe just a little of both.

At one point, critics were saying that Dominique was trying to do too much. This complaint was especially common immediately after the All-Star break. Wilkins felt he was robbed on his final slam dunk (so do I). As if to prove he was better than billed, he went out and averaged 41 points a game during his next 11 games. Unfortunately, Atlanta lost more than they won. With help from the off-guards, Wilkins can take off the asbestos gloves. A one/two punch like Theus and Wilkins might be the envy of the league next year. Assuming a Theus/Wilkins combo, the two would be the league's top off-guard/small forward scoring duo based on the 1987-88 season.

Small Forward/Off Guard

Wilkins/Theus	Atla	52.24
McDaniel/Ellis	Seat	47.24
Kersey/Drexler	Port	46.17
Bird/Ainge	Bost	45.67
Sellers/Jordan	Chic	44.46

Up front, Atlanta had some solid players with Rollins and Koncak at center, and Willis, Levingston, and Carr at the power positions. There's that depth again. Rollins ranked #26 at center, last in the NBA in assists, and third to last in scoring among regulars. If it weren't true that Atlanta had other weapons, Rollins' offensive woes would have been unacceptable. As it is, he was the focal point of a defense which ranked among the league leaders in scoring and field goal percentage. When Cleveland backed the Brinks truck under Rollins' tree last summer, he hopped on. Wouldn't you?

Koncak's performance was also vital to the team last season. Atlanta was 32-17 when he played, but only 18-15 when he did not. Levingston had similar influence on the team's success. The Hawks were 29-12 when Cliff scored in double figures, but only 21-20 when he did not. Antoine Carr came on strong late in the season hitting 60% from the field the last 30 games. Kevin Willis' production dropped substantially from two years ago - mostly because of lower scoring and rebounding outputs. Willis has the distinction of being the runaway winner in the "black hole" contest. During the season Kevin McHale of Boston was tagged the "black hole", meaning passes go in, but never come out. It's cute, but inaccurate. The real black holes are two other Kevins - Willis and Duckworth. The black hole rating is derived from (FGA\AST).

1. Kevin Willis	Atla	24.54
2. Kevin Duckworth	Port	13.74
3. Wayne Rollins	Atla	13.00
4. Mel Turpin	Utah	12.16
5. Mike Mitchell	S.A.	11.53

Prediction - best case: 65-17

If everything works out with Theus so that Wilkins is free to move more freely, this club will be improved - even unstoppable. Such are the benefits of great depth. I would be remiss if I didn't add, however, that Detroit, Chicago, Cleveland, and Indiana of the same division should all be better too. Only the Bucks are likely to drop.

Prediction - worst case: 53-29

Even if the Theus/Malone experiment fails miserably, Atlanta has way too much talent not to win at least 53 games. Admittedly, however, Reggie and 'Nique could get into a shooting battle which could kill chemistry - an element lacking all too often as it was last year. If that were to happen, the worst case scenerio might prevail.

Boston Celtics ....History

The Boston Celtics are one of the original clubs in the NBA. Having begun in 1946, the Celtics, along with the Knicks and Warriors, enter their 43rd season this year and rank as charter members of the 25 team association.

The 1960's were dominated by the Celtics. They won 9 of 10 championships during the decade. In fact, from 1957-1969, Boston won 11 of 13. Not coincidentally, these 13 years coincide with Bill Russell's career. Russell was injured in 1958 and Boston finished second. The "worst" year of the 13 was 1967, when Boston was defeated in the division finals. Ironically, in the midst of the greatest *dynasty* ever, many consider the greatest *team* ever as the team that beat the Celts that season - the Philadelphia 76ers.

Apart from the success of the 60's, the best period for the franchise has been the Larry Bird era. Bird only joined the team in 1979/80 and has led his team to three championships thus far. In some ways the 80's Celtics have been as dominant as the 60's club. Bird's teams have won 75% of their regular season games while Russell won at *only* a 71% clip. Both players have won at a 63%- 64% level in the playoffs.

Red Auerbach is, arguably, the greatest professional coach in any sport in history. He came to the Celtics in 1950-51 and led the team to 9 titles, retiring in 1966 having won 8 in a row. He posted a winning record in each of his 16 years. The Celtics won more than they lost the next 3 years as well. That 19 year span is the longest consecutive streak of winning seasons ever.

Auerbach holds the record for the most victories in a career - 938 (regular season) and 99 (playoffs) and was duly elected to the Hall-Of-Fame in 1968. Incredibly, ten of his former players have achieved the same honor. Three of them - Bill Russell, Tommy Heinsohn, and K.C. Jones - have each won two championships as coach of the Celtics.

Trivia: The Celtics were the first franchise to have a black player, the first to have an all-black starting five, and the first to have a black coach... The club holds the record for most consecutive home wins (38), most home wins in a season (40), and most road wins in a season (32)... Of the eight "original" continually operating franchises, only the Celtics have failed to have an annual scoring leader... The Celts are the only team who failed to make the playoffs following a championship (1970).

> **Quiz: Who was the first player to hit a 3-pointer in an All-Star Game?**

ALL TIME CELTICS' TEAM

Player	Span	Yrs	CRD
Bill Russell	1957-69	13	30,533
John Havlicek	1963-78	16	25,310
Larry Bird	1980-88	9	21,691
Dave Cowens	1971-80	10	18,664
Bob Cousy	1951-63	13	17,251
Robert Parish	1981-88	8	14,447
Sam Jones	1958-69	12	13,748
Kevin McHale	1981-88	8	12,945
Jo Jo White	1970-79	10	11,761
Tommy Heinsohn	1957-65	9	11,542

ALL TIME CELTICS' COACH

Red Auerbach	16 Years
90-58 Playoffs	16 Playoffs
795-397 Reg. Season	9 Championships

HISTORICAL PROFILE

Category	Data
Celtics' Coach	Jimmy Rodgers
Years coached Boston	0
# of franchise years	42
# of coaches	10
# of winning seasons	34
# of playoff years	35
# of runner's up	3
# of championships	16
Regular season win %	64.2
Playoff win %	60.8

> **Answer:**
> **Larry Bird (1980)**

Boston Celtics ....1987-88 Highlights

Celts 140-139 Bullets   Sat.   November 7, 1987

It was the most points Washington had allowed in 8 1/2 years and the most points they allowed at home...ever. Furthermore, it was the most points Boston had allowed on the road since 1979 when the Celtics lost to these same Bullets 119-145. That was the 4th to last game of the year. Boston only played 3 more games before the Bird era began. In this game Bird had 47 points. Ironically, however, Bird missed two free throws in the game - it's ironic because he wouldn't miss again for a month - after he set a Celtic record of 59 straight.

Celts 111-109 Knicks (2 OT)   Wed.   November 18, 1987

It was the 15th straight home court victory by Boston over New York. Ironically, it was the first game Larry Bird missed this season and the first time both Bird and McHale have both missed a Celtic game. Amazingly, Boston overcame a 28 point deficit and won on a last second tip-in by Bird's replacement - Darren Daye.

Celts 130-99 Nets   Wed.   December 2, 1987

The Celtics won their 34th straight regular season game at Boston Garden, and won the game by the largest margin during a regular season game since 1984. Larry Bird went 6 for 6 and thus passed Bill Sharman for the Celtics all-time consecutive free-throws-made record. Bird increased his total to 59, well ahead of Sharman's 55, but one shy of Rick Barry's 60. Barry is third all-time to Calvin Murphy and Dan Issel. Murphy hit 78 straight in 1981. Issel hit on 63 straight in 1982.

Celts 124-87 76ers   Sun.   December 20, 1987

The Boston Celtics destroyed the Philadelphia 76ers, thus preventing the Sixers from tying the Celts for the division lead. Philly had won 3 straight and 6 of 7. The 37 point margin was the most decisive regular season win by Boston over Philadelphia in the history of the two franchises. Ironically, the earlier meeting last year was won by Philly by 31 points. That was the largest margin by the Sixers over the Celtics in over 6 years.

Celts 143-105 Pistons   Wed.   January 13, 1988

The Boston Celtics used a 43 point 3rd quarter (biggest of the year) to humiliate the Detroit Pistons. It was the first return to the Boston Garden for Dennis Rodman since his famous quote about Larry Bird. Bird had 28 points by quarter's end and watched the last 12 minutes while Detroit lost its 20th straight at the Garden. The victory margin (38) was the largest since Boston beat Detroit 129-88 in 1981.

Celts 122-86 Kings   Fri.   January 15, 1988

The 23 point first quarter lead was the season's largest to date in the NBA. Ironically, the Celtics did it to their former greatest player. The trip to the Garden was the first by Bill Russell (Kings coach) since 1977. As an opposing coach at Seattle, Russell was 2-2 each of his 4 years vs Boston.

Celts 106-100 Bullets   Wed.   January 27, 1988

The Boston Celtics used the scoring power of Larry Bird to defeat the Washington Bullets. Bird scored 49 points - his highest in 2 years. Ironically, Bernard King scored 32 points in the game for Washington. It was his highest game in 3 years. Boston won on a last minute steal by Danny Ainge, who fed Robert Parish for the lay in. Coincidentally, just the night before Boston had won on a last minute steal by *Parish* who fed *Ainge* for the lay in.

Boston Celtics . . . . Influence on Winning

TEAM RECORD BY ... SCR Leader   ... REB Leader   ... AST Leader

PLAYER	GAMES	HOME	ROAD	HOME	ROAD	HOME	ROAD
Larry Bird	76	29-4	17-10	20-2	5-10	9-1	3-6
Kevin McHale	64	3-0	2-6	9-1	4-6	1-1	1-0
Robert Parish	74	---	---	10-2	15-5	---	0-1
Danny Ainge	81	2-0	1-2	---	---	9-1	5-5
Dennis Johnson	77	0-1	0-1	---	---	23-2	15-9
Jim Paxson	28	---	---	---	---	---	---
Fred Roberts	74	---	---	---	---	---	---
Dirk Minniefield	61	---	---	---	---	1-0	0-1
Fred Acres	79	1-0	0-1	2-0	0-3	---	---
Artis Gilmore	47	---	---	---	---	---	---

TEAM RECORD BY SCORING *

PLAYER	PLAY	DNP	0-9	10-19	20-29	30-39	40+
Larry Bird	55-21	2-4	1-0	5-5	17-10	23-4	9-2
Kevin McHale	45-19	12-6	---	10-5	31-11	4-3	---
Robert Parish	51-23	6-2	6-6	31-16	14-1	---	---
Danny Ainge	57-24	0-1	6-5	34-13	16-6	1-0	---
Dennis Johnson	54-23	3-2	12-10	36-10	6-3	---	---
Jim Paxson	19-9	38-16	11-4	8-5	---	---	---
Fred Roberts	50-24	7-1	38-18	11-6	1-0	---	---
Dirk Minniefield	44-17	13-8	41-16	3-1	---	---	---
Fred Acres	56-23	1-2	51-21	5-2	---	---	---
Artis Gilmore	32-15	25-10	29-15	3-0	---	---	---

TEAM RECORD BY STARTING POSITION *

PLAYER	GAMES	STARTS	PG	OG	SF	PF	C
Larry Bird	76	75	---	---	53-19	1-2	---
Kevin McHale	64	63	---	---	---	45-18	---
Robert Parish	74	73	---	---	---	---	51-22
Danny Ainge	81	81	---	57-24	---	---	---
Dennis Johnson	77	74	52-22	---	---	---	---
Jim Paxson	28	2	1-1	---	---	---	---
Fred Roberts	74	14	---	---	0-2	9-3	---
Dirk Minniefield	61	6	4-2	---	---	---	---
Fred Acres	79	5	---	---	---	---	4-1
Artis Gilmore	47	4	---	---	---	---	2-2

* For further definition of each category and column heading see pages 38 & 39.

Boston Celtics . . . . 1987-88 Statistics

RAW NUMBERS *

PLAYER	2pt%	3pt%	FT%	MIN	PF	DQ	HI	TO	RB	AS	BL	ST
Larry Bird	.546	.414	**.916**	2965	157	0	**49**	213	703	467	57	125
Kevin McHale	**.604**	0-0	.797	2390	179	1	33	141	536	171	**92**	27
Robert Parish	.590	0-1	.734	2312	198	**5**	26	154	628	115	84	55
Danny Ainge	.534	**.415**	.878	**3018**	203	1	33	153	249	503	17	115
Dennis Johnson	.449	.261	.856	2670	**204**	0	24	195	240	**598**	29	93
Jim Paxson	.477	.238	.861	801	73	0	19	39	45	76	5	30
Fred Roberts	.497	0-6	.776	1032	118	0	20	68	162	81	15	16
Dirk Minniefield	.507	.250	.745	1070	133	0	16	93	96	228	3	59
Mark Acres	.532	0-0	.640	1151	198	2	19	54	270	42	27	29
Artis Gilmore	.547	0-0	.523	893	148	0	15	67	211	21	30	15

OVERALL RANKINGS *

PLAYER	G	GS	PPG	PR	RANK	SC	SH	RB	AS	BL	ST
Larry Bird	76	75	**29.93**	**34.01**	2	3	4	46	37	66	43
Kevin McHale	64	63	22.59	**26.28**	9	11	2	55	94	29	158
Robert Parish	74	73	14.34	**19.15**	41	62	5	20	120	32	121
Danny Ainge	**81**	**81**	15.68	**18.26**	48	50	3	143	34	124	55
Dennis Johnson	77	74	12.61	**16.13**	68	83	117	135	13	100	66
Jim Paxson	45	3	7.71	**6.49**	DNQ						
Fred Roberts	74	14	6.08	**6.08**	DNQ						
Dirk Minniefield	72	6	3.63	**5.93**	DNQ						
Mark Acres	79	5	3.63	**5.90**	DNQ						
Artis Gilmore	71	27	3.73	**4.68**	DNQ						

POSITION RANKINGS *

PLAYER	POSITION	RANK	SC	SH	RB	AS	BL	ST
Larry Bird	Small Forward (SF)	1	2	1	3	1	17	7
Kevin McHale	Power Forward (PF)	3	3	1	26	8	10	35
Robert Parish	Center (C)	7	9	1	10	11	17	8
Danny Ainge	Off Guard (OG)	9	14	1	25	5	26	15
Dennis Johnson	Point Guard (PG)	16	16	21	20	13	6	30
Jim Paxson	Off Guard (OG)	DNQ						
Fred Roberts	Power Forward (PF)	DNQ						
Dirk Minniefield	Point Guard (PG)	DNQ						
Mark Acres	Power Forward (PF)	DNQ						
Artis Gilmore	Center (C)	DNQ						

*For further definition of each category and column heading see pages 38 & 39.

Boston Celtics ....Team Info

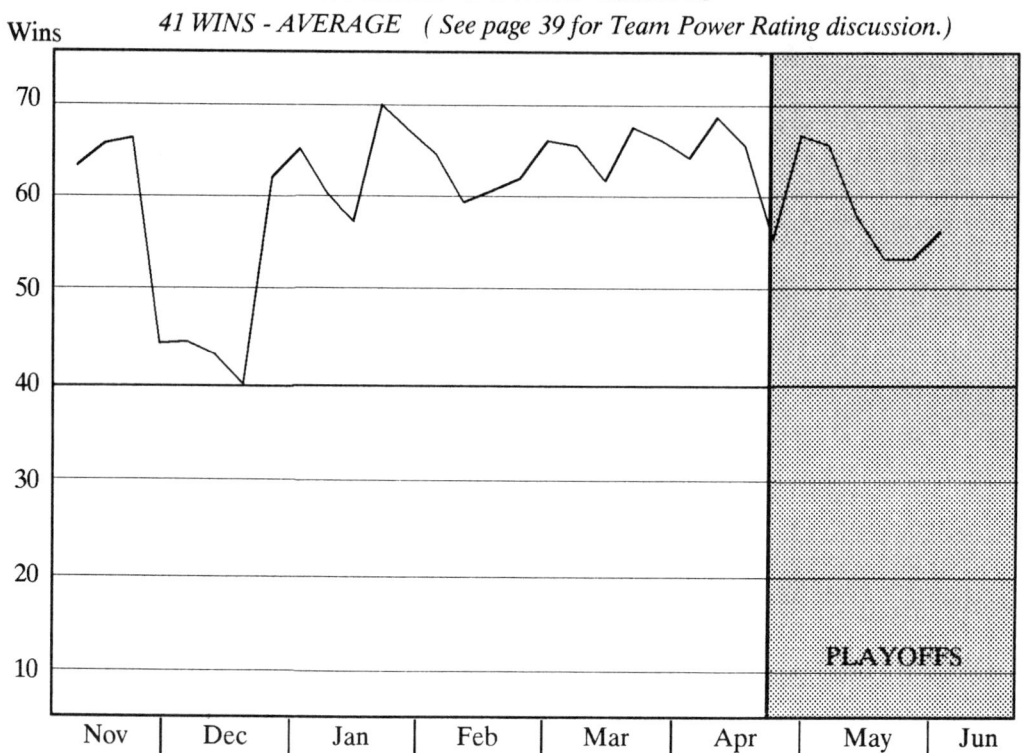

WEEKLY POWER RATING
41 WINS - AVERAGE (See page 39 for Team Power Rating discussion.)

[Weekly Power Rating chart showing wins from Nov through Jun, with values fluctuating between 40-70, and a shaded PLAYOFFS region from late April through June]

Miscellaneous Categories	Data	Rank	Performance Categories	Data	Rank
Attendance	611K	6	Offensive Scoring (per game)	113.6	3
Key-Man Games Missed	42	8	Defensive Scoring (per game)	107.7	14
Season Record	57-25	2	Scoring Margin (per game)	5.9	1
- Home	36-5	1	Defensive FG%	.482	15
- Road	21-20	2	Offensive 2-point%	.537	1
Eastern Conference	39-19	3	Offensive 3-point%	.384	1
Western Conference	18-6	2	Offensive Free Throw %	.803	2
Overtime Record	2-0	2	Offensive Rebs (Off REB/Opp Def REB)		22
Record 5 Pts. or Less	13-6	3	Defensive Rebs (Def REB/Opp Off REB)		3
Record 10 Pts. or More	32-13	3	Offensive Assists (AST/FGMade)		2
Games Won By Bench	3	14	Offensive Blocks (BLK/Opp FGAttempted)		14
Games Won By Starters	37	1	Offensive Steals (STL/Game)		20
Winning Streak	8	6	Turnover Margin (Off T.O. - Def T.O.)		21
Losing Streak	3	1	Finesse (BLK + STL) / PF		12
Home Winning Streak	15	2	Rebounding Record	41-38-3	10
Road Winning Streak	4	5	Assists Record	57-22-3	2
Home Losing Streak	2	2	Field Goal Pct. Record	54-28-0	2
Road Losing Streak	4	1	Free Throw Pct. Record	55-26-1	1

Boston Celtics .... Miscellaneous

ADMINISTRATIVE INFORMATION

Team Offices: 150 Causeway Street
Boston, Massachusetts
02114

Telephone: (617) 523-6050
Head Coach: Jimmy Rodgers
Home Arena: Boston Garden
Capacity: 14,890

1988-89 ROSTER*

J#	VETERANS	COLLEGE	POS	R#	D#	HT	WT	Bost	NBA
42	Mark Acres	ORU	F-C	2	40	6-11	220	1	1
44	Danny Ainge	BYU	G	2	31	6-5	185	7	7
33	Larry Bird	Indiana State	F	1	6	6-9	220	9	9
20	Darrin Daye	UCLA	F	3	57	6-8	221	2	5
3	Dennis Johnson	Pepperdine	G	2	29	6-4	202	5	12
35	Reggie Lewis	Northeastern	G-F	1	22	6-7	195	1	1
54	Brad Lohaus	Iowa	F	2	45	7-0	235	1	1
32	Kevin McHale	Minnesota	F-C	1	3	6-10	225	8	8
10	Dirk Minniefield	Kentucky	G	2	33	6-3	180	1	3
00	Robert Parish	Centenary	C	1	8	7-0	230	8	12
5	Bill Walton	UCLA	C	1	1	6-11	235	3	14
4	Jim Paxson	Dayton	G	1	12	6-6	210	1	9

	ROOKIES	COLLEGE	POS	R#	D#	HT
	Brian Shaw	UC-Santa Barbara	G	1	24	6-6
	Gerald Paddio	UNLV	F-G	3	74	6-7

* For further definition of category and column headings, see pages 38 & 39.

Boston Celtics .... Overview

The Boston Celtics of the 1980's are clearly one of the all time great teams. In fact, a valid argument could be made that they have been the best, though not greatest, team ever. I developed a simple formula for evaluating how dominant a team was for a given year. Without going into details, it measures winning percentage during the regular season and playoffs as well as points scored and points allowed. The results show the Russell-led Celtics of the 60's and the Bird-led Celtics of the 80's as the top two dynasties. Each team placed 6 seasons in the top-30 best seasons ever in the NBA. The 80's Lakers have placed 4 seasons in the group. The top three teams (1972 Lakers, 1971 Bucks, 1967 Sixers) were not part of any dynasty.

What makes this team so special is the fantastic shooting statistics it has racked up. Impressively, Boston's last 4 years are among the 10 best shooting seasons by an NBA club. The rating below is based on a shooting index which I explain on page 29.

1. LA Lakers	1985	1.082
2. Boston Celtics	**1988**	**1.078**
3. Boston Celtics	1987	1.066
4. LA Lakers	1986	1.057
5. LA Lakers	1984	1.055
6. LA Lakers	1987	1.054
7. Denver Nuggets	1982	1.050
8. Boston Celtics	1985	1.042
9. Boston Celtics	1986	1.041
10. LA Lakers	1988	1.036

Incredibly, four Celts were among the league's top-5 shooters last season. Immediately behind John Stockton of Utah were #2 Kevin McHale, #3 Danny Ainge, #4 Larry Bird, and #5 Robert Parish. Each is #1 at his position. The 5th starter? Dennis Johnson ranked #21 at his position (point guard). That's pretty good evidence that DJ truly isn't a good shooter (except in clutch situations). The simple reality is that Bird & Co. make everyone shoot better than they would on another team. A position rank of #21 sticks out like a sore thumb.

Bird, McHale, and Ainge have all set shooting marks the last two years. Bird is the only player in NBA history to shoot 50%+ from the field and 90%+ from the line the same year. He's done it twice in a row. McHale is the only player ever to shoot 60%+ from the field and 80%+ from the line. He did it in 1987, but fell ever so short in 1988 (.604, .797). Ainge, of course, set an NBA record for made 3-pointers last season (148), a 61% increase over the old record of 92 set by Darrell Griffith in 1985.

Boston's present team may be the best half court team ever. That seems apparent enough, considering the club was, as usual, tops in the league in 2-point FG%, 3-point FG%, and free throw %. These achievements are possible only if a team has a finely tuned half court offense. One could argue that these high percentages came off of easy buckets on fast breaks, but Boston ranked dead last in forcing turnovers - one of the key elements to initiating the break. Another argument might be that percentages this good had to come from stickbacks. The only flaw in this logic is that the Celtics ranked last as well in offensive rebounds. What is the conclusion then? It's simple. They move the ball brilliantly to find the open man and they **never** take bad shots. Additionally, they ranked second in assists divided by field-goal-attempts.

By now everyone knows how strong Boston's starters are and how weak their bench is. Since the first five average well over 30 years of age, a respectable bench would be nice. And although the bench increased from 17% of points scored in 1987 to 24% in 1988, it still remains unable to provide quality help at critical moments. Amazingly, only one of Boston's first round picks since 1980 was still on the team last season (Reggie Lewis). The hard and cold reality is that the most valuable person on the bench is Ed Lacerte (trainer). As long as he has a good supply of denture cream and preparation H, he'll provide the most relief on the team.

Boston Celtics . . . . Overview

Boston's starters averaged more points than any others, primarily because of the excessive number of minutes (also a league high) they played. Considering their age, that's almost cruel and unusual punishment.

	Min/Game
Boston	**35.90**
New York	34.66
Dallas	34.31
LA.L	34.06
Detroit	33.24
Portland	32.43
Indiana	31.66

The Celtics' record by quarters gives some indication of wearing down during games. Their quarter #1 record was 54-25-3, quarter #2 (35-43-4), quarter #3 (53-27-2), and quarter #4 (48-35-1). When you look at those records, it seems reasonable to think that Boston would wear down in quarters 2 and 4. Of course, we know how they tired out in the playoffs. That's two years in a row that they have hit a treadmill when it mattered the most. One has to wonder where they will be in June of 1989. Nevertheless, the starters won 37 games compared to 3 by the bench. (I have a complicated formula to determine if a game is won by the starters, the bench, both, or neither.) The 37 wins are a mile above second place Denver (13 wins).

Larry Bird is among the top three or four greatest players ever. If K.C. Jones was the heart of the club, then Bird was at least the Central Artery. Virtually everything good that happened to this team passed through Larry. In 1987-88, he set consecutive FT streaks of 59 and 53; he scored at a career high rate 29.93 points per game; and he proved how essential he was when he was out. The team was 18-19 when he scored 27 points or less. When he scored 28 or more, Boston sizzled, winning 39 and losing only 6. Tellingly, when he led in scoring on the road, the club went 17-10. When a teammate led in scoring on the road, the club was a paltry 3-10. That's what I call valuable!

During one 9 game stretch he scored 49 points, 17 rebounds, managed his only triple double, averaged 37 ppg, passed Bob Cousy (#2 all-time Celtics list), hit a game winning 3-pointer on the road over Dallas, and led Boston to its largest victory ever over Milwaukee. That's impressive, but that's Bird. I did a poll of NBA coaches last season. They voted Larry #1 as best player to start a team with, best off-balance outside shooter, best at moving without the ball, and best team leader.

K.C. Jones has left to go fishing, but Jimmy Rodgers will fill in adequately. Jones took a little heat for not substituting more. Maybe that's justified. His laissez faire methods were not particularly admired or copied, but truthfully the X's and O's just weren't necessary with this bunch. Other questions were asked. Did Paxson get to play enough? Why did he pull the starters in the final game of the playoffs down by only 8 with a minute to play? I suppose these questions were enough to make Case want to quit. Who can blame him. He's the single most successful basketball individual ever! As player and coach, he's been more than a winner. He's simply been fantastic. He won an NCAA championship, 8 NBA titles, and he's the only coach to record 60+ win seasons in two different cities (Boston and Washington, 1975). His .706 winning percentage trails only Pat Riley's for the best ever.

Prediction - best case: 56-26

There is no way the Celtics can get better than they have been without new people. They have to slip. Of course they could pick up a free agent or two which could push them back to 60 wins, but that's unlikely. It's Geritol time.

Prediction - worst case: 51-31

Though 51 wins is good, it would be an enormous plummet for this group. Unless help comes, however, 51 wins is a real possibility. If any injuries should prevent Bird or McHale from playing a combined 30 games or more, then even 51 wins may be tough to reach.

# Charlotte Hornets .... Miscellaneous

ADMINISTRATIVE INFORMATION

Team Offices: Two First Union Center
Suite 2600
Charlotte, North Carolina
28282
Telephone: (704) 376-6430
Head Coach: Dick Harter
Home Arena: Charlotte Coliseum
Capacity: 23,500

1988-89 ROSTER*

J#	VETERANS	COLLEGE	POS	R#	D#	HT	WT	Char	NBA
	Tyrone Bogues	Wake Forest	G	1	12	5-4	140	0	1
	Michael Brooks	LaSalle	F	1	9	6-7	220	0	6
	Dell Curry	Virginia Tech	G	1	15	6-5	195	0	2
	Rickey Green	Michigan	G	1	16	6-0	172	0	10
	Michael Holton	UCLA	G	3	53	6-4	195	0	4
	David Hoppen	Nebraska	C	3	65	6-11	235	0	1
	Ralph Lewis	La Salle	F-G	6	139	6-6	205	0	1
	Kurt Rambis	Santa Clara	F	3	58	6-8	218	0	7
	Bernard Thompson	Fresno State	G-F	1	19	6-6	211	0	4
	Sedric Toney	Dayton	G	3	59	6-2	178	0	2
	Kelly Tripucka	Notre Dame	F	1	12	6-6	220	0	7

ROOKIES	COLLEGE	POS	R#	D#	HT
Rex Chapman	Kentucky	G	1	8	6-5
Tom Tolbert	Arizona	F	2	34	6-7
Jeff Moore	Auburn	F	3	58	6-7

*For further definition of category and column headings, see pages 38 & 39.

Charlotte Hornets .... Overview

The Charlotte Hornets may be an expansion team, but a great deal about the franchise would make one think it had been around a long time. George Shinn, a dynamic and energetic individual, personally took the NBA by storm and literally forced the city down the league's throat. His tenacity set the stage for several events.

To begin with, the Hornets will be moving into a brand new arena seating 23,500, the largest in the league. The way season ticket reservations have been going, attendance in Charlotte may very well be the highest in the NBA. Now, if they can just keep the scoreboard from falling.

In a way it's surprising that the NBA would be so in-demand in a state like North Carolina. After all, this is the state with Smith's Tar Heels, Valvano's Wolfpack, Coach K's Blue Devils, and Wake Forest (all ACC members). It seems hard to imagine a vacuem existing for the NBA to fill. A closer look, however, reveals that each of these universities is at least two hours from Charlotte. Even more exciting is that the club can draw from nearly 6 million people within 100 miles. It's a perfect marriage. A basketball crazy, growth-oriented city and an exciting, increasingly popular professional league. Without the NFL or Major League Baseball, this franchise should really thrive.

Interestingly, there used to be a professional club in the state. From 1970-74, the Carolina Cougars played ball in the ABA. A slightly better than average club, they won big in 1973. The team not only had 57 victories, but Larry Brown (UNC) was named Coach-of-the-Year (his first year as a head coach - a sign of things to come) and Billy Cunningham (UNC) was named league MVP.

The club did a marvelous job of picking up talent in the expansion draft. Though they are likely to wallow in the Atlantic Division basement in 1989, something tells me they won't be cellar-dwellers for long. With Dallas as the only NBA expansion team since the Jazz in 1975, the league hasn't been depleted of talent. Using Dallas as a model, the Hornets could become successful in just a few seasons. As new coach, **Dick Harter** (former Indiana assistant) said, "It may take a year, it may take two years, it may take three years, but some day we're going to have some fun beating people."

They will start off with **Kelly Tripucka** who was obtained from the Jazz for Mike Brown (formerly of Chicago). In his five seasons with Detroit, he averaged 21.6 ppg. After being traded to Utah, his one-dimensional play was exposed. In two years under Frank Layden, he played sparingly while maintaining a scoring average of just 9.1... **Dell Curry** is another former Jazz who excelled away from Utah. After being shipped to Cleveland, he averaged over 15 ppg as a starter... **Dave Hoppen** had a decent rookie season with the Bucks and Warriors. If there is a big man who will surprise a lot of people it's this guy... **Kurt Rambis** was picked up from the Lakers and will probably start at power forward... **Tyrone Bogues** is not only the league's shortest player, but quickest as well. Bogues ranked #2 among point guards in steals (per minute). Additionally, he ranked best among the outstanding group of rookie PG's (M. Jackson, K. Smith, K. Johnson, W. Garland) in assist-to-turnover ratio... **Rex Chapman** was probably the top undergraduate picked in the draft. He's a great athlete with unlimited range. So what if it takes him a year or two to get oriented... **Rickey Green** is an excellent playmaker (another Utah product). His only problem is that he played behind John Stockton. Add to these players **Michael Holton, Michael Brooks** (CBA MVP), **Bernard Thompson**, etc. and the Hornets have a real shot at respectability.

When all the ticker tape has been swept, when the last season ticket is sold, when the curtain goes up, the fans will be asking "Dean who? Jimmy who? Mike who?" Then, after a moment of silence, comes the chant "George, George, George".

Chicago Bulls . . . . History

Though the Chicago Bulls franchise began in 1966-67, it was not the first professional basketball team in the windy city. The original Chicago franchise was named the Stags, and began in the old BAA in 1946-47. However, after 4 seasons the team disbanded, leaving Chicago teamless until 1961-62 when a new team began. That club was called the Packers and remained for two years.

Dick Motta joined the club in 1968-69 and certainly has to be regarded as the team's all-time finest coach. Motta won well over twice as many games as any other coach at Chicago. Prior to last year, the Bulls had only won over 50 games four times - all in succession - all under Motta, from 1971-1974. The first of those 4 years Motta was also named Coach-of-the-Year.

Ironically, Chicago's best year in the playoffs was the year following their last 50+ win season. In 1975, the Bulls won only 47 games, but managed to advance to the Western Conference championships. That series was very close and went down to the last few minutes of game 7 vs Golden State. There the championship dreams were lost 83-79. Consequently, by virtue of never having reached the finals, Chicago is the oldest club to be so thwarted (23 years). San Antonio (22) is second.

The franchise has experienced lean times since their glory days of the early 1970's. In the last 11 years Chicago has only had two winning seasons; however, they have gone to the playoffs six times, including the last four. They lost each first-round series prior to last year's victory over Cleveland. The Bulls rank # 15 in regular season winning percentage (47%), but rank last (#23) in playoff winning percentage (32%). Interestingly, the next worse playoff record is Cleveland's at 37%.

The club's fortunes turned sharply in 1984 when Chicago drafted Michael Jordan 3rd. Jordan has been superhuman in his first four years. He was named Rookie-of-the-Year and has been voted to the all-star game each season. His excellence was further rewarded last year as he scored the second highest total ever during an all-star game (40) and captured the MVP award. Additionally, Jordan has been named all-NBA 1st team the last two years - the only Bull to achieve that honor. Michael even managed to be selected as Defensive Player-of-the-Year last season despite the lofty 35 ppg scoring average.

Quiz: Michael Jordan holds the record for highest PPG for a guard at 37.1. Whose record did he break?

ALL TIME BULLS' TEAM

Player	Span	Yrs	CRD
Artis Gilmore	1977-87	7	12,076
Jerry Sloan	1967-76	10	11,150
Bob Love	1969-76	8	9,914
Tom Boerwinkle	1969-78	10	9,522
Chet Walker	1970-75	6	9,227
Norm Van Lier	1972-78	7	8,278
Michael Jordan	1985-88	4	8,229
David Greenwood	1980-85	6	8,108
Reggie Theus	1979-84	6	7,496
Dave Corzine	1983-88	6	6,659

ALL TIME BULLS' COACH

Dick Motta   8 Years
18-25 Playoffs   6 Playoffs
356-300 Reg. Season   0 Championships

HISTORICAL PROFILE

Category	Data
Bulls' Coach	Doug Collins
Years coached Chicago	2
# of franchise years	22
# of coaches	11
# of winning seasons	8
# of playoff years	14
# of runner's up	0
# of championships	0
Regular season win%	47.4
Playoff win %	32.1

Answer: Nate Archibald - 34.0 (1980)

Chicago Bulls ....1987-88 Highlights

Bulls 107-102 Celts   Mon.   November 23, 1987

By defeating the Celtics, the Bulls ended Boston's 33 game home-court winning streak. The streak was the third longest in NBA history. These same Celtics have the longest (38) which ran from Dec. 10, 1985 to Nov. 28, 1986. Rookie Scottie Pippen was the difference as he had a career high 20 points. Boston was playing only its second home game of the 1980's without Bird or McHale. The win also broke a 10 game losing streak to the Celts.

Bulls 116-93 Nets   Sat.   January 2, 1988

The win ended a 5 game losing streak and represented the largest margin of victory (23 points) of the season for the Bulls. At the same time, Michael Jordan *only* scored 25 points, but registered his first triple double of the season. Meanwhile, the Nets remained winless on the road (0-11).

Bulls 113-101 Suns   Thur.   February 4, 1988

The victory was especially notable for Chicago, as it represented their first win in Phoenix since March of 1977 and required a great comeback to do it. Chicago, trailing by 16 points halfway through the 3rd quarter, used a furious rally to take the lead as the quarter ended. The loss was the 10th in a row for Phoenix as both teams ended the first half of the season on very opposite notes.

Bulls 95-93 Bucks   Fri.   February 12, 1988

It was only the third time in the previous 15 games that the Bulls had defeated another team on the road. Prior to that, their road record was 8-1. In an interesting bit of irony, Jack Sikma had only 1 point for Milwaukee. Sikma, who had a scoring average of 18 ppg and who led the NBA in FG% at .943, hit his only point with 6 seconds remaining to tie the score. His second FTA (a miss) cost Milwaukee the win.

Bulls 128-107 Lakers   Thur.   March 10, 1988

The 21 point margin represented the Lakers worst defeat of the season. Magic Johnson was injured in the game and only played 10 minutes. The win was the Bulls first over the Lakers at Chicago Stadium since 1984. Michael Jordan scored 38 points while Magic Johnson was limited to a mere 7 points.

Bulls 113-103 Celtics   Fri.   March 18, 1988

The loss prevented the Celtics from becoming the first eastern team to be guaranteed a playoff spot. Chicago had lost 10 straight at home against Boston. The 10 point margin, though modest, was the most devastation inflicted by the Bulls over the Celts since 1984. In the battle between the league's top two players by Production Rating, Larry Bird was physically roughed up twice, shut out in quarters 1 and 3, and finished with 19 points. Michael Jordan scored 50 - the third time last season that he reached that plateau.

Bulls 118-102 76ers   Wed.   March 23, 1988

The victory broke the Bulls' 6 game road losing streak. Interestingly, Chicago's longest losing streak of 9 was also broken at the Spectrum. The 16 point margin was Chicago's largest win on the road vs. Philly in 15 years. As usual, Michael Jordan had 49 points and 13 rebounds, but Charles Oakley's 19 rebounds and Sam Vincent's 12 assists might have made the difference. Vincent's assist total was the second highest of his career to this point, but his 22 points represented a career high.

Chicago Bulls .... Influence on Winning

TEAM RECORD BY ... SCR Leader ... REB Leader ... AST Leader

PLAYER	GAMES	HOME	ROAD	HOME	ROAD	HOME	ROAD
Michael Jordan	82	30-11	19-21	4-1	1-1	13-6	9-10
Charles Oakley	82	0-1	---	20-10	16-17	2-1	---
Dave Corzine	80	---	---	4-0	3-3	---	---
Sam Vincent	29	---	---	---	---	8-3	8-5
Horace Grant	81	---	1-0	2-0	2-1	---	---
Brad Sellers	82	---	---	---	---	1-0	0-1
Scottie Pippen	79	---	---	---	---	---	1-1
John Paxson	81	---	---	---	---	7-1	1-3
Rory Sparrow	55	---	---	---	---	1-1	1-1
Mike Brown	46	---	---	1-0	---	---	---

TEAM RECORD BY SCORING *

PLAYER	PLAY	DNP	0-9	10-19	20-29	30-39	40+
Michael Jordan	50-32	---	---	1-2	9-11	27-14	13-5
Charles Oakley	50-32	---	15-10	31-18	4-4	---	---
Dave Corzine	50-30	0-2	20-10	28-19	2-1	---	---
Sam Vincent	19-10	31-22	4-3	13-6	2-1	---	---
Horace Grant	49-32	1-0	26-23	23-8	0-1	---	---
Brad Sellers	50-32	---	22-18	26-14	2-0	---	---
Scottie Pippen	49-30	1-2	27-22	20-8	2-0	---	---
John Paxson	50-31	0-1	30-23	20-7	0-1	---	---
Rory Sparrow	31-24	19-8	23-21	8-3	---	---	---
Mike Brown	25-21	25-11	23-19	2-2	---	---	---

TEAM RECORD BY STARTING POSITION *

PLAYER	GAMES	STARTS	PG	OG	SF	PF	C
Michael Jordan	82	82	---	50-32	---	---	---
Charles Oakley	82	82	---	---	---	50-32	---
Dave Corzine	80	32	---	---	---	---	19-13
Sam Vincent	29	27	19-8	---	---	---	---
Horace Grant	81	6	---	---	3-3	---	---
Brad Sellers	82	76	---	---	47-29	---	---
Scottie Pippen	79	0	---	---	---	---	---
John Paxson	81	30	17-13	---	---	---	---
Rory Sparrow	55	25	14-11	---	---	---	---
Mike Brown	46	27	---	---	---	---	16-11

* For further definition of each category and column heading see pages 38 & 39.

TEAM BY TEAM ANALYSIS 61

Chicago Bulls . . . . 1987-88 Statistics

RAW NUMBERS *

PLAYER	2pt%	3pt%	FT%	MIN	PF	DQ	HI	TO	RB	AS	BL	ST
Michael Jordan	**.546**	.132	.841	**3311**	270	2	**59**	252	449	485	131	259
Charles Oakley	.487	.250	.727	2816	**272**	2	26	241	**1066**	248	28	68
Dave Corzine	.486	.111	.752	2328	149	1	21	109	527	154	95	36
Sam Vincent	.459	**.381**	**.868**	1501	145	0	23	136	152	381	16	55
Horace Grant	.503	0-2	.626	1827	221	3	20	86	447	89	53	51
Brad Sellers	.460	.143	.790	2212	174	0	24	91	250	141	66	34
Scottie Pippen	.475	.174	.576	1650	214	3	24	131	298	169	52	91
Jon Paxson	.522	.347	.733	1888	154	2	22	64	104	303	1	49
Rory Sparrow	.411	.154	.727	1044	79	1	19	58	72	167	3	41
Mike Brown	.451	0-1	.577	591	85	0	15	38	159	28	4	11

OVERALL RANKINGS *

PLAYER	G	GS	PPG	PR	RANK	SC	SH	RB	AS	BL	ST
Michael Jordan	**82**	**82**	**34.98**	**35.05**	1	1	15	97	42	26	4
Charles Oakley	**82**	**82**	12.37	**20.54**	29	84	104	2	76	105	119
Dave Corzine	80	32	10.05	**13.72**	91	106	103	53	102	23	149
Sam Vincent	72	27	7.96	**10.67**	122	136	85	123	7	101	60
Horace Grant	81	6	7.68	**10.56**	124	141	120	34	125	39	99
Brad Sellers	**82**	76	9.48	**9.22**	138	120	137	115	104	37	150
Scottie Pippen	79	0	7.91	**9.22**	139	137	147	79	63	35	22
Jon Paxson	81	30	7.90	**8.96**	142	138	37	158	36	158	110
Rory Sparrow	58	25	4.48	**5.17**	DNQ						
Mike Brown	46	27	4.28	**5.11**	DNQ						

POSITION RANKINGS *

PLAYER	POSITION	RANK	SC	SH	RB	AS	BL	ST
Michael Jordan	Off Guard (OG)	1	1	4	6	9	1	2
Charles Oakley	Power Forward (PF)	8	17	23	2	4	32	24
Dave Corzine	Center (C)	18	20	20	23	6	13	20
Sam Vincent	Point Guard (PG)	25	26	16	12	7	7	29
Horace Grant	Power Forward (PF)	29	30	27	15	17	13	18
Brad Sellers	Small Forward (SF)	27	26	30	30	23	7	32
Scottie Pippen	Small Forward (SF)	28	31	32	17	7	5	3
Jon Paxson	Point Guard (PG)	29	27	9	32	30	31	32
Rory Sparrow	Point Guard (PG)	DNQ						
Mike Brown	Center (C)	DNQ						

*For further definition of each category and column heading see pages 38 & 39.

Chicago Bulls ....Team Info

WEEKLY POWER RATING
41 WINS - AVERAGE (See page 39 for Team Power Rating discussion.)

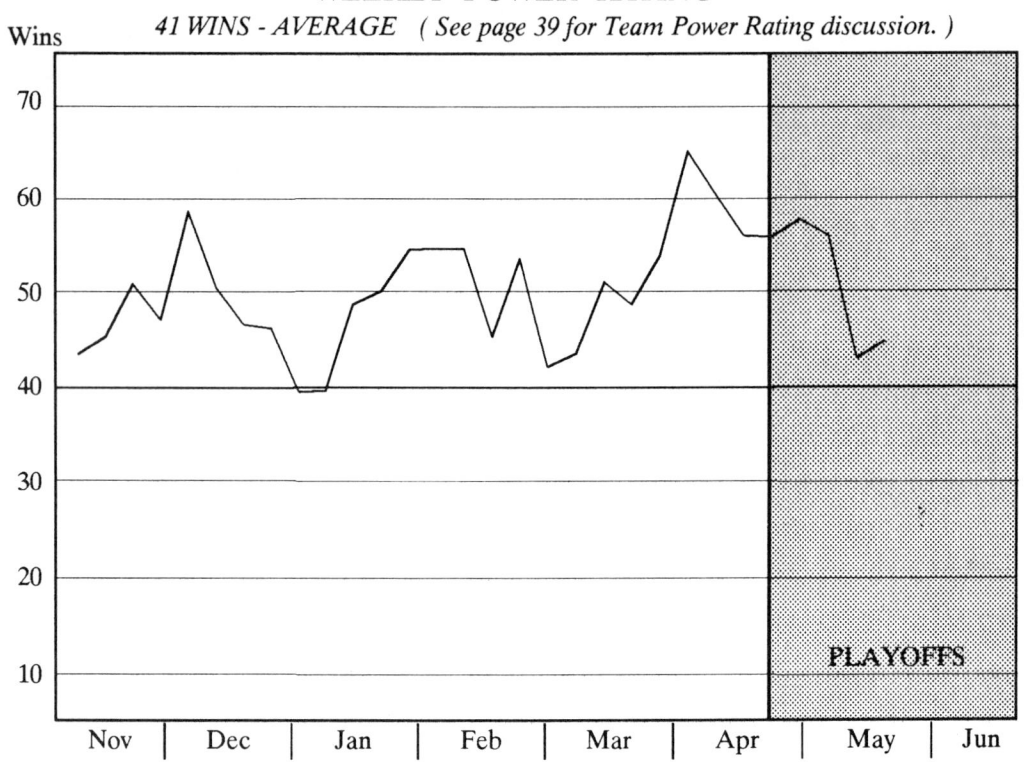

Miscellaneous Categories	Data	Rank
Attendance	740K	2
Key-Man Games Missed	10	1
Season Record	50-32	7
- Home	30-11	11
- Road	20-21	3
Eastern Conference	34-24	9
Western Conference	16-8	4
Overtime Record	4-3	7
Record 5 Pts. or Less	15-13	9
Record 10 Pts. or More	25-12	5
Games Won By Bench	7	5
Games Won By Starters	9	6
Winning Streak	6	10
Losing Streak	5	10
Home Winning Streak	7	15
Road Winning Streak	7	2
Home Losing Streak	2	2
Road Losing Streak	9	14

Performance Categories	Data	Rank
Offensive Scoring (per game)	105.0	19
Defensive Scoring (per game)	101.6	1
Scoring Margin (per game)	3.4	9
Defensive FG%	.470	4
Offensive 2-point%	.499	6
Offensive 3-point%	.230	22
Offensive Free Throw %	.759	16
Offensive Rebs ..... (Off REB/Opp Def REB)		9
Defensive Rebs .... (Def REB/Opp Off REB)		1
Offensive Assists .... (AST/FGMade)		8
Offensive Blocks .. (BLK/Opp FGAttempted)		6
Offensive Steals .... (STL/Game)		11
Turnover Margin .... (Off T.O. - Def T.O.)		13
Finesse .... (BLK + STL) / PF		5
Rebounding Record	47-29-6	6
Assists Record	41-32-9	8
Field Goal Pct. Record	49-33-0	6
Free Throw Pct. Record	41-38-3	11

Chicago Bulls . . . . Miscellaneous

ADMINISTRATIVE INFORMATION

Team Offices: One Magnificent Mile
980 North Michigan Avenue
Suite 1600
Chicago, Illinois 60611
Telephone: (312) 943-5800
Head Coach: Doug Collins
Home Arena: Chicago Stadium
Capacity: 17,458

1988-89 ROSTER*

J#	VETERANS	COLLEGE	POS	R#	D#	HT	WT	Chic	NBA
	Bill Cartwright	USF	C	1	3	7-1	245	0	8
40	Dave Corzine	DePaul	C	1	18	6-11	265	6	10
23	Michael Jordan	North Carolina	G	1	3	6-6	198	4	4
54	Horace Grant	Clemson	F-C	1	10	6-10	215	1	1
5	John Paxson	Notre Dame	G	1	19	6-2	185	3	5
33	Scott Pippen	C. Arkansas	F	1	5	6-7	210	1	1
6	Brad Sellers	Ohio State	F	1	9	7-0	212	2	2
2	Rory Sparrow	Villanova	G	4	75	6-2	175	1	8
21	Elston Turner	Mississippi	G	2	43	6-5	220	2	7
11	Sam Vincent	Michigan State	G	1	20	6-2	185	1	3
31	Granville Waiters	Ohio State	C	2	39	6-11	225	2	6

	ROOKIES	COLLEGE	POS	R#	D#	HT
	Will Perdue	Vanderbilt	C	1	11	7-0
	Derrick Lewis	Maryland	F	3	62	6-7

* For further definition of category and column headings, see pages 38 & 39.

Chicago Bulls .... Overview

When Michael Jordan entered the league as a rookie in 1984, it was quickly apparent that he would become another player in the mold of Magic Johnson or Larry Bird. Actually, Jordan has already reached that lofty status. If he continues to play as he has, he'll be remembered as one of the greatest, if not *the* greatest player ever. But since I claim a player must play 10+ years to be considered among the all-time greatest, he's got a lot of proving yet to do. I thought it would be interesting to look at the first four-year totals for Jordan, Bird, and Johnson. Here they are.

```
       PR   PPG  2P%  3P%  FT   SH    RB   AS   BL   ST
Jordan 31.17 32.69 .517 .164 .848 1.052 6.96 6.57 1.63 3.43
Bird   27.76 22.23 .500 .321 .850 1.026 13.70 6.85 1.00 2.36
Magic  28.14 18.30 .548 .163 .785 1.069 11.21 11.69 .71 3.33
```
See page 39 for explanation of column headings.

What Jordan hasn't yet done is to take his team to outstanding levels. During the regular season, Bird averaged 60.5 wins during his first four years, Magic 57.3 wins, Jordan 39.5 wins. Johnson won 33 playoff games and Bird 26 while Jordan won only 5. Of course, there is an obvious argument as to why Jordan has not won more games. After all, the only group playing in Chicago since 1984 has been Michael and the Kryptonites. In some cases he's had to actually *overcome* his own teammates to win. Although he is yet to prove that he is as capable as Bird or Johnson with respect to making his teammates better, he is clearly more dominant individually.

Jordan is the only player ever to register 200+ steals and 100+ blocks in a season. He's done it two years in a row. He even managed to swipe the ball 10 times in one game - a Chicago team record. He was the first person ever to win the scoring and steals (per game basis) titles in the same year. He even became the first player to score 50+ points in back-to-back playoff games. To top it off he won the slam dunk competition in his own arena and was named the All-Star MVP after he scored a game high 40 points. And if all that wasn't enough, he was voted the league's defensive player of the year. Wow! No wonder he was named the NBA's MVP for 1987-88.

Defensive Player	Votes
Michael Jordan	37
Mark Eaton	9
Akeem Olajuwon	7
Alvin Robertson	6

Some argue that Jordan tries to do too much. Considering that 3 years ago Chicago won 30 games, 2 years ago 40 games, and last year 50 games, I'll take a wait-and-see approach. If they win 60 games next year, no one will make that argument. Still, an amazing stat is that Jordan had almost as many 40+ games (18) as his teammates combined had 20+ games (20). And he did make more field goals than any other teammate attempted. Nevertheless, Chicago was 27-14 when Michael scored in the 30's, 10-4 when he scored in the 40's and 3-1 in the 50's. Can anyone seriously suggest they would rather he scored in the 20's where Chicago's record was 10-13? If he is wrong for being too involved in Chicago's offense then I guess four of the other All-NBA 1st and 2nd team players are in the same boat.

	PTS + (2 x AST)	% of his team's points involved in
1. **Jordan**	3838	.446
2. Stockton	3460	.389
3. Bird	3209	.344
4. Magic	3124	.338
5. Drexler	3119	.328

Of course, the big off-season news for Chicago was the trade with New York. Charles Oakley, who lost the rebounding title on the last day of the season to Michael Cage (also traded), was sent packing to the Big Apple while the Knicks sent Bill Cartwright west. We'll find out who has the broader shoulders in Chicago. The Bulls also picked up New York's 1st round draft pick (#11 Will Perdue) while sacrificing the #19 pick - Rod Strickland. It should be a good swap for both teams. The

TEAM BY TEAM ANALYSIS 65

Chicago Bulls .... Overview

Knicks desperately need a power forward, while no team needed a center more than Chicago.

Cartwright was one of six players to hit more FT's than FG's. Interestingly, they are all among the league's older players.

	FTs-FGs	DIFF	AGE
B. Cartwright	340-287	(+53)	30
A. Dantley	492-444	(+48)	32
D. Schayes	407-361	(+46)	29
C. Maxwell	110- 80	(+30)	32
B. Hanzlik	129-109	(+20)	30
M. Malone	543-531	(+12)	33

Three main players manned the post during 1988 for the Bulls. If Mike Brown is the answer, someone's asking the wrong question; Artis Gilmore proved he didn't belong anymore (He should have retired 2 years ago.); and Dave Corzine would be an excellent backup center and possibly a decent power forward. Yet, the three each had their moments. Gilmore began the season as the starter. Chicago went 12-3 before winning only 3 of the next 12. When Mike Brown became the starter the club won 11 of 15, but then slipped to 5-8. Next it was Dave Corzine's turn. Although the team went 19-7 to end the season, it was only after it had lost the first 6 games he started. Clearly, the Bulls need a consistent center day in and day out. It remains to be seen whether Mr. Bill can provide that stability. If not, it's "Oh nooooo!" time.

The Bulls may have problems on the boards without Oakley. Cartwright and Corzine may yet be the reincarnation of CC Revival, but the simple truth is they ranked #22 and #23 at rebounding among centers - not good. Grant and Pippen were 15th and 17th in rebounding at their forward positions while Sellers ranked #30 at small forward. Where will the rebounding come from? This club was #1 in defensive rebounding last season by the standards enumerated on page 62. That will change in 1989 just as sure as the Jordan road show will draw even more fans. Nevertheless, Charles "I'll do anything for the team, but they should give something back" Oakley had to go. He was just unwilling to accept his role as a mop-up artist.

The guard position is set pretty well with Jordan and Vincent. When Vincent was traded to Chicago he quickly moved into the starting point-guard spot where he led the team to a 19-8 record. With Paxson and Sparrow (the NBA's last two players by FTA's per 48 minutes) backing up, there is potential to win 60 games someday.

The two rookies, Grant and Pippen, had average rookie years for players picked #5 and #10, but their FT% was a problem. If they are going to take some heat off Michael, they are going to have to hit their freebies at better than the combined 60% they were at last season. Even without some of those easy points, Chicago improved their record on 3-point margin games from 5-16 in 1987 (last) to 10-10 in 1988. With better shooting at the line, the Bulls may be near the top next season.

Misc: The team was an incredible 8-1 on the road to begin the season and 7-2 at season's end. However during the 23 games in the middle they were only 5-18. With some consistency there who knows?... The club missed only 10 key-man games (#1 in the league). That's great, but odds of repeating that feat are slim... Chicago was 27-0 when leading at home after quarter 3, but only 1-11 at home when trailing after quarter 3... When any two of the four (Grant, Pippen, Paxson, and Sellers) scored in double figures, Chicago was 35-11. When less than two hit that magic mark the team was only 15-21.

Prediction - best case: 57-25

If Chicago can stay healthy like last year, and Cartwright can provide inside offense and someone can pick up the rebounding slack, this club can win it all.

Prediction - worst case: 46-36

If Jordan suffers any injuries or no rebounder can be found, 46 wins is a possibility. Cartwright hasn't proven himself a winner yet and Vincent's late season leadership may have just been a coincidence.

Cleveland Cavaliers ....History

The Cleveland Cavaliers began as an NBA franchise in 1970-71. Though the club has experienced a great deal of difficulty, one particular period from 1976-78 was fairly respectable. During this 3 year span, the Cavs won 49, 43 and 43 games, reaching the playoffs all three seasons. Considering the fact that Cleveland has only reached the playoffs two other times in 18 years, it's easy to see why this period is so fondly recalled by Cleveland partisans.

In 1975-76 the Cavaliers achieved their highest victory total yet - 49. They also won the Central Division title over Washington by one game. The two met again in the playoffs, where Cleveland won its only playoff series in history, (4 games to 3, 87-85 in game 7). After defeating Washington, the team lost to the Celtics for the Eastern Conference championship, 4 games to 2.

Cleveland has had a number of solid players, but has failed to win on a consistent basis, at least in part, because of an absence of excellence. Among the major statistical categories Cleveland is the only franchise among the twenty-three without at least one annual leader.

Cleveland's first owner was Nick Mileti. Mileti did a fairly good job, but nonetheless must bear the blame for the team's poor drafts. From 1975-1981, Cleveland only got one good first pick - Mike Mitchell. Three of the first round picks were John Lambert, Chuckie Williams and Chad Kinch. These players won very few games for the Cavs.

Cleveland's next owner was a disaster. Ted Stepien took over in 1980. During his ownership, the Cavs made some of the worst trades ever. Without wasting space on the details, Cleveland traded draft picks with the Lakers, meaning the Cavaliers got Kinch while LA got James Worthy. Later, they effectively traded the #3 pick in the draft (Rodney McCray) for Terry Furlow. They then traded Kenny Carr and Bill Laimbeer for John Bagley and Phil Hubbard. Finally, they traded two first round draft picks (Derek Harper and Roy Tarpley) for Jerome Whitehead and Richard Washington. See what I mean?

Mercifully, Stepien sold out in 1984. The new owners - George and Gordon Gund - have begun to turn the team around. A series of sound decisions have established a very good, very young nucleus of players. In fact, two years ago, three of their players were named on the all-rookie team.

> **Quiz: Can you name any of the four Cleveland head coaches in the 1981-82 season?**

ALL TIME CAVS' TEAM

Player	Span	Yrs	CRD
Bingo Smith	1971-80	10	8,614
Austin Carr	1972-80	9	8,341
World Free	1983-86	4	6,918
Jim Chones	1975-79	5	6,784
Jim Brewer	1974-79	6	5,641
John Johnson	1971-73	3	5,184
Phil Hubbard	1982-88	7	5,021
Foots Walker	1975-80	6	4,724
John Bagley	1983-87	5	4,524
Campy Russell	1975-84	7	3,689

ALL TIME CAVS' COACH

Bill Fitch   9 Years
7-11 Playoffs   3 Playoffs
341-479 Reg. Season   0 Championships

HISTORICAL PROFILE

Category	Data
Cavs' Coach	Lenny Wilkens
Years coached Cleveland	2
# of franchise years	18
# of coaches	9
# of winning seasons	4
# of playoff years	5
# of runner's up	0
# of championships	0
Regular Season win %	38.8
Playoffs win %	37.0

> **Answer: The history making four were Don Delaney (4-11), Bob Kloppenburg (0-3), Chuck Daly (9-32), and Bill Musselman (2-21)**

Cleveland Cavaliers . . . . .1987-88 Highlights

Cavs 97-95 Lakers   Sat.   December 5, 1987

By defeating the Lakers, the Cavaliers won their third game in a row. It was also the third loss in a row for LA - their longest losing streak in two years. The game was unique because it represented the first time the Cavs had won over LA at home since 1980 when they won one of the NBA's biggest scoring games 154-153 in 3 OT's.

Cavs 119-111 Knicks   Tue.   January 12, 1988

Cleveland's win avenged an earlier loss at home 101-104 to the Knicks. That was New York's only road win to date, upping their present record to 1-14. The Cleveland victory was also #600 for Lenny Wilkens (see page 271). Wilkens' milestone came largely because of Mark Price who scored a career high 29 points. In his prior 11 starts after coming off injury, Price had averaged over 20 ppg. Ironically, Price, a rookie two years before, had outscored his 3 first-team all-rookie selection teammates during this 11 game span. Daugherty had scored 16 ppg, Williams 11 ppg, and Harper 10 ppg.

Cavs 109-85 Rockets   Thur.   January 28, 1988

The win broke Houston's seven game home winning streak. The 24 point margin of victory was the largest of the season to date for Cleveland, while it was also Houston's worst loss. Additionally, it tied the Cavs all-time largest margin of victory over the Rockets. The defense was the key, as Cleveland prevented Houston from scoring a single field goal for an unbelievable 11 minutes and 41 seconds - only 19 seconds short of a full quarter.

Cavs 128-126 Bullets (OT)   Sat.   January 30, 1988

Cleveland's rookie foursome of 1987 all had notable games. Although this was game #42 for the club, Ron Harper scored a season high 27 points; Brad Daugherty tied his season high with 29; Mark Price had his 2nd highest total (26); and John Williams collected a season high 14 rebounds.

Cavs 107-106 Bullets   Wed.   February 3, 1988

The win was the 5th in a row for Cleveland, while the loss broke an 8 game home winning streak since Wes Unseld took over. The Cavs went 3-0 vs the Bullets to this point last year, winning all three by a total of only 7 points. Cleveland won the game on the strength of Brad Daugherty's first triple double and John Williams' nine blocks which tied a Cavs record. Cleveland's previous *team* record for blocks (15) fell on the last play of the game, when Craig Ehlo blocked Muggsy Bogues' shot to preserve the victory.

Cavs 117-91 Bucks   Wed.   March 9, 1988

The 26 point margin was the most for Cleveland over Milwaukee since 1976. In fact, in the last 9 years Cleveland has only won 5 games vs losing 42 against the Bucks - including 0-3 up to this game in 1988. The win was even more critical for the Cavs because it broke a 6 game losing streak. Cleveland was 0-4 since the trade with Phoenix.

Cavs 120-109 Celtics   Fri.   April 15, 1988

The Cleveland Cavaliers came from 17 points behind to win going away over the Boston Celtics. The win gave the Cavs a 3-2 edge over the Celtics in the season series - the first time that had happened since the 1977-78 season (see page 229). The victory also broke Boston's 8 game winning streak and effectively clinched a playoff spot for Cleveland. Brad Daugherty scored a career high 44 points while Ron Harper scored a season high 30.

Cleveland Cavaliers . . . . Influence on Winning

TEAM RECORD BY

PLAYER	GAMES	... SCR Leader HOME	ROAD	... REB Leader HOME	ROAD	... AST Leader HOME	ROAD
Larry Nance	27	1-1	1-3	4-1	1-6	---	---
Brad Daugherty	79	10-5	3-13	15-5	6-15	4-5	1-4
Mark Price	80	7-1	3-5	---	---	19-5	9-11
Ron Harper	57	6-1	1-5	3-0	---	6-0	5-10
John Williams	77	4-0	1-1	12-3	0-5	---	0-1
Craig Ehlo	79	1-0	0-1	2-1	1-1	2-0	0-7
Dell Curry	79	2-0	0-3	1-0	1-0	0-2	0-1
Phil Hubbard	78	4-1	0-1	---	1-1	---	---
Michael Sanders	24	---	0-1	---	---	---	---
Chris Dudley	55	---	---	---	0-1	---	---

TEAM RECORD BY SCORING *

PLAYER	PLAY	DNP	0-9	10-19	20-29	30-39	40+
Larry Nance	14-13	28-27	2-0	7-8	5-5	---	---
Brad Daugherty	41-38	1-2	1-0	26-22	12-16	1-0	1-0
Mark Price	41-39	1-1	2-12	24-19	14-8	1-0	---
Ron Harper	30-27	12-13	4-7	16-14	9-6	1-0	---
John Williams	41-36	1-4	16-13	18-23	7-0	---	---
Craig Ehlo	40-39	2-1	29-30	9-9	2-0	---	---
Dell Curry	41-38	1-2	24-18	13-16	4-4	---	---
Phil Hubbard	41-37	1-3	29-26	8-10	4-1	---	---
Michael Sanders	12-12	30-28	8-10	4-1	0-1	---	---
Chris Dudley	30-25	12-15	29-22	1-3	---	---	---

TEAM RECORD BY STARTING POSITION *

PLAYER	GAMES	STARTS	PG	OG	SF	PF	C
Larry Nance	27	26	---	---	0-3	14-9	---
Brad Daugherty	79	78	---	---	---	---	40-38
Mark Price	80	79	40-39	---	---	---	---
Ron Harper	57	52	---	25-23	3-1	---	---
John Williams	77	50	---	---	0-2	25-23	---
Craig Ehlo	79	27	---	15-11	1-0	---	---
Dell Curry	79	8	---	2-6	---	---	---
Phil Hubbard	78	59	---	---	28-29	1-1	---
Michael Sanders	24	11	---	---	8-3	---	---
Chris Dudley	55	1	---	---	---	---	0-1

* For further definition of each category and column heading see pages 38 & 39.

Cleveland Cavaliers .... 1987-88 Statistics

RAW NUMBERS *

PLAYER	2pt%	3pt%	FT%	MIN	PF	DQ	HI	TO	RB	AS	BL	ST
Larry Nance	**.531**	.333	.779	2383	**242**	**10**	45	155	607	207	**159**	63
Brad Daugherty	.511	0-2	.716	**2957**	235	2	44	**267**	**665**	333	56	48
Mark Price	.510	**.486**	**.877**	2626	119	1	32	184	180	**480**	12	99
Ron Harper	.473	.150	.705	1830	157	3	30	158	223	281	52	**122**
John Williams	.477	0-1	.756	2106	203	2	24	104	506	103	145	61
Craig Ehlo	.485	.344	.674	1709	182	0	20	107	274	206	30	82
Dell Curry	.472	.346	.782	1499	128	0	27	108	166	149	22	94
Phil Hubbard	.494	0-5	.749	1631	167	1	25	118	281	81	7	50
Michael Sanders	.507	0-1	.776	883	131	1	29	50	109	56	9	31
Chris Dudley	.474	0-0	.563	513	87	2	14	31	144	23	19	13

OVERALL RANKINGS *

PLAYER	G	GS	PPG	PR	RANK	SC	SH	RB	AS	BL	ST
Larry Nance	67	60	**19.10**	**24.51**	11	29	29	28	77	12	107
Brad Daugherty	79	78	18.73	20.70	25	32	74	54	54	69	147
Mark Price	**80**	**79**	15.99	16.92	55	46	9	155	29	136	57
Ron Harper	57	52	15.42	16.23	67	53	139	107	38	40	9
John Williams	77	50	10.95	14.79	80	99	105	43	124	10	92
Craig Ehlo	79	27	7.13	9.44	133	149	114	89	51	73	31
Dell Curry	79	8	9.96	8.68	146	110	110	116	67	87	13
Phil Hubbard	78	59	8.41	8.31	149	134	88	83	121	138	85
Michael Sanders	59	16	6.19	5.98	DNQ						
Chris Dudley	55	1	3.09	4.27	DNQ						

POSITION RANKINGS *

PLAYER	POSITION	RANK	SC	SH	RB	AS	BL	ST
Larry Nance	Small Forward (SF)	2	11	5	2	14	1	23
Brad Daugherty	Center (C)	4	4	15	24	1	24	18
Mark Price	Point Guard (PG)	12	4	2	29	26	17	28
Ron Harper	Off Guard (OG)	11	15	28	10	7	2	4
John Williams	Power Forward (PF)	18	20	24	20	16	3	16
Craig Ehlo	Off Guard (OG)	25	33	23	5	17	6	9
Dell Curry	Off Guard (OG)	29	23	22	15	23	10	6
Phil Hubbard	Small Forward (SF)	30	30	20	20	30	31	15
Michael Sanders	Small Forward (SF)	DNQ						
Chris Dudley	Center (C)	DNQ						

*For further definition of each category and column heading see pages 38 & 39.

Cleveland Cavaliers ....Team Info

WEEKLY POWER RATING
41 WINS - AVERAGE (See page 39 for Team Power Rating discussion.)

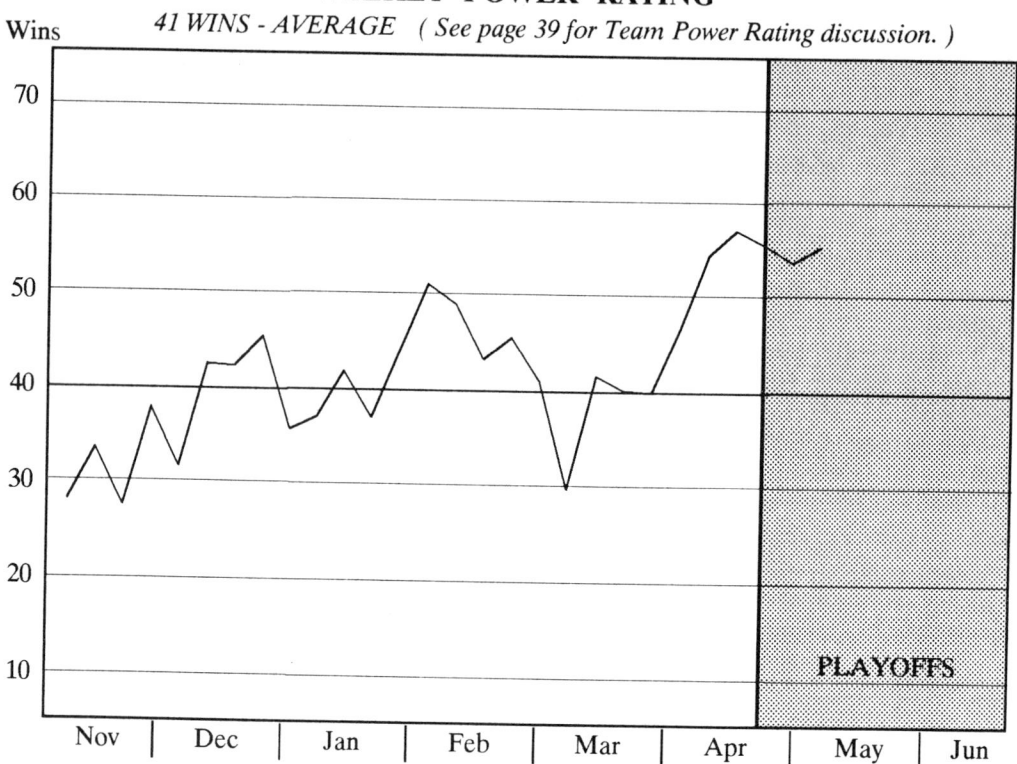

Miscellaneous Categories	Data	Rank
Attendance	504K	12
Key-Man Games Missed	49	9
Season Record	42-40	12
- Home	31-10	9
- Road	11-30	15
Eastern Conference	30-28	11
Western Conference	12-12	14
Overtime Record	2-2	10
Record 5 Pts. or Less	14-15	11
Record 10 Pts. or More	22-15	10
Games Won By Bench	4	12
Games Won By Starters	5	11
Winning Streak	5	12
Losing Streak	6	17
Home Winning Streak	7	15
Road Winning Streak	3	9
Home Losing Streak	2	2
Road Losing Streak	12	17

Performance Categories	Data	Rank
Offensive Scoring (per game)	104.5	21
Defensive Scoring (per game)	103.7	2
Scoring Margin (per game)	.8	12
Defensive FG%	.476	9
Offensive 2-point%	.496	8
Offensive 3-point%	.378	2
Offensive Free Throw %	.744	20
Offensive Rebs (Off REB/Opp Def REB)		17
Defensive Rebs (Def REB/Opp Off REB)		18
Offensive Assists (AST/FGMade)		9
Offensive Blocks (BLK/Opp FGAttempted)		3
Offensive Steals (STL/Game)		7
Turnover Margin (Off T.O. - Def T.O.)		10
Finesse (BLK + STL) / PF		2
Rebounding Record	36-43-3	18
Assists Record	43-37-2	11
Field Goal Pct. Record	43-39-0	10
Free Throw Pct. Record	28-53-1	21

Cleveland Cavaliers ....Miscellaneous

ADMINISTRATIVE INFORMATION

Team Offices: The Coliseum
2923 Streetsboro Rd.
Richfield, Ohio
44286
Telephone: (216) 659-9100
Head Coach: Lenny Wilkens
Home Arena: The Coliseum
Capacity: 20,900

1988-89 ROSTER*

J#	VETERANS	COLLEGE	POS	R#	D#	HT	WT	Clev	NBA
43	Brad Daugherty	North Carolina	C	1	1	7-0	245	2	2
22	Chris Dudley	Yale	C	4	75	6-11	235	1	1
3	Craig Ehlo	Washington State	G	3	48	6-7	185	2	5
4	Ron Harper	Miami (Ohio)	G	1	8	6-6	205	2	2
35	Phil Hubbard	Michigan	F	1	15	6-8	225	7	9
22	Larry Nance	Clemson	F	1	20	6-10	217	2	7
25	Mark Price	Georgia Tech	G	2	25	6-1	174	2	2
	Wayne Rollins	Clemson	C	1	14	7-1	240	0	11
11	Michael Sanders	UCLA	F	4	74	6-6	210	2	6
	Darnell Valentine	Kansas	G	1	16	6-1	183	0	7
18	John Williams	Tulane	F	2	45	6-11	230	2	2

ROOKIES	COLLEGE	POS	R#	D#	HT
Randolph Keys	Southern Mississippi	F	1	22	6-9
Winston Bennet	Kentucky	F	3	64	6-7

* For further definition of category and column headings, see pages 38 & 39.

Cleveland Cavaliers .... Overview

There's a renaissance happening in Cleveland these days. In baseball, football, and now basketball, the city has teams to be proud of. I think it's great. For too long this blue collar town has been the butt of everyone from economists to stand-up comedians. The changes are apparent not only in won/lost records, but in the rebuilding of the city. Part of the vision is represented in the arenas the teams play in. Both the Indians and Cavaliers have facilities which seat more than any other team (the expansion Hornets will end up seating more than the Cavs). Even the Browns are within a few hundred seats of being #1 in seating capacity in the NFL. A lot of winning and losing is related to the atmosphere the teams play in, the number of fans, and the pride those fans have in their city. That may seem like a small psychological edge at best, but it should continue to have an effect on winning and losing for the next few years anyway.

The biggest news of the season was the trade with Phoenix. The Cavs sent Kevin Johnson, Tyrone Corbin, and Mark West to the Suns for Larry Nance and Mike Sanders. It will probably end up being a good trade for both teams, but I have to believe it is most favorable to Cleveland in the short run. Nance is a star in my book and Sanders was just gravy. Kevin Johnson may end up being great, (In fact, I predict he will be an All-Star by the 1989-90 season.) but Nance was the missing piece Cleveland needed. I've argued for some time that Larry Nance was underrated. Here is a guy who has ranked among the top-11 players in Production Rating four years in a row. Despite this, he has only been selected to one All-Star game. Considering 24 players are voted in every year - that's a joke. Outside of his rookie season, the 7-year veteran has been ranked in the top-20 every year. I polled the NBA coaches for their "most underrated" list. Not surprisingly, Nance was there, along with Rodney McCray, John Stockton, Danny Ainge, and Terry Porter.

Though Nance "slipped" to #11 last season, I don't think there is any doubt that the trade was the reason. For several weeks after Larry came to Cleveland, both he and the team struggled. Nance managed a Production Rating of *only* 22.50 in his first 14 games as a Cav, while Cleveland's record was only 3-11. Once he got on track and the team got used to the changes, they won 11 of 13 and lost a close series to Chicago in the playoffs. The team's power rating on page 70 shows graphically this late-season rise. Common sense says that that should continue next year since none of the key players has reached, much less passed, their peaks. Amazingly, the team's players averaged less than one year of playoff experience each. That's young!

What makes Nance so good? To begin with, he's consistent. He's improved every year, he's not a mistake player, and he's versatile. Other than his rank at steals (#107) and assists (#77), Nance ranks very near the top in the other four performance categories - scoring, shooting, rebounding, and blocks. In fact, his lowest rank on any of those four is #29 (shooting). Only three players have four categories that rank higher than #29.

Akeem Olajuwon	#18	Steals
Pat Ewing	#24	Shooting
Michael Jordan	#26	Blocks
Larry Nance	**#29**	**Shooting**
Charles Barkley	#34	Blocks
Magic Johnson	#40	Steals
Clyde Drexler	#40	Assists
Jack Sikma	#42	Blocks

Mike Sanders was an unexpected surprise in the trade. His Production Rating for the season was 6.19, but during a 12 game stretch at the end of the season, Sanders rated 12.00 on the PR scale. Other than Kevin Johnson, Cleveland gave up some rebounding strength in Corbin and blocked shots ability in West. Nevertheless, Nance and Sanders more than compensated.

Led by Brad Daugherty, three others - Mark Price, Ron Harper, and John Wil-

Cleveland Cavaliers .... Overview

liams - will all be entering their third year. This is a remarkable group. To remember these four were rookies together, along with Johnny Newman of New York, is truly an amazing thought.

Daugherty came into the league as the number 1 pick. Do you think anyone in Philadelphia laments trading that pick for Roy Hinson, who was then traded for Mike Gminski - a second year All-Star center for an eighth year center? I'll take that trade every day. Daugherty showed his value beginning at game #54. Ironically, it was due to a tragedy in his own life. Daugherty left the team for a short while to see his dying father. Prior to that departure, Cleveland was 11-5 in 16 games. In the 16 games immediately following his leaving, the Cavs were 3-13. His tag of being too "soft" is diminishing quickly. It's true that he isn't a Hulk Hogan on the boards or in blocking shots, but his rank of #4 among centers is excellent nonetheless.

Mark Price was not supposed to be a factor at all this year. That's why Kevin Johnson was drafted. His brilliant play as a sophomore is why Johnson was expendable. What's even more exciting is where Price can go from here. His rookie year yielded a Production Rating (PR) of 6.79. In his first seventy games last season he had a PR of 16, but in his last ten games he managed a PR of 20. The best part of all is that in the playoffs he had a brilliant Production Rating of 25. When Price led the team in assists, the Cavs were 28-16; when someone else led, they were 18-30. This Price is right!

The fifth piece of the puzzle is Ron Harper. Harper was #2 in the Rookie-of-the-Year voting two years ago. Last season he struggled somewhat because of injuries. However, late in the year he had a stretch where he scored 20.5 points/game, 5.2 assists/game and 2.5 steals/game while shooting 59% from the field. If he can become a little more disciplined, and play more under control, he'll be a star for sure. Even without being classified as one of the league's very best, he is still an explosive player with enormous athletic ability.

With the hope that Randolph Keys (1st round draft pick), John Williams (14.79 Production Rating), Phil Hubbard (59 starts), Chris Dudley (#3 in offensive rebounds/48 minutes), Craig Ehlo (16-11 as a starter), and Tree Rollins (Atlanta's starting center - picked up as free agent) will provide strength on the bench, this is going to be a tough team to beat.

With Lenny Wilkens at the helm, Cleveland has everything it needs. Wilkins has made this team into one of the top defensive clubs in the league - a truly impressive feat for young players. Cleveland was #2 in defensive scoring, and #9 in defensive scoring average. Offensively, the team has a few weaknesses. Their offensive scoring is 21st and FT% 20th. When their offense did click, however, they were unbeatable. Sixteen times they scored 115 or more points. Sixteen times they won.

Flip side: The Cavaliers had the league's top FT% game (22 of 22) as well as the worst (9 of 24)... Cleveland was 1-6 in 1 point games but 6-1 in 2 point games... The club was 20-1 when they won the FG% battle at home, but was only 1-20 when they lost the FG% battle on the road... After years of losing late in the game the Cavs were 10-5 (#3 in NBA) in comebacks vs blown leads.

Prediction - best case: 55-27

I know, I know. It sounds outrageous for me to suggest Cleveland could win 55 games in the rugged Central Division. Admittedly, it's not likely, but only because of youth. In two years, I'd say its not only likely, but probable.

Prediction - worst case: 45-37

I would consider 45 wins disappointing. If that is all the victories Cleveland can muster (assuming no major injuries), the future will be clear. There will be no championships with this bunch. I really can't see this happening, though. There is just too much talent here for them not to improve substantially over last season's 42-40 record.

Dallas Mavericks ....History

The Dallas Mavericks became the 23rd NBA team in 1980-81. The expansion Mavericks, while facing 22 superior clubs, had an advantage in the early 80's. Unlike the expansion in the late 1980's with four new teams, Dallas did not have to compete with any other expansion teams for the best available players. By being the NBA's only expansion club from 1970 to present, Dallas was in the best position any new team has been in yet.

As a result, the Mavs have been able to draft several great young players. During this period, the NBA draft procedures were such that the team with the poorest record could do no worse than pick second in the draft. Without the lottery restrictions, Dallas drafted players like Mark Aguirre, Rolando Blackman, and Derek Harper. Add to that first-rounders Sam Perkins, Roy Tarpley, and Detlef Schrempf and the club has picked players capable of winning championships for years.

The Mavericks have done just about every thing right since inception. The draft is a big part of the success story, but the Mavs first coach, Dick Motta, was instrumental as well. Motta, who retired two years ago, ranks #3 in the NBA in wins. His slow and methodical building of the team paid dividends as Dallas got better and better.

The club has shown consistent improvement in the NBA. In fact, prior to last year, Dallas had won at least as many regular season games as the previous year for 6 straight years - an NBA record. The 76ers, Celtics, and Hawks have each had streaks of improvement for 5 straight years.

The Mavs have gone to the playoffs each of the last 5 years. It has really been a mixed bag for the team. In 1984, they lost to the Lakers in round two. In 1985, they were upset in round one. In 1986, they again lost to the Lakers in round two. In 1987, they again were upset in round one. Both first-round losses were similar. In each case, they won the first game only to lose the next three. On just four occasions in NBA history has a club won the first game of a best-of-five series before losing three straight. Besides Dallas having done it twice, Rochester (1952) and Minneapolis (1951) were equally disappointed.

Only one Maverick has received an award in the brief history of the franchise. The person is Roy Tarpley, who was the NBA's top 6th man in 1987-88.

> **Quiz:** Dale Ellis set a Western Conference mark for consecutive 3-pointers during his rookie season (1984). How many?

ALL TIME MAVS' TEAM

Player	Span	Yrs	APR
Mark Aguirre	1982-88	7	10,947
Rolando Blackman	1982-88	7	9,340
Brad Davis	1981-88	8	8,458
Jay Vincent	1982-86	5	6,270
Derek Harper	1984-88	5	5,995
Sam Perkins	1985-88	4	5,516
James Donaldson	1986-88	3	3,974
Kurt Nimphius	1982-85	5	3,413
Pat Cummings	1983-84	2	2,553
Detlef Schrempf	1986-88	3	2,106

ALL TIME MAVS' COACH

Dick Motta   7 Years
11-17 Playoffs   4 Playoffs
267-307 Reg. Season 0 Championships

HISTORICAL PROFILE

Category	Data
Mavs' coach	John MacLeod
Years coached Dallas	1
# of franchise years	8
# of coaches	2
# of winning seasons	5
# of playoff years	5
# of runner's up	0
# of championships	0
Regular season win %	48.8
Playoff win %	46.7

> **Answer:** Eight

Dallas Mavericks . . . . 1987-88 Highlights

Mavs 117-101 Sonics   Tue.   November 10, 1987

In the season's first matchup of the two teams, the Mavericks "got even" by defeating the Sonics. Dallas continued their dominance over Seattle in the regular season (in 1987 Dallas was 5-0 and averaged winning by 19.6 ppg). However, Seattle won the playoff series 3 games to 1 to eliminate the highly favored Mavs. Although Dale Ellis scored 28 points against his former team, the home Sonics got destroyed in the second quarter 40-21.

Mavs 109-96 Nuggets   Sat.   December 5, 1987

The Dallas Mavericks won their fifth game in six attempts when they defeated the Denver Nuggets. Interestingly, their only loss had been to the Nuggets a few days earlier. By winning, the Mavericks accomplished something they had failed to do in the previous 43 meetings between the two clubs - they held Denver below 100 points. By winning the game, Dallas passed Denver by percentage points to take over the division lead.

Mavs 110-108 Pacers   Wed.   January 13, 1988

The win made 1988 the 6th consecutive year that one or the other of the two clubs has swept the home and away series. Amazingly, Dallas' earlier win over Indiana was by a virtually identical score 110-109. Coach MacLeod won his 600th game (see page 271), Brad Davis scored his 6,000th point, Roy Tarpley gathered in a career (and Maverick's record) 23 rebounds, and Dallas won despite Vern Fleming's first triple double.

Mavs 114-107 Suns   Mon.   February 22, 1988

The win was the 11th straight for the Mavs over teams from the Pacific Division while it was the team's 5th straight overall. The win was also personally significant for John MacLeod. It ran his record to 4-0 vs his former club. Roy Tarpley had a brilliant game off the bench. His 27 points was a career high while his 23 rebounds tied a career high. It was only the 3rd 20/20 by a Maverick in the club's 8 years. Even more impressively, it was the only 20/20 by a bench player in the NBA during the 87/88 season.

Mavs 108-106 Rockets   Thur.   February 25, 1988

It's ironic that the Mavericks won at Houston. In the club's last match-up at Dallas, the Rockets prevailed, breaking the Mavs' 7 game winning streak. By winning this game, Dallas reached another 7 game winning streak. The two streaks were the club's longest in 5 years to this point. Rolando Blackman was the primary star of the game. Blackman, coming off a milestone in his previous game (10,000th career point), scored 29 - his highest point total in 3 months.

Mavs 124-105 Knicks   Tue.   March 22, 1988

The game produced several records. Roy Tarpley had his 2nd 20/20 in three games -both as a starter. His 24 rebounds set a team record. Tarpley also scored 29 points - a career high. Finally, Dallas tied a team record by having four players score 20+ points.

Mavs 135-109 Nuggets   Sat.   April 9, 1988

The Mavericks used a strong second half surge to knock off the Denver Nuggets. Though tied at 71-71, the Mavs outscored the Nuggets 51-18 over the next 12 minutes. The 135 points were a season high for Dallas. The win was especially significant since the division lead was at stake. Even more impressive, the win broke Denver's 10 game winning streak - the longest in 6 years. Derek Harper tied a career high 35 points.

Dallas Mavericks . . . . Influence on Winning

TEAM RECORD BY

		... SCR Leader		... REB Leader		... AST Leader	
PLAYER	GAMES	HOME	ROAD	HOME	ROAD	HOME	ROAD
Mark Aguirre	77	21-5	12-12	1-2	3-0	5-0	2-3
Roy Tarpley	81	5-1	0-1	22-4	10-8	---	-----
Derek Harper	82	5-1	2-3	---	---	27-6	13-15
Sam Perkins	75	1-1	1-1	4-2	2-2	---	---
Rolando Blackman	71	5-2	4-4	---	0-1	4-1	2-2
James Donaldson	81	---	---	9-1	8-11	---	---
Brad Davis	75	---	---	---	---	0-1	2-2
Detlef Schrempf	82	---	---	1-0	---	---	0-1
Uwe Blab	73	---	---	---	---	---	---
Steve Alford	28	---	---	---	---	1-0	---

TEAM RECORD BY SCORING *

PLAYER	PLAY	DNP	0-9	10-19	20-29	30-39	40+
Mark Aguirre	51-26	2-3	1-1	10-4	27-12	13-9	---
Roy Tarpley	52-29	1-0	16-8	28-17	8-4	---	---
Derek Harper	53-29	---	4-6	31-16	16-7	2-0	---
Sam Perkins	50-25	3-4	6-7	38-14	6-4	---	---
Rolando Blackman	44-27	9-2	3-3	22-15	15-7	4-2	---
James Donaldson	52-29	1-0	35-24	16-5	1-0	---	---
Brad Davis	49-26	4-3	33-21	15-5	1-0	---	---
Detlef Schrempf	53-29	---	31-18	21-11	1-0	---	---
Uwe Blab	48-25	5-4	47-25	1-0	---	---	---
Steve Alford	20-8	33-21	19-8	1-0	---	---	---

TEAM RECORD BY STARTING POSITION *

PLAYER	GAMES	STARTS	PG	OG	SF	PF	C
Mark Aguirre	77	77	---	---	51-26	---	---
Roy Tarpley	81	9	---	---	---	4-5	---
Derek Harper	82	82	53-29	---	---	---	---
Sam Perkins	75	75	---	---	2-1	48-24	---
Rolando Blackman	71	69	---	43-26	---	---	---
James Donaldson	81	81	---	---	---	---	52-29
Brad Davis	75	12	---	9-3	---	---	---
Detlef Schrempf	82	4	---	1-0	0-2	1-0	---
Uwe Blab	73	1	---	---	---	---	1-0
Steve Alford	28	0	---	---	---	---	---

* For further definition of each category and column heading see pages 38 & 39.

Dallas Mavericks . . . . 1987-88 Statistics

RAW NUMBERS *

PLAYER	2pt%	3pt%	FT%	MIN	PF	DQ	HI	TO	RB	AS	BL	ST
Mark Aguirre	.496	.302	.770	2610	223	1	**38**	203	434	278	57	70
Roy Tarpley	.503	0-5	.740	2307	**313**	**8**	29	172	**959**	86	86	103
Derek Harper	.488	.313	.759	**3032**	164	0	35	190	246	**634**	35	**168**
Sam Perkins	.460	.167	.822	2499	227	2	26	119	601	118	54	74
Rolando Blackman	.476	0-5	.873	2580	112	0	32	144	246	262	18	64
James Donaldson	**.558**	0-0	.778	2523	175	2	20	113	755	66	**104**	40
Brad Davis	.522	**.405**	.843	1480	149	0	25	91	102	303	18	51
Detlef Schrempf	.475	.156	.756	1587	189	0	22	108	279	159	32	42
Uwe Blab	.439	0-0	.708	658	108	1	12	49	134	35	29	8
Steve Alford	.426	.125	**.941**	197	23	0	10	12	23	23	3	17

OVERALL RANKINGS *

PLAYER	G	GS	PPG	PR	RANK	SC	SH	RB	AS	BL	ST
Mark Aguirre	77	77	**25.09**	21.13	24	8	79	87	60	55	102
Roy Tarpley	81	9	13.49	20.23	31	73	76	1	148	30	37
Derek Harper	**82**	**82**	16.99	19.17	39	41	91	145	20	97	21
Sam Perkins	75	75	14.21	16.71	57	65	121	42	127	58	90
Rolando Blackman	71	69	18.66	16.48	64	33	66	129	64	117	115
James Donaldson	81	81	7.05	14.98	78	152	13	13	156	22	148
Brad Davis	75	12	7.16	9.28	136	146	16	153	23	96	67
Detlef Schrempf	**82**	4	8.51	9.07	141	130	127	81	65	62	105
Uwe Blab	73	1	2.22	3.10	DNQ						
Steve Alford	28	0	2.11	2.79	DNQ						

POSITION RANKINGS *

PLAYER	POSITION	RANK	SC	SH	RB	AS	BL	ST
Mark Aguirre	Small Forward (SF)	6	3	17	22	5	12	21
Roy Tarpley	Power Forward (PF)	9	14	17	1	31	11	2
Derek Harper	Point Guard (PG)	9	3	18	25	20	5	11
Sam Perkins	Power Forward (PF)	12	13	28	19	19	19	15
Rolando Blackman	Off Guard (OG)	10	10	15	22	22	22	29
James Donaldson	Center (C)	14	23	3	5	24	12	19
Brad Davis	Off Guard (OG)	26	31	5	32	2	12	18
Detlef Schrempf	Small Forward (SF)	29	28	29	19	8	15	22
Uwe Blab	Center (C)	DNQ						
Steve Alford	Off Guard (OG)	DNQ						

*For further definition of each category and column heading see pages 38 & 39.

Dallas Mavericks ....Team Info

WEEKLY POWER RATING
41 WINS - AVERAGE (See page 39 for Team Power Rating discussion.)

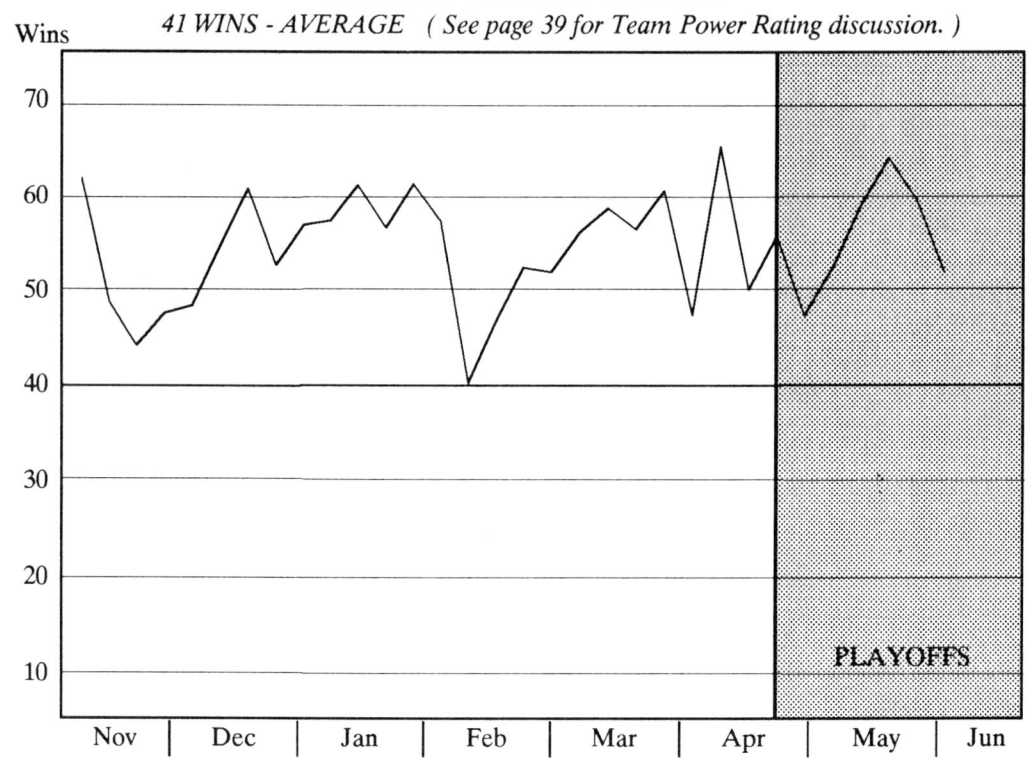

Miscellaneous Categories	Data	Rank
Attendance	696K	4
Key-Man Games Missed	32	5
Season Record	53-29	5
- Home	33-8	5
- Road	20-21	3
Eastern Conference	12-10	10
Western Conference	41-19	3
Overtime Record	3-0	1
Record 5 Pts. or Less	11-8	6
Record 10 Pts. or More	29-15	7
Games Won By Bench	2	17
Games Won By Starters	12	4
Winning Streak	11	2
Losing Streak	4	4
Home Winning Streak	11	6
Road Winning Streak	5	4
Home Losing Streak	2	2
Road Losing Streak	5	6

Performance Categories	Data	Rank
Offensive Scoring (per game)	109.3	7
Defensive Scoring (per game)	104.9	6
Scoring Margin (per game)	4.4	5
Defensive FG%	.470	4
Offensive 2-point%	.489	12
Offensive 3-point%	.293	17
Offensive Free Throw %	.789	4
Offensive Rebs (Off REB/Opp Def REB)		1
Defensive Rebs (Def REB/Opp Off REB)		11
Offensive Assists (AST/FGMade)		17
Offensive Blocks (BLK/Opp FGAttempted)		13
Offensive Steals (STL/Game)		18
Turnover Margin (Off T.O. - Def T.O.)		15
Finesse (BLK + STL) / PF		6
Rebounding Record	53-26-3	1
Assists Record	24-53-3	20
Field Goal Pct. Record	46-36-0	7
Free Throw Pct. Record	46-35-1	8

Dallas Mavericks . . . . Miscellaneous

ADMINISTRATIVE INFORMATION

Team Offices: Reunion Arena
777 Sports Street
Dallas, Texas 75207

Telephone: (214) 748-1808
Head Coach: John MacLeod
Home Arena: Reunion Arena
Capacity: 17,007

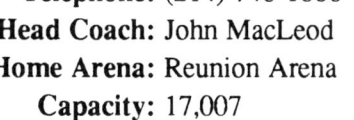

1988-89 ROSTER*

J#	VETERANS	COLLEGE	POS	R#	D#	HT	WT	Dall	NBA
2	Steve Alford	Indiana	G	2	26	6-2	190	1	1
24	Mark Aguirre	DePaul	F	1	1	6-6	235	7	7
33	Uwe Blab	Indiana	C	1	17	7-1	252	3	3
22	Rolando Blackman	Kansas State	G	1	9	6-6	194	7	7
15	Brad Davis	Maryland	G	1	15	6-3	180	8	11
40	James Donaldson	Washington State	C	4	73	7-2	277	3	7
20	Jim Farmer	Alabama	G	1	20	6-4	190	1	1
12	Derek Harper	Illinois	G	1	11	6-4	203	5	5
44	Sam Perkins	North Carolina	F	1	4	6-9	238	4	4
32	Detlef Schrempf	Washington	F-G	1	8	6-10	214	3	3
42	Roy Tarpley	Michigan	F-C	1	7	7-0	244	2	2
23	Bill Wennington	St. Johns	C	1	16	7-0	240	3	3

ROOKIES	COLLEGE	POS	R#	D#	HT
Morlon Wiley	Long Beach St.	G	2	46	6-4
Jose Vargas	LSU	C	2	49	6-10
Jerry Johnson	Florida Southern	G	3	70	5-11

* For further definition of category and column headings, see pages 38 & 39.

Dallas Mavericks .... Overview

After six consecutive years of at least tying the number of wins they'd garnered the year before, the Mavericks fell last season from 55 victories in 1987 to 53 in 1988. In one sense that would seem to be a reason for concern. After all, the club ranked #5 for fewest key-man games missed (they were the only team with the same dozen players all season); had all of the major players from the year before (none of whom had passed their prime); and they saw the emergence of a monster off the bench (Roy Tarpley). Yet, they lost two more games. One could justifiably assume that this group was incapable of exceeding 55 wins or even 53 wins. That may be true, but not automatically assumed. Remember the Celtics in 1983? Larry Bird's first three years were great for Boston. They won 61, 62, and 63 games. Then in 1983 they won only 56. They had few injuries and the same cast of characters. If anything they should have won 64 not 56. There may have been reason to panic. They didn't. As we know they went on to win 62, 63, and 67 their next three years.

The Mavericks had another streak broken last season. After leading the NBA in fewest turnovers for five straight years, Dallas dropped to 3rd. (The club was actually 15th by TO's minus opponent's TOs.) On the positive side, Dallas set two club records in 1987-88. For one thing, they won five consecutive road games at one point. For another, they held three consecutive opponents to below 100 points. This enabled the Mavs to finish 4th in defensive FG% and 6th in defensive scoring.

In a season with more fluctuations than the stock market, the Mavericks were the rule - not the exception. At one point Dallas won 10 of 11, then lost 6 of 7, and followed that up with 11 wins in a row. Explain that! They seemed to rebound well from a big loss, however. After four of the season's biggest losses to the likes of the Celtics, Lakers, and Hawks, the Mavericks subsequently won 8 of 9, 10 of 11, 7 in a row, and 11 in a row.

Like most teams, the Mavs were very tough at home (33-8). In fact, their second quarter record was a league best 31-9-1 at Reunion Arena. The Lakers were 2nd at 32-10. Dallas was the last team to play a game and lose the rebounding, assists, FG% and FT% battles. It didn't come until game #58 and was ironically played at home and played against the Lakers. As friendly as Reunion Arena was to the home team, it's probably no surprise that it was voted as the top arena in the NBA by my exclusive coaches poll. Also on the list were The Coliseum in Cleveland, Madison Square Garden in New York, The Summit in Houston, and The Forum in L.A. As is the case with most teams who excel at home, the club won the war in the trenches. Dallas had the highest margin of fouls committed by opponents minus fouls committed by your team.

1. Dallas	+263
2. Philadelphia	+252
3. LA Lakers	+225
4. Detroit	+207
5. Cleveland	+185
6. New York	+185

When I think of the reason for success by the club, I think first of all about...(drum roll)...James Donaldson. Donaldson came to the club early in the 1985-86 season. At the time, they were 6-7. They went on to go 38-31 the rest of the year. Two years ago the Mavericks were 55-27, but lost the first round of the playoffs when Donaldson was injured. Last season, they were again successful with the big guy. Donaldson missed a game late in the year, breaking his streak of 586 consecutive regular season games - 2nd longest ongoing to Bill Laimbeer. That consistency has been critical to Dallas the last 3 years. Donaldson also leads a unique group of 17 players who had more rebounds than points. James was at +184 followed by four other non-scoring centers - Alton Lister (+166), Mark Eaton (+146), Tree Rollins (+123), and Manute Bol (+99).

Dallas Mavericks .... Overview

The team has an excellent set of starting guards. Both Derek Harper and Rolando Blackman were defensive specialists in college and both have been more than adequate in the NBA. Blackman was ranked in the coaches' poll as one of the top-5 NBA players who move best without the ball. Rolando was joined by Larry Bird, Jim Paxson, Michael Jordan, and Alex English. I know I should be biased towards Blackman since we both went to Kansas State, but the reality is that Harper is more valuable. Whoa, what's that you say? I know Rolando has been selected to three All-Star Games, averaged nearly 20 ppg in them, and hit the winning free throws in 1987. Yes, I haven't forgotten Harper's folly - "the stall". Nevertheless, Dallas went 9-2 when Blackman was injured. Brad Davis is a good outside shooter and filled in admirably during Ro's absence. On the other hand, Harper is very difficult to replace. Considering all the responsibilities of the point guard, he definitely doesn't get the recognition he deserves. Harper led the team in assists 61 of 82 games. In one stretch he actually led the team in assists 29 consecutive games. Their record was 19-10. When he followed that streak by leading the team in 4 of 14 games, Dallas only compiled a record of 7-7. That's evidence of his value.

At forward, Dallas is loaded - perhaps overly so. Sam Perkins is another defensive specialist and a respectable offensive player. Perkins redefined his value to the team when he was injured late in the season. The Mavericks went 2-4 during this stretch, but clearly struggled, losing 4 games by nine points or more. One would think that a Roy Tarpley substitution would have solved that in a hurry. After all, Tarpley was voted top 6th man of the year, gathering 67 votes to Thurl Bailey's 13 (see page 240 for my 6th man rankings). Even so, Tarpley was far superior coming off the bench than as a starter. When he led the team in rebounding, Dallas was 32-12. When someone else led the team, they were only 28-19. He became the first non-starter to be ranked among the league rebound leaders and his 23 bounds in one game is a club record. Additionally, he was named NBA Player-of-the-Week during February - the only non-starter to achieve that honor as well. Despite his heroics, he does get into foul trouble. His 313 fouls ranked him among the league's worst.

Mark Aguirre is somewhat of an enigma. His clashes with Dick Motta were well-known. When he began to have problems with the mild-mannered John MacLeod, it became clear that Aguirre was trouble. That doesn't mean, however, that he's not valuable. He is. Sometimes he's brilliant, like when he hit 27 third quarter points in a playoff game. Not unexpectedly, he took exception to being benched late in games and I wouldn't be surprised to see him packing sometime in the near future. As a 3-time All-Star, his best bet would be to move to shooting guard. The problem is, of course, the club already has one 3-time All-Star at that position. They don't need two.

Detlef Schrempf is another player anxious to move on. With all the talent on the team, he has failed to get much of a shot at P.T. Doesn't he kind of remind you of another 3-point shooting star who was a "tweener" sized player for Dallas? Dale Ellis had very similar stats after 3 years before he got the chance to excel in Seattle.

Prediction - best case: 58-24

This is high because I doubt that the key players will stay as injury free or be that much more productive than last year. Even so, with the talent the team has and a second year under MacLeod, they sure have the potential to nail down the best record in the West.

Prediction - worst case: 50-32

There is virtually little way, barring major problems, that this team is not going to win 50+ games. Even if Aguirre and Schrempf are traded, they will do at least that well. The Achilles Heel remains Donaldson. If he has more problems with his legs, the club could get walked on 32 times or more.

Denver Nuggets ....History

The Denver Nuggets were one of only four teams to survive the ABA. The Nuggets have been successful in both leagues. In fact, the franchise has never had more than two consecutive losing seasons - an NBA record. Four teams have had losing streaks of only three seasons in a row. Surprisingly, they do not include the Lakers, Celtics, or 76ers, but rather belong to Milwaukee, Dallas, Phoenix, and San Antonio.

Denver is the only ABA team to win 60+ wins two consecutive years. Only 4 NBA teams have accomplished that feat. Denver's success in the ABA led to a championship series berth in 1975-76. However, the club lost to New York (New Jersey Nets) two games to four.

The team has been fortunate to have two great coaches in its history. Since 1974, either Larry Brown or Doug Moe has coached most all of Denver's games. Together they combined to coach 11 complete seasons for Denver. In each case, they went on to post-season play. Brown increased Denver's wins +28 in his first year while Moe is distinguished by having led one team longer than any other present NBA coach. Ironically, the two have an incredibly similar history (see page 125, Basketball Heaven, 1987/88).

The franchise has made two major trades in the last few years, and both have proven enormously successful for Denver. In 1984, the Nuggets traded Kiki Vandeweghe to Portland for Calvin Natt, Wayne Cooper, Fat Lever and a later first-round pick - Blair Rasmussen. Trade II, as it's now being called, was made last year with Washington, and resulted in swapping Mark Alarie and Darrel Walker for Jay Vincent and Michael Adams.

Fortunately for Denver, they have had great coaching and great trades, because the drafts have been unbelievably bad. Perhaps the most staggering statistic in this entire book is that from 1972 to 1987, of all the players Denver drafted in every round - only 1 player in 1 year ever scored as many as 10 ppg for the club. In 1982, the Nuggets drafted Rob Williams. Two years later he scored 10.2 ppg. Big deal! That performance was so unspectacular he was waived before the next season began. Finally, however, Denver may have struck gold. Blair Rasmussen, a 1985 pick, scored 13.3 ppg in 1988.

> **Quiz:** Denver is the only team to go an entire season having never failed to break the 100 point scoring barrier. What year was it?

ALL TIME NUGGETS' TEAM

Player	Span	Yrs	CRD
Dan Issel	1976-85	10	17,910
Alex English	1980-88	9	17,134
David Thompson	1976-82	7	10,434
Byron Beck	1968-77	10	10,284
Ralph Simpson	1971-78	7	7,872
Bobby Jones	1975-78	4	7,627
Dave Robisch	1972-83	8	7,259
Lafayette Lever	1985-88	4	7,237
T.R. Dunn	1981-88	8	6,210
Kiki Vandeweghe	1981-84	4	6,376

ALL TIME NUGGETS' COACH

Doug Moe   8 Years
25-31 Playoffs   7 Playoffs
345-280 Reg. Season   0 Championships

HISTORICAL PROFILE

Category	Data
Nuggets' coach	Doug Moe
Years coached Denver	8
# of franchise years	21
# of coaches	8
# of winning seasons	15
# of playoff years	17
# of runner's up	1 (ABA)
# of championships	0
Regular season win %	54.6
Playoff win %	43.6

> **Answer:**
> 1981-82 season

Denver Nuggets ....1987-88 Highlights

Nuggets 132-104 Nets   **Tue.**   **November 24, 1987**

Fat Lever recorded his second straight triple double and third of the season. The Nuggets had 10 players score 10 or more points in the game. This is believed to be an all-time record. Not only that, they set another team record with 19 blocked shots, eight each from Wayne Cooper and Blair Rasmussen.

Nuggets 124-119 Celtics   **Wed.**   **December 9, 1987**

The victory broke Boston's 34 game winning streak at the Boston Garden. Lever's league-leading 5th triple-double, as well as a career high 31 points by Michael Adams, were the major reasons why. The win was the first by a Midwest Division team at the Garden since 1981, breaking a 36 game streak.

Nuggets 151-142 Pistons   **Sat.**   **January 2, 1988**

This was the NBA's second highest scoring game of the year. It is worth mentioning that the highest game was also won by Denver by an almost identical score of 156-142 over San Antonio. The 151 points were the most scored by Denver against the Pistons on the road, while they also represented the most ever allowed by Detroit at home. Ironically, the highest scoring game in NBA history featured the same two teams. Detroit won in 3 OT's 186-184 at Denver on the strength of Isiah Thomas' 47 points and 17 assists. Thomas just wasn't up to it in the latest matchup. He *only* had 40 points and 17 assists.

Nuggets 138-125 Celtics   **Wed.**   **February 17, 1988**

Blair Rasmussen had a brilliant game. Not only did he score a career high 34 points, a full 9 points better than his previous high, but he also secured 11 rebounds. Perhaps even more importantly, he (unintentionally, of course) broke Larry Bird's nose. That accident affected the game's outcome because Bird had been averaging nearly 40 ppg since the all-star break. Rasmussen's "defensive maneuver" held Bird to only 13.

Nuggets 99-81 Cavs   **Wed.**   **March 2, 1988**

The Denver Nuggets, coming off their worst loss of the season to Dallas, soundly defeated the Cleveland Cavaliers. What was most amazing about the game was the dominance of Fat Lever. Lever recorded his 9th triple-double of the season. He not only had 20 points and 12 assists, but managed to find time to corral 20 rebounds. He is believed to be the shortest player in modern times to achieve a 20/20 (via points and rebounds).

Nuggets 116-115 Trail Blazers   **Thur.**   **March 17, 1988**

The win was ironic, as Denver's previous game was lost by the same score. The win broke Portland's 9 game winning streak and was the club's first overtime loss in two years. Michael Adams was the hero, scoring a game high 29 points and a game winning 3-pointer. Ironically, Adams set a 3-point record during the game, scoring at least one shotput from left field in 24 consecutive games and breaking Danny Ainge's record set earlier in the year.

Nuggets 120-119 Lakers   **Fri.**   **March 25, 1988**

The Denver Nuggets came from behind in quarter 4 to upset the Los Angeles Lakers at the Forum in LA. Once again the hero was Michael Adams. He scored a career high 32 points. Included were two 3-pointers, making 29 straight games in which Adams has hit at least one trey. Ironically, Magic Johnson, Adams' point-guard counterpart for LA, scored only 2 points - the fewest in his career.

Denver Nuggets .... Influence on Winning

TEAM RECORD BY

		... SCR Leader		... REB Leader		... AST Leader	
PLAYER	GAMES	HOME	ROAD	HOME	ROAD	HOME	ROAD
Lafayette Lever	82	6-0	4-3	16-2	5-9	18-3	13-13
Alex English	80	10-4	10-11	1-1	1-2	5-2	2-2
Danny Schayes	81	2-2	0-3	13-3	9-8	---	---
Michael Adams	82	4-0	1-1	---	---	14-1	6-9
Blair Rasmussen	79	4-0	0-1	5-1	1-7	---	---
Jay Vincent	73	1-0	3-3	1-1	1-1	3-0	---
Wayne Cooper	45	---	---	---	2-1	---	---
Calvin Natt	27	1-0	---	---	---	---	---
T.R. Dunn	82	---	---	---	1-0	---	---
Bill Hanzlik	77	---	---	---	---	---	---

TEAM RECORD BY SCORING *

PLAYER	PLAY	DNP	0-9	10-19	20-29	30-39	40+
Lafayette Lever	54-28	---	1-2	22-18	29-7	2-1	---
Alex English	52-28	2-0	---	9-9	30-13	13-6	---
Danny Schayes	53-28	1-0	8-10	35-11	9-7	1-0	---
Michael Adams	54-28	---	9-10	32-13	11-5	2-0	---
Blair Rasmussen	52-27	2-1	15-13	24-12	10-2	3-0	---
Jay Vincent	49-24	5-4	14-6	21-13	10-5	4-0	---
Wayne Cooper	29-16	25-12	23-11	5-5	1-0	---	---
Calvin Natt	19-8	35-20	10-4	7-3	2-1	---	---
T.R. Dunn	54-28	---	53-28	1-0	---	---	---
Bill Hanzlik	51-26	3-2	44-26	7-0	---	---	---

TEAM RECORD BY STARTING POSITION *

PLAYER	GAMES	STARTS	PG	OG	SF	PF	C
Lafayette Lever	82	82	4-3	50-25	---	---	---
Alex English	80	80	---	---	52-28	---	---
Danny Schayes	81	74	---	---	---	26-11	23-14
Michael Adams	82	75	50-25	---	---	---	---
Blair Rasmussen	79	45	---	---	---	21-8	11-5
Jay Vincent	73	8	---	---	2-0	3-3	---
Wayne Cooper	45	32	---	---	---	0-3	20-9
Calvin Natt	27	7	---	---	---	4-3	---
T.R. Dunn	82	1	---	1-0	---	---	---
Bill Hanzlik	77	0	---	---	---	---	---

* For further definition of each category and column heading see pages 38 & 39.

TEAM BY TEAM ANALYSIS 85

Denver Nuggets . . . . 1987-88 Statistics

RAW NUMBERS *

PLAYER	2pt%	3pt%	FT%	MIN	PF	DQ	HI	TO	RB	AS	BL	ST
Lafayette Lever	.484	.211	785	**3061**	214	0	32	**182**	665	639	21	223
Alex English	.496	0-6	.828	2818	193	1	37	181	373	377	23	70
Danny Schayes	**.542**	0-2	**.836**	2166	**323**	9	32	155	662	106	92	62
Michael Adams	.505	**.367**	.834	2778	138	0	32	144	223	503	16	168
Dennis Rasmussen	.492	0-0	.776	1779	241	2	35	73	437	78	81	22
Jay Vincent	.466	.250	.805	1755	198	1	**42**	37	309	143	26	46
Wayne Cooper	.439	0-1	.746	865	145	3	23	59	270	30	**94**	12
Calvin Natt	.493	0-1	.740	533	43	0	26	30	96	47	3	13
T.R. Dunn	.452	0-1	.769	1534	152	0	10	26	240	87	11	101
Bill Hanzlik	.391	.188	.791	1334	185	1	16	95	171	166	17	64

OVERALL RANKINGS *

PLAYER	G	GS	PPG	PR	RANK	SC	SH	RB	AS	BL	ST
Lafayette Lever	**82**	**82**	18.85	**25.94**	10	31	101	59	21	119	7
Alex English	80	80	**25.00**	21.70	22	9	60	101	48	111	114
Danny Schayes	81	74	13.94	**18.63**	45	67	10	11	123	21	97
Michael Adams	**82**	75	13.87	**16.57**	63	68	27	146	30	123	14
Dennis Rasmussen	79	45	12.68	**13.42**	95	81	80	33	136	19	157
Jay Vincent	73	8	15.40	**12.92**	99	54	11	80	86	86	108
Wayne Cooper	45	32	6.36	**10.31**	DNQ						
Calvin Natt	27	7	9.56	**9.70**	DNQ						
T.R. Dunn	82	1	2.20	**6.04**	DNQ						
Bill Hanzlik	77	0	4.55	**5.99**	DNQ						

POSITION RANKINGS *

PLAYER	POSITION	RANK	SC	SH	RB	AS	BL	ST
Lafayette Lever	Off Guard (OG)	3	9	20	1	1	23	3
Alex English	Small Forward (SF)	5	4	11	28	2	27	26
Danny Schayes	Center (C)	8	10	2	4	13	11	4
Michael Adams	Point Guard (PG)	15	10	4	26	27	11	7
Dennis Rasmussen	Power Forward (PF)	20	15	18	14	23	8	34
Jay Vincent	Small Forward (SF)	21	18	24	18	18	22	24
Wayne Cooper	Center (C)	DNQ						
Calvin Natt	Small Forward (SF)	DNQ						
T.R. Dunn	Off Guard (OG)	DNQ						
Bill Hanzlik	Off Guard (OG)	DNQ						

*For further definition of each category and column heading see pages 38 & 39.

Denver Nuggets ....Team Info

WEEKLY POWER RATING
41 WINS - AVERAGE (See page 39 for Team Power Rating discussion.)

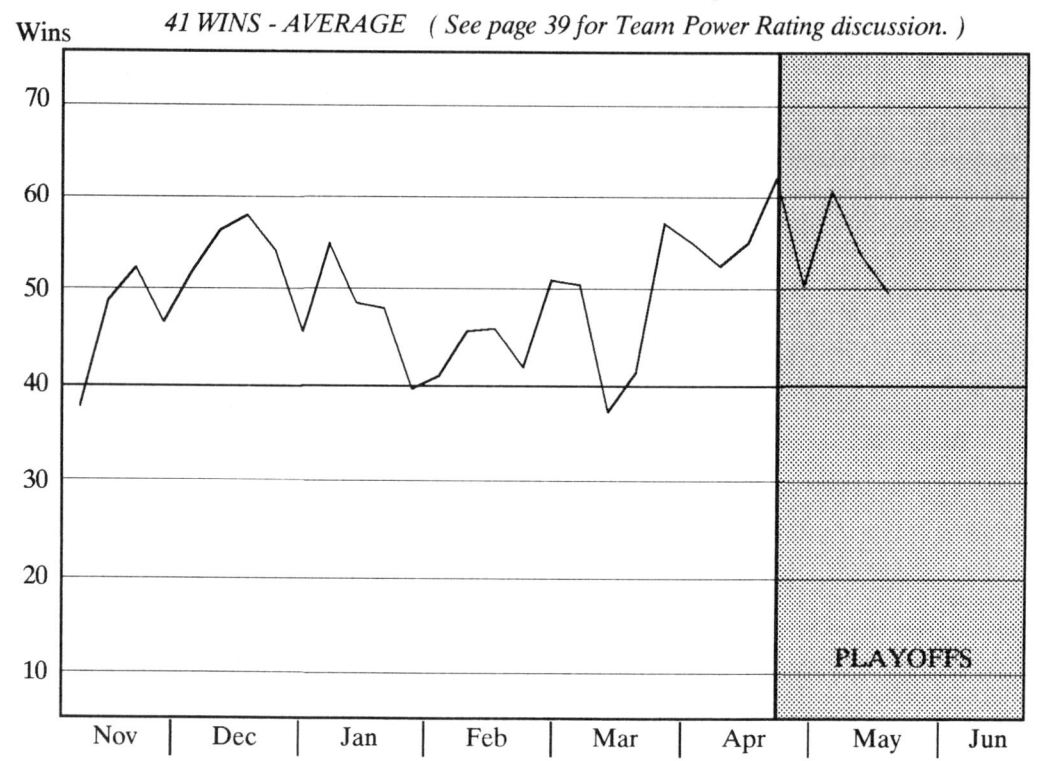

Miscellaneous Categories	Data	Rank
Attendance	521K	9
Key-Man Games Missed	125	15
Season Record	54-28	3
- Home	35-6	3
- Road	19-22	8
Eastern Conference	15-7	2
Western Conference	39-21	5
Overtime Record	2-2	10
Record 5 Pts. or Less	13-5	2
Record 10 Pts. or More	32-17	8
Games Won By Bench	7	5
Games Won By Starters	13	2
Winning Streak	10	3
Losing Streak	3	1
Home Winning Streak	10	8
Road Winning Streak	6	3
Home Losing Streak	2	2
Road Losing Streak	4	1

Performance Categories	Data	Rank
Offensive Scoring (per game)	116.7	1
Defensive Scoring (per game)	112.7	19
Scoring Margin (per game)	4.0	6
Defensive FG%	.490	17
Offensive 2-point%	.484	16
Offensive 3-point%	.342	4
Offensive Free Throw %	.804	1
Offensive Rebs (Off REB/Opp Def REB)		23
Defensive Rebs (Def REB/Opp Off REB)		12
Offensive Assists (AST/FGMade)		11
Offensive Blocks (BLK/Opp FGAttempted)		17
Offensive Steals (STL/Game)		1
Turnover Margin (Off T.O. - Def T.O.)		1
Finesse (BLK + STL) / PF		9
Rebounding Record	26-49-7	20
Assists Record	48-31-3	4
Field Goal Pct. Record	33-49-0	19
Free Throw Pct. Record	51-31-0	2

Denver Nuggets . . . . Miscellaneous

ADMINISTRATIVE INFORMATION

Team Offices: McNichols Sports Arena
1635 Clay Street
Denver, Colorado
80204
Telephone: (303) 893-6700
Head Coach: Doug Moe
Home Arena: McNichols Sports Arena
Capacity: 17,022

1988-89 ROSTER*

J#	VETERANS	COLLEGE	POS	R#	D#	HT	WT	Denv	NBA
14	Michael Adams	Boston College	G	3	66	5-11	165	1	3
42	Wayne Cooper	New Orleans	C	2	40	6-10	220	4	10
	Walter Davis	North Carolina	G	1	5	6-6	200	0	11
23	T.R. Dunn	Alabama	G	2	41	6-4	193	8	11
2	Alex English	South Carolina	F	2	23	6-7	190	8	12
5	Mike Evans	Kansas State	G	1	21	6-1	170	6	9
24	Bill Hanzlik	Notre Dame	F-G	1	20	6-7	200	6	8
12	Lafayette Lever	Arizona State	G	1	11	6-3	175	4	6
33	Calvin Natt	N.E. Louisiana	F	1	8	6-6	220	4	9
41	Blair Rasmussen	Oregon	C	1	15	7-0	250	3	3
34	Danny Schayes	Syracuse	C	1	13	6-11	245	6	7
31	Jay Vincent	Michigan State	F	2	24	6-7	220	1	7

ROOKIES	COLLEGE	POS	R#	D#	HT
Jerome Lane	Pittsburgh	F	1	23	6-6
Todd Mitchell	Purdue	F	2	43	6-7
Dwight Boyd	Memphis State	G	3	66	6-4

* For further definition of category and column headings, see pages 38 & 39.

Denver Nuggets .... Overview

There's gold in them thar hills! At least there was last season, and more than a nugget or two. This team surprised everyone by winning 54 games and the Midwest Division title.

Denver's 54 wins was a net gain of +17 - the NBA's best. Behind Denver were New York +14, Cleveland +11, and Chicago +10. There are many reasons for the radical improvement, but the one most logical when the season began would have been the return of Calvin Natt. As it turns out, Natt was virtually insignificant. He only played in 27 games, started 7 (4-3 as a starter) and averaged only 9.6 points per game. Had fans known that going into the season, it would have been reasonable to suggest that Denver might not match 1986-87's 37 wins. Apparently, Doug Moe thought differently. Moe made what was probably the second boldest prediction in the league when he declared prior to the opening game "We're going to be good. I know people will say I'm crazy, but I promise you we'll be back." Moe went on to be named Coach-of-the-Year in the NBA - a more than deserved honor.

	Votes
1. Doug Moe	**41**
2. Pat Riley	25
3. Doug Collins	5
4. Mike Schuler	5
5. Rick Pitino	2

Despite coming off such a rewarding season, the Nuggets will have to overcome the Midwest title jinx. (No team has repeated since 1981 and 1982.) They will also have to overcome the fact, that a team averages losing -5.7 games more the year after its coach wins Coach-of-the-Year than the season he won it for. With that stat in mind, and realizing that only 5 of 25 times has a team improved that next year, Denver fans should not automatically expect better things to come. Nevertheless, if you look only at the 2nd half of last season (30-11, #1), the Nuggets should win 60 games next year.

What makes the team's victory total all the more impressive is that Denver ranked last (#23) in offensive rebounding and only won the total rebounding battle 25 of 82 games (20th worst). Not only that, but the club ranked #19 in that they only won the FG% battle 32 of 82 games. How can a team that ranks so poorly in these two critical categories win 54 games? I know of no other 54 win team that has ever ranked so low in two such important areas.

Despite these weaknesses, the Nuggets had some very real strengths. For one thing Denver's assist record was 48-31-3 (#4) and their FT% record was 51-31-0 (#2). When the club won assists at home they were 23-0. Of the top-10 players on the team, the worst free throw shooter was Wayne Cooper at a league average 74%. The team average of 80.4% was #1 in the NBA.

That explains part of the 54 wins, but the primary reason has to be steals and turnovers. Denver ranked #1 in steals which led to fast breaks which led to high scoring. As they have been accustomed to do so, the Nuggets led the NBA in scoring per game (116.7 - the lowest high since 1978). Denver clinched the #1 position by scoring 132 points or more the last 5 games of the season. As far as turnovers go, the team ranked #1 in the margin between turnovers committed and turnovers created. Actually, they dominated everyone else in the league. Part of it is quick hands and part of it is great ball handling. This team has both.

If there was one more major reason why Denver won more games this year than last, it was the trade with Washington. Trade II as it has been called was as great as Trade I (Vandeweghe for Lever, Cooper and Natt). The Nuggets sent Mark Alarie and Darrell Walker (Production Ratings of 5.21 and 5.96 respectively) to the Bullets for Michael Adams and Jay Vincent. Adams was a season long starter, set a club record for 3 pointers, hit at least one trey in each of his last 43 games, ranked in the top-30 in the league in shooting, assists,

Denver Nuggets .... Overview

and steals, and had a Production Rating of 16.57. Jay Vincent had a midseason injury, but still scored over 15 points per game and came off the bench to score over 25 points 9 times. This trade will long be remembered as a steal for Denver, barring something unforeseen.

Along with Adams at guard is Fat Lever. Lever was named to the All-NBA second team for his second year; he ended up second in the league in triple-doubles (11 - one behind Magic's 12); he broke the team record for steals (223); and he surpassed 600 assists and 600 rebounds for the second time. Only 13 times in NBA history has a player reached the lofty 600/600 list. Oscar Robertson did it 5 times, Wilt Chamberlain, John Havlicek, Magic Johnson, and now Fat Lever have done it twice. Think about it for a minute. Is that company or what? A commonly heard question is "How can a 6'3" guard rack up so many rebounds?" There are several reasons. The up tempo game, the perimeter and 3-point shooting which causes long rebounds, and the general lack of good rebounding teammates all go into it, but he still deserves tremendous credit for getting more rebounds than all but 8 of the NBA's starting centers!

Alex English scored 27 points in his last game in 1988. In doing so he ended up with exactly 2,000 points - his 7th consecutive year which ties him with Wilt Chamberlain and Oscar Robertson. There's that company again. Seven players scored 2,000+ points last season, the most since 1972. Alex also passed the magical 20,000 point plateau into 10th all time. I'm not going into detail about English slipping any, but he is entering his 13th season.

Danny Schayes and Blair Rasmussen both improved dramatically last season. Especially Schayes. The two interchanged between power forward and center depending on whether the team was at home or on the road. With the club playing a motion offense as opposed to a more traditional set offense, most of the players' positions were less defined than would normally be the case. After 6 years of Production Ratings of 14.35 or less, Schayes responded by registering a very respectable 18.63.

The bench is outstanding as well. With All-Star Walter Davis coming over from Phoenix to provide the perimeter shooting and rookie Jerome Lane (NCAA rebounding champ as a sophomore) joining the team to provide muscle underneath, this club shouldn't have any real weaknesses. Davis has a career scoring average of over 20 ppg while Lane (6'6") is the first sophomore to lead the NCAA in rebounding since the "short" 6'7" Xavier McDaniel. Bill Hanzlik led the coaches' poll for "Most Willing To Sacrifice Body". Also on the team were Bird, Barkley, Stockton, and Ainge. Michael Brooks was the MVP of the CBA last year, but was picked up by Charlotte during the off-season. T.R. Dunn (+75) led a group of 13 players who had more steals than turnovers.

Team notes: Denver was 30-0 when leading at halftime in McNichols Arena... When they shot 50%+ their record was 18-0... The starters were responsible for 13 victories (#2 in the league behind the Celtics' 37 wins)... The team was 15-6 in games decided by 6 points or less (#2 behind the Lakers 18-6 record)... They were the first team since Denver did it in 1979 to defeat both Boston and L.A. in the season series.

Prediction - best case: 59-23

If the two jinxes (repeating and C.O.Y. honors) don't get to Denver, English doesn't slip too much, Davis is as valuable as he should be, and the injuries are few then this may be the best team in the league. Since not all that could possibly come true, I say 59 wins max.

Prediction - worst case: 46-26

Davis and English could have shooting problems; Schayes '88 season could have been a one-time phenomenon; or Lever could get injured. This is a finely woven team. A few holes in the dike and the whole thing could crumble. Even so, a minimum of 46 wins seems assured.

Detroit Pistons ....History

The Detroit Pistons began as a franchise in the National Basketball League in 1941-42. Seven years later they defected to the rival Basketball Association of America. In 1949, the two leagues merged to form the NBA. During these years the Pistons were located in Fort Wayne, Indiana. In 1957 the club moved to Detroit.

The Pistons are one of the "original" NBA clubs - that is clubs who have been in existence longer than 40 years. Arguably, they are the least successful of the bunch. As a matter of fact, the Pistons have had the poorest ratio of winning vs losing seasons. Of the eight teams, each has reached the championship series at least three times and won once, except for Detroit, which has attained that lofty level only twice - losing both times.

Detroit suffered a long dry spell from 1963 to 1984. During this span, the Pistons experienced only 3 winning seasons. During one 10 year stretch, the club went to only one playoff. The franchise had 12 different coaches during this period. In fact, they have hired a total of 20 coaches in 41 years. This represents the second highest number in the NBA.

Prior to the arrival of Chuck Daly, only three coaches had regular season winning records with the club. The best of the three, Ray Scott, still ended with a winning percentage of just barely over .500 (51.9%). In Daly's five years he has not only won at a 60%+ rate, but has won 32 playoff games. Charles Eckman is the second best with 10. In fact, during Detroit's 41 years and 20 coaches, only once has a coach led the Pistons to back-to-back winning seasons (including playoff record). Chuck Daly is the coach and he is five for five. His *worst* season is 10 games over .500.

The franchise has the distinction of being at both ends of several statistical spectrums. The Pistons have the record for the most blocks in a game (21 - Atla - 1980) as well as the fewest (0 - N.Y. - 1975). The same pattern prevails for rebounding. The team holds the NBA record for most rebounds combined between two teams in a game (109 - Boston - 1960) as well as the least (20 - N.Y. vs Ft. Wayne - 1955). Probably the most unique dichotomy would be in scoring. The Pistons have played in the highest scoring game of all time and the lowest of all time. In 1983, they defeated Denver 186-184. Twenty three years earlier (1950) the Pistons nipped Minneapolis 19-18.

Quiz: What famous T.V. analyst once coached the Pistons?

ALL TIME PISTONS' TEAM

Player	Span	Yrs	CRD
Bob Lanier	1971-80	10	18,822
Dave Bing	1967-75	9	13,582
Isiah Thomas	1982-88	7	12,412
Bill Laimbeer	1982-88	7	11,893
Bailey Howell	1960-64	5	9,754
Larry Foust	1951-57	7	8,803
Dave DeBusschere	1963-69	7	8,721
Terry Tyler	1979-85	7	8,427
Ray Scott	1962-67	6	7,806
Gene Shue	1958-62	5	7,374

ALL TIME PISTONS' COACH

Chuck Daly 5 Years
32-24 Playoffs 5 Playoffs
247-163 Reg. Season 0 Championships

HISTORICAL PROFILE

Category	Data
Pistons' coach	Chuck Daly
Years coached Detroit	5
# of franchise years	47
# of coaches	21
# of winning seasons	21
# of playoff years	32
# of runner's up	3
# of championships	0
Regular season win %	47.5
Playoffs win %	47.2

Answer:
Dick Vitale (1978-79, 34-60)

Detroit Pistons ....1987-88 Highlights

Pistons 127-117 Trail Blazers   Tue.   December 8, 1987

The victory ended Portland's franchise high nine game winning streak. The streak was broken on the strength of a season high 30 points by Bill Laimbeer, a career high 20 rebounds by Rick Mahorn, and a history making basket by Adrian Dantley. Dantley scored his career 20,000th point with just 13 seconds left - the 13th player in NBA history to do so.

Pistons 127-123 Bulls (OT)   Tue.   December 15, 1987

The game was virtually a carbon copy of their earlier meeting. In both cases missed free throws allowed the visiting team a three point shot at the buzzer to take the game into overtime. In game 1 Detroit went on to win in Chicago, overcoming Jordan's 49 points. In game 2 Detroit went on to win at home despite Jordan's last second 3-pointer at regulation. In both games Jordan fouled out in O.T. That may be the reason Detroit won both games, but the success may also have been the result of Adrian Dantley's performance. He scored a season high 45 points in game 1 and tied an NBA record by going 19 for 19 from the line in game 2.

Pistons 117-112 Mavericks   Fri.   December 18, 1987

The two division leaders evened the season rivalry at one game each. Interestingly, both Isiah Thomas and Mark Aguirre hit five 3-point shots. What makes this coincidence even more remarkable is that both players put up 7 shots, missing twice. By accomplishing the feat, the two offseason friends are tied for the most 3-point shots made in a game thus far in 1987/88.

Pistons 125-108 Celtics   Fri.   January 29, 1988

The win was the 7th straight for Detroit at home vs Boston. Interestingly, the Celtics have a 20 game streak over Detroit at Boston. The 17 point winning margin was the greatest since a 160-117 win over the Celtics in 1979. The best thing about this game, however, was a new NBA record attendance (61,983). Only once has basketball been watched by more people live in person - the NCAA finals in the Superdome, when 64,959 watched.

Pistons 89-74 Bulls   Tue.   February 9, 1988

The 15 point margin reflected Chicago's worst loss at home. The 74 points represented both a season defensive low for Detroit as well as a season offensive low by Chicago. This excellent defensive effort was primarily due to quarter #2 in which Detroit won 23-8. Chicago's 8 points tied a team record low. This was the first game since the All-Star game for both teams. Merely 48 hours earlier on the same court, Michael Jordan scored 40 points and won the MVP award. In this game he had *only* 20 - his lowest of the year at home.

Pistons 107-95 Nets   Tue.   April 5, 1988

By winning, the Pistons broke a 4 game losing streak (their longest in 3 years). The loss was the 7th consecutive for the Nets. Adrian Dantley was the hero. He not only scored a game high 27 points, which were his most since early in the year, but also scored his 20,871st point to pass Bob Pettit for 12th on the all-time scoring list.

Pistons 114-96 Nets   Sat.   April 16, 1988

The Detroit Pistons accomplished 2 major milestones while Adrian Dantley moved up one more notch on the NBA's scoring list. The victory gave Detroit the club's first division title since moving to Detroit in 1957. The game was also special for the fans. The 22,767 fans who watched the game became part of history as the Pistons became the first team to go over one million in attendance. Dantley also passed the 21,000 barrier during the game (#11 all time).

Detroit Pistons .... Influence on Winning

TEAM RECORD BY

PLAYER	GAMES	... SCR Leader HOME	ROAD	... REB Leader HOME	ROAD	... AST Leader HOME	ROAD
Bill Laimbeer	82	5-0	2-2	15-5	12-8	1-0	0-1
Isiah Thomas	81	8-4	7-11	---	---	23-5	14-16
Adrian Dantley	69	15-2	7-5	1-0	---	2-0	1-0
Dennis Rodman	82	3-0	2-2	14-1	9-10	---	---
Rick Mahorn	67	1-0	1-0	9-1	1-4	---	---
Joe Dumars	82	4-1	1-3	---	---	3-2	6-5
John Salley	82	---	1-0	3-0	---	---	---
James Edwards	26	---	---	0-1	---	---	---
Vinnie Johnson	82	3-0	1-3	---	---	5-0	1-2
William Bedford	38	---	---	---	---	---	---

TEAM RECORD BY SCORING *

PLAYER	PLAY	DNP	0-9	10-19	20-29	30-39	40+
Bill Laimbeer	54-28	---	15-7	31-18	7-3	1-0	---
Isiah Thomas	53-28	1-0	7-3	22-13	22-6	2-4	0-2
Adrian Dantley	44-25	10-3	5-0	14-15	18-10	6-0	1-0
Dennis Rodman	54-28	---	19-14	29-10	6-3	0-1	---
Rick Mahorn	43-24	11-4	17-12	23-12	2-0	1-0	---
Joe Dumars	54-28	---	12-3	34-22	8-3	---	---
John Salley	54-28	---	25-23	28-5	1-0	---	---
James Edwards	17-9	37-19	14-8	3-1	---	---	---
Vinnie Johnson	54-28	---	22-9	27-15	5-4	---	---
William Bedford	28-10	26-18	28-9	0-1	---	---	---

TEAM RECORD BY STARTING POSITION *

PLAYER	GAMES	STARTS	PG	OG	SF	PF	C
Bill Laimbeer	82	82	---	---	---	---	54-28
Isiah Thomas	81	81	53-28	---	---	---	---
Adrian Dantley	69	50	---	---	31-19	---	---
Dennis Rodman	82	32	---	---	23-9	---	---
Rick Mahorn	67	64	---	---	---	43-21	---
Joe Dumars	82	82	---	54-28	---	---	---
John Salley	82	16	---	---	---	10-6	---
James Edwards	26	2	---	---	---	1-1	---
Vinnie Johnson	82	1	1-0	---	---	---	---
William Bedford	38	0	---	---	---	---	---

* For further definition of each category and column heading see pages 38 & 39.

Detroit Pistons . . . . 1987-88 Statistics

RAW NUMBERS *

PLAYER	2pt%	3pt%	FT%	MIN	PF	DQ	HI	TO	RB	AS	BL	ST
Bill Laimbeer	.500	.333	**.874**	2897	284	**6**	30	136	**832**	199	78	66
Isiah Thomas	.475	.309	.774	**2927**	217	0	42	**273**	278	**678**	17	**141**
Adrian Dantley	.516	0-2	.860	2144	144	0	**45**	135	227	171	10	39
Dennis Rodman	.568	.294	.535	2147	273	5	30	156	715	110	45	75
Rick Mahorn	**.574**	**.500**	.756	1963	262	4	34	119	565	60	42	43
Joe Dumars	.477	.211	.815	2732	155	1	25	172	200	387	15	87
John Salley	.566	0-0	.709	2003	**294**	4	21	120	402	113	**137**	53
James Edwards	.470	0-1	.654	1705	216	2	32	130	412	78	37	16
Vinnie Johnson	.449	.208	.677	1935	164	0	27	152	231	267	18	58
William Bedford	.436	0-0	.565	298	47	0	14	19	65	4	17	8

OVERALL RANKINGS *

PLAYER	G	GS	PPG	PR	RANK	SC	SH	RB	AS	BL	ST
Bill Laimbeer	**82**	**82**	13.54	**20.17**	32	74	42	16	98	46	123
Isiah Thomas	81	81	19.47	**19.86**	35	27	107	131	11	122	30
Adrian Dantley	69	50	**20.00**	17.29	53	22	20	119	88	135	142
Dennis Rodman	**82**	32	11.62	15.84	70	95	58	6	117	60	65
Rick Mahorn	67	64	10.70	15.67	72	102	8	15	154	59	128
Joe Dumars	**82**	**82**	14.16	13.59	92	66	89	149	46	127	80
John Salley	**82**	16	8.55	12.34	104	131	26	67	112	11	106
James Edwards	69	44	11.80	11.23	117	91	143	41	130	57	159
Vinnie Johnson	**82**	1	12.22	10.00	129	87	148	109	47	107	87
William Bedford	38	0	2.66	2.87	DNQ						

POSITION RANKINGS *

PLAYER	POSITION	RANK	SC	SH	RB	AS	BL	ST
Bill Laimbeer	Center (C)	6	11	8	7	4	19	10
Isiah Thomas	Point Guard (PG)	6	2	20	16	11	10	16
Adrian Dantley	Small Forward (SF)	11	7	3	31	19	30	30
Dennis Rodman	Small Forward (SF)	17	23	9	1	29	13	13
Rick Mahorn	Power Forward (PF)	16	21	3	8	34	20	26
Joe Dumars	Off Guard (OG)	16	17	18	29	13	27	21
John Salley	Power Forward (PF)	23	26	5	32	13	4	20
James Edwards	Center (C)	25	16	24	21	16	23	26
Vinnie Johnson	Off Guard (OG)	23	19	30	12	14	17	23
William Bedford	Center (C)	DNQ						

*For further definition of each category and column heading see pages 38 & 39.

Detroit Pistons .... Team Info

WEEKLY POWER RATING
41 WINS - AVERAGE   (See page 39 for Team Power Rating discussion.)

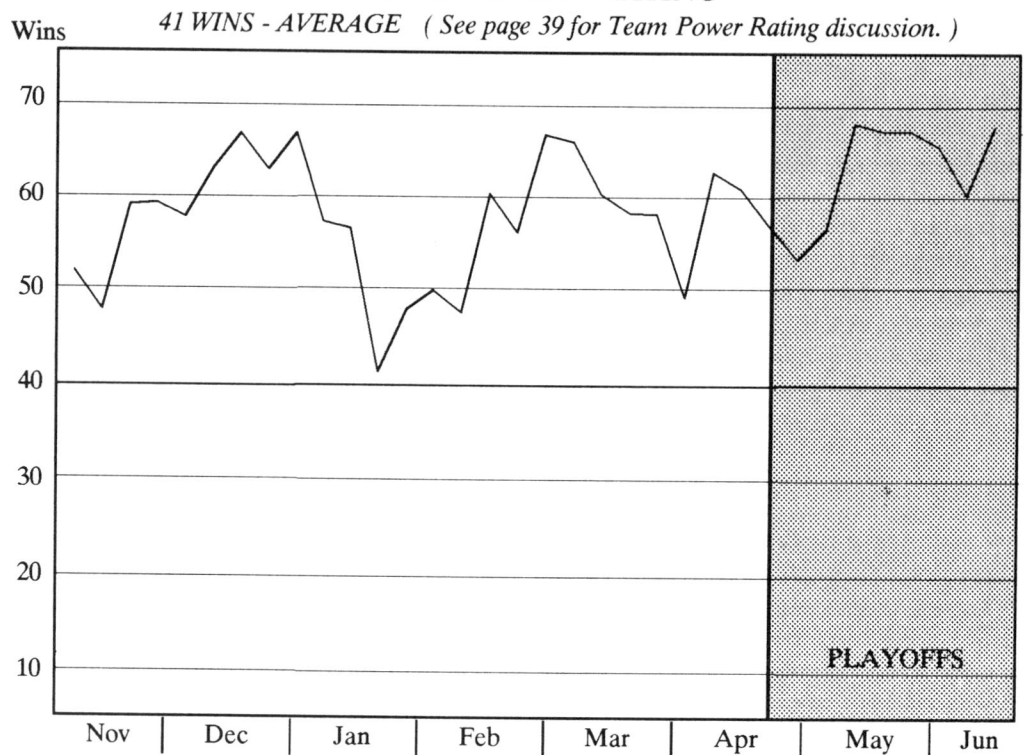

Miscellaneous Categories	Data	Rank	Performance Categories	Data	Rank
Attendance	1,067K	1	Offensive Scoring (per game)	109.2	8
Key-Man Games Missed	29	4	Defensive Scoring (per game)	104.1	3
Season Record	54-28	3	Scoring Margin (per game)	5.1	3
- Home	34-7	4	Defensive FG%	.467	3
- Road	20-21	3	Offensive 2-point%	.499	6
Eastern Conference	39-19	3	Offensive 3-point%	.287	19
Western Conference	15-9	8	Offensive Free Throw %	.757	17
Overtime Record	3-1	3	Offensive Rebs (Off REB/Opp Def REB)		8
Record 5 Pts. or Less	13-11	8	Defensive Rebs (Def REB/Opp Off REB)		4
Record 10 Pts. or More	35-12	2	Offensive Assists (AST/FGMade)		18
Games Won By Bench	8	2	Offensive Blocks (BLK/Opp FGAttempted)		16
Games Won By Starters	6	9	Offensive Steals (STL/Game)		22
Winning Streak	10	3	Turnover Margin (Off T.O. - Def T.O.)		14
Losing Streak	4	4	Finesse (BLK + STL) / PF		21
Home Winning Streak	10	8	Rebounding Record	52-27-3	2
Road Winning Streak	4	5	Assists Record	45-29-8	5
Home Losing Streak	2	2	Field Goal Pct. Record	52-30-0	3
Road Losing Streak	4	1	Free Throw Pct. Record	37-44-1	17

Detroit Pistons .... Miscellaneous

ADMINISTRATIVE INFORMATION

Team Offices: 3777 Lapeer Rd.
Auburn Hills, Mich
48057

Telephone: (313) 377-0100
Head Coach: Chuck Daly
Home Arena: Palace of Auburn Hills
Capacity: 20,000

1988-89 ROSTER*

J#	VETERANS	COLLEGE	POS	R#	D#	HT	WT	Detr	NBA
50	William Bedford	Memphis State	C	1	6	7-1	235	1	2
45	Adrian Dantley	Notre Dame	F	1	6	6-5	210	2	12
4	Joe Dumars	McNeese State	G	1	18	6-3	190	3	3
53	James Edwards	Washington	C	3	46	7-1	252	6	11
15	Vinnie Johnson	Baylor	G	1	7	6-2	200	7	9
40	Bill Laimbeer	Notre Dame	C	3	65	6-11	260	7	8
44	Rick Mahorn	Hampton, Va.	F	2	35	6-10	255	3	8
42	Chuck Nevitt	N. Carolina State	C	3	63	7-5	237	3	5
10	Dennis Rodman	S.E. Oklahoma	F	2	27	6-8	210	2	2
22	John Salley	Georgia Tech	F-C	1	11	6-11	231	2	2
11	Isiah Thomas	Indiana	G	1	2	6-1	185	7	7

ROOKIES	COLLEGE	POS	R#	D#	HT
Fennis Dembo	Wyoming	F	2	30	6-6
Michael Williams	Baylor	G	2	48	6-2
Lee Johnson	Norfolk State	F	3	72	6-9

* For further definition of category and column headings, see pages 38 & 39.

Detroit Pistons .... Overview

After 31 years in Detroit, the Pistons finally won their first divisional title, their first conference title, and came within one game of winning it all. If Isiah Thomas hadn't been hurt...well, who knows? After coming so close to the precipice of success, it will be very interesting to see how this team responds. On the one hand, the taste of victory might only linger until next year when it can be gulped. On the other hand, the disappointment may cause finger-pointing and chemistry problems. That last notion is a real possibility. The Pistons are the antithesis of a mixed bag of goodies. They've got everything you could want and more. It's the "and more" that concerns most of their fans. What happened on occasion, and seemed as if it were about to happen all the time, was a certain amount of ego clashing. Role playing was not an easy thing to enforce and Chuck Daly deserves enormous credit for controlling such strong personalities. When the Pistons did play under control they often clicked on all cylinders and rarely ran out of gas.

Attendance was at record levels in the motor city during 1987-88. The franchise set NBA records for home fans in a playoff game (41,732), a regular season game (61,893) and a season (1,066,550). Ironically, the club will be moving into a new facility next season, making all of those records unachievable. The new arena (Palace of Auburn Hills) will seat 20,000 - big by NBA standards, but small potatoes compared to the cavernous Silverdome. Given the new arena, the company jet the club flies in, and the popularity of the team (unprecedented 5 years leading NBA in attendance), this group has just about every luxury you could want.

Although they came close to a championship with their existing weaknesses, I think they will have to improve a few things to go one more step. To begin with, the club lacks continuity. Their ratio of assists-to-field-goals-made was 18th in the league. That implies too much one-on-one activity. They ranked #22 in steals, #17 in free throw pct, and #19 in 3-point percentage. This poor shooting of triples (.287) is very significant. The NBA is radically increasing in the use of the trey (see page 252 for discussion). Any team which does not concentrate on it is going to pay the price.

Inconsistency was sometimes a problem. In one 8 game stretch, the Pistons were 0-8 in the third quarter, losing each by an average of 10 points. Included in that span were quarter #3 losses by 21, 20, 17, and 15 points. That's embarassing! When they survived and led after Q3, their record reached a sparkling 38-0 before they hdropped four of their last eight.

The team has its share of strengths, led by their rebounding record. At 52-27-3, only one other team (Dallas 53-26-3) did better on the boards. The club's FG% record was almost as good as their rebounding at 52-30-0 (#3). Detroit's defense was among the NBA's best as well. They were 3rd in defensive FG% and defensive scoring. In fact, they held their opponents to below 100 points six consecutive games in one stretch during the regular season and held the league's best teams below the century mark 15 of 23 games in the playoffs. The Pistons have what many have said is the strongest bench in the league. Nine players played a lot, with eight of them in double figures. The eight ties Detroit with 6 other teams for the NBA record.

Isiah Thomas continues to be the most pivotal player on the club. I know I'm running the risk of alienating 1 million Detroit fans, but his being the most pivotal player is scary, for Thomas is inconsistent and always has been. Unfortunately, for a point guard, that's a serious problem. From a production point of view, Thomas ranks #6 at his position, behind Magic, Stockton, Porter, Jackson and Rivers. From a leadership standpoint, he rates exceptionally high, but in terms of being pivotal he ranks *too* high. The reason is because he doesn't make very good decisions at times, plays out of control, and takes too many bad shots. In his 7 years in the league, he has

Detroit Pistons .... Overview

had huge numbers of turnovers, but the biggest concern is his shot selection decisions. Perhaps the most telling statistic in this book is Detroit's record (26-23) when Isiah attempts 16 or more field goals. However, when he shot less than 16 times, the team was an excellent 27-5. The problem with this is that it is controllable. He could *choose* to be more of a playmaker and less of a shooter. Even in the playoffs last year, the principle was the same. When he shot 20+ times Detroit was 4-6. When he shot less than 20, they were 10-3. Hum? One more stat. When Thomas led the team in scoring they were only 15-15. When someone else led the team they were 46-17. As fans, what we tend to remember are the 25 third quarter points Thomas scored in game 6 vs the Lakers. What we tend to forget is that Detroit lost the game.

Joe Dumars and Vinnie Johnson are the other guards. Little Joe is commonly on most experts' all-underrated lists. Both he and Johnson can play either guard spot. V.J. had a relatively poor year. His red hot shooting streaks have earned him the nickname "Microwave", but in October of 1987 somebody just forgot to plug him in. Consequently, Vinnie was the 2nd most inefficient shooter in the league last season. (See page 32 for discussion of efficiency and inefficiency points.)

1. Mark Eaton	-107
2. Vinnie Johnson	**-105**
3. Reggie Williams	-105
4. Joe Barry Carroll	-104
5. Herb Williams	-103

Coincidentally, Johnson and Eaton are two of the top-5 rated by the coaches as having the flattest shots. The others are Clyde Drexler, Dennis Johnson, and James Worthy. I'd throw in Rodney McCray.

The forwards - Dantley, Rodman, Mahorn, and Salley - all bring their own value to the team. Detroit went 22-7 when Adrian Dantley led the team in scoring. In a similar vein they won every playoff game in which he scored 20+ points. Despite this, he was possibly more valuable in the 19 games he came off the bench. During those games he shot 60% from the field. Dennis Rodman may be the most opportunistic player in the league. If the truth be known, he creates most of these opportunities with hustle and energy. One area must improve, however. That is his free throw shooting. At 53.5%, it can lose some games. Only three players had a higher FG% than FT%. Rodman had a net difference of 2.6%, Artis Gilmore 2.4%, and Danny Vranes 1.1%. A little more maturity will eliminate the kind of mistakes he made in the closing seconds of game 7 vs the Lakers. Rick Mahorn (McNasty), along with Bill Laimbeer, were voted as two of the most physical in the league. The other three were Barkley, Oakley, and Buck Williams. John Salley filled in well off the bench. His best trait was consistency. In one 5 game stretch he scored 14 points in each.

At center, Bill Laimbeer leads the way, with James Edwards as back-up. Notably, Laimbeer backed up Edwards in 1981-82 from game #19 to game #50 with Cleveland. Interestingly, the Cleveland coach was none other than... Chuck Daly. Laimbeer has been the league's leading rebounder the last 5 years. Considering that rugged track record, it's remarkable that he leads the NBA in consecutive starts (521) and consecutive games (646).

Prediction - best case: 63-19

This is lofty, but possible. Unfortunately with Isiah coming off a bunch of scoring in the playoffs, I doubt that he'll tone it down to the degree necessary. If he does, there is no reason 63 wins is not possible.

Prediction - worst case: 51-31

I doubt that Detroit can lose more than 31 games. If Daly becomes side-tracked and he loses control (an unlikely event), the fragile psyche on this team could come apart. Dissension is just around the next bend and it will take a concentrated effort by all to hold it at bay during the 1988-89 season.

Golden State Warriors .... History

The Philadelphia Warriors were one of the original NBA franchises. Their initial season, along with that of the Celtics and Knicks, was in 1946-47. At that time, the league was called the Basketball Association of America. The Warriors moved to San Francisco in 1962 and later (1971) changed their name from the San Francisco Warriors to the Golden State Warriors.

The club certainly started off on the right foot, as they won the first championship in the BAA. However, since 1977 they have only gone to the playoffs once. In fact, from 1978-1986, the team failed to reach the playoffs at all. This 9-year stretch is the second longest in history. The Clippers present 12-year playoffless streak is the worst. Despite the recent failures, the Warriors, with the exception of the Lakers, Celtics, and Sixers, have reached the finals more often (6) and won more championships (3) than any other team.

The franchise has developed what has become a very disturbing coaching trend. On eight occasions a first-time coach has entered his second year with the team after coaching the team for the entire previous season. Every time the coach won fewer games in his second year than his first (George Karl is the latest). The average for each of these coaches is 14 wins *less* in year 2. Only one of these coaches lasted more than 3 seasons.

One of the highlights for the franchise were Wilt Chamberlain's years - especially 1962. The big center not only set the all-time NBA record of 100 points in a game, but also averaged an all-time high 50.1 points per game. In addition Chamberlain averaged an incredible 48.5 minutes per game (possible only because of overtime games). Wilt managed to play in every single minute for 79 of 82 games, including 47 straight.

The most notable point of interest for Golden State might be their penchant for individual scoring. Five separate Warriors have won the title. During the NBA's 41 years, a Warrior's player has been the scoring champ twelve times. The Lakers (two players - four years) and the Spurs (one player - four years) come the closest to equalling the Warrior's dominance in scoring. All twelve titles were accumulated in the first 21 years. The closest a Warrior came after that period was the last year the club won the title (1974-75). Rick Barry finished second that year at 30.6 ppg, well behind Bob McAdoo (34.5 ppg).

> **Quiz: Which Warrior listed below leads the club in triple-doubles?**

ALL TIME WARRIORS' TEAM

Player	Span	Yrs	CRD
Wilt Chamberlain	1960-65	6	20,024
Nate Thurmond	1964-74	11	19,745
Paul Arizin	1951-62	10	15,209
Rick Barry	1966-78	8	13,759
Jeff Mullins	1967-76	10	12,148
Neil Johnston	1952-59	8	11,386
Purvis Short	1979-87	9	10,271
J.B. Carroll	1981-88	7	9,893
Guy Rodgers	1959-66	8	9,681
Tom Gola	1956-62	7	9,508

ALL TIME WARRIORS' COACH

Al Attles	13 Years
31-30 Playoffs	6 Playoffs
519-518 Reg. Season	1 Championship

HISTORICAL PROFILE

Category	Data
Warriors' coach	Don Nelson
Years coached Golden State	0
# of franchise years	42
# of coaches	13
# of winning seasons	21
# of playoff years	23
# of runner's up	3
# of championships	3
Regular season win %	48.1
Playoff win %	47.1

> **Answer:**
> **Guy Rodgers (8), Rick Barry (6), Wilt Chamberlain (5)**

Golden State Warriors . . . . .1987-88 Highlights

Warriors 129-119 Spurs   Tue.   January 5, 1988

This was one of those bizarre games for the record books. The Warriors used 5 individual milestones to overcome San Antonio's trio of records. Robertson, Sundvold, and Mitchell all had season high games for the Spurs. Their composite score was 68 points. Golden State responded in kind: Rod Higgins registered his second highest game in a month, Tellis Frank his second highest game in his career, Otis Smith his second highest game as a Warrior, Winston Garland his highest game of his career and Terry Teagle his season high. Whew! The five combined their efforts for 98 points.

Warriors 103-101 Nets   Wed.   January 20, 1988

The victory was the first road win by the Warriors this season, breaking a 17 game losing streak. Ironically, the Nets were left as the only remaining winless road team. The Warriors overcame another negative 17 during the game as they rallied from 17 points behind in the 3rd quarter to clinch the victory. The comeback was fueled by Tony White, whose career high 24 points led all scorers.

Warriors 96-90 Cavaliers   Thur.   February 4, 1988

The win was the second in four games since Chris Mullin's return to the team. His 22 points was his high since November. The road victory was only the second Warrior win in 23 games, while the loss broke the Cav's 5 game winning streak, largely through Golden State's brilliant "defense" against Cleveland at the free throw line. Cleveland hit only 9-24.

Warriors 117-99 Kings   Tue.   February 9, 1988

The win pulled the Warriors out of last place in the Pacific Division for the first time last season. The 18 point margin of victory was a season high. Ironically, Sacramento's biggest win had been against the Warriors by 28 points. Golden State's victory came on the strength of stellar performances by Ralph Sampson and Chris Mullin. Sampson scored 34 points, while Mullin had 27.

Warriors 126-122 Spurs   Mon.   February 15, 1988

The Warriors staged a great comeback in winning. They trailed by 25 in the second quarter, 22 at halftime and 20 in quarter #3. The Warriors went to 4-1 in their last 5 games - the point at which Higgins, Sampson, and Mullin began starting together. Even their one loss was by only 1 point. During this 5 game span, the three players averaged nearly 22 ppg each. Coincidentally, the Spurs' losing streak went to five games.

Warriors 126-118 Kings   Wed.   March 23, 1988

The win broke a five game losing streak for the Warriors. More importantly, however, it was the first game for new coach Ed Gregory. Just two hours before game time George Karl announced his resignation. The three heroes in the game were Chris Mullin (29 pts) Steve Harris (21) and Dave Feitl (20). In Mullins' previous 4 games he averaged 31 ppg. Harris scored his 2nd highest total of the season and Fietl managed to score a career high.

Warriors 112-110 Mavericks   Wed.   April 13, 1988

Golden State played the spoiler with the victory, as it may have cost the Mavs the division title. What made it most amazing was that Higgins, Teagle, Sampson, and Larry Smith missed the game while Dallas was completely healthy and had won 4 straight games by an average of 21 points each.

Golden State Warriors . . . . . . Influence on Winning

TEAM RECORD BY

PLAYER	GAMES	... SCR Leader HOME	ROAD	... REB Leader HOME	ROAD	... AST Leader HOME	ROAD
Chris Mullin	60	4-9	3-8	1-1	1-0	5-4	1-2
Ralph Sampson	29	1-3	0-2	6-4	2-7	0-1	0-2
Rod Higgens	68	2-2	0-9	0-5	0-2	0-1	2-1
Winston Garland	67	1-3	0-4	1-3	---	9-16	3-19
Otis Smith	57	1-4	0-4	0-2	0-2	1-0	0-3
Ben McDonald	81	---	---	2-1	0-3	---	0-1
Tellis Frank	78	1-1	0-1	2-2	0-8	1-0	0-2
Steve Harris	44	1-0	0-1	---	---	---	0-1
Terry Teagle	47	4-0	0-4	---	---	---	---
Jerome Whitehead	72	0-1	---	3-3	1-1	---	---

TEAM RECORD BY SCORING *

PLAYER	PLAY	DNP	0-9	10-19	20-29	30-39	40+
Chris Mullin	15-45	5-17	0-4	4-14	11-25	0-2	---
Ralph Sampson	10-19	10-43	1-4	7-10	2-5	---	---
Rod Higgens	17-51	3-11	2-8	8-32	6-8	1-2	0-1
Winston Garland	17-50	3-12	3-17	13-26	1-7	---	---
Otis Smith	15-42	5-20	4-15	8-20	3-7	---	---
Ben McDonald	19-62	1-0	9-46	10-14	0-2	---	---
Tellis Frank	19-59	1-3	8-45	6-11	5-3	---	---
Steve Harris	11-33	9-29	5-16	4-16	2-1	---	---
Terry Teagle	11-36	9-26	3-11	5-21	3-4	---	---
Jerome Whitehead	15-57	5-5	14-42	1-15	---	---	---

TEAM RECORD BY STARTING POSITION *

PLAYER	GAMES	STARTS	PG	OG	SF	PF	C
Chris Mullin	60	55	---	12-40	0-3	---	---
Ralph Sampson	29	25	---	---	---	---	8-17
Rod Higgens	68	67	---	---	17-50	---	---
Winston Garland	67	62	17-45	---	---	---	---
Otis Smith	57	12	---	2-8	0-2	---	---
Ben McDonald	81	41	---	---	3-7	9-22	---
Tellis Frank	78	29	---	---	---	6-23	---
Steve Harris	44	16	---	6-10	---	---	---
Terry Teagle	47	4	---	0-4	---	---	---
Jerome Whitehead	72	27	---	---	---	4-11	3-9

* For further definition of each category and column heading see pages 38 & 39.

TEAM BY TEAM ANALYSIS 101

Golden State Warriors . . . . 1987-88 Statistics

RAW NUMBERS *

PLAYER	2pt%	3pt%	FT%	MIN	PF	DQ	HI	TO	RB	AS	BL	ST
Chris Mullin	.526	.351	**.885**	2033	136	3	38	156	205	290	32	113
Ralph Sampson	.443	.182	.760	1663	164	3	34	**171**	**462**	122	**88**	41
Rod Higgens	**.528**	**.487**	.848	**2188**	188	2	**41**	111	293	188	31	70
Winston Garland	.444	.333	.879	2122	188	2	27	167	227	**429**	7	**116**
Otis Smith	.502	.317	.777	1549	160	0	29	107	247	155	42	91
Ben McDonald	.482	.257	.784	2039	246	4	22	93	335	138	8	39
Tellis Frank	.429	0-1	.725	1597	**267**	5	23	109	330	111	23	53
Steve Harris	.465	0-7	.788	1084	89	0	24	56	126	87	8	50
Terry Teagle	.460	.111	.802	958	95	0	28	80	81	61	4	32
Jerome Whitehead	.483	0-0	.720	1221	209	3	19	49	321	39	21	32

OVERALL RANKINGS *

PLAYER	G	GS	PPG	PR	RANK	SC	SH	RB	AS	BL	ST
Chris Mullin	60	55	20.22	20.17	33	20	18	124	4	82	20
Ralph Sampson	48	44	15.60	17.94	51	51	144	17	92	16	116
Rod Higgens	68	67	15.50	16.65	58	52	11	99	80	92	79
Winston Garland	67	62	12.40	14.76	82	85	134	118	24	147	23
Otis Smith	72	18	11.68	12.24	107	92	59	90	66	44	15
Ben McDonald	81	41	7.56	8.90	145	142	108	88	101	143	139
Tellis Frank	78	29	8.13	8.49	148	135	151	63	96	89	72
Steve Harris	58	26	9.22	7.97	DNQ						
Terry Teagle	47	4	12.64	7.87	DNQ						
Jerome Whitehead	72	27	5.65	7.81	DNQ						

POSITION RANKINGS *

PLAYER	POSITION	RANK	SC	SH	RB	AS	BL	ST
Chris Mullin	Off Guard (OG)	7	7	6	20	11	8	7
Ralph Sampson	Center (C)	11	7	25	8	3	9	7
Rod Higgens	Small Forward (SF)	13	17	2	27	15	23	14
Winston Garland	Point Guard (PG)	19	17	28	11	22	24	12
Otis Smith	Small Forward (SF)	22	22	10	23	9	9	2
Ben McDonald	Power Forward (PF)	33	31	25	35	10	35	30
Tellis Frank	Power Forward (PF)	34	28	32	30	9	30	7
Steve Harris	Off Guard (OG)	DNQ						
Terry Teagle	Off Guard (OG)	DNQ						
Jerome Whitehead	Center (C)	DNQ						

*For further definition of each category and column heading see pages 38 & 39.

Golden State Warriors..................Team Info

WEEKLY POWER RATING
41 WINS - AVERAGE   (See page 39 for Team Power Rating discussion.)

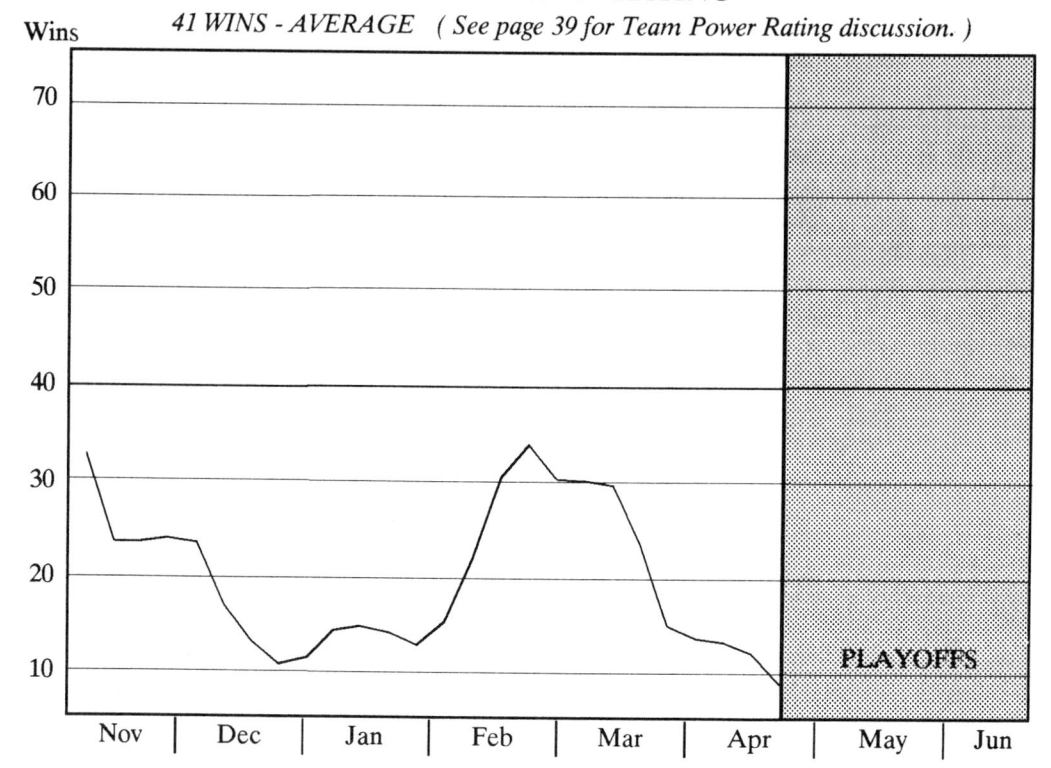

Miscellaneous Categories	Data	Rank	Performance Categories	Data	Rank
Attendance	465K	17	Offensive Scoring (per game)	107.0	14
Key-Man Games Missed	240	23	Defensive Scoring (per game)	115.3	22
Season Record	20-62	21	Scoring Margin (per game)	-8.3	22
- Home	16-25	21	Defensive FG%	.501	22
- Road	4-37	21	Offensive 2-point%	.475	21
Eastern Conference	5-17	20	Offensive 3-point%	.292	18
Western Conference	15-45	22	Offensive Free Throw %	.796	3
Overtime Record	1-2	19	Offensive Rebs (Off REB/Opp Def REB)		16
Record 5 Pts. or Less	9-17	22	Defensive Rebs (Def REB/Opp Off REB)		22
Record 10 Pts. or More	7-34	21	Offensive Assists (AST/FGMade)		19
Games Won By Bench	5	9	Offensive Blocks (BLK/Opp FGAttempted)		23
Games Won By Starters	3	15	Offensive Steals (STL/Game)		5
Winning Streak	2	21	Turnover Margin (Off T.O. - Def T.O.)		8
Losing Streak	8	19	Finesse (BLK + STL) / PF		22
Home Winning Streak	3	20	Rebounding Record	20-58-4	23
Road Winning Streak	2	14	Assists Record	21-59-12	22
Home Losing Streak	5	20	Field Goal Pct. Record	24-58-0	22
Road Losing Streak	17	20	Free Throw Pct. Record	48-33-1	5

Golden State Warriors .... Miscellaneous

ADMINISTRATIVE INFORMATION

Team Offices: Oakland Coliseum Arena
Oakland, California
94621

Telephone: (415) 638-6300
Head Coach: Don Nelson
Home Arena: Oakland Coliseum Arena
Capacity: 15,025

1988-89 ROSTER*

J#	VETERANS	COLLEGE	POS	R#	D#	HT	WT	G.St	NBA
	Manute Bol	Bridgeport	C	2	31	7-6	225	0	3
32	Tellis Frank	W. Kentucky	F	1	14	6-10	240	1	1
12	Winston Garland	S.W. Missouri St.	G	2	40	6-2	170	1	1
20	Steve Harris	Tulsa	G	1	19	6-5	195	1	3
40	Rod Higgens	Fresno State	F	2	31	6-7	205	2	6
55	Ben McDonald	Irvine	F	3	50	6-8	225	2	3
17	Chris Mullin	St. Johns	G	1	7	6-7	220	3	3
50	Ralph Sampson	Virginia	C	1	1	7-4	230	1	5
13	Larry Smith	Alcorn State	F	2	24	6-8	235	8	8
22	Otis Smith	Jacksonville	G	2	41	6-5	210	1	2
20	Terry Teagle	Baylor	G	1	16	6-5	195	4	6
4	Tony White	Tennessee	G	2	33	6-2	170	1	1
33	Jerome Whitehead	Marquette	C-F	2	44	6-10	240	4	10

	ROOKIES	COLLEGE	POS	R#	D#	HT
	Mitch Richmond	Kansas State	G	1	5	6-5
	Keith Smart	Indiana	G	2	41	6-2

* For further definition of category and column headings, see pages 38 & 39.

Golden State Warriors .... Overview

The stock market wasn't the only thing that crashed in late October 1987. That's also when the Golden State Warriors began their preseason. After reaching a 10 year high (first trip to the playoffs) just the summer before, the 1987-88 season started low and dropped faster than Don Ameche could yell "Sell! Sell! Sell!". The Warriors did sell, of course, but much too late - well after the damage had been done. Like most of us, they sold short and bought long. Well actually, they sold Short before the season began, but teammates Sleepy Floyd and J.B. Carroll soon followed him to Houston. The long is Ralph Sampson - the "prize" for waiting until Floyd and Carroll's stock had plunged. It's ironic that these two should be traded, as they had both been voted first time All-Stars just the season before. What they left behind on the trading floor was nothing short of a carnage - 15 losers and 3 gainers.

Unfortunately, it could get worse and it did. The team went on to a record of 20-62. The 22 game drop (from 42 wins) was by far the biggest in the league last year and the largest single season crash in the NBA since Wall Street's Knicks plunged 23 wins from 1984 to 1985.

Drops from 1986-87 to 1987-88
1. **Golden St. Warriors   -22 wins**
2. Philadelphia   -9 wins
3. Milwaukee   -8 wins
4. Phoenix   -8 wins
5. Atlanta   -7 wins

The reaction of fans to the 22 win drop ranged from very disappointed to stunned, since two of the country's leading publications had picked Golden State to finish 2nd in the division. Despite all of this, I actually rank Indiana's season as more disappointing. If you want to know why, read pages 120-121.

The Warriors were the busiest team last year with respect to personnel. Amazingly, 22 different players suited up. None wore #24, however. That was retired during the season in honor of the club's last great player - Rick Barry. Barry retired in 1981 - the same year as Kermit Washington. Wait a minute. Didn't a Kermit Washington start Golden State's first game of last season? "Yup!" Is it the same..."Yup!" How many points did he ..."Four". How many starts did he..."One". Maybe that's part of why the Warriors nose dived. Still, you wouldn't think any team could be so bad on the boards that they would jump that far off the deep end. Well, they were and they did. It didn't help either. Golden State ended up last (#23) with a rebounding record of 20-58-4. Of course, part of the reason for that dismal stat was Larry Smith's constant yo-yoing in and out of the lineup. Smith had been the #1 rebounder in the NBA on a 48 minute basis just the season before. His 62 missed games due to injury were a significant, yet small, part of Golden State's injury woes. The club ranked dead last with 240 key-man games missed during the season. That's the main reason the team needed more players on its roster than any other. It's also why no consistency was achieved during the season and ultimately had to be a big reason why George Karl just couldn't take it anymore.

Karl tried to fight the inevitable, but with injuries mounting, a 16-48 record, and the big shadow of Don Nelson hanging over the team, what else could he do? There will be those who will say "I told you so." regarding Nelson's taking over. Nelson enters next season as one of the winningest coaches ever. He reached 500 victories faster than any other (a record soon to be broken by Pat Riley) and his teams have won 50+ games seven straight years.

The club ranked last in blocks, next to last in defensive FG%, and next to last in defensive scoring. (The last 23 games their opponents scored 110 or more points.) With a defense that bad, it's no surprise that the club was 0-17 in games decided by 20 points or more and 0-18 in games where their opponents scored 123+ points. Due to the number of blowouts the team endured, the bench got its share of playing

Golden State Warriors .... Overview

time. In fact, in 10 games, the bench actually scored 55 or more points. That's tops in the league. If you're saying "So what?", take a look at the benches this group beat out.

	Games where bench scored 55+ points	Wins
1. **Golden State**	10	22
2. Denver	9	54
3. Utah	9	47
4. Washington	8	38
5. Seattle	7	44
6. Atlanta	5	50
7. Portland	5	53

There were a few bright spots for the club last year. Among others, the Warriors ranked #3 in FT% (.796). One would think that might lead to winning some close games. Well, maybe it did in a few cases, but not enough, as the team ranked #22 in games decided by 5 points or less (9-17). The club also ranked high in steals (#5) and turnover margin (#8).

The natives are restless, but there is hope that the trim towers (Sampson and Manute Bol) will lead them into the promised land. I, for one, am a strong critic of Ralph. I've never believed that he had the heart to win. I've always thought he was too selfish. As far as I'm concerned, I proved it last season by charting his shots. At Houston he shot .785 from within 5', .344 6'-8', .169 9'-12', .238 13'-15', and .200 from 16' out. Despite this obvious bricklaying, he chose to shoot, shoot, shoot. The reality is that over 50% of his shots were from 9+ feet out. From that distance he might as well be pitching nickels into Coke bottles. If the problem had been left behind in Houston that would be fine, but not so. His excessive interest in seeing the ball shotput from his hands cost his new club victories as well. When he took less than 10 field goal attempts, they were an excellent 4-1; when he shot 10-18 times they were a poor 6-13; and finally, when he air-balled his way to 19+ FGA's, his poor teammates never won (0-5). It's really a sad commentary on a player as gifted as he is. Maybe Don Nelson can do something with him. If so, Ralph could be great as a defensive center, a rebounder, and a stickback artist. Just don't give him the ball 6 feet or more from the hoop. It should be no shock to anyone that the NBA coaches I surveyed rated him the league's most overrated player.

The best player on the team was clearly Chris Mullin. Hopefully, he's rehabilitated from his alcohol addiction. If so, he's valuable. "Air Mullin", as he jokingly calls himself, can't run or jump (sounds like Larry Bird), but he can do one other thing - shoot. Mullin came very close to matching Bird as the only player ever to shoot 50%+ from the field (.508) and 90%+ from the line (.885). Still, when your shooting guard is by far and away your best player, either you're the Chicago Bulls or you're in trouble!

Ironically, or stupidly, depending on your viewpoint, the Warriors took a shooting guard as the #5 pick in the draft. I'll have to argue here that the team was smart - assuming Mullin can make the transition to small forward. I think he can. If he cannot, he may be out of a job or used for trade bait. That's how good Richmond is. I saw him play a lot at Kansas State and I would agree completely with Bob Lanier who said "If Mitch Richmond doesn't make it in the NBA, I'll eat my shoes." If you don't remember Lanier's feet, let me assure you, he's going on the line.

Prediction - best case: 33-49

If this team exceeds 33 victories it will be a miracle. I'll certainly tip my hat to Don Nelson. He'll deserve it because it will mean he disciplined Sampson or at least he trimmed a few of his locks. Nevertheless, Garland is so young at point guard - though he has potential - and the power forward position is weak, weak, weak.

Prediction - worst case: 20-62

The same as last year. It can't get any worse. Richmond will see to that alone. Even so, if Ralph doesn't change and the usual injuries occur, not even Don Nelson will be able to subsidize this crop.

Houston Rockets ....History

The Houston Rockets were one of the NBA's two expansion teams in 1967-68. The other was Seattle. From 1967 to 1971, eight new teams joined the league. The club's record is better than the Clippers and the Cavaliers of this group, but not as good as that of the other five.

The Rockets have had their moments, however, especially in the 1980's. Houston advanced to the championship series twice. In 1981, they entered the playoffs with a relatively poor 40-42 record, but managed to climb to the finals by winning on the road. Coincidentally, Houston's opponent in the Western Conference finals was Kansas City. The Kings had also been 40-42 during the season and had also won big on the road. In the 25 games played in the Western Conference playoffs during 1981, an incredible 17 were won by the road team. After upsetting the defending champion Lakers, the Rockets lost to the Celtics 4 games to 2.

In 1986, the club also made it to the championship round. Again they had to upset the defending champion LA Lakers along the way. Again the championship series was against the Boston Celtics. Again Houston lost 2 games to 4. Ironically, Houston's coach in 1986 was Boston's coach in 1981 - Bill Fitch.

Fitch is, among other things, the only coach to have won a title in three different divisions in addition to being named Coach-of-the-Year twice. Finally, he ended 1987-88 with 997 career victories (NBA plus college). Only Jack Ramsay (1,104) and Red Auerbach (1,037) have won more.

The Rockets had a 15-67 record in 1967-68. The 15 wins tied Cleveland and Dallas for the fewest wins by an NBA club in their initial season. Houston improved dramatically in 1969 to 37-45 with the addition of Elvin Hayes. This 22 game improvement is the third best by an NBA team in its second year, trailing Milwaukee (+29 wins) and Phoenix (+23 wins).

Calvin Murphy holds many franchise records including the single game scoring record of 57 points... Murphy also holds the NBA all-time record for consecutive FT's made (78)... Additionally, he ranks #4 in most regular season games played with one franchise. Murphy played in 1002 games. Only John Havlicek (1220 - Boston), Hal Greer (1122 - Philadelphia), and Dolph Schayes (1059 - Syracuse) have played more games with one team.

> **Quiz:** Besides Sampson for Carroll, when was the last time two #1 picks in a draft were traded for each other?

ALL TIME ROCKETS' TEAM

Player	Span	Yrs	CRD
Calvin Murphy	1971-83	13	15,626
Rudy Tomjanovich	1971-81	11	14,133
Moses Malone	1977-82	6	13,340
Elvin Hayes	1969-84	7	12,612
Robert Reid	1978-88	10	10,121
Akeem Olajuwon	1985-88	4	8,393
Mike Newlin	1972-79	8	8,262
Allen Leavell	1980-88	9	7,316
Rodney McCray	1984-88	5	7,001
Ralph Sampson	1984-88	5	6,794

ALL TIME ROCKETS' COACH

Bill Fitch   4 Years
20-15 Playoffs   3 Playoffs
170-158 Reg. Season   0 Championships

HISTORICAL PROFILE

Category	Data
Rockets' coach	Don Chaney
Years coached Houston	0
# of franchise years	21
# of coaches	8
# of winning seasons	7
# of playoff years	11
# of runner's up	2
# of championships	0
Regular season win %	45.3
Playoff win %	48.0

> **Answer:** Never

Houston Rockets . . . . 1987-88 Highlights

Rockets 121-96 Warriors   Sat.   December 5, 1987

Houston defeated Golden State on the strength of Purvis Short's 27 points. It was the most points Short had scored all year and came at an appropriate time. Purvis spent his first nine years in the NBA with Golden State, making this his first game ever against his former team. The 25 point margin of victory was Houston's largest of the season to date.

Rockets 101-91 Pistons   Tue.   December 29, 1987

The Rockets made use of an explosive 3rd quarter to win by 10 points over the Detroit Pistons. During the third quarter, both Akeem Olajuwon and J.B. Carroll scored 10 points each - the same as Detroit. Houston won the quarter 30-10 by scoring the first 16 points after intermission. The 10 point quarter was Detroit's low of the season. The loss also snapped Detroit's 10 game home-court winning streak and their overall 10 game winning streak - the NBA's longest of the year to this point and tying the longest in Piston's history.

Rockets 102-93 Bucks   Wed.   December 30, 1987

Houston won their third straight game over the top three Central Division leaders, including two on the road. The Rockets averaged defeating Atlanta, Detroit, and Milwaukee by 13 points each to end 1987 on a high note. Ironically, the win in Milwaukee was Houston's first since 1980 when Houston's coach was Del Harris - presently Milwaukee's coach.

Rockets 111-100 Bullets   Sat.   January 2, 1988

The Rockets used a 16-0 spurt at the start of the second half to take a 32 point lead (72-40). The victory was the 3rd in a row on the road and was so crushing that it became the straw that broke Kevin Loughery's back. Loughery was fired before the Bullets next game. The Rockets 3rd quarter starts were awesome during this 3 game stretch. They outscored Detroit 16-0, Milwaukee 16-3, and Washington 16-0 to start second halves.

Rockets 120-113 Warriors   Thur.   January 7, 1988

The Rockets met the Warriors for the first time since "THE TRADE". The unique individual matchup of the year was at center with Ralph Sampson vs his former teammate Akeem Olajuwon. As it turned out, it was Akeem's best game of the year to date, as he scored 30 points and collected 20 rebounds. Sampson scored 14 points and collected 14 rebounds. Ironically, Purvis Short playing against his former team for the second time in his career, scored 27 points. The irony is that in his first game vs the Warriors, he also scored 27 points. The two games were his season highs up to this point.

Rockets 102-100 Pacers   Thur.   March 31, 1988

The win was Houston's 7th consecutive vs Indiana. The two heroes for the Rockets were Joe Barry Carroll and Cedric Maxwell. Carroll, starting for an injured Akeem Olajuwon, scored a season high 29 points, including the game winning shot. Maxwell, though, was the big hero. He scored 23 points, 15 rebounds, and 10 assists. All were easily season highs, while it represented his first-ever triple-double and a career high in assists.

Rockets 127-119 Lakers   Sun.   April 17, 1988

The victory was Houston's first after 8 consecutive losses against the defending champs. The loss was LA's 5th in a row on the road - the longest losing stint in 7 years. Akeem Olajuwon scored a season high 38 points to fend off the Lakers. Magic Johnson registered his league-leading 12th triple-double.

Houston Rockets .... Influence on Winning

TEAM RECORD BY

		... SCR Leader		... REB Leader		... AST Leader	
PLAYER	GAMES	HOME	ROAD	HOME	ROAD	HOME	ROAD
Akeem Olajuwon	79	21-5	10-18	24-8	10-14	2-0	---
Rodney McCray	81	2-0	---	6-0	2-6	4-0	2-2
Eric Floyd	59	3-2	0-1	0-1	1-0	16-6	6-14
Joe Barry Carroll	63	0-1	2-3	3-0	2-1	---	---
Allen Leavell	80	3-0	1-1	---	---	15-1	5-14
Jim Petersen	69	---	---	2-1	1-2	1-0	---
Purvis Short	81	5-0	0-4	---	---	0-1	1-1
Buck Johnson	70	---	0-1	1-0	---	---	0-1
Robert Reid	62	---	---	---	---	---	0-1
Cedric Maxwell	71	---	---	---	1-0	1-0	1-0

TEAM RECORD BY SCORING *

PLAYER	PLAY	DNP	0-9	10-19	20-29	30-39	40+
Akeem Olajuwon	45-34	1-2	0-1	12-9	26-21	7-3	---
Rodney McCray	46-35	0-1	13-13	25-22	8-0	---	---
Eric Floyd	32-27	14-9	5-9	20-15	7-3	---	---
Joe Barry Carroll	35-28	11-8	10-11	22-13	3-4	---	---
Allen Leavell	46-34	0-2	26-16	15-18	5-0	---	---
Jim Petersen	39-30	7-6	20-15	18-15	1-0	---	---
Purvis Short	45-36	1-0	8-15	23-17	11-4	3-0	---
Buck Johnson	39-31	7-5	34-24	5-7	---	---	---
Robert Reid	36-26	10-10	27-17	8-8	1-1	---	---
Cedric Maxwell	42-29	4-7	38-26	3-3	1-0	---	---

TEAM RECORD BY STARTING POSITION *

PLAYER	GAMES	STARTS	PG	OG	SF	PF	C
Akeem Olajuwon	79	79	---	---	---	---	45-34
Rodney McCray	81	80	---	---	45-35	---	---
Eric Floyd	59	55	26-21	4-4	---	---	---
Joe Barry Carroll	63	16	---	---	---	5-8	1-2
Allen Leavell	80	54	18-14	15-7	---	---	---
Jim Petersen	69	50	---	---	---	30-20	---
Purvis Short	81	11	---	6-5	---	---	---
Buck Johnson	70	2	---	---	1-1	---	---
Robert Reid	62	31	---	15-16	---	---	---
Cedric Maxwell	71	0	---	---	---	---	---

* For further definition of each category and column heading see pages 38 & 39.

Houston Rockets — 1987-88 Statistics

RAW NUMBERS *

PLAYER	2pt%	3pt%	FT%	MIN	PF	DQ	HI	TO	RB	AS	BL	ST
Akeem Olajuwon	.516	0-4	.695	2825	324	7	38	243	959	163	214	162
Rodney McCray	.484	0-4	.785	2689	166	2	24	144	631	264	51	57
Eric Floyd	.453	.194	.850	2514	190	1	37	223	296	544	12	95
Joe Barry Carroll	.436	0-2	.764	2004	195	1	29	164	489	113	106	50
Allen Leavell	.471	.216	.869	2150	162	1	26	130	148	405	9	124
Jim Petersen	.515	.167	.745	1793	203	3	22	119	436	106	40	36
Purvis Short	.486	.238	.858	1949	197	0	33	118	222	162	14	58
Buck Johnson	.531	.125	.736	879	127	0	19	54	168	49	26	30
Robert Reid	.472	.382	.794	980	118	0	21	41	125	67	5	27
Cedric Maxwell	.473	0-2	.769	848	75	0	23	54	179	60	12	22

OVERALL RANKINGS *

PLAYER	G	GS	PPG	PR	RANK	SC	SH	RB	AS	BL	ST
Akeem Olajuwon	79	79	22.85	28.10	4	10	72	5	110	6	18
Rodney McCray	81	80	12.42	17.27	54	86	84	48	68	68	130
Eric Floyd	77	73	15.00	16.58	62	56	129	110	18	134	56
Joe Barry Carroll	77	30	12.68	12.92	98	82	146	37	113	17	113
Allen Leavell	80	54	10.24	12.09	109	105	98	154	27	139	17
Jim Petersen	69	50	8.88	12.09	110	126	53	39	108	54	137
Purvis Short	81	11	14.31	11.74	113	63	69	113	84	116	88
Buck Johnson	70	2	5.40	6.14	DNQ						
Robert Reid	62	31	6.34	6.00	DNQ						
Cedric Maxwell	71	0	3.80	5.14	DNQ						

POSITION RANKINGS *

PLAYER	POSITION	RANK	SC	SH	RB	AS	BL	ST
Akeem Olajuwon	Center (C)	1	1	14	2	8	5	1
Rodney McCray	Small Forward (SF)	12	21	18	4	10	18	28
Eric Floyd	Point Guard (PG)	14	6	26	8	18	16	27
Joe Barry Carroll	Power Forward (PF)	22	16	31	16	14	7	22
Allen Leavell	Point Guard (PG)	23	20	19	28	25	19	9
Jim Petersen	Power Forward (PF)	25	25	11	17	12	17	29
Purvis Short	Off Guard (OG)	19	16	16	13	30	21	24
Buck Johnson	Small Forward (SF)	DNQ						
Robert Reid	Off Guard (OG)	DNQ						
Cedric Maxwell	Small Forward (SF)	DNQ						

*For further definition of each category and column heading see pages 38 & 39.

Houston Rockets ....Team Info

WEEKLY POWER RATING
41 WINS - AVERAGE (See page 39 for Team Power Rating discussion.)

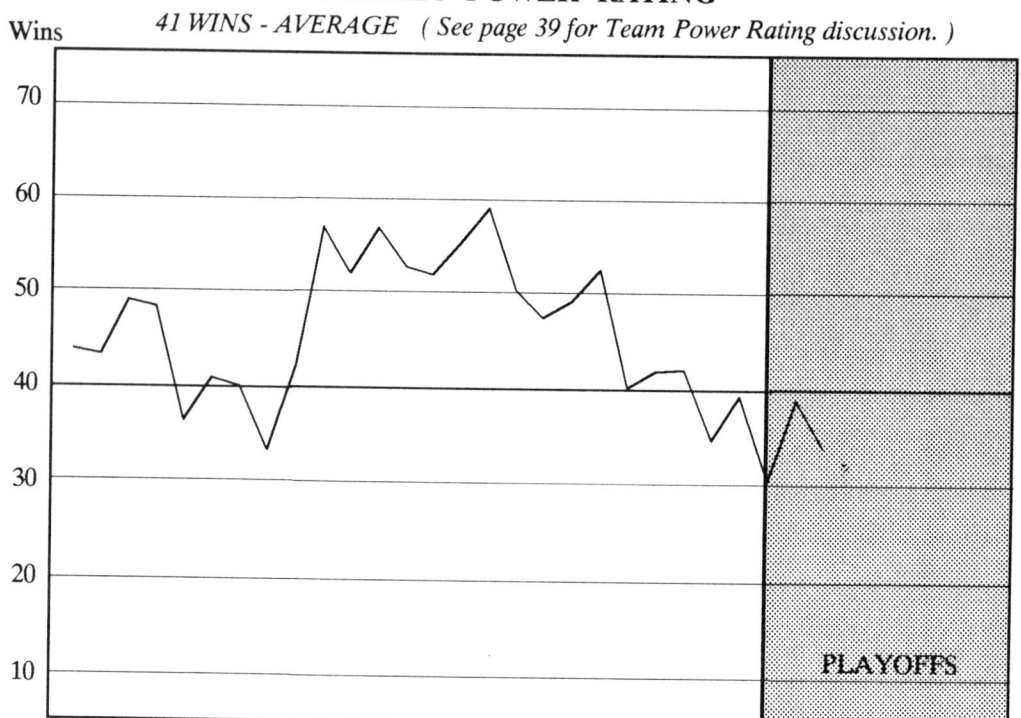

Miscellaneous Categories	Data	Rank	Performance Categories	Data	Rank
Attendance	681K	5	Offensive Scoring (per game)	109.0	9
Key-Man Games Missed	39	7	Defensive Scoring (per game)	107.6	13
Season Record	46-36	10	Scoring Margin (per game)	1.4	11
- Home	31-10	9	Defensive FG%	.465	2
- Road	15-26	9	Offensive 2-point%	.481	17
Eastern Conference	13-9	7	Offensive 3-point%	.237	21
Western Conference	33-27	11	Offensive Free Throw %	.780	7
Overtime Record	0-0	10	Offensive Rebs (Off REB/Opp Def REB)		11
Record 5 Pts. or Less	8-11	19	Defensive Rebs (Def REB/Opp Off REB)		15
Record 10 Pts. or More	19-16	12	Offensive Assists (AST/FGMade)		23
Games Won By Bench	8	2	Offensive Blocks (BLK/Opp FGAttempted)		7
Games Won By Starters	0	22	Offensive Steals (STL/Game)		11
Winning Streak	4	14	Turnover Margin (Off T.O. - Def T.O.)		7
Losing Streak	4	4	Finesse (BLK + STL) / PF		3
Home Winning Streak	7	15	Rebounding Record	40-40-2	13
Road Winning Streak	3	9	Assists Record	40-37-5	13
Home Losing Streak	2	2	Field Goal Pct. Record	43-39-0	10
Road Losing Streak	6	8	Free Throw Pct. Record	41-37-4	9

Houston Rockets .... Miscellaneous

ADMINISTRATIVE INFORMATION

Team Offices: The Summit
Ten Greenway Plaza
Houston, Texas
77046
Telephone: (713) 627-0600
Head Coach: Don Chaney
Home Arena: The Summit
Capacity: 16,279

1988-89 ROSTER*

J#	VETERANS	COLLEGE	POS	R#	D#	HT	WT	Hous	NBA
2	Joe Barry Carroll	Purdue	C	1	1	7-1	255	1	7
7	Lester Conner	Oregon St.	G	1	14	6-4	185	1	5
21	Eric Floyd	Georgetown	G	1	13	6-3	175	1	6
1	Buck Johnson	Alabama	F	1	20	6-7	190	2	2
30	Allen Leavell	Oklahoma City	G	5	104	6-2	190	9	9
18	Cedric Maxwell	UNCC	F	1	12	6-8	224	2	11
22	Rodney McCray	Louisville	F-G	1	3	6-8	235	5	5
34	Akeem Olajuwon	Houston	C	1	1	7-0	250	4	4
43	Jim Petersen	Minnesota	F-C	3	51	6-10	236	4	4
33	Robert Reid	St. Marys (Tx)	F-G	2	40	6-8	215	10	10
45	Purvis Short	Jackson State	F	1	5	6-7	215	1	10

ROOKIES	COLLEGE	POS	R#	D#	HT
Derrick Chievous	Missouri	F	1	16	6-7

* For further definition of category and column headings, see pages 38 & 39.

Houston Rockets .... Overview

"They ought to throw us in jail for making that trade!" At least in jail one gets two dollars a day plus room and board. That's $2/day plus room and board more than Bill Fitch is getting now. When Fitch made the statement quoted above, it's clear he did not anticipate that it would be used to bring about his own dismissal just months later. Nevertheless, that's exactly what happened. When the trade, which should have moved the Rockets to the top, fizzled, Fitch became more and more personanongrata. Oh, well, it will give the captain more time to watch his videos.

Houston was 11-8 when the big trade was made. Most Rocket fans felt, as Fitch did, that the club should win 50 of their next 63 games (that would have meant a final record of 61 wins). Of course, we know the Rockets went 35-28 after the trade - hardly world beaters - and finished 4th in the division with 46 wins and 36 losses.

What was most interesting about the trade was what happened after it. The Rockets lost their first three games by an average of 10 points each. They looked sluggish and unsure. Then came one of the most dominant stretches in the NBA during 1987-88. During a six game period, Houston went 5-1 despite playing four games on the road against six teams which had been to the playoffs the year before (5 had won 50+ games). The club's 3rd quarters during this stretch were simply incredible. The Rockets came out of the halftime locker room rolling. Amazingly, they used runs of 16-0, 16-0, and 16-3 to take insurmountable leads (see Houston highlights, page 107). This power surge was short-lived as the Rockets sputtered for two months before going 8-12 to close out the regular season. A subsequent first round playoff loss sealed Fitch's fate.

I want to make it clear that the trade was a good one to make. In fact, I, like most people, thought the team might be great. What I expected to happen was an immediate trade of Joe Barry Carroll for a solid power forward. Instead, the Rockets used J.B.C. and Jim Petersen interchangeably at that spot. In my opinion, this strategy failed. Houston was led in rebounding by its starting power forward only 14 times; an abysmally low performance. The whole purpose of that position is to rebound. Only Portland's Caldwell Jones and Washington's Charles Jones (Caldwell's brother) were less effective (11 times for each team). It's pretty bad when players like Carroll and Petersen can't keep up with the Joneses.

I was always a big fan of Jim Petersen when Ralph Sampson was around. I guess my affection for Pete was based on the fact that the team played better when this unknown 3rd round pick was in the game and the #1 player picked in the draft was on the bench. Unfortunately, however, when Petersen had to carry the load after Ralph was gone, his weaknesses became glaring. He not only lacks the rebounding necessary to be a solid starting power forward, but his defense is hopelessly inadequate against many of the quicker forwards he matched up against. Having the human eraser (Olajuwon) behind him to wipe the boards helped, but it became clear that Jimbo wasn't the answer. That's when Carroll got the nod. But even he failed to break the club's fall (see page 110 to note Houston's slide the last two-thirds of the season).

As I said, the trade was essential because Ralph Sampson had to go. He proved he could not play more than 5' from the basket as he shot only 23% from 6' out vs 79% from 5' in. This would only be just *bad* except that a whopping 67% of his shots were from 6' out! Sampson was selfish and did nothing for the team's chemistry. Though Fitch had finally broken Ralph of leading the break, he could not convince him to play in close to the basket, crash the boards, play tight defense, and pass the ball. Ralph's poor shooting cost Houston dearly over the last couple years. In the 19 games as a Rocket in the 87-88 season, Houston went 8-3 when he shot less than 15 times. When he threw up 15 or more

Houston Rockets .... Overview

garbage shots a game, the team went 3-5. I'd bet Fitch wanted to throw up even more than Ralph!

Of course the "prize" of the trade was to be Sleepy Floyd. Floyd was the long sought-after point guard that Houston has needed so long. If the move from Golden State to a contending team was a "dream come true" for Sleepy, then somebody forgot to set the alarm, because he never woke up. Among other problems, he failed to become the true point guard Houston needed; rather, he was more of a shooting playmaker in the mold of Reggie Theus or Isiah Thomas. Not bad company, but not what Houston needed. To make matters worse, Houston could not keep defenses honest by the outside shot. Both Floyd and Leavell shot only about 20% from 3-point country. In fact, both players were among the league's worst at 3-pt inefficiency points (see definition of inefficiency points on page 32).

1. Michael Jordan	-31
2. Sleepy Floyd	**-28**
3. Allen Leavell	**-28**
4. Mark Jackson	-25
5. John Williams	-22

Akeem Olajuwon is this team's one man Salvation Army. Yet, despite his winning most of his battles, the Rockets lost far too many wars. Only one player (A.O.) in the NBA ranked in the top-20 in 4 of the 6 performance categories. Amazingly, Olajuwon had one more top-20 ranking than all his teammates combined. Akeem made first team All-NBA and All-Defense as well as leading the league in 20/20's with six. Charles Barkley and Buck Williams were next with 4. Despite all these laurels, there were the usual voiced concerns (those that go with all superstars) that he tried to do too much. As the season wore on, Akeem became increasingly offensive minded. Interestingly, it was at season's end that he was complaining more often about not getting the ball. That's starting to border on "Sampsonitis" disease. Let's just hope we're seeing only the symptoms.

Purvis Short and Rodney McCray covered time at the swing position. Houston's record was 13-23 when Purvis scored 13 points or less. When he hit 14 or more, the team was rocking at 33-13. That's what I call pivotal! Short made the coaches' "All High Arching Shot" team, and he's on my "All Fun To Watch" team along with superstars Jordan, Wilkins, Drexler, and Bird.

McCray is a tough call. I've always said he was underrated. The coaches apparently agree, placing him on both the All-Underrated and All-Unselfish teams. The problem with Rodney McDangerfield (he gets no respect) is that at times he's just not aggressive enough. When McCray wants to bang and crash and take the ball to the hoop (a' la James Worthy), he can be extremely complementary to Olajuwon. In one 10 game stretch, R-Mac averaged 16.2 points per game and nearly 12 rebounds. Excluding those games, his season's average was 11.9 ppg and 7.3 rpg. In truth, he can lead a break as well as anyone in the NBA. Unfortunately, he rarely seems to be in a position to capitalize on his ability to take it to the hole. On defense, he's as good as it gets - 1st team NBA with Akeem. He has a good attitude and he never seems to get hurt. So, given the givens, I'd take him any day.

Prediction - best case: 50-32

With the talent on this team, they should win 55-60 games. Of course, that was true last year too and they only won 46. Without a "real" point guard, they're not going very far this season either. Derrick Chievous (an inconsistent, often troubled, collegian) won't help at all and Akeem can't do anymore than he already has. Without another trade, it's repeat city.

Prediction - worst case: 44-38

No matter how poorly the molecules come together, this team can't lose more than 38 games. Well, assuming Akeem plays at least half the season anyway. With McCray, Carroll, Short, Peterson, and Floyd, any team should be able to claim at least 44 wins, chemistry or no chemistry.

Indiana Pacers .... History

The Indiana Pacers were one of four ABA teams to join the NBA in 1976, which survived the league's folding. The Pacers were the most successful ABA team of the group. The Spurs, Nuggets, and Nets all had winning records in the ABA, but the Pacers won three titles and reached the finals five times. Though their winning percentage of 57% in the regular season and 58% in the playoffs was outstanding, they have not yet been able to carry that over into the NBA.

The club experienced its worst year up to that point in its first NBA season when it won only 36 times while losing 46. That trend has continued. The Pacers have now failed to reach the playoffs in nine of their first ten years in the NBA. Since joining the league, Indiana has won only 40% of their regular season matchups and only one playoff contest. The logical reason for the decline is that the NBA with 22-23 teams is significantly more difficult to compete in than the ABA with 7-10 teams.

Indiana has the distinction of having the fewest coaches in its franchise history (except for Dallas, of course). Though 14 clubs have been in existence since Indiana's first year (1967-68), the Pacers have seen just five coaches. Only the Bullets have also had as few as five during this period. The interesting point about the Bullets, however, is that in the 6 years before the Pacers franchise was established, the Bullets had made seven coaching changes. Coincidentally, of the group, the coach with the most wins was Bob Leonard. Leonard, went on to coach Indiana for 12 years. (see below for Leonard's stats)

The club boasts of having made two of the longest shots in history. In one of the first ABA games ever played, Jerry Harkness of the Pacers hit an 88 footer - the longest ever in professional basketball. Amazingly, Indiana trailed by two when this 3-pointer (one of the league's first) won the game. Herb Williams hit the NBA's second longest - an 81 footer just before half-time of a game in 1986.

The Pacers have had some interesting rookie records. Chuck Person, who was Rookie-of-the-Year in 1987, holds the NBA record for most 3-point field goals without a miss in a game (6). Dudley Bradley set the rookie record for steals (211) in 1979-80. And last year Reggie Miller surpassed Larry Bird's record for most 3-pointers made during a rookie season (61).

> **Quiz: What two stars from the old Indianapolis Olympians were banned from the league?**

ALL TIME PACERS' TEAM

Player	Span	Yrs	CRD
Mel Daniels	1969-74	6	12,835
George McGinnis	1972-82	7	11,154
Billy Knight	1975-83	8	10,324
Roger Brown	1968-74	8	10,059
Herb Williams	1982-87	6	9,312
Bob Netolicky	1968-75	8	9,062
Fred Lewis	1968-77	8	8,640
Billy Keller	1970-76	7	8,421
Don Buse	1973-82	7	7,096
Darnell Hillman	1972-77	6	7,070

ALLTIME PACERS' COACH

Bob Leonard   12 Years
69-47 Playoffs   8 Playoffs
529-456 Reg. Season   3 Championships

HISTORICAL PROFILE

Category	Data
Pacers' coach	Jack Ramsay
Years coached Indiana	2
# of franchise years	21
# of coaches	5
# of winning seasons	8
# of playoff years	11
# of runner's up	2 (ABA)
# of championships	3 (ABA)
Regular season win %	47.5
Playoffs win %	56.0

> **Answer:
> Alex Groza and Ralph Beard**

Indiana Pacers . . . . .1987-88 Highlights

Pacers 110-108 Lakers Tue. February 9, 1988

The win by Indiana broke a couple Lakers' streaks, including a 13 game home-court winning streak, and a 7 game winning streak overall. It also broke a 7 game road losing streak by the Pacers. Interestingly, Indiana won without its last two heralded rookies. Chuck Person did not play for only the 3rd game in his career, while Reggie Miller failed to score for only the second time. As a result, an unlikely hero emerged. Stuart Gray scored a season high 10 points and set career highs in rebounds and assists.

Pacers 107-102 Suns Sat. February 13, 1988

The win was the third straight road win for the Pacers. Additionally, Indiana went to three games over .500 for only the third time since joining the NBA. Only one time, 1981, when Indiana went 44-38 has the team been three games over .500 this late in the season. Impressively, the team had won 4 straight games without Chuck Person.

Pacers 130-112 Kings Sun. February 21, 1988

Wayman Tisdale replaced last year's Rookie-of-the-Year Chuck Person in the starting lineup the last 5 games - all wins. Tisdale responded by scoring his season high of 26 points while Person, ironically, had his season high in assists off the bench. The win was actually Indiana's 7th straight - an NBA high for the club. It also represented the team's 9th straight home win - passing last year's mark of 8.

Pacers 117-104 Pistons Tue. March 8, 1988

The 13 point margin equalled Indy's biggest win over Detroit in 7 years and 40 games in the series. The win broke a 4 game losing streak at home, the longest of the year - surprising, since it immediately followed a 9 game home winning streak - a club NBA record. Vern Fleming was the hero as he put together his 3rd triple-double of the season, moving him into 3rd behind Magic Johnson and Fat Lever in this category.

Pacers 95-93 Nets Mon. April 11, 1988

The Pacers trailed by as many as 16 points in the first half and 11 in the fourth quarter, but won on a last second shot by John Long. Long wasn't the only hero as Wayman Tisdale scored a season high 32 points to lead both teams. The win was the 9th straight by Indiana over New Jersey, but its significance was in keeping Indiana in the playoff race. By winning, the Pacers stayed 1/2 game in front of New York and Philadelphia. A loss would have dropped them from 7th to 9th place.

Pacers 126-92 76ers Sat. April 16, 1988

The victory couldn't have come at a better time, as Indiana had dropped into a tie for the final playoff spot - their lowest level to date. The 34 point victory margin was the Pacers' largest of the season and largest ever vs Philly. Rookie Reggie Miller performed the heroics. He not only scored a career high 31 points, but also hit four 3-point shots. In doing so, he tied and passed Larry Bird's rookie record for made 3-pointers.

Pacers 116-98 Hawks Wed. April 20, 1988

The win moved Indy into a tie for the final playoff spot while the 18 point victory margin was the Pacers largest ever at Atlanta. Herb Williams was the game's MVP. Williams led all scorers with 20 points. In his most recent two games he had scored 24 and 20 - his highest totals of the season. The victory also broke an 11 game road losing streak.

Indiana Pacers .... Influence on Winning

TEAM RECORD BY

PLAYER	GAMES	... SCR Leader HOME	ROAD	... REB Leader HOME	ROAD	... AST Leader HOME	ROAD
Vern Fleming	80	2-3	2-2	2-1	1-2	19-13	11-15
Steve Stipanovich	80	4-2	1-4	11-4	4-11	0-1	---
Chuck Person	79	9-4	4-13	2-6	3-6	5-4	2-4
Wayman Tisdale	79	8-3	2-5	6-6	4-5	---	0-2
Herb Williams	75	1-0	0-1	5-3	2-9	---	---
John Long	81	2-3	4-2	---	---	---	1-4
Reggie Miller	82	2-1	1-1	---	---	0-1	---
Ron Anderson	74	---	0-2	0-1	1-2	---	---
Scott Skiles	51	---	---	---	---	2-0	2-6
Stuart Gray	74	---	---	1-0	3-1	---	---

TEAM RECORD BY SCORING *

PLAYER	PLAY	DNP	0-9	10-19	20-29	30-39	40+
Vern Fleming	38-42	0-2	4-13	28-24	5-5	1-0	---
Steve Stipanovich	38-42	0-2	4-13	28-22	6-7	---	---
Chuck Person	36-43	2-1	7-7	16-23	13-10	0-3	---
Wayman Tisdale	36-43	2-1	4-10	22-20	9-12	1-1	---
Herb Williams	35-40	3-4	17-17	17-22	1-1	---	---
John Long	38-43	0-1	9-18	21-18	7-7	1-0	---
Reggie Miller	38-44	---	16-21	17-20	4-3	1-0	---
Ron Anderson	36-38	2-6	23-28	13-9	0-1	---	---
Scott Skiles	22-29	16-15	20-23	2-6	---	---	---
Stuart Gray	36-38	2-6	34-36	2-2	---	---	---

TEAM RECORD BY STARTING POSITION *

PLAYER	GAMES	STARTS	PG	OG	SF	PF	C
Vern Fleming	80	80	38-42	---	---	---	---
Steve Stipanovich	80	80	---	---	---	---	38-42
Chuck Person	79	71	---	---	31-40	---	---
Wayman Tisdale	79	57	---	---	7-4	18-28	---
Herb Williams	75	37	---	---	---	20-15	0-2
John Long	81	81	---	38-43	---	---	---
Reggie Miller	82	1	---	0-1	---	---	---
Ron Anderson	74	1	---	---	---	0-1	---
Scott Skiles	51	2	0-2	---	---	---	---
Stuart Gray	74	0	---	---	---	---	---

* For further definition of each category and column heading see pages 38 & 39.

Indiana Pacers .... 1987-88 Statistics

RAW NUMBERS *

PLAYER	2pt%	3pt%	FT%	MIN	PF	DQ	HI	TO	RB	AS	BL	ST
Vern Fleming	.531	0-13	.802	2733	225	0	30	175	364	**568**	11	115
Steve Stipanovich	.502	.200	.809	2692	**302**	8	26	156	**662**	183	69	90
Chuck Person	.480	.333	.670	**2807**	266	4	**35**	210	536	309	8	73
Wayman Tisdale	.513	0-2	.783	2378	274	5	32	145	491	103	34	54
Herb Williams	.428	0-6	.737	1966	244	1	24	119	469	98	**146**	37
John Long	.478	**.442**	**.907**	2022	164	1	32	127	229	173	11	84
Reggie Miller	**.538**	.355	.801	1840	157	0	31	101	190	132	19	53
Ron Anderson	.500	0-2	.766	1097	98	0	25	73	216	78	6	41
Scott Skiles	.423	.300	.833	760	97	0	6	76	66	180	3	22
Stuart Gray	.469	0-1	.603	807	152	1	15	50	250	44	32	11

OVERALL RANKINGS *

PLAYER	G	GS	PPG	PR	RANK	SC	SH	RB	AS	BL	ST
Vern Fleming	80	80	13.89	**19.19**	38	69	32	100	22	141	44
Steve Stipanovich	80	80	13.49	**18.13**	49	75	50	32	100	49	69
Chuck Person	79	71	**16.97**	16.65	59	42	124	72	56	149	109
Wayman Tisdale	79	57	16.05	15.82	71	45	44	64	37	91	124
Herb Williams	75	37	9.97	12.17	108	112	153	45	119	8	141
John Long	81	**81**	12.77	11.42	115	79	47	114	81	128	46
Reggie Miller	**82**	1	10.02	9.23	137	111	21	122	93	103	93
Ron Anderson	74	1	7.32	7.54	DNQ						
Scott Skiles	51	2	4.37	5.61	DNQ						
Stuart Gray	74	0	3.03	5.12	DNQ						

POSITION RANKINGS *

PLAYER	POSITION	RANK	SC	SH	RB	AS	BL	ST
Vern Fleming	Point Guard (PG)	8	11	6	5	21	20	23
Steve Stipanovich	Center (C)	9	12	10	17	5	22	3
Chuck Person	Small Forward (SF)	14	16	26	12	3	33	25
Wayman Tisdale	Power Forward (PF)	15	8	9	31	24	31	25
Herb Williams	Power Forward (PF)	24	24	34	22	15	2	31
John Long	Off Guard (OG)	21	18	12	14	28	28	13
Reggie Miller	Off Guard (OG)	27	24	7	19	31	14	25
Ron Anderson	Small Forward (SF)	DNQ						
Scott Skiles	Point Guard (PG)	DNQ						
Stuart Gray	Center (C)	DNQ						

*For further definition of each category and column heading see pages 38 & 39.

118 BASKETBALL HEAVEN 1989

Indiana Pacers ....Team Info

WEEKLY POWER RATING
41 WINS - AVERAGE (See page 39 for Team Power Rating discussion.)

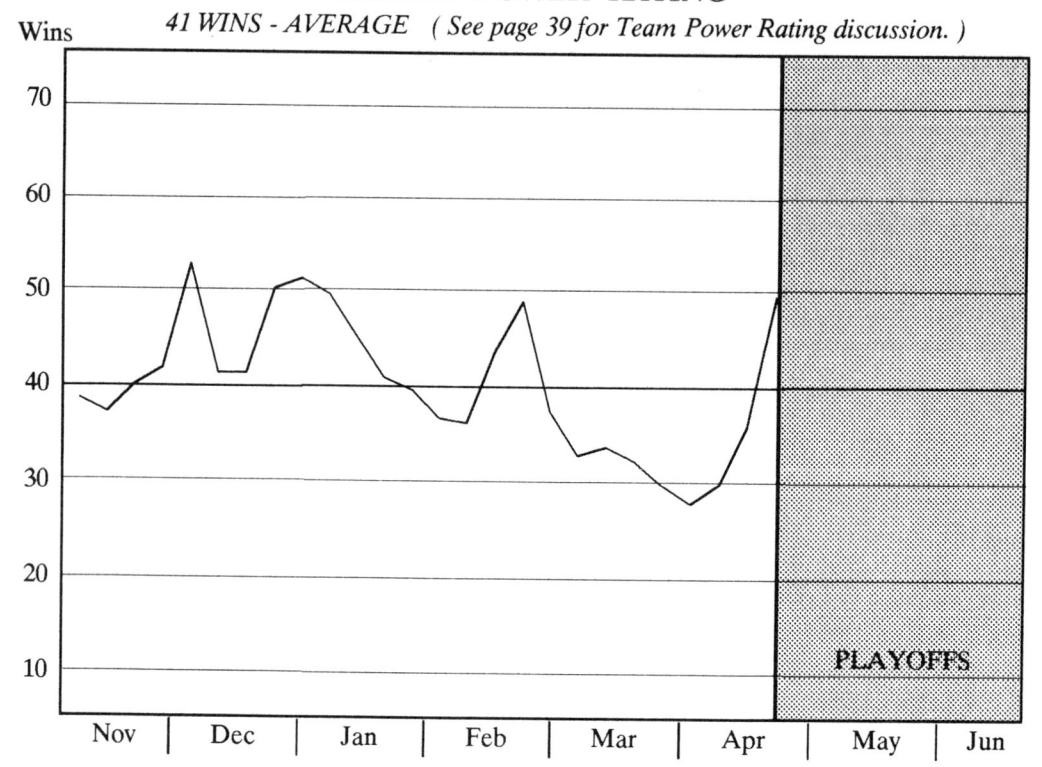

Miscellaneous Categories	Data	Rank	Performance Categories	Data	Rank
Attendance	502K	14	Offensive Scoring (per game)	104.6	20
Key-Man Games Missed	26	3	Defensive Scoring (per game)	105.4	7
Season Record	38-44	14	Scoring Margin (per game)	-.8	15
- Home	25-16	16	Defensive FG%	.472	7
- Road	13-28	11	Offensive 2-point%	.491	11
Eastern Conference	25-33	15	Offensive 3-point%	.336	5
Western Conference	13-11	12	Offensive Free Throw %	.780	6
Overtime Record	0-1	21	Offensive Rebs (Off REB/Opp Def REB)		21
Record 5 Pts. or Less	17-15	10	Defensive Rebs (Def REB/Opp Off REB)		9
Record 10 Pts. or More	16-20	15	Offensive Assists (AST/FGMade)		20
Games Won By Bench	4	12	Offensive Blocks (BLK/Opp FGAttempted)		20
Games Won By Starters	2	19	Offensive Steals (STL/Game)		21
Winning Streak	7	7	Turnover Margin (Off T.O. - Def T.O.)		16
Losing Streak	4	4	Finesse (BLK + STL) / PF		23
Home Winning Streak	9	12	Rebounding Record	37-44-1	17
Road Winning Streak	3	9	Assists Record	36-42-4	14
Home Losing Streak	4	15	Field Goal Pct. Record	44-37-1	9
Road Losing Streak	7	12	Free Throw Pct. Record	47-35-0	7

TEAM BY TEAM ANALYSIS   119

Indiana Pacers .... Miscellaneous

ADMINISTRATIVE INFORMATION

Team Offices: Two West Washington St.
Suite 510
Indianapolis, Indiana
46204
Telephone: (317) 263-2100
Head Coach: Jack Ramsay
Home Arena: Market Square Arena
Capacity: 16,910

1988-89 ROSTER*

J#	VETERANS	COLLEGE	POS	R#	D#	HT	WT	Indi	NBA
15	Ron Anderson	Fresno State	F	2	27	6-7	215	3	4
54	Greg Dreiling	Kansas	C	2	26	7-1	250	2	2
10	Vern Fleming	Georgia	G	1	18	6-5	195	4	4
55	Stuart Gray	UCLA	C	2	29	7-0	245	4	4
25	John Long	Detroit	G	2	29	6-5	195	2	10
31	Reggie Miller	UCLA	G-F	1	11	6-7	190	1	1
45	Chuck Person	Auburn	F	1	4	6-8	225	2	2
3	Scott Skiles	Michigan State	G	1	22	6-1	190	1	2
40	Steve Stipanovich	Missouri	C-F	1	2	7-0	250	5	5
23	Wayman Tisdale	Oklahoma	F	1	2	6-9	240	3	3
32	Herb Williams	Ohio State	F-C	1	14	6-11	240	7	7

	ROOKIES	COLLEGE	POS	R#	D#	HT
	Rick Smits	Marist	C	1	2	7-4
	Herbert Crook	Louisville	F	3	61	6-7
	Michael Anderson	Drexel	G	3	73	5-11

* For further definition of category and column headings, see pages 38 & 39.

Indiana Pacers .... Overview

Atlanta, Philadelphia, and especially Golden State had disappointing seasons during 1987-88. However, not even the Warriors (22 less wins than the year before) were as big a disappointment as Indiana. The Pacers won only 38 games and failed to make the playoffs. The final game loss at home to the Knicks in the battle for the last playoff spot was just the icing on the cake.

Three years ago, Indiana won 26 games. Two years ago, they won 41. Given a maturing club and one of the game's all-time great coaches, any reasonable person might have assumed that the Pacers would win 45-50 games. Had you told me that the team would rank #3 at season's end for fewest key-man games missed, I'd have told you there was no way in the world this team would end up 38-44. I would have been eating my words. The question is "How could this have happened?" Moreover, "What happened?" I think there are some reachable conclusions.

First and foremost, it's probably true that the club overachieved in 1986-87. Assuming that they did, it may be more understandable why they found it so hard to reach 41 wins again. Another possibility is the sophomore jinx. Chuck Person won the Rookie-of-the-Year award in 1986-87. Becoming an All-Star could hardly be far away. Who would have thought that his Production Rating would drop from 19.63 to a mediocre 16.65 and that he would slide from 10th to 14th at his position.

The third probable cause for the decline was the very real possibility that most of the Pacer's top players were too often playing the wrong positions. What's that you're saying? It may sound presumptous to suggest that Ramsay should have done something different - especially something so basic as start players at other positions. In chapter 4, I discuss a statistical rating system to determine what position a player is most ideal for. First, I established the league averages for twelve categories including shooting percentages, scoring, rebounds, assists, height, weight, etc. I then ranked each player by how close they were to each position on a 100 point scale. Herb Williams played primarily at power forward - starting 35 games at the position. On the 100 point scale he ranks a 20 power forward and 80 center. What does that mean? It means he's a center. That's simple. But Indiana already has a center - Steve Stipanovich. However, although Stipo has always played the post, he ranks a 36 center and 64 power forward. Clearly, in my opinion, these two players should change positions. Vern Fleming ranks a 41 point guard and 59 off-guard. Chuck Person could play off-guard as well. With his outside shooting ability, he could be more valuable at that position. The problem is that no club needs four off-guards (Fleming, Person, Long, and Miller). Without a solid starting point guard, a slightly dissatisfied and miscast small forward, and a power forward and center who should switch, the number of wins are going to be restricted and the offense is going to be lacking (Indiana ranked #20 in scoring).

The club's offensive woes were evident by their assist-to-field-goals-made ratio which ranked #20, but the most telling stat was that Indiana had the most games in the league (excluding the Clippers, naturally) where not one single starter scored 20+ points. The Pacers failed to manage this level 23 times, Golden State 20, New York 19, and Cleveland 19. This represents too much parity in the lineup and not enough individuality. I know that's anathema to Ramsay, the ultimate pacer, but one has to wonder if his triathlon experience has taught him to pace himself and his team too much. If so, it's a questionable strategy in the NBA. Teams win with explosive outbursts - a 15-3 run, a 12-0 spurt, a 18-6 lead to start the second half. Most of these stretches happen in the third quarter where Indiana was the victim far more often than the victor. Their winning percentage for all four quarters was Q1 56%, Q2 52%, Q3 37%, Q4 54%. See what I

Indiana Pacers .... Overview

mean? If the Pacers don't develop someone to take charge, they will always be mediocre. I think Ramsay should encourage more independent and aggressive play from Person. Look what has happened with Clyde Drexler in Portland's post-Ramsay era. Person ranked dead last among starting NBA small forwards in FTA's per minute. In fact, this club was far behind the second lowest team in total FTA's (1982 to Phoenix's 2200). Now, having criticized Ramsay so much, it's time to tell it like it is. He's proven that he's a great coach over and over again. Maybe he'll find a way to win with this group too. We'll see. One thing is for sure. If he continues to coach, Ramsay will pass Red Auerbach as the league's all time winningest coach sometime around March 1st, 1990.

Reggie Miller was one of the top rookies in the league. His long bomb shooting from "Reggie Range" established a rookie record of 61 3-point field goals and surpassed Larry Bird's 1980 record (58). Wayman Tisdale was, at times, the catalyst this team needs (Indiana was 20-15 with Tisdale as a starting power forward), yet he still remains somewhat of an underachiever as an NBA player. The big question is "How will Rik Smits fit in at center?" The 7'4" giant could be the real key to this club's success. He's a project, but you can't coach 88 inches. Like most tall white guys, he's a little slow and needs more strength, but he does have good shooting touch, averaging 24.7 ppg. Unfortunately, he only averaged 8.7 reb/game. At a small school like Marist, one would think a 7'4" center could do better. Nevertheless, the Pacers will probably try to move some of their front line people (Williams, Tisdale, Stipanovich) to make room for Smits or to bring in point guard help or both.

Only five times in league history has an entire division finished above .500. And only the central has failed to do so. Ironically, it could have happened and should have happened in 1987-88. Only the Pacers of the division's six teams missed this level. Shown below are the five divisions and the number of teams in each.

1983	Atlantic	5
1978	Pacific	5
1971	Midwest	4
1957	Eastern	4
1948	Western	4

If Indiana can improve and Milwaukee can stem their tide, this division could again challenge being the first 6-team division over .500. As it is, it's a guarantee to be the league's best again next year. That's pretty impressive, considering just three years ago they were the worst.

1982	.447	4th
1983	.411	4th
1984	.447	4th
1985	.478	3rd
1986	.434	4th
1987	.551	1st
1988	**.561**	**1st**

It's reasonable to believe the fans will remain loyal despite the question marks on the team and despite this being college basketball country. Indiana led all other franchises in ratio of customers who attended home games and population of the area. One person for every 14.4 locals attended a home game last season. Utah was second, with one for every 13.4, while Portland was third at one per 10.3.

Prediction - best case: 47-35

I haven't given up on this team. I'm convinced that if Smits can work out, Stipo can move to power forward, Tisdale can be traded for a solid point guard, and Person is given a free reign, that the Pacers can be a competitive force in the division, possibly even challenging 50 wins. That's a lot of if's, however.

Prediction - worst case: 39-43

I have to believe Indiana will do better than last year - even in the worst case. Other than an expendable John Long, this team is still relatively young. One more year of maturity has got to be worth at least one more win over last season.

Los Angeles Clippers .... History

The Los Angeles Clippers came into the NBA as an expansion team in 1970-71. The Braves, as they were called at the time, spent their first 8 years in Buffalo. In 1978 the team was moved to San Diego and became known as the Clippers. The Clippers remained in San Diego until 1984. At that time they moved up the coast to LA where they have remained. Only four times has an existing NBA club moved in the last 10 years. As noted, the Clippers have done it twice, while the Kings and Jazz have each moved once.

The club has only made the playoffs three times in its 18 year history - by far the fewest of any NBA team in the same period. Not surprisingly, the Clippers have the worst regular season winning percentage of any team. The last 12 years have been unparalleled in terms of futility. LA has not gone to the playoffs even once during this period, which represents the longest dry spell in NBA history. The club has experienced a 19 game losing streak, a 12 win season, 12 coaching changes and two moves. The 29 wins in the last two years is the fewest two-year total ever.

Despite these failures, the Clippers managed to attend the post-season party three consecutive years from 1974-1976. During that period, Bob McAdoo won his three scoring titles, and the club had three of its only four winning seasons. Of the four playoff series, the Clippers won only one - a 2 game to 1 victory over the 76ers. The series was highlighted by a 124-123 O.T. victory in the final game.

The franchise has been widely criticized the past 10 years or so for giving up young talent at the expense of the future. Present stars, Adrian Dantley, Tom Chambers, Byron Scott and Terry Cummings were, at one time, the property of the Clippers. It's easy to be critical of the decisions which allowed these players to get away.

Misc... The club has had four Rookie-of-the-Year award winners since 1971, twice the number of the next closest team... Of the five offensive categories kept by the NBA since 1971, the Clippers have had a league leader in all five. In that same 18 year period only Washington has had a player lead the NBA in as many as four of the five... LA has a winning record against only one other club (Utah Jazz 39-29). The team that has presented the Clippers with the most difficulties is, perhaps surprisingly, the San Antonio Spurs (10-44).

> **Quiz: Who are the only father/son duos where the dad won an NBA championship while the son won an NCAA title?**

ALL TIME CLIPPERS' TEAM

Player	Span	Yrs	CRD
Randy Smith	1972-83	9	12,072
Bob McAdoo	1973-76	5	9,951
Swen Nater	1978-82	6	7,233
Michael Cage	1985-88	4	4,761
Garfield Heard	1974-81	4	4,326
Norm Nixon	1984-86	3	4,101
Jim McMillian	1974-76	3	3,917
Terry Cummings	1983-84	2	3,622
Benoit Benjamin	1986-88	3	3,597
Elmore Smith	1972-73	2	3,515

ALL TIME CLIPPERS' COACH

Jack Ramsay   4 Years
9-13 Playoffs   3 Playoffs
158-170 Reg. Season   0 Championships

HISTORICAL PROFILE

Category	Data
Clippers' coach	Gene Shue
Years coached Los Angeles	1
# of franchise years	18
# of coaches	11
# of winning seasons	4
# of playoff years	3
# of runner's up	0
# of championships	0
Regular season win %	36.4
Playoff win %	40.9

> **Answer:**
> **Rick and Scooter Barry,**
> **Ed and Danny Manning**

Los Angeles Clippers . . . . 1987-88 Highlights

Clippers 100-88 Jazz   Tue.   November 10, 1987

Benoit Benjamin registered a career high 9 assists (old record - 6) as the Clippers broke a 16 game losing streak dating back to 1987. The streak tied the previous season's 16 gamer. Both losing streaks were the longest for the club since it moved to Los Angeles in 1978. It was also Gene Shue's first win as head coach and a welcome relief, as the Clippers had lost their first two games of the season by an average of over 35 points each.

Clippers 97-106 Celtics   Sat.   December 26, 1987

The good news is that the Clippers led by seven going into quarter #4. The bad news is they lost by nine. The game was remarkable in several ways. The win was Boston's 5th in 6 games while the loss was also the Clipper's 5th in 6 games. Though consistent, the starters for the Clippers had a horrible shooting night. The five shot 35%, 33%, 31%, 29%, and 28%. Because of the 72 missed Clippers FGA's (39-111), Michael Cage had plenty of opportunities for offensive boards. He took advantage and gathered in 14 offensive (a league high to this point) and 9 defensive rebounds. The 23 bounds tied his career high set three games earlier.

Clippers 110-109 Lakers (OT)   Wed.   January 13, 1988

The Clippers stunned their crosstown rivals as they beat the Lakers 110-109 in OT. The win has to go down as the year's biggest upset and perhaps one of the biggest upsets ever. The Clippers entered the game on an 11 game losing streak while the Lakers had not lost in the last 15, the NBA's longest since Boston's 18 game streak in 1982. Despite Magic Johnson's 4th triple-double, the Clippers won the battle down the stretch. Interestingly, it had been a month since the NBA had an overtime game - the longest "dry spell" in many years.

Clippers 97-96 Cavs   Sat.   February 27, 1988

The triumph was significant because the Clippers had to rally from a double-digit deficit. In doing so, they broke a 7 game losing streak. The Clippers can probably thank their top two draft picks in 1987 for the win. Joe Wolf had his season high as a reserve - 17pts, while Reggie Williams played in his first game after missing twenty-one. He scored 15 points.

Clippers 113-98 Warriors   Fri.   March 25, 1988

The 15 point margin was their second highest of the year. The interesting feature of this game was that both teams were led by a rookie who had recently joined the team. For the Warriors, Dave Hoppen scored a career high 11 points and 13 rebounds. For the Clippers, it was Claude Gregory who also had a career high 15 points and 12 rebounds.

Clippers 105-103 Kings   Sat.   April 2, 1988

Trailing by 21 points midway through the 3rd quarter, the Clippers rallied to capture their first road win after 27 straight losses. Stunningly, the winning free throws were made by Claude Gregory. Gregory came into the game shooting sub 30% from the line. Benoit Benjamin scored a career high 30 points while corralling 14 rebounds.

Clippers 122-105 Rockets   Sun.   April 10, 1988

The Los Angeles Clippers blew out the Houston Rockets early and went on to win by 17. The margin of victory matched the season's largest. Surprisingly, both were against teams with winning records. Darnell Valentine was the hero, as he outscored his opposing point guard Sleepy Floyd 30-2. In his last two games Valentine set consecutive career highs of 27 and 30 while shooting 67% from the field.

Los Angeles Clippers . . . . . . Influence on Winning

TEAM RECORD BY

PLAYER	GAMES	... SCR Leader HOME	ROAD	... REB Leader HOME	ROAD	... AST Leader HOME	ROAD
Michael Cage	72	1-6	0-4	9-18	1-23	---	---
Benoit Benjamin	66	1-3	1-2	1-4	2-8	2-0	0-1
Michael Woodson	80	8-9	1-13	---	---	2-2	1-5
Larry Drew	74	0-1	0-5	---	0-1	8-16	3-11
Darnell Valentine	79	1-0	0-2	---	---	4-11	0-20
Ken Norman	66	0-1	0-3	2-1	0-1	0-1	---
Quintin Dailey	67	4-5	1-9	---	---	0-1	0-1
Joe Wolf	42	---	---	1-0	---	0-1	0-2
Reggie Williams	35	0-1	0-3	---	---	---	---
Earl Cureton	69	0-1	---	0-2	0-2	0-1	0-1

TEAM RECORD BY SCORING *

PLAYER	PLAY	DNP	0-9	10-19	20-29	30-39	40+
Michael Cage	16-56	1-9	1-14	12-29	3-13	---	---
Benoit Benjamin	14-52	3-13	2-15	10-29	1-8	1-0	---
Mike Woodson	16-64	1-1	1-9	5-33	7-19	3-3	---
Larry Drew	16-58	1-7	7-29	8-25	1-4	---	---
Darnell Valentine	15-64	2-1	9-46	4-16	1-2	1-0	---
Ken Norman	14-52	3-13	9-30	4-17	1-3	0-2	---
Quintin Dailey	14-53	3-12	4-15	7-29	3-8	0-1	---
Joe Wolf	8-34	9-31	2-26	6-7	0-1	---	---
Reggie Williams	8-27	9-38	5-15	2-8	1-2	0-2	---
Earl Cureton	13-56	4-9	11-48	2-7	0-1	---	---

TEAM RECORD BY STARTING POSITION *

PLAYER	GAMES	STARTS	PG	OG	SF	PF	C
Michael Cage	72	70	---	---	---	16-53	0-1
Benoit Benjamin	66	59	---	---	---	---	12-47
Mike Woodson	80	77	---	15-60	0-2	---	---
Larry Drew	74	51	11-40	---	---	---	---
Darnell Valentine	79	31	6-25	---	---	---	---
Ken Norman	66	28	---	---	7-21	---	---
Quintin Dailey	67	7	---	2-5	---	---	---
Joe Wolf	42	26	---	---	5-18	0-3	---
Reggie Williams	35	14	---	---	3-11	---	---
Earl Cureton	69	11	---	---	---	0-6	1-4

* For further definition of each category and column heading see pages 38 & 39.

TEAM BY TEAM ANALYSIS 125

Los Angeles Clippers .... 1987-88 Statistics

RAW NUMBERS *

PLAYER	2pt%	3pt%	FT%	MIN	PF	DQ	HI	TO	RB	AS	BL	ST
Michael Cage	.471	0-1	.688	**2660**	194	1	26	160	**938**	110	58	91
Benoit Benjamin	**.496**	0-8	.706	2171	203	2	30	**223**	530	172	**225**	50
Michael Woodson	.459	.231	**.868**	2534	**210**	1	**36**	186	190	273	26	109
Larry Drew	.479	.289	.769	2024	114	0	27	152	119	**383**	0	65
Darnell Valentine	.416	**.455**	.743	1636	135	0	30	148	156	382	8	**122**
Ken Norman	.492	0-10	.512	1435	123	0	31	103	263	78	34	44
Quintin Dailey	.439	.167	.776	1282	128	1	33	123	154	109	4	69
Joe Wolf	.417	.200	.833	1137	139	**8**	23	76	187	98	16	38
Reggie Williams	.377	.224	.727	857	108	1	34	63	118	58	21	29
Earl Cureton	.433	0-3	.524	1128	135	1	21	58	271	63	36	32

OVERALL RANKINGS *

PLAYER	G	GS	PPG	PR	RANK	SC	SH	RB	AS	BL	ST
Michael Cage	72	70	14.53	**21.24**	23	61	140	3	140	56	68
Benoit Benjamin	66	59	13.03	17.97	50	78	102	35	89	2	122
Mike Woodson	**80**	**77**	**17.97**	13.80	89	35	119	148	59	104	41
Larry Drew	74	51	10.34	10.31	127	104	123	157	26	159	77
Darnell Valentine	79	31	7.11	9.33	134	150	150	130	10	132	6
Ken Norman	66	28	8.62	8.23	151	129	149	74	116	51	86
Quintin Dailey	67	7	13.45	9.21	DNQ						
Joe Wolf	42	26	7.62	8.95	DNQ						
Reggie Williams	35	14	10.43	6.71	DNQ						
Earl Cureton	69	11	4.33	6.32	DNQ						

POSITION RANKINGS *

PLAYER	POSITION	RANK	SC	SH	RB	AS	BL	ST
Michael Cage	Power Forward (PF)	7	12	30	3	26	18	5
Benoit Benjamin	Center (C)	10	13	19	18	2	2	9
Mike Woodson	Off Guard (OG)	15	11	25	28	20	15	11
Larry Drew	Point Guard (PG)	26	19	24	31	24	32	31
Darnell Valentine	Point Guard (PG)	28	30	31	15	10	15	3
Ken Norman	Small Forward (SF)	32	27	33	14	28	10	16
Quintin Dailey	Off Guard (OG)	DNQ						
Joe Wolf	Small Forward (SF)	DNQ						
Reggie Williams	Small Forward (SF)	DNQ						
Earl Cureton	Power Forward (PF)	DNQ						

*For further definition of each category and column heading see pages 38 & 39.

Los Angeles Clippers ....Team Info

WEEKLY POWER RATING
41 WINS - AVERAGE (See page 39 for Team Power Rating discussion.)

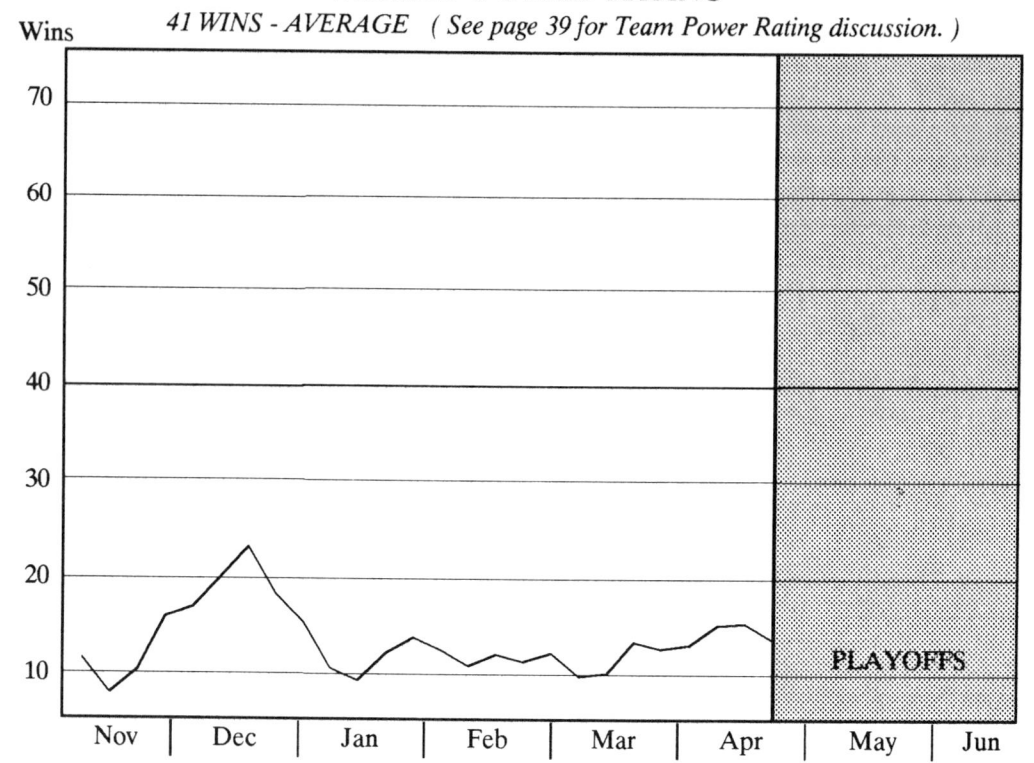

Miscellaneous Categories	Data	Rank
Attendance	360K	22
Key-Man Games Missed	157	21
Season Record	17-65	23
- Home	14-27	23
- Road	3-38	22
Eastern Conference	4-18	23
Western Conference	13-47	23
Overtime Record	2-2	10
Record 5 Pts. or Less	8-9	15
Record 10 Pts. or More	6-43	23
Games Won By Bench	1	19
Games Won By Starters	3	15
Winning Streak	2	21
Losing Streak	11	22
Home Winning Streak	2	23
Road Winning Streak	2	14
Home Losing Streak	5	20
Road Losing Streak	25	23

Performance Categories	Data	Rank
Offensive Scoring (per game)	98.8	23
Defensive Scoring (per game)	109.1	16
Scoring Margin (per game)	-10.3	23
Defensive FG%	.477	12
Offensive 2-point%	.452	23
Offensive 3-point%	.249	20
Offensive Free Throw %	.713	23
Offensive Rebs (Off REB/Opp Def REB)		18
Defensive Rebs (Def REB/Opp Off REB)		20
Offensive Assists (AST/FGMade)		15
Offensive Blocks (BLK/Opp FGAttempted)		4
Offensive Steals (STL/Game)		10
Turnover Margin (Off T.O. - Def T.O.)		19
Finesse (BLK + STL) / PF		4
Rebounding Record	21-58-3	22
Assists Record	21-56-5	21
Field Goal Pct. Record	32-50-0	20
Free Throw Pct. Record	26-56-0	22

Los Angeles Clippers .... Miscellaneous

ADMINISTRATIVE INFORMATION

Team Offices: L.A. Memorial Sports Arena
3939 Figueroa Street
Los Angeles, California
90037
Telephone: (213) 748-8000
Head Coach: Gene Shue
Home Arena: L.A. Memorial Sports Arena
Capacity: 15,167

1988-89 ROSTER*

J#	VETERANS	COLLEGE	POS	R#	D#	HT	WT	LA.C	NBA
00	Benoit Benjamin	Creighton	C	1	3	7-0	245	3	3
25	Earl Cureton	Detroit	F	3	58	6-9	215	2	8
20	Quintin Dailey	USF	G	1	7	6-3	210	2	6
22	Larry Drew	Missouri	G	1	17	6-2	190	2	8
	Greg Kite	BYU	C	1	21	6-11	250	1	5
33	Ken Norman	Illinois	F	1	19	6-8	225	1	1
	Eric White	Pepperdine	G	3	65	6-0	180	1	1
34	Reggie Williams	Georgetown	G-F	1	4	6-7	180	1	1
24	Joe Wolf	North Carolina	F-C	1	13	6-11	230	1	1
42	Mike Woodson	Indiana	G	1	12	6-5	198	2	8

ROOKIES	COLLEGE	POS	R#	D#	HT
Danny Manning	Kansas	F	1	1	6-10
Charles Smith	Pittsburgh	F	1	3	6-10
Gary Grant	Michigan	G	1	15	6-3
Tom Garrick	Rhode Island	G	2	45	6-2
Rob Lock	Kentucky	F-C	3	51	6-9

* For further definition of category and column headings, see pages 38 & 39.

Los Angeles Clippers .... Overview

Quiz: What do Byron Scott, Tom Chambers, Terry Cummings, and Adrian Dantley have in common? Well, despite the fact that they are All-Stars, they each were drafted in the first round by the Clippers and each was gone within 2 years. Yes, I know that they have virtually all been called "gunners" sometime in their career (not so much Scott), but it's hard to believe none of them were worth keeping. Had the Clippers traded them for other All-Stars who were still contributing - fine, but not so. They traded Scott *and* his NBA career for 3 years from Norm Nixon. They traded Chambers *and* 4+ years in the NBA for 2 1/2 years of James Donaldson. They traded Cummings *and* 3+ years in the NBA for 2 years of Marques Johnson. And they traded Dantley *and* 10+ years for 1 year of Billy Knight. Barring miracle comebacks by Nixon or Johnson, not one of these traded-for players is still in the NBA.

If you're a Clippers fan, I'm sure it's painful to hear such a horror story. The reason I bring up this example of futility now is because Los Angeles will have had six first round draft picks in the last two years (Williams, Wolf, Norman in 1987 and Manning, Smith, and Grant in 1988). I hope the temptation to trade will remain only that - a temptation and nothing more.

Despite the great expectations of last year's rookie crop, only Kenny Norman (#19) performed adequately. Joe Wolf (#13) was a big disappointment and Reggie Williams (#4) was a major fiasco. Nevertheless, few expect Wolf and Williams to repeat their 1987 performance next season. It's not unusual for rookies to struggle - especially in shooting the ball. Williams and Wolf shot 35.6% and 40.7% from the field while Norman was bricklaying his way to a 51.2% success rate at the line. Consequently, of the 230 players I analyze in statistical detail in this book (10 for each team), Ken Norman ranked #207, Joe Wolf #216, and Reggie Williams dead last at #230 in overall shooting. (See page 28 for explanation of shooting formula.)

A quick look at the three's statistics reveal many deficiencies and few strengths, but again remember, they're rookies. If they fail to improve next season, I won't be so kind.

	PR	**SC**	**RB**	**AS**	**BK**	**ST**
Norman	8.2	8.6	8.8	2.6	1.1	1.5
Wolf	9.0	7.6	7.9	4.1	0.7	1.6
Williams	6.7	10.4	6.6	3.2	1.2	1.6

PR = Production Rating, SC = Points per game. The other four are based on 48 minute averages.

The single reason to be excited about next year will be the maturing of this group and the incoming rookies, led by Player-of-the-Year Danny Manning. Joining Manning are Charles Smith and Gary Grant. Manning was easily the country's top player the second half of the season. When he carried the Kansas Jayhawks on his back to the NCAA title (see page x, xi for story), he was suddenly being compared with Larry Bird and Magic Johnson as the type of player who could make those players around him better. In these cases, much better. Of course being a big KU fan (I only live a few miles away), I'm probably prejudiced. However, I don't think there is any doubt that Manning will be an NBA bonafide superstar the minute he sets foot on the court. Admittedly, that's a risky comment to make, but that's how confident I am. Apparently, the Clippers feel the same. They drafted him knowing his price tag would be $30 million. Manning, after striking gold in the heartland, had told them that L.A. is where he wanted to be. So he loaded up his truck and he moved to Beverly. Hills that is - swimming pools, movie stars.

Although I can't understate how great Manning may become, he didn't really mature until midway through his senior season. Prior to that, he and his teammates had let many games slip away late; they played poorly on the road in pressure situations; and the chemistry just wasn't there. Part of it is because Danny is so unassuming, so unselfish that he didn't feel comfort-

Los Angeles Clippers .... Overview

able taking charge. When he finally had no choice and began to assert himself, it became clear that he had everything it takes to become one of the greats of the game.

There is some talk about Manning at power forward. That's a joke. There is no way he'll play that position. Name one power forward in the NBA with the kind of finesse skills Manning has. Only Tom Chambers and Charles Barkley come to mind at all and many call them small forwards anyway. No, let's be clear. Manning is a small forward in the same mold of Larry Bird. He could conceivably play point as Magic has done, but it's doubtful that he will. You won't see him at shooting guard because it's almost impossible for a shooting guard to make others around him better. Besides, shooting guards are rarely used for rebounding, and at 6'10", Manning isn't going to waste that skill.

A lot of people were surprised to see the top rebounder in the league - Michael Cage - traded to Seattle. I'm not. Cage will be entering his 4th year in the NBA. Whereas that is young, it's still true that his best 3 years are behind him (on an average). That's the way it is with most rebounders - they peak early (you know, young legs). Secondly, Cage was not a good shooter and truthfully, he got a lot of rebounds because his teammates were equally pathetic in their shooting. Nevertheless, if L.A. doesn't replace Cage's rebounding they will be in trouble. As it was, when they lost the backboard battle on the road, they were a wretched 0-30.

For Cage, the Clippers got Gary Grant. Grant has enormous potential and the Clippers desperately need a point-guard. Larry Drew, whose best ranking at the point guard position was #19 (scoring) and who is the only player of 230 who failed to block a single shot last season, isn't the answer. Neither would have been former Jayhawk, Darnell Valentine who led the team to an 0-20 record when he was the assist leader. Valentine was left unprotected and was lost in the expansion draft.

Benoit Benjamin remains an enigma. On the one hand he's capable of scoring 30 points and 14 rebounds while on the other he's gone 18 consecutive games without once leading the team in boards. I honestly think of all the assets Manning will bring to this team, his capability to light a fire under Benoit and make him consistent could be Danny's greatest contribution. Ironically, Benjamin scored 12 points five consecutive games - a misleading statistic (inferring consistency) if I ever heard one. Benjamin can be tough on defense, however. He led the league with 10 blocks in a game and rejected 9 on two more occasions.

This is a team without an identity and a team that has become much too used to being blown out. (In games decided by 20+ points, the Clippers were 0-19.) That leads to becoming much too used to losing. The Clippers' 29 wins the last two seasons rank as the all time lowest for back-to-back seasons since the NBA was formed in 1950.

	2 seasons	Wins
1. **L.A. Clippers**	1987, 88	29
2. Philadelphia 76ers	1973, 74	34
3. Cleveland Cavaliers	1971, 72	38
4. Cincinnati Royals	1959, 60	38
5. Portland Trailblazers	1972, 73	39
6. Philadelphia Warriors	1953, 54	41
7. Houston Rockets	1983, 84	43

Prediction - best case: 34-48

The Clippers could very well double their number of wins from a year ago. I'm calling that a best case scenario. Yet somehow in the back of my crystal ball, I vaguely see a 41-41 record, a playoff spot, and Coach-of-the-Year honors for Gene Shue. It would be his 3rd time to receive this tribute - the first person ever to secure such kudos.

Prediction - worst case: 26-56

There is only one way that this team could do this bad. That's if there is something in the air in Memorial Arena which eats up quality players and spits them out. With Nixon, Johnson, Wolf and Williams, it's starting to be more than a coincidence.

Los Angeles Lakers ....History

The Los Angeles Lakers originally began as a franchise in Minneapolis in 1947-48 as part of the NBL. In 1960 the club moved from the land of 10,000+ lakes to the city of angels.

The Lakers have continuously been among the best in the league during the franchise's 41 years - having only missed the playoffs three times - the best ratio for post season play of any team. Not surprisingly, LA holds the record for most playoff victories ever (273). The Celtics are #2 with 257. Though Boston's 16 championships are well known, the Lakers have won 11. In fact, LA has appeared in 22 finals - three more than Boston. The franchise holds many NBA records, including the longest winning streak (33) and the best record ever put together during the regular season (69-13).

Despite these many accomplishments, Los Angeles has almost always played second fiddle to Boston. At one point the Lakers lost seven consecutive championship series to the Celtics. Interestingly, LA lost the 7th game of the series three times by razor thin margins (107-110 OT, 93-95, and 106-108). It wasn't until 1985 that Los Angeles finally defeated Boston for the championship. Again, just two years later, the Lakers again knocked off the Celtics.

The club has had more than its share of superstars. Six of the top greatest players in NBA history spent most or all of their careers with the team. Wilt Chamberlain, Magic Johnson, George Mikan, Kareem Abdul-Jabbar, Jerry West and Elgin Baylor have combined for forty-two 1st team All-NBA awards just among themselves as Lakers. This is eight more than any other entire franchise. In fact, at least one player from tinseltown has made the 1st team each of the last 13 years - the longest ongoing streak for any franchise.

Lakers' coach, Pat Riley, holds the NBA record for winning percentage among coaches at 73.4%. Only former Celtic's coach, K.C. Jones, also has a career percentage of 70%+. (technically 70.6%) Speaking of Lakers' coaches, the coach with the worst record for Los Angeles in its 40-year history was, ironically, possibly its greatest player. George Mikan led the Minneapolis Lakers to six titles in the 40's and 50's, but only managed a 9-30 coaching record during the Lakers worst year - 1957-58 (19-53). It was Mikan's only NBA's coaching experience.

> **Quiz: What former Laker is the only championship series MVP despite his team losing?**

ALL TIME LAKERS' TEAM

Player	Span	Yrs	CRD
Kareem Abdul-Jabbar	1976-88	13	28,831
Elgin Baylor	1959-72	14	25,156
Jerry West	1961-73	13	25,149
Earvin Johnson	1980-88	9	18,462
George Mikan	1948-56	9	12,796
Vern Mikkelsen	1950-59	10	12,044
Gail Goodrich	1966-76	9	11,368
Wilt Chamberlain	1969-73	5	11,031
Rudy LaRusso	1960-67	8	10,319
Jamaal Wilkes	1978-85	8	10,147

ALL TIME LAKERS' COACH

John Kundla   12 Years
68-37 Playoffs   11 Playoffs
466-349 Reg. Season 6 Championships

HISTORICAL PROFILE

Category	Data
Lakers' coach	Pat Riley
Years coached Los Angeles	7
# of franchise years	41
# of coaches	12
# of winning seasons	32
# of playoff years	38
# of runner's up	11
# of championships	12
Regular season win %	61.0
Playoff win %	60.5

> **Answer:**
> **Jerry West (1969)**

Los Angeles Lakers ....1987-88 Highlights

Lakers 147-120 Spurs   Sun.   November 15, 1987

Magic Johnson entered the game with San Antonio only one assist shy of Jerry West's club record (6238 regular season). Not surprisingly, Johnson quickly surpassed the record on his way to his fifth straight game of double figures for assists. Coincidentally, James Worthy also had 10 assists in the game - a career high. By winning, the Lakers set a club record for wins to start a season. The previous record since the team moved to Los Angeles was a 5-0 start in 1980-81. As of this game, LA was 6-0.

Lakers 115-114 Celtics   Fri.   December 11, 1987

Celtics/Lakers? A controversial finish? What's new? With Boston leading 114-113, Danny Ainge missed the second of two free throws. While the ball was in the air on the rebound, several Lakers were calling time out. The official, assuming the Lakers would get the rebound, blew the whistle the moment it touched Mychal Thompson's hand. The controversy was that the ball bounced off his hand into Kevin McHale's, where presumably the game would have ended. Instead, LA got the ball in bounds and to Magic Johnson. Johnson hit a running one hander to win the game for the Lakers as time expired.

Lakers 117-109 Jazz . . .Pistons 110-75 Nets   Sat.   December 26, 1987

The two top teams in the NBA, Detroit and L.A. Lakers, had similar streaks on the same day. The Pistons (17-5) won their 10th straight by defeating the Nets 110-75. The 10 in a row tied a club record. They did it on the strength of a 15-0 scoring burst to *start* the game. Ironically, the Laker's (19-6) used a 15-0 scoring spurt to *end* their game against Utah. It enabled them to change a 102-109 deficit into a 117-109 win. The win was the 8th straight for LA.

Lakers 121-110 Rockets   Mon.   January 18, 1988

The Lakers' 41 1st quarter points were a season high, while their 19 point 1st quarter lead not only represented LA's high, but also Houston's low. During that pivotal quarter, the Lakers hit 18 straight field goals - believed to be an all-time record. Magic Johnson had his best game of the year as he scored 37 points and 17 assists.

Lakers 116-109 Sonics   Sun.   January 24, 1988

The game pitted the team with the best road record (LA) vs the team with the best home record (Seattle). In fact, Seattle had won a franchise record 18 straight at home prior to the loss. LA won largely because of the outstanding defense on Dale Ellis. Ellis had his worst game of the year on 5-21 shooting. Ironically, Ellis was coming off his career high 47 pts in the previous game while defensive player of the year Michael Cooper - who would have guarded Ellis - missed his first game in over 5 years. The defensive hero was Byron Scott who played all 48 minutes.

Lakers 115-106 Celtics   Sun.   February 14, 1988

The Lakers were awesome 3/4 of the time in defeating the Celtics. Using a ferocious running game, Los Angeles built a 20 point halftime lead, 64-44. But, in what was among the most dominating 3rd quarters of the year for any NBA team, the Celtics outscored the Lakers 36-12 to lead by 4 at the quarter break. Once again the Lakers went to work, scoring the first 9 points in the 4th quarter, and coasted to victory. Both starting guards had noteworthy performances. The Lakers' Byron Scott hit a career high 38 points while Boston's Danny Ainge hit the last 5 points of that incredible third quarter, including a three pointer which set an NBA season record (passing Darrell Griffith's 92), as well as a running one hander at the buzzer.

Los Angeles Lakers .... Influence on Winning

TEAM RECORD BY

PLAYER	GAMES	... SCR Leader HOME	ROAD	... REB Leader HOME	ROAD	... AST Leader HOME	ROAD
Earvin Johnson	72	11-0	8-3	1-0	5-6	29-3	24-9
Byron Scott	81	13-1	11-4	1-0	---	4-1	0-2
James Worthy	75	10-2	7-4	2-1	3-1	2-0	1-0
A.C. Green	82	1-0	---	17-3	13-7	---	---
K. Abdul-Jabbar	80	1-0	2-1	2-0	3-0	---	---
Mychal Thompson	80	2-0	1-2	11-1	3-3	---	---
Michael Cooper	61	0-1	---	---	0-1	1-1	2-1
Tony Campbell	13	1-0	0-1	---	---	---	---
Kurt Rambis	70	---	---	6-0	0-1	---	---
Wes Matthews	51	---	---	---	---	3-0	0-3

TEAM RECORD BY SCORING *

PLAYER	PLAY	DNP	0-9	10-19	20-29	30-39	40+
Earvin Johnson	57-15	5-5	6-3	19-7	28-4	4-1	---
Byron Scott	62-19	0-1	1-2	16-9	36-7	9-1	---
James Worthy	57-18	5-2	4-1	21-8	29-8	3-1	---
A.C. Green	62-20	---	26-5	31-14	5-1	---	---
K. Abdul-Jabbar	60-20	2-0	9-4	40-13	11-3	---	---
Mychal Thompson	60-20	2-0	24-8	32-10	4-2	---	---
Michael Cooper	49-13	13-7	29-7	19-6	1-0	---	---
Tony Campbell	9-4	53-16	7-1	0-3	2-0	---	---
Kurt Rambis	51-19	11-1	42-19	9-0	---	---	---
Wes Matthews	39-12	23-8	32-8	7-4	---	---	---

TEAM RECORD BY STARTING POSITION *

PLAYER	GAMES	STARTS	PG	OG	SF	PF	C
Earvin Johnson	72	70	56-14	---	---	---	---
Byron Scott	81	81	---	62-19	---	---	---
James Worthy	75	72	---	---	55-17	---	---
A.C. Green	82	64	---	---	1-1	49-13	---
K. Abdul-Jabbar	80	80	---	---	---	---	60-20
Mychal Thompson	80	0	---	---	---	---	---
Michael Cooper	61	8	---	0-1	5-2	---	---
Tony Campbell	13	1	---	---	1-0	---	---
Kurt Rambis	70	20	---	---	---	13-7	---
Wes Matthews	51	8	4-4	---	---	---	---

* For further definition of each category and column heading see pages 38 & 39.

Los Angeles Lakers .... 1987-88 Statistics

RAW NUMBERS *

PLAYER	2pt%	3pt%	FT%	MIN	PF	DQ	HI	TO	RB	AS	BL	ST
Earvin Johnson	.510	.196	.853	2637	147	0	**39**	269	449	**858**	13	114
Byron Scott	.554	**.346**	**.858**	3048	204	2	38	161	333	335	27	**155**
James Worthy	.537	.125	.796	2655	175	1	38	155	374	289	55	72
A.C. Green	.505	0-2	.773	2636	204	0	28	120	**710**	93	45	87
K. Abdul-Jabbar	.532	0-1	.762	2308	216	1	27	159	478	135	**92**	48
Mychal Thompson	.515	0-3	.634	2007	**251**	1	28	113	489	66	79	38
Michael Cooper	.434	.320	**.858**	1793	136	1	21	101	228	289	26	66
Tony Campbell	**.571**	.333	.718	242	41	0	28	26	27	15	2	11
Kurt Rambis	.548	0-0	.785	845	103	0	17	59	268	54	13	39
Wes Matthews	.491	.233	.831	706	65	0	18	69	66	138	3	25

OVERALL RANKINGS *

PLAYER	G	GS	PPG	PR	RANK	SC	SH	RB	AS	BL	ST
Earvin Johnson	72	70	19.56	**27.71**	6	24	36	85	2	130	40
Byron Scott	**81**	**81**	21.65	21.73	21	12	7	117	57	109	25
James Worthy	75	72	19.71	20.09	34	23	25	94	58	61	101
A.C. Green	82	64	11.43	16.44	65	97	54	21	149	75	74
K. Abdul-Jabbar	80	80	14.56	15.90	69	60	31	62	109	24	131
Mychal Thompson	80	0	11.56	12.81	101	96	96	38	152	27	140
Michael Cooper	61	8	8.72	11.98	111	128	130	103	35	88	59
Tony Campbell	13	1	11.00	9.00	DNQ						
Kurt Rambis	70	20	3.96	6.97	DNQ						
Wes Matthews	51	8	5.67	6.02	DNQ						

POSITION RANKINGS *

PLAYER	POSITION	RANK	SC	SH	RB	AS	BL	ST
Earvin Johnson	Point Guard (PG)	1	1	8	1	2	14	21
Byron Scott	Off Guard (OG)	5	4	2	16	19	18	8
James Worthy	Small Forward (SF)	7	8	4	25	4	14	20
A.C. Green	Power Forward (PF)	14	19	12	10	32	24	8
Kareem Abdul-Jabbar	Center (C)	12	8	7	26	7	14	14
Mychal Thompson	Center (C)	21	18	18	20	21	16	16
Michael Cooper	Off Guard (OG)	18	30	26	8	6	11	16
Tony Campbell	Small Forward (SF)	DNQ						
Kurt Rambis	Power Forward (PF)	DNQ						
Wes Matthews	Point Guard (PG)	DNQ						

*For further definition of each category and column heading see pages 38 & 39.

Los Angeles Lakers .... Team Info

WEEKLY POWER RATING
41 WINS - AVERAGE (See page 39 for Team Power Rating discussion.)

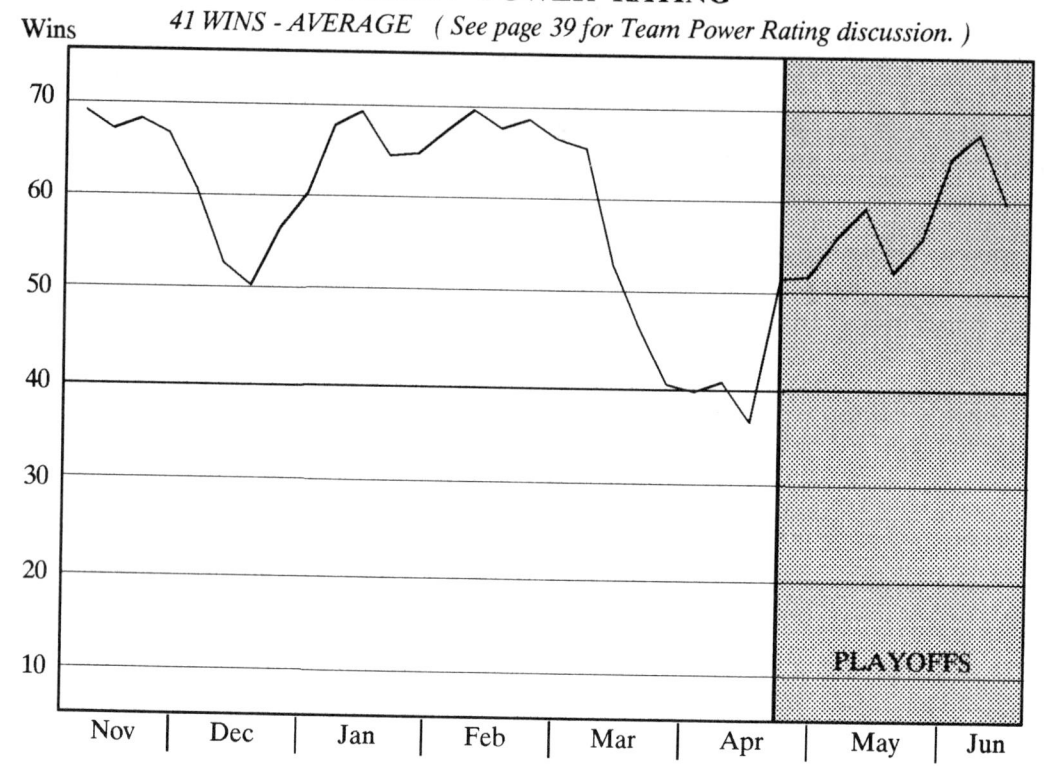

Miscellaneous Categories	Data	Rank
Attendance	714K	3
Key-Man Games Missed	55	10
Season Record	62-20	1
- Home	36-5	1
- Road	26-15	1
Eastern Conference	16-6	1
Western Conference	46-14	1
Overtime Record	2-3	18
Record 5 Pts. or Less	16-6	1
Record 10 Pts. or More	29-9	1
Games Won By Bench	3	14
Games Won By Starters	12	4
Winning Streak	15	1
Losing Streak	3	1
Home Winning Streak	13	4
Road Winning Streak	8	1
Home Losing Streak	1	1
Road Losing Streak	5	6

Performance Categories	Data	Rank
Offensive Scoring (per game)	112.8	5
Defensive Scoring (per game)	107.0	11
Scoring Margin (per game)	5.8	2
Defensive FG%	.476	9
Offensive 2-point%	.520	2
Offensive 3-point%	.297	16
Offensive Free Throw %	.789	5
Offensive Rebs (Off REB/Opp Def REB)		12
Defensive Rebs (Def REB/Opp Off REB)		8
Offensive Assists (AST/FGMade)		4
Offensive Blocks (BLK/Opp FGAttempted)		18
Offensive Steals (STL/Game)		15
Turnover Margin (Off T.O. - Def T.O.)		18
Finesse (BLK + STL) / PF		7
Rebounding Record	48-29-5	5
Assists Record	41-35-6	10
Field Goal Pct. Record	51-31-0	4
Free Throw Pct. Record	49-32-1	4

Los Angeles Lakers .... Miscellaneous

ADMINISTRATIVE INFORMATION

Team Offices: The Forum
3900 West Manchester Blvd.
Inglewood, California
90306
Telephone: (213) 674-6000
Head Coach: Pat Riley
Home Arena: The Forum
Capacity: 17,505

1988-89 ROSTER*

J#	VETERANS	COLLEGE	POS	R#	D#	HT	WT	LA.L	NBA
33	Kareem Abdul-Jabbar	UCLA	C	1	1	7-2	250	13	19
19	Tony Campbell	Ohio State	F	1	20	6-7	215	1	4
21	Michael Cooper	New Mexico St.	G-F	3	60	6-7	176	10	10
45	A.C. Green	Oregon State	F	1	23	6-9	224	3	3
32	Earvin Johnson	Michigan State	G	1	1	6-9	220	9	9
1	Wes Matthews	Wisconsin	G	1	14	6-1	170	2	8
4	Byron Scott	Arizona State	G	1	4	6-4	193	5	5
52	Mike Smrek	Canasius	C	2	25	7-0	263	2	3
43	Mychal Thompson	Minnesota	F-C	1	1	6-10	235	2	9
20	Milt Wagner	Louisville	G	2	35	6-4	180	1	1
	Orlando Woolridge	Notre Dame	F	1	6	6-9	215	0	7
42	James Worthy	North Carolina	F	1	1	6-9	235	6	6

ROOKIES	COLLEGE	POS	R#	D#	HT
David Rivers	Notre Dame	G	1	25	6-0

* For further definition of category and column headings, see pages 38 & 39.

Los Angeles Lakers .... Overview

In my opinion it will go down as one of the great predictions of all time. After winning the 1986-87 NBA title, coach Pat Riley was heard saying "I know this is going to sound crazy, but I guarantee that we're going to win the championship again." All season long Riley was berated for having made that comment. In some cases even his own players were upset with their leader for the added pressure. As time went on, however, it became clear that Riley's tactic had been brilliant. No team had repeated since the late 1960's and no team was going to again without having that carrot dangling. In last year's book I discussed the difficulty of repeating. Probably the biggest single reason is that once the prize has been obtained, the motivation is gone. What Riley did was to lessen the thrill of the prize by making the job seem incomplete. I can understand why some of the players resented it at the time, but if he hadn't thrown down the gauntlet, odds are exceptional that it would have been some other team wearing the crown last June.

The championship gave Los Angeles five titles in this decade. Most of the nine seasons since Magic joined the club have been very successful. The fewest wins in any year was 54 in 1984. This group has produced the 7th greatest (1987) and 8th greatest (1985) teams of all time (by my rating system in last year's book). The 62 regular-season wins gave the Lakers four consecutive 60+ win seasons. It's the first time any team has accomplished that feat. Moreover, the club's 251 victories over the last 4 seasons ties Los Angeles with Boston as the all-time top 4-year teams.

	4 years	Win%
Los Angeles Lakers	**1985-88**	**.765**
Boston Celtics	1984-87	.765
Milwaukee Bucks	1971-74	.756
Boston Celtics	1962-65	.747
Philadelphia 76ers	1980-83	.744
Boston Celtics	1980-83	.737
Boston Celtics	1972-75	.731

The 1988 Lakers set many records in addition to the four consecutive 60+ win seasons. The 106 games they played including the playoffs was one more than the previous high (Boston, 105, 1987). They were also the first team to survive three 7th games. Winning the 7th game of the championship series broke an 0-5 streak by the Lakers since they'd moved to L.A.

7th games in championship series
1988	L.A. vs Detroit	108-105	**Win**
1984	L.A. vs Boston	102-111	Loss
1970	L.A. vs New York	99-113	Loss
1969	L.A. vs Boston	106-108	Loss
1966	L.A. vs Boston	93-95	Loss
1962	L.A. vs Boston	107-110(ot)	Loss

Pat Riley is on his way to becoming one of, if not, *the* most successful coach in NBA history. He's off to a faster start than any other coach, having reached 400 victories in only 540 games. Billy Cunningham had reached 400 wins the quickest (572 games). Besides being rated as either the #1 or #2 best-dressed coach (depending on which poll you look at), he is rated as #1 in ability by his fellow coaches. Though he has not won a Coach-of-the-Year award, he is consistently in the running. The trouble is that it is difficult to measure how good a job he's done in any given year when the team varies only slightly from the previous season. Just because he hasn't won the C.O.Y. award isn't a good argument to support those who say he isn't given enough credit or that he's underrated. No coach who's won as much as he has and who coaches in Los Angeles is going to be underrated!

Magic Johnson continues to be the Lakers primary star. At this point in his career he's acting as a liaison between the "fossilique" Jabbar and the younger Green, Worthy, and Scott. Although he didn't have his greatest year, he was still magnificent. Magic has been ranked #1 at his position every year he's been in the league. Being injured and missing 10 games last season just gave him an opportunity to emphasize his

Los Angeles Lakers . . . . Overview

value. (The Lakers were only 5-5 without him.) Johnson was gracious in saying they were "forgetting how to win", but the truth is they were playing without a healthy Magic. As further evidence of how pivotal he is, consider that the team was 25-10 when he scored 19 points or less and 32-5 when he scored 20 or more. The Lakers were 53-12 when he led the team in assists, 9-8 when he did not. Johnson also led the NBA in triple doubles, with 12. Ten of those dozen were on the road - nearly as many as the rest of the league combined.

2+	Triple Doubles	Road
Magic Johnson	12	10
Fat Lever	11	5
Kevin Johnson	3	2
Vern Fleming	3	1
Terry Porter	2	1
Doc Rivers	2	1
Paul Pressey	2	0
Mark Jackson	2	0
Michael Jordan	2	0
Others	11	5

Byron Scott had his best season yet in 1987-88. His scoring (21.65) and production (21.73) were both substantially ahead of his previous years. In one eight game stretch Scott averaged nearly 30 ppg. Like Magic, Scott's value was apparent in his scoring. When he scored 16 points or less, LA was only 8-9. When he scored 17 or more they were 54-10. When Scott and Johnson both scored 20 or more points Los Angeles was a sparkling 25-1.

Michael Thompson continued to add to the team. Since his arrival, the Lakers are 81-17 in games where the top 7 players all played.

James Worthy has finally begun to shake the "one-dimensional" tag that has plagued him so long. Symbolically, his first career triple double came in his final game of the season (game 7 vs Detroit) and won him individual recognition as the championship MVP.

A.C. Green began the season on an outstanding note, but gradually became less and less valuable, ultimately returning the starting power forward spot to Kurt Rambis in game #65. Rambis, the Clark Kent look alike, has since flown off to Charlotte.

Orlando Woolridge will be coming over from the Nets. He has the tag of being one-dimensional and selfish. Besides that, he's coming off substance abuse. If he lives up to his potential, great. I've got my doubts.

Michael Cooper lost a bit of durability when he missed his first games in 6 years. The Lakers managed to win the first few games without Cooper, but then hit a tailspin, going 8-8. After he came back, the club re"cooped" and won 8 of 11 to close the regular season strong.

With the late-season injuries to Johnson and Cooper, Los Angeles had its share of difficulties. Consider these examples. In the 4th quarter on the road, LA was 15-6-0 in the first half of the season, but only 3-16-1 in the second half. The club won the rebounding battle over their opponents at a 3 to 1 rate in the first half before slipping to 18-19-1. Nevertheless, LA went 29-12 in their last 41 games.

Notes: The Lakers were 21-0 when leading on the road after Q3... When they won the rebounding at home they went 23-0... Los Angeles had a dozen 4th quarter comebacks while only losing two leads - the NBA's best... The club's worst category is blocks (#18)... The franchise set a new attendance high - one of seven teams in the league to do so.

Prediction - best case: 64-18

If everyone is healthy there is no reason this team can't reach at that lofty pinnacle again. Rebounding will be the key. Green needs to regain his early 1987-88 form and Scott and Worthy must continue to improve. Sixty-four wins is very difficult!

Prediction - worst case: 52-30

If Magic has injury problems and Kareem drops to a Production Rate of 13 or less, this team will have major holes. Already the bench is weak. If Cooper and Thompson are unable to perform up to par, a record of 52-30 is not improbable.

Miami Heat ....Miscellaneous

ADMINISTRATIVE INFORMATION

Team Offices: Miami Arena
Miami, Florida
33136-4102

Telephone: (305) 577-4328
Head Coach: Ron Rothstein
Home Arena: Miami Arena
Capacity: 16,500

1988-89 ROSTER*

J#	VETERANS	COLLEGE	POS	R#	D#	HT	WT	Miami	NBA
	Hansi Gnad	Alaska-Anchorage	C	3	57	6-10	230	0	0
	Scott Hastings	Arkansas	F-C	2	29	6-10	235	0	6
	Conner Henry	Santa Barbara	G	4	89	6-7	195	0	3
	Arvid Kramer	Augustana	F	3	45	6-9	220	0	1
	John Stroeder	Minnesota	C	8	168	6-10	250	0	1
	Jon Sundvold	Missouri	G	1	16	6-2	170	0	5
	Billy Thompson	Louisville	F	1	19	6-7	210	0	2
	Andre Turner	Memphis State	G	3	69	5-11	160	0	2
	Dwayne Washington	Syracuse	G	1	13	6-2	195	0	2
	Kevin Williams	St. Johns	G	2	45	6-2	180	0	4

ROOKIES	COLLEGE	POS	R#	D#	HT
Rony Seikaly	Syracuse	C-F	1	9	6-11
Kevin Edwards	DePaul	G	1	20	6-3
Grant Long	Eastern Michigan	F	2	33	6-8
Sylvester Gray	Memphis State	F	2	35	6-6
Orlando Graham	Auburn-Montgomery	F	2	40	6-7
Nate Johnson	Tampa	F	3	59	6-8

* For further definition of category and column headings, see pages 38 & 39.

Miami Heat .... Overview

The expansion of the NBA is very exciting to me. Four new teams, an opportunity for many players to make their mark instead of riding a bench, and visible proof of the growth in the NBA. Nevertheless, I do have some questions about expansion (see page 253 for discussion of parity). I also have some questions about expansion in Miami. One would expect the locals to be enthusiastic about the possibility of bringing in the likes of Michael Jordan, Larry Bird, or Magic Johnson. Of course, many are. Surprisingly, however, there is a fair amount of criticism.

To begin with, the city is made up of such a diverse group of people, Cubans, natives, retirees, vacationers, that it makes it hard to rally around one cause. Secondly, the state has always been football crazy. The Miami Dolphins and Miami University Hurricanes command a lot of local and national attention. Competing for their following will be tough. Thirdly, even after football is over, spring training begins for baseball and Florida is home for the majority of major league teams. A fourth problem is the location of the new arena. It's downtown and parking is a serious problem. The team took a lot of *heat* for the decision to move there. Maybe that's where the name came from. The final concern is the fact that the Floridians of the ABA failed, albeit many years ago. In their final game only 3,000 fans showed up to watch Dr. J score 37 points and 27 rebounds. Hopefully, we'll never see a repeat of that. Perhaps these are the reasons why Miami barely made the league season ticket requirements (10,000 by December 31st, 1987).

Zen Bufman and Ted Arison were ultimately responsible for putting together the financial package which brought the town its team. When you have to pay 32.5 million to join this elite club, a good financial base is a must. Arison's net worth (estimated at 350 million) more than makes the club solvent. Joining these two are Billy Cunningham - the former NBA/ABA great. Cunningham's NBA ties were instrumental in the club getting its chance.

The Heat will have some good players to build around. Their two first round draft picks should both provide instant help. **Ron Siekely** improved every year in college and should be an excellent power forward in the Kevin McHale mold... **Kevin Edwards** is a very athletic guard with a very accurate shot and should start at off-guard... **Billy Thompson**, who has sat on the Laker's bench for 2 years, comes into town with the distinction of having played for a championship team 3 consecutive years (Louisville, L.A., L.A.). Do you think that streak will end?... **Scott Hastings** failed to get much playing time at Atlanta. Though the unprotected players were not made public, can anyone tell me how Hastings (a 6-year career 3ppg scorer) is the 9th best player on Atlanta's team (each team protected eight)?... **Jon Sundvold** will be the leading candidate at point guard. Jon is one of the top 3-point shooters in the league and averaged 13 ppg as a late season starter for the Spurs... **Kevin Williams** is a very respectable player. Just knowing that he scored 31 ppg in the CBA in 1986 heightens the expectations... With additional players like **Hansi Gnad, Pearl Washington**, and **Andre Turner**, the Heat should have a decent bench.

Of course, what's even more important to the club's future were the six pre-draft deals they made. The net result was an additional first round pick in last year's draft and five additional second rounders, three of which will come in the next few years.

The coach will be **Ron Rothstein**, assistant to Chuck Daly at Detroit. Blessed with a sense of humor (he'll need one), he realized just how tough times might be when he signed on with Miami. "I have a great lawyer who negotiated my contract", he said. "And in my contract, it says three wins." Although they'll be replacing Sacramento in the very tough Midwest Division, I'll bet they end up with at least four marks in the "W" column.

Milwaukee Bucks .... History

The Milwaukee Bucks came into the NBA as an expansion team in 1968. Four other NBA clubs came into existence during the next two years. Including the four ABA teams who are now part of the NBA, nine of the league's franchises got their start during this 3 year period. Of the group, Milwaukee leads in total regular season victories (992 to 944 for Denver) and playoff victories (81 vs 70 for Indiana). Of the nine, only Seattle has also won an NBA championship.

Without doubt, the franchise has been very successful. In fact, the Bucks have averaged 49.6 victories per year - more than any other team. Even the Celtics (49.4), Lakers (47.5), and Sixers (45.2) have not won as many games each season. Only Boston (64.2%) and LA (62.0%) have won at a higher rate than Milwaukee - but just barely (60.5%).

The Bucks can lay claim to making the most dominant trip through the playoffs in a given year. In 1971, the team went 12-2 to secure their only championship. In doing so, they won each game by an average of 14.5 points - a margin nearly twice that of the next best champion. It's interesting that the Bucks would have such a dominant playoff considering their generally poor showing in post season play. Of the eleven teams who have won an NBA championship, Milwaukee is last in ratio of championships per 50+ win seasons (1 to 6) followed by Portland (1 to 2), Philly (1 to 1.75) and Seattle (1 to 1.5).

Milwaukee leads in one other category as well - ratio of franchise years per coach (6.67). Only 3 individuals have headed the club in 20 years. Larry Costello was the club's first coach and lasted 8.5 years. Don Nelson followed by coaching 10.5 seasons. Del Harris spent his first year with the Bucks last year. Don Nelson holds the record for reaching 500 victories faster than any other coach (817 games). Boston's Red Auerbach took 821 games to reach the same milestone.

Coming into 1987-88 season, four teams had won 60+ games three years in a row - However none had achieved four straight. In 1974, Milwaukee won 59 games in what would have been their fourth straight. The Bucks with Abdul-Jabbar lost their 23rd and last loss to the Lakers that year. Ironically, Jabbar and the Lakers became the first team to win four straight 60+ seasons last year.

Quiz: What Bucks player holds the NBA record for the quickest DQ in playoff history?

ALL TIME BUCKS' TEAM

Player	Span	Yrs	CRD
Kareem Abdul-Jabbar	1970-75	6	17,608
Bob Dandridge	1970-81	9	12,035
Marques Johnson	1978-84	7	12,023
Sidney Moncrief	1980-88	9	11,878
Junior Bridgeman	1976-87	10	8,994
Brian Winters	1976-83	8	8,378
Paul Pressey	1983-88	6	7,385
Terry Cummings	1983-88	6	6,924
Jon McGlocklin	1969-76	8	7,256
Oscar Robertson	1971-74	4	5,967

ALL TIME BUCKS' COACH

Don Nelson   11 Years
42-46 Playoffs   9 Playoffs
540-344 Reg. Season   0 Championships

HISTORICAL PROFILE

Category	Data
Bucks' coach	Del Harris
Years coached Milwaukee	1
# of franchise years	20
# of coaches	3
# of winning seasons	15
# of playoff years	16
# of runner's up	1
# of championships	1
Regular season win %	60.5
Playoff win %	52.9

Answer:
Paul Mokeski, May 7, 1986, after playing just 6 minutes, (113-108 win over Philly).

Milwaukee Bucks ....1987-88 Highlights

Bucks 115-100 Bullets   Tue.   November 10, 1987

Randy Breuer had a career high 16 rebounds and 22 points, extending his scoring average to 18 ppg - slightly better than the 6.4 average he had accumulated his first 4 years in the league. The 7'3" Breuer helped the Bucks overcome the heroics of 5'3" Mugsy Bogues. The Bullet guard hit the season's longest shot to date at the end of the half - 60 feet. It whimsically became known as "the Mug Shot".

Bucks 124-116 Lakers (OT)   Sun.   November 22, 1987

The Milwaukee Bucks had not won at Los Angeles against the Lakers since Jan. 1982. It was the 7th win in 10 games for Milwaukee and was the first loss of the season for L.A., ending the best start in Laker's history. The game represented the second most consistent scoring by an NBA team's starters (18, 19, 19, 20, 24 - Milwaukee). Interestingly, the Lakers have the best this year (19, 23, 23, 24, 25).

Bucks 85-83 Lakers   Fri.   December 4, 1987

This victory marked the first time the Bucks have won the home and away series since 1981/82. Ironically, the Bucks brought to an end one of the NBA's longest streaks as they held their former center to only 7 points. It was exactly 10 years to the day since Kareem began his streak of games where he scored in double figures. Amazingly, Jabbar kept it going in the first meeting of the two teams by scoring his 10th point in overtime. A Laker missed FG attempt at the buzzer ruined his chance to repeat that performance in this game.

Bucks 114-110 Bullets   Mon.   February 15, 1988

The victory was traceable to Jack Sikma, who went 9-10 from the field and 9-12 from the line. Coincidentally, Sikma was coming off his lowest scoring game in many years - 1 point. Sikma may have indirectly won the game in the first quarter when he got Moses Malone ejected for fighting with him. Malone ended up with 6 points, Sikma with 27. Even so, Washington nearly pulled off the season's biggest comeback. The Bullets trailed by 30 (84-54), but fought back on the strength of John Williams' career high 28 points.

Bucks 119-108 Pistons   Fri.   February 19, 1988

The win broke Detroit's six game winning streak. Apparently the Pistons didn't appreciate it. Detroit's coach Chuck Daly, assistant coach Dick Versace, and center Bill Laimbeer were all ejected from the game. Additionally, Detroit's other assistant, Ron Rothstein, had one technical. The NBA's leading FT% shooter, Jack Sikma, hit all 7 technicals. Surprisingly, the Pistons had one more FTA than did Milwaukee.

Bucks 104-101 Hawks   Sat.   March 5, 1988

The Bucks were hot, having won 8 of 10 while the Hawks were not, having lost their 3rd straight home game. Milwaukee broke a 6 game losing streak at the Omni, losing by an average of 12 ppg. The heroes were Terry Cummings, who tied his season high of 15 rebounds, and Sidney Moncrief, who had a season high 29 points.

Bucks 132-94 Bullets   Wed.   April 20, 1988

The 132 points tied a season high. The 38 point victory margin was the Buck's largest ever over Washington, and broke a 5 game Bucks losing streak. Interestingly, the Malones were held to only a combined 13 points (7+6). This is the fewest they have combined to score as teammates. The previous fewest (14, 8+6) was earlier last year vs these same Bucks.

Milwaukee Bucks . . . . Influence on Winning

TEAM RECORD BY

		... SCR Leader		... REB Leader		... AST Leader	
PLAYER	GAMES	HOME	ROAD	HOME	ROAD	HOME	ROAD
Jack Sikma	82	6-2	3-4	13-2	5-14	2-0	3-1
Terry Cummings	76	15-5	4-14	7-5	4-8	1-1	1-1
Paul Pressey	75	3-2	2-3	1-2	1-3	17-8	5-17
Randy Breuer	81	2-1	1-3	11-2	1-4	---	---
Jay Humphries	18	---	---	---	---	---	1-0
Sidney Moncrief	56	2-0	1-1	---	---	6-2	0-4
John Lucas	81	1-0	0-2	---	---	8-4	3-10
Larry Krystowiak	50	1-0	---	1-1	0-4	---	---
Ricky Pierce	37	1-3	0-4	---	---	----	0-1
Jerry Reynolds	62	1-0	1-1	---	---	---	0-2

TEAM RECORD BY SCORING *

PLAYER	PLAY	DNP	0-9	10-19	20-29	30-39	40+
Jack Sikma	42-40	---	4-7	22-22	15-11	1-0	---
Terry Cummings	39-37	3-3	1-1	12-18	20-16	6-2	---
Paul Pressey	40-35	2-5	12-10	18-22	10-3	---	---
Randy Breuer	41-40	1-0	13-20	20-16	8-3	0-1	---
Jay Humphries	10-8	32-32	10-8	---	---	---	---
Sidney Moncrief	27-29	15-11	13-14	11-13	3-2	---	---
John Lucas	41-40	1-0	24-20	16-19	1-1	---	---
Larry Krystowiak	24-26	18-14	16-16	6-10	2-0	---	---
Ricky Pierce	19-18	23-22	3-2	11-7	5-9	---	---
Jerry Reynolds	34-28	8-12	18-17	14-10	2-1	---	---

TEAM RECORD BY STARTING POSITION *

PLAYER	GAMES	STARTS	PG	OG	SF	PF	C
Jack Sikma	82	82	---	---	---	38-36	4-4
Terry Cummings	76	76	---	---	37-36	2-1	---
Paul Pressey	75	75	32-28	6-6	2-1	---	---
Randy Breuer	81	73	---	---	---	---	38-35
Jay Humphries	18	0	---	---	---	---	---
Sidney Moncrief	56	51	---	25-26	---	---	---
John Lucas	81	22	10-12	---	---	---	---
Larry Krystowiak	50	7	---	---	0-1	2-3	0-1
Ricky Pierce	37	0	---	---	---	---	---
Jerry Reynolds	62	21	---	10-7	2-2	---	---

* For further definition of each category and column heading see pages 38 & 39.

Milwaukee Bucks — 1987-88 Statistics

RAW NUMBERS *

PLAYER	2pt%	3pt%	FT%	MIN	PF	DQ	HI	TO	RB	AS	BL	ST
Jack Sikma	.489	.214	**.922**	2923	316	11	35	157	**709**	279	80	93
Terry Cummings	.485	.333	.665	2629	274	6	**36**	170	553	181	46	78
Paul Pressey	.508	.205	.798	2484	233	6	25	**198**	375	**523**	34	112
Randy Breuer	.495	0-0	.657	2258	198	3	33	107	551	103	**107**	46
Jay Humphries	**.540**	.167	.732	1809	177	1	26	127	174	395	5	81
Sidney Moncrief	.513	.161	.837	1428	109	0	29	86	180	204	14	41
John Lucas	.479	.338	.802	1766	102	1	25	125	159	392	3	88
Larry Krystkowiak	.487	0-3	.811	1050	137	0	23	57	231	50	8	18
Ricky Pierce	.519	.214	.877	965	94	0	29	57	83	73	7	21
Jerry Reynolds	.449	**.429**	.773	1161	97	0	24	104	160	104	32	74

OVERALL RANKINGS *

PLAYER	G	GS	PPG	PR	RANK	SC	SH	RB	AS	BL	ST
Jack Sikma	**82**	**82**	16.49	**21.77**	20	44	38	40	72	42	82
Terry Cummings	76	76	**21.33**	**19.16**	40	15	126	61	97	74	89
Paul Pressey	75	75	13.11	**18.67**	44	77	52	91	19	94	35
Randy Breuer	81	73	11.95	**14.47**	83	88	115	36	131	18	135
Jay Humphries	68	33	10.04	**13.47**	93	113	35	28	17	151	36
Sidney Moncrief	56	51	10.77	**12.45**	103	101	46	105	43	106	94
John Lucas	81	22	9.17	**10.84**	120	124	81	134	14	154	27
Larry Krystkowiak	50	7	7.18	**8.94**	143	147	70	58	126	114	145
Ricky Pierce	37	0	16.38	**12.97**	DNQ						
Jerry Reynolds	62	21	8.03	**8.03**	DNQ						

POSITION RANKINGS *

PLAYER	POSITION	RANK	SC	SH	RB	AS	BL	ST
Jack Sikma	Power Forward (PF)	6	7	7	18	3	14	12
Terry Cummings	Small Forward (SF)	9	6	28	6	21	20	17
Paul Pressey	Point Guard (PG)	10	15	13	2	19	3	19
Randy Breuer	Center (C)	15	14	21	19	17	10	15
Jay Humphries	Point Guard (PG)	20	21	7	14	17	26	20
Sidney Moncrief	Off Guard (OG)	17	21	11	9	10	16	26
John Lucas	Point Guard (PG)	24	24	15	19	14	29	15
Larry Krystkowiak	Power Forward (PF)	31	33	16	28	18	33	32
Ricky Pierce	Off Guard (OG)	DNQ						
Jerry Reynolds	Off Guard (OG)	DNQ						

*For further definition of each category and column heading see pages 38 & 39.

Milwaukee Bucks ....Team Info

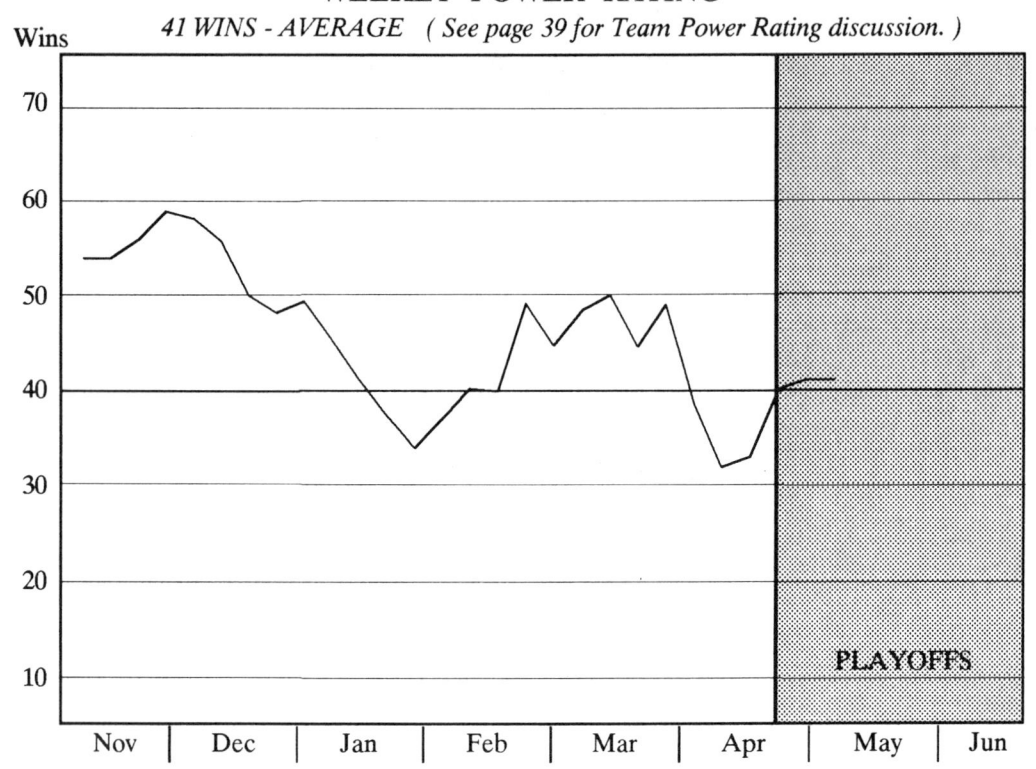

WEEKLY POWER RATING
41 WINS - AVERAGE   (See page 39 for Team Power Rating discussion.)

Wins

(Chart showing weekly power rating from Nov through Jun, with PLAYOFFS shaded region in May-Jun)

Miscellaneous Categories	Data	Rank
Attendance	452K	19
Key-Man Games Missed	159	22
Season Record	42-40	12
- Home	30-11	11
- Road	12-29	13
Eastern Conference	28-30	12
Western Conference	14-10	10
Overtime Record	3-1	3
Record 5 Pts. or Less	15-12	7
Record 10 Pts. or More	21-18	13
Games Won By Bench	3	14
Games Won By Starters	3	15
Winning Streak	4	14
Losing Streak	5	10
Home Winning Streak	10	8
Road Winning Streak	2	14
Home Losing Streak	2	2
Road Losing Streak	8	13

Performance Categories	Data	Rank
Offensive Scoring (per game)	106.1	15
Defensive Scoring (per game)	105.5	8
Scoring Margin (per game)	.6	13
Defensive FG%	.473	8
Offensive 2-point%	.485	14
Offensive 3-point%	.324	7
Offensive Free Throw %	.775	8
Offensive Rebs (Off REB/Opp Def REB)		14
Defensive Rebs (Def REB/Opp Off REB)		17
Offensive Assists (AST/FGMade)		5
Offensive Blocks (BLK/Opp FGAttempted)		19
Offensive Steals (STL/Game)		17
Turnover Margin (Off T.O. - Def T.O.)		6
Finesse (BLK + STL) / PF		16
Rebounding Record	35-46-1	19
Assists Record	46-30-6	6
Field Goal Pct. Record	40-41-1	12
Free Throw Pct. Record	51-31-0	3

Milwaukee Bucks .... Miscellaneous

ADMINISTRATIVE INFORMATION

Team Offices: 1001 North Fourth Street
Milwaukee, Wisconsin
53203

Telephone: (414) 272-6030
Head Coach: Del Harris
Home Arena: Bradley Center
Capacity: 18,578

1988-89 ROSTER*

J#	VETERANS	COLLEGE	POS	R#	D#	HT	WT	Milw	NBA
45	Randy Breuer	Minnesota	C	1	18	7-3	230	5	5
34	Terry Cummings	DePaul	F	1	2	6-10	220	4	6
24	Jay Humphries	Colorado	G	1	13	6-3	182	1	4
42	Larry Krystowiak	Montana	F	2	28	6-10	245	1	1
10	John Lucas	Maryland	G	1	1	6-3	185	2	12
44	Paul Mokeski	Kansas	C	2	42	7-1	255	6	9
4	Sidney Moncrief	Arkansas	G	1	5	6-5	183	9	9
22	Ricky Pierce	Rice	G-F	1	18	6-5	205	4	6
25	Paul Pressey	Tulsa	F-G	1	20	6-5	201	6	6
35	Jerry Reynolds	LSU	F	1	22	6-8	198	3	3
	Fred Roberts	BYU	F	2	27	6-10	220	0	5
43	Jack Sikma	Ill. Wesleyan	C	1	8	6-11	250	2	11

ROOKIES	COLLEGE	POS	R#	D#	HT
Jeff Grayer	Iowa State	G	1	13	6-5
Tito Horford	Miami	C	2	39	7-1
Mike Jones	Auburn	F	3	63	6-7

* For further definition of category and column headings, see pages 38 & 39.

Milwaukee Bucks .... Overview

"Everyone" expected the Milwaukee Bucks to slide last year. To begin with, they were the oldest team in the league, with an average age approaching 30; their record-setting coach, Don Nelson, had moved on to greener pastures; and the club didn't have a first round draft choice. If that weren't enough, they had to face a contract dispute with Sidney Moncrief, late resignings by John Lucas and Craig Hodges, and the holdout of their 4th guard Ricky Pierce. As it turns out "everyone" was right. The team did fall. As a matter of fact, their streak of 52 consecutive winning months finally fell in January (record 6-9) as did their streak of 7 consecutive years of 50+ wins. Interestingly, four of the five longest 50+ win streaks have been in the 1980's.

	Span	# Years
Boston	1959-68	10
Boston	1980-88	9
Los Angeles	1980-88	9
Milwaukee	**1981-87**	**7**
Philadelphia	1980-86	7

When the season began, it didn't look as though the Bucks were going to slip at all. They were 9-4 at one point and 15-9 at another, but age and a deteriorating bench eventually got the best of them. A visual look at the December/January decline can be seen on page 144. There was a brief resurgence after the All-Star break, but that didn't last either. The cold truth is that this team is going nowhere with its present personnel. Logically, one would expect continued decline.

Two rookies, Jeff Grayer #13, and Tito Horford #39 offer some future potential. Grayer, a swingman type player, may have been the steal of the draft. The former Iowa State star has very few weaknesses. He should be able to move right in at the #2 guard spot. As far as Horford is concerned, he's a project. Nevertheless, he has great potential. The last player I noted in that category was Chris Washburn. Well, that's the chance you take with the #39 pick. (As you may recall, Golden State took that chance with the #3 pick) No matter how well Grayer and Horford perform, this team will do well to keep pace with last year.

I wouldn't be saying that had Jack Sikma continued all season at the rate he began. Sikma was among the league's elite in every phase of the game during the first quarter of the season, but whether it was age or something else, he just could not maintain the same level. Breaking the season into fourths, Sikma's Production Rating was Q1 28.89, Q2 21.17, Q3 19.50, and Q4 18.09. Despite the decline, Sikma's worst performance category was steals, where he ranked #82. That may seem high, but only four other players ranked #82 or better in all six performance categories.

	Worst Ranking	Performance Category
Larry Bird	#66	Blocks
Frank Brickowski	#79	Blocks
Jack Sikma	**#82**	**Steals**
Jerome Kersey	#82	Assists
Clyde Drexler	#82	Rebounds

These are truly versatile players. The concern with Sikma is that he's entering his 12th year. If his decline continues, he'll be of less and less value. (Gee, that's profound!) Maybe his lowest performance category will be #100 or so. The problem is that if his *best* category is #60, he won't help the team all that much. Coincidentally, Sikma and Brickowski tied for the most disqualifications last season (11). Only one time in NBA history has the DQ leader been that low. In 1963-64 Zelmo Beatty and Gus Johnson also tied with 11.

Randy Breuer had a frustrating year as well. He was my early season leader as most improved player. Unfortunately, injury and a lack of confidence hurt his production significantly. He finally lost his starting spot as the season came to an end. Randy had been moved into the starting lineup in an effort to gain rebounding help. By starting Breuer, Sikma moved to power forward and Cummings to small forward.

Milwaukee Bucks .... Overview

Of course, with limited guard help at the beginning of the season, possible small forwards Paul Pressey and Jerry Reynolds had to be in the back court. In the first 25 games Breuer averaged 16 points per game and Milwaukee was 15-10. When he was injured and had to begin wearing a flack jacket, the Bucks went only 27-30 and Breuer averaged only 9 ppg.

At the tail end of the regular season Larry Krystowiak replaced Breuer in the lineup. Krysto started at PF while Sikma moved back to center. All of this was designed to help rebounding, but little worked. The club's rebounding record was 35-46-1 (#19) despite a starting lineup that averaged over 6'9". This is a classic case where inches don't make up for age.

I don't want to harp on gray hair and wrinkles, but it is so significant with this club that everything else pales in comparison. A perfect example is the breakdown by quarters. In quarter #1 at home the Bucks were 29-9-3 (.763), quarter #2 27-12-2 (.692), quarter #3 22-18-1 (.550) and quarter #4 15-24-2 (.385). Even on the *road*, quarters #2 and #4 were the worst, whereas those quarters after being rested (#1 and #3), they did OK in.

Ironically, Terry Cummings - a youngster to Moncrief, Sikma, and Lucas - has the most serious endurance problem. His heart ailment only allows him to play at most 35 minutes a game; this puts even more pressure on the bench. T.C. has always been a little streaky, but last season he was even more so. Six of his eight 30+ scoring games came back-to-back. Early in the season he scored 33 and 34 in consecutive games; at midseason he hit 30 and 30 back-to-back; later on he hit 36 and 36 two games in a row.

Rickey Pierce finally joined the team at midseason, but his presence didn't seem to affect winning or losing. Pierce had a good year shooting and scoring, but he is of no value at all in rebounding, assists, blocks or steals. Had he qualified (see page 272 for qualification requirements), he would have joined Mike Mitchell as the only player in the NBA who ranked #100 or below in those four performance categories. Besides scoring at 16.38 ppg, Pierce shot 51% from the field and 88% from the line. Only seven others reached the 50/85 plateau last year.

	FG%	FT%
Ricky Pierce	**.510**	**.877**
Larry Bird	.527	.916
Chris Mullin	.508	.885
Byron Scott	.527	.858
Adrian Dantley	.514	.860
Tree Rollins	.512	.815
Mark Price	.506	.877
Kiki Vandeweghe	.508	.878

Notes: John Lucas had the highest performance category rank on the team (#14 assists). Every other team had at least one PC rank higher. The closest was Sacramento (Reggie Theus #13 scoring)... When the team didn't run out of gas prematurely and scored 115+ points, they were 17-0... Only 12 players from the Central Division were playing with their same teams in 1983. Three Bucks (Moncrief, Pressey, Mokeski) along with three Hawks, three Pistons, a Pacer, a Cavalier, and a Bull make up the list... Larry Krystowiak ranked last in the, admittedly incomplete, defensive category [(Blocks + Steals) / Fouls].

Prediction - best case: 41-41

I'm sorry, but I cannot see how this team can break .500 in the rugged Central Division no matter what happens. Although the team came off a new attendance high and will be moving into a $53 million arena next season, I doubt that it will help the bottom line (wins and losses).

Prediction - worst case: 30-52

The club dropped 8 games from 1987 to 1988. There is no reason not to think it can't happen again. It could even be worse. They lost their last 8 road games and 13 of 14. With an aged cast and nagging injuries, anything is possible. Still, there is enough talent that 30 wins would have to be considered a nightmare season.

New Jersey Nets ....History

The Nets were one of the original franchises in the ABA. The first year (1968) the club was located in New Jersey. They were called the Americans at the time. In their second year, the Americans moved to New York and became the Nets. The team remained in New York for nine years, returning to New Jersey in 1977-78, their second NBA year.

The Nets won two championships in the ABA (1974 and 1976) and were runner's up once (1972). The period from 1974-76 not only produced two championship teams, but also represents the only 3 years the Nets won over 50 games. Interestingly, the Nets best regular season (1975 - 58 wins) was the only year of the three in which the club failed to win the title. That year the highly favored Nets were upset by the 32-52 St. Louis Spirits.

The same 3-year period produced three Most Valuable Player awards for Julius Erving. It was his only 3 years with the team. Dr. J was clearly the force who led the Nets to the playoffs each year. In fact, he led sixteen straight teams to playoffs - a professional sports record.

Four teams went from the ABA to the NBA in 1976-77. Though all four were successful in the ABA, the Nets just barely compiled a winning record (374-370). It's been more of the same in the NBA with respect to the other three former ABA teams. Whereas New Jersey has a losing record against Indiana (29-33), their record against the other two is much worse. The Nets have lost the head-to-head matchups to Denver and San Antonio by records of 8-22 and 7-27 respectively.

In 1982, the Nets won 44 games. What was impressive about that year is that the average attendance was 13,875 - up over 6,000 from the previous year. However, since then, attendance has slipped back to 11,611. This is especially disconcerting considering that NBA attendance has risen enormously throughout the league during the same period.

1982 was also Larry Brown's first year as coach. The 44 wins were +20 more than the year before. Only ten times in NBA or ABA history has a first year coach guided his team to 20 or more victories over the previous year's team. Amazingly, Larry Brown has done it three times - improving the Denver Nugget's record +28 wins, the Carolina Cougars +22 wins, and the Nets +20 wins - all in his first year.

> **Quiz: The franchise record for points in one game is 52. By whom?**

ALL TIME NETS' TEAM

Player	Span	Yrs	CRD
Buck Williams	1982-88	7	12,629
Billy Paultz	1971-75	5	8,640
Julius Erving	1974-76	3	8,082
Mike Gminski	1981-88	8	7,167
John Williamson	1974-79	6	6,348
Albert King	1982-87	6	5,270
Darwin Cook	1981-86	6	5,249
Otis Birdsong	1982-88	7	4,877
M.R. Richardson	1983-86	4	4,593
Jan van Breda Kolff	1977-83	7	3,897

ALL TIME NETS' COACH

Kevin Loughery — 7.5 Years
21-13 Playoffs — 4 Playoffs
297-318 Reg. Season — 2 Championships

HISTORICAL PROFILE

Category	Data
Nets' coach	Willis Reed
Years coached New Jersey	1
# of franchise years	21
# of coaches	11
# of winning seasons	8
# of playoff years	13
# of runner's up	1 (ABA)
# of championships	2 (ABA)
Regular season win %	45.0
Playoff win %	45.2

> **Answer:
> Ray Williams (1982)
> Mike Newlin (1979)**

New Jersey Nets . . . . 1987-88 Highlights

Nets 104-98 Spurs   Tue.   December 15, 1987

The New Jersey Nets began their game with San Antonio on an 11 game losing streak. The Spurs had won 4 straight. Beyond that, the Nets' top player - Buck Williams - had to miss the game due to an ankle injury. It was his first "no show" in 4 years. Considering that the Spurs' center, Frank Brickowski, had a career high 29 points and 15 rebounds, it is impressive that the Nets won the game. The win was the first for interim coach Bob MacKinnon.

Nets 106-95 Jazz   Mon.   December 21, 1987

New Jersey staged a furious 4th quarter rally to win going away over Utah. The Nets outscored the Jazz 35-10 in the final period to overcome an 18 point deficit. An even more soaring statistic was Pearl Washington's season high 24 points, accompanied by 7 assists, 7 rebounds, and 4 steals while leading one of the season's best comebacks - one which saw the Nets score the final 16 points of the game.

Nets 116-104 Pistons   Sat.   January 30, 1988

The victory was especially notable for New Jersey, since Detroit was coming off its biggest win of the year - a 17 point victory the night before over Boston (in front of the largest crowd in NBA history). The game featured a season high 26 points by Otis Birdsong, a season high 21 rebounds by Buck Williams and a season high foursome of 20+ point scorers.

Nets 108-103 Mavs   Mon.   February 1, 1988

The win broke a 26 game road losing streak dating back to 1987, while it was the second home loss in a row for Dallas, the first time that has happened in two years. The game also sported a stellar performance by John Bagley, who led the team in assists and rebounds, registering his first triple double. At 6'0" he is the shortest person to record a triple double.

Nets 109-105   76ers   Sun.   February 14, 1988

The game was significant in that it was the first match-up between the two clubs since their big trade. Charles Barkley was ejected in quarter 2 with 16 points and 12 rebounds while his counterpart, Buck Williams, had his league leading third 20/20 game (26 pts, 21 reb). The final exclamation point on the game came as the Nets overcame a 16 point 4th quarter deficit to win. Perhaps even more historic was the play-by-play broadcast by Leandra Reilly. Reilly became the first female ever to broadcast a live NBA game.

Nets 104-75 Clippers   Tue.   March 1, 1988

The winning margin (29) was 11 points more than any other Nets win this year. Ironically, the game was the first for new coach Willis Reed. The margin of victory was surprising since New Jersey had lost 6 in a row. Both clubs entered the game as the league's worst (12 wins and 40+ losses). The lopsided victory really came down to three things - holding the Clippers to 39% FG pct, outrebounding them 49-29, and registering a monstrous 21 steals. The Nets hold the NBA record of 28 steals in a game.

Nets 117-107 Celtics   Wed.   March 2, 1988

Amazingly, the loss was the first home loss for the Celtics in 67 regular season games against an Eastern Conference team. The win came despite an injury to Buck Williams who only played 4 minutes. Roy Hinson made up for the loss by scoring 21 points and a season high 15 rebounds while new coach Willis Reed remained undefeated (2-0).

New Jersey Nets .... Influence on Winning

TEAM RECORD BY

PLAYER	GAMES	SCR Leader HOME	SCR Leader ROAD	REB Leader HOME	REB Leader ROAD	AST Leader HOME	AST Leader ROAD
Buck Williams	70	3-8	1-14	10-15	0-22	---	---
Roy Hinson	48	4-4	0-4	1-3	1-3	---	---
Tim McCormick	47	1-0	1-7	1-4	1-4	---	0-3
John Bagley	82	2-0	1-0	---	1-0	11-15	3-23
Otis Birdsong	67	2-1	0-3	---	---	0-3	0-7
Dudley Bradley	65	0-1	---	---	---	0-4	0-2
Pearl Washington	68	1-2	0-3	---	---	3-4	0-9
Dennis Hopson	61	0-1	0-1	---	---	1-1	0-1
Orlando Woolridge	19	3-2	0-3	---	---	2-1	0-4
Dallas Comegys	75	0-1	0-2	1-0	0-2	0-1	---

TEAM RECORD BY SCORING *

PLAYER	PLAY	DNP	0-9	10-19	20-29	30-39	40+
Buck Williams	14-56	5-7	2-0	6-32	6-24	---	---
Roy Hinson	12-36	7-27	0-3	4-21	8-12	---	---
Tim McCormick	11-36	8-27	5-9	3-21	3-6	---	---
John Bagley	19-63	---	3-25	11-34	4-4	1-0	---
Otis Birdsong	15-52	4-11	5-22	8-27	2-3	---	---
Dudley Bradley	16-47	3-16	12-35	3-11	1-1	---	---
Pearl Washington	14-54	5-9	8-34	3-17	3-3	---	---
Dennis Hopson	12-49	7-14	7-26	4-18	1-5	---	---
Orlando Woolridge	6-13	13-50	2-3	1-6	3-4	---	---
Dallas Comegys	17-58	2-5	15-46	2-11	0-1	---	---

TEAM RECORD BY STARTING POSITION *

PLAYER	GAMES	STARTS	PG	OG	SF	PF	C
Buck Williams	70	70	---	---	---	14-56	---
Roy Hinson	48	47	---	---	7-27	2-2	2-7
Tim McCormick	47	38	---	---	---	---	9-29
John Bagley	82	74	17-57	---	---	---	---
Otis Birdsong	67	59	---	13-46	---	---	---
Dudley Bradley	63	15	---	0-2	5-8	---	---
Pearl Washington	68	10	2-6	1-1	---	---	---
Dennis Hopson	61	19	---	5-12	0-2	---	---
Orlando Woolridge	19	12	---	---	3-9	---	---
Dallas Comegys	75	17	---	---	4-12	---	1-0

* For further definition of each category and column heading see pages 38 & 39.

New Jersey Nets — 1987-88 Statistics

RAW NUMBERS *

PLAYER	2pt%	3pt%	FT%	MIN	PF	DQ	HI	TO	RB	AS	BL	ST
Buck Williams	.560	1.000	.668	2637	266	5	30	189	**834**	109	44	68
Roy Hinson	.488	0-2	.775	2592	**275**	**6**	27	169	517	99	**140**	69
Mike McCormick	.539	0-2	.674	2114	234	3	27	111	467	118	23	32
John Bagley	.471	.292	**.822**	**2774**	162	0	**31**	201	257	**479**	10	110
Otis Birdsong	.461	.360	.511	1882	143	2	26	129	167	222	11	54
Dudley Bradley	.452	.363	.763	1437	172	1	22	88	127	151	43	**114**
Pearl Washington	.470	.224	.698	1379	163	2	27	141	118	206	4	91
Dennis Hopson	.417	.267	.740	1365	145	0	25	119	143	118	25	57
Orlando Woolridge	.449	0-2	.708	622	73	2	29	48	91	71	20	13
Dallas Comegys	.431	0-1	.707	1122	175	3	21	116	218	65	70	36

OVERALL RANKINGS *

PLAYER	G	GS	PPG	PR	RANK	SC	SH	RB	AS	BL	ST
Buck Williams	70	70	**18.27**	**22.96**	14	34	41	8	141	77	111
Roy Hinson	77	57	15.30	16.60	61	55	83	68	147	15	103
Mike McCormick	70	55	12.01	14.29	85	89	43	57	115	99	152
John Bagley	**82**	**74**	11.96	13.43	94	90	122	133	32	145	54
Otis Birdsong	67	59	10.90	9.12	140	100	145	136	53	121	96
Dudley Bradley	65	15	6.51	8.28	150	154	106	137	62	36	3
Pearl Washington	68	10	9.31	8.12	154	123	142	140	41	148	11
Dennis Hopson	61	19	9.62	7.18	157	118	154	120	79	71	45
Orlando Woolridge	19	12	16.42	14.95	DNQ						
Dallas Comegys	75	17	5.57	5.87	DNQ						

POSITION RANKINGS *

PLAYER	POSITION	RANK	SC	SH	RB	AS	BL	ST
Buck Williams	Power Forward (PF)	5	6	8	4	27	25	21
Roy Hinson	Power Forward (PF)	13	10	20	33	30	6	19
Mike McCormick	Center (C)	16	15	9	25	9	26	21
John Bagley	Point Guard (PG)	21	18	23	18	28	22	26
Otis Birdsong	Off Guard (OG)	28	20	29	23	18	25	27
Dudley Bradley	Small Forward (SF)	31	33	23	33	6	6	1
Pearl Washington	Point Guard (PG)	31	23	30	22	32	25	5
Dennis Hopson	Off Guard (OG)	31	26	31	17	27	5	12
Orlando Woolridge	Small Forward (SF)	DNQ						
Dallas Comegys	Small Forward (SF)	DNQ						

*For further definition of each category and column heading see pages 38 & 39.

New Jersey Nets ....Team Info

WEEKLY POWER RATING

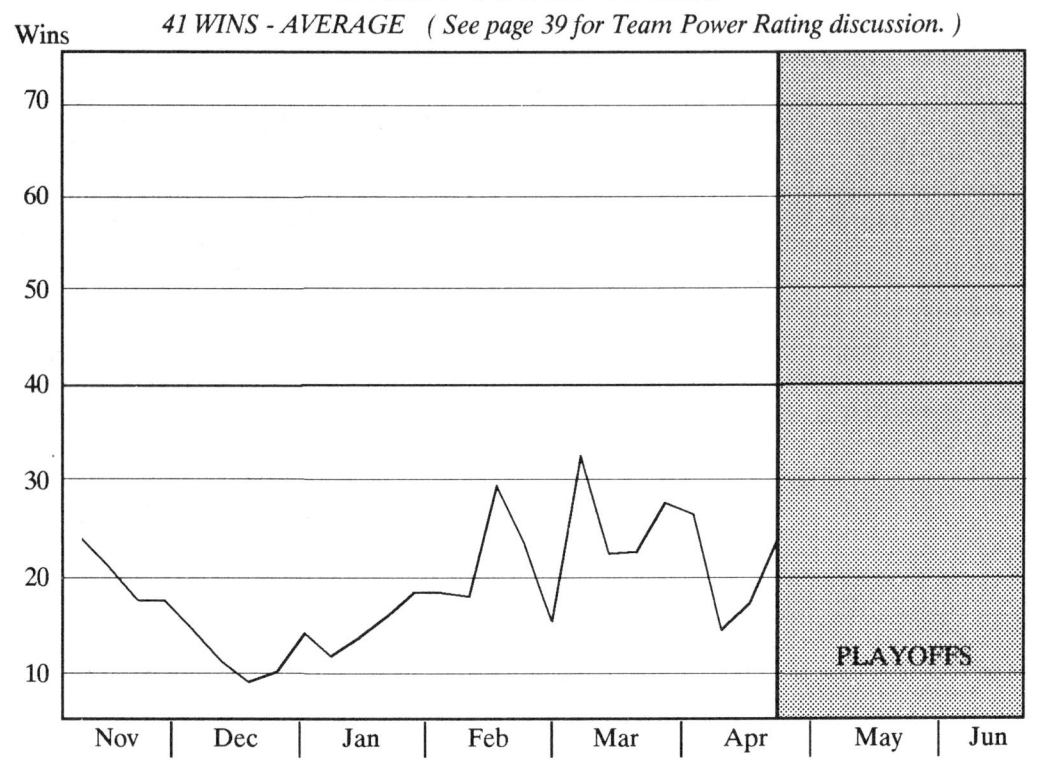

41 WINS - AVERAGE (See page 39 for Team Power Rating discussion.)

Miscellaneous Categories	Data	Rank	Performance Categories	Data	Rank
Attendance	476K	16	Offensive Scoring (per game)	100.4	22
Key-Man Games Missed	136	18	Defensive Scoring (per game)	108.5	15
Season Record	19-63	22	Scoring Margin (per game)	-8.1	21
- Home	16-25	21	Defensive FG%	.497	19
- Road	3-38	22	Offensive 2-point%	.480	19
Eastern Conference	11-47	22	Offensive 3-point%	.301	14
Western Conference	8-16	20	Offensive Free Throw %	.729	22
Overtime Record	0-4	21	Offensive Rebs (Off REB/Opp Def REB)		19
Record 5 Pts. or Less	8-15	21	Defensive Rebs (Def REB/Opp Off REB)		2
Record 10 Pts. or More	7-34	21	Offensive Assists (AST/FGMade)		21
Games Won By Bench	0	22	Offensive Blocks (BLK/Opp FGAttempted)		15
Games Won By Starters	6	9	Offensive Steals (STL/Game)		8
Winning Streak	3	19	Turnover Margin (Off T.O. - Def T.O.)		17
Losing Streak	15	23	Finesse (BLK + STL) / PF		15
Home Winning Streak	3	20	Rebounding Record	37-43-2	16
Road Winning Streak	1	21	Assists Record	33-46-3	18
Home Losing Streak	6	23	Field Goal Pct. Record	24-58-0	22
Road Losing Streak	18	21	Free Throw Pct. Record	23-59-0	23

New Jersey Nets .... Miscellaneous

ADMINISTRATIVE INFORMATION

Team Offices: Meadowlands Arena
East Rutherford, New Jersey
07073

Telephone: (201) 935-8888
Head Coach: Willis Reed
Home Arena: Meadowlands Arena
Capacity: 20,149

1988-89 ROSTER*

J#	VETERANS	COLLEGE	POS	R#	D#	HT	WT	N.J.	NBA
5	John Bagley	Boston College	G	1	12	6-0	192	1	6
	Walter Berry	St. Johns	F	1	14	6-8	215	0	2
24	Dudley Bradley	North Carolina	G	1	13	6-6	195	1	8
10	Otis Birdsong	Houston	G	1	2	6-4	195	7	11
50	Chris Engler	Wyoming	C	3	60	7-0	248	2	5
23	Roy Hinson	Rutgers	F-C	1	20	6-10	215	1	5
23	Dennis Hopson	Ohio State	G	1	3	6-5	200	1	1
40	Tim McCormick	Michigan	C	1	12	7-0	240	1	4
52	Buck Williams	Maryland	F	1	3	6-8	225	7	7

ROOKIES	COLLEGE	POS	R#	D#	HT
Chris Morris	Auburn	F	1	4	6-8
Charles Shackleford	N.C. State	F	2	32	6-10
Derek Hamilton	Southern Mississippi	F	3	52	6-6

* For further definition of category and column headings, see pages 38 & 39.

New Jersey Nets .... Overview

The New Jersey Nets are a team I wouldn't want to have any stock in right now. Just about every other team in the NBA can give me reason to be optimistic. But try as I may, I find it hard to see the light at the end of the (Lincoln) tunnel. I'm sure I'm not alone. I would be surprised if any of the major prognosticators were to pick the N.E.T.S. (Nothing Expected This Season) anything but last in the Atlantic Division. Come to think of it, if New Jersey finishes ahead of any team in the Eastern Conference (excluding Charlotte) it'll be a shock to everyone. Whenever I write about a team I try to evaluate the good and bad, find a balance, and go from there. Truthfully, with the Nets I can only find a few reasons to be anything other than discouraged. What's more, the biggest single positive (Buck Williams) isn't as big an advantage as most people think.

I've argued before that the power forward position is overrated. It's not that anyone is calling it the most valuable position, but the facts are that it ranks *last* as far as I'm concerned. I argue this proposition on page 232. I certainly don't mean to belittle Buck Williams or the power forward position. Nevertheless, the PF tends to benefit disproportionately as his team declines. Since he will usually get more than his share of rebounds, then it's true that the more his teammates miss, the better his potential stats. Since the Nets were 19th in 2-pt FG% and 22nd in FT%, there were a lot of opportunities for rebounds.

Interestingly, New Jersey was 5-7 when Buck didn't play - not too bad. When he was in there cleaning the glass, the club was 14-56. That's got to be coincidence, of course. Clearly, the Nets are better with him than without him. However, in the twelve games he missed, his replacement - either Ben Coleman or Roy Hinson - averaged over 17 points and nearly 10 boards. Both totals were only slightly below those accumulated by Williams. Even if the PF position is the weakest, Buck still ranked #5. Considering the fact that the highest rated Net at any of the other four positions is Tim McCormick at center (#16), having Buck Williams is a breath of fresh air. Despite this, New Jersey would be wise to trade him for as much point guard, small forward, and center as they can get.

Dave Wohl survived longer than I thought he would. He was fortunate to make it to this season, but when New Jersey struggled to a 2-13 record, he was history. Bob MacKinnon became interim manager, going 10-29, before Willis Reed took over. The team certainly had its share of moments with Reed at the helm, winning the first three, but ultimately it could do little better than earlier in the season (7-21). Even though Reed didn't change the nature of the team all that much, he at least added excitement. A look at the club's power rating chart on page 152 shows the radical changes (up and down) the team went through once Reed took over. Hopefully, Willis will be successful. He'll need all the help he can get. It's commonly believed that he saw the writing on the wall in Sacramento, that Russell would be canned. Knowing he had little future there, he chose the head job for the Nets. Before next season is over, he may wish he was back on the west coast. I doubt it, however, since the only non-expansion teams likely to challenge New Jersey for fewest wins next year are Sacramento and possibly Golden State.

At guard, the club has serious if not major problems. John Bagley leads the way at point, but is truly not very good. His best rank at any of the six performance categories is 18th at his position (scoring and rebounding). On the few occasions where he had outstanding games (20+ points) the team was 5-4. The rest of the time? Forget it! Pearl Washington could have been the point guard for this team if not for the fact that he's as bad as it gets. Other than his ability to swipe the ball on occasion, he's not worth having. It's clear after two years that those tools aren't

New Jersey Nets .... Overview

enough. There was a brief four-game stretch this year where he looked like an NBA player. Playing primarily at off-guard he averaged 23 ppg starting the last game. When he was injured early in the fifth game, his streak ended. We may never know what would have happened were it not for the injury.

At the 2 guard spot, the club is just as desperate. No, I'd say more desperate. For the second year in a row the Nets used their top pick on a guard - Dennis Hopson. Considered a "can't miss" player by nearly every scout, he missed! That's putting it mildly. He rarely contributed to the team's success and virtually never looked like the player he was supposed to be. Most people felt that Hopson would be the most likely Rookie-of-the-Year as he would get plenty of playing time. As it turns out he was way down the list. The primary starter at off-guard was veteran Otis Birdsong. He was a little more valuable than Hopson, but not much. Both players averaged only 10 ppg and were terribly inconsistent. Birdsong had to miss from 1 to 3 games on an incredible nine different occassions because of nagging problems.

With these needs, wouldn't you think the team would go for guard help? Guess what? They didn't. Of course I don't blame them. They've been burned recently on guards. What they got was 6'8" Chris Morris of Auburn. Given the type of forwards coming out of that school recently (Barkley, Person), it's probably a good risk. Morris will bring that same type of intensity and dominance. The second pick was Charles Shackleford, a 6'11" forward/center from N.C. State. Let's see, a 6'11" center, underclassman from N.C. State. Hum! Does that remind you of anyone? Since 1981, this team has gotten absolutely nothing of value in the draft. No wonder they've dropped from 49 wins in 1983 to 45 to 42 to 39 to 24 to 19. And yes, it can go lower.

The most interesting aspect of last season was the trade which sent Mike Gminski and Ben Coleman to Philadelphia for Mike McCormick and Roy Hinson. G-man is the best of the group, but it's probably an equal trade. Gminski and Coleman had a combined Production Rating of 16.10 before the swap while McCormick and Hinson managed a rating of 12.10. After the two exchanged teams, Gminski and Coleman had a Production Rating of 15.27 while McCormick and Hinson increased to 17.36. New Jersey gave up more initially, but gained more after the fact.

A couple players would have been very valuable to the Nets. As fate would have it, considering all the key-man games missed in recent years, both Orlando Woolridge and Michael Ray Richardson - easily the two most gifted players the Nets have had - have drug problems. Though both are apparantly over their addictions, neither stayed with the Nets.

Dallas Comegys has left town too, but at least New Jersey got something in return. That "something" is Walter Berry, formerly of the Spurs. Berry averaged 17.4ppg and ranked 4th in blocks, 6th in shooting, and 7th in rebounding at his position. Not bad.

Notes: The Nets were 15-26-3 in the 3rd quarter during the first portion of the season. During the last half they came out of the locker room to win Q3 at a rate of 24-12-2... Every lottery team ended the season on a losing note except New Jersey. The Nets won their final game. Ironically, the victory broke the league's longest losing streak (15)... When the club's opponents scored 114+ points the Nets were horrendous, going 0-27.

Prediction - best case: 20-62

In truth, it's just too much to ask for this team to be competitive. Maybe a few more drafts, some maturity, sprinkle in a miracle or two and...who knows?

Prediction - worst case: 12-70

With the injury profile the Nets seem to have and the unknown situation with Woolridge, this team is pretty poor. The "16W" of Exit 16W may stand for 16 wins and the "Exit" may stand for Willis Reed long before 82 games have been played.

New York Knicks . . . . History

The New York Knicks, along with the Celtics and Warriors, began in 1946-47 in the original BAA. The Knicks have reached the finals six times over the years. Interestingly, the six fit into two groups. The first three were from 1951-53, while the last three were 20 years later from 1970-73.

The club won two championships of the six. Both were in the Knick's "Golden Era" (1970 and 1973). From 1972-1974, five famous NBA stars played together for New York. All five have had their numbers retired by the club (the only five). The quintet was Walt Frazier (10), Earl Monroe (15), Willis Reed (19), Dave DeBusschere (22), and Bill Bradley (24). Hall of Famer Jerry Lucas also played with the group during these three years. Understandably, the span from 1972-74 represents the three seasons with the largest attendance.

The Knicks have established four distinct periods during their franchise history. The club went to the playoffs its first 9 years. During the next 11 years, however, the team went to the playoffs only once. They then had another streak of nine straight appearances. Finally, the last 13 years have produced only five playoff teams. The winning percentages and number of coaches for each period are inversely related - period one (57%, 2 coaches), period 2 (39%, 7 coaches), period 3 (60%, 2 coaches), period 4 (44%, 6 coaches).

Speaking of coaches, the Knicks have had two of the greatest. Only Red Auerbach has more total years with the same franchise (16-Boston) without a single losing season, than does Joe Lapchick. Lapchick coached 8 straight winning years with New York. Additionally, only Red Auerbach has more regular season wins with the same franchise (795 Boston) than Red Holzman. Holzman won 613 games with New York.

Odds & Ends: The Knicks (1965) are one of only two clubs (Cleveland 1987) to place three players on the all-rookie team... Bernard King holds the team record for most points scored in a game. He scored 60 points on Christmas Day in 1984... New York has had a total of 18,129,619 fans since 1946, rivaling the population of the Big Apple... The Knicks scored the last 19 points vs Milwaukee in 1972. Though they trailed by 18 points with 5 minutes left, they ended up winning 88-86... In the last 20 years, the Knicks are 11-9 in home openers *and* 11-9 in Christmas day games.

> **Quiz:** The New York Knicks played in the first-ever BAA game on Nov. 1, 1946. Name their opponent and did they win?

ALL TIME KNICKS' TEAM

Player	Span	Yrs	CRD
Walt Frazier	1968-77	10	17,100
Willis Reed	1965-74	10	15,607
Harry Gallatin	1949-57	9	11,701
Richie Guerin	1957-63	8	10,350
Bill Cartwright	1980-88	8	10,344
Dave DeBusschere	1969-74	6	8,733
Willie Naulls	1957-63	7	8,597
Earl Monroe	1972-80	9	8,335
Carl Braun	1948-60	12	8,297
Bill Bradley	1968-77	10	8,264

ALL TIME KNICKS' COACH

Red Holzman
54-43 Playoffs
613-484 Reg. Season
13.5 Years
9 Playoffs
2 Championships

HISTORICAL PROFILE

Category	Data
Knicks' coach	Rick Pitino
Years coached New York	1
# of franchise years	42
# of coaches	13
# of winning seasons	21
# of playoff years	24
# of runner's up	4
# of championships	2
Regular season win %	48.7
Playoff win %	50.3

> **Answer:**
> The Toronto Huskies. Yes, 68-66

New York Knicks . . . . 1987-88 Highlights

Knicks 116-92 Bullets Tue. December 8, 1987

The winning margin (24) was twice as substantial as New York's previous largest to this point in the season. The game was ironic in that New York broke a four game losing streak, while Washington's losing streak was extended to four. Also, by winning, the Knicks moved from 1/2 game behind to 1/2 game ahead of the Bullets. Despite the team battle, it was Pat Ewing and Bernard King who commanded the crowd's attention. Ewing had a season high (so far) 29 points against the team from his old college stomping ground, while Bernard King returned to New York as an opponent for the first time since becoming a Knick in 1982. His 19 points and the crowd's standing ovation helped take some of the sting out of the loss.

Knicks 123-110 Trail Blazers Tue. December 29, 1987

The Knicks used a season high 25 points by Kenny Walker to upset the Portland Trailblazers. The 13 point winning margin broke a 9 game losing streak to the Blazers and was the largest winning margin by New York over Portland since 1978. The Knicks, who trailed by 8 early, used a 12-0 run at the end to seal the victory. Walker's heroics overcame a second best career 29 points by his small forward counterpart Jerome Kersey.

Knicks 89-87 Bucks Tue. February 23, 1988

Coming into the game, the Bucks had won 4 straight - their season high. Additionally, Terry Cummings had had back-to-back 36 point performances - his season highs. Although Milwaukee lead after the first two quarters, the Knicks battled back to eventually win on Gerald Wilkins' 3-point play. Kenny Walker scored his most points as a starter (21). New York won their 10th straight at home; that's significant because it represented the longest home court winning streak since the world champion Knicks in 1973.

Knicks 106-96 Clippers Thur. February 25, 1988

By winning, the Knicks ended an 18 game road losing streak. The 10 point margin was the largest on the road in exactly 100 games. The loss was the 7th in a row for the Clippers, who started rookie Kenny Norman for only the second time and Greg Kite for the first.

Knicks 125-119 Warriors Fri. February 26, 1988

After losing 18 straight road games, the Knicks had now won 2 straight. The normally poor FT shooting Knicks really won the game at the stripe, hitting 31 of 32. That's ironic, considering the Warriors were the best in the NBA in that area. Gerald Wilkins had 34 points. He averaged nearly 28 ppg in his previous 5 games. Johnny Newman tied his career high with 26 points. It took both efforts to overcome the Warriors' Winston Garland. Garland had the first triple double of his career.

Knicks 118-98 Bullets Sun. April 10, 1988

The Knicks won two critical games on the road the previous few days - upsetting both Washington and Philadelphia. Both wins were by large margins, and both second quarters were the reason why (45-26) and (36-16) - biggest in both cases since the early 1970's.

Knicks 88-86 Pacers Sat. April 23, 1988

New York won their biggest game of the year over Indiana. The game was as critical as it gets. A Knicks' loss meant the lottery; a win meant the playoffs. The fact that they defeated Indiana on the road, immediately after the Pacers had defeated Detroit and Atlanta, made it all the sweeter. The final twist was that Indiana had exactly the same things at stake.

New York Knicks .... Influence on Winning

TEAM RECORD BY ... SCR Leader ... REB Leader ... AST Leader

PLAYER	GAMES	HOME	ROAD	HOME	ROAD	HOME	ROAD
Patrick Ewing	82	12-6	1-13	14-5	5-13	---	---
Mark Jackson	82	5-3	1-2	2-0	0-3	30-12	9-29
Gerald Wilkins	81	8-2	5-9	---	---	1-0	0-2
Bill Cartwright	82	0-1	0-3	1-0	1-7	---	---
Sidney Green	82	---	0-1	14-4	3-11	---	---
Kenny Walker	82	4-0	0-3	2-3	0-2	---	---
Johnny Newman	77	2-0	1-4	---	---	---	---
Trent Tucker	71	---	0-1	---	---	---	1-1
Pat Cummings	62	---	---	1-0	0-1	---	---
Billy Donavan	44	---	---	---	---	---	---

TEAM RECORD BY SCORING *

PLAYER	PLAY	DNP	0-9	10-19	20-29	30-39	40+
Patrick Ewing	38-44	---	0-1	20-21	15-20	2-1	1-1
Mark Jackson	38-44	---	7-14	25-26	5-4	1-0	---
Gerald Wilkins	38-43	0-1	0-8	22-23	14-12	2-0	---
Bill Cartwright	38-44	---	16-16	18-26	4-2	---	---
Sidney Green	38-44	---	23-34	14-10	1-0	---	---
Kenny Walker	38-44	---	17-21	17-22	4-1	---	---
Johnny Newman	38-39	0-5	18-24	15-11	5-4	---	---
Trent Tucker	33-38	5-6	21-28	12-10	---	---	---
Pat Cummings	29-33	9-11	26-29	3-4	---	---	---
Billy Donavan	21-23	17-21	20-22	1-1	---	---	---

TEAM RECORD BY STARTING POSITION *

PLAYER	GAMES	STARTS	PG	OG	SF	PF	C
Patrick Ewing	82	82	---	---	---	---	38-44
Mark Jackson	82	80	38-42	---	---	---	---
Gerald Wilkins	81	78	---	36-42	---	---	---
Bill Cartwright	82	4	---	---	---	2-2	---
Sidney Green	82	65	---	---	---	31-34	---
Kenny Walker	82	61	---	---	28-29	2-2	---
Johnny Newman	77	25	---	---	10-15	---	---
Trent Tucker	71	4	---	2-2	---	---	---
Pat Cummings	62	9	---	---	---	3-6	---
Billy Donavan	44	0	---	---	---	---	---

* For further definition of each category and column heading see pages 38 & 39.

TEAM BY TEAM ANALYSIS 159

New York Knicks . . . . 1987-88 Statistics

RAW NUMBERS *

PLAYER	2pt%	3pt%	FT%	MIN	PF	DQ	HI	TO	RB	AS	BL	ST
Patrick Ewing	**.556**	0-3	.716	2546	**332**	5	**42**	287	**676**	125	**245**	104
Mark Jackson	.458	.254	.774	**3249**	244	2	33	258	396	**868**	6	**205**
Gerald Wilkins	.462	.302	.786	2703	183	1	39	212	270	326	22	90
Bill Cartwright	.544	0-0	.798	1676	234	4	23	135	384	85	43	43
Sidney Green	.443	0-2	.663	2049	318	9	20	148	142	93	32	65
Kenny Walker	.473	0-1	.775	2139	290	5	25	83	389	86	59	63
Johnny Newman	.463	.280	**.841**	1589	204	5	29	103	159	62	11	72
Trent Tucker	.431	**.413**	.718	1248	158	3	18	47	119	117	6	53
Pat Cummings	.458	0-1	.738	946	143	0	17	65	235	37	10	20
Billy Donavan	.431	0-7	.810	364	33	0	14	42	25	87	1	16

OVERALL RANKINGS *

PLAYER	G	GS	PPG	PR	RANK	SC	SH	RB	AS	BL	ST
Pat Ewing	**82**	**82**	20.16	22.61	17	21	24	22	122	3	51
Mark Jackson	**82**	80	13.59	**20.68**	26	72	141	106	6	152	12
Gerald Wilkins	81	78	17.43	13.86	88	38	133	126	50	112	70
Bill Cartwright	**82**	4	11.15	12.28	106	98	19	51	118	48	112
Sidney Green	**82**	65	7.83	11.40	116	140	152	9	133	84	83
Kenny Walker	**82**	61	10.07	11.17	118	107	113	77	142	41	91
Johnny Newman	77	25	10.04	7.60	156	114	100	125	146	118	34
Trent Tucker	71	4	7.13	6.65	DNQ						
Pat Cummings	62	9	5.47	6.26	DNQ						
Billy Donavan	44	0	2.39	2.80	DNQ						

POSITION RANKINGS *

PLAYER	POSITION	RANK	SC	SH	RB	AS	BL	ST
Patrick Ewing	Center (C)	2	3	5	11	12	3	2
Mark Jackson	Point Guard (PG)	4	14	29	7	6	27	6
Gerald Wilkins	Off Guard (OG)	14	13	27	21	16	19	19
Bill Cartwright	Center (C)	23	19	4	22	10	21	6
Sidney Green	Power Forward (PF)	26	29	33	5	21	29	13
Kenny Walker	Small Forward (SF)	23	24	25	16	32	8	18
Johnny Newman	Small Forward (SF)	33	25	22	32	33	28	5
Trent Tucker	Off Guard (OG)	DNQ						
Pat Cummings	Power Forward (PF)	DNQ						
Billy Donavan	Point Guard (PG)	DNQ						

*For further definition of each category and column heading see pages 38 & 39.

New York Knicks ....Team Info

WEEKLY POWER RATING
41 WINS - AVERAGE (See page 39 for Team Power Rating discussion.)

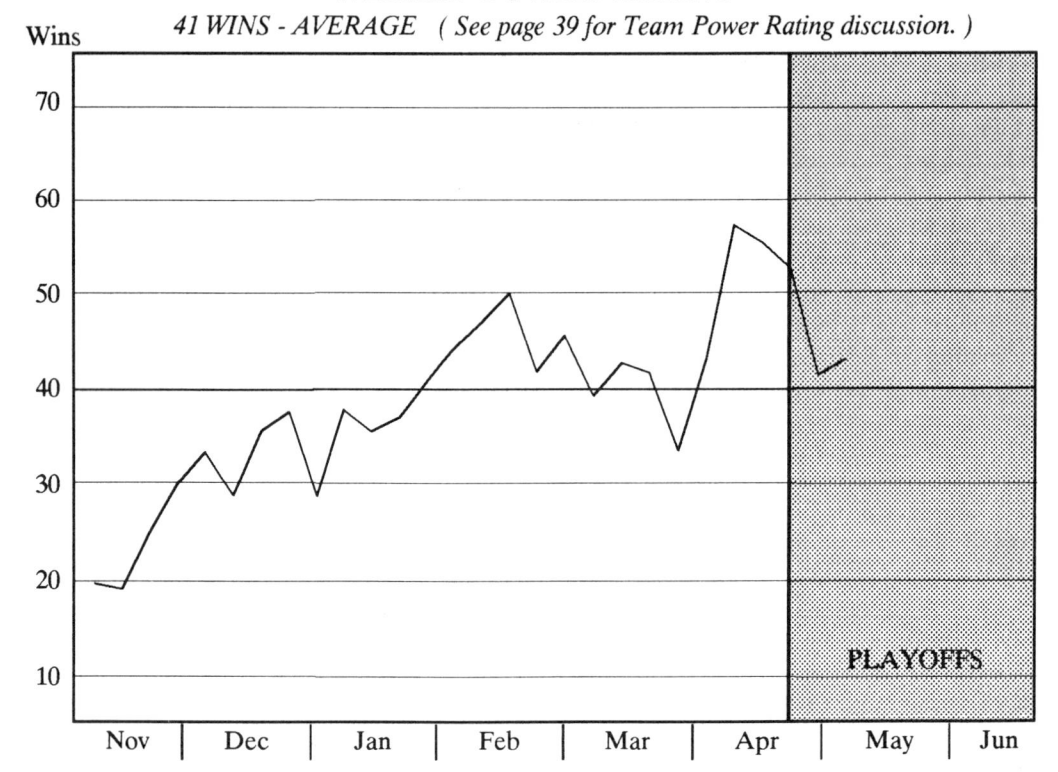

Miscellaneous Categories	Data	Rank	Performance Categories	Data	Rank
Attendance	587K	7	Offensive Scoring (per game)	105.5	17
Key-Man Games Missed	37	6	Defensive Scoring (per game)	106.0	9
Season Record	38-44	14	Scoring Margin (per game)	-.5	14
- Home	29-12	14	Defensive FG%	.477	12
- Road	9-32	16	Offensive 2-point%	.478	20
Eastern Conference	27-31	13	Offensive 3-point%	.316	12
Western Conference	11-13	16	Offensive Free Throw %	.759	15
Overtime Record	2-2	10	Offensive Rebs (Off REB/Opp Def REB)		3
Record 5 Pts. or Less	14-15	11	Defensive Rebs (Def REB/Opp Off REB)		19
Record 10 Pts. or More	16-16	14	Offensive Assists (AST/FGMade)		14
Games Won By Bench	5	9	Offensive Blocks (BLK/Opp FGAttempted)		8
Games Won By Starters	0	22	Offensive Steals (STL/Game)		2
Winning Streak	3	19	Turnover Margin (Off T.O. - Def T.O.)		3
Losing Streak	5	10	Finesse (BLK + STL) / PF		17
Home Winning Streak	13	4	Rebounding Record	40-37-5	9
Road Winning Streak	2	14	Assists Record	35-42-5	15
Home Losing Streak	2	2	Field Goal Pct. Record	37-44-1	16
Road Losing Streak	18	21	Free Throw Pct. Record	37-44-1	17

New York Knicks .... Miscellaneous

ADMINISTRATIVE INFORMATION

Team Offices: Madison Square Garden
Four Pennsylvania Plaza
New York, New York
10001
Telephone: (212) 563-8000
Head Coach: Rick Pitino
Home Arena: Madison Square Garden
Capacity: 19,591

1988-89 ROSTER*

J#	VETERANS	COLLEGE	POS	R#	D#	HT	WT	N.Y.	NBA
42	Pat Cummings	Cincinnati	F-C	3	59	6-10	220	4	9
33	Patrick Ewing	Georgetown	C	1	1	7-0	240	3	3
2	Sidney Green	UNLV	F	1	5	6-9	220	1	4
18	Mark Jackson	St. Johns	G	1	18	6-3	205	1	1
22	Johnny Newman	Richmond	G	2	29	6-7	190	1	2
	Charles Oakley	Virginia Union	F	1	9	6-9	245	0	3
55	Louis Orr	Syracuse	F	2	29	6-9	200	6	8
6	Trent Tucker	Minnesota	G	1	6	6-5	190	6	6
34	Kenny Walker	Kentucky	F	1	5	6-8	210	2	2
21	Gerald Wilkins	Tennessee-Chatt.	F	2	47	6-6	195	3	3

ROOKIES	COLLEGE	POS	R#	D#	HT
Rod Strickland	DePaul	G	1	19	6-3
Greg Butler	Stanford	F-C	2	37	6-11
Phil Stinnie	Va. Commonwealth	F	3	69	6-8

*For further definition of category and column headings, see pages 38 & 39.

New York Knicks . . . . Overview

"Pat Ewing is a $30 million bad movie." Who could make such a statement? Who could have been so wrong? Oh, I remember. It was former coach, Hubie Brown. (You thought I'd let him off the hook, didn't you?) In fairness, Brown wasn't that wrong at the time he said it, but year-by-year his statements have seemed more and more far-fetched.

Ewing had a Production Rating of 20.56 in his rookie year as a big leaguer, 21.90 as a sophomore, and 22.61 as a junior. His rank at center has gone from #7 to #5 to #2. Although it's unlikely that he will pass Akeem Olajuwon anytime soon, he could remain at #2 and increase his production for several years to come. OK, it's true that he's not the second coming of Bill Russell, but #2 at your position ain't bad! I thought it would be interesting to look at the #1 draft picks the last 10 years and compare their Production Rating (PR) and position rank (PS) in their 3rd year.

3rd yr	#1 pick	PR	PS
1981	Mychal Thompson	20.35	9
1982	Magic Johnson	29.65	1
1983	Joe B. Carroll	23.62	6
1984	Mark Aguirre	25.04	4
1985	James Worthy	19.59	12
1986	Ralph Sampson	22.85	4
1987	Akeem Olajuwon	28.99	1
1988	**Pat Ewing**	**22.61**	**2**

Notably, with the exception of Magic Johnson and Akeem Olajuwon, every one of these players has been criticized - in some cases severely. What's ironic is that Magic lost the Rookie-of-the-Year award and has lived in the shadow of Larry Bird. Similarly, Akeem lost the Rookie-of-the-Year award and has lived in the shadow of Michael Jordan. My point is, Pat Ewing is perfectly respectable and will only get better. Get off his back!

Who is this Ewing character? His hands are too small to catch the ball; he can't rebound - supposedly his strong suit out of college (he ranks #22 in the NBA); and he led the league in fouls. I just thought I'd temper my partisanship with a few hard, cold realities. Nevertheless, I like him; I'd take him; and so would you.

Ewing isn't the only good thing going for the Knicks. Rookie Mark Jackson may be the best thing to hit the Big Apple since the government bailout a decade ago. "Action" Jackson was a simply brilliant rookie. Very rarely does a first year player show the maturity and poise of this one. Jackson, though drafted #18, won the Rookie-of-the-Year award by a landslide (77 of 80 votes). In doing so, he became the lowest ranked rookie to win the award since Woody Sauldsberry, an 8th rounder, in 1957.

With so little expected out of him, it's all the more remarkable what he accomplished. Jackson set an NBA record for rookies in assists, recording 868 and thereby dwarfing the previous record by Oscar Robertson (690). He also passed the Knicks team record of 832 set by Michael Ray Richardson in 1980. Beyond those accomplishments he managed 205 steals - the 3rd best by a rookie. Only Dudley Bradley (1980 - 211) and Ron Harper (1987 - 209) ever recorded more in their first season. Not surprisingly, Jackson led the All-Rookie team with 22 votes. Joining him were Armon Gilliam (16), Kenny Smith (16), Greg Anderson (15) and Derrick McKey (11).

I wouldn't be objective if I let it go at that, however. Truthfully, Jackson has a few weaknesses. As a rookie they're probably expected, but he had an abnormally high number of assists at home (12.02 per game) vs on the road (9.20 per game). Some suggested the stat man was overly generous at Madison Square Garden. Without more evidence, I doubt it. The NBA has strict guidelines and I can't imagine poor statkeeping going unchecked. Jackson's biggest weakness is, of course, his shooting. At 43.2%, it's nothing to write home about. In fact, common sense says that any player who shoots 43.2% would be more valuable shooting less often. In Mark's case, though, it is less true than nor-

TEAM BY TEAM ANALYSIS 163

New York Knicks .... Overview

mal for two reasons: The first is offensive rebounding. The Knicks ranked 15th in total rebounding, (This is great considering that in the previous three years New York registered the lowest rebounding totals in NBA history.) and an incredible 3rd in offensive rebounding. When you clean the offensive boards that well, why not spray the Windex wherever you want? The second reason is that the Knicks had no one else to turn to from out front. Gerald Wilkins shot only 44.6%, Johnny Newman 43.5%, Trent Tucker 42.4%, and Billy Donavan 40.4%. Annie, get your gun. We need ya!

The Knicks should really be tough rebounding next year, as the backboard eater himself, Charles Oakley, joins the team. The off-season trade with the Bulls is one that should benefit both teams. New York sent Bill Cartwright to Chicago. Cartwright was miscast at power forward, too expensive as a back-up center, and not very happy. He'll have a great opportunity at Chicago, though he'll have to hit the boards harder. Oakley will give New York an imposing twosome with Ewing. They're still razor thin up front, but then maybe those two can play 48 minutes per game.

The Knicks also picked up the 19th pick in the draft, Rod Strickland. Although he's a point guard (some said the best in the draft), New York desperately needs help on the perimeter. At the minimum, Jackson and Wilkins can use a backup. The small forward position is bad news! Kenny Walker is no better than a 7th or 8th player off the bench - nothing more. The same appears to be true of Johnny Newman. Newman had two distinctions last season. At one point he was 35/90 from the field before hitting an unbelievable 19 straight! The second oddity is that Newman led a group of four players in having more offensive rebounds than defensive rebounds. Newman was +10, Otis Smith +5, Chris Dudley +4, and Terry Teagle +1.

New York was anemic on the road last season. At one point early on they lost a club record 18 straight and 23 of 24. Things changed, however, when they went 8-9 to close out the season. The most important road victory was the final one - an 88-86 triumph over Indiana to clinch a playoff spot.

The Knicks struggled at home early in the season as well. Yet, their overall record of 4-12 at one point was misleading and actually showed the team was ready to excel. At the time they had won 33 quarters, lost 30, and tied 1. Furthermore, more than half their losses were by margins of 1, 4, 2, 1, 5, 3, and 6. It proved to be just a matter of time, as the Knicks won 13 consecutive home games - the most by the club since they'd won the 1973 world championship.

Rick Pitino was almost as outstanding a rookie coach as his point guard was a player. It took a while for the team to adjust to his unusual full court defenses, but once they did, they generally tore up their opponents. The Knicks ranked #2 in steals and #3 in turnover ratio. Because of the constant substitutions, New York rarely wore down late in the game. Even so, the bench is weak and needs help if this team is going to advance.

Notes: In the second half of the season the Knicks werer 1-16-3 in quarter #1, but 13-4-3 in quarter #4... In February, the club was 8-4, the first winning month in four years... When Rick Pitino begins his second year on November 4, he'll have the longest tenure of any coach in his 6-team division.

Prediction - best case: 48-34

No matter what happens, the Knicks have too many serious holes to do much better than 48 wins. Outside shooting, small forward, and depth are tough to overcome. They have strengths to be sure, but Pitino can only hope to climb one more step up the ladder in 1988-89.

Prediction - worst case: 41-41

New York is too talented to do worse. Unless Ewing or Jackson combine to miss over half the season, there is no way they won't at least break even. Unfortunately, the record crowds of 1988 won't be happy with 41 wins in 1989.

Philadelphia 76ers ....History

The Philadelphia 76ers were originally located in Syracuse, NY. At the time they were called the Nationals. The club began in 1946-47 in the National Basketball League (NBL). Three years later, the NBL merged with the rival Basketball Association of America (BAA) to form the NBA. The team stayed in Syracuse for 17 years before coming to the city of brotherly love. The Sixers celebrated their silver anniversary in Philly last year.

Philadelphia's first year in the NBA was a good one. In 1950 they registered the league's best record (51-13). Their .797 winning percentage was the highest from the time the league merged until 1967. Despite the great regular season, the Nationals lost in the first round of the playoffs.

Interestingly, the franchise has had eight finals participants. Three times they gained the championship round in the early 50's. Their losses in 1950 and 1954 set the stage for the team's first championship in 1955. Five other times the club made it to the final dance. Four of those were in the Dr. J era. The Sixers were runners-up in 1977, 1980 and 1982 before winning it all in 1983.

That team went 12-1 in the playoffs - the best winning percentage ever by an NBA team. The only other appearance in the finals was between the 1955 and 1977 teams. The 1967 Philadelphia team won that championship and was later voted the greatest team ever to play the game.

The 76ers franchise holds the record for 25 consecutive playoff appearances. The next longest streak is held by Boston (19). After the Sixers completed their 25 year stretch, they then missed four straight. The second year of the four (1973) produced only 9 wins and 73 losses - the worst single season in NBA history. Included in the debacle was a 20 game losing streak - another record. Immediately after the 4 year dry spell, Philadelphia went back to being a routine post-season participant. For 12 consecutive years, Philadelphia made the playoffs - until last year.

Notes: The 76ers have been a very successful franchise. Their having reached the playoffs 37 of 42 years represents an 88% ratio which only one other club (L.A. Lakers) can match... Former coach, Billy Cunningham, has a winning percentage of 70% - third highest ever to K.C. Jones and Pat Riley... Since the NBA was formed, the Sixers, Celtics, & Lakers have had the most players (7) claim NBA first team honors.

> Quiz: Dr. J is the only person to win the MVP in both the NBA and ABA. How many times did he do it?

ALL TIME SIXERS' TEAM

Player	Span	Yrs	CRD
Dolph Schayes	1949-64	16	22,991
Hal Greer	1959-73	15	20,345
Julius Erving	1977-87	11	19,237
John Kerr	1955-65	11	15,603
Billy Cunningham	1966-76	9	15,085
Maurice Cheeks	1979-88	10	13,980
Wilt Chamberlain	1965-68	4	12,220
Chet Walker	1963-69	7	9,704
Larry Costello	1958-68	10	9,216
Bobby Jones	1979-86	8	8,779

ALL TIME SIXERS' COACH

Billy Cunningham   8 Years
54-43 Playoffs   8 Playoffs
454-196 Reg. Season 1 Championship

HISTORICAL PROFILE

Category	Data
Sixers' coach	Jim Lynam
Years coached Philadelphia	1
# of franchise years	42
# of coaches	12
# of winning seasons	29
# of playoff years	37
# of runner's up	5
# of championships	3
Regular season win%	57.4
Playoffs win %	53.4

> **Answer:**
> NBA (1981), ABA (1974, 75, 76)

Philadelphia 76ers ....1987-88 Highlights

76ers 106-100 Jazz Mon. November 30, 1987

The Jazz, after winning seven straight, were the last team in the NBA to lose at home. John Stockton had his second straight 16-assist game for his season high. His 9 third quarter assists tied a Jazz record. Despite his brilliant efforts, Philadelphia won by Charles Barkley's scoring 43 points and grabbing 14 rebounds.

76ers 94-86 Trail Blazers Wed. December 9, 1987

The Philadelphia 76ers ended an 11 game stretch which was as bizarre as any. The win came as a result of Charles Barkley's 38 points and 24 rebounds. The game was also significant in that Philadelphia's defense forced Portland into shooting only 31 of 91 from the field. The Blazers were the only NBA team shooting above 50% coming into the game. The 11 game stretch was illuminating because it showed a lot of Sixer's inconsistency. Philly won 7 games while losing 4. Oddly enough, however, the record of Philly's *losing* opponents was an excellent 70-49, while the record of their 4 *winning* opponents was only 18-45.

76ers 119-113 Bucks Thur. February 11, 1988

Charles Barkley, who had scored 47 points in his previous game, totalled 46 against the Bucks, including 38 in the second half. Barkley also had 16 rebounds, one short of Mike Gminski's 17. The victory was the first for new coach Jim Lynam, who had replaced Matt Guokas a few days earlier.

76ers 102-101 Bulls Mon. February 29, 1988

The win came on a driving layup by Gerald Henderson as time expired. The last 4 seconds were filled with controversy over the clock, prompting Bulls' coach, Doug Collins, to charge the official timekeeper after the game. The win broke a 5 game losing streak for the Sixers - tying their season's longest. The 1 point win was Philly's first win of a close game (3 pts or less) last year. The team's record had been 0-9. Rookie Horace Grant of Chicago *achieved* a career high in points (20) by one, but *missed* a career high in rebounds (11) by one.

76ers 105-100 Pacers Sun. March 6, 1988

Prior to the victory, the Sixers had lost 3 1/2 games to Washington and 4 1/2 games to New York since the All-Star break to slip behind the other two in the battle for the 8th playoff spot. The win also broke another slide. Going into the game, Philadelphia had lost a club record 20 straight road games. Indiana had now lost 3 straight at home after setting a club record for consecutive home wins.

76ers 97-93 Celtics Fri. March 25, 1988

The 76ers pulled off a miracle comeback against the Celtics. Philadelphia trailed by a whopping 27 points at halftime. The comeback was the season's largest in the NBA. The 4th quarter was most special, as Philly outscored Boston by an incredible 30-9. By winning, the 76ers also broke a 14 game road losing streak at Boston Garden.

76ers 97-96 Bullets Wed. April 13, 1988

The 76ers came from 20 points behind to defeat the Bullets 97-96. The win not only broke a 4 game home losing streak (the longest since 1979), but kept the Sixers alive in their attempt at a playoff berth. The game was special for Charles Barkley. His 35 second half points (38 total) and 20 rebounds kept Philly in the game, and it was his off balance 30 footer at the buzzer which won it in overtime.

Philadelphia 76ers .... Influence on Winning

TEAM RECORD BY ... SCR Leader ... REB Leader ... AST Leader

PLAYER	GAMES	HOME	ROAD	HOME	ROAD	HOME	ROAD
Charles Barkley	80	24-11	7-25	17-7	7-21	---	1-3
Mike Gminski	47	2-0	0-4	7-3	1-9	---	0-1
Maurice Cheeks	79	1-1	0-2	---	0-1	24-9	9-21
Cliff Robinson	62	2-0	1-4	1-1	0-3	1-0	---
Ben Coleman	43	---	---	---	0-1	---	---
Gerald Henderson	69	---	---	---	---	2-1	1-5
Albert King	72	---	---	---	---	---	---
David Wingate	61	---	---	---	---	---	0-3
Mark McNamara	42	---	---	0-2	1-3	---	---
Danny Vranes	57	---	---	---	---	---	---

TEAM RECORD BY SCORING *

PLAYER	PLAY	DNP	0-9	10-19	20-29	30-39	40+
Charles Barkley	35-45	1-1	0-2	1-8	16-20	14-13	4-2
Mike Gminski	18-29	18-17	1-1	11-19	5-9	1-0	---
Maurice Cheeks	34-43	1-2	6-8	23-28	5-7	---	---
Cliff Robinson	30-32	6-14	4-4	8-14	16-13	2-1	---
Ben Coleman	17-26	19-20	15-17	2-9	---	---	---
Gerald Henderson	30-39	6-7	18-26	12-13	---	---	---
Albert King	31-41	5-5	18-28	13-13	---	---	---
David Wingate	26-35	10-11	12-21	13-14	1-0	---	---
Mark McNamara	19-23	17-23	19-20	0-3	---	---	---
Danny Vranes	25-32	11-14	24-31	1-1	---	---	---

TEAM RECORD BY STARTING POSITION *

PLAYER	GAMES	STARTS	PG	OG	SF	PF	C
Charles Barkley	80	80	---	---	4-6	31-39	---
Mike Gminski	47	47	---	---	---	---	18-29
Maurice Cheeks	79	79	35-44	---	---	---	---
Cliff Robinson	62	51	---	---	26-25	---	---
Ben Coleman	43	14	---	---	4-10	---	---
Gerald Henderson	69	3	1-2	---	---	---	---
Albert King	72	44	---	20-22	1-1	---	---
David Wingate	61	22	---	11-11	---	---	---
Mark McNamara	42	18	---	---	---	---	9-9
Danny Vranes	57	5	---	---	1-4	---	---

* For further definition of each category and column heading see pages 38 & 39.

Philadelphia 76ers — 1987-88 Statistics

RAW NUMBERS *

PLAYER	2pt%	3pt%	FT%	MIN	PF	DQ	HI	TO	RB	AS	BL	ST
Charles Barkley	.630	.280	.751	3170	278	6	47	304	951	254	103	100
Mike Gminski	.449	0-2	.906	2961	176	0	30	177	814	139	118	64
Maurice Cheeks	.504	.136	.825	2871	116	0	25	160	253	635	22	167
Cliff Robinson	.466	.222	.717	2110	192	4	32	161	405	131	39	79
Ben Coleman	.502	0-3	.762	1498	230	5	23	127	350	62	41	43
Gerald Henderson	.431	.423	.812	1505	187	0	18	133	107	231	5	69
Albert King	.395	.347	.757	1593	219	4	17	93	216	109	18	39
David Wingate	.412	.250	.750	1419	125	0	28	104	101	119	22	47
Mark McNamara	.391	0-0	.727	581	67	0	17	26	157	18	12	4
Danny Vranes	.449	0-3	.429	772	100	0	10	25	117	36	33	27

OVERALL RANKINGS *

PLAYER	G	GS	PPG	PR	RANK	SC	SH	RB	AS	BL	ST
Charles Barkley	80	80	28.30	32.51	3	4	6	12	87	34	84
Mike Gminski	81	81	16.85	20.56	27	43	93	18	128	25	129
Maurice Cheeks	79	79	13.75	19.22	37	71	49	138	15	113	16
Cliff Robinson	62	51	19.00	16.61	60	30	138	70	107	70	58
Ben Coleman	70	24	8.47	9.87	130	132	68	49	139	43	95
Gerald Henderson	75	5	7.93	7.77	155	139	45	151	39	146	33
Albert King	72	44	7.18	6.28	158	148	157	98	99	98	117
David Wingate	61	22	8.93	6.07	159	127	155	150	83	85	73
Mark McNamara	42	18	3.62	5.19	DNQ						
Danny Vranes	57	5	2.12	3.88	DNQ						

POSITION RANKINGS *

PLAYER	POSITION	RANK	SC	SH	RB	AS	BL	ST
Charles Barkley	Power Forward (PF)	1	1	2	7	6	12	14
Mike Gminski	Center (C)	5	5	16	9	14	15	13
Maurice Cheeks	Point Guard (PG)	7	13	12	21	15	9	8
Cliff Robinson	Small Forward (SF)	15	12	31	10	25	19	10
Ben Coleman	Power Forward (PF)	30	27	15	24	25	15	17
Gerald Henderson	Point Guard (PG)	32	28	11	27	31	23	18
Albert King	Off Guard (OG)	32	32	33	7	33	13	30
David Wingate	Off Guard (OG)	33	29	32	30	29	9	20
Mark McNamara	Center (C)	DNQ						
Danny Vranes	Small Forward (SF)	DNQ						

*For further definition of each category and column heading see pages 38 & 39.

Philadelphia 76ers ....Team Info

WEEKLY POWER RATING
41 WINS - AVERAGE (See page 39 for Team Power Rating discussion.)

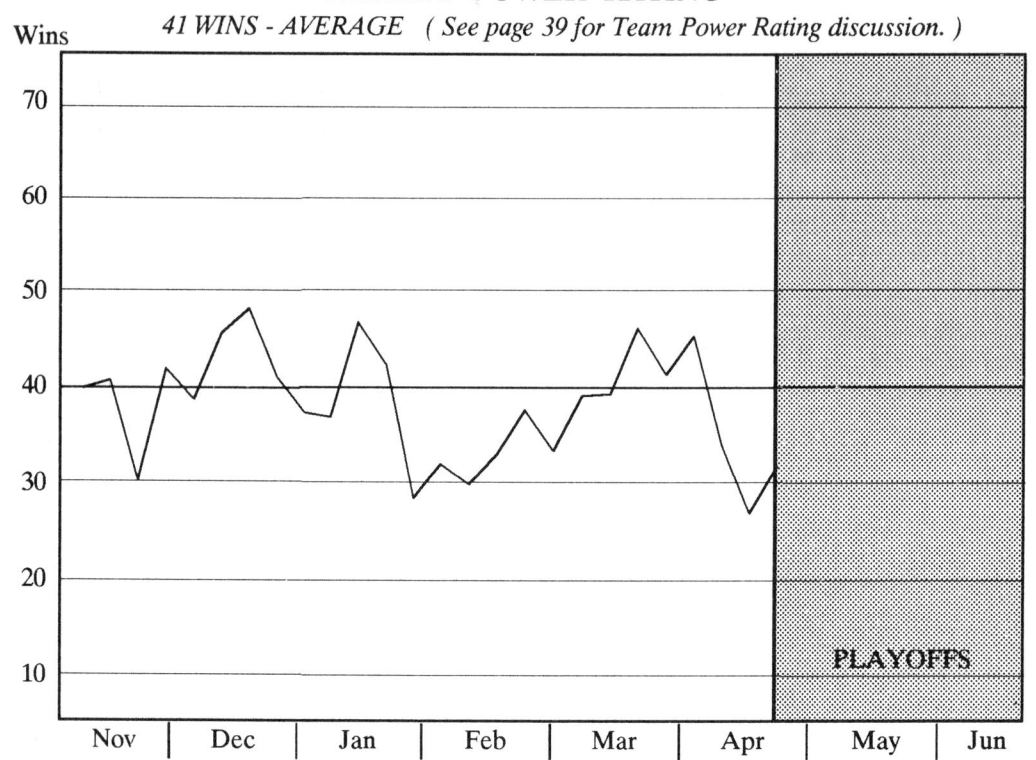

Miscellaneous Categories	Data	Rank	Performance Categories	Data	Rank
Attendance	513K	11	Offensive Scoring (per game)	105.7	16
Key-Man Games Missed	131	16	Defensive Scoring (per game)	107.1	12
Season Record	36-46	17	Scoring Margin (per game)	-1.4	17
- Home	27-14	15	Defensive FG%	.496	18
- Road	9-32	16	Offensive 2-point%	.485	14
Eastern Conference	25-33	15	Offensive 3-point%	.323	8
Western Conference	11-13	16	Offensive Free Throw %	.764	13
Overtime Record	2-7	20	Offensive Rebs (Off REB/Opp Def REB)		4
Record 5 Pts. or Less	11-15	17	Defensive Rebs (Def REB/Opp Off REB)		10
Record 10 Pts. or More	17-24	17	Offensive Assists (AST/FGMade)		16
Games Won By Bench	1	19	Offensive Blocks (BLK/Opp FGAttempted)		10
Games Won By Starters	4	14	Offensive Steals (STL/Game)		15
Winning Streak	4	14	Turnover Margin (Off T.O. - Def T.O.)		22
Losing Streak	5	10	Finesse (BLK + STL) / PF		10
Home Winning Streak	6	18	Rebounding Record	50-30-2	4
Road Winning Streak	2	14	Assists Record	18-57-7	23
Home Losing Streak	4	15	Field Goal Pct. Record	34-48-0	17
Road Losing Streak	15	19	Free Throw Pct. Record	42-38-2	10

Philadelphia 76ers .... Miscellaneous

ADMINISTRATIVE INFORMATION

Team Offices: Veterans Stadium
P.O. Box 25040
Philadelphia, Pennsylvania
19147-0240
Telephone: (215) 339-7600
Head Coach: Jim Lynam
Home Arena: The Spectrum
Capacity: 17,967

1988-89 ROSTER*

J#	VETERANS	COLLEGE	POS	R#	D#	HT	WT	Phil	NBA
34	Charles Barkley	Auburn	F	1	5	6-6	253	4	4
10	Maurice Cheeks	West Texas State	G	2	36	6-1	181	10	10
40	Ben Coleman	Maryland	F	2	37	6-9	235	1	2
42	Mike Gminski	Duke	C	1	7	6-11	260	1	8
7	Gerald Henderson	VCU	G	3	64	6-2	175	1	9
55	Albert King	Maryland	F	1	10	6-6	205	1	7
31	Mark McNamara	California	C	1	22	6-11	235	2	5
4	Cliff Robinson	USC	F	1	11	6-9	240	2	9
22	Andrew Toney	S.W. Louisiana	G	1	8	6-3	190	8	8
20	Danny Vranes	Utah	F	1	5	6-8	220	2	7
44	Chris Welp	Washington	C	1	16	7-0	245	1	1
25	David Wingate	Georgetown	G-F	2	44	6-5	185	2	2

ROOKIES	COLLEGE	POS	R#	D#	HT
Hersey Hawkins	Bradley	G	1	6	6-3
Everette Stephens	Purdue	G	2	31	6-3
Hernan Montenegro	LSU	F	3	57	6-10

* For further definition of category and column headings, see pages 38 & 39.

Philadelphia 76ers .... Overview

Boy, have times changed in the city of brotherly love. The once proud Sixers slumped to a seldom seen level of 36 wins in 1988. It was the club's first losing season-since 1975. For you youngsters, that was way back in the olden days; way back when the ABA was still a thorn in the NBA's side; back when Billy Cunningham and Doug Collins were teammates; when Kareem Abdul-Jabbar was just *one* of the oldest players on his team; yes, back when the Golden State Warriors were NBA champions! Say what? That's right. It was that long ago. Going into last season, Philadelphia had won 651 games since 1975, while the "elite" teams fared no better. (Boston 652, Los Angeles 657) The club's streak of twelve consecutive playoff appearances, now over, was the longest ongoing. But like Dr. J's playing career, all good things must come to an end. Unlike the unforgettable way Erving went out, however, the 1987-88 Sixers are easy to erase from memory.

In analyzing why Philadelphia has declined from 58 wins just 4 years ago or 54 victories only 3 years ago, one need look no farther than the trading floor. Two disastrous trades have left the team weak, old, and shallow (With one notable exception, of course). Remember when Moses Malone (3400 points in the last 2 years) was traded for Jeff Ruland (47 points) and the #1 pick (Brad Daugherty) was traded for Roy Hinson? Daugherty has a 2-year Production Rating of 20, while Hinson's PR was so disappointing that he was traded.

Speaking of trades, one of the league's biggest last season was the Hinson and McCormick swap for Gminski and Coleman. On the surface, this looks like a better deal for Philadelphia, and it may be, but upon closer observation it appears to be fairly even. Mike Gminski is entering his 9th year this season while Ben Coleman begins his third. Philly gave up a little youth with McCormick and Hinson. Together they've combined for 9 years of professional ball. Though G-man is the best of the bunch, odds are he's only going to go a few more rounds.

Gminski not only had a career high Production Rating (20.56), but actually ranked #5 among centers. Considering the fact that his best position rank prior to this season was 10th, such a large rise up the ladder in one season so late in his career is quite amazing. I'm sure some will say, "How can he rank 5th at center? I've hardly heard of him." The reason is simple - he ranks no worse than 16th in any of the six performance categories. His general lack of weaknesses makes him valuable. Interestingly, he is the first center in NBA history to shoot over 90% from the line (90.6%). If you're wondering about Jack Sikma who shot 92.2% last season, he started 74 games at power forward and only 8 at center.

Maurice Cheeks has always been such a pleasant player. He's a good leader, consistent, and excellent in all phases of the game. Cheeks was voted most coachable by my exclusive NBA coaches' poll. Joining him were Stockton, Moncrief, Bird, and Buck Williams. He also led in a couple other unusual categories. One which I call "Finesse" [(Blocks + Steals) / Fouls], showed Cheeks at 1.629. Michael Jordan (1.444) and Benoit Benjamin (1.355) are second and third. Only five players had more steals than fouls.

	Steals	- Fouls	= Diff.
Maurice Cheeks	167	116	+51
Michael Adams	168	138	+30
Fat Lever	223	214	+9
Lester Conner	38	31	+7
Derek Harper	168	164	+4

Charles Barkley is without a doubt one of the more amazing physical specimens ever. At 6'5" he became the shortest rebounding leader since the 1950's two seasons ago. Charles was third in Production Rating, behind Jordan and Bird, last year and finally made 1st team NBA. At times he so completely dominated that many of his teammates became bystanders. Of course, some

Philadelphia 76ers .... Overview

argue that he is too involved in the offense, that too much depends on him. I think that's somewhat true. Let's face it, when you're playing your best hand every time down court, the defense cheats. The more you play it, the more it cheats. Considering that only three players besides Barkley reached the century mark or better in rebounds, assists, blocks, and steals, (Olajuwon, Jordan, and Ewing are the others) it's no surprise to the opposition that Charles is in charge of the 76ers when it counts.

Arguably, Barkley is the most passionate and competitive person in the league. When he only played a handful of minutes in the All-Star game, he defiantly declared he would never come back except as a starter. In an effort to justify his inference that he was better than he was given credit for, he came out smoking after the All-Star break, scoring 47 points and 15 rebounds in his first game and 46 points and 16 rebounds in his second. Ironically, though Charles led the league in technicals, he also led the league in free throw attempts per 48 minutes (His 26 FTA's in one game last season were the most in the NBA). So it's not as though the officials were only calling them one way. Not surprisingly, he led the coaches' poll for being most expressive. The others on that team were Magic Johnson, Isiah Thomas, Karl Malone, and Michael Jordan.

Cliff Robinson had a decent season (excluding injuries), but he still ranked 15th at small forward while continuing to try to shed the "selfish" and "loser" labels. Robinson has never been accused of inspiring good chemistry either. Strangely, the team did better without most of the players than with them. Only Robinson (30-32 when he played, but 6-14 when he didn't) and Mark McNamara seem to have been more valuable on the court than off.

This team is not that bad until you look at the off guard position. The three players regularly used were Andrew Toney, David Wingate, and Albert King. Truthfully, these three taken together don't represent a decent player. Toney shot only 42.1%, Wingate 41.2%, and King 39.1%. This is wretched and cost the Sixers a lot of games. I suppose the ultimate is to be able to plug such a huge hole with the college Player-of-the-Year. That's exactly what Hersey Hawkins was, according to several polls. Beyond that, he led the nation in scoring, at 36.3 ppg, and was impossible to defend. If he doesn't do some major league scoring in the NBA, I'll be shocked. He couldn't ask for a better situation than to get to play with the 76ers.

Notes: the Sixers had the worst record in the NBA in assists. They won 18, lost 57 and tied 7... Philadelphia lost a club record 20 straight road games in 1988... The only two categories in which Philly was ranked better than #10 were defensive rebounding (#4) and rebounding record (#4)... The club placed three players in the bottom six according to how inefficient they were at shooting 2-point shots (see inefficiency discussion on page 32).

Joe Barry Carroll	-110
Albert King	**-95**
Mike Gminski	**-94**
Herb Williams	-92
Reggie Williams	-85
David Wingate	**-84**

Prediction - best case: 39-43

This 3 game improvement over last year is possible only if Hawkins performs up to the level expected out of him. Additionally, turnovers must be reduced. Their 2-7 overtime record as well as the 3-11 record on margins of 3 points or less must be corrected as well.

Prediction - worst case: 28-54

If Hawkins is a Dennis Hopson-type disappointment, then this club will lose even more ground to .500. If Cheeks or Barkley or Gminski suffer any serious injuries, it could be even worse. With no bench, a semi-new coach, and an unhappy Barkley, what chemistry they have now may seem like a lot later.

Phoenix Suns ....History

The Phoenix Suns became an NBA expansion team in 1968-69 along with the Milwaukee Bucks. The Suns have really straddled the fence between winning and losing in their 20 year existence. The club's regular season record has been 811-829. Additionally, they have gone to the playoffs 10 times while missing on 10 other occasions. Interestingly, Phoenix made the playoffs in 1970 with a 39-43 record, but failed to qualify the following two years despite glossy records of 48-34 and 49-33.

Although the Suns have reached the NBA finals only once, losing two games to four to Boston (1976), they have reached the conference finals two additional times. In 1978-79 Phoenix lost to Seattle three games to four (110-114 in game 7). In 1983-84, the Suns lost to the Lakers two games to four.

When the club made the finals in 1976, it capped an impressive playoff run. Phoenix had entered post-season play with a less-than-dazzling 42-40 record, but proceeded to upset favored Seattle and defending champion Golden State on their way to making the championship round versus Boston. Though they lost, game 5 of the series with the Celtics - a triple overtime battle - is considered the most exciting basketball game ever played.

In 1969, the Suns lost the flip, but won the draw. After posting a dismal 16-66 record in their initial year, Phoenix squared off against Milwaukee in the most important coin flip in NBA history. The Suns called "heads". The coin showed "tails". Milwaukee got Lew Alcindor (Abdul-Jabbar), while Phoenix got Neal Walk. Later that summer, when Connie Hawkins came over from the ABA, Phoenix and Seattle drew to obtain Hawkins' rights. This time the Suns won. As it turns out, the Jabbar-led Bucks gained +29 wins while the Hawkins-led Suns registered an increase of +23 wins. Ironically, these are the two largest improvements in year 2 by any franchise.

Notes: For 11 straight years, the home attendance has been between 11,000 and 12,000 despite an arena which holds 14,500... Jerry Colangelo has twice been named Executive-of-the-Year. Only Bob Ferry (Washington) and Stan Kasten (Atlanta) have also accomplished this feat... John MacLeod is second only to Red Auerbach for most consecutive seasons coaching the same club. MacLeod coached Phoenix for 14 straight years from 1974-87. Red Auerbach coached Boston 16 straight years from 1951-66.

> **Quiz: Phoenix is 16-4 in home openers, and 5-0 against what team?**

ALL TIME SUNS' TEAM

Player	Span	Yrs	CRD
Alvan Adams	1976-88	13	17,397
Walter Davis	1978-88	11	16,424
Dick Van Arsdale	1969-77	9	10,805
Larry Nance	1982-88	7	10,551
Paul Westphal	1976-84	6	8,535
Connie Hawkins	1970-73	5	7,436
Paul Silas	1970-72	3	5,202
Truck Robinson	1979-82	4	5,055
Kyle Macy	1981-85	5	4,882
Maurice Lucas	1983-85	3	4,210

ALL TIME SUNS' COACH

John Macleod   14.5 Years
33-44 Playoffs   9 Playoffs
579-543 Reg. Season   0 Championships

HISTORICAL PROFILE

Category	Data
Suns' coach	Cotton Fitzsimmons
Years coached Phoenix	0
# of franchise years	20
# of coaches	7
# of winning seasons	9
# of playoff years	10
# of runner's up	1
# of championships	0
Regular season win %	49.5
Playoff win %	45.5

> **Answer:
> Golden State Warriors**

Phoenix Suns ....1987-88 Highlights

Suns 121-102 Clippers   Wed.   December 31, 1987

Though the Suns trailed by as many as 20 points in the third quarter, they won going away largely on the coattails of Eddie Johnson. The newly-acquired Sun scored 43 points - a career high. It was a full 20 points more than his previous high since being traded to Phoenix. Interestingly, his 43 points matched the point total Phoenix scored in their 4th quarter comeback while his own 19 4th quarter points matched the victory margin.

Suns 128-108 Nuggets   Sat.   February 20, 1988

The win was important as it was only the second home win for Phoenix in the club's last 9 games. Significantly, it was also the largest winning margin of the season - 20 pts. Phoenix's top two scorers of the previous season were Walter Davis and Larry Nance. Although both players started a majority of the games, both came off the bench in this one to score 29 and 28 points. It was the most points either had scored since 1987.

Suns 109-103 Cavs   Thur.   February 25, 1988

The Suns and Cavaliers made a blockbuster trade before the two teams clashed. None of the five players who were traded played in the game. Larry Nance was the key to the trade. Three of his former teammates picked up the slack. Armon Gilliam hit a career high 24 points, Jeff Hornacek had a season high 15 assists and Walter Davis managed to have season highs in both scoring and assists (35,11)

Suns 111-90 Sonics   Tue.   March 15, 1988

The victory was impressive for many reasons. 1) It broke the Suns' 9 game losing streak. 2) It was the first win since the trades. 3) The 21 point margin was the largest of the year for Phoenix. 4) To make the victory even sweeter, the Suns came from 20 points behind, trailing at one point 31-11. 5) Finally, on one of those rare occasions, Phoenix held Seattle's bench scoreless. The Suns won the bench battle 47-0. This was the only time last year a bench was held scoreless in a game.

Suns 107-99 Clippers   Mon.   March 21, 1988

Phoenix won a season high 4th straight game in dumping the LA Clippers. The loss was the 26th straight on the road by LA. The Suns trailed late in the game, but scored 14 of the final 16 points to win. Phoenix went to 6-0 when holding their opponents under 100 points - the best record in the NBA!

Suns 123-116 Spurs   Wed.   April 13, 1988

The Suns, fighting to make the playoffs, beat the team they were trying to catch. As impressive as the Johnsons' offensive efforts were (Eddie scored 37 points, while Kevin had a triple double) the key was defense. Coming into the game the Spurs starting forwards, Frank Brickowski and Mike Mitchell, had scored 120 points in their previous two games - an average of 30 per game each. Brickowski only scored 9 and Mitchell 11.

Suns 121-119 Sonics   Sat.   April 16, 1988

The win was the first O.T. victory of the season for the Suns and kept their playoff hopes mathematically alive. The game became a battle between guards. Phoenix overcame a career high 31 points by Sedale Threatt on the strength of a career high 31 by their own Kevin Johnson. Johnson also had double figure rebounds and assists, giving him his third triple double of the season and second in 3 games.

Phoenix Suns . . . . Influence on Winning

TEAM RECORD BY

PLAYER	GAMES	... SCR Leader HOME	ROAD	... REB Leader HOME	ROAD	... AST Leader HOME	ROAD
Walter Davis	68	6-6	2-8	---	---	2-1	0-4
Armon Gilliam	55	4-0	0-5	7-8	2-7	---	---
Eddie Johnson	73	4-4	1-11	---	0-3	0-1	0-1
Jeff Hornacek	82	---	0-1	0-1	---	9-6	2-13
Mark West	29	---	0-1	4-1	0-6	---	---
Kevin Johnson	28	2-0	0-2	1-0	1-0	8-3	1-9
Alvan Adams	82	---	---	1-1	0-3	---	---
Tyrone Corbin	30	---	---	---	0-3	---	0-1
Craig Hodges	23	---	---	---	---	---	----
James Bailey	65	---	---	1-0	0-2	---	---

TEAM RECORD BY SCORING *

PLAYER	PLAY	DNP	0-9	10-19	20-29	30-39	40+
Walter Davis	22-46	6-8	2-8	8-19	8-19	4-0	---
Armon Gilliam	17-38	11-16	0-8	14-25	3-5	---	---
Eddie Johnson	23-50	5-4	1-10	10-19	10-18	1-3	1-0
Jeff Hornacek	28-54	---	13-28	14-25	1-1	---	---
Mark West	11-18	17-36	3-5	8-12	0-1	---	---
Kevin Johnson	11-17	17-37	2-8	7-7	1-2	1-0	---
Alvan Adams	28-54	---	12-16	16-38	---	---	---
Tyrone Corbin	11-19	17-35	8-12	3-7	---	---	---
Craig Hodges	9-14	19-40	4-7	5-7	---	---	---
James Bailey	23-42	5-12	22-39	1-3	---	---	---

TEAM RECORD BY STARTING POSITION *

PLAYER	GAMES	STARTS	PG	OG	SF	PF	C
Walter Davis	68	48	---	16-32	---	---	---
Armon Gilliam	55	53	---	---	---	17-36	---
Eddie Johnson	73	59	---	0-2	21-36	---	---
Jeff Hornacek	82	49	12-20	6-11	---	---	---
Mark West	29	29	---	---	---	---	10-19
Kevin Johnson	28	25	10-15	---	---	---	---
Alvan Adams	82	25	---	---	3-4	4-6	4-4
Tyrone Corbin	30	1	---	---	0-1	---	---
Craig Hodges	23	0	---	---	---	---	---
James Bailey	65	0	---	---	---	---	---

* For further definition of each category and column heading see pages 38 & 39.

Phoenix Suns — 1987-88 Statistics

RAW NUMBERS *

PLAYER	2pt%	3pt%	FT%	MIN	PF	DQ	HI	TO	RB	AS	BL	ST
Walter Davis	.483	.375	**.887**	1951	131	0	35	126	159	278	3	86
Armon Gilliam	.475	0-0	.679	1807	143	1	25	123	434	72	29	58
Eddie Johnson	.501	.255	.850	2177	190	0	**43**	139	318	180	9	33
Jeff Hornacek	.528	.293	.822	**2243**	151	0	21	156	262	**540**	10	**107**
Mark West	**.552**	0-1	.596	2098	**265**	4	23	173	523	74	**147**	47
Kevin Johnson	.472	.208	.839	1917	155	1	31	146	191	437	24	103
Alvan Adams	.496	**.500**	.844	1646	245	3	18	140	365	183	41	82
Tyrone Corbin	.493	.167	.797	1739	181	2	23	104	350	115	18	72
Craig Hodges	.448	.491	.831	1445	118	1	22	77	78	153	2	46
James Bailey	.460	0-4	.787	869	180	1	12	70	210	42	28	17

OVERALL RANKINGS *

PLAYER	G	GS	PPG	PR	RANK	SC	SH	RB	AS	BL	ST
Walter Davis	68	48	**17.90**	15.41	74	36	51	144	45	155	38
Armon Gilliam	55	53	14.82	15.36	75	58	135	44	143	80	78
Eddie Johnson	73	**59**	17.73	14.82	79	37	61	93	85	140	151
Jeff Hornacek	82	49	9.52	14.78	81	122	30	111	9	137	32
Mark West	83	41	9.66	12.63	102	116	71	29	150	9	125
Kevin Johnson	80	28	9.15	12.32	105	125	90	127	12	95	24
Alvan Adams	82	25	7.45	10.57	123	144	48	56	55	50	28
Tyrone Corbin	**84**	5	7.44	9.29	135	145	75	66	103	102	47
Craig Hodges	66	0	9.53	8.15	153	121	12	159	61	156	81
James Bailey	65	0	4.43	5.60	DNQ						

POSITION RANKINGS *

PLAYER	POSITION	RANK	SC	SH	RB	AS	BL	ST
Walter Davis	Off Guard (OF)	12	12	13	26	12	32	10
Armon Gilliam	Power Forward (PF)	17	11	29	21	28	27	11
Eddie Johnson	Small Forward (SF)	18	13	12	24	17	32	33
Jeff Hornacek	Point Guard (PG)	18	22	5	9	9	18	17
Mark West	Center (C)	22	22	13	16	20	7	11
Kevin Johnson	Point Guard (PG)	22	25	17	13	12	4	13
Alvan Adams	Power Forward (PF)	28	32	10	27	2	16	1
Tyrone Corbin	Small Forward (SF)	26	32	14	8	22	25	8
Craig Hodges	Off Guard (OG)	30	28	3	33	21	33	22
James Bailey	Power Forward (PF)	DNQ						

*For further definition of each category and column heading see pages 38 & 39.

176 BASKETBALL HEAVEN 1989

Phoenix Suns ....Team Info

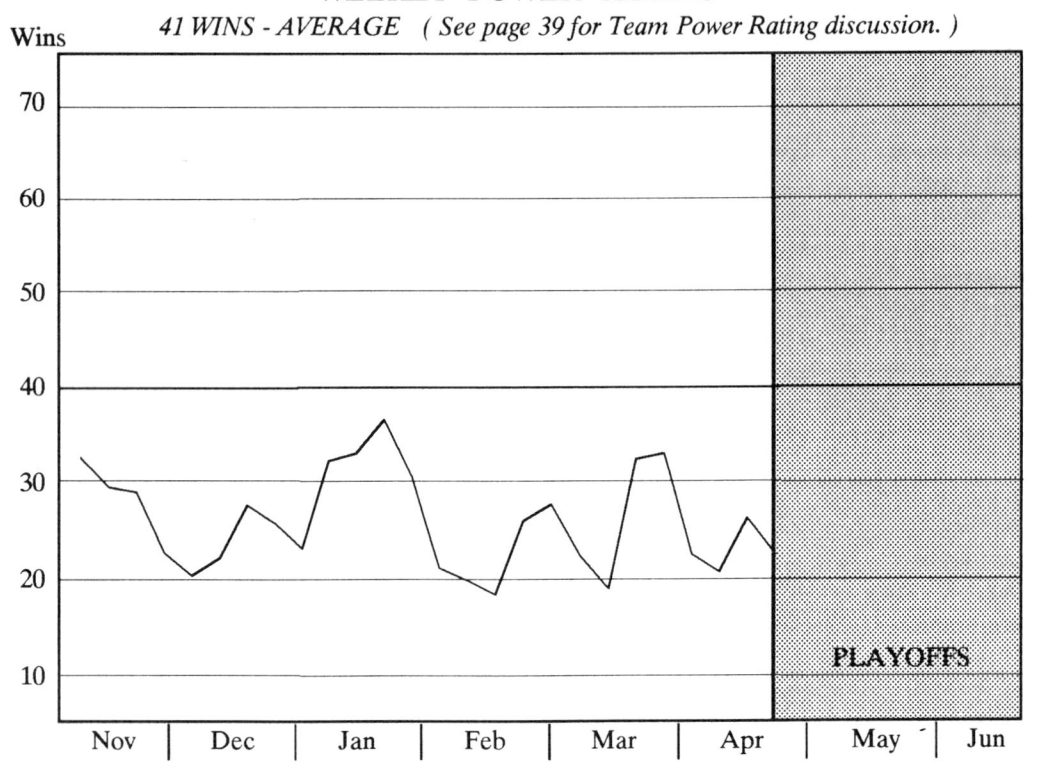

WEEKLY POWER RATING
41 WINS - AVERAGE   (See page 39 for Team Power Rating discussion.)

Wins

[Line graph showing weekly power rating from Nov through Jun, with values fluctuating between approximately 18 and 36. Playoffs region shaded from May to Jun.]

Miscellaneous Categories	Data	Rank	Performance Categories	Data	Rank
Attendance	461K	18	Offensive Scoring (per game)	108.5	10
Key-Man Games Missed	74	14	Defensive Scoring (per game)	113.0	20
Season Record	28-54	19	Scoring Margin (per game)	-4.5	18
- Home	22-19	19	Defensive FG%	.498	20
- Road	6-35	19	Offensive 2-point%	.494	9
Eastern Conference	7-15	18	Offensive 3-point%	.331	6
Western Conference	21-39	19	Offensive Free Throw %	.764	14
Overtime Record	1-1	10	Offensive Rebs (Off REB/Opp Def REB)		15
Record 5 Pts. or Less	7-15	23	Defensive Rebs (Def REB/Opp Off REB)		6
Record 10 Pts. or More	13-28	18	Offensive Assists (AST/FGMade)		3
Games Won By Bench	2	17	Offensive Blocks (BLK/Opp FGAttempted)		21
Games Won By Starters	7	8	Offensive Steals (STL/Game)		14
Winning Streak	4	14	Turnover Margin (Off T.O. - Def T.O.)		20
Losing Streak	10	21	Finesse (BLK + STL) / PF		20
Home Winning Streak	4	19	Rebounding Record	37-40-5	15
Road Winning Streak	1	21	Assists Record	42-37-3	12
Home Losing Streak	4	15	Field Goal Pct. Record	38-44-0	14
Road Losing Streak	9	14	Free Throw Pct. Record	39-43-0	15

Phoenix Suns . . . . Miscellaneous

ADMINISTRATIVE INFORMATION

Team Offices: 2910 N. Central
Phoenix, Arizona
85012

Telephone: (602) 266-5753
Head Coach: Cotton Fitzsimmons
Home Arena: Arizona Veterans' Memorial Coliseum
Capacity: 14,471

1988-89 ROSTER*

J#	VETERANS	COLLEGE	POS	R#	D#	HT	WT	Phoe	NBA
2	James Bailey	Rutgers	F	1	6	6-9	220	1	9
24	Tom Chambers	Utah	F	1	8	6-10	230	0	7
23	Tyrone Corbin	DePaul	F	2	35	6-6	222	1	3
35	Armon Gilliam	UNLV	F	1	2	6-9	245	1	1
15	Craig Hodges	Long Beach	G	3	48	6-3	190	1	6
14	Jeff Hornacek	Iowa State	G	2	46	6-4	191	2	2
8	Eddie A. Johnson	Illinois	F	2	29	6-7	210	1	7
10	Kevin Johnson	California	G	1	7	6-1	180	1	1
53	Ron Moore	W. Virginia State	C	2	25	7-0	260	1	1
41	Mark West	Old Dominion	F-C	2	30	6-10	226	1	5

ROOKIES	COLLEGE	POS	R#	D#	HT
Tim Perry	Temple	F	1	7	6-9
Dan Majerle	Central Michigan	F	1	14	6-6
Andrew Lang	Arkansas	C	2	28	6-11
Dean Garrett	Indiana	F-C	2	38	6-10
Steve Kerr	Arizona	G	2	50	6-3
Rodney Johns	Grand Canyon	G	3	55	6-2

* For further definition of category and column headings, see pages 38 & 39.

Phoenix Suns .... Overview

At one point in the 1987-88 season the Phoenix Suns were 13-19 and healthy. Believe it or not, I was excited about their chances. Consider my reasons: The Suns had won their last two games over Denver and Houston (two hot teams); Armon Gilliam had returned from injury and started the previous two games - looking strong; James Edwards was scoring at a career high rate of 17 ppg; Walter Davis had returned from injury just six games earlier and was averaging over 20 ppg; Eddie Johnson had been scoring at a 20 point clip his past eight games; Larry Nance had just come off the Player-of-the-Month award in the NBA; and Jay Humphries had averaged 16 points and 9 assists for his last half dozen games. There was no reason not to expect good things from there on out. One of the best arguments for such optomism was that the six players listed above are prototype position players. James Edwards is a typical center, Larry Nance a perfect small forward, Armon Gilliam a tenacious power forward, Walter Davis a hot shooting guard, Jay Humphries a playmaking point guard, and Eddie Johnson the quintessential 6th man. So, after a 13-19 start and a good looking future, Phoenix proceeded to go out and... lose 10 straight games - one of the worst streaks in team history. Who'd a thunk it?

As a result of this failure, the team finished 28-54 - their worst record in 20 years. Only the expansion season of 1968-69 was worse (16-66). It wasn't exactly a shock when John Wetzel was let go at season's end. It would have been a miracle had he survived to this season. In fairness, he inherited a team fractured by disputes, a drug scandal, the unexpected death of their future center, and three consecutive losing seasons. It would have been unrealistic to have expected the Suns to have done much better than 28 victories. Given their circumstances, they did better than anyone had thought they would. Of the thirteen major preseason polls for the Pacific Division, Phoenix was picked 5th in eight and 6th in five. For what it's worth, they finished in 4th place - a full eight games ahead of the 5th place Warriors. Actually, they almost slid into the playoffs, but lost the spotlight to the Spurs. No, I'm not saying Wetzel was unfairly dismissed. When a team finishes 28-54 and misses the playoffs, the management has every right to make any decision they want for the sake of the team without expecting criticism.

Due to the problems the club was experiencing, they initiated the biggest trade in franchise history in late February. Phoenix sent their star forward, Larry Nance, and reserve Mike Sanders to Cleveland for the trio of Mark West, Kevin Johnson, and Tyrone Corbin. As I argued in Cleveland's overview (pg 72), I believe the Cavs got the better end of the deal for the short run - but only because Nance was the missing piece to Cleveland's puzzle and they didn't need two young, potentially great, point guards. Phoenix, however, may gain in the long run. After all, Nance will be entering his 8th season this October. The youth and potential is something Phoenix needed desperately. I saw enough of Kevin Johnson to believe he's going to be a star - and soon; Mark West is a reject artist; and Tyrone Corbin adds depth.

The Suns traded Edwards about the same time to Detroit for Ron Moore. That's a tough call, but it's a decision based on youth vs age. James was in his 11th, though arguably his best, year. Moore is high risk and unproven. Phoenix cleaned house a little further when they traded Jay Humphries to Milwaukee for Craig Hodges. Hodges is an outstanding 3-point shooter. As a matter of fact, he set an all-time NBA record last season for 3-pt percentage (.491). The previous record was held by Kiki Vandeweghe (1987 - .481). All in all, the trades gave them youth and a few new weapons.

Alvan Adams retired at season's end. It was a quiet and unspectacular close to an outstanding career. Adams was one of those remarkably versatile players similar

Phoenix Suns .... Overview

to a Bill Walton or a Larry Bird. He was named Rookie-of-the-Year in 1976 and consistently led all centers in steals and assists. Even last season, his 13th, he managed to rank #1 among centers in steals and #2 in assists. What this proves is that he wasn't really a center, but rather a 1990's small forward. On more than one occasion Alvan lamented that he was unable to play forward more in the NBA. Had he been able to, he very likely would have been an annual All-Star. At center, too many of his talents went unnoticed. Adams has the distinction of being the only player in NBA history to place in the top 20% of all six performance categories sometime during his career (see discussion page 304). In my mind he deserves a real tribute.

Jeff Hornacek started a little over half of the time at both guard positions. Though hardly the most important player on the team (who was?), Hornacek led the club in minutes-played, with 2243. This is a very low number. Every other team (except the Clippers) had at least two players with more than 2243 minutes. It's clear from that statistic that the Suns were a club in disarray - various lineups, several injuries, and a lot of immaturity. Those areas can always change. As a parallel stat, Eddie Johnson started 59 games - the team high. That's ironic since I call him my "quintessential 6th man". In any event, every other team had at least two players with more than 59 starts. This is just one more piece of evidence that Phoenix was in turmoil.

Armon Gilliam was the #2 pick in the 1987 draft, behind David Robinson. Gilliam played one game before being injured and missing 27. That's a tough way to start, but he rebounded (in more ways than one) nicely and made the All-Rookie team. Gilliam is a stereotypical power forward.

As if the Suns didn't have enough problems last season, they finished 7-15 in games decided by 5 points or less (last in the NBA). Part of that was due to their poor success rate down the stretch. Phoenix also ranked last in the unenviable category of comebacks (wins after trailing going into the fourth quarter) minus blown games (losses after leading going into the fourth quarter).

	Comebacks	- Blown	= Deficit
Phoenix	**3**	**-9**	**-6**
Milwaukee	2	-7	-5
New Jersey	4	-9	-5
L.A. Clippers	6	-10	-4
Utah	8	-12	-4

Not all was gloomy. Phoenix did have two rookies who showed promise. Both Armon Gilliam and Kevin Johnson received a Rookie-of-the-Month award and should be dynamite next year.

November	Mark Jackson	New York
December	Mark Jackson	New York
January	**Armon Gilliam**	**Phoenix**
February	Mark Jackson	New York
March	Greg Anderson	San Antonio
April	**Kevin Johnson**	**Phoenix**

Add to those players the #7 and #14 picks in the recent draft (Tim Perry, Dan Mejerle) and the core of a good team has been formed. Either one of the two could become the replacement for Nance at small forward. It's too bad that Walter Davis left for Denver, but in his 12th year, his longevity is in serious doubt - especially since he has announced his retirement once already.

Prediction - best case: 36-46

It will be difficult to win 36 games, but with KJ, Armon, and Perry this should be a very exciting team. They're building, and they have already poured what appears to be a sound foundation. If so, new coach, Cotton Fitzsimmons, has something good to look forward to.

Prediction - worst case: 20-62

I'm not sure why this team should do worse than 28 wins. Nevertheless, the replacement of Nance, Edwards, Sanders, and Humphries, will mean a lot of new faces on the club. A couple of injuries and a lot of inexperience ...well, it would have to be bad, but 62 losses is possible.

Portland Trail Blazers .... History

The Portland Trail Blazers came into the NBA as an expansion team in 1970-71. At the time, the league expanded from 14 to 17 teams. The other two new entries were Cleveland and Buffalo (LA Clippers). In the 18 years since these three clubs joined the NBA, the Blazers have been far more successful than either the Cavaliers or Braves. Portland has won 725 games to 573 for Cleveland and 537 for Los Angeles. The Blazers also have recorded more winning seasons (10) than the other two combined (8). Not surprisingly, the club has won the head-to-head matchups against both teams (67 to 33 over LA and 38 to 26 over Cleveland).

Two of those 38 victories over Cleveland are of special significance. Twice the two clubs met in season openers (1971 and 1974). The '71 encounter was the NBA debut for both teams. Portland won 115-112. The 1974 opener was even closer - a 131-129 four O.T. victory for the Blazers. That game represents the longest overtime game in club history.

The club has been especially successful since the beginning of their championship season. In the last dozen years, Portland has won 555 games. Only the Lakers, Celtics, Sixers, and Bucks have won more. As well as they have done against other teams in the league, however, they have yet to be big winners during the regular season. Whereas the previously mentioned four teams have averaged 7+ seasons at 54+ victories since 1978, the Blazers have failed to do this even once.

Odds and Ends: Terry Porter has 7 of the club's 9 highest assist totals in a game. Six of the seven occurred during the calendar year of 1987. The only one that did not was last season. Porter's 19 assists in that game was a franchise high... The 50 point barrier has only been broken twice by a Blazer. Both times it was Geoff Petrie. Both occasions occurred in early 1973. Moreover, both opponents were the same team - Houston... Houston was also the opponent in Portland's record setting overtime victory in 1984. The Blazers outscored the Rockets 17-0 during the extra session - an NBA all-time high... The club also *benefitted* at Houston's expense in FT shooting. The Rockets hit an NBA low percentage from the line vs Portland (3 of 14, 10 FT minimum). Coincidentally, Portland was the *victim* in the NBA's best FT performance. It was the the same year (1982) and Utah hit 39 straight to defeat the Blazers.

Quiz: Who was the first Blazer to have his number retired?

ALL TIME BLAZERS' TEAM

Player	Span	Yrs	CRD
Mychal Thompson	1979-86	7	10,945
Sidney Wicks	1972-76	5	9,382
Jim Paxson	1980-88	9	8,897
Clyde Drexler	1984-88	5	8,353
Geoff Petrie	1971-76	6	7,333
Calvin Natt	1980-84	5	6,188
Lloyd Neal	1973-78	7	6,148
Bob Gross	1976-82	7	6,061
Bill Walton	1975-78	4	5,620
Larry Steel	1972-80	9	5,573

ALL TIME BLAZERS' COACH

Jack Ramsay   10 Years
29-30 Playoffs   9 Playoffs
453-367 Reg. Season   1 Championship

HISTORICAL PROFILE

Category	Data
Blazers' coach	Mike Schuler
Years coached Portland	2
# of franchise years	18
# of coaches	5
# of winning seasons	10
# of playoff years	11
# of runner's up	0
# of championships	1
Regular season win %	49.1
Playoff win %	46.3

**Answer:
Lloyd Neal, #36**

Portland Trail Blazers . . . . 1987-88 Highlights

Blazers 117-104 Lakers   Wed.   December 2, 1987

The Trail Blazers won their 7th game in a row by defeating the Lakers. The streak is the club's longest since Portland won 8 straight in 1984 and the first time the Blazers had beaten the Lakers in LA since the final game of the 1983 season. Clyde Drexler scored 28 points while Jerome Kersey scored a career high 32 points.

Blazers 136-91 Warriors   Tue.   December 22, 1987

The winning margin (45) was Portland's largest since Nov. 82 and third biggest in franchise history, while it tied with three other games Golden State's worst losses in the 80's. Amazingly, it could have been worse. Portland led by 50 going into the last quarter.

Blazers 119-111 Pistons   Sun.   January 24, 1988

It was a game of similarities as Portland defeated Detroit. The win was the 18th straight home win by the Blazers over the Pistons. In fact, Detroit had not won at Portland since 1974. The similarity is that the Portland win left both clubs in second place in their divisions, 3rd place in their conferences, and 9 games over .500. Ironically, two replacement starters were the stars. Dennis Rodman had career highs in points (30) and rebounds (18), but it was Kevin Duckworth's career highs in points (22) and rebounds (15) that made the difference.

Blazers 120-105 Nuggets   Fri.   February 12, 1988

Portland won going away after being tied entering quarter #4. The win came despite a triple double by Fat Lever - his league leading 7th of the season - and 24 3rd quarter points by Alex English. Three Blazers scored 28+ points - only the second time this season that has been accomplished by an NBA team (Seattle did it once). Kevin Duckworth tied his career high 28 points while Jerome Kersey had the second highest scoring game of his career (34) and a career high 20 rebounds. Ironically, Kiki Vandeweghe, who is averaging nearly 25 ppg, failed to reach double figures for the first time in 128 games.

Blazers 104-96 Bulls   Fri.   February 26, 1988

The Portland Trail Blazers defeated the Bulls in a shoot out of two of the league's top players. Portland won on the strength of a career high 42 points by Clyde Drexler. Michael Jordan scored 52 points - tying his NBA high for the season to date. Incredibly, only one other Bull scored in double figures. Charles Oakley barely made it by scoring 10.

Blazers 123-120 Hawks   Sat.   February 27, 1988

The Blazers entered the game against Atlanta as big underdogs. It was the 4th game of a road trip for Portland; Atlanta was 20-3 at home; Portland was playing without Steve Johnson, Kiki Vandeweghe & Jim Paxson; Dominique Wilkins scored 47 points for the Hawks; Portland's coach, Mike Schuler, was ejected from the game; And Portland trailed by 15 points entering the 4th quarter. The fact that they won is incredible!

Blazers 112-95 Lakers   Tue.   March 15, 1988

The 17 point margin was Portland's largest over LA since 1984. The Blazers beat the Lakers at their own game, outscoring LA on fast break points by an astonishing 40-6. The Lakers were playing without Magic Johnson. His point guard counterpart, Terry Porter, hit 11 straight FG's at one point and scored a career high 33 points. The win was Portland's 9th in a row. There were 7 technicals in the game. In two straight nights Jack Madden and Steve Javie whistled 15 T's - despite no fights.

Portland Trail Blazers . . . . . . Influence on Winning

TEAM RECORD BY

PLAYER	GAMES	... SCR Leader HOME	ROAD	... REB Leader HOME	ROAD	... AST Leader HOME	ROAD
Clyde Drexler	81	21-4	11-9	7-0	3-3	6-2	3-2
Terry Porter	82	2-0	0-1	---	1-2	29-6	18-21
Jerome Kersey	79	6-1	3-4	9-2	5-6	---	---
Kevin Duckworth	78	4-2	1-3	9-2	6-6	---	---
Caldwell Jones	79	---	---	2-1	3-1	---	---
Kiki Vandeweghe	37	3-0	1-3	---	0-1	---	---
Steve Johnson	43	3-0	0-4	4-1	1-2	---	---
Maurice Lucas	73	---	---	2-1	---	---	---
Richard Anderson	74	---	---	4-0	1-1	1-0	---
Michael Holton	82	---	---	1-0	---	1-0	---

TEAM RECORD BY SCORING *

PLAYER	PLAY	DNP	0-9	10-19	20-29	30-39	40+
Clyde Drexler	53-28	0-1	1-0	1-6	28-19	18-3	5-0
Terry Porter	53-29	---	10-2	35-23	5-4	2-0	1-0
Jerome Kersey	50-29	3-0	0-3	24-14	20-12	6-0	---
Kevin Duckworth	52-26	1-3	11-11	19-5	20-7	2-3	---
Caldwell Jones	51-28	2-1	46-26	5-2	---	---	---
Kiki Vandeweghe	22-15	31-14	2-0	11-6	5-8	4-0	0-1
Steve Johnson	27-16	26-13	8-4	10-6	8-5	1-1	---
Maurice Lucas	48-25	5-4	34-19	14-6	---	---	---
Richard Anderson	41-21	12-8	28-19	11-2	2-0	---	---
Michael Holton	53-29	---	45-23	8-6	---	---	---

TEAM RECORD BY STARTING POSITION *

PLAYER	GAMES	STARTS	PG	OG	SF	PF	C
Clyde Drexler	81	80	---	51-28	1-0	---	---
Terry Porter	82	82	53-29	---	---	---	---
Jerome Kersey	79	75	---	---	49-23	0-3	---
Kevin Duckworth	78	50	---	---	---	---	33-17
Caldwell Jones	79	77	---	---	---	51-25	0-1
Kiki Vandeweghe	37	7	---	---	2-5	---	---
Steve Johnson	43	33	---	---	---	1-1	20-11
Maurice Lucas	73	0	---	---	---	---	---
Richard Anderson	62	3	---	---	1-1	1-0	---
Michael Holton	82	2	---	2-0	---	---	---

* For further definition of each category and column heading see pages 38 & 39.

Portland Trailblazers .... 1987-88 Statistics

RAW NUMBERS *

PLAYER	2pt%	3pt%	FT%	MIN	PF	DQ	HI	TO	RB	AS	BL	ST
Clyde Drexler	.515	.212	.811	3060	250	2	**42**	236	533	467	52	**203**
Terry Porter	**.533**	.348	.846	2991	204	1	40	**244**	378	**831**	16	150
Jerome Kersey	.502	.200	.735	2888	**302**	**8**	36	161	**657**	243	65	127
Kevin Duckworth	.496	0-0	.770	2223	280	5	32	177	576	66	32	31
Caldwell Jones	.494	0-4	.736	1778	251	0	14	82	408	81	**99**	29
Kiki Vandeweghe	.523	**.379**	**.878**	1038	68	0	41	48	109	71	7	21
Steve Johnson	.530	0-1	.586	1050	151	4	36	122	242	57	32	17
Maurice Lucas	.454	0-3	.736	1191	188	0	18	73	315	94	10	33
Richard Anderson	.426	.320	.753	1350	137	1	22	61	303	112	16	51
Michael Holton	.473	.200	.829	1279	154	0	18	86	149	211	10	41

OVERALL RANKINGS *

PLAYER	G	GS	PPG	PR	RANK	SC	SH	RB	AS	BL	ST
Clyde Drexler	81	80	**26.98**	27.94	5	6	40	82	40	76	10
Terry Porter	**82**	**82**	14.90	22.87	16	57	17	104	5	129	26
Jerome Kersey	79	75	19.19	21.87	19	28	77	52	82	53	39
Kevin Duckworth	78	50	15.78	15.42	73	48	67	26	155	90	156
Caldwell Jones	79	77	4.23	8.94	144	158	94	50	132	14	146
Kiki Vandeweghe	37	7	20.19	16.51	DNQ						
Steve Johnson	43	33	15.40	12.91	DNQ						
Maurice Lucas	73	0	6.10	7.95	DNQ						
Richard Anderson	74	3	6.05	7.86	DNQ						
Michael Holton	**82**	2	5.32	6.70	DNQ						

POSITION RANKINGS *

PLAYER	POSITION	RANK	SC	SH	RB	AS	BL	ST
Clyde Drexler	Off Guard (OG)	2	2	10	3	8	7	5
Terry Porter	Point Guard (PG)	3	7	3	6	5	13	14
Jerome Kersey	Small Forward (SF)	4	10	5	5	16	11	6
Kevin Duckworth	Center (C)	13	6	12	14	23	25	25
Caldwell Jones	Power Forward (PF)	32	34	21	25	20	5	33
Kiki Vandeweghe	Small Forward (SF)	DNQ						
Steve Johnson	Center (C)	DNQ						
Maurice Lucas	Power Forward (PF)	DNQ						
Richard Anderson	Small Forward (SF)	DNQ						
Michael Holton	Point Guard (PG)	DNQ						

*For further definition of each category and column heading see pages 38 & 39.

184 BASKETBALL HEAVEN 1989

Portland Trail Blazers ....Team Info

WEEKLY POWER RATING

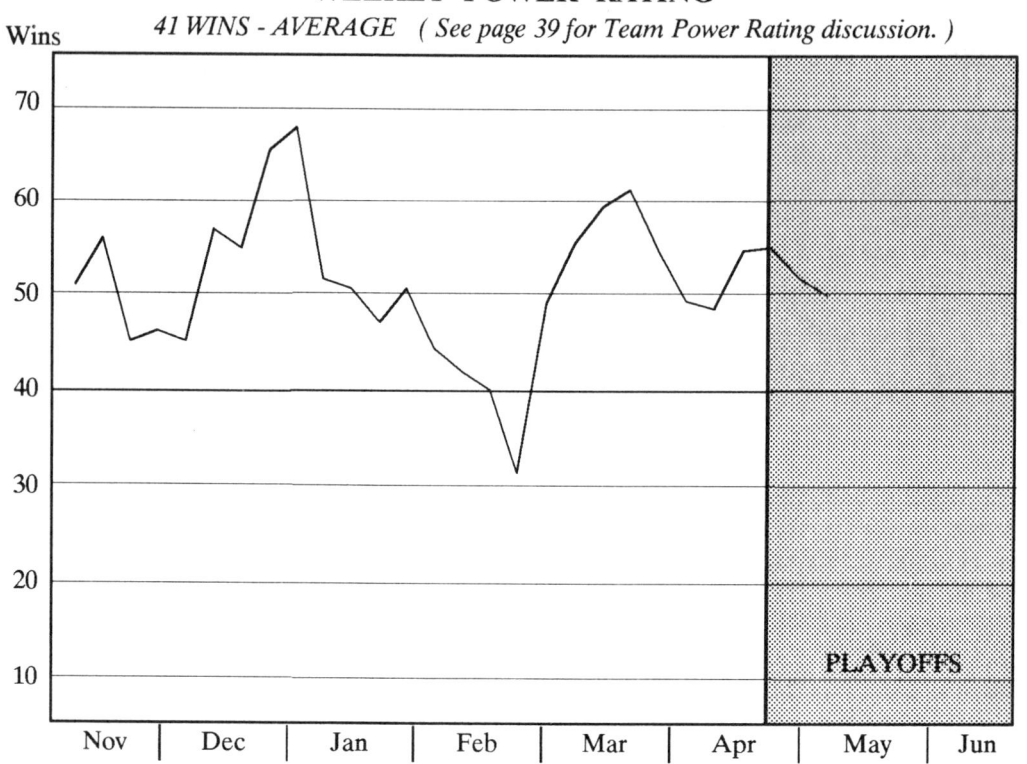

41 WINS - AVERAGE   (See page 39 for Team Power Rating discussion.)

Miscellaneous Categories	Data	Rank
Attendance	519K	10
Key-Man Games Missed	136	18
Season Record	53-29	5
- Home	33-8	5
- Road	20-21	3
Eastern Conference	14-8	5
Western Conference	39-21	5
Overtime Record	1-1	10
Record 5 Pts. or Less	13-8	4
Record 10 Pts. or More	30-15	6
Games Won By Bench	5	9
Games Won By Starters	13	2
Winning Streak	9	5
Losing Streak	5	10
Home Winning Streak	11	6
Road Winning Streak	3	9
Home Losing Streak	2	2
Road Losing Streak	4	1

Performance Categories	Data	Rank
Offensive Scoring (per game)	116.1	2
Defensive Scoring (per game)	111.5	18
Scoring Margin (per game)	4.6	4
Defensive FG%	.476	9
Offensive 2-point%	.501	4
Offensive 3-point%	.308	13
Offensive Free Throw %	.770	11
Offensive Rebs (Off REB/Opp Def REB)		6
Defensive Rebs (Def REB/Opp Off REB)		5
Offensive Assists (AST/FGMade)		7
Offensive Blocks (BLK/Opp FGAttempted)		22
Offensive Steals (STL/Game)		9
Turnover Margin (Off T.O. - Def T.O.)		5
Finesse (BLK + STL) / PF		19
Rebounding Record	44-36-2	8
Assists Record	45-35-2	7
Field Goal Pct. Record	46-36-0	7
Free Throw Pct. Record	40-41-1	12

Portland Trail Blazers .... Miscellaneous

ADMINISTRATIVE INFORMATION

Team Offices: Suite 950
Lloyd Building
700 N.E. Multnomah Street
Portland, Oregon 97232
Telephone: (503) 234-9291
Head Coach: Mike Schuler
Home Arena: Memorial Coliseum
Capacity: 12,666

1988-89 ROSTER*

J#	VETERANS	COLLEGE	POS	R#	D#	HT	WT	Port	NBA
10	Richard Anderson	U.C. Santa Barbara	F	2	32	6-10	240	1	4
31	Sam Bowie	Kentucky	C	1	2	7-1	240	4	4
22	Clyde Drexler	Houston	G-F	1	13	6-7	215	5	5
00	Kevin Duckworth	Eastern Illinois	C	2	33	7-0	280	2	2
33	Steve Johnson	Oregon State	C-F	1	7	6-10	235	2	7
27	Caldwell Jones	Albany State	C	2	32	6-11	225	3	15
8	Charles A. Jones	Louisville	F	2	36	6-8	232	1	2
25	Jerome Kersey	Longwood	F	2	46	6-7	222	4	4
34	Ronnie Murphy	Jacksonville	G-F	1	17	6-5	225	1	1
30	Terry Porter	Wisc. St. Point	G	1	24	6-3	195	3	3
12	Jerry Sichting	Purdue	G	4	82	6-1	180	1	8
55	Kiki Vandeweghe	UCLA	F	1	11	6-8	220	4	8

ROOKIES	COLLEGE	POS	R#	D#	HT
Mark Bryant	Seton Hall	F	1	21	6-9
Rolando Ferreira	Houston	C	2	26	7-1
Anthony Mason	Tennessee State	F	3	53	6-7
Craig Neal	Georgia Tech	G	3	71	6-5

* For further definition of category and column headings, see pages 38 & 39.

Portland Trail Blazers .... Overview

Talk about bad luck! This club has had it the last two years - especially at the beginning of the season. Just as in 1986-87, last season's team lost five consecutive games in addition to losing one of their starters to injury. And just like the prior year, that player (in this case Kiki Vandeweghe) wouldn't start another game the rest of the season. If that were the only problem, it wouldn't have been so bad. But it wasn't. Immediately before the season began, Sam Bowie went down once again with a broken leg, casting doubt on the team's front line.

Though there were a lot of heroes, head coach Mike Schuler deserves much of the credit for minimizing the damage. The 1986-87 Coach-of-the-Year substituted brilliantly to overcome the loss of Bowie and the injuries to Vandeweghe (45 games missed) and All-Star Steve Johnson (39 games missed). The result was that the Blazers gained 4 wins from 1987 to 1988 (49 and 53). What is significant about this is that only five coaches have ever won more games the year following their C.O.Y. honors than in the year they won the award.

	Wins	C.O.Y.
Mike Fratello	+7	1986
Dick Motta	+6	1971
Hubie Brown	+5	1978
Mike Schuler	**+4**	**1987**
Bill Fitch	+1	1980

As a result of his back-to-back performances, Schuler became only the 8th NBA coach to win 100+ games in his first two years. Interestingly, four of the top six did it with the Lakers.

	Wins	Two Years	
Bill Sharman	129	72/73	Lakers
Bill Russell	114	67/68	Celtics
Pat Riley	108	82/83	Lakers
Bill van BredaKolff	107	68/69	Lakers
K.C. Jones	107	74/75	Bullets
Paul Westhead	104	80/81	Lakers
Mike Schuler	**103**	**87/88**	**Blazers**
Billy Cunningham	100	78/79	76ers

Portland was 1987-88's ultimate team for low draft picks, castoffs, and elder statesmen. Of the top-20, the three lowest drafted players who ranked high for production were Terry Porter (22.87, drafted #24), Jerome Kersey (21.87, drafted #46), and Kevin Duckworth (20.23 as a starter, drafted #33). It's no coincidence that these three "surprises" were from schools like Wisconsin Stevens-Point, Longwood College, and Eastern Illinois. Portland management deserves tremendous credit for realizing the potential of these little-known players. Even Steve Johnson, who had been with three other clubs in 5 years, has become an All-Star in just 2 years in Portland. Clyde Drexler was drafted only 14th - amazingly low for such a magnificent player. How would you like to have Russell Cross or Ennis Whatley instead? Both were picked ahead of Clyde the Glide. These brilliant choices more than make up for the mistakes of the Natt, Cooper, Lever for Vandeweghe trade (1984) and the drafting of Sam Bowie in front of Michael Jordan (1984). Add to this group ABA veteran Caldwell Jones, (the only other present players in the NBA to also play in the ABA are Moses Malone and Artis Gilmore) and you have a seemingly unlikely group to be winning 53+ games in 1987-88.

Clyde Drexler ended up #5 in Production Rating at 27.94, 2nd team All-League, and was only one of two players (Jordan was the other) who ranked in the top-10 at his position in each of the six performance categories. Portland can be very thankful that they didn't make the 1987 trade with Houston for Ralph Sampson! The Blazers were 28-3 when Clyde scored 29+ points and only 26-25 when he didn't. (See Golden State and Houston overviews to see Ralph's opposite influence on winning.) Probably the biggest reason for Drexler's improvement was his outside shot. Though still flatter than Dave Schlueter's footprint, Clyde's shot was successful 50.6% of the time - his best yet.

Portland Trail Blazers .... Overview

Speaking of improvement, none was greater than that of Kevin Duckworth. How much is a Duck worth? Well, in terms of Most-Improved-Player voting, it's worth 33 votes. John Stockton was next with 15, Mark Price 11, Michael Adams 7, and teammate Jerome Kersey 5. Kevin had a season Production Rating of 15.42, which makes him the 13th best center. However, as a starter his production was 20.23 and would have ranked him #6 at his position. When he failed to make double figures, the club was only 11-11. When he hit 10+ ppg, they blazed their way to a 41-15 record.

Jerome Kersey was another thrilling surprise last year. Kersey's best rank in his first 3 years was #72. Last season he rocketed his way up to #19 overall. Kersey fit into an interesting group of players who ranked worse in all six performance categories at his position than he did in Production Rating at his position. What this means is that these players were multi-talented, versatile, and displayed few weaknesses. The other guys who fit that mold were Sam Perkins, Mark Jackson, and Maurice Cheeks.

All-Stars Steve Johnson and Kiki Vandeweghe may end up being the NBA's version of Wally Pipp. Both were injured last season. They returned to the team only to find their replacements (Kersey and Duckworth) playing outstanding basketball. Consequently, neither could regain their starting positions. What's more, neither ever will - at least not on this team. Unless there are even more injuries, Kiki and Stevie will have to help out on the bench. There is a chance that SJ will move into the starting power forward spot, and KV could be one of the best off-guards in the NBA. The only problem with both is that the team plays better with Caldwell Jones at PF, and then there's Clyde Drexler at the 2 guard spot. Besides, it's always been argued that Vandweghe is not a player that inspires his team to win. The fact that Portland was only 9-9 when he scored 20+ points, but 12-4 when he scored less is evidence of this.

Terry Porter has become one of the NBA's brightest young stars. He ranked #3 at the point behind Magic and Stockton. His 831 assists were well ahead of his previous season's 715. The improvement came as a result of several factors, but having Kersey and Drexler as two of the five best "closers" on the break (Along with Jordan, Worthy, and Karl Malone.) didn't hurt.

If Sam Bowie ever gets healthy (which is very, very doubtful) and Ronnie Murphy gets his act together (which is very questionable) and Jerry Sichting averages 63% from the field as he did his last 11 games (which is unlikely), this team will have magnificent depth. Maurice Lucas has retired, but Vandeweghe, Johnson, and rookies Mark Bryant and Rolando Ferreira may make this the best bench in the league.

Let's face it. Schuler had a cast of characters that would have put a broadway show to shame. With athletes like Drexler, Porter, Kersey, and Duckworth, this team can slam and jam with the best of them. Every time these guys took to the stage, 12,666 watched. In fact, that same number have jammed the theater for 480 consecutive 4-act plays - an NBA record. The Blazers rarely disappointed their fans, as they won 27 of 28 when they went into the final act with the lead. When you go to Memorial Coliseum, settle in. Get ready for ballet, orchestrated harmony, and superb direction. Turn the lights down, raise the curtains, cause it's showtime!

Prediction - best case: 60-22

This would be the best record in Blazer history. Nevertheless, it is very reachable, but only if everything goes right. It requires help from the rookies as well as the acceptance of KV and SJ to their relegation to the bench. Should they unseat LA, well... ...Rip city!

Prediction - worst case: 50-32

I don't see how this team can lose more than 32 games. With Golden State, the L.A. Clippers, Sacramento, Phoenix, and Miami in the conference, it should be feeding time more often than not for Portland.

Sacramento Kings ....History

The Sacramento Kings began in the NBL (National Basketball League) in 1945-46 as the Rochester Royals, making them one of six clubs 42+ years old. The franchise has gradually moved West over the years. After 12 seasons in Rochester, the club moved to Cincinnati. Still known as the Royals, the team spent the next 15 years in Ohio. In 1972, the Royals moved to Kansas City where they remained for 13 years as the Kings. Three years ago, the Kings continued their move west in search for gold - ending up in Sacramento. By virtue of having four homes at one time or another, the club ties the Hawks for transience.

The move west has been less than favorable for the Kings. In Rochester, the Royals were winners 60% of the time, securing ten playoffs and two championships. In Cincinnati, they won at 47%, with six playoffs and zero championships. In Kansas City, the club managed to win but 46% of their games, with only five playoff appearances. The Sacramento Kings have been to only one post-season party while winning at only 37%.

While at Rochester and Cincinnati, the club had players make either the NBA 1st or 2nd team thirty times. At KC and Sacramento, the same award was garnered only five times. Eighteen times a Royal led the league in a major category (FG%, FT%, Ast, Blk, Stl, Reb), but never has a King won the same honor.

As of 1960, the franchise could boast of more wins than any other club, with over 500 victories. Even the Lakers and Celtics were less successful. On the other hand, since 1968, the Kings have won only eleven playoff games. Of the eighteen NBA clubs in existence since 1968, the Kings' eleven wins are by far the fewest. The Chicago Bulls have won the next fewest (25).

The Royals reached the finals in 1946, 1947, and 1948 - their first three years. In 1946, they captured the NBL title; the next two years however, they lost the final series one game to three. The only other time the franchise has managed to make the finals was in 1951 when the Royals defeated the New York Knicks four games to three (79-75 in game 7) to become World Champions. Since then, the club has reached the conference finals twice. In 1963, they lost to Boston three games to four (131-142 in game 7). In 1981, the Kings lost to Houston one game to four.

Quiz: Who is the only NBA player in history to average a triple-double for an entire season?

ALL TIME KINGS' TEAM

Player	Span	Yrs	CRD
Oscar Robertson	1961-70	10	26,764
Sam Lacey	1971-81	12	17,277
Jerry Lucas	1964-69	7	15,204
Jack Twyman	1956-66	11	14,530
Wayne Embry	1959-66	8	10,556
Nate Archibald	1971-76	6	10,042
Scott Wedman	1975-81	7	9,013
Arnie Risen	1948-55	8	8,334
Bobby Wanzer	1948-57	10	7,231
LaSalle Thompson	1983-87	5	7,062

ALL TIME KINGS' COACH

Les Harrison
19-19 Playoffs
295-181 Reg. Season

6 Years
6 Playoffs
1 Championship

HISTORICAL PROFILE

Category	Data
Kings' coach	Jerry Reynolds
Years coached Sacramento	2
# of franchise years	43
# of coaches	16
# of winning seasons	18
# of playoff years	23
# of runner's up	2
# of championships	2
Regular season win %	48.9
Playoff win %	41.9

Answer:
Oscar Robertson (1962)
30.8 points, 11.4 assists, & 12.5 rebounds

Sacramento Kings ....1987-88 Highlights

Kings 134-106 Warriors   Fri.   November 6, 1988

The victory was one of the most impressive of the year for Sacramento as they opened the season, winning by 28 points over Golden State. The margin ended up being a season's high. The 134 points tied two other games as the club's highest scoring ones. LaSalle Thompson's 20 points were the most he would score all season.

Kings 107-105 Jazz   Sat.   January 2, 1988

Sacramento's victory over Utah was special as the team had to overcome two important elements. Not only did John Stockton of Utah record a career high 19 assists, but the Kings had lost 5 consecutive home games vs the Jazz. Reggie Theus led the team with a season high 36 points, as well as the game winning shot.

Kings 118-115 Hawks   Tue.   February 16, 1988

This game was a major upset. Going into it the Kings were 2-18 on the road, while the Hawks were 18-3 at home. Kenny Smith had one of his best games of the season with 24, but Reggie Theus' 3-pointer at the buzzer won the game. The loss dropped Atlanta out of sole possession of 1st place for the first time in 2 months. Amazingly, the Kings won despite Dominique Wilkins. Wilkins scored 51 points - the second highest total of the season thus far. In fact, Wilkins scored 28 points in the third period alone, which broke the single-quarter club scoring record set 30 years earlier by Cliff Hagan.

Kings 118-101 Mavericks   Thur.   February 4, 1988

The Sacramento Kings pulled a major upset by defeating the division-leading Dallas Mavericks. The 17 point margin was the 3rd largest win by the Kings. At the same time, it represented Dallas' 3rd largest loss. The loss was also the 4th in a row for the Mavs - their longest losing streak in two years.

Kings 116-114 Nuggets   Mon.   March 7, 1988

The significance of the win was that it was the first for new coach Jerry Reynolds. Reynolds replaced Bill Russell just 8 hours prior the game. The Kings played inspired ball to upset Denver which had won 7 of 8 while Sacramento had lost 4 straight at home. Reggie Theus provided the heroics as he hit two foul shots with two seconds left in regulation to tie the game. He then sank three more free throws in the final 8 seconds of overtime. Theus ended with 33 points - his most in two months.

Kings 114-92 Lakers   Sat.   March 26, 1988

By winning, Sacramento broke an unbelievable 27 game losing streak vs LA. The Kings hadn't beat the Lakers in over 5 years. Ironically, the 22 point loss for Los Angeles was their biggest margin of defeat in the regular season. Rookie Kenny Smith was the hero as he scored a career high 30 points while registering an equally impressive 12 assists. Smith had free rein in the backcourt offensively and defensively. Missing the game were Reggie Theus and Derek Smith of Sacramento as well as Magic Johnson and Michael Cooper of L.A.

Kings 115-109 Spurs   Wed.   April 6, 1988

The Kings defeated the Spurs 115-109 due to a great individual performance by Harold Pressley. Pressley, who was starting because of the injuries to Derek Smith and Kenny Smith, scored a career high 29 points and tied a club record by hitting five 3-pointers. It was the 13th straight game that Pressley has hit at least one 3-pointer.

Sacramento Kings . . . . Influence on Winning

TEAM RECORD BY

PLAYER	GAMES	... SCR Leader HOME	ROAD	... REB Leader HOME	ROAD	... AST Leader HOME	ROAD
Otis Thorpe	82	4-10	2-17	12-10	3-18	0-2	1-0
Reggie Theus	73	10-7	1-9	---	---	10-7	1-10
Kenny Smith	61	1-3	1-2	---	---	7-10	3-19
Joe Kleine	82	---	0-1	8-3	1-8	---	0-1
Harold Pressley	80	2-1	0-1	0-1	0-3	0-1	0-3
Derek Smith	35	1-1	0-5	---	---	---	0-1
LaSalle Thompson	69	---	0-1	3-4	0-3	---	----
Mike McGee	48	2-1	0-5	---	---	1-0	---
Ed Pinckney	79	---	0-1	---	0-2	---	---
Terry Tyler	74	---	---	---	0-2	---	0-1

TEAM RECORD BY SCORING *

PLAYER	PLAY	DNP	0-9	10-19	20-29	30-39	40+
Otis Thorpe	24-58	---	0-2	11-23	11-24	2-9	---
Reggie Theus	23-50	1-8	0-2	5-21	13-22	5-5	---
Kenny Smith	17-44	7-14	1-12	10-25	5-7	1-0	---
Joe Kleine	24-58	---	10-34	13-21	1-3	---	---
Paul Pressley	24-56	0-2	14-29	7-24	2-3	1-0	---
Derek Smith	11-24	13-34	5-7	4-12	2-4	0-1	---
LaSalle Thompson	20-49	4-9	14-30	5-19	1-0	---	---
Mike McGee	13-24	11-34	4-10	5-9	3-5	1-0	---
Ed Pinckney	24-55	0-3	16-41	8-12	0-2	---	---
Terry Tyler	21-53	3-5	13-48	8-5	---	---	---

TEAM RECORD BY STARTING POSITION *

PLAYER	GAMES	STARTS	PG	OG	SF	PF	C
Otis Thorpe	82	82	---	---	---	24-58	---
Reggie Theus	73	73	4-7	19-43	---	---	---
Kenny Smith	61	60	17-43	---	---	---	---
Joe Kleine	82	60	---	---	---	---	19-41
Harold Pressley	80	49	---	5-11	12-21	---	---
Derek Smith	35	18	---	0-2	3-13	---	---
LaSalle Thompson	69	9	---	---	---	---	2-7
Mike McGee	37	0	---	---	---	---	---
Ed Pinckney	79	7	---	---	0-7	---	---
Terry Tyler	74	28	---	0-2	9-17	---	---

* For further definition of each category and column heading see pages 38 & 39.

Sacramento Kings .... 1987-88 Statistics

RAW NUMBERS *

PLAYER	2pt%	3pt%	FT%	MIN	PF	DQ	HI	TO	RB	AS	BL	ST
Otis Thorpe	.510	0-6	.755	**3072**	**264**	3	35	228	**837**	266	56	62
Reggie Theus	.479	.271	**.831**	2653	173	0	**36**	234	232	**463**	16	59
Kenny Smith	.487	.308	.819	2170	140	1	30	184	138	434	8	**92**
Joe Kleine	.472	0-0	.814	1999	228	1	23	107	579	93	59	28
Harold Pressley	.476	.327	.792	2029	211	**4**	31	135	369	185	55	84
Derek Smith	.487	.348	.770	899	108	2	30	48	103	89	17	21
LaSalle Thompson	.472	**.400**	.720	1257	217	1	20	109	427	68	**73**	54
Mike McGee	.459	.331	.745	1003	81	0	30	65	128	71	6	52
Ed Pinckney	**.525**	0-2	.747	1177	118	0	24	77	230	66	32	39
Terry Tyler	.457	.143	.641	1185	85	0	18	43	242	56	47	43

OVERALL RANKINGS *

PLAYER	G	GS	PPG	PR	RANK	SC	SH	RB	AS	BL	ST
Otis Thorpe	**82**	**82**	20.78	**23.71**	13	16	56	19	78	72	136
Reggie Theus	73	73	**21.56**	18.44	46	13	86	139	31	120	126
Kenny Smith	61	60	13.79	**15.23**	77	70	7	156	25	144	42
Joe Kleine	**82**	60	9.77	12.88	100	115	95	14	129	38	155
Harold Pressley	80	49	9.69	11.52	114	117	97	78	74	45	48
Derek Smith	35	18	12.66	11.69	DNQ						
LaSalle Thompson	69	9	7.97	11.25	DNQ						
Mike McGee	48	0	11.98	9.04	DNQ						
Ed Pinckney	79	7	6.22	7.24	DNQ						
Terry Tyler	74	28	5.54	6.88	DNQ						

POSITION RANKINGS *

PLAYER	POSITION	RANK	SC	SH	RB	AS	BL	ST
Otis Thorpe	Power Forward (PF)	4	4	13	9	5	23	28
Reggie Theus	Off Guard (OG)	8	5	17	24	4	24	31
Kenny Smith	Point Guard (PG)	17	12	14	30	23	21	22
Joe Kleine	Center (C)	20	21	17	6	15	18	24
Harold Pressley	Off Guard (OG)	20	25	19	2	25	3	14
Derek Smith	Small Forward (SF)	DNQ						
LaSalle Thompson	Power Forward (PF)	DNQ						
Mike McGee	Off Guard (OG)	DNQ						
Ed Pinckney	Small Forward (SF)	DNQ						
Terry Tyler	Small Forward (SF)	DNQ						

*For further definition of each category and column heading see pages 38 & 39.

Sacramento Kings ....Team Info

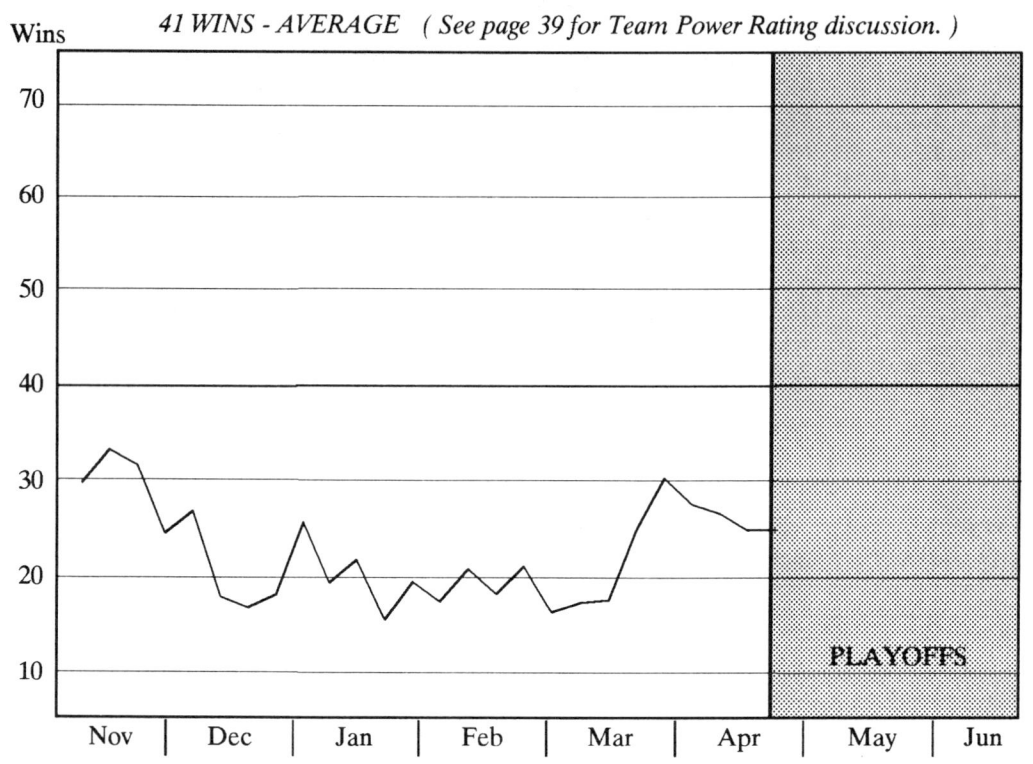

WEEKLY POWER RATING
41 WINS - AVERAGE (See page 39 for Team Power Rating discussion.)

Wins

[Line chart showing weekly power rating from Nov through Jun, with values mostly between 15-30, ending around 25 going into the shaded PLAYOFFS region from May-Jun]

Miscellaneous Categories	Data	Rank	Performance Categories	Data	Rank
Attendance	424K	21	Offensive Scoring (per game)	108.0	12
Key-Man Games Missed	153	20	Defensive Scoring (per game)	113.7	21
Season Record	24-58	20	Scoring Margin (per game)	-5.7	20
- Home	19-22	20	Defensive FG%	.498	20
- Road	5-36	20	Offensive 2-point%	.481	17
Eastern Conference	5-17	20	Offensive 3-point%	.320	10
Western Conference	19-41	21	Offensive Free Throw %	.772	10
Overtime Record	2-2	10	Offensive Rebs (Off REB/Opp Def REB)		10
Record 5 Pts. or Less	10-18	20	Defensive Rebs (Def REB/Opp Off REB)		7
Record 10 Pts. or More	9-29	19	Offensive Assists (AST/FGMade)		10
Games Won By Bench	1	19	Offensive Blocks (BLK/Opp FGAttempted)		9
Games Won By Starters	5	11	Offensive Steals (STL/Game)		23
Winning Streak	2	21	Turnover Margin (Off T.O. - Def T.O.)		23
Losing Streak	8	19	Finesse (BLK + STL) / PF		14
Home Winning Streak	3	20	Rebounding Record	47-32-1	7
Road Winning Streak	1	21	Assists Record	35-43-4	16
Home Losing Streak	4	15	Field Goal Pct. Record	31-51-0	21
Road Losing Streak	13	18	Free Throw Pct. Record	40-42-0	13

Sacramento Kings .... Miscellaneous

ADMINISTRATIVE INFORMATION

Team Offices: One Sports Parkway
Sacramento, California
95834

Telephone: (916) 648-0000
Head Coach: Jerry Reynolds
Home Arena: Arco Arena
Capacity: 16,400

1988-89 ROSTER*

J#	VETERANS	COLLEGE	POS	R#	D#	HT	WT	Sacr	NBA
2	Michael Jackson	Georgetown	G	2	47	6-2	185	1	1
35	Joe Kleine	Arkansas	C-F	1	6	6-11	240	3	3
7	Mike McGee	Michigan	G	1	19	6-5	207	1	7
44	Jawann Oldham	Seattle	C	2	41	7-1	245	1	8
54	Ed Pinckney	Villanova	F	1	10	6-9	215	1	3
21	Harold Pressley	Villanova	F	1	17	6-7	210	2	2
18	Derek Smith	Louisville	G	2	35	6-7	225	2	6
30	Kenny Smith	North Carolina	G	1	6	6-3	170	1	1
41	LaSalle Thompson	Texas	C	1	5	6-10	250	6	6
33	Otis Thorpe	Providence	F	1	9	6-10	235	4	4
40	Terry Tyler	Detroit	F	2	23	6-7	220	3	10
10	Randy Wittman	Indiana	G	1	22	6-6	210	0	5

	ROOKIES	COLLEGE	POS	R#	D#	HT
	Ricky Berry	San Jose State	G	1	18	6-8
	Vinny Del Negro	N.C. State	G	2	29	6-5

* For further definition of category and column headings, see pages 38 & 39.

Sacramento Kings .... Overview

When Bill Russell took the Sacramento head coaching position, he was heard to prophesy "If you want a team to make the playoffs, I'm not your guy..." that part was right. The trouble is, he took the prediction a little farther. "...but, if you want an NBA championship, I am." At the risk of estranging all the Bill Russell lovers out there, I say, "Give me a break!" I, like everyone, respect Bill Russell the player. There may never be another like him. But as a coach... forget it. As a player he was known for analyzing the game in detail and always trying to figure a way to gain an edge. As a coach, at least with the Kings, he was known for exactly the opposite traits. Was he bored or burned out? Was it just the money? I think we'll eventually find out.

The Kings tied for the best record in the Midwest Division during preseason and were anxious to turn 1987-88 into a success. It didn't happen. To be blunt, one would have to look back on the season as a failed experiment. I sure don't blame Gregg Luckenbill for trying something different, but that doesn't change the facts. The Russell-led Kings limped to a 17-41 record before the change was made. Replacing Russell was Jerry Reynolds. Sacramento was 7-17 under Reynolds. Though Russell's winning percentage was .293 and Reynolds .292, this near-identity is misleading. The Kings had 153 key-man games missed (20th worst). Under Russell they had 69 in 58 games or 1.19 KMGM/game. Reynolds had the misfortune of 84 key-man games missed in only 24 games, or 3.50 KMGM/game. During one two week period, six players, including Theus, K. Smith, Thompson, McGee, D. Smith, and Oldham, all went out with injuries. That's more snap, crackle and pop than a California brush fire. With no one to douse the flames, Reynolds was at a major disadvantage. Assuming 3.5 KMGM/game over an 82 game season, it would be 287 total missed games. That would have put the Kings in last for every year I've kept this stat!

When Russell was let go as coach, the termination was disguised as a "move-up". (He was named vice president and allowed to announce Reynolds as his successor.) That's fine, but no one bought it. As Roy Firestone commented "The vice president tag is just a fancy name for chief scout."

As a player, Russell was known for excelling defensively. It seems reasonable, then, that he should have at least made his teams successful in defensive scoring and defensive FG%. I decided to see how his four Seattle teams and one Sacramento team fared in these two categories as compared to their overall winning percentage.

		Record Rank	Def SCR Rank	Def FG% Rank
1974	Seattle	10	13	9
1975	Seattle	7	13	12
1976	Seattle	7	16	14
1977	Seattle	14	8	9
1988	**Sacramento**	**20**	**21**	**21**

As you can see, his teams were worse in these defensive categories than they were as a whole. What does that mean? Well, logically, it should at least imply that he may not be able to teach that which he did well as a player.

Jerry Reynolds has the distinction of being the second best known person from French Lick, Indiana (Larry Bird is first), the second best known person with that name in the NBA (Jerry Reynolds of Milwaukee is first) and the second best known leader in a Midwest Division town with the initials J.R. (Ewing of Dallas is first). He may be #2 in the central part of the United States, but he's #1 in Sacramento. His bow ties, unassuming style, and friendly nature have made him very popular with the fans and players. The Kings need to have a stable coaching situation. For their sake I hope Reynolds works out.

Reggie Theus was, of course, traded to Atlanta for Randy Wittman and the Hawks' #1 pick, which turned out to be Ricky Berry of San Jose State. Only time will tell which team the trade was better

Sacramento Kings .... Overview

for. Other than his rookie season (1979) and 1984, Reggie has been pretty consistent. Despite this, he's entering his 11th season and it's never unreasonable to question how much longer someone in this situation will be able to play. Wittman was expendable to Atlanta, and will probably be of limited value to Sacramento. If he can consistently pop the perimeter shot (something he was unable to do last season), he could help the club. Berry averaged 24.2 ppg his senior year. He's an excellent shooter. Between Wittman and Berry, the Kings should be able to field a respectable off-guard. Not a Reggie Theus, at least not in 1989, but what about 1990 and beyond? If there is hope for this club, it will come by building the team with youth.

Kenny Smith was a nice surprise last year, and subsequently made the All-Rookie team. There were two problems, however. First, it was tough for him to maintain consistency with his injuries. Kenny missed 11 games early in the season as well as the last 10. The other concern was that Reggie Theus has been a point guard himself. He regularly wanted control, and ranked #4 in assists among off-guards. It should be a little more cut and dried next season for Smith.

Otis Thorpe was this team's superstar last season. His Production Rating of 23.71 placed him #4 among power forwards. Since I hold that the PF position is the least critical of the five (see discussion on page 232), my recommendation would be to trade him for center and small forward help. Some will question my sanity. After all, Otis is young, aggressive, consistent, and he always brings his lunch pail. He's *the* prototype power forward. Still, he can only help the team so much from that position. After all, Sacramento had the 20th best record despite ranking a team-best 4th in total rebounds. If Thorpe's production was so critical, then why is it true that the team's record was 12-30 when he scored 21 points or less and a nearly identical 12-28 when he scored 22 points or more?

Derek Smith still may become an important member of the team. The problem is his health. In 6 NBA seasons he's only played in 266 games, or 44 per year. 1988 was the same story (35 games). As luck would have it, he averaged 26 points per game in the five game period before his last injury. Just when you thought it was safe to go into the water...

Best of the rest: With Kenny Smith out, Harold Pressley started the last 15 games and looked pretty good. He not only averaged 17.3 ppg, but 1+ 3-pointer per game as well... Joe Kleine gave it 100% every night and ranked #6 at rebounding among centers... Michael Jackson was the only regular in the NBA with more assists than points (179 to 157). That's unselfish!

Sacramento will be permanently moving into the Pacific Division in 1988. That shift, plus a new arena (ARCO II), will give the club something to look forward to. For three seasons the Kings have played before sellout crowds. It will be interesting to see if they can fill up 16,400 seats as easily as 10,333. Three existing teams and two expansion clubs will begin in new arenas next year. That's one more than have moved to new homes since 1979. Interestingly, these four all won more games at home the year before the move than the year after.

		Before	-After	= Diff.
1979	Jazz	+18	+10	+8
1985	**Kings**	**+15**	**+13**	**+2**
1981	Nets	+8	+6	+2
1984	Clippers	+10	+9	+1

Prediction - best case: 29-53

If Derek Smith comes on strong and remains healthy, that will help enormously. If Ricky Berry and Kenny Smith progress, as expected, then 29 wins is probable.

Prediction - worst case: 20-62

So many things are unknown about the Kings. So many injuries to overcome, Theus traded, coaching change, etc. If more than a couple of these question marks turn out to have bad answers, there won't be a happy ending to the 1989 story.

San Antonio Spurs .... History

The San Antonio Spurs were originally known as the Dallas Chaparrals in 1968, their first year in the ABA. After 6 years, the club changed their name for one season to the Texas Chaparrals. The club moved to San Antonio in 1973 and have, for 16 years, had the distinction of being the ABA/NBA's southernmost franchise.

The Spurs were relatively successful in the ABA, and even more so in the NBA. By virtue of having gone to the playoffs 18 of 21 years, the club has a higher ratio (86%) of post-season play than twenty of the other twenty-two clubs. Only Los Angeles (93%) and Philadelphia (88%) have been playoff bound more consistently.

Though the team has had excellent regular season success, they have not been a good playoff club. Of the 18 seasons in which the Spurs have advanced, only once (1983, 6-5) did they win more games than they lost. Consequently, their playoff record is an extremely poor 42-72 (37%). Only Chicago (32%) has a lower percentage in the playoffs. A perfect example of the dichotomy between the regular season success and post-season failure is an eight-year period from 1974-81. During this span the Spurs won 383 games, second only to Boston (398). Even so, they lost in the first round every year but one.

These post-season failures might help explain why San Antonio has the third highest ratio of coaching changes per year of all twenty-three clubs. Only the Los Angeles Clippers and Cleveland Cavaliers have a higher ratio.

Seven Spurs have merited a major statistical category in the NBA. George Gervin has won four scoring titles (1978, 79, 80, and 82). Artis Gilmore was the FG% king in 1983 and 1984, while Steve Johnson occupied the same category in 1986. Alvin Robertson was the leader in steals in 1986 and 1987; Johnny Moore was the assist leader in 1982; Mike Dunleavy was the 3-point king in 1983; and George Johnson led in blocks in both 1981 and 1982. The 11 titles won by these players in the 80's, trails only Utah.

Odds and ends: In the NBA, San Antonio is 27-7 vs their former ABA chums - the Nets... The Spurs hold the NBA FG% record for a single game (.707) versus Dallas in 1983... San Antonio played in the second highest scoring game ever - a 171-166 victory over the Milwaukee Bucks.

Quiz: The Texas Chapparrals existed only 1 year (1970-71). They played "home" games in Dallas, Ft. Worth, and what other Texas town?

ALL TIME SPURS' TEAM

Player	Span	Yrs	CRD
George Gervin	1974-85	12	20,394
Larry Kenon	1976-80	5	9,271
James Silas	1973-81	9	8,853
Artis Gilmore	1983-87	5	8,250
Johnny Moore	1981-87	8	7,755
Mike Mitchell	1982-88	7	7,574
Mark Olberding	1976-82	7	7,177
Rich Jones	1970-75	6	7,031
Billy Paultz	1976-83	4	6,431
Alvin Robertson	1985-88	4	6,205

ALL TIME SPURS' COACH

Stan Albeck 3 Years
13-14 Playoffs 3 Playoffs
153-93 Reg. Season 0 Championships

HISTORICAL PROFILE

Category	Data
Spurs' coach	Larry Brown
Years coached San Antonio	0
# of franchise years	21
# of coaches	12
# of winning seasons	11
# of playoff years	18
# of runner's up	0
# of championships	0
Regular season win %	51.4
Playoff win %	37.5

Answer: Lubbock

San Antonio Spurs ....1987-88 Highlights

Spurs 140-108 Kings   Wed.   December 30, 1987

The Spurs 61% shooting and 42 assists defeated the Kings by 32 points. The winning margin was easily the largest of the year. Even more impressive was the fact that the win was the 10th straight at home for the Spurs and pushed their overall record over .500, to 13-12.

Spurs 110-104 Bucks   Tue.   January 19, 1988

The Bucks' record dropped to 19-15 while the Spurs record improved to 15-19. Surprisingly, the quote "This is one of the best games we've played all year" was from Del Harris (Milwaukee) while the quote "This might have been the worst game played this season." was from Bob Weiss (San Antonio).

Spurs 123-121 76ers   Wed.   February 24, 1988

The Spurs broke a season high 5 game home losing streak by defeating the Philadelphia 76ers. The loss for Philly was the 16th consecutive on the road - a team record. San Antonio had five players score between 18-23 points, including 2-20+ reserves (the 5th time in the NBA this happened during 1987/88). Every point was needed to overcome Charles Barkley's 37 points and 21 rebounds.

Spurs 111-107 Rockets   Fri.   February 26, 1988

The 16 point 3rd quarter margin equaled San Antonio's biggest winning margin in any quarter last year while it was Houston's worst quarter #3 of the season. It's ironic because Houston's best quarter had been quarter 3. Their Q3 record was 31-16-4 coming into the game. Speaking of irony, the Spurs' top two players in the game were Walter Berry and Greg Anderson. Berry had 30 points, while Anderson had 19 points and 12 rebounds. What is interesting is that both players played college ball in Houston. Berry played at San Jacinto Juco while Anderson played with Akeem Olajuwon at the University of Houston.

Spurs 107-106 Pistons   Fri.   March 25, 1988

The Spurs overcame Isiah Thomas' 34 points - his second highest total of the season. The heroes for San Antonio were Alvin Robertson who registerd his first triple-double of the year and tied his season high in assists while fellow guard, Jon Sundvold, came off the bench to tie his career high of 25 points. By winning, San Antonio prevented Detroit from tying the Boston Celtics for the best record in the Eastern Conference. In 41 years, Detroit has never had the best record in the conference after the All-Star break!

Spurs 127-119 Rockets   Tue.   April 12, 1988

The Spurs started the 4th quarter with an 18-2 spurt on their way to a victory over Houston. Frank Brickowski achieved his second consecutive career high in the game with 34 points. Brickowski had scored 33 points just a few nights earlier against Denver. Ironically, it was Brickowski who ignited the 18-2 run in quarter 4. With one second left at the end of quarter 3, he hit a 35 foot bank shot to get it started. It was his first career 3-pointer.

Spurs 117-116 Rockets   Thur.   April 21, 1988

The San Antonio Spurs scored a last second field goal to upset Houston. The interesting thing about the final shot was that it was the result of an Olajuwon block. With 3 seconds left Olajuwon rejected Ricky Wilson's shot into the hands of Mitchell who immediately hit a 15 footer for the win. Ironically, Akeem's block was his 10th of the game, giving him an odd triple-double with points, rebounds and blocks - the only such triple-double last season.

San Antonio Spurs . . . . Influence on Winning

TEAM RECORD BY ... SCR Leader ... REB Leader ... AST Leader

PLAYER	GAMES	HOME	ROAD	HOME	ROAD	HOME	ROAD
Alvin Robertson	82	5-6	5-9	3-4	0-3	11-8	5-11
Frank Brickowski	70	3-3	1-2	9-4	3-5	---	0-2
Johnny Dawkins	65	4-1	2-4	---	0-1	13-8	3-11
Walter Berry	73	5-5	0-3	1-5	2-6	---	---
Greg Anderson	82	1-1	0-3	9-3	4-10	---	0-1
Mike Mitchell	68	2-4	0-5	---	0-1	---	---
David Greenwood	45	---	0-1	5-1	1-3	1-0	---
Peter Gudmundson	69	---	0-2	1-1	1-9	---	0-1
Jon Sundvold	52	2-0	0-1	---	---	2-2	1-3
Kurt Nimphius	72	1-0	0-1	---	---	---	---

TEAM RECORD BY SCORING *

PLAYER	PLAY	DNP	0-9	10-19	20-29	30-39	40+
Alvin Robertson	31-51	---	0-6	13-17	15-24	3-3	0-1
Frank Brickowski	28-42	3-9	1-11	16-21	10-9	1-1	---
Johnny Dawkins	25-40	6-11	5-8	11-20	8-12	1-0	---
Walter Berry	28-45	3-6	2-7	12-23	12-13	2-2	---
Greg Anderson	31-51	---	10-21	16-26	5-3	0-1	---
Mike Mitchell	26-42	5-9	12-13	10-17	3-11	1-1	---
David Greenwood	20-25	11-26	11-15	9-9	0-1	---	---
Peter Gudmundson	23-46	8-5	20-36	3-9	0-1	---	---
Jon Sundvold	18-34	13-17	12-23	3-8	3-3	---	---
Kurt Nimphius	27-45	4-6	21-39	5-6	1-0	---	---

TEAM RECORD BY STARTING POSITION *

PLAYER	GAMES	STARTS	PG	OG	SF	PF	C
Alvin Robertson	82	82	---	31-51	---	---	---
Frank Brickowski	70	68	---	---	1-1	8-23	17-18
Johnny Dawkins	65	61	23-38	---	---	---	---
Walter Berry	73	56	---	---	22-34	---	---
Greg Anderson	82	45	---	---	---	5-9	11-20
Mike Mitchell	68	20	---	---	7-13	---	---
David Greenwood	45	40	---	---	1-2	18-19	---
Peter Gudmundsson	69	9	---	---	---	---	0-9
John Sundvold	52	12	5-7	---	---	---	---
Kurt Nimphius	72	7	---	---	---	---	3-4

* For further definition of each category and column heading see pages 38 & 39.

San Antonio Spurs .... 1987-88 Statistics

RAW NUMBERS *

PLAYER	2pt%	3pt%	FT%	MIN	PF	DQ	HI	TO	RB	AS	BL	ST
Alvin Robertson	.478	.284	.748	**2978**	300	4	40	251	498	**557**	69	243
Frank Brickowski	.530	.200	.768	2227	275	11	34	207	483	266	36	74
Johnny Dawkins	.499	.311	**.896**	2179	95	0	30	154	204	480	2	88
Walter Berry	**.563**	0-0	.600	1922	207	2	31	162	395	110	63	55
Greg Anderson	.503	.200	.604	1984	228	1	31	143	**513**	79	**122**	54
Mike Mitchell	.486	.250	.825	1501	101	0	36	52	198	68	13	31
David Greenwood	.463	0-2	.748	1236	134	2	23	74	300	97	22	33
Peter Gudmundsson	.498	0-1	.807	1017	197	5	21	103	323	86	61	18
Jon Sundvold	.476	**.406**	**.896**	1024	54	0	25	57	48	183	2	27
Kurt Nimphius	.500	0-1	.723	919	141	2	25	49	153	53	56	22

OVERALL RANKINGS *

PLAYER	G	GS	PPG	PR	RANK	SC	SH	RB	AS	BL	ST
Alvin Robertson	**82**	82	19.63	**22.94**	15	25	116	86	28	52	2
Frank Brickowski	70	68	15.99	**18.71**	43	47	33	60	52	79	71
Johnny Dawkins	65	61	15.80	**18.37**	47	49	39	132	16	157	52
Walter Berry	73	56	17.42	**16.23**	66	39	34	65	111	33	98
Greg Anderson	**82**	45	11.67	**13.11**	97	93	132	27	144	13	100
Mike Mitchell	68	20	13.51	**10.84**	121	76	78	102	134	110	133
David Greenwood	45	40	8.56	**12.40**	DNQ						
Peter Gudmundsson	69	9	5.72	**8.86**	DNQ						
Jon Sundvold	52	12	8.10	**8.00**	DNQ						
Kurt Nimphius	72	7	4.39	**5.54**	DNQ						

POSITION RANKINGS *

PLAYER	POSITION	RANK	SC	SH	RB	AS	BL	ST
Alvin Robertson	Off Guard (OG)	4	8	24	4	3	4	1
Frank Brickowski	Power Forward (PF)	10	9	6	29	1	26	6
Johnny Dawkins	Point Guard (PG)	11	5	10	17	16	30	25
Walter Berry	Small Forward (SF)	16	14	6	7	26	4	19
Greg Anderson	Center (C)	19	17	22	15	19	8	5
Mike Mitchell	Small Forward (SF)	24	19	16	29	31	26	29
David Greenwood	Power Forward (PF)	DNQ						
Peter Gudmundsson	Center (C)	DNQ						
Jon Sundvold	Point Guard (PG)	DNQ						
Kurt Nimphius	Power Forward (PF)	DNQ						

*For further definition of each category and column heading see pages 38 & 39.

200 BASKETBALL HEAVEN 1989

San Antonio Spurs ....Team Info

WEEKLY POWER RATING

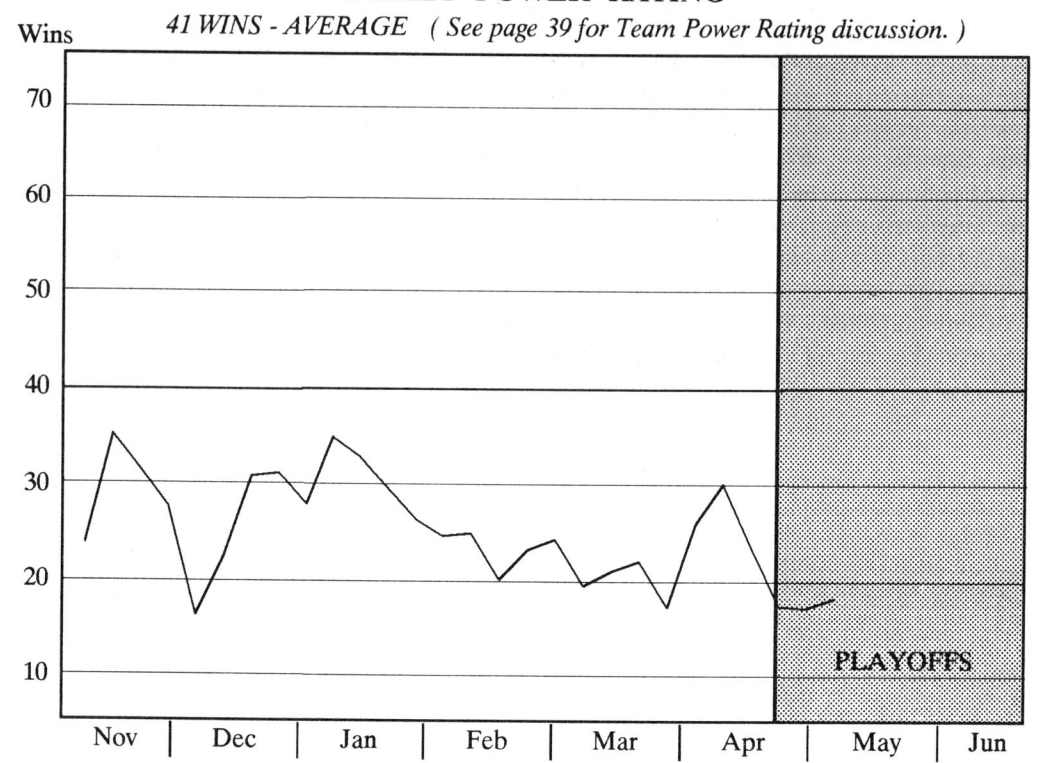

41 WINS - AVERAGE (See page 39 for Team Power Rating discussion.)

Wins

[Line graph showing weekly power rating from Nov through Jun, with values fluctuating between approximately 16 and 35 wins. Shaded PLAYOFFS region covers May-Jun.]

Miscellaneous Categories	Data	Rank	Performance Categories	Data	Rank
Attendance	347K	23	Offensive Scoring (per game)	113.6	3
Key-Man Games Missed	132	17	Defensive Scoring (per game)	118.5	23
Season Record	31-51	18	Scoring Margin (per game)	-4.9	19
- Home	23-18	18	Defensive FG%	.502	23
- Road	8-33	18	Offensive 2-point%	.500	5
Eastern Conference	6-16	19	Offensive 3-point%	.323	8
Western Conference	25-35	18	Offensive Free Throw %	.733	21
Overtime Record	3-2	6	Offensive Rebs ..... (Off REB/Opp Def REB)		13
Record 5 Pts. or Less	16-10	5	Defensive Rebs .... (Def REB/Opp Off REB)		23
Record 10 Pts. or More	9-30	20	Offensive Assists .... (AST/FGMade)		6
Games Won By Bench	0	22	Offensive Blocks .. (BLK/Opp FGAttempted)		12
Games Won By Starters	5	11	Offensive Steals .... (STL/Game)		6
Winning Streak	4	14	Turnover Margin ....(Off T.O. - Def T.O.)		9
Losing Streak	7	18	Finesse .... (BLK + STL) / PF		11
Home Winning Streak	10	8	Rebounding Record	25-54-3	21
Road Winning Streak	2	14	Assists Record	34-42-6	17
Home Losing Streak	5	20	Field Goal Pct. Record	34-48-0	17
Road Losing Streak	11	16	Free Throw Pct. Record	29-53-0	20

San Antonio Spurs .... Miscellaneous

ADMINISTRATIVE INFORMATION

Team Offices: 600 East Market Street
Suite 102
San Antonio, Texas
78205
Telephone: (512) 224-4611
Head Coach: Larry Brown
Home Arena: HemisFair Arena
Capacity: 15,786

1988-89 ROSTER*

J#	VETERANS	COLLEGE	POS	R#	D#	HT	WT	S.A.	NBA
33	Greg Anderson	Houston	C-F	1	23	6-10	2309	1	1
43	Frank Brickowski	Penn State	F	3	57	6-10	240	2	4
	Dallas Comegys	DePaul	F	1	21	6-9	205	0	1
24	Johnny Dawkins	Duke	G	1	10	6-2	165	2	2
10	David Greenwood	UCLA	F	1	2	6-9	225	3	9
34	Peter Gudmundsson	Washington	C	3	61	7-2	270	1	3
34	Mike Mitchell	Auburn	F	1	15	6-7	215	7	10
32	Ed Nealy	Kansas State	F	8	166	6-7	238	2	5
41	Kurt Nimphius	Arizona State	C-F	3	47	6-10	218	1	7
21	Alvin Robertson	Arkansas	G	1	7	6-4	190	4	4
15	Ricky Wilson	George Mason	G	3	52	6-3	185	1	1

ROOKIES	COLLEGE	POS	R#	D#	HT
Willie Anderson	Georgia	G	1	10	6-7
Shelton Jones	St. John's	F	2	27	6-9
Vernon Maxwell	Florida	G	2	47	6-5
Barry Sumpter	Austin Peay	C	3	56	7-0
Archie Marshall	Kansas	F	3	75	6-7

* For further definition of category and column headings, see pages 38 & 39.

San Antonio Spurs . . . . Overview

If any team could use a quick fix, it's the San Antonio Spurs. Though the club's not that bad, they nonetheless ranked #23 in attendance. Too few people paid too little money to watch too few wins. One would guess that the sporadic attendance had an effect on the home-court advantage. At one point the Spurs won ten straight at home before dropping four in a row. Later they lost five consecutive at the HemisFair before winning three straight. Even later in the season at home, they went, win, loss, win, loss, win, loss, win, loss. Sound confusing? It was.

What should you do in a case like this? You go out and hire the best coach in America. That's what. Just weeks after Larry Brown had taken the Kansas Jayhawks to the NCAA title, and shortly after he had turned down the UCLA coaching job, the Spurs made him an offer he couldn't refuse. In round numbers, it was... a fortune. Brown will become the highest paid coach in America. A look at his record reveals why.

1st Year	Team	Record Before	1st Year
1972-73	Carolina ABA	34-50	57-27
1974-75	Denver ABA	37-47	65-19
1979-80	UCLA	25- 5	22-10*
1981-82	New Jersey NBA	24-58	44-38
1983-84	Kansas	13-14	22-10
		133-174	210-104
		.433	.669

* UCLA is the only case where the team's record declined after Brown. The silver lining is that he took his 22-10 team to the NCAA championship game!

Only ten times in NBA or ABA history has a first year coach guided his team to 20 or more victories over the previous year's team. Larry Brown has done it an incredible three of those ten. He was named ABA Coach-of-the-Year three times as well. There is no way that this team is not going to win more games than last year.

Many have called Brown an opportunist. Maybe so, but what of it. Why wouldn't anyone want to take the best position available at any moment? As a big KU Jayhawk fan, I'm glad we had Larry as long as we did. I held no resentment towards him for leaving. Anyone who thought he would be here longer than 5 years was nuts anyway. Need I repeat that statement by substituting San Antonio? If the Spurs get Brown for 5 or 6 years they will have won at least one NBA title. If he leaves then, who can complain?

It's too bad that David Robinson won't be starting his career until 1989-90. That doesn't mean, however, that the club can't win some games. As a fairly young team they did make the playoffs. As a Brown-led, slightly more mature club, and with the addition of rookie Willie Anderson, they may be quite a bit to handle in their pre-D.R. days.

Quiz: Who was the last group of Texans to fail badly on defense despite their sharp shooting? Answer: Remember the Alamo? The team's highest rankings were in offensive scoring (#3) and 2-pt FG% (#5). They even ranked #8 at shooting 3-pointers. But defensively, they couldn't hold the fort down. The Spurs ranked dead last in defensive scoring, defensive FG%, and defensive rebounds. A perfect example of the problem was a game played with Boston March 9, 1988. Though every single player on the team shot 50%+ from the field, the Spurs allowed 119 points and lost.

Because of the high scoring affairs, many games were decided by a streak late in the game. Consequently, San Antonio ranked #2 in most games won (11) when *trailing* after three quarters. Only the Lakers had more (12). Interestingly, they ranked #2 in most games lost (10) when *leading* after three quarters. The Utah Jazz had the most, with 12. Despite these wild 4th quarter variations, there was one point of consistency. The Spurs were 16-10 (#5) in games decided by five points or less. Not bad.

Despite the positives, one rather negative statistic was that the team was swept by

San Antonio Spurs .... Overview

both Los Angeles and Portland. In eleven NBA years prior to 1988, the Spurs had only been swept in the season series (3 or more games) three times. In fact, since 1977 (0-4 to Boston and Atlanta) the club had only been swept once. In 1984 Phoenix did the trick five games to zero.

Frank Brickowski was a very pleasant surprise last year. Consequently, he was the NBA's most improved player (1988 Production Rating (PR) minus 1987 Production Rating). Johnny Dawkins was #5.

	1988 PR	1987 PR	
1. **Brickowski**	**18.71**	**5.05**	**+13.66**
2. Stockton	25.64	14.80	+11.74
3. Tarpley	20.23	10.68	+9.55
4. Duckworth	15.42	5.89	+9.53
5. **J. Dawkins**	**18.37**	**9.58**	**+8.79**
6. Price	16.92	8.52	+8.40
7. Schayes	18.63	11.22	+7.41
8. M. Adams	16.57	9.19	+7.38

Brickowski scored more points and had more rebounds, assists, blocks, and steals than he did in his first 3 years combined. It's very similar to the Dale Ellis story the year before. Though the Spurs were better when he played center (17-18) than when he played power forward (8-23), he will have to go at PF once Robinson arrives. Bricko had the most influence on winning. When he scored 18+ points, the team was a respectable 16-15. When he scored 17 or less, they struggled to a 12-27 record. He ranked #1 among power forwards in assists, but undermined his finesse image by tying Jack Sikma as the league's leader in disqualifications (11 times).

Greg Anderson was another surprise. He was the only rookie to register a 20/20, and subsequently made the All-Rookie team. His free throw shooting is pretty bad, though, at 60.4%. In fact, he ranked 2nd for most inefficiency points at the line (see page 32 for discussion). Nevertheless, he's got a bright future. Add Anderson to a front line of Brickowski/Robinson and you're talking P-O-T-E-N-T-I-A-L.

The small forward duo of Dallas Comegys and Mike Mitchell isn't bad either. It is imperative that Comegys pay off. After all, the Spurs gave up Walter Berry for him and Berry averaged 17.4ppg. Before that they gave up Kevin Duckworth for Berry and Duckworth is becoming one of the NBA's top centers. Duckworth for Comegys? I'll wait to be critical of these trades.

The guards are going to be great - if not quite yet, then in another year or so. By adding both player's Production Ratings, Robertson and Dawkins rank 5th among NBA starting guard duo's - no small honor since each of those ahead of them have more NBA experience.

Guard Duo's	PR	Combined Years in NBA
Drexler/Porter	50.81	8
Johnson/Cooper	49.44	14
Jordan/Vincent	45.72	7
Lever/Adams	42.51	9
Robertson/Dawkins	**41.31**	**6**

When Dawkins was injured late in the season, Jon Sundvold filled in admirably. In 12 games, he averaged 13 points and 7 assists. Even so, he was left unprotected in the expansion draft and picked up by Miami.

Prediction - best case: 45-37

This is the hardest prediction in this book. Given Brown's track record and the great guard talent he has, this team should improve substantially. The biggest problem will be announcer Sam Smith's. He'll be the one who has to say: "Robertson brings the ball down court, passes into Robinson (next season), flips it over to Anderson, out to Anderson, over to Gudmundson."

Prediction - worst case: 37-45

Trying to repeat the 16-10 record in close games will be difficult. If the Spurs can't ignore the distractions of who's *not* on the team, they may manage *only* 37 wins. Even so, that would be a substantial improvement. Maybe I'm just blinded by Brown's magic, but I expect a miracle down south.

Seattle SuperSonics .... History

The Seattle Supersonics began as an NBA expansion franchise in 1967 along with the Houston Rockets. Comparing the two franchises, Seattle leads in regular season and playoff wins as well as the head-to-head matchup. The Rockets have made the playoffs one more year - eleven to ten, but the Sonics have won a championship in two final appearances. Houston, although they too have reached the finals twice, has come up short both times.

Seattle won the NBA title in 1979. Except for Portland and Milwaukee, the Sonics are the only expansion team to win it all. In 1978, Seattle reached the championship round against Washington. The Sonics led three games to two, but ended up losing in the seventh game 99-105. The following year the Sonics won the championship over the Bullets four games to one. Since then, the closest Seattle has come to the championship was one year later. In 1980 the club lost one game to four to the Lakers in the conference finals. During this 3-year period from 1978-80, the team won more total games (187) than any other club in the league. The Sixers were close behind with 184 wins.

Seattle also has a winning playoff record which only six of twenty-two other clubs can boast of. Only two teams have combined losing regular season records, yet combined winning post-season records: Indiana (48% and 56%) and Seattle (49% and 51%).

The Sonics have enjoyed use of the Kingdome in the playoffs. Because of the size of the stadium, Seattle managed to draw the five largest crowds in NBA playoff history prior to Detroit in 1988. Though Seattle won three of those five games, the two they lost were the two with the highest attendance (1980 vs Milwaukee - 40,172) and (1978 vs Washington - 39,457).

Since 1967, there have been 144 individual titles in the NBA for everything from blocks to free throw percentage. A relatively small number of Sonics are among those leaders. In 1980, Fred Brown won the NBA's first 3-point FG% crown. Joining Brown with league honors were Lenny Wilkens and Slick Watts. Both were leaders in assists. Wilkens led the NBA in 1971, while Watts was the top playmaker in 1976. Again, from rebounding to steals and everything in between, Jack Sikma has won the most team titles (16). Gus Williams (15) and Fred Brown (14) are close behind.

> **Quiz: Besides Tom Chambers in 1987, what other Sonic was named MVP of the All-Star game?**

ALL TIME SONICS' TEAM

Player	Span	Yrs	CRD
Jack Sikma	1978-86	9	15,370
Fred Brown	1972-84	13	12,617
Gus Williams	1978-84	6	9,117
Spencer Haywood	1971-75	5	8,640
Tom Chambers	1984-88	5	7,284
Lenny Wilkens	1969-72	4	7,161
Dick Snyder	1970-79	6	6,744
Tom Meschery	1968-71	4	5,383
Lonnie Shelton	1979-83	5	5,099
Xavier McDaniel	1986-88	3	4,809

ALL TIME SONICS' COACH

Lenny Wilkens   11 Years
37-32 Playoffs   6 Playoffs
478-402 Reg. Season   1 Championship

HISTORICAL PROFILE

Category	Data
Sonics' coach	Bernie Bickerstaff
Years coached Seattle	3
# of franchise years	21
# of coaches	7
# of winning seasons	10
# of playoff years	10
# of runner's up	1
# of championships	1
Regular season win %	48.7
Playoff win %	50.5

> **Answer:
> Lenny Wilkens (1971)**

Seattle SuperSonics . . . . 1987-88 Highlights

Sonics 111-105 Celtics   Wed.   December 30, 1987

Tom Chambers scored 31 points to lead the upset. The win was the 9th in a row at home for Seattle and ended Boston's six game winning streak. Even though the contest was at Seattle, the Sonics had not defeated the Celtics at home in six years.

Sonics 141-133 Spurs   Sat.   January 9, 1988

The Sonics 141 points (the most since 1983) were bolstered by Dale Ellis' record performance. The Sonics ran their home winning streak to 12 games, but the last three home games were the most profound. Win #10 was significant for Xavier McDaniel, as he scored a season high 35 points. Win #11 was noteworthy for Tom Chambers, as he hit a career high 46 points. Win #12 resulted from Ellis' 47 points - also a career high.

Sonics 108-96 Knicks   Wed.   January 20, 1988

The Sonics defeated the New York Knicks on the strength of a 38-16 first quarter run. The win was the 16th consecutive at home for the Sonics, tying a franchise single season record. Xavier McDaniel bettered his career scoring and rebounding totals for one game as he hit 41 points and gathered 18 rebounds. His old records were 40 and 17. The loss dropped New York's road record to 1-16 despite a career high of 26 points by Johnny Newman.

Sonics 133-130 Kings   Fri.   February 26, 1988

The SuperSonics held off a late rally by the Kings. The Sonics did it by using their usual 3-pronged attack: Dale Ellis scored 37 points, Xavier McDaniel racked up 31, and Tom Chambers hit 30. This was the only time last year a team had 3-30+ scorers in the same game. Even so, the hero for the Sonics might not have been any of the three, but rather Nate McMillan, who nailed down a 13 rebound, 14 assist game. He missed a triple double by scoring only 9 points. An oddity in the game was Sacramento's "th-boys". The top five scorers were **Th**orpe, D. Smith, **Th**eus, K. Smith, and **Th**ompson - the only time they've ranked 1-5.

Sonics 114-100 Lakers   Tue.   March 1, 1988

The victory ended LA's 10 game winning streak. Ironically, despite the loss, and despite only 2 points by Kareem Abdul-Jabbar, the Lakers became the first NBA team to clinch a playoff spot. Kareem's 2 points equalled the lowest offensive output of his NBA career (19 years, 1658 games). The only other time he scored as low as 2 points is part of an amazing story. (see page 15) Nate McMillan was the key to Seattle's success, contributing 17 assists.

Sonics 106-97 Kings   Wed.   March 9, 1988

The win was a direct result of free throw percentage. Sacramento, which trailed the entire game, had a chance to finally tie it up as late as 74 all, but Kenny Smith missed his last two FTA's. An 86% FT shooter, Smith went only 1 of 8 while his point guard counterpart, Nate McMillan, went 10 for 10. For the game, Seattle missed only 1 FT while Sacramento missed 16. The loss was new coach Jerry Reynold's first this year.

Sonics 151-107 Suns   Sat.   April 2, 1988

The SuperSonics swamped the Suns 151-107. The 151 points were the most ever scored by the Sonics while the 44 point loss was the worst in Phoenix's history. Going into the game, Ellis, McDaniel, and Chambers had scored 20 or more points 135 times. In this game, Williams and McKey hit that plateau for career highs. Ironically, three weeks earlier Seattle's bench had gone scoreless vs Phoenix. In this rematch they scored 63 points!

Seattle SuperSonics . . . . Influence on Winning

TEAM RECORD BY   ... SCR Leader   ... REB Leader   ... AST Leader

PLAYER	GAMES	HOME	ROAD	HOME	ROAD	HOME	ROAD
Dale Ellis	75	12-4	8-18	1-0	0-4	---	0-2
Xavier McDaniel	78	13-1	3-5	8-2	5-5	1-0	0-4
Tom Chambers	82	6-3	1-8	4-3	2-4	---	0-1
Nate McMillan	82	---	---	5-0	0-1	27-6	9-21
Alton Lister	82	1-0	---	12-2	3-16	---	---
Derrick McKey	82	1-0	---	2-0	1-1	---	---
Sedale Threatt	26	---	0-1	---	---	1-0	1-1
Olden Polynice	82	---	---	4-1	2-4	---	---
Danny Young	77	---	---	---	---	1-0	3-2
Clemon Johnson	74	---	---	---	---	1-0	---

TEAM RECORD BY SCORING *

PLAYER	PLAY	DNP	0-9	10-19	20-29	30-39	40+
Dale Ellis	41-34	3-4	---	8-8	20-16	9-9	4-1
Xavier McDaniel	41-37	3-1	1-2	11-18	15-16	13-1	1-0
Tom Chambers	44-38	---	3-2	20-13	11-22	8-1	2-0
Nate McMillan	44-38	---	26-28	17-10	1-0	---	---
Alton Lister	44-38	---	37-33	7-5	---	---	---
Derrick McKey	44-38	---	25-24	18-14	1-0	---	---
Sedale Threatt	15-11	29-27	8-6	7-4	---	0-1	---
Olden Polynice	44-38	---	37-34	7-4	---	---	---
Danny Young	42-35	2-3	41-34	1-1	---	---	---
Clemon Johnson	39-35	5-3	39-35	---	---	---	---

TEAM RECORD BY STARTING POSITION *

PLAYER	GAMES	STARTS	PG	OG	SF	PF	C
Dale Ellis	75	73	---	39-34	---	---	---
Xavier McDaniel	78	77	---	---	41-35	0-1	---
Tom Chambers	82	82	---	---	2-0	42-37	0-1
Nate McMillan	82	82	44-38	---	---	---	---
Alton Lister	82	55	---	---	---	---	27-28
Derrick McKey	82	4	---	---	1-3	---	---
Sedale Threatt	26	0	---	---	---	---	---
Olden Polynice	82	0	---	---	---	---	---
Danny Young	77	0	---	---	---	---	---
Clemon Johnson	74	26	---	---	---	---	17-9

* For further definition of each category and column heading see pages 38 & 39.

Seattle SuperSonics — 1987-88 Statistics

RAW NUMBERS *

PLAYER	2pt%	3pt%	FT%	MIN	PF	DQ	HI	TO	RB	AS	BL	ST
Dale Ellis	.521	.413	.767	**2790**	221	1	**47**	172	340	197	11	74
Xavier McDaniel	.496	.280	.715	2703	230	2	41	**223**	518	263	52	96
Tom Chambers	.461	.303	**.807**	2680	297	4	46	209	490	212	53	87
Nate McMillan	.479	.375	.707	2453	238	1	21	189	338	**702**	47	**169**
Alton Lister	.504	**.500**	.606	1812	**319**	**8**	19	90	**627**	58	**140**	27
Derrick McKey	.499	.367	.772	1706	237	3	20	108	328	107	63	70
Sedale Threatt	**.535**	.111	.803	1055	100	0	31	63	88	160	8	60
Olden Polynice	.468	0-2	.639	1080	215	1	15	81	330	33	26	32
Danny Young	.475	.286	**.811**	949	69	0	13	37	75	218	2	52
Clemon Johnson	.467	0-0	.688	723	104	0	8	29	174	17	24	13

OVERALL RANKINGS *

PLAYER	G	GS	PPG	PR	RANK	SC	SH	RB	AS	BL	ST
Dale Ellis	75	73	**25.84**	20.55	28	7	23	108	95	142	104
Xavier McDaniel	78	77	21.40	19.78	36	14	92	71	70	65	63
Tom Chambers	**82**	**82**	20.41	17.73	52	18	112	76	90	63	76
Nate McMillan	**82**	**82**	7.61	16.71	56	143	118	95	4	67	8
Alton Lister	**82**	55	5.62	11.94	112	155	136	4	153	5	154
Derrick McKey	**82**	4	8.46	10.23	128	133	57	69	105	31	49
Sedale Threatt	71	0	6.93	7.35	DNQ						
Olden Polynice	**82**	0	4.11	5.90	DNQ						
Danny Young	77	0	3.16	5.38	DNQ						
Clemon Johnson	74	26	1.62	3.42	DNQ						

POSITION RANKINGS *

PLAYER	POSITION	RANK	SC	SH	RB	AS	BL	ST
Dale Ellis	Off Guard (OG)	6	3	9	11	32	30	28
Xavier McDaniel	Small Forward (SF)	8	5	21	11	11	16	11
Tom Chambers	Power Forward (PF)	11	5	26	34	7	21	10
Nate McMillan	Point Guard (PG)	13	29	22	4	4	1	4
Alton Lister	Center (C)	24	25	23	1	22	4	23
Derrick McKey	Small Forward (SF)	25	29	8	9	24	3	9
Sedale Threatt	Off Guard (OG)	DNQ						
Olden Polynice	Center (C)	DNQ						
Danny Young	Point Guard (PG)	DNQ						
Clemon Johnson	Center (C)	DNQ						

*For further definition of each category and column heading see pages 38 & 39.

208 BASKETBALL HEAVEN 1989

Seattle SuperSonics ....Team Info

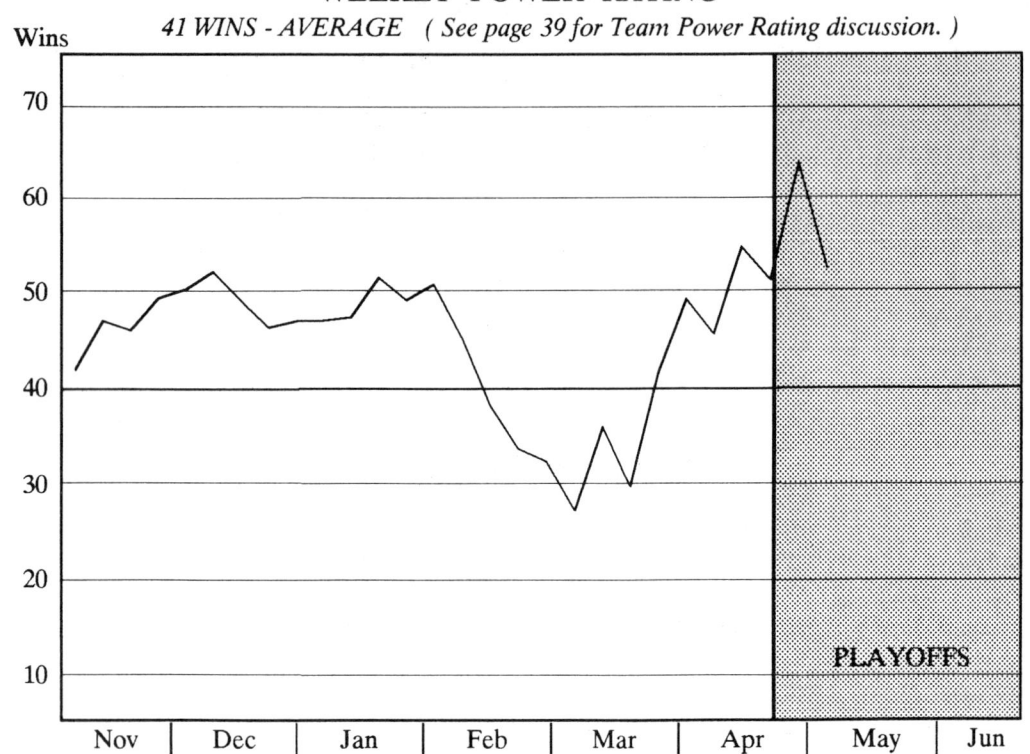

WEEKLY POWER RATING
41 WINS - AVERAGE (See page 39 for Team Power Rating discussion.)

Wins

[Line chart showing weekly power rating from Nov through Jun, with values fluctuating between about 27 and 64. Playoffs period (May-Jun) is shaded.]

Miscellaneous Categories	Data	Rank
Attendance	492K	15
Key-Man Games Missed	22	2
Season Record	44-38	11
- Home	32-9	8
- Road	12-29	13
Eastern Conference	13-9	7
Western Conference	31-29	13
Overtime Record	3-4	17
Record 5 Pts. or Less	12-13	13
Record 10 Pts. or More	24-19	11
Games Won By Bench	8	2
Games Won By Starters	9	6
Winning Streak	6	10
Losing Streak	5	10
Home Winning Streak	17	1
Road Winning Streak	2	14
Home Losing Streak	2	2
Road Losing Streak	6	8

Performance Categories	Data	Rank
Offensive Scoring (per game)	111.4	6
Defensive Scoring (per game)	109.3	17
Scoring Margin (per game)	2.1	10
Defensive FG%	.485	16
Offensive 2-point%	.488	13
Offensive 3-point%	.346	3
Offensive Free Throw %	.748	19
Offensive Rebs (Off REB/Opp Def REB)		2
Defensive Rebs (Def REB/Opp Off REB)		14
Offensive Assists (AST/FGMade)		12
Offensive Blocks (BLK/Opp FGAttempted)		11
Offensive Steals (STL/Game)		3
Turnover Margin (Off T.O. - Def T.O.)		2
Finesse (BLK + STL) / PF		18
Rebounding Record	49-28-5	3
Assists Record	48-30-4	3
Field Goal Pct. Record	40-42-0	13
Free Throw Pct. Record	38-43-1	16

Seattle SuperSonics .... Miscellaneous

ADMINISTRATIVE INFORMATION

Team Offices: 190 Queen Anne Avenue
Box 900911
Seattle, Washington
98109-9711
Telephone: (206) 281-5800
Head Coach: Bernie Bickerstaff
Home Arena: Coliseum
Capacity: 14,200

1988-89 ROSTER*

J#	VETERANS	COLLEGE	POS	R#	D#	HT	WT	Seat	NBA
	Michael Cage	San Diego State	F	1	14	6-9	235	0	4
3	Dale Ellis	Tennessee	G	1	9	6-7	215	2	5
53	Alton Lister	Arizona State	C	1	21	7-0	240	2	7
34	Xavier McDaniel	Wichita State	F	1	4	6-7	205	3	3
31	Derrick McKey	Alabama	F	1	9	6-9	210	1	1
10	Nate McMillan	N.Carolina State	G	2	30	6-5	197	2	2
23	Olden Polynice	Virginia	C	1	8	6-11	245	1	1
40	Russ Schoene	Tennessee-Chatt.	F	2	45	6-10	215	2	3
3	Sedale Threatt	W. Virginia Tech	G	6	139	6-2	177	1	5
22	Danny Young	Wake Forest	G	2	39	6-4	175	4	4

ROOKIES	COLLEGE	POS	R#	D#	HT
Corey Gaines	Loyola Marymount	G	3	65	6-3

* For further definition of category and column headings, see pages 38 & 39.

Seattle SuperSonics . . . . Overview

There are only a few times when a team gains five victories from the season before and it's considered a disappointment. This was one of those occasions. It's not that the 39 victories in 1986-87 were reason to believe Seattle would be good. No, it's what happened in the following playoffs that had hungry fans licking their chops. The Sonics devoured the Mavericks 3 games to 1, before chewing up the Rockets 4 games to 2. Most prognisticators chose Seattle to finish second in the Pacific to the Lakers. As we know, they finished third with 44 wins - a full 9 games behind second place Portland. So, although expectations may have been unreasonably high, the 1987-88 season was somewhat of a letdown.

There were other reasons for the faithful to expect to be blessed last season. The miracle worker himself, Bernie Bickerstaff, had become so revered in such a short time that the modern day Sampson (Ralph) was heard to say, when commenting about his own coach, Bill Fitch, "He ain't no Bernie Bickerstaff." Where did this guy come from? Remember, in two years of NBA coaching his record was only 70-94. Was it the surprising 39 wins in 1987; the ensuing playoffs; or perhaps some unknown mystical trance that made everyone assume he could produce another faith healing season? I suppose it may have been all those things. In retrospect, there probably wasn't a particularily good reason to assume the Sonics would win many more than 44 games in 1988.

Another reason expectations were high was because of the two incoming rookies. Any team who picks up the 8th and 9th players of a draft has to feel excited. Nevertheless, it's rare that rookies make a lot of difference. A few wins a year - maybe, but not much more. Olden Polynice ended up as one of the more unfulfilling rookies of the season. What makes it worse is that Polynice came into the season with a year of pro experience (Europe) and had ample opportunity to prove himself. With Seattle's deficits at center and power forward, he could have been a star. Given what we now know, his 82 game scoring average of 4.1 and 16.3 fouls per 48 minutes are dismal to say the least.

Derrick McKey was a different story. From early in the season it became clear that McKey had the potential to become a top notch player. Though he subbed behind the league's 4th highest scoring forward duo (Chambers, McDaniel), he managed to excel enough to make the All-Rookie team. Surprisingly, (again, rookies rarely make a difference) McKey managed to have a very positive influence on winning. The Sonics were 11-4 when McKey scored 14 or more points, but only 33-34 when he failed to reach 14.

Probably the biggest single problem this club had last year was the disproportionate number of fouls committed vs fouls drawn.

	Team Fouls -	Opps Fouls =	Diff.	Wins
Seattle	2380	1963	417	44
New York	2361	1969	392	38
Golden St.	2155	1811	344	20
Indiana	2038	1859	179	38
Phoenix	2045	1901	144	28

Actually, it's exciting that the Sonics won 44 games considering how overwhelming their disadvantage at the line was. On page 18 I discuss the "negativity" of a foul. I estimate a foul costs 5/24ths of a point. Using this standard, Seattle lost 87 points (5/24 times 417) off the league's average. That's roughly a point per game. Using admittedly questionable methods of deduction, it could be argued that this cost the Sonics a minimum of four victories. That's the number of overtime losses Seattle suffered. The assumption is that they would not have gone to overtime with just one more point.

It's clear that when the club did draw fouls, they won at an exceptionally high rate. The Sonics were 7-2 when X-man had 10+ FTA's at home. They were 7-0 when Chambers did the same thing. And when either of the two shot double figure FT's on the road their record was again 7-0.

Seattle SuperSonics .... Overview

When your team wins 21 of 23 games just by having one of your starting forwards shoot 10 free throws or more, then you figure out a way to get to the line.

Chambers and McDaniel are two of the big three (Dale Ellis is the third member of the "Three Basketeers".) All three scored over 20 points per game - a relatively unusual event, though not rare. What is rare is having three teammates score 20+ ppg two years in a row! That has only happened on two other occasions.

English, Issel, Vandeweghe - Denver 1982-1983, 24.40 ppg
Pettit, Hagan, Lovellette - St. Louis 1960-1961, 24.03 ppg
Ellis, McDaniel, Chambers - Seattle 1987-1988, 23.12 ppg

The scoring was so dominated by the three that it wasn't until game #56 that another player on the team scored 20 points or more. By that time, Ellis had passed 20 points 45 times, McDaniel 32, and Chambers 31. Despite these soaring numbers, the three's average of 22.47 ppg fell just short of the Celtics' Bird, McHale, and Ainge (22.58). McDaniel led the team to a 14-1 record when he exceeded 30 points. Chambers took the Sonics to a similar 10-1 record by the same criterion. Perhaps surprisingly, Seattle was only 13-10 when Ellis achieved that mark.

Chambers is, of course, no longer a resident alien. A sometimes loved, oftentimes criticized player, Tom Terrific has taken his show on the road. By the time he got to Phoenix, the fans in Seattle had forgotten his name. Why? Michael Cage. The Sonics picked up the league's leading rebounder in a trade for draft rights to Gary Grant. Cage is exactly what Seattle had to have for two reasons. First of all, going back to the discussion on FTA's vs fouls, the Sonics had a ratio of 1.03 (the league's lowest). The average NBA team had a ratio of 1.21. Cage had a spectacular ratio of 2.44. He's a banger who draws a lot of fouls. The best part is that he only fouled out once. The second advantage of Cage over Chambers was defense. It's not that Cage's fortress was tantamount to putting iron bars around the basket, but compared to Tom (Stevie Wonder) Chambers, his protection of his turf could be likened to a German Shepherd at a junkyard.

Danny Young led the league in assists-to-turnover ratio - the ultimate "good hands" award. Nate McMillan was 6th. If I were to try to statistically evaluate the most unselfish players in the NBA, I'd say the formula should read assists/fga. By that standard, McMillan was #2, Young #4.

Most Unselfish	Ast/FGA
Stockton	.701
McMillan	**.707**
Minniefield	.969
Young	**1.000**
Bogues	1.054

Notes: Seattle was 37-39-6 in quarters 1 & 4 on the road. They really failed in quarters 2 & 3, however. Their record in those two quarters was 25-52-5... The club's home wins minus road wins after the All-Star break were higher than any other club. This is part of the reason why the league home court win percentage was the 2nd highest ever (.679, 2nd to 1977's .685)... The Sonics had the largest rise in attendance in 1988 (+38%). Detroit (17%) and Chicago (14%) were next... Though it's probably an anomoly, the team was a very good 17-9 when Clemon Johnson (since departed) started at center.

Prediction - best case: 54-28

This team will definitely be improved. Cage, whose biggest contribution will be his fouls/fta ratio, will fit the club's needs much better than Chambers. Very seldom does a team need three high-powered scorers. Another year of maturity by everyone else and this becomes a very good club. If Alton "Listless" can regain his 1987 form - watch out.

Prediction - worst case: 47-35

I suppose with major injuries, the club could lose more than 35 games, but with Phoenix, Golden State, and Sacramento in the division, Seattle's schedule alone could heal a lot of wounds.

Utah Jazz .... History

The Utah Jazz is the second youngest franchise in the NBA (13 years). Only the Dallas Mavericks (7 years) and the new Miami and Charlotte franchises have been around more briefly. The Jazz were either bad or very bad their first nine seasons. During that stretch, the club never had a winning season and subsequently never played a single playoff game. This established Utah as the NBA's worst team from 1975-1983. In that 9 year period, Utah won only 268 regular season games while the next worse team, Detroit, won 301 and went to the playoffs three times.

Since 1983, the Jazz have been relatively successful. The club has not had a single losing season and has been to the playoffs all 5 years. Only nine of twenty-two other teams have had more victories during this period. The dramatic turnaround has to be due to Frank Layden, who in 1984 became only the second person to win both Coach-of-the-Year and Executive-of-the-Year honors (Red Auerbach is the other).

The Jazz have had several top performers in their short history. Besides Layden's two awards, Darrell Griffith also was selected as the top representative twice. Griffith won the 3-point FG% crown in 1984 and was named Rookie-of-the-Year in 1981. Adrian Dantley was named Comeback-Player-of-the-Year in 1984 and was scoring champ in 1981 and 1984. Mark Eaton has won 4 blocked shot titles while being named the 1985 Defensive-Player-of-the-Year. Finally, point guards Ricky Green and John Stockton have led the league in steals and assists respectively. Green was honored in 1984, Stockton last season. The 14 titles and awards are the most by any team this decade. Truck Robinson and Pete Maravich won the club's only other titles (rebounding - 1978 & scoring - 1977).

Trivia: Stockton is the only player since the 1984 draft who has not missed a game (328)... The club's 28 consecutive road losses (1975) are a one-season record. It was the club's first 28 road games. The streak was finally broken by Pete Maravich's 47 points... Assistant coach Jerry Sloan's #4 is the only number ever retired by Chicago... Frank Layden and former NBA coach Hubie Brown were college roommates at Niagra University from 1951-1955... Kelly Tripucka is 4-0 on his birthday (Feb. 16) in the NBA, 2-0 at Notre Dame, and he scored his 1,000th and 2,000th points on this day as well.

> **Quiz: Besides Utah, which two NBA teams have a nickname which does not end in "s"?**

ALL TIME JAZZ' TEAM

Player	Span	Yrs	CRD
Adrian Dantley	1980-86	7	12,419
Rickey Green	1981-88	8	9,075
Darrell Griffith	1981-88	8	7,615
Rich Kelley	1976-85	7	7,262
Pete Maravich	1975-79	5	7,140
Mark Eaton	1983-88	6	6,709
Thurl Bailey	1984-88	5	6,135
Karl Malone	1986-88	3	5,379
John Stockton	1985-88	4	5,248
Jeff Wilkins	1981-85	5	4,215

ALL TIME JAZZ' COACH

Frank Layden   7 Years
19-22 Playoffs   5 Playoffs
266-288 Reg. Season   0 Championships

HISTORICAL PROFILE

Category	Data
Jazz' coach	Frank Layden
Years coached Utah	7
# of franchise years	14
# of coaches	5
# of winning seasons	4
# of playoff years	5
# of runner's up	0
# of championships	0
Regular season win %	42.4
Playoff win %	43.9

> **Answer:**
> **Miami Heat & Orlando Magic**

TEAM BY TEAM ANALYSIS 213

Utah Jazz ....1987-88 Highlights

Jazz 118-96 Rockets   Fri.   November 27, 1987

The Utah Jazz won their 7th straight home game to remain the only NBA team to be undefeated at home. In each of the seven home wins Utah had streaks to break the games open. Those streaks added up to a total of 146 points for the Jazz to 23 for their opponents in a period less than a 48 minute game. The 22 point margin was the largest over the Rockets in three years.

Jazz 119-96 Cavaliers   Mon.   January 25, 1988

Although the win was nice, as it represented the first back-to-back wins at home in over a month, the third quarter was what will be remembered. Utah led by only one point at half, but outscored the Cavs 40-16 in quarter 3. That 24 point margin was Utah's largest of the year for a quarter as well as one of the most decisive in the NBA. Ironically, at the very end of the quarter Ricky Green made a long bomb as time expired to cap the scoring. The irony was that the shot represented the 5 millionth point scored in the NBA's 41 seasons.

Jazz 112-94 Trail Blazers   Mon.   February 15, 1988

Thurl Bailey continued a hot scoring streak. For the 4th time to this point in the season Bailey had come off the bench to score 30+ points. His 32 points vs Portland improved his average in his previous 9 games to 25.1 ppg. In addition to his scoring, Bailey gathered in a career high 17 rebounds. The win was made a little easier for Utah by Portland's injuries. Drexler, Vandeweghe, Johnson, and Lucas all missed the game. Though he tried, Kevin Duckworth's career high 31 points were not enough to overcome the Jazz.

Jazz 98-88 & 120-103 Clippers   F/S   February 19-20, 1988

The Utah Jazz swept the Clippers in back-to-back games. The second win gave the surging Jazz their 4th straight victory while it extended the Clippers' losing streak to six games. Amazingly, John Stockton not only had 21 assists in the first game, but 21 assists in the second game as well. By this performance, Stockton became the first person in NBA history to accumulate 20+ assists on back-to-back nights. Not only that, the two games climaxed a week in which Stockton took over the league leadership in assists from Magic Johnson and was named NBA Player-of-the-Week.

Jazz 116-115 Nuggets   Mon.   March 14, 1988

Superstar forward Karl Malone was ejected after playing only 3 minutes, while coach Frank Layden soon followed him to the shower. In fact, before half the first quarter had been played, the Jazz had been whistled for 6 technicals. Still, John Stockton's 20 assists and Thurl Bailey's career high 41 points, including 16 of the last 19 and a game winning bucket, secured the victory. The 41 points by a bench player was an NBA high last season. Utah overcame the Nuggets' guards' best efforts. Fat Lever had 17 rebounds and Michael Adams set an NBA record 15 3-pt FGA's - hitting 5. It was his 23rd straight game having hit at least one 3-pointer. That tied Danny Ainge's record. The victory was so dramatic it prompted Jazz announcer Hot Rod Hundley to call it "The greatest win I've ever seen by the Jazz."

Jazz 125-107 Rockets   Sat.   April 23, 1988

The Utah Jazz stomped the Houston Rockets to finish the regular season with five straight wins - a season high. The Jazz had four players score 20 or more points for the first time last year. John Stockton led the way with a career high 27 points, but his 14th assist in the game set an NBA single season record, eclipsing Isiah Thomas' mark.

Utah Jazz . . . . Influence on Winning

TEAM RECORD BY ... SCR Leader ... REB Leader ... AST Leader

PLAYER	GAMES	HOME	ROAD	HOME	ROAD	HOME	ROAD
Karl Malone	82	25-6	10-22	27-6	13-14	---	---
John Stockton	82	---	0-3	---	---	30-8	13-26
Thurl Bailey	82	9-1	2-2	2-1	0-4	---	---
Mark Eaton	82	---	---	9-1	2-8	---	---
Bobby Hansen	81	---	1-0	---	---	---	---
Darrell Griffith	52	1-0	0-2	---	---	---	---
Kelly Tripucka	49	---	---	---	---	---	---
Mel Turpin	79	---	---	---	1-3	---	---
Rickey Green	81	---	---	---	---	3-0	1-1
Marc Iavaroni	81	---	---	2-0	0-1	---	---

TEAM RECORD BY SCORING *

PLAYER	PLAY	DNP	0-9	10-19	20-29	30-39	40+
Karl Malone	47-35	---	1-1	2-5	22-17	19-12	3-0
John Stockton	47-35	---	5-7	34-24	8-4	---	---
Thurl Bailey	47-35	---	4-4	16-17	21-13	6-1	---
Mark Eaton	47-35	---	36-26	11-9	---	---	---
Bobby Hansen	47-34	0-1	22-21	15-12	10-1	---	---
Darrell Griffith	26-26	21-9	14-12	10-12	2-0	0-2	---
Kelly Tripucka	27-22	20-13	19-18	8-3	0-1	---	---
Mel Turpin	45-34	2-1	35-26	9-6	1-2	---	---
Rickey Green	47-34	0-1	39-30	8-4	---	---	---
Marc Iavaroni	47-34	0-1	41-30	6-4	---	---	---

TEAM RECORD BY STARTING POSITION *

PLAYER	GAMES	STARTS	PG	OG	SF	PF	C
Karl Malone	82	82	---	---	---	47-35	---
John Stockton	82	79	46-33	---	---	---	---
Thurl Bailey	82	10	---	---	4-6	---	---
Mark Eaton	82	82	---	---	---	---	47-35
Bobby Hansen	81	51	---	30-21	---	---	---
Darrell Griffith	52	11	---	6-5	---	---	---
Kelly Tripucka	49	21	---	11-9	0-1	---	---
Mel Turpin	79	0	---	---	---	---	---
Rickey Green	81	3	1-2	---	---	---	---
Marc Iavaroni	81	71	---	---	43-28	---	---

* For further definition of each category and column heading see pages 38 & 39.

Utah Jazz — 1987-88 Statistics

RAW NUMBERS *

PLAYER	2pt%	3pt%	FT%	MIN	PF	DQ	HI	TO	RB	AS	BL	ST
Karl Malone	.522	0-5	.700	**3198**	296	2	**41**	325	**986**	199	50	117
John Stockton	**.594**	.358	.840	2842	247	5	27	262	237	**1128**	16	**242**
Thurl Bailey	.493	.333	.826	2804	186	1	**41**	190	531	158	125	49
Mark Eaton	.418	0-0	.623	2731	**320**	**8**	16	131	717	55	**304**	41
Bob Hansen	.553	.330	.743	1796	193	2	28	91	187	175	5	65
Darrell Griffith	.462	.275	.641	1052	102	0	32	67	127	91	5	52
Kelly Tripucka	.472	**.419**	.868	976	68	1	25	68	117	105	4	34
Mel Turpin	.513	.333	.724	1011	157	2	22	71	236	32	68	26
Rickey Green	.436	.211	**.904**	1116	83	0	18	94	80	300	1	57
Marc Iavaroni	.467	0-2	.788	1238	162	1	17	83	268	67	25	23

OVERALL RANKINGS *

PLAYER	G	GS	PPG	PR	RANK	SC	SH	RB	AS	BL	ST
Karl Malone	**82**	**82**	**27.66**	**27.63**	7	5	64	10	106	83	61
John Stockton	**82**	79	14.68	**26.54**	8	59	1	142	1	125	1
Thurl Bailey	**82**	10	19.56	18.94	42	26	55	73	114	20	144
Mark Eaton	**82**	**82**	6.96	14.27	86	153	158	23	157	1	153
Bob Hansen	81	51	9.59	9.68	131	119	22	121	69	150	62
Darrell Griffith	52	11	11.33	8.27	DNQ						
Kelly Tripucka	49	21	7.51	7.90	DNQ						
Mel Turpin	79	0	5.95	6.89	DNQ						
Rickey Green	81	3	4.85	6.37	DNQ						
Marc Iavaroni	81	71	4.49	5.90	DNQ						

POSITION RANKINGS *

PLAYER	POSITION	RANK	SC	SH	RB	AS	BL	ST
Karl Malone	Power Forward (PF)	2	2	14	6	11	28	4
John Stockton	Point Guard (PG)	2	8	1	24	1	12	1
Thurl Bailey	Small Forward (SF)	10	9	7	13	27	2	31
Mark Eaton	Center (C)	17	24	26	12	25	1	2?
Bob Hansen	Off Guard (OG)	24	27	8	18	24	31	17
Darrell Griffith	Off Guard (OG)	DNQ						
Kelly Tripucka	Off Guard (OG)	DNQ						
Mel Turpin	Center (C)	DNQ						
Rickey Green	Point Guard (PG)	DNQ						
Marc Iavaroni	Small Forward (SF)	DNQ						

*For further definition of each category and column heading see pages 38 & 39.

Utah Jazz ....Team Info

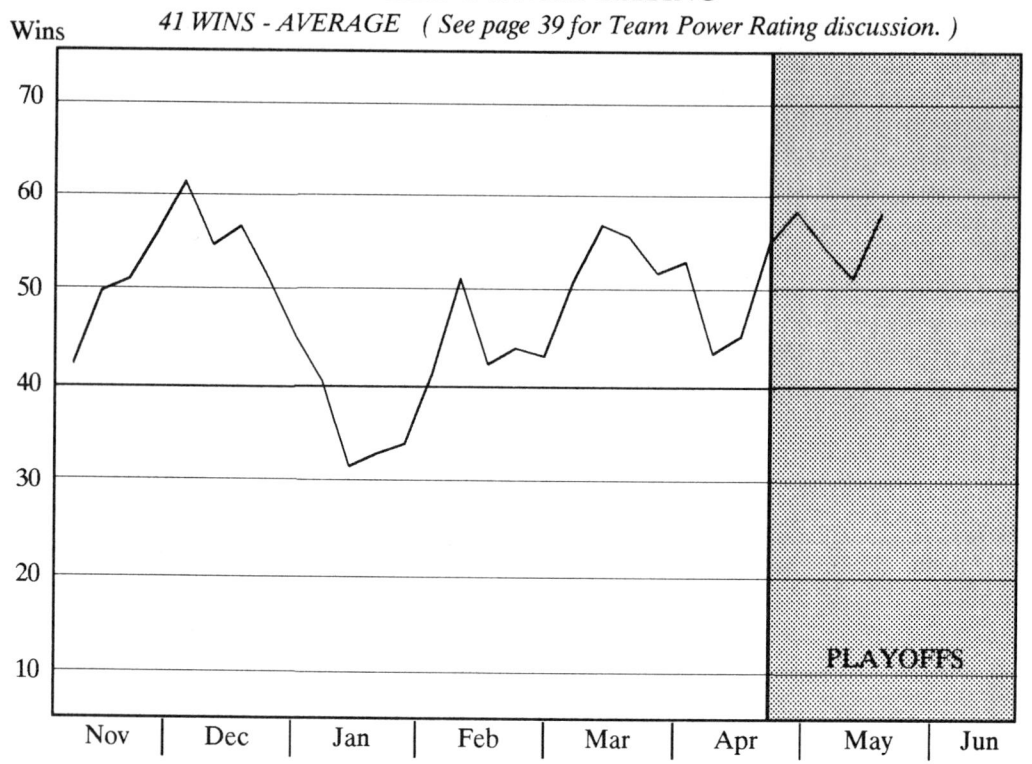

WEEKLY POWER RATING
41 WINS - AVERAGE (See page 39 for Team Power Rating discussion.)

Wins

[Chart showing weekly power rating from Nov through Jun, with playoffs shaded region in May-Jun]

Miscellaneous Categories	Data	Rank
Attendance	504K	12
Key-Man Games Missed	69	11
Season Record	47-35	9
- Home	33-8	5
- Road	14-27	10
Eastern Conference	9-13	17
Western Conference	38-22	7
Overtime Record	0-1	21
Record 5 Pts. or Less	11-15	17
Record 10 Pts. or More	28-13	4
Games Won By Bench	13	1
Games Won By Starters	3	15
Winning Streak	5	12
Losing Streak	4	4
Home Winning Streak	9	12
Road Winning Streak	4	5
Home Losing Streak	2	2
Road Losing Streak	6	8

Performance Categories	Data	Rank
Offensive Scoring (per game)	108.5	10
Defensive Scoring (per game)	104.8	5
Scoring Margin (per game)	3.7	7
Defensive FG%	.449	1
Offensive 2-point%	.502	3
Offensive 3-point%	.319	11
Offensive Free Throw %	.750	18
Offensive Rebs (Off REB/Opp Def REB)		20
Defensive Rebs (Def REB/Opp Off REB)		16
Offensive Assists (AST/FGMade)		1
Offensive Blocks (BLK/Opp FGAttempted)		1
Offensive Steals (STL/Game)		4
Turnover Margin (Off T.O. - Def T.O.)		12
Finesse (BLK + STL) / PF		1
Rebounding Record	39-38-5	12
Assists Record	62-16-4	1
Field Goal Pct. Record	57-25-0	1
Free Throw Pct. Record	37-45-0	19

TEAM BY TEAM ANALYSIS 217

Utah Jazz .... Miscellaneous

ADMINISTRATIVE INFORMATION

Team Offices: 5 Triad Center
Suite 500
Salt Lake City, Utah
84180
Telephone: (801) 575-7800
Head Coach: Frank Layden
Home Arena: Salt Palace
Capacity: 12,212

1988-89 ROSTER*

J#	VETERANS	COLLEGE	POS	R#	D#	HT	WT	Utah	NBA
41	Thurl Bailey	N. Carolina State	F	1	7	6-11	222	5	5
	Mike Brown	G. Washington	F	3	69	6-9	250	0	2
53	Mark Eaton	UCLA	C	4	72	7-4	290	6	6
35	Darrell Griffith	Louisville	G	1	2	6-4	190	7	7
20	Bob Hansen	Iowa	G-F	3	54	6-6	195	5	5
43	Marc Iavaroni	Virginia	F	3	55	6-10	225	3	6
11	Bart Kofoed	Kearney State	G	5	107	6-5	210	1	1
32	Karl Malone	Louisiana Tech	F	1	13	6-9	256	3	3
12	John Stockton	Gonzaga	G	1	16	6-1	175	4	4
54	Mel Turpin	Kentucky	C	1	6	6-11	260	1	4

ROOKIES	COLLEGE	POS	R#	D#	HT
Eric Leckner	Wyoming	C	1	17	6-11
Jeff Moe	Iowa	G	2	42	6-4
Ricky Grace	Oklahoma	G	3	67	6-1

* For further definition of category and column headings, see pages 38 & 39.

Utah Jazz .... Overview

OK, OK, let's get the Frank "In India they worship my body" Layden jokes out of the way. Yes, Frank is a little overweight; yes, he's listed as the worst-dressed coach in the league; and yes, the following story is true. (Well, you know...) One day Layden was at a carnival. Thinking he'd see what the weight scales had to say, he got on. After putting in his quarter, he expected to read his fortune. What he got was a modest little note that read "Look, I'll give you your fortune, just come back next time and come back alone!"

We may have been laughing *with* him, but no one was laughing *at* him. Layden did his best job of coaching yet. By season's end he had put together the most well-defined collection of players in the league. Frank has always been big on discipline and role playing. The obvious positives which result from this are consistency and chemistry. The Jazz had a lot of both. Nevertheless, the whole season wasn't a walk in the park. At one point, just prior to the All-Star game, the team was on a 4 win, 8 loss run. Layden made no bones about it. If he was going to suffer the consequences, so would those players who were not giving it their best. It must have worked. From then on, Utah went 29-13, the league's second best record over the same period.

The Jazz waltzed into the playoffs on a high note before dancing all over Portland 4 games to 1. Other than being walked on in the first quarter of game 1 vs the Lakers (8 points scored - a playoff record low), they more than kept pace with the world champions in round 2. Talk about consistency. In the seven game series with L.A., Karl Malone scored 29, 29, 29, 29, 27, 27, and 31. That's incredible. John Stockton set a 7 game series record for most assists (115) and steals (28). That's incredible too! By the time Los Angeles survived Utah, it had become clear there would be a new challenger in 1988-89.

When talking about the team's strengths, I think you have to start with John Stockton. John came out of nowhere two seasons ago to make All-NBA 2nd team in 1987-88. As Layden said "Last year you didn't know his name. You didn't know if he was Stockton from Gonzaga or Gonzaga from Stockton." Every expert in the country could have been given the opportunity to list 50 players during the preseason who might make the league's 1st or 2nd team. I'm confident that none would have chosen John Stockton. Perhaps, upon reflection, this oversight was a little surprising. After all, he ranked #1 in assists and #2 in steals on a 48 minute basis in the whole NBA during the 1986-87 season. Whether his 87-88 success could have been predicted or not really doesn't change anything. The simple fact is that he ranked #1 in assists (per minute), #1 in steals (per minute), and #1 in shooting (See page 40 for explanation of formula). No player in the history of the game has led three of the six performance categories the same season. (Blocks, rebounds, and scoring are the other three.) That's no one, folks. Not Mikan, Chamberlain, Russell, Havlicek, Robertson, Abdul-Jabbar, Erving, Magic, or Bird. No one!

Stockton barely triumphed in the shooting battle with Kevin McHale: 1.1614 to 1.1608. Had John missed just 1 more free throw than he did, he would have dropped to second. Additionally, he shot 59.4% on his 2-pt shots (the highest ever for a point guard) and dished off 1128 assists. Guess what? Another NBA record. He passed Isiah Thomas' mark of 1123 in his last game. Stockton led the Jazz in assists the last 57 games. That's consistency! There is a real possibility that he could be even more valuable than Magic by the end of next season. His stock is rising - that's for sure.

As remarkable as Stockton's season was, the average person on the street would say the best player on the team was Karl Malone. I can't argue with that either. Both players were brilliant; both got better as the season went on; both made 2nd team All-NBA; and both were named back-to-back Player's-of-the-Month.

Utah Jazz .... Overview

November	Michael Jordan
December	Larry Nance
January	Michael Jordan
February	**John Stockton**
March	**Karl Malone**
April	Lafayette Lever

Malone led the team in scoring at 27.66 points per game. Add 12+ rebounds per contest to his stats and you're talking about not just a star, but a supernova. No player in the NBA went to the hoop with more authority than Malone. Karl averaged 37 points and 15 rebounds over his last eight games. If he does that well over the course of next season, he'll be the unanimous league MVP. Though the Post Office may shut down on Saturdays, this "mailman" delivered. Malone average 31 points and 14 boards on thirteen Saturdays in 1988. Though he entered last season with a career FT% of only 54.8%, he managed to hit a very respectable 70% during 1987-88. His most noteworthy accomplishment on defense was when he held Ralph Sampson scoreless in an early season matchup. It was so embarassing to the Rockets that they traded Ralph shortly thereafter.

Thurl Bailey was voted the #2 6th man behind Roy Tarpley. Though Tarpley had a great season, Bailey actually led him 36 to 27 in games where, if his scoring were discounted, his team would have lost. That is a good formula for value. His seven 30+ point games were easily the high among nonstarters. In fact, he actually played more minutes than 80% of the league's starters. I put together a very interesting comparison between T.B. and perennial All-Star James Worthy on page 233. How do the two compare? Take a look.

At times there have been cries to replace Mark Eaton at center. It's true that he only gets about as high off the ground as the Spruce Goose, and he ranked 158th out of 159 regulars in overall shooting, but I say the Jazz would be nuts to let him go. Though the team has several good defensive players, they are good largely because Eaton is great! With the possible exception of fellow-UCLA alumnus Kareem Abdul-Jabbar, Eaton is likely going to end his career as the all-time leader in blocked shots. His rebounding is respectable and he takes up a ton of space. Despite being voted behind Akeem Olajuwon as the league's top defensive center, he generally won the battle when the two met head-to-head. His many blocks that started fast breaks as well as his unsurpassed ability to set picks are intangibles that are hard to measure. What *is* measurable is the team defensive FG%. At .449, it's the lowest in the NBA since Cleveland in 1977.

Bobby Hansen had one late-season stretch where he hit an amazing 44 of 54 FGA's. His Production Rating, like that of his teammates, was substantially superior in the 2nd half of the season to the first.

	1st half	**2nd half**
Stockton	21.98	31.10
Malone	25.51	29.76
Bailey	16.56	21.32
Hansen	7.80	11.51

Misc: The Jazz ranked #1 in the league in games won by the bench... Utah set a new attendance high of 12,056 per game... This was the only team in the NBA to beat the Denver Nuggets in the season series... Utah went 9-0 vs the three Texas teams at home, but was shut out (0-9) while playing in the Lone Star State.

Prediction - best case: 58-24

This team can be the best in the NBA. They won 29 games the 2nd half of last season and could double that number in 1988-89. If rookies Eric Leckner and Jose Ortiz can contribute as expected and veteran Darrell Griffith can help keep the Jazz on track, very little will stop this train.

Prediction - worst case: 49-33

The club must improve in one area or *only* 49 wins is possible. The Jazz ranked last, having lost 12 games after leading going into the final quarter. Additionally, they were lucky, lucky, lucky on injuries. Of their top-5 players, they only lost 1 game.

Washington Bullets .... History

The Washington Bullets became an NBA franchise in 1961-62. At the time it was the first new NBA franchise in twelve years and it increased from eight to nine the number of teams in the league.

The Bullets were initially known as the Chicago Packers. Interestingly, Walt Bellamy scored 31.6 ppg that year - the most impressive achievement the windy city would see for 25 years until Michael Jordan scored 37.0 ppg. In 1963, the club changed their name to the Zephyrs. Prior to their 3rd year, the team moved to Baltimore. Since then, the club has changed names twice. In 1973, they were known as the Capital Bullets. The following year, the Bullets finally settled with Washington. An earlier franchise from 1948-54 was called the Baltimore Bullets, but there is no relationship between the two clubs. The present day Bullets have had five different names - more than any other franchise.

The club went to the finals four times between 1971 and 1972 - more than any other NBA club. In 1971, the Bullets lost to the Bucks, zero games to four. Again, the team was shut out zero to four in 1975 against the Warriors. What is intriguing here is that present coach Wes Unseld played in both final series losses - thus becoming the only player in NBA history to play in two championship shut-outs. Unseld just missed playing in a third (1979). That year the Bullets lost to Seattle one game to four. The lone victory was by a slim two points (99-97). Washington's only title came in 1978, also against Seattle, four games to three (105-99 in game 7). Though they have been to the playoffs six of the last seven years, the Bullets have won only one playoff series (2-0 over New Jersey, 1982).

Trivia: The Bullets are the only NBA team to win over 35 games every season during the last 21 years. The Lakers have won 35+ games 20 of 21... The club is one of two NBA teams to have back-to-back seasons of 15 or more wins from the previous year (1967 and 1968). Houston was the other (1985 and 1986)... Although he did not coach the Bullets every year from 1967 to 1986, Gene Shue holds the record for coaching the same team over the longest span (20 years, 1967-73 and 1981-86)... The Bullets hold the record for most playoff losses in one season (10). They did it twice... Six different Bullets have led the club in steals the last 6 seasons.

> **Quiz: Besides Unseld, what other player was the Rookie-of-the-Year and MVP the same season?**

ALL TIME BULLETS' TEAM

Player	Span	Yrs	APR
Wes Unseld	1969-81	13	22,572
Elvin Hayes	1973-81	9	17,612
Gus Johnson	1964-72	9	12,694
Walt Bellamy	1962-65	4	10,908
Greg Ballard	1978-85	8	9,964
Kevin Loughery	1964-71	9	8,132
Jack Marin	1967-72	6	8,054
Phil Chenier	1972-79	9	7,795
Jeff Ruland	1982-86	5	7,086
Earl Monroe	1968-71	4	6,353

ALL TIME BULLETS' COACH

Gene Shue — 13 Years
19-36 Playoffs — 8 Playoffs
522-505 Reg. Season — 0 Championships

STATISTICAL INFORMATION

Category	Data
Bullets' coach	Wes Unseld
Years coached Washington	1
# of franchise years	27
# of coaches	12
# of winning seasons	13
# of playoff years	20
# of runner's up	3
# of championships	1
Regular season win %	50.0
Playoff win %	42.3

> **Answer:**
> **Wilt Chamberlain**

Washington Bullets ....1987-88 Highlights

Bullets 108-101 Knicks Fri. November 13, 1987

The Washington Bullets set an NBA record against the New York Knicks in their 108-101 victory. The Bullets hit 60 of 69 free throws, eclipsing the old mark of 59 set in 1949 by the Syracuse Nationals in a 5-overtime game against the Anderson Packers. Whereas Washington shot 87% for the game, the Nationals only shot 69%, despite an NBA record 86 attempts. Not surprisingly, Knicks' coach Rick Pitino was ejected for disputing fouls.

Bullets 120-112 Lakers Wed. December 9, 1987

The Washington Bullets, who have really struggled so far this year, looked like world beaters when they defeated the defending champion L.A. Lakers. The victory broke a four game losing streak for the Bullets. The win was attributable to a strong first quarter. Coming into the game, the Bullets had won the first quarter only once out of 16 games. Their 34 1st quarter points vs the Lakers represented a season high to this point.

Bullets 101-97 Nets Tue. January 5, 1988

This was Wes Unseld's first head coaching experience. Unseld went back to the starting lineup used by former coach, Kevin Loughery, at the beginning of the season. That lineup was 0-3 for Loughery. As of this date, Unseld can claim to be the only undefeated coach in NBA history.

Bullets 136-107 Bucks, Bullets 108-76 Clippers Thur. January 14, 1988

The Washington Bullets were on a roll. In two consecutive games they won by 32 and 29 points - their largest margins of victory since 1981. The Bullets have not lost at home to LA since 1979 and the win extended the Clipper's losing streak to 10 games. The win was also the largest margin of victory ever over the Clippers. Amazingly, the 136-107 victory over Milwaukee was also the largest margin of victory ever over the Bucks. The Bullets remain undefeated at home for new coach Wes Unseld (3-0).

Bullets 131-99 76ers Sun. January 24, 1988

The Bullets continued their roll since Wes Unseld took over the coaching reins - this time by beating up on Philadelphia. The win was the 6th straight win vs no losses at home by the Bullets, while Philly was winless in their last 7 road games. The 32 point victory margin was the largest Bullet victory over Philadelphia since 1974. During Unseld's 6 home victories, the Bullets have averaged winning by an astonishing 23 ppg.

Bullets 115-111 Suns Wed. March 9, 1988

The victory was the 7th in a row for the Bullets - the longest winning streak since 1983. Meanwhile, the loss represented the 7th straight for Phoenix - all 7 coming since the Suns cleaned house with three big trades. Noteworthy was the play of Steve Colter and Charles Jones. Colter was just 1 point and 1 assist (16,8) shy of his tops for the Bullets, while Jones hit double figures (11) the first time this season.

Bullets 86-85 Hawks Mon. April 11, 1988

The Washington Bullets jumped off to a big lead early and held off an Atlanta rally to win at the Omni. It was the first Bullets road win vs Atlanta since 1985. The importance was that it kept Washington tied with New York for the #8 position in the playoff race. Darrell Walker was the man. His 19 points were the game's high and his second highest of the season, but it was his last second shot that snatched victory from the jaws of defeat.

Washington Bullets .... Influence on Winning

TEAM RECORD BY

PLAYER	GAMES	...SCR Leader HOME	ROAD	...REB Leader HOME	ROAD	...AST Leader HOME	ROAD
Moses Malone	79	11-4	5-5	20-13	8-18	---	0-1
Jeff Malone	80	7-5	3-13	---	0-1	3-0	3-6
John S. Williams	82	2-2	1-2	1-2	2-2	1-3	3-3
Bernard King	69	8-2	2-7	1-0	---	2-1	1-2
Terry Catledge	70	1-1	1-2	2-0	2-4	---	0-1
Steve Colter	68	---	0-1	1-0	---	3-3	4-8
Tyrone Bogues	79	---	---	---	---	15-10	2-12
Charles Jones	69	---	---	1-0	0-3	---	---
Frank Johnson	75	---	0-1	---	---	1-0	1-2
Darrell Walker	52	---	1-1	---	---	1-1	0-3

TEAM RECORD BY SCORING *

PLAYER	PLAY	DNP	0-9	10-19	20-29	30-39	40+
Moses Malone	37-42	1-2	1-2	12-25	17-13	7-2	---
Jeff Malone	37-43	1-1	1-4	17-14	16-19	2-6	1-0
John S. Williams	38-44	---	8-19	24-18	6-7	---	---
Bernard King	30-39	8-5	8-8	4-18	15-11	3-2	---
Terry Catledge	33-37	5-7	13-19	18-15	2-3	---	---
Steve Colter	29-27	9-17	15-22	14-3	0-2	---	---
Tyrone Bogues	36-43	2-1	31-35	5-8	---	---	---
Charles Jones	32-37	6-7	31-37	1-0	---	---	---
Frank Johnson	33-42	5-2	26-36	5-6	2-0	---	---
Darrell Walker	23-29	15-15	17-22	5-7	1-0	---	---

TEAM RECORD BY STARTING POSITION *

PLAYER	GAMES	STARTS	PG	OG	SF	PF	C
Moses Malone	79	78	---	---	---	---	37-41
Jeff Malone	80	80	---	36-44	---	---	---
John S. Williams	82	37	---	---	18-12	3-4	---
Bernard King	56	38	---	---	16-22	---	---
Terry Catledge	70	40	---	---	0-1	15-24	---
Steve Colter	56	53	29-24	---	---	---	---
Tyrone Bogues	79	14	5-9	---	---	---	---
Charles Jones	69	49	---	---	4-9	20-16	---
Frank Johnson	75	17	4-11	2-0	---	---	---
Darrell Walker	52	0	---	---	---	---	---

* For further definition of each category and column heading see pages 38 & 39.

Washington Bullets — 1987-88 Statistics

RAW NUMBERS *

PLAYER	2pt%	3pt%	FT%	MIN	PF	DQ	HI	TO	RB	AS	BL	ST
Moses Malone	.488	.286	.788	**2692**	160	0	36	**249**	**884**	112	72	59
Jeff Malone	.478	**.417**	**.882**	2655	198	1	**47**	172	206	237	13	51
John Williams	.484	.132	.734	2428	217	3	28	145	444	232	34	117
Bernard King	.503	.167	.762	2044	202	3	34	211	280	192	10	49
Terry Catledge	**.508**	0-2	.655	1610	172	0	27	101	397	63	9	33
Steve Colter	.464	.300	.789	1513	132	0	29	88	173	261	14	62
Tyrone Bogues	.398	.188	.784	1628	138	1	16	101	136	**404**	3	**127**
Charles Jones	.409	0-1	.707	1313	**226**	5	11	57	325	59	**113**	53
Frank Johnson	.440	.111	.812	1258	120	0	23	99	121	188	4	70
Darrell Walker	.400	0-6	.781	940	105	2	20	69	127	100	10	62

OVERALL RANKINGS *

PLAYER	G	GS	PPG	PR	RANK	SC	SH	RB	AS	BL	ST
Moses Malone	79	78	20.34	22.53	18	19	65	7	138	47	127
Jeff Malone	80	**80**	20.51	15.24	76	17	62	147	75	131	138
John Williams	**82**	37	12.77	14.37	84	80	125	75	71	93	29
Bernard King	69	38	17.22	13.96	87	40	63	96	73	133	120
Terry Catledge	70	40	10.66	11.10	119	103	99	31	145	126	134
Steve Colter	68	53	7.12	9.53	132	151	128	112	33	108	50
Tyrone Bogues	79	14	4.97	8.68	147	156	159	141	8	153	5
Charles Jones	69	49	2.86	8.16	152	159	156	30	135	4	53
Frank Johnson	75	17	7.39	7.04	DNQ						
Darrell Walker	52	0	5.96	6.54	DNQ						

POSITION RANKINGS *

PLAYER	POSITION	RANK	SC	SH	RB	AS	BL	ST
Moses Malone	Center (C)	3	2	11	3	18	20	12
Jeff Malone	Off Guard (OG)	13	6	14	27	26	29	33
John Williams	Small Forward (SF)	19	20	27	15	12	24	4
Bernard King	Small Forward (SF)	20	15	13	26	13	29	27
Terry Catledge	Power Forward (PF)	27	22	22	13	29	34	27
Steve Colter	Point Guard (PG)	27	31	25	10	29	8	24
Tyrone Bogues	Point Guard (PG)	30	32	32	23	8	28	2
Charles Jones	Power Forward (PF)	35	35	35	12	22	1	3
Frank Johnson	Point Guard (PG)	DNQ						
Darrell Walker	Off Guard (OG)	DNQ						

*For further definition of each category and column heading see pages 38 & 39.

Washington Bullets .... Team Info

WEEKLY POWER RATING
41 WINS - AVERAGE (See page 39 for Team Power Rating discussion.)

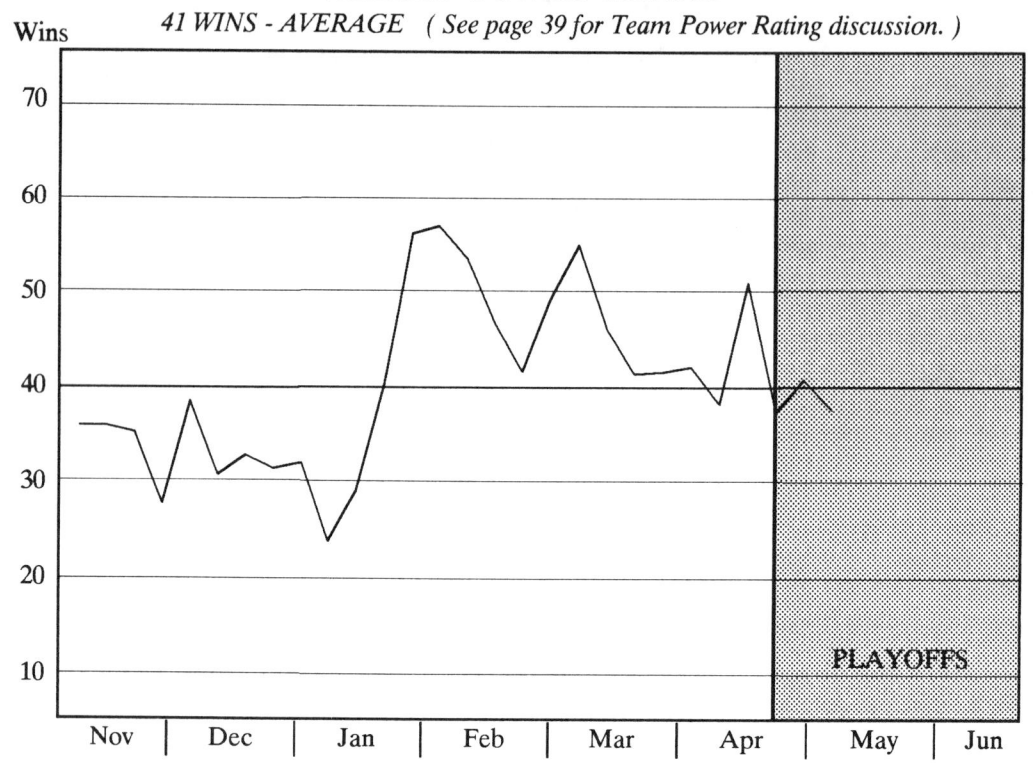

Miscellaneous Categories	Data	Rank
Attendance	433K	20
Key-Man Games Missed	73	13
Season Record	38-44	14
- Home	25-16	16
- Road	13-28	11
Eastern Conference	26-32	14
Western Conference	12-12	14
Overtime Record	4-3	7
Record 5 Pts. or Less	13-15	16
Record 10 Pts. or More	16-22	16
Games Won By Bench	6	8
Games Won By Starters	2	19
Winning Streak	7	7
Losing Streak	5	10
Home Winning Streak	8	14
Road Winning Streak	4	5
Home Losing Streak	4	15
Road Losing Streak	6	8

Performance Categories	Data	Rank
Offensive Scoring (per game)	105.5	17
Defensive Scoring (per game)	106.3	10
Scoring Margin (per game)	-.8	15
Defensive FG%	.478	14
Offensive 2-point%	.473	22
Offensive 3-point%	.210	23
Offensive Free Throw %	.773	9
Offensive Rebs (Off REB/Opp Def REB)		7
Defensive Rebs (Def REB/Opp Off REB)		21
Offensive Assists (AST/FGMade)		22
Offensive Blocks (BLK/Opp FGAttempted)		5
Offensive Steals (STL/Game)		13
Turnover Margin (Off T.O. - Def T.O.)		10
Finesse (BLK + STL) / PF		8
Rebounding Record	38-39-5	14
Assists Record	26-52-4	19
Field Goal Pct. Record	38-44-0	14
Free Throw Pct. Record	48-33-1	5

Washington Bullets .... Miscellaneous

ADMINISTRATIVE INFORMATION

Team Offices: Capital Centre
Landover, Maryland
20785

Telephone: (301) 773-2255
Head Coach: Wes Unseld
Home Arena: Capital Centre
Capacity: 19,411

1988-89 ROSTER*

J#	VETERANS	COLLEGE	POS	R#	D#	HT	WT	Wash	NBA
31	Mark Alarie	Duke	F	1	18	6-8	217	1	2
33	Terry Catledge	South Alabama	F	1	21	6-8	230	2	3
14	Steve Colter	New Mexico State	G	2	33	6-3	175	1	4
5	Dave Feitl	UTEP	C	2	43	7-0	240	0	2
15	Frank Johnson	Wake Forest	G	1	11	6-3	185	7	7
23	Charles Jones	Albany State	F	8	165	6-9	215	4	5
30	Bernard King	Tennessee	F	1	7	6-7	205	1	10
24	Jeff Malone	Mississippi State	G	1	10	6-4	205	5	5
5	Darrell Walker	Arkansas	G	1	12	6-4	180	1	5
34	John Williams	LSU	F	1	12	6-9	237	2	2

ROOKIES	COLLEGE	POS	R#	D#	HT
Harvey Grant	Oklahoma	F	1	12	6-9
Ledell Eackles	New Orleans	G	2	36	6-5
Ed Davender	Kentucky	G	3	60	6-3

* For further definition of category and column headings, see pages 38 & 39.

Washington Bullets .... Overview

Question: What club is less aptly named than the Washington Bullets? Answer: None. Of all the images I think of when I think of this team, a bullet is far down the list. Most would agree that Washington's offense was the ugliest in the NBA. There was such a wide divergence of players in both size and style that it rarely looked as if the club was "in sync" or "flowing". It's true that they had their moments, but even then, they looked more like the spray from a water pistol than the bullet from a gun. Even Tyrone Bogues, though small enough and fast enough, never went in a straight line.

There were several reasons why the Bullets were sluggish offensively. To begin with, their shooting was by far the worst among clubs who made the playoffs; their 3-point shooting was last in the league; and they ranked next to the bottom in assists. Throw in the league's top garbage man and... well, you see what I mean.

At one point in the season, they were so bad at getting out of the blocks they were virtually assured of a loss. In their first 22 games, the team won quarter #1 only once! In fact, the Bullets' opponents were so geared up against the likes of Bol and Bogues that they won 20 of the 22 games played immediately after facing Washington.

It's understandable why the club has been known as average for so long. With the NFL's Redskins to compete against, the less than exciting Cap Center to play in, and the endless parade of politicians grabbing headlines, it's a wonder the Bullets had time to win at all. In spite of this, the club entered the last game of the year with 1101 regular season wins and 1101 regular season losses. That's what I call average! As it turns out, they won their final game against Atlanta. This victory not only gave the Bullets an all-time winning record, but more importantly, made the difference on a playoff berth.

After an 8-19 beginning, the playoffs seemed remote, to say the least. Nevertheless, Bob Ferry (GM) wasn't giving up hope. Ferry replaced Kevin Loughery with Wes Unseld. It proved to be a great move. Unseld was 30-25 the rest of the way and nearly upset Detroit in round 1 of the playoffs. Unseld ranks #2 all-time for turning a team around in mid-season. Using the admittedly obscure criterion that a team had to have played 27+ games (1/3 of the season), but less than 55 games (2/3 of the season) when the coaching change was made, Wes led the team to a .545 winning percentage. Before he took over, it was only .296. The net difference is +.249.

			PRE/POST/NET
1970 Joe Belmont	Denver	9-19 42-14	+.429
1988 Wes Unseld	**Washington**	**8-19 30-25**	**+.249**
1968 Red Holzman	New York	15-22 28-17	+.217
1984 Bob Bass	San Antonio	11-20 26-25	+.155
1981 Doug Moe	Denver	11-20 26-25	+.155
1970 Jerry Colangelo	Phoenix	15-23 24-20	+.151
1982 Rod Thorn	Chicago	19-33 15-15	+.135
1987 Jerry Reynolds	Sacramento	14-32 15-21	+.112

Belmont accomplished his feat in the ABA.

Under Loughery, the Bullets were 3-19-5 in the first quarter. Unseld changed that stat to 30-21-4. The Bullets were horrible in their last four home games under Loughery, losing by margins of -4, -5, -15, and -11. Under Wes, the club won its first six home games by spreads of +4 (it took a little getting used to), +32, +29, +17, +24, +32. That is an unbelievable reversal. Unseld's influence is depicted graphically on page 226. It's probably no surprise that he was named Coach-of-the-Month for January.

At this point, it's probably fair to say the club made two big **Boo Boo**'s when they drafted **Bol** and **Bogues** - the league's tallest and shortest players. Manute Bol was drafted as an undergraduate early in the second round. Although a 2nd round pick is no guarantee in the NBA, his 3-year Production Ratings have dropped from 12.05 to 8.96 to 6.94. If Bullet management thought Bol would help out, do you think

Washington Bullets .... Overview

he would have been traded away after 3 years of investment? Tyrone Bogues was clearly more disappointing than Bol. Drafted in 1987 as the 12th pick, he managed only a .398 fg% and 5 points/game. I'm sure fans are less than thrilled when they think of some of those players picked after Bogues (Mark Jackson and Greg Anderson are just two of many). Again, if Bogues was a success, then why, with his career ahead of him, was he left unprotected in the expansion draft? Worth mentioning is the fact that, two years ago, Bol didn't get his first assist until game #44. Last season, Bogues was blockless until game #38. The two are just too one-dimensional. In any event they're both gone. With no Mutt and Jeff to kick around anymore, I guess the critics will have to go elsewhere.

On second thought, as long as Darrell Walker and Mark Alarie remain, it will be a constant reminder of what the club lost in its trade with Denver. As you may recall, the Bullets sent Michael Adams and Jay Vincent to the Nuggets. For a club that ranked dead last in 3-point percentage, imagine how valuable Adams would have been. Michael hit 139 treys last season - the 2nd highest in NBA history! Jay Vincent ranked #2 among 6th men in scoring. Again, for a team that so desperately needed strong offensive players, this trade has to be considered a mistake. Outside of Walker's 10.5 ppg scoring average his last dozen games (including playoffs), his season was a bitter disappointment. Both he and Alarie averaged barely over 5 ppg.

One trade which was as good as this one was bad was the trade of Jeff Ruland and Cliff Robinson for Moses Malone and Terry Catledge. The keys are that Ruland played only a handful of games before retiring while Malone has been very productive the last 2 years. Moses once again proved his value to his team. When he scored 24+ points, the Bullets were 19-5; when he didn't they struggled at 18-37. As always, he had a lot of turnovers, ranking third worst among centers. Interestingly, the league's other two Malones, including his teammate Jeff, ranked worst in the league at turnovers per minute. Bernard King also ranked worst at his postion.

Pat Ewing	Center	.113
Bernard King	Small Forward	**.103**
Magic Johnson	Point Guard	.102
Jeff Malone	**Off Guard**	**.102**
Karl Malone	Power Forward	.092

The best of the rest: Bernard King had a successful comeback season. After missing two years, he averaged over 17 ppg. He has slowed just a bit, but that doesn't mean he's not valuable. When he scored in the teens, Washington was a terrible 4-18. When he scored 20 or more, they were a robust 18-13... Jeff Malone has consistently been on everyone's "gunner" list. His .476 shooting percentage isn't great, but then considering the shots he takes, it's not bad either. Malone made my exclusive coaches' poll as one of the best off-balance outside shooters. The others were Bird, Magic, Jordan, and Mike Evans... John Williams is easily the most versatile player on the team. He too made the coaches' poll as one of the best non-guards to lead the break. Joining him were Bird (again), McCray, Barkley, and Worthy... Steve Colter was instrumental in Washington's late-season surge. After averaging only 3 ppg the first half, he averaged a respectable 10 ppg thereafter.

Prediction - best case: 40-42

Though a lot has to go right, including a contribution by rookie Harvey Grant, for the team to win 40 games, it's not that hard to imagine. At the rate they played under Unseld, they would win 45. Still, that was with Moses parting the waters.

Prediction - worst case: 28-54

With Malone gone to Atlanta (free agent), a mere 28 wins is easily imaginable. If Bernard King struggles or gets injured, if Grant fails to help, if Colter doesn't continue at his late-season pace, then 34 wins could be tops.

Larry Bird of the Boston Celtics
- The Celtics of the Bird era are the winningest group in NBA history
- Basketball Hall of Fame -

CHAPTER 4

PLAYERS' POSITIONS

CLEVELAND VS BOSTON

During the last few years, the Cleveland Cavaliers have had inexplicable success vs the Boston Celtics. In 1987 and 1988 the Cavs won only 73 games compared to the Celts 116 victories - not to mention two division titles. However, both teams won 5 games against each other. The Cavs, by winning last season's series 3-2, are the only team with a regular season losing record in the Larry Bird era (1980-87) to defeat the Celtics in a season series (1988). Even more impressively, Cleveland has actually outscored Boston the past two years 1087-1085.

Since Bob Cousy's first year (1950-51), Boston has played in 31 playoffs. They have outscored their first round opponent an incredible 30 times. Ironically, the one time they failed to achieve this standard, their opponent was Cleveland in 1985. It was the only time the Cavs have met the Celts in round 1. The total score of the series was 459-459.

PLAYERS POSITIONS

Any discussion of positions in the NBA needs to be prefaced with a disclaimer or two. Basketball, unlike baseball, has less definabled qualities which make up each position. Many times a player plays more than one position throughout the season. In fact, half the time a player plays more than one position in a given game. A team such as Denver makes little distinction between Adams and Lever at point or off guard. For that matter, Schayes and Rasmussen interchange regularly between center and power forward. The point is that some players play out of position because of the team's needs.

Then too, are there only five positions? What about a power center (Malone) vs a perimeter center (Laimbeer) or a finesse center (Jabbar) vs a defensive center (Eaton)? I call them all one thing - a center. A small forward is also a finesse forward, a quick forward or even a shooting forward; an off-guard is often referred to as a shooting guard or a two-guard; a point guard is called a lead guard; and a power forward is synonymous with a rebounding forward.

Despite the multitude of names associated with the five positions, it is generally accepted that only five positions exist. Although point forward (Pressey), swingman (McCray), and power guard (Jordan) are terms which have gained popularity. Nevertheless, until the NBA offices pick the All-NBA team by parameters other than guards, forwards and center, I will accept what is traditional.

POSITION AVERAGES

Certainly, some players can reasonably be listed at either of several positions, however, I generally chose the position they played at most often during the 1987-88 season. To help me determine what position a player "really" was, I developed a formula which identified the average center, power forward, etc. Once that was accomplished, I evaluated each player by those averages to determine how closely each was to his position.

I decided that to the degree a player came closer to one position than another on a scale of 100, he was most like the average player at that position. More precisely, I chose to compare each player to the average of each position by twelve categories - 2-pt %, FT%, 3-pt FGA's per minute, Pts/min, Reb/min, Ast/min, Blk/min, Stl/min, T.O./min, Fouls/min, height, and weight. When you think about it, some categories are more likely to indicate whether a player is of one position or another. For example, if a player shoots 2 pointers at 48.3% or 50.3% which is he? Is he a point guard or a center? That's not too easy to say. On the other hand if a player is 7'0" or 6'2", is he most likely a point guard or a center? That's easy. Therefore, I gave different values to the twelve categories. These values are not for the purpose of diciding which category is most *important*, but rather which is most *telling* about what position a player plays. Shown below are the averages for the twelve positions.

	2pt%	FT%	3-pt* FGA	* PPG	* RB	* AS	* BK	* ST	* T.O.	* FL	HT	WT
Center	50.3	72.5	.1	20.2	12.8	2.3	2.3	1.1	3.3	5.5	7'0"	247 lbs.
Power Forward	50.2	74.6	.3	20.9	12.3	2.8	1.4	1.3	3.2	5.6	6'9"	232 lbs.
Small Forward	49.5	76.6	.9	24.8	8.6	3.9	1.0	1.5	3.1	4.6	6'8"	216 lbs.
Off Guard	48.4	80.7	1.9	24.2	5.5	5.8	.5	2.1	3.1	4.0	6'5"	197 lbs.
Point Guard	48.3	81.3	1.6	18.8	4.8	10.8	.3	2.4	3.6	3.7	6'2"	183 lbs.
Points	**1**	**2**	**13**	**3**	**11**	**12**	**13**	**11**	**1**	**5**	**14**	**14**

*based on 48 minute averages.

PLAYERS' POSITIONS 231

The trends are obvious and unmistakable. Since they are, it is reasonable to say that a player who is very close to the average small forward and quite aways from the other four positions is, in fact, a small forward - regardless of what position he plays.

As I mentioned earlier, I gave a possible 100 points to each player. These points were distributed according to the above chart. Suppose a power player were more like a center in the first two categories (up to fouls), but more like a power forward in height and weight. He would rate a 72 center 28 power forward.

The reason the twelve categories have different values is because of what I said earlier. Some categories are far more telling than others [height (14) vs FG% (1) or weight (14) vs T.O. (1)]. Therefore, the telling categories must carry the most weight.

Lets use an example. Rickey Green of Utah is a point guard. He always has been. He plays that position virtually exclusively. However, should he? Maybe he's more of an off-guard. Here's a look at his twelve stats. * based on 48 minute averages.

	2pt%	FT%	3-pt* FGA	PPG*	RB	AS*	BK	ST*	T.O.*	FL*	HT	WT
Rickey Green	42.4	90.4	.8	16.9	3.4	12.9	.04	2.5	4.0	3.6	6'0"	172 lbs.

If you care to work it out, you will see that Green is closer to the average point guard vs off-guard in every single category. That means his rating is 100 point guard vs 0 (zero) off-guard. Therefore, the answer is "yes, he should definitely be playing the point".

I thought it would be interesting to see which players are most *like* the positions they play. Of course, even more interesting are the players who are most *unlike* the positions they play. Shown below are the top-10 at each position and their rating (100 scale) vs the two closest positions. Where two choices are given, the numbers in bold are the lowest.

Center	PF	Power Forward	C	SF	Small Forward	PF	OG	Off Guard	SF	PG	Point Guard	OG
Donaldson	97	Cureton	82	84	McDaniel	97	**81**	Long	85	**84**	Green	100
Lister	94	Perkins	80	**78**	RAnderson	85	**79**	Scott	96	**82**	Cheeks	98
Eaton	93	J. Bailey	**73**	83	O. Smith	85	**75**	Curry	82	87	Thomas	95
Gminski	93	Greenwood	79	**73**	Kersey	**73**	88	M. Cooper	75	75	Stockton	94
Blab	83	M. Lucas	73	73	Pippen	76	**73**	Tripucka	**74**	76	Valentine	93
Kleine	83	A. Carr	**72**	87	J. Vincent	**70**	84	Harris	75	**73**	Minniefield	92
Koncak	82	Coleman	**71**	98	D. Smith	84	**70**	Woodson	96	**72**	Bogues	92
Rollins	81	Grant	**69**	85	Norman	92	**69**	R. Harper	**71**	74	K. Smith	88
Gray	81	Petersen	**67**	87	Schrempf	**66**	96	V. Johnson	**70**	71	Leavell	86
Ewing	81	Sikma	**67**	73	D. Wilkins	99	**65**	G. Wilkins	83	**69**	J. Dawkins	85

Some players are miscast at their positions. Usually this is just because the team has unique needs. Shown below are the top players who are out of position and the reason why.

	PP	RT	AP	
Lever	OG	18	PG	1987-88 was Michael Adams' best year at point guard.
H. Williams	PF	20	C	Plays some center. Should trade with Stipo.
Bradley	SF	20	OG	Plays both off guard and small forward.
Rasmussen	PF	23	C	Plays both center and power forward.
Dumars	OG	24	PG	Isiah Thomas plays the point in Motown.
Iavaroni	SF	27	PF	Some argue Karl Malone is a small forward. Not me.
Short	OG	28	SF	Houston is desperate for a shooting guard.
S. Johnson	C	28	PF	Filled in for Bowie's annual injury.
Battle	OG	29	PG	Doc Rivers and Spud Webb man the point for Atlanta.
Carroll	PF	29	C	Akeem Olajuwon is the NBA's #1 center.
Pressley	PG	30	OG	Part of Milwaukees "big" movement.

	PP	RT	AP	
Drexler	OG	30	SF	Kersey and Vandeweghe are already one too many SF's.
Newman	SF	31	OG	Gerald Wilkins is solid, Kenny Walker is not.
Holton	PG	32	OG	Drexler had Paxson as backup. Porter needed someone.
Chambers	PF	34	SF	McDaniel is also a small forward. Trade time?
Sellers	SF	34	PF	Grant and Oakley are enough at PF.
Tarpley	PF	34	C	Plays some center, but Donaldson is always there.
Mahorn	PF	35	C	Laimbeer has NBA's longest consecutive game streak.
Stipanovich	C	36	PF	Should trade positions with Williams.

PP = Present Position
RT = Rating
AP = Appropriate Position

POSITION VALUE

Once in a while a discussion comes up as to which position is the most important. There was a time (as in every year in the NBA until the early '80s) that the answer was "the center". However, many changes have taken place in the game. Johnson, Bird, Jordan, Drexler, Wilkens, Barkley and others have proven beyond question that the center is not necessarily the most critical position.

I decided to try to determine what position was the most valuable. To do this I evaluated the relationship between the best players at each position and the number of games their team's won. The long and the short of it is that the point guard (.586) is the most critical position in the 1980's. The small forward (.580), center (.568), off guard (.521) and power forward (.498) are next.

If you want the quick answer to position value, I've just given it. If you want to see how I came up with it, here goes. What I did was to look at the top-10 players at each position for every year in the 1980's. I then looked at that player's team's wins and losses. What I did was multiply the best player's team's wins times 10 and losses times 10, the second best player's team's wins times 9 and losses times 9, etc. As you can see, this gave more weight to the top players and less to those at the bottom. I then determined the winning percentage for each position for each year.

Next, I followed the same principle again. There have been 9 years in the 1980's. I took the most recent winning percentage times 9, the second most recent winning percentage times 8, etc. This gave more weight to recent years. Subsequently, I came up with the winning percentages I mentioned earlier for each of the five positions.

What does it mean? Well, lets look at 1987-88 only. Last year every one of the top-10 *small* forwards played on teams with winning records, but only five of the top-10 *power* forwards were winners as well. Coincidence? I don't think so. The facts are that power forwards are good or great (excellent stats) largely because of the inadequacies of their team. The more a team misses from the field, the more chances the power forward has to get a rebound (1 positive credit) and a stick back (2 positive credits). A classic example was earlier in the year when the Clippers shot 39-111 in a game - an abysmal 35%. Michael Cage, who won the rebounding title by 1 rebound over Charles Oakley, had 23 rebounds, including a season high 14 offensive. Simply stated, the *better* the team, the less for the power forward to "achieve", while the *worse* the team, the more "potential" for the power forward. Because of the wide open style so prevalent in the NBA, the point guard has become essential. A team without a very good point guard has almost no chance to be the league's best, whereas a team can win with just a banger at power forward. The other three positions fall somewhere in between.

COMPARISONS

Some interesting comparisons are the three gravity defiers, the four defensive centers, the four rookie point guards, the two ACC alumnus, the top two rebounders, the two best assists seasons in history, and Bird vs Johnson.

GRAVITY DEFIERS
No one would argue who these three should be classified as such. It is interesting to see how high Drexler rates on rebounds and assists per 48 minutes. Also noteworthy is how much Wilkins trails Jordan in most categories.

	PR	2PT%	3PT%	FT%	SC	SH*	RB*	AS*	BK*	ST*
M. Jordan	**35.05**	**.546**	.132	**.841**	**34.98**	**1.088**	6.51	7.03	**1.90**	**3.75**
C. Drexler	27.94	.515	.212	.811	26.98	1.034	**8.36**	**7.33**	.82	3.18
D. Wilkins	24.27	.464	**.295**	.826	30.73	.986	8.17	3.65	.77	1.68

*based on 48 minute averages
PR = Production Rating

DEFENSIVE CENTERS
All four of the centers below played for teams with winning records in 1987-88, yet none of the four averaged scoring in double figures. In fact, the highest any ranks on his own team in scoring is Eaton (7th). Their value is in clogging up the middle on defense and rebounding. What is interesting to note is the 87.5% FT shooting by Rollins (surprisingly high) and the 41.8% FG shooting by Eaton (surprisingly low).

	PR	2PT%	3PT%	FT%	SC	SH	RB*	AS*	BK*	ST*
T. Rollins	10.39	.512	0-0	**.875**	4.42	1.056	12.48	.54	3.59	**.84**
J. Donaldson	**14.98**	**.558**	0-0	.778	**7.05**	**1.090**	14.36	1.26	1.98	.76
M. Eaton	14.27	.418	0-0	.623	6.96	.834	12.60	.97	**5.34**	.72
A. Lister	11.94	.504	**1-2**	.606	5.62	.940	**16.61**	**1.54**	3.71	.72

*based on 48 minute averages
PR = Production Rating

ROOKIE POINT GUARDS
Last season's rookie crop of point guards was one of the best in quite a while. Mark Jackson deserved the Rookie-of-the-Year award with a Production Rating of 20.68. Amazingly, he only leads in one category among these players (steals per 48 minutes). Kevin Johnson's stats are based on what he did at Phoenix only.

	PR	2PT%	3PT%	FT%	SC	SH	RB*	AS*	BK*	ST*
M. Jackson	**20.68**	.458	.254	.774	13.59	.925	5.85	12.82	.09	**3.03**
K. Johnson	19.07	.478	.200	.859	12.57	.990	**6.54**	**13.40**	**.38**	2.36
K. Smith	15.23	**.487**	.308	.819	**13.79**	**.999**	3.05	9.60	.18	2.04
W. Garland	14.76	.444	**.333**	**.879**	12.40	.941	5.13	9.70	.16	2.62

*based on 48 minute averages
PR = Production Rating

ACC ALUMNUS
James Worthy and Thurl Bailey were both freshman in college in 1980. Worthy was at North Carolina, Bailey was at North Carolina State. Both players won a national championship in their final year (Worthy went hardship his senior year). Most will be surprised to learn that their NBA stats last year were very similar as well.

	PR	2PT%	3PT%	FT%	SC	SH	RB*	AS*	BK*	ST*
T. Bailey	18.94	.493	1-3	.826	19.56	1.013	**9.09**	2.70	**2.14**	.84
J. Worthy	**20.09**	**.537**	2-16	.796	**19.71**	**1.064**	6.76	**5.22**	.99	**1.30**

*based on 48 minute averages
PR = Production Rating

Interestingly, the Lakers and the Jazz met in the playoffs for the first time last season. The series went to seven games and highlighted the head-to-head matchup between Bailey and Worthy. Coincidentally, they both had Production Ratings of 18.14 for the series.

	PR	2PT%	3PT%	FT%	SC	SH	RB*	AS*	BL*	ST*
T. Bailey	18.14	.479	0-1	**.882**	**20.29**	.993	**6.66**	1.20	**2.22**	.85
J. Worthy	18.14	**.490**	1-2	.730	18.86	.972	6.02	**4.28**	1.66	**2.33**

*based on 48 minute averages
PR = Production Rating

There is only one logical reason in the world why Worthy is an All-Star while no one has heard of Bailey; Worthy plays for the Lakers and Bailey plays for the Jazz.

REBOUNDERS

Michael Cage needed 30 rebounds in his final game to win the rebounding title over Charles Oakley. He got 30 exactly. Cage finished at 13.03 RPG while Oakley could *only* manage 13.00 RPG.

	PR	2PT%	3PT%	FT%	SC	SH	RB*	AS*	BK*	ST*
M. Cage	**21.24**	.471	0-1	.688	**14.53**	.931	16.93	1.98	**1.05**	**1.64**
C. Oakley	20.54	**.487**	**.250**	**.727**	12.37	**.970**	**18.17**	**4.23**	.48	1.16

*based on 48 minute averages
PR = Production Rating

ASSIST LEADERS

John Stockton set an NBA record in his final game surpassing Isiah Thomas' mark of 1123 assists in a season. Stockton finished with 1128. Shown below is Isiah's best year (1985 - the year he set the assist record) as well as Stockton's 1988 season.

	PR	2pt%	3pt%	FT%	SC	SH	RB*	AS*	BL*	ST*
Stockton (88)	26.53	**.594**	**.358**	**.840**	14.68	**1.161**	4.00	**19.05**	.27	**4.09**
Thomas (85)	**27.85**	.476	.257	.809	**21.23**	.990	**5.61**	17.45	**.39**	2.91

*based on 48 minute averages
PR = Production Rating

BIRD VS JOHNSON

Larry Bird had his third most productive season during the 1987-88 campaign, while Magic Johnson had his second lowest productive year - ahead of only his rookie season. Also shown are Bird's best season (1985) and Magic's best year (1987).

	PR	2pt%	3pt%	FT%	SC	SH	RB*	AS*	BL*	ST*
Bird (88)	34.01	**.546**	.414	**.916**	**29.93**	**1.136**	11.38	7.56	.92	2.02
Magic (88)	27.71	.510	.196	.853	19.56	1.042	8.17	15.62	.24	2.08
Bird (85)	**34.39**	.529	**.427**	.882	28.69	1.096	**12.78**	8.06	**1.49**	1.96
Magic (87)	31.79	.532	.205	.848	23.86	1.076	8.33	**16.15**	.60	**2.28**

*based on 48 minute average
PR = Production Rating

RANKINGS AMONG CENTERS *

RK	PLAYER	TEAM	PR	PPG	2pt%	3pt%	FT%	SC	SH	RB	AS	BL	ST
1.	A. Olajuwon	Hous	**28.10**	**22.85**	.516	0-4	.695	1	14	2	8	5	1
2.	Pat Ewing	N.Y.	22.61	20.16	.556	0-3	.716	3	5	11	12	3	2
3.	Moses Malone	Wash	22.53	20.34	.488	.286	.788	2	11	3	18	20	12
4.	Brad Daugherty	Clev	20.70	18.73	.511	0-2	.716	4	15	24	1	24	18
5.	Mike Gminski	Phil	20.56	16.85	.449	0-2	**.906**	5	16	9	14	15	13
6.	Bill Laimbeer	Detr	20.17	13.54	.500	.333	.874	11	8	7	4	19	10
7.	Robert Parish	Bost	19.15	14.34	**.590**	0-1	.734	9	1	10	11	17	8
8.	Danny Schayes	Denv	18.63	13.94	.542	0-2	.836	10	2	4	13	11	4
9.	S. Stipanovich	Indi	18.13	13.49	.502	.200	.809	12	10	17	5	22	3
10.	B. Benjamin	LA.C	17.97	13.03	.496	0-8	.706	13	19	18	2	2	9
11.	Ralph Sampson	G.St	17.94	15.60	.443	.182	.760	7	25	8	3	9	7
12.	Abdul-Jabbar	LA.L	15.90	14.56	.532	0-1	.762	8	7	26	7	14	14
13.	K. Duckworth	Port	15.42	15.78	.496	0-0	.770	6	12	14	23	25	25
14.	J. Donaldson	Dall	14.98	7.05	.558	0-0	.778	23	3	5	24	12	19
15.	Randy Breuer	Milw	14.47	11.95	.495	0-0	.657	14	21	19	17	10	15
16.	M. McCormick	N.J.	14.29	12.01	.539	0-2	.674	15	9	25	9	26	21
17.	Mark Eaton	Utah	14.27	6.96	.418	0-0	.623	24	26	12	25	1	22
18.	Dave Corzine	Chic	13.72	10.05	.486	.111	.752	20	20	23	6	13	20
19.	Greg Anderson	S.A.	13.11	11.67	.503	.200	.604	17	22	15	19	8	5
20.	Joe Kleine	Sacr	12.88	9.77	.472	0-0	.814	21	17	6	15	18	24
21.	M. Thompson	LA.L	12.81	11.56	.515	0-3	.634	18	18	20	21	16	16
22.	Mark West	Phoe	12.63	9.66	.552	0-1	.596	22	13	16	20	7	11
23.	B. Cartwright	N.Y.	12.28	11.15	.544	0-0	.798	19	4	22	10	21	6
24.	Alton Lister	Seat	11.94	5.62	.504	**.500**	.606	25	23	1	22	4	23
25.	James Edwards	Detr	11.23	11.80	.470	0-1	.654	16	24	21	16	23	26
26.	Wayne Rollins	Atla	10.39	4.42	.512	0-0	.875	26	6	13	26	6	17

* Only players who qualify. See qualification requirements on page 272.
* Numbers in **bold** are the best for each category.

RK = Rank by Production Rating
PR = Production Rating (see page 3)
PPG = Points Per Game
SC = Rank for scoring (points per game)
SH = Rank for shooting (composite shooting formula - see page 29 for explanation)
RB = Rank for rebounds per 48 minutes
AS = Rank for assists per 48 minutes
BL = Rank for blocks per 48 minutes
ST = Rank for steals per 48 minutes

RANKINGS AMONG POWER FORWARDS *

RK	PLAYER	TEAM	PR	PPG	2pt%	3pt%	FT%	SC	SH	RB	AS	BL	ST
1.	Charles Barkley	Phil	**32.51**	**28.30**	**.630**	.280	.751	**1**	2	7	6	12	14
2.	Karl Malone	Utah	27.63	27.66	.522	0-5	.700	2	14	6	11	28	4
3.	Kevin McHale	Bost	26.28	22.59	.604	0-0	.797	3	**1**	26	8	10	35
4.	Otis Thorpe	Sacr	23.71	20.78	.510	0-6	.755	4	13	9	5	23	28
5.	Buck Williams	N.J.	22.96	18.27	.560	1.000	.668	6	8	4	27	25	21
6.	Jack Sikma	Milw	21.77	16.49	.489	.214	**.922**	7	7	18	3	14	12
7.	Michael Cage	LA.C	21.24	14.53	.471	0-1	.688	12	30	3	26	18	5
8.	Charles Oakley	Chic	20.54	12.37	.487	.250	.727	17	23	2	4	32	24
9.	Roy Tarpley	Dall	20.23	13.49	.503	0-5	.740	14	17	**1**	31	11	9
10.	F. Brickowski	S.A.	18.71	15.99	.530	.200	.768	9	6	29	**1**	26	6
11.	Tom Chambers	Seat	17.73	20.41	.461	.303	.807	5	26	34	7	21	10
12.	Sam Perkins	Dall	16.71	14.21	.460	.167	.822	13	28	19	19	19	15
13.	Roy Hinson	N.J.	16.60	15.30	.488	0-2	.775	10	20	33	30	6	19
14.	A.C. Green	LA.L	16.44	11.43	.505	0-2	.773	19	12	10	32	24	8
15.	Wayman Tisdale	Indi	15.82	16.05	.513	0-2	.783	8	9	31	24	31	25
16.	Rick Mahorn	Detr	15.67	10.70	.574	**.500**	.756	21	3	8	34	20	26
17.	Armon Gilliam	Phoe	15.36	14.82	.475	0-0	.679	11	29	21	28	27	11
18.	John Williams	Clev	14.79	10.95	.477	0-1	.756	20	24	20	16	3	16
19.	Cliff Levingston	Atla	13.78	9.99	.557	**.500**	.772	23	4	23	33	9	23
20.	B. Rasmussen	Denv	13.42	12.68	.492	0-0	.776	15	18	14	23	8	34
21.	Kevin Willis	Atla	13.33	11.61	.520	0-2	.649	18	19	11	35	22	9
22.	J. B. Carroll	Hous	12.92	12.68	.436	0-2	.764	16	31	16	14	7	22
23.	John Salley	Detr	12.34	8.55	.566	0-0	.709	26	5	32	13	4	20
24.	Herb Williams	Indi	12.17	9.97	.428	0-6	.737	24	34	22	15	2	31
25.	Jim Petersen	Hous	12.09	8.88	.515	.167	.745	25	11	17	12	17	29
26.	Sidney Green	N.Y.	11.40	7.83	.443	0-2	.663	29	33	5	21	29	13
27.	Terry Catledge	Wash	11.10	10.66	.508	0-2	.655	22	22	13	29	34	27
28.	Alvin Adams	Phoe	10.57	7.45	.496	**.500**	.844	32	10	27	2	16	**1**
29.	Horace Grant	Chic	10.56	7.68	.503	0-2	.626	30	27	15	17	13	18
30.	Ben Coleman	Phil	9.87	8.47	.502	0-3	.762	27	15	24	25	15	17
31.	L. Krystkowiak	Milw	8.94	7.18	.487	0-3	.811	33	16	28	18	33	3
32.	Caldwell Jones	Port	8.94	4.23	.494	0-4	.736	34	21	25	20	5	33
33.	B. McDonald	G.St	8.90	7.56	.482	.257	.784	31	25	35	10	35	30
34.	Tellis Frank	G.St	8.49	8.13	.429	0-1	.725	28	32	30	9	30	7
35.	Charles Jones	Wash	8.16	2.86	.409	0-1	.707	35	35	12	22	**1**	3

* Only players who qualify. See qualification requirements on page 272.
* Numbers in **bold** are the best for each category.

RK = Rank by Production Rating
PR = Production Rating (see page 3)
PPG = Points Per Game
SC = Rank for scoring (points per game)
SH = Rank for shooting (composite shooting formula - see page 29 for explanation)
RB = Rank for rebounds per 48 minutes
AS = Rank for assists per 48 minutes
BL = Rank for blocks per 48 minutes
ST = Rank for steals per 48 minutes

RANKINGS AMONG SMALL FORWARDS *

RK	PLAYER	TEAM	PR	PPG	2pt%	3pt%	FT%	SC	SH	RB	AS	BL	ST
1.	Larry Bird	Bost	**34.01**	29.93	.546	.414	**.916**	2	1	3	1	17	7
2.	Larry Nance	Clev	24.51	19.10	.531	.333	.779	11	5	2	14	**1**	23
3.	D. Wilkins	Atla	24.27	**30.73**	.476	.295	.826	**1**	19	21	20	21	12
4.	Jerome Kersey	Port	21.87	19.19	.502	.200	.735	10	15	5	16	11	6
5.	Alex English	Denv	21.70	25.00	.496	0-6	.828	4	11	28	2	27	26
6.	Mark Aguirre	Dall	21.13	25.09	.496	.302	.770	3	17	22	5	12	21
7.	James Worthy	LA.L	20.09	19.71	.537	.125	.796	8	4	25	4	14	20
8.	X. McDaniel	Seat	19.78	21.40	.496	.280	.715	5	21	11	11	16	11
9.	T. Cummings	Milw	19.16	21.33	.485	.333	.665	6	28	6	21	20	17
10.	Thurl Bailey	Utah	18.94	19.56	.493	.333	.826	9	7	13	27	2	31
11.	Adrian Dantley	Detr	17.29	20.00	.516	0-2	.860	7	3	31	19	30	30
12.	Rodney McCray	Hous	17.27	12.42	.484	0-4	.785	21	18	4	10	18	28
13.	Rod Higgens	G.St	16.65	15.50	.528	**.487**	.848	17	2	27	15	23	14
14.	Chuck Person	Indi	16.65	16.97	.480	.333	.670	16	26	12	3	33	25
15.	Cliff Robinson	Phil	16.61	19.00	.466	.222	.717	12	31	10	25	19	10
16.	Walter Berry	S.A.	16.23	17.42	.563	0-0	.600	14	6	7	26	4	19
17.	Dennis Rodman	Detr	15.84	11.62	**.568**	.294	.535	23	9	**1**	29	13	13
18.	Eddie Johnson	Phoe	14.82	17.73	.501	.255	.850	13	12	24	17	32	33
19.	J.S. Williams	Wash	14.37	12.77	.484	.132	.734	20	27	15	12	24	4
20.	Bernard King	Wash	13.96	17.22	.503	.167	.762	15	13	26	13	29	27
21.	Jay Vincent	Denv	12.92	15.40	.466	.250	.805	18	24	18	18	22	24
22.	Otis Smith	G.St	12.24	11.68	.502	.317	.777	22	10	23	9	9	2
23.	Kenny Walker	N.Y.	11.17	10.07	.473	0-1	.775	24	25	16	32	8	18
24.	Mike Mitchell	S.A.	10.84	13.51	.486	.250	.825	19	16	29	31	26	29
25.	Derrick McKey	Seat	10.23	8.46	.499	.367	.772	29	8	9	24	3	9
26.	Tyrone Corbin	Phoe	9.29	7.44	.493	.167	.797	32	14	8	22	25	8
27.	Brad Sellers	Chic	9.22	9.48	.460	.143	.790	26	30	30	23	7	32
28.	Scottie Pippen	Chic	9.22	7.91	.475	.174	.576	31	32	17	7	5	3
29.	D. Schrempf	Dall	9.07	8.51	.475	.156	.756	28	29	19	8	15	22
30.	Phil Hubbard	Clev	8.31	8.41	.494	0-5	.749	30	20	20	30	31	15
31.	Dudley Bradley	N.J.	8.28	6.51	.452	.363	.763	33	23	33	6	6	**1**
32.	Ken Norman	LA.C	8.23	8.62	.492	0-10	.512	27	33	14	28	10	16
33.	Johnny Newman	N.Y.	7.60	10.04	.463	.280	.841	25	22	32	33	28	5

* Only players who qualify. See qualification requirements on page 272.
* Numbers in **bold** are the best for each category.

RK = Rank by Production Rating
PR = Production Rating (see page 3)
PPG = Points Per Game
SC = Rank for scoring (points per game)
SH = Rank for shooting (composite shooting formula - see page 29 for explanation)
RB = Rank for rebounds per 48 minutes
AS = Rank for assists per 48 minutes
BL = Rank for blocks per 48 minutes
ST = Rank for steals per 48 minutes

RANKINGS AMONG OFF GUARDS *

RK	PLAYER	TEAM	PR	PPG	2pt%	3pt%	FT%	SC	SH	RB	AS	BL	ST
1.	Michael Jordan	Chic	**35.05**	34.98	.546	.132	.841	1	4	6	9	1	2
2.	Clyde Drexler	Port	27.94	26.98	.515	.212	.811	2	10	3	8	7	5
3.	Fat Lever	Denv	25.94	18.85	.484	.211	.785	9	20	1	1	23	3
4.	A. Robertson	S.A.	22.94	19.63	.478	.284	.748	8	24	4	3	4	1
5.	Byron Scott	LA.L	21.73	21.65	**.554**	.346	.858	4	2	16	19	18	8
6.	Dale Ellis	Seat	20.55	25.84	.521	.413	.767	3	9	11	32	30	28
7.	Chris Mullin	G.St	20.17	20.22	.526	.351	.885	7	6	20	11	8	7
8.	Reggie Theus	Sacr	18.44	21.56	.479	.271	.831	5	17	24	4	24	31
9.	Danny Ainge	Bost	18.26	15.68	.534	.415	.878	14	1	25	5	26	15
10.	R. Blackman	Dall	16.48	18.66	.476	0-5	.873	10	15	22	22	22	29
11.	Ron Harper	Clev	16.23	15.42	.473	.150	.705	15	28	10	7	2	4
12.	Walter Davis	Phoe	15.41	17.90	.483	.375	.887	12	13	26	12	32	10
13.	Jeff Malone	Wash	15.24	20.51	.478	.417	.882	6	14	27	26	29	33
14.	Gerald Wilkins	N.Y.	13.86	17.43	.462	.302	.786	13	27	21	16	19	19
15.	Mike Woodson	LA.C	13.80	17.97	.459	.231	.868	11	25	28	20	15	11
16.	Joe Dumars	Detr	13.59	14.16	.477	.211	.815	17	18	29	13	27	21
17.	Sidney Moncrief	Milw	12.45	10.77	.513	.161	.837	21	11	9	10	16	26
18.	Michael Cooper	LA.L	11.98	8.72	.434	.320	.858	30	26	8	6	11	16
19.	Purvis Short	Hous	11.74	14.31	.486	.238	.858	16	16	13	30	21	24
20.	Paul Pressley	Sacr	11.52	9.69	.476	.327	.792	25	9	2	25	3	14
21.	John Long	Indi	11.42	12.77	.478	.442	**.907**	18	12	14	28	28	13
22.	Randy Wittman	Atla	10.39	10.04	.478	0-0	.798	22	21	31	15	20	32
23.	Vinnie Johnson	Detr	10.00	12.22	.449	.208	.677	19	30	12	14	17	23
24.	Bobby Hansen	Utah	9.68	9.59	.553	.330	.743	27	8	18	24	31	17
25.	Craig Ehlo	Clev	9.44	7.13	.485	.344	.674	33	23	5	17	6	9
26.	Brad Davis	Dall	9.28	7.16	.522	.405	.843	31	5	32	2	12	18
27.	Reggie Miller	Indi	9.23	10.02	.538	.355	.801	24	7	19	31	14	25
28.	Otis Birdsong	N.J.	9.12	10.90	.461	.360	.511	20	29	23	18	25	27
29.	Dell Curry	Clev	8.68	9.96	.472	.346	.782	23	22	15	23	10	6
30.	Craig Hodges	Phoe	8.15	9.53	.448	**.491**	.831	28	3	33	21	33	22
31.	Dennis Hopson	N.J.	7.18	9.62	.417	.267	.740	26	31	17	27	5	12
32.	Albert King	Phil	6.28	7.18	.395	.347	.757	32	33	7	33	13	30
33.	David Wingate	Phil	6.07	8.93	.412	.250	.750	29	32	30	29	9	20

* Only players who qualify. See qualification requirements on page 272.
* Numbers in **bold** are the best for each category.

RK = Rank by Production Rating
PR = Production Rating (see page 3)
PPG = Points Per Game
SC = Rank for scoring (points per game)
SH = Rank for shooting (composite shooting formula - see page 29 for explanation)
RB = Rank for rebounds per 48 minutes
AS = Rank for assists per 48 minutes
BL = Rank for blocks per 48 minutes
ST = Rank for steals per 48 minutes

PLAYERS' POSITIONS 239

RANKINGS AMONG POINT GUARDS *

RK	PLAYER	TEAM	PR	PPG	2pt%	3pt%	FT%	SC	SH	RB	AS	BL	ST
1.	Earvin Johnson	LA.L	**27.71**	**19.56**	.510	.196	.853	1	8	1	2	14	21
2.	John Stockton	Utah	26.54	14.68	**.594**	.358	.840	8	1	24	1	12	1
3.	Terry Porter	Port	22.87	14.90	.533	.348	.846	7	3	6	5	13	14
4.	Mark Jackson	N.Y.	20.68	13.59	.458	.254	.774	14	29	7	6	27	6
5.	Glenn Rivers	Atla	20.36	14.17	.460	.273	.758	9	27	3	3	2	10
6.	Isiah Thomas	Detr	19.86	19.47	.475	.309	.774	2	20	16	11	10	16
7.	Maurice Cheeks	Phil	19.22	13.75	.504	.136	.825	13	12	21	15	9	8
8.	Vern Fleming	Indi	19.19	13.89	.531	0-13	.802	11	6	5	21	20	23
9.	Derek Harper	Dall	19.17	16.99	.488	.313	.759	3	18	25	20	5	11
10.	Paul Pressey	Milw	18.67	13.11	.508	.205	.798	15	13	2	19	3	19
11.	Johnny Dawkins	S.A.	18.37	15.80	.499	.311	**.896**	5	10	17	16	30	25
12.	Mark Price	Clev	16.92	15.99	.510	**.486**	.877	4	2	29	26	17	28
13.	Nate McMillan	Seat	16.71	7.61	.479	.375	.707	29	22	4	4	1	4
14.	Eric Floyd	Hous	16.58	15.00	.453	.194	.850	6	26	8	18	16	27
15.	Michael Adams	Denv	16.57	13.87	.505	.367	.834	10	4	26	27	11	7
16.	Dennis Johnson	Bost	16.13	12.61	.449	.261	.856	16	21	20	13.	6	30
17.	Kenny Smith	Sacr	15.23	13.79	.487	.308	.819	12	14	30	23	21	22
18.	Jeff Hornacek	Phoe	14.78	9.52	.528	.293	.822	22	5	9	9	18	17
19.	W. Garland	G.St	14.76	12.40	.444	.333	.879	17	28	11	22	24	12
20.	Jay Humphries	Milw	13.47	10.04	.540	.167	.732	21	7	14	17	26	20
21.	John Bagley	N.J.	13.43	11.96	.471	.292	.822	18	23	18	28	22	26
22.	Kevin Johnson	Phoe	12.32	9.15	.472	.208	.839	25	17	13	12	4	13
23.	Allen Leavell	Hous	12.09	10.24	.471	.216	.869	20	19	28	25	19	9
24.	John Lucas	Milw	10.84	9.17	.479	.338	.802	24	15	19	14	29	15
25.	Sam Vincent	Chic	10.67	7.96	.459	.381	.868	26	16	12	7	7	2
26.	Larry Drew	LA.C	10.31	10.34	.479	.289	.769	19	24	31	24	32	31
27.	Steve Colter	Wash	9.53	7.12	.464	.300	.789	31	25	10	29	8	24
28.	D. Valentine	LA.C	9.33	7.11	.416	.455	.743	30	31	15	10	15	3
29.	John Paxson	Chic	8.96	7.90	.522	.347	.733	27	9	32	30	31	32
30.	Tyrone Bogues	Wash	8.68	4.97	.398	.188	.784	32	32	23	8	28	2
31.	P. Washington	N.J.	8.12	9.31	.470	.224	.698	23	30	22	32	25	5
32.	G. Henderson	Phil	7.77	7.93	.431	.423	.812	28	11	27	31	23	18

* Only players who qualify. See qualification requirements on page 272.
* Numbers in **bold** are the best for each category.

RK = Rank by Production Rating
PR = Production Rating (see page 3)
PPG = Points Per Game
SC = Rank for scoring (points per game)
SH = Rank for shooting (composite shooting formula - see page 29 for explanation)

RB = Rank for rebounds per 48 minutes
AS = Rank for assists per 48 minutes
BL = Rank for blocks per 48 minutes
ST = Rank for steals per 48 minutes

RANKINGS AMONG 6TH MEN *

RK	PLAYER	TEAM	PR	PPG	2pt%	3pt%	FT%	SC	SH	RB	AS	BL	ST
1.	Roy Tarpley	Dall	**20.23**	13.49	.503	0-5	.740	4	20	**1**	43	9	16
2.	Thurl Bailey	Utah	18.94	**19.56**	.493	.333	.826	1	11	18	33	5	44
3.	Dennis Rodman	Detr	15.84	11.62	**.568**	.294	.535	10	13	2	35	19	22
4.	John Williams	Wash	14.37	12.77	.484	.132	.734	6	33	20	21	28	11
5.	Cliff Levingston	Atla	13.78	9.99	.557	**.500**	.772	14	2	8	45	8	39
6.	Dave Corzine	Chic	13.72	10.05	.486	.111	.752	13	27	11	28	6	46
7.	Jay Humphries	Milw	13.47	10.04	.540	.167	.732	18	7	36	6	42	15
8.	J.B. Carroll	Hous	12.92	12.68	.436	0-2	.764	7	37	5	32	4	38
9.	Jay Vincent	Denv	12.92	15.40	.466	.250	.805	2	30	22	25	24	35
10.	M. Thompson	LA.L	12.81	11.56	.515	0-3	.634	11	25	6	46	7	42
11.	Mark West	Phoe	12.63	9.66	.552	0-1	.596	20	18	3	44	2	40
12.	John Salley	Detr	12.34	8.55	.566	0-0	.709	30	6	16	31	3	34
13.	Kevin Johnson	Phoe	12.32	9.15	.472	.208	.839	25	24	35	4	29	8
14.	Bill Cartwright	N.Y.	12.28	11.15	.544	0-0	.798	12	4	10	36	16	37
15.	Otis Smith	GoSt	12.24	11.68	.502	.317	.777	9	14	25	19	15	6
16.	Herb Williams	Indi	12.17	9.97	.428	0-6	.737	17	43	7	37	**1**	43
17.	Michael Cooper	LA.L	11.98	8.72	.434	.320	.858	27	35	27	8	26	20
18.	Purvis Short	Hous	11.74	14.31	.486	.238	.858	3	16	29	24	37	29
19.	John Lucas	Milw	10.84	9.17	.479	.338	.802	24	22	38	5	44	9
20.	Mike Mitchell	S.A.	10.84	13.51	.486	.250	.825	5	21	26	40	35	41
21.	Sam Vincent	Chic	10.67	7.96	.459	.381	**.868**	34	23	33	1	31	21
22.	Alvan Adams	Phoe	10.57	7.45	.496	.500	.844	39	10	12	14	17	10
23.	Horace Grant	Chic	10.56	7.68	.503	0-2	.626	38	32	4	38	13	32
24.	Derrick McKey	Seat	10.23	8.46	.499	.367	.772	32	12	17	30	10	19
25.	Vinnie Johnson	Detr	10.00	12.22	.449	.208	.677	8	39	28	12	34	28
26.	Ben Coleman	Phil	9.87	8.47	.502	0-3	.762	31	15	9	41	14	31
27.	Craig Ehlo	Clev	9.44	7.13	.485	.344	.674	43	31	24	13	22	12
28.	D. Valentine	LA.C	9.33	7.11	.416	.455	.743	44	41	37	3	39	3
29.	Tyrone Corbin	Phoe	9.29	7.44	.493	.167	.797	40	19	15	29	32	18
30.	Brad Davis	Dall	9.28	7.16	.522	.405	.843	41	3	44	7	30	23
31.	Reggie Miller	Indi	9.23	10.02	.538	.355	.801	16	5	32	26	33	30
32.	Scottie Pippen	Chic	9.22	7.91	.475	.174	.576	35	38	21	17	11	7
33.	D. Schrempf	Dall	9.07	8.51	.475	.156	.756	29	34	23	18	20	33
34.	John Paxson	Chic	8.96	7.90	.522	.347	.733	36	8	45	9	46	36
35.	L. Krystowiak	Milw	8.94	7.18	.487	0-3	.811	42	17	13	39	36	45

* Only players who qualify. See qualification requirements on page 272.
* Numbers in **bold** are the best for each category.

RK = Rank by Production Rating
PR = Production Rating (see page 3)
PPG = Points Per Game
SC = Rank for scoring (points per game)
SH = Rank for shooting (composite shooting formula - see page 29 for explanation)
RB = Rank for rebounds per 48 minutes
AS = Rank for assists per 48 minutes
BL = Rank for blocks per 48 minutes
ST = Rank for steals per 48 minutes

RANKINGS AMONG ROOKIES *

RK	PLAYER	TEAM	PR	PPG	2pt%	3pt%	FT%	SC	SH	RB	AS	BL	ST
1.	Mark Jackson	N.Y.	**20.68**	13.58	.458	.254	.774	3	10	9	1	2	14
2.	Armon Gilliam	Phoe	15.36	**14.82**	.475	0-0	.679	1	9	3	14	10	7
3.	Kenny Smith	Sacr	15.23	13.79	.487	.308	.819	2	4	15	5	6	12
4.	W. Garland	G.St	14.76	12.40	.444	.333	**.879**	4	8	10	4	4	13
5.	Greg Anderson	S.A.	13.11	11.67	.503	.200	.604	5	7	1	15	14	1
6.	Kevin Johnson	Phoe	12.33	9.15	.472	.208	.839	8	5	13	3	5	9
7.	Horace Grant	Chic	10.56	7.68	.503	0-2	.626	13	6	2	12	13	4
8.	Derrick McKey	Seat	10.23	8.46	.499	**.367**	.772	10	2	6	10	8	2
9.	Reggie Miller	Indi	9.23	10.02	**.538**	.355	.801	6	1	12	8	12	10
10.	Scottie Pippen	Chic	9.22	7.91	.475	.174	.576	12	11	8	6	3	3
11.	L. Krystowiak	Milw	8.94	7.18	.487	0-3	.811	14	3	4	13	15	11
12.	Tyrone Bogues	Wash	8.68	4.97	.398	.188	.784	15	15	14	2	1	15
13.	Tellis Frank	G.St	8.49	8.13	.429	0-1	.725	11	13	5	9	9	8
14.	Ken Norman	LA.C	8.23	8.62	.492	0-10	.512	9	12	7	11	11	5
15.	Dennis Hopson	N.J.	7.18	9.62	.417	.267	.740	7	14	11	7	7	6

* Only players who qualify. See qualification requirements on page 272.
* Numbers in **bold** are the best for each category.

RK = Rank by Production Rating
PR = Production Rating (see page 3)
PPG = Points Per Game
SC = Rank for scoring (points per game)
SH = Rank for shooting (composite shooting formula - see page 29 for explanation)
RB = Rank for rebounds per 48 minutes
AS = Rank for assists per 48 minutes
BL = Rank for blocks per 48 minutes
ST = Rank for steals per 48 minutes

Dominique Wilkins of the Atlanta Hawks
- Wilkins has scored more points in the last 4 years than any other player.
- Basketball Hall of Fame -

CHAPTER 5

DISCUSSION AND DEBATE

DETR. VS ATLA.
DALL. VS DENV.

Every so often a similarity of amazing proportion takes place in the NBA. Late in this previous season, the NBA's two best divisions - the Central and the Midwest - both had nearly identical showdowns. In both cases the number 1 teams met the number 2 teams. In the Central, the leader was Detroit and in the Midwest, it was Dallas. Both teams, with identical 48-25 records, faced off against their nearest rivals. Both Atlanta and Denver were within 1 game of the top.

What made the matchups all the more dramatic was that both leaders came into the game hanging on for dear life. Both had gone 2-4 in their last 6 games while both second place clubs had gone 6-0 and were closing fast. Both Detroit and Denver had held the top spot for at least 6 weeks. The last club to lead the division were the two challengers now attempting to retake the throne.

Ironically, both games were played the same night - Sunday April 10, 1988 and followed a similar course. Both games were close. In fact, each game was tied late in the third quarter, but didn't stay that way. Both of the leaders, Detroit and Dallas, rallied to win going away.

DISCUSSION AND DEBATE

On the following pages are seven subjects. Each is worthy of analysis. In most cases, I make an attempt to prove or disprove certain widely-held views on everything from home-court advantage to parity. Subsequent to getting into those areas, however, I would like to discuss a variety of minor questions.

Is Tommy Heinsohn biased in favor of the Celtics?

Frankly, I have always thought so. In recent years I've watched him on satellite as he does the Celtics games. At one time I could hardly take it. But when he did the CBS games - even those involving the Celtics - I was amazed at how impartial he was. Clearly, he went out of his way to be objective. Yes, he appears a little stilted when he tries to be "colorful" or "cute", but he's brilliant at strict analysis and, in my opinion, he's fair on national T.V.

Is the four point turn around really worth four points?

How many times do you hear someone say "That was a 4-pt play." when they are referring to a block on one end of the court which led to a fast break lay in on the other? I've heard it a thousand times. Psychologically it may be worth 4 points or 10 points or no points. Who knows? But technically it is worth, at best, two points. Let's say the score is 8-4. The leading team has the ball. Since one possession = one point, on an average, the most that can be attributed to the block is that it took possession away from the leading team (1 point) and led to 2 points on the offensive end. Since the normal expectation would be one point anyway, this also represents the net gaining of 1 point. Therefore, the score is now 8-6 with the ball back in the hands of the leading team - just where it was before this play began. That is a 2-point play folks, not a 4 point play.

Are there too many teams in the playoffs?

Of course not. Would any real fan want only 8 teams in the post season? If parity were so bad that the first round were boring, I might agree. But the facts are that Washington, Cleveland, Milwaukee and Seattle came within 1 win of upsets in round one while Utah did upset Portland. Only the Spurs were swept by the Lakers. It represents more money, more exposure, and keeps teams playing for something of value late into the season.

What are the ramifications of the new player's contract?

There are many, but the most interesting is what will happen to rookies? Lots of lower round rookies make teams who won't in the future. The reason is because there will not be the built in opportunity which being drafted creates. Since the draft will only go two rounds, expect very few third-rounders to make a team. They will have their opportunity to make the NBA via the CBA, but few will make it prior to that.

Why isn't there an All-6th man team?

Since there is a Rookie-of-the-Year and an all-rookie team; since there is an MVP and an all-league team; and since there is a Defensive Player-of-the-Year and an all-defensive team, I ask "Why isn't there an All-6th man team." After all, there is a 6th Man-of-the-Year award. My five would be Roy Tarpley, Thurl Bailey, Dennis Rodman, John Williams (Wash), and Cliff Levingston.

SALARIES

Shown on the opposite page are three top-20 lists comparing Production with salary during the 1987-88 season. Admittedly, these choices are somewhat subjective in nature, yet appear to me to be common sensical. The reason why I chose two lists for the overpaid group is because I wanted to make a distinction between types of players who fit into that category. In overpaid, I have shown those players who probably everyone would agree got more last year than their production justifies. However, in OVERPAID II, I have listed the players who produced reasonably well (in some cases, as well as they were expected to). However, their salaries are just too out of line with respect to their own teammates and the league in general. Pat Ewing is a good example. I'm one of his biggest fans, but at 2.75 million per year, he was the highest paid NBA player last season. Few would claim he was the best player. Even if he was, would he be worth half again as much as Larry Bird (1.8 million) or three times what Michael Jordan got (850 grand)? Obviously not.

Of course, there are other reasons besides skill for players getting paid what they do. Longevity (Abdul-Jabbar), long term contracts (Ewing), drawing power (Magic Johnson), or draft location (Mark Jackson) all figure in the process. Because of these subjective elements, as well as salary caps and trades, all kinds of anomalies will result.

You might notice that most of the top-paid players in OVERPAID II are centers. Up until the early to mid-1980's, the center position was essential to success. That is just no longer true. With the increased use of the 3-pointer, the fast break, pressure defense, etc., the center is just another of the five positions. In fact, the Production Ratings leader was a center 33 of the first 37 years in the NBA. Times have changed. Since Moses Malone won in 1983, not one center has captured that spot. The closest any center has come since 1983 was in 1986 when Akeem Olajuwon was third. In fact, the center position was the least productive position in the NBA during the 1987-88 season. My point is that, although I understand how these salaries for centers have developed, what baffles me is why one more team would agree to continue to pay abnormally more for a player at that position (see page 232 for discussion on value of each position).

I should also say that I excluded from these lists five players who missed the season entirely (Benson played 12 minutes). Because of this, these players were radically more overpaid than anyone else. Even so, I think they should be kept out of this discussion since it wasn't necessarily any inability which prevented them from justifying what they got paid. The five are Sam Bowie (1,055,000), Norm Nixon (985,000), Bill Walton (425,000), Kent Benson (350,000), and Scott Wedman (175,000).

The fact that the first player under OVERPAID II is Kareem Abdul-Jabbar seems almost sacrilegious. OK, OK, I'm sorry. The devil made me do it. No one would argue that Kareem is a great player, perhaps the greatest player who has ever played the game. Yet even so, his case is a classic example of a player being paid for what he's already done. Add to that his drawing ability and the fact that he lives in LA., and you have a formula for being overpaid with respect to production only. The truth is, his salary to production ratio was higher than anyone else on the list. Maybe I could remove his name by .... hmm ... maybe some kind of new math?

As you can see, the players in the underpaid group produced dramatically more than the others, yet got paid substantially less. Curiously, four Trailblazers are in the underpaid group while four Clippers are in the overpaid group (including Nixon). The four Blazers averaged 22.03 credits per game (Production Rating), but only got paid $242,000 per year apiece. The Clippers (excluding Nixon) averaged just 11.66 credits per game, yet an astonishing 761,000 per year. (I'm sure the guys writing the checks in Portland appreciate my using this particular comparison.)

246   BASKETBALL HEAVEN 1989

MOST UNDERPAID			MOST OVERPAID I			MOST OVERPAID II		
	PR	$/YR		PR	$/YR		PR	$/YR
M. Jackson	20.68	*115	C. Washburn	2.95	*777	Abdul-Jabbar	15.90	*2,000
J. Hornacek	14.78	94	W. Bedford	2.87	638	P. Ewing	22.61	2,750
N. McMillan	16.71	129	A. Gilmore	4.68	863	W. Rollins	10.39	1,117
J. Kersey	21.87	190	M. Turpin	6.89	1,000	R. Parish	19.15	2,038
R. Higgins	16.65	150	Ji. Paxson	6.49	875	J.B. Carroll	12.92	1,325
M. Adams	16.57	160	D. Vranes	3.88	517	R. Sampson	17.94	1,735
D. Rodman	15.84	160	K. Tripucka	7.90	971	B. Cartwright	12.28	1,135
M. Price	16.92	175	P. Cummings	6.26	712	M. Malone	22.53	2,067
J. Stockton	26.54	278	C. Maxwell	5.14	551	H. Williams	12.17	983
T. Porter	22.87	252	A. Toney	7.55	700	O. Woolridge	14.95	1,200
K. Duckworth	15.42	175	R. Williams	6.71	600	D. Smith	11.69	900
C. Drexler	27.94	350	C. Natt	9.70	808	J. Sikma	21.77	1,600
A.C. Green	16.44	219	D. Griffith	8.27	685	B. King	13.96	1,000
O. Thorpe	23.71	338	S. Pippen	9.22	725	A. Lister	11.94	835
D. Ellis	20.55	325	K. Rambis	6.97	525	T. Cummings	19.16	1,333
G. Wilkins	13.86	247	M. Mitchell	10.84	750	A. English	21.70	1,500
C. Oakley	20.54	465	V. Johnson	10.00	633	W. Tisdale	15.82	1,000
M. Jordan	35.05	845	W. Cooper	10.31	650	B. Benjamin	17.97	1,082
C. Barkley	32.51	823	S. Green	11.40	700	K. Vandeweghe	16.51	961
K. Malone	27.63	835	L. Drew	10.31	600	D. Greenwood	12.40	700
AVERAGE	**21.15**	**316**	**AVERAGE**	**7.42**	**714**	**AVERAGE**	**16.19**	**1,363**

*All salaries are shown in thousands (2,000 for Abdul-Jabbar is actually 2,000,000).

HOME COURT ADVANTAGE

There are a lot of interesting facets to home-court advantage (HCA) in the NBA. Does it exist? If so, why? How much is it worth? What causes one team to have a greater HCA than another?

Home-court advantage is a very important element in the NBA game. The average HCA is roughly equivalent to 5 points. When you consider that at least 30% of the games played in the NBA are decided by a margin less than or equal to a team's HCA, this factor is indeed critical.

There are probably other ways to determine HCA, but I use a relatively simple method. In effect, what I do is to take the difference between the points a team scores at home vs points scored on the road. This number is always positive. I then divide by 82 games to get the home-court advantage for that club.

This works pretty well, but it is not perfect, since all clubs are not always giving 100% all the time. The most obvious examples are the Lakers and Celtics and Clippers. Let me give a hypothetical situation. Suppose a team was so great that it never lost. At home they would get out to a 20 point lead and then coast. Let's suppose they ended winning by 15 at home. On the road they were so good they always won. But since it was much harder, they had to leave the starters in most of the game. Thus, they ended up winning on the road by 10 points. Consequently, their HCA would only be 2.5 points figuring it as I have. The Lakers and Celtics are analogous to the above team. The Clippers' stats are also skewed. The difference is that they play their starters more at home, but rest them on the road.

What happens is that these three teams do not show a true relationship between home and road because, being so dominant, they rest their best players a lot at home, but can't afford to do so on the road. With the Clippers, it's the other way around. In either case, it is comparing apples to oranges. Because of this, I used a complicated conversion formula which adjusts a team's HCA depending on how close or far from 41 wins the team was. Forty-one wins is, of course, average and ideal for evaluating a true relationship of home vs road performance throughout the season. Shown below is each team's HCA for the past several years.

		HCA			HCA			HCA
1.	Utah	7.26	9.	Indiana	5.34	17.	Houston	4.98
2.	Denver	7.00	10.	Atlanta	5.29	18.	Detroit	4.94
3.	Boston	6.63	11.	LA Clippers	5.24	19.	Chicago	4.52
4.	Milwaukee	5.77	12.	Dallas	5.15	20.	Portland	4.45
5.	Phoenix	5.71	13.	Cleveland	5.09	21.	Washington	4.29
6.	Golden State	5.60	14.	New Jersey	5.05	22.	New York	3.84
7.	Seattle	5.58	15.	Sacramento	5.00	23.	Philadelphia	3.71
8.	LA Lakers	5.37	16.	San Antonio	4.98			

What this is measuring is not specifically home-court advantage, but rather [(home-court advantage + road-court disadvantage) / 2]. You see, HCA is really the differential between how a team plays at home vs on the road. If the team plays well at home, but great on the road - their HCA may be the same as that of a team who plays poor at home, but well on the road. The issue is not how well a team plays at home, but rather how much better they play at home versus on the road.

GEOGRAPHICAL ISOLATION:

In my research I discovered a couple of very interesting correlations between HCA and geography. The first is isolation. The premise might read: *To the degree a team is isolated from the other NBA teams - that is how far away geographically they are - their HCA is higher.*

This premise is only an approximation and does not hold true in every case, but it is, without any question whatsoever, somewhat valid. Shown below are the 23 teams in order of their GIR (geographical isolation rank).

The way I figured GIR was to add up the total mileage as a plane flies for the three closest cities. Why three? No particular reason except that it would have taken too much time to figure all 22 opponent's mileage from each team. I've also shown the team's HCA rank (HCAR).

	GIR	HCAR		GIR	HCAR		GIR	HCAR
1.	Denver	2	9.	Dallas	12	17.	Detroit	18
2.	Atlanta	10	10.	Sacramento	15	18.	Milwaukee	4
3.	Seattle	7	11.	Golden State	6	19.	Washington	21
4.	Utah	1	12.	LA Lakers	8	20.	Chicago	19
5.	Phoenix	5	13.	LA Clippers	11	21.	New York	22
6.	Portland	20	14.	Cleveland	13	22.	New Jersey	14
7.	Houston	17	15.	Indiana	9	23.	Philadelphia	23
8.	San Antonio	16	16.	Boston	3			

Though exceptions exist, it is clear that the wider the difference between cities, the wider the difference between home-court advantage and road-court disadvantage. As you can see, three of the top-5 by HCA are also among the top-5 by GI. At the same time, four of the bottom-5 by HCA are among the bottom-5 by GI as well. Despite this relationship, three major exceptions to this rule exist. The three are Portland, Boston, and Milwaukee. I think I can explain at least two of the three.

The Blazers are 6th by geographical isolation, yet they only rank #20 by HCA. The possible **explanation might** be that Portland's home-court is unique. Memorial Coliseum has been sold out now for almost 500 games over 10 years - easily league highs. Perhaps due to this, the fans have become very sophisticated and not easily excitable. In fact, many opposing broadcasters have commented throughout recent seasons that the Portland fans made less noise than any other team in the league. If that is so, then it might be understandable why their HCA is abnormally low. (I should say that even a low HCA is extremely meaningful - in Portland's case 4.45 point advantage.)

The Celtics are 16th by geographical isolation. Even so, their HCA is a very high 3rd. Why? Do Bill Russell, John Havlicek, Bob Cousy, and Red Auerbach ring any bells? Boston Garden is by far the oldest arena in the NBA. Add to that the intimidating presence of 16 championship banners and you have all the ingredients necessary for a large HCA.

The Bucks rank #18 by geographical isolation and #4 by home-court advantage. Yes, I realize Milwaukee is widely known for a strong HCA. I'm just not sure why it is so high. In any event, it is the most inexplicable discrepancy between the two lists. Got any ideas?

I suppose I should try to speculate on why this relationship between GI and HCA exists. Though I'm not certain, I do feel like I've got a good idea as to the reason. The farther from other cities a team is, the farther one's opponents have to travel. It is also true that the teams with high GI's have farther to travel themselves when they go on the road. Remember, HCA measures both home-court advantage *and* road-court disadvantage. All of this means more jet lag and more living out of the suitcase. Consequently, more isolation means more home-court advantage. Additionally, when teams are close to each other, less advantage exists because the players are more likely to be familiar with the surroundings and the visiting team is likelier to have more fans of their own on hand.

GEOGRAPHICAL ELEVATION:

The other correlation between geography and HCA is elevation. The premise here is: *To the degree that a team's elevation is high, so is their HCA.*

I decided to establish three categories for elevation - sea level, inland (including Great Lakes teams) and mountain. If my premise is correct, then I should expect the average HCA for sea level to be the lowest and mountain to be the highest. Having gone this far with it, I'm sure it will be no surprise to hear that the average HCA for sea level teams is 4.98 while inland teams average 5.12 and mountain teams average 6.66. Even the spread from sea level to inland makes sense. It is small, but then so is the change in elevation. As the elevation changes dramatically, so does the HCA.

The most apparent reason for this phenomenon is less oxygen. The home team is used to it, the visiting team isn't. Result - big advantage to the mountain teams.

PERFORMANCE CATEGORIES:

I thought if I was going to research HCA to this degree I should determine what influence the home-court has on the performance categories. As you might expect, virtually every category was helped by the home-court.

Assists were influenced the most. The home team won the assists matchup 68% of the time. Field goal percentage was second at 62%. Then came fouls and turnovers. The home team had fewer fouls called on them in 56% of the games and made fewer turnovers in 55% of the games. The home team led in rebounds 54%, blocks 52%, and steals 52% of the time.

The most interesting part of this research is free throw percentage. It seems hard to believe that any category would do better on the road than at home. Hard to believe or not, FT% is just such a category. As it turns out, the home team only won the FT% battle in 47% of the games. The only explanation for it that I can think of is based on lack of concentration. As a team gets a big lead (at home that happens a lot), the leading team tends to let up. As a result, they miss a lot of meaningless FT's and thus, contribute toward a weaker FT% at home.

SCHEDULE

When you consider that the National Basketball Association schedules 943 regular season games throughout the country and that the average team takes around 20 road trips per year, then I think the final result of the schedule is excellent. Add to that the difficulty of meeting local team's needs, arena availabilities, television contracts, fixed numbers of games for intra-division and intra-conference teams and even someone like me finds it impressive that it can all be coordinated so well.

Even so, the NBA schedule is not perfect; at least in part, because there is no such animal. There are many possible ways that a schedule can hurt a team; the most obvious problem is posed by numerous road games on consecutive nights; a second, by the number of games a team plays against severe competition.

Back-to-back:

It is generally regarded as the most difficult game in the NBA to play - the second game of two in two days, especially when the game is on the road. As you can imagine, this means the team must play a game (generally at night) go to bed, get up very early, travel, and then play again that night. If it seems like this would be harder on a team than a normal road game, then you're right.

Over the last several years in the NBA, the visiting team has only won 32.5% of the time. However, when a team played two games in two days, their winning record for the second game (when it was on the road) has only been 29.5%. That may not seem like much of a difference, but the actual way to look at it is to remove from all road games those that are the second of back-to-back games. This means that of all *other* road games which are not part of the 29.5%, the visiting team wins 34.2% of the time.

What we have, then, is a situation where a team can normally expect to win 34.2% of their road games. However, in some cases, a road game is the second of back-to-back games. When it is, the probability of winning is only 29.5%. In essence, every time a team is forced to play 2 games in 2 nights, they can assume their chances of winning game 2 on the road are 15.9% lower than a normal road game [(34.2/29.5) minus 1].

Considering the disadvantage of playing one of these travel terrors, it seems logical that no team would want to have to play more than their share. The average team plays nearly 14 of these per year, yet some have had to face this difficult proposition more often. Shown below are the teams who have played the second of back-to-back games on the road the most times in the last 3 years. Also shown are those who've faced these games the least.

Most		**Least**	
Utah	50	Indiana	34
Chicago	48	Golden State	37
Phoenix	47	San Antonio	39
Dallas	46	Portland	39
Denver	46	Philadelphia	39

What interests me is that it really matters little whether you're Indiana or Utah. Remember, a road game which does not include the above games is usually won by the visiting team 34.2% of the time. The 2nd of a back-to-back set is 29.5%. That means Indiana played 16 less "potentially harder" games than did Utah. If we assume the above percentages, Indiana should have won 5.47 of those games (16 times .342), while Utah should have only won 4.72 (16 times .295). Because of scheduling only then, Indiana, in these years, won .75 more games (5.47 - 4.72) than Utah. Simply put, that represents only a potential of 1/4 of a win more per year for Indiana - and that is the *most* fortunate vs the *least* fortunate in the NBA.

Competition:

The second aspect of scheduling I want to look at is the quality level of the competition. During 1987/88, the Central Division had the best record. Shown below are the four division's season records and winning percentages.

Central	276-216	56.10%
Midwest	255-237	51.83%
Atlantic	188-222	45.85%
Pacific	224-268	45.28%

Common sense says that if a team is in the Central vs the Pacific they will have a more difficult schedule. The simple way to view the difference is to take a hypothetical average Central Division team and compare it to an average Pacific division team. Shown below are the two hypothetical teams and the number of games they play against the four divisions as well as the likelihood of winning a game vs each division.

	Central	Midwest	Atlantic	Pacific
Hypothetical Central Division Team	30	12	28	12
Hypothetical Pacific Division Team	12	30	10	30
% of time any team will defeat a team in the following divisions	43.90%	48.17%	54.15%	54.72%

Considering the givens, the average number of wins for both teams in all divisions are shown below...

	Central	Midwest	Atlantic	Pacific	Total
Central Division Team	13.17	5.78	15.16	6.57	40.68
Pacific Division Team	5.27	14.45	5.42	16.42	41.56

What the above charts indicate is that the average Central Division team has a disadvantage of .88 wins (41.56 - 40.68) just because of the dissimilarity in competition. Again, that is not a major difference, but the Indiana Pacers will probably disagree. Indiana tied Washington and New York for the last two playoff positions last year, but lost out on the tie breakers. If the Pacers had not played in the Central Division, +.88 wins could have given them a playoff birth. Oh well, them's the breaks.

LUCK

Imagine you're John MacLeod and you just received word that Magic Johnson went down with an injury against Chicago and would miss playing against your team (the Dallas Mavericks) the next day. Now imagine your team is coming into the match with a two game losing streak, including a double digit home court loss to these same Lakers just a few days before. Consider also that prior to Magic's injury, LA was 21-2 over the last 7 weeks. When you see that the Lakers, without Magic, went on to get blown out by Chicago 107-128, how do you think you would feel? How do you think MacLeod felt? If you say he felt bad - give me a break. There is more chance of J.R. Ewing feeling sorry for Magic than either MacLeod or you as the top dog in Dallas.

Not surprisingly, the Mavericks traveled to the Forum and won 110-101. Does this mean Dallas was better than LA? Clearly not. It simply means the Mavericks were lucky. No other word is appropriate. Had Magic been healthy, the Lakers probably would have won.

Many times throughout the season teams will happen to play another club whose star is out with an injury or who happens to be in a shooting slump. Of course, the opposite is also true. Often a team has the misfortune to play another club which is peaking at that very time for whatever reason. I'm sure most coaches feel as if they are nearly always playing hot teams and seldom cold ones.

I decided to take a look at each team and see which ones were luckier - that is, which ones had the higher percentage of games that fell during their opponent's cold streaks as opposed to their opponent's hot streaks.

Shown below are the 16 teams who went to the playoffs. I did not include the lottery teams for two reasons: 1) These teams' losses strongly contributed to other teams' "hot" streaks. Thus they were skewed to being "unlucky" when, in actuality, they were merely losing a lot of games, as would be expected; 2) There were more hot streaks in the NBA last year than cold streaks. Consequently, the lottery teams appear to have been unlucky far more than they really were.

Also shown below are how many games each played during their opponent's streaks (hot and cold), how lucky they were (advantage), and how many more or less wins for the season they might have recorded had they had average luck.

	Lucky Games	Unlucky Games	Col. 1 - Col. 2 (Advantage)	+/- 1988 wins with Average Luck
Atlanta	17	10	+7	-2.0
Cleveland	15	10	+5	-1.4
Portland	16	12	+4	-1.1
Utah	11	7	+4	-1.1
Denver	14	11	+3	-.9
Milwaukee	12	11	+1	-.3
LA Lakers	13	12	+1	-.3
Boston	11	11	-	-
Chicago	10	12	-2	+.6
Seattle	11	13	-2	+.6
Dallas	10	13	-3	+.9
Houston	11	14	-3	+.9
New York	10	14	-4	+1.1
San Antonio	8	12	-4	+1.1
Detroit	10	15	-5	+1.4
Washington	11	18	-7	+2.0

As you can see, Atlanta was the "luckiest" team by this criterion in the NBA, while Washington was the "unluckiest". Since these 16 teams won 88% of their lucky games (column 1) and only 31% of the unlucky games (column 2), it is relatively easy to determine how much advantage in terms of wins Atlanta had over Washington. That can be calculated by looking first at each team independently. Without going into the specifics, the formula would read...

Projected +/- wins (col. 4) = Advantage (col. 3) * [(.88 - .31)/-2]

As I show in the chart, Atlanta would have won 2 less games given average luck, while Washington would have won 2 more games given the same set of circumstances. Once again, this is not major, but it does say that the concerns over Atlanta's 1987/88 performance are even more justified than before. It also says that the Bullets were probably better than most people realized.

3-POINTERS

The 3-point shot has increased in popularity every year since the league first adopted it in 1979. The reasons are simple and I'll get into those, but first I want to say that even though it has increased in both numbers-attempted as well as percentage-made, it is not as popular as it should be. The 3-pointer is a big advantage and should be used more effectively by NBA teams.

There has been an overall upward trend in both attempts and percentage in the NBA - especially since 1983. In that year the San Antonio Spurs shot the most 3-pointers (308). Last year 18 of the 23 teams and two players exceeded that number. The Spurs also led in team 3-pt% in 1983, at .305. Even that *high* mark was below the league *average* in 1988.

If you have read chapter 2, you might remember that Boston was the most efficient 3-point shooting team in the league last year, and only partly because they had the league's highest percentage (.384). The major reason was because they took 705 rainbows - easily the most ever taken by an NBA team in a season.

It is probably no surprise that in 1988 Danny Ainge set a mid-season record for the most consecutive games in which he hit at least one trey. As you may recall, Michael Adams went on to surpass Ainge's streak. Adams hit at least one 3-pointer in every game the entire second half of the season! In addition to these noteworthy accomplishments, Reggie Miller of Indiana established a new record for most 3-pointers made by a rookie.

With this much increase, why should I argue for more long range shooting? There are really two reasons. The first is a simple argument that is being adhered to more and more often. I dealt with it in last year's book in detail. The primary argument was that when your team trails by two points and you have the ball with 10 seconds left on both clocks, then you should (there are always exceptions) shoot the 3-pointer for the win - as opposed to the 2-pointer and the tie. Expect to see that happen at an increasing rate in the years ahead. (see pages 151-152 Basketball Heaven 1987/88)

The other reason is one that I also analyzed a little bit last year. The premise is that when a team hits 49.0% of it's 2-point shots (league average for 2-pointers), then it need only shoot 29.8% from 3-point range.

The traditional argument is that 50% from 2-point land equals 33.33% from 3-point country. This seems so plainly apparent. After all, if a team takes 100 2-pt shots and hits 50%, then they scored 100 points (2 X 50). On the other hand, if a team shoots 100 3-pt shots and makes 33.33% then they managed to rack up 100 points as well (3 X 33.33). How can there be a difference?

The difference is the number of offensive rebound possibilities available. You see, if TEAM A takes 100 trips up the court and shoots 31.6% (NBA average) on its threes, then that team will score 124.54 points. "What's that you're saying?" I know it seems like 100 trips should equal 31.6 made 3-pointers, which equals 94.8 points (31.6 X 3). What needs to be realized, however, is that 68.4 shots missed! This means there are a lot of offensive rebounds available. When an offensive board occurs, another 3-pointer is taken, etc., etc. By the time every trip up the court yielded either a bucket or a defensive rebound, TEAM A will score 124+ points.

On the other hand, if TEAM B were to bring the ball down court 100 times, but always shoot a 2-point shot at 49.0% then they will end up scoring *only* 117.34 points. Again, this is because of offensive rebounds.

Therefore, based on the league averages, the 3-pointer could be successfully shot at only a 29.8% clip - not 31.6% - to equal the 2-pointer at 49.0%. *The simple reason why this works is because more misses means more chances.*

There is one more element to this discussion. I will not work out the numbers for you here, but when I calculated the above scenarios I used two different offensive rebounding percentages. On a missed 3-pointer, I said that a team will get the offensive rebound 35.0% of the time. On a missed 2-pointer I used 32.5% as the offensive rebound ratio. Why?

Well, I always suspected that 3-pointers were rebounded a little more often by the offensive team than a 2-pointer. It makes sense, after all. A 3-pointer will bound out further, on an average, making it more of a "jump ball" than if it were to roll off the rim. On 2-pt shots, the defender should generally have better position - denying the offensive board. Despite this suspicion, I knew of no compiled statistics which would prove it. Consequently, I chose to figure out the two percentages.

If you're interested in the details - here goes. I decided to produce three columns of numbers. I would show how many missed 2-pt FG's, missed 3-pt FG's and offensive rebounds for each team. When I say offensive rebounds, I really mean to an adjusted offensive rebound total. That number was arrived at by the following method of calculation:

The first thing I needed to do was multiply offensive rebounds times 1.20. The reason for this is because the *player* rebound totals do not include *team* rebounds. These are rebounds which go out of bounds off of a player, but are not ascribable to a specific opposing player, only to his team.

A few offensive rebounds are the result of missed FT's. Therefore, I needed to remove those, but how? As you may recall from a previous discussion in this chapter, I talked about the percentage of FT's which give an opportunity for a rebound. I determined that 6/10ths of all FTA's present that opportunity. Even then it is only on missed FTA's. Causing the number to be reduced still further is the fact that the offensive rebound on a missed FT is only about 25% compared to the overall 32.8%. The formula for this column then is...

**Offensive Adjusted Rebounds =
(Actual Offensive Rebounds X 1.20) - [(FTA - FTM) X .6 X .25]**

What is left are only the offensive rebounds which come as a result of either a 2 or 3-point missed FG. I have removed all offensive rebounds via the missed FT.

What I did next was put my computer to work. I ran through every combination of offensive rebound percentages from 27.0% to 37.0% for both the missed 2-pt FG's column and the 3-pt FG's column. I then added up the hypothetical offensive rebounds created by these two columns. Next, I compared this figure to the adjusted offensive rebounds in column 3. The two percentages I wanted were the two that most closely approximated the following...

(Missed 2-pt FG's times y) + (Missed 3-pt FG's times z) = Adjusted Offensive Rebounds

Without going into more detail, when y = 32.5% and z = 35.0% this formula comes closest to working. I will continue to use these percentages until I either "discover" a better method or until someone starts keeping offensive rebounds by the various types of shots.

PARITY

With expansion in the NBA, I was curious to know how much parity there was. After all, it surely wouldn't make sense to expand if there was already a too-wide divergence between the good and bad teams, would it? Well, with $130+ million pouring into the league from four new teams, who can blame them if parity wasn't at an ideal level?

I decided in a rudimentary way to evaluate how close to being the same all the teams in the league were for a given year. My thinking was that I would then compare the years to discover trends. What I decided to do was to measure how far each team was from the average (since 1968 that is 41 wins). I then added up all these differences for each of the teams and divided by the number of teams. What I ended up with is a number I call Annual Parity Level (APL). The closer to zero, the more parity.

To give you an example, consider 1965. The nine teams in the league at that time are shown below. Each team played 80 games that season. Other than the Celtics and the Warriors, the league was relatively balanced.

1964-65	# Of Wins	Distance From 40 Wins
Boston Celtics	62	22
Los Angeles Lakers	49	9
Cincinnati Royals	48	8
St. Louis Hawks	45	5
Philadelphia 76ers	40	-
Baltimore Bullets	37	3
New York Knicks	31	9
Detroit Pistons	31	9
San Francisco Warriors	17	23
Total Distance From 40 Wins		**88**

Average Distance From 40 Wins = Annual Parity Level (APL) 88/9 = 9.78

Obviously, if all nine teams were 40-40 then the APL would be zero (perfect parity). On the other hand, if 4 teams won 60 games, 1 won 40, and 4 won 20, the APL would be a huge 17.78. The highest APL ever was in 1973, at 13.29.

What is interesting is how APL has generally decreased. This means more parity. However, over the course of 30 years (I am not considering pre-1960 seasons for various reasons), a slight trend is irrelevant at any given time. In 1966, the league had a fairly low APL (8.67). Therefore, it was reasonable to expand. Over the next 3 years five new teams were added. The APL climbed immediately, as one might expect, peaking in 1968 at 10.67, but had dropped back to only 8.00 two years later. This was a new low APL. Could expansion be far off? That answer was and is "no". The following year the NBA added 3 more teams. At this point the league had 17 teams - including 8 new clubs in just a half dozen years. It seemed logical to think the APL would soar. It did.

In 1971 and 1972 the APL was over 13 - the most in any year. However, as usual, the dynamic of parity began to be manifested and by 1976 the APL had dropped to the lowest levels yet, 6.56. Of course 1976 was the last year of the ABA. When it folded, four of its teams joined the NBA. The APL began rising again. With the addition of Dallas in 1980, the APL reached a new recent high of 10.78 in 1983. In the five years since then it has only dropped slightly, to 10.52.

The question that any reasonable person might ask is, "How can the league expand when there is a relatively high Annual Parity Level? In other words, when eight teams won over 50 games during the 1987-88 season (the first time in league history), but the bottom six teams averaged only 22 wins versus 60 losses, does expansion make *cents*? Oh, I mean, does it make *sense*?

Well, my thoughts are that expansion is generally desirable for the league. It's not good to stifle growth and the NBA is certainly growing, while the additional revenue and exposure is hard to ignore. The problem is that it may take until the mid 1990's or even later before a good Annual Parity Level can be reached again, yet the temptation to expand again in a few years may be just too great to ignore. One LA Clippers is enough. A half dozen of them could be a serious problem.

ONE-DIMENSIONAL PLAYERS

It's a common expression throughout sports that a particular player is one-dimensional. In the NBA, obvious examples might be Kiki Vandeweghe (scoring), Manute Bol (blocks), or Mugsy Bogues (steals). I thought it would be interesting to come up with a simple formula for determining this, then list who such players are.

Although I could conceive of a more complicated formula, I thought this simplistic endeavor would suffice...

One Dimensional Assists = Assists / (Pts + Reb + Ast + Blk + Stl)

Of course, if I want to look at one dimensional-blocks, I would just substitute a player's blocks into the numerator. In effect, what is happening here is that each of the five performance categories are being viewed as a percent of the player's whole game. It doesn't matter how much or little he plays since his assists (for example) are evaluated with respect only to his own stats. You might notice that the denominator consists of the positive CREDITS in the Production Rating formula. On the following page(s), I have shown the most one-dimensional players in the NBA in 1987-88 for each of the 5 categories. I have also shown the most multi-dimensional for each category. What's that? I mean only that they are the *least* one-dimensional for a specific category. For example, Jeff Hornacek is last among scorers despite many others having scored less than Hornacek. It only means that scoring was a smaller percent of his positive CREDITS than of any other player. It probably also implies that he is relatively high in the other categories. In fact, he is #6 in assists.

ONE-DIMENSIONAL SCORERS

TOP 10			BOTTOM 10		
1. Vandeweghe	Port	.782	1. Ch. Jones	Wash	.264
2. Teagle	Gost	.769	2. Dunn	Denv	.291
3. Pierce	Milw	.767	3. McMillan	Seat	.332
4. J. Malone	Wash	.764	4. Eaton	Utah	.338
5. Ellis	Seat	.757	5. Rollins	Atla	.344
6. Dantley	Detr	.755	6. C. Johnson	Seat	.345
7. Mitchell	Sant	.748	7. Ca. Jones	Port	.351
8. D. Wilkins	Atla	.732	8. Lister	Seat	.351
9. Dailey	LACl	.728	9. Vranes	Phil	.362
10. Campbell	LALa	.722	10. Bogues	Wash	.370

ONE-DIMENSIONAL REBOUNDERS

TOP 10			BOTTOM 10		
1. C. Johnson	Seat	.500	1. Sundvold	Sant	.070
2. Donaldson	Dall	.492	2. Stockton	Utah	.084
3. Lister	Seat	.478	3. Hodges	Phoe	.086
4. Rollins	Atla	.469	4. Price	Clev	.088
5. Koncak	Atla	.461	5. Ji. Paxson	Bost	.089
6. McNamara	Phil	.458	6. Drew	LACl	.089
7. Gray	Indi	.446	7. W. Davis	Phoe	.091
8. Oakley	Chic	.440	8. K. Smith	Sacr	.091
9. S. Green	NYor	.436	9. Woodson	LACl	.093
10. Ch. Jones	Wash	.435	10. Jo. Paxson	Chic	.095

ONE-DIMENSIONAL ASSISTS

TOP 10				BOTTOM 10			
1.	Stockton	Utah	.399	1.	Willis	Atla	.018
2.	Bogues	Wash	.380	2.	Rollins	Atla	.020
3.	McMillan	Seat	.373	3.	Bedford	Detr	.021
4.	Donavan	NYor	.372	4.	Koncak	Atla	.026
5.	Young	Seat	.369	5.	Eaton	Utah	.033
6.	Skiles	Indi	.364	6.	Duckworth	Port	.034
7.	R. Green	Utah	.361	7.	Tarpley	Dall	.037
8.	Minniefield	Bost	.352	8.	Turpin	Utah	.038
9.	Jackson	NYor	.335	9.	Gilmore	Bost	.039
10.	S. Vincent	Chic	.324	10.	M. Thompson	LALa	.041

ONE-DIMENSIONAL BLOCKS

TOP 10				BOTTOM 10			
1.	Bol	Wash	.305	1.	Drew	LACl	.000
2.	Eaton	Utah	.180	2.	Jo. Paxson	Chic	.001
3.	Ch. Jones	Wash	.151	3.	Dawkins	Sant	.001
4.	W. Cooper	Denv	.136	4.	R. Green	Utah	.001
5.	Rollins	Atla	.135	5.	J. Lucas	Milw	.002
6.	Benjamin	LACl	.122	6.	Jackson	NYor	.002
7.	Lister	Seat	.107	7.	W. Davis	Phoe	.002
8.	Ca. Jones	Port	.104	8.	Hodges	Phoe	.002
9.	Vranes	Phil	.099	9.	Dailey	LACl	.003
10.	H. Williams	Indi	.097	10.	Sundvold	Sant	.003

ONE-DIMENSIONAL STEALS

TOP 10				BOTTOM 10			
1.	Dunn	Denv	.163	1.	McHale	Bost	.012
2.	Alford	Dall	.136	2.	Edwards	Detr	.012
3.	Bradley	NJer	.133	3.	McNamara	Phil	.012
4.	Bogues	Wash	.119	4.	Rasmussen	Denv	.014
5.	D. Walker	Wash	.102	5.	Duckworth	Port	.016
6.	Valentine	LACl	.099	6.	W. Cooper	Denv	.017
7.	Minniefield	Bost	.091	7.	S. Johnson	Port	.017
8.	McMillan	Seat	.090	8.	Ed. Johnson	Phoe	.018
9.	Young	Seat	.088	9.	Kleine	Sacr	.018
10.	P. Washington	NJer	.087	10.	Daugherty	Clev	.019

The 4 greatest centers of all time
- Read account of each in Basketball Heaven 1987-88 ppg. 24,25
- Basketball Hall of Fame -

CHAPTER 6

THE TRENDS

CENTERS

The NBA has spanned 4 decades of centers. First George Mikan (1947-57); then Wilt Chamberlain & Bill Russell (1957-73); finally Kareem Abdul-Jabbar (1970-present).

Interestingly, highlights of the other three can be charted by looking at each decade of Kareem's life. Kareem was born April 16, 1947 - the same day the very first NBA championship began.

George Mikan's 10 year career coincided with the first 10 years of Kareem's life. During this period, Mikan won 7 championships and was voted the greatest player of the 1st half century.

Just days from Kareem's 10th birthday Bill Russell won his first of 11 championships to begin the greatest dynasty ever in professional sports. Russell was voted the NBA's greatest player in 1981.

On the day Kareem turned 20 (April 16, 1967), Wilt Chamberlain grabbed 26 rebounds in one half, for an NBA finals record. His 76ers team went on to rout the Warriors 126-95 and broke Boston's streak of 8 straight championships. Chamberlain's Philadelphia team that year was later voted the greatest team in NBA history.

Just a few days prior to Kareem's 30th birthday. Bill Russell coached his final NBA game (prior to Sacramento). Ironically, his Seattle Supersonics played that game against Abdul-Jabbar and the Lakers. Jabbar scored 30 points to match his age while leading the Lakers to victory.

Finally, April 16, 1987 was Kareem's 40th birthday. The Lakers defeated Utah 110-97. Kareem had 15 points. He is now the oldest player to ever play in the NBA and, not surprisingly, many consider him the game's greatest center.

OFFENSIVE TRENDS

On the opposite page are the annual averages for the NBA by various offensive categories since 1950. Just as society has changed in 40 years - so has the game of basketball. In 1950, the game was much slower, more methodical, less stylized and much less sophisticated. A lot has happened in the intervening years to change the game. Statistical information such as that on the next page merely reflects the development of the game. In most cases the trends that have developed are obvious. There are some surprises, however.

In the early years, the lane was 6 feet wide, there was no shot clock, goal tending was legal, and there was no limit on fouls per quarter. Because of these rules and others, the game varied from one decade to another. Later on, of course, the 3-point shot was added which also significantly affected the game.

By observing free throw and field goal percentages, it's clear that both have risen since 1950. It is also understandable. Players have grown up playing basketball, have had excellent coaching in grade school, high school and college, and have developed better training techniques. Since 1950, field goal percentage has risen continually, from 34% to 49%, while free throw percentage has been more volatile. In the most extreme scenario, free throw percentage has barely risen since 1959 when it was 75.6%. Since then it has been as low as 71.4% in 1969 and as high as 77.1% in 1974.

Virtually every category rose when the 24 second clock was introduced in 1955. Even free throw percentage rose sharply. The reason why is because fouling became less selective. Before the shot clock, primarily only *poor* free throw shooters were fouled to stop the clock. After 1955 fouls became evenly distributed. Field goal percentage also rose in 1955, proving those wrong who said the shot clock would force bad shots.

Somewhat surprisingly, scoring actually reached its peak in the early 1960's at over ten points per game more than today. Perhaps today's defenses are more sophisticated, or perhaps the offenses are more structured to take advantage of an opponent's weaknesses. In either event the result is more additional time off the clock and less scoring.

Assists have continually increased while rebounds have continually declined. Both patterns can be attributed to better field goal percentages. Since a good pass only becomes an assist if the other player scores, he will clearly register less assists when his teammate shoots field goals at 37% as opposed to 49% like he might do today. Furthermore, the reason more successful shots were not the result of an assist was largely because of stick-backs. The more misses, the more offensive rebounds and the less assists. Obviously, rebounds, both offensive and defensive, would be greater with lower field goal percentages as well. As a result, assists and rebounds are inversely proportionate.

Three point percentages have risen sharply since they were introduced in 1980. The trey has gone from an occasional event (1 attempt per team per game in 1980) to a regular part of the offense (5 attempts per team per game in 1989). Players like Michael Adams and Danny Ainge went long periods of time last season where they hit at least one 3-pointer in each game. I go into more detail on the rise of this shot on page 252.

The NBA began distinguishing between offensive and defensive rebounds in 1974. Although they have varied and no clear trend exists, offensive rebounds constituted from 30% to 33% of all rebounds.

I have explained why the trends exist, but it is also noteworthy that not that much has changed since 1980. Take a look at the stats for the decade's first year. Compare them with 1988. You'll see very little difference other than 3-point FG%. Clearly the league has reached a certain equilibrium.

OFFENSIVE TRENDS

YEAR	SCORING	ASSISTS	REBOUNDS	2-PT FG%	3-PT FG%	FT%
1950	80.0	19.6	---	34.0	---	71.4
1951	84.1	21.0	46.8	35.7	---	73.2
1952	83.7	21.9	51.8	36.7	---	73.5
1953	82.7	21.0	48.9	37.0	---	71.6
1954	79.5	20.3	48.4	37.2	---	70.9
1955	93.9	23.6	53.1	38.5	---	73.8
1956	99.0	24.3	56.5	38.7	---	74.5
1957	99.6	18.9	58.0	38.0	---	75.1
1958	106.6	19.6	65.9	38.3	---	74.6
1959	108.2	19.6	62.3	39.5	---	75.6
1960	115.3	22.6	66.2	40.9	---	73.5
1961	118.1	24.2	66.0	41.5	---	73.3
1962	118.8	23.9	64.3	42.6	---	72.7
1963	115.3	22.7	60.1	44.1	---	72.7
1964	111.0	21.4	59.3	43.3	---	72.2
1965	110.6	21.0	60.5	42.6	---	72.1
1966	115.5	22.9	61.4	43.3	---	72.7
1967	117.4	22.4	60.6	44.1	---	73.2
1968	116.6	22.8	59.6	44.6	---	72.0
1969	112.3	23.1	56.9	44.1	---	71.4
1970	116.7	24.7	52.9	46.0	---	75.1
1971	112.4	24.3	53.1	44.9	---	74.5
1972	110.2	24.1	51.1	45.5	---	74.8
1973	107.6	25.2	50.3	45.6	---	75.8
1974	105.7	24.6	48.2	45.9	---	77.1
1975	102.6	23.8	47.1	45.7	---	76.5
1976	104.5	23.0	47.4	45.8	---	75.1
1977	106.6	22.8	47.1	46.5	---	75.1
1978	108.5	25.0	47.1	46.9	---	75.2
1979	110.3	25.8	45.2	48.5	---	75.2
1980	109.3	25.8	44.9	48.8	28.0	76.4
1981	110.1	25.5	43.5	49.1	24.5	75.1
1982	108.6	25.2	43.5	49.7	26.2	74.6
1983	108.5	25.9	42.6	49.2	23.8	74.0
1984	110.3	26.2	41.2	49.9	25.0	76.0
1985	110.8	26.3	43.5	49.9	28.2	76.4
1986	110.2	26.0	43.6	49.5	28.2	75.6
1987	109.9	26.0	44.0	49.0	30.1	76.3
1988	108.2	25.8	43.4	49.0	31.6	76.6

MISCELLANEOUS TRENDS

On the opposite page are six miscellaneous trends in the NBA since 1950. As the NBA has grown and developed over the years, these numbers have also inflated. There are few surprises, but some explanation is necessary.

You will see that there are seventeen teams listed in 1950, but only eleven in 1951. There is a logical explanation. The National Basketball League (NBL) began back in 1937. The league, along with the American Basketball League, the negro leagues, and amateur leagues set the stage for a post World War II unification.

The Basketball Association of America (BAA) began in 1946-47. During the next three years, the NBL and BAA battled for the same players and franchises. In 1949 (1949-50 season) the two leagues finally merged to form the NBA.

Seventeen of the twenty clubs survived the merger to play in the 1950 season. Unfortunately for six of them, the first season in the NBA did not prove profitable. Their disbanding made the new league much stronger. Over the next five years three more teams would fold. Since 1955, no NBA team has gone under and the league has tripled in size.

DISBANDED TEAMS (1950-55)

1950	Anderson Packers
1950	Chicago Stags
1950	Denver Nuggets
1950	St. Louis Bombers
1950	Sheroygan Redskins
1950	Waterloo Hawks
1951	Washington Capitols
1953	Indianapolis Olympians
1955	Baltimore Bullets

It's no surprise that players' heights have increased consistently over the years. What is strange is that players' weights have not substantially risen since 1969. Strangely, the wieghts dropped during the 1970's to bottom out in 1979. Once again, they began rising in the 1980's to reach an all time high 216 pounds - only 2 more than in 1969.

The average players' salary has risen dramatically (50%) the last two years. At the current rate, the 1989 average annual salary in the league will be well over 650 thousand dollars.

Also rising at a rapid pace is the NBA's popularity. Average game attendance has increased substantially the last five years to record levels. In fact, the last three years are two of the top years with respect to largest gains.

TOP YEARS
INCREASED ATTENDANCE

YEAR	GAIN	PCT.
1956	+ 1,153	34.47%
1970	+ 1,079	16.64%
1975	+ 960	10.14%
1987	**+ 902**	**7.58%**
1976	+ 840	8.99%
1977	+ 795	7.81%
1986	**+ 752**	**6.75%**
1988	**+ 624**	**4.88%**

This is all the more impressive considering capacity levels. Clearly, at some point the average per-game attendance cannot continue to rise. When every arena is sold out, increases will no longer happen. In 1988 the NBA sold out at 82.3% capacity. In 1987 it was 78.6% of capacity. In 1986 it was 73.1% of capacity and in 1985 - 68.5%. By dividing the change in capacity levels by the amount available to grow, [Example: (82.3 - 78.6) / (100 - 78.6) = 17.3%] 1988 was the 2nd most impressive year ever in attendance just behind 1987. In 1987 attendance rose at 20.5% its available capacity to grow. The years 1988 and 1987, as well as 1986 (14.74% availability), are the top three years in history.

I believe the attendance levels are representative of the popularity of the sport. I see basketball as the sport of the future simply because player identification is easy, it's fast paced, it's indoors and under ideal conditions, it's conducive to statistical analysis, and its easy for anyone to play - even by themselves.

MISCELLANEOUS TRENDS

YEAR	TEAM	GAMES	HEIGHT	WEIGHT	ATTEN.	SALARY
1950	17	68	6'4"	197	U/A	U/A
1951	11	68	6'4"	198	U/A	U/A
1952	10	66	6'4.5"	198	U/A	U/A
1953	10	71	6'4.5"	200	3,210	U/A
1954	9	72	6'5"	205	3,583	U/A
1955	8	72	6'5"	203	3,345	U/A
1956	8	72	6'5"	206	4,498	U/A
1957	8	72	6'5"	207	4,895	U/A
1958	8	72	6'5"	205	4,824	U/A
1959	8	72	6'5"	208	5,077	U/A
1960	8	75	6'5.5"	206	5,008	U/A
1961	8	79	6'5.5"	207	5,494	U/A
1962	9	80	6'5.5"	208	4,566	U/A
1963	9	80	6'5.5"	208	5,054	U/A
1964	9	80	6'6"	211	5,266	U/A
1965	9	80	6'6"	213	5,371	U/A
1966	9	80	6'6"	211	6,019	U/A
1967	10	81	6'6"	210	6,631	U/A
1968	12	82	6'6"	211	5,967	U/A
1969	14	82	6'6"	214	6,484	U/A
1970	14	82	6'6"	211	7,563	U/A
1971	17	82	6'6"	210	7,648	U/A
1972	17	82	6'6"	211	8,061	U/A
1973	17	82	6'6"	211	8,396	U/A
1974	17	82	6'6"	210	8,479	U/A
1975	18	82	6'6"	208	9,339	U/A
1976	18	82	6'6.5"	209	10,179	U/A
1977	22	82	6'6.5"	208	10,974	130K
1978	22	82	6'6.5"	207	10,947	139K
1979	22	82	6'6.5"	206	10,822	148K
1980	22	82	6'6.5"	208	11,017	170K
1981	23	82	6'6.5"	209	10,021	171K
1982	23	82	6'6.5"	210	10,567	212K
1983	23	82	6'7"	211	10,220	249K
1984	23	82	6'7"	211	10,620	275K
1985	23	82	6'7"	212	11,141	325K
1986	23	82	6'7.5"	214	11,893	375K
1987	23	82	6'7.5"	215	12,795	440K
1988	23	82	6'7.5"	216	13,419	550K

POSITION LEADERS

Listed below are the annual Production Ratings leaders regardless of position and the annual Production Ratings leaders at the forward position. I began making a distinction between small forwards with power forwards in 1974. A lack of statistical information makes Production Ratings prior to 1950 highly suspect.

	PRODUCTION LEADER		FORWARD	
1950	G. Mikan	28.13	D. Schayes	25.20
1951	G. Mikan	30.16	D. Schayes	25.80
1952	P. Arizin	27.06	P. Arizin	27.06
1953	N. Johnston	26.99	D. Schayes	23.31
1954	N. Johnston	25.53	H. Gallatin	23.61
1955	N. Johnston	29.00	B. Pettit	24.85
1956	B. Pettit	29.74	B. Pettit	29.74
1957	D. Schayes	27.44	D. Schayes	27.44
1958	B. Russell	30.71	D. Schayes	29.07
1959	B. Pettit	32.99	B. Pettit	32.99
1960	W. Chamberlain	43.83	B. Pettit	32.29
1961	W. Chamberlain	45.58	E. Baylor	40.19
1962	W. Chamberlain	52.29	E. Baylor	39.31
1963	W. Chamberlain	50.59	E. Baylor	35.98
1964	W. Chamberlain	44.60	B. Pettit	32.41
1965	W. Chamberlain	40.62	J. Lucas	34.26
1966	W. Chamberlain	45.76	J. Lucas	33.66
1967	W. Chamberlain	45.54	R. Barry	31.32
1968	W. Chamberlain	42.80	J. Lucas	34.37
1969	W. Chamberlain	34.68	J. Lucas	33.66
1970	K. Abdul-Jabbar	33.63	B. Cunningham	30.48
1971	K. Abdul-Jabbar	38.88	J. Havlicek	30.40
1972	K. Abdul-Jabbar	42.63	J. Havlicek	29.11
1973	K. Abdul-Jabbar	39.12	S. Haywood	30.81

	PRODUCTION LEADER		SMALL FORWARD		POWER FORWARD	
1974	K. Abdul-Jabbar	35.91	R. Tomjanovich	25.73	S. Haywood	26.92
1975	K. Abdul-Jabbar	35.62	R. Barry	26.26	E. Hayes	25.70
1976	K. Abdul-Jabbar	39.65	J. Drew	22.14	G. McGinnis	25.05
1977	K. Abdul-Jabbar	35.16	L. Kenon	25.17	E. Hayes	26.87
1978	K. Abdul-Jabbar	34.39	M. Johnson	24.13	T. Robinson	24.77
1979	K. Abdul-Jabbar	34.68	M. Johnson	26.64	E. Hayes	24.56
1980	K. Abdul-Jabbar	32.87	J. Erving	27.78	L. Bird	25.26
1981	M. Malone	31.67	A. Dantley	28.23	L. Bird	26.74
1982	M. Malone	33.12	A. Dantley	27.81	L. Bird	29.16
1983	M. Malone	30.08	A. English	28.30	L. Bird	30.04
1984	E. Johnson	30.30	L. Bird	29.99	J. Ruland	27.67
1985	L. Bird	34.39	L. Bird	34.39	T. Cummings	24.39
1986	L. Bird	31.30	L. Bird	31.30	C. Barkley	28.26
1987	L. Bird	34.28	L. Bird	34.28	C. Barkley	33.46
1988	M. Jordan	35.05	L. Bird	34.01	C. Barkley	32.51

THE TRENDS   265

POSITION LEADERS

Listed below are the annual Production Ratings leaders at the center and guard positions. I began making a distinction between off guards and point guards in 1974. A lack of statistical information makes Production Ratings prior to 1950 highly suspect. ABA ratings are not

	CENTER			GUARD	
1950	G. Mikan	28.13		A. Phillip	14.83
1951	G. Mikan	30.16		A. Phillip	17.00
1952	G. Mikan	24.88		B. Cousy	20.03
1953	N. Johnston	26.99		B. Cousy	20.27
1954	N. Johnston	25.53		B. Cousy	19.56
1955	N. Johnston	29.00		B. Cousy	22.27
1956	N. Johnston	27.36		B. Cousy	22.49
1957	N. Johnston	27.20		B. Cousy	19.39
1958	B. Russell	30.71		T. Gola	21.81
1959	B. Russell	32.70		B. Cousy	21.25
1960	W. Chamberlain	43.83		T. Gola	22.44
1961	W. Chamberlain	45.58		O. Robertson	36.42
1962	W. Chamberlain	52.29		O. Robertson	40.51
1963	W. Chamberlain	50.59		O. Robertson	36.81
1964	W. Chamberlain	44.60		O. Robertson	39.15
1965	W. Chamberlain	40.62		O. Robertson	37.49
1966	W. Chamberlain	45.76		O. Robertson	36.41
1967	W. Chamberlain	45.54		O. Robertson	35.13
1968	W. Chamberlain	42.80		O. Robertson	33.46
1969	W. Chamberlain	34.68		O. Robertson	30.51
1970	K. Abdul-Jabbar	33.63		J. West	30.01
1971	K. Abdul-Jabbar	38.88		J. West	29.62
1972	K. Abdul-Jabbar	42.63		N. Archibald	28.21
1973	K. Abdul-Jabbar	39.12		N. Archibald	33.18

	CENTER		OFF GUARD		POINT GUARD	
1974	K. Abdul-Jabbar	35.91	P. Maravich	20.62	W. Frazier	23.46
1975	K. Abdul-Jabbar	35.62	G. Goodrich	18.11	W. Frazier	23.56
1976	K. Abdul-Jabbar	39.65	P. Maravich	20.39	W. Frazier	22.15
1977	K. Abdul-Jabbar	35.16	G. Gervin	21.68	P. Westphal	18.86
1978	K. Abdul-Jabbar	34.39	G. Gervin	24.93	P. Westphal	20.67
1979	K. Abdul-Jabbar	34.68	G. Gervin	25.31	P. Westphal	21.89
1980	K. Abdul-Jabbar	32.87	G. Gervin	27.19	E. Johnson	25.13
1981	M. Malone	31.67	G. Gervin	22.10	M. Richardson	21.81
1982	M. Malone	33.12	G. Gervin	24.82	E. Johnson	29.65
1983	M. Malone	30.08	S. Moncrief	22.80	E. Johnson	28.63
1984	M. Malone	25.85	S. Moncrief	22.76	E. Johnson	30.30
1985	M. Malone	27.30	M. Jordan	29.24	E. Johnson	28.77
1986	A. Olajuwon	28.40	A. Robertson	22.48	E. Johnson	28.50
1987	A. Olajuwon	28.99	M. Jordan	31.91	E. Johnson	31.79
1988	A. Olajuwon	28.10	M. Jordan	35.05	E. Johnson	27.71

CATEGORY LEADERS

Listed below are the annual leaders in three different categories. Scoring is based on points-per-game. Shooting is based on equally analyzing 2 pt. FG%, 3 pt. FG% and FT%. A rating of 1.000 means average shooting (50% - 2 pt FG%, 33% - 3pt FG%, 75% - FT%). The formula for shooting is equal to (points + 1/3 FTs made) / shots attempted. The third category is rebounds based on 48 minutes per game.

	SCORING		SHOOTING		REBOUNDS	
1950	G. Mikan	27.43	A. Groza	.962	Unavailable	
1951	G. Mikan	28.41	A. Groza	.978	D. Schayes	16.36
1952	P. Arizin	25.36	B. Wanzer	.974	D. Schayes	18.51
1953	N. Johnston	22.34	B. Sharman	.951	H. Gallatin	18.85
1954	N. Johnston	24.43	E. Macauley	.987	G. Mikan	20.89
1955	N. Johnston	22.65	L. Foust	.992	C. Share	19.48
1956	B. Pettit	25.68	N. Johnston	.974	M. Stokes	22.61
1957	P. Arizin	25.59	N. Johnston	.968	B. Russell	26.70
1958	G. Yardley	27.79	K. Sears	.954	B. Russell	28.44
1959	B. Pettit	29.24	K. Sears	1.042	B. Russell	25.97
1960	W. Chamberlain	37.60	K. Sears	1.021	W. Chamberlain	27.91
1961	W. Chamberlain	38.39	O. Robertson	.995	W. Chamberlain	27.34
1962	W. Chamberlain	50.36	O. Robertson	.994	W. Chamberlain	25.37
1963	W. Chamberlain	44.83	O. Robertson	1.050	B. Russell	25.28
1964	W. Chamberlain	36.85	J. Lucas	1.049	B. Russell	26.61
1965	W. Chamberlain	34.71	J. West	1.026	B. Russell	26.01
1966	W. Chamberlain	33.53	J. West	1.018	B. Russell	25.22
1967	R. Barry	35.58	O. Robertson	1.045	W. Chamberlain	25.21
1968	O. Robertson	29.17	O. Robertson	1.054	W. Chamberlain	24.43
1969	E. Hayes	28.38	J. Lucas	1.079	W. Unseld	24.10
1970	J. West	31.20	J. McGlocklin	1.071	T. Boerwinkle	20.89
1971	K. Abdul-Jabbar	31.66	K. Abdul-Jabbar	1.091	T. Boerwinkle	22.95
1972	K. Abdul-Jabbar	34.84	K. Abdul-Jabbar	1.087	C. Ray	22.68
1973	N. Archibald	33.99	M. Guokas	1.134	W. Chamberlain	20.68
1974	B. McAdoo	30.55	R. Tomjanovich	1.086	E. Hayes	19.50
1975	B. McAdoo	34.52	L. Steele	1.099	H. Hairston	19.89
1976	B. McAdoo	31.12	J. McMillian	1.086	K. Abdul-Jabbar	19.65
1977	P. Maravich	31.14	D. Twardzik	1.183	S. Nater	21.18
1978	G. Gervin	27.22	D. Twardzik	1.132	M. Malone	20.18
1979	G. Gervin	29.56	S. Nater	1.124	M. Malone	20.45
1980	G. Gervin	33.14	K. Abdul-Jabbar	1.159	S. Nater	20.41
1981	A. Dantley	30.65	A. Gilmore	1.182	L. Smith	18.51
1982	G. Gervin	32.29	A. Gilmore	1.194	L. Smith	17.63
1983	A. English	28.37	A. Gilmore	1.157	M. Malone	19.61
1984	A. Dantley	30.61	C. Natt	1.139	L. Thompson	17.77
1985	B. King	32.89	J. Donaldson	1.176	B. Walton	17.49
1986	D. Wilkins	30.33	J. Sichting	1.166	C. Oakley	17.99
1987	M. Jordan	37.09	K. McHale	1.182	L. Smith	18.54
1988	M. Jordan	34.98	J. Stockton	1.161	R. Tarpley	19.95

CATEGORY LEADERS

Listed below are the annual leaders in three different categories. All three are based on 48 minutes per game. The purpose of using this statistic, as opposed to a per-game-only statistic, is that it reveals those players who really excel in a particular area. For role players, a statistic based on 48 minutes is much more meaningful. Steals and blocks were not kept by the NBA until 1974.

Year	ASSISTS		BLOCKS		STEALS	
1950	A. Phillip	5.80	Unavailable		Unavailable	
1951	A. Phillip	6.27	Unavailable		Unavailable	
1952	D. McGuire	9.23	Unavailable		Unavailable	
1953	B. Cousy	8.92	Unavailable		Unavailable	
1954	B. Cousy	8.70	Unavailable		Unavailable	
1955	D. McGuire	11.26	Unavailable		Unavailable	
1956	B. Cousy	11.14	Unavailable		Unavailable	
1957	B. Cousy	9.71	Unavailable		Unavailable	
1958	B. Cousy	10.00	Unavailable		Unavailable	
1959	B. Cousy	11.13	Unavailable		Unavailable	
1960	B. Cousy	13.26	Unavailable		Unavailable	
1961	B. Cousy	11.42	Unavailable		Unavailable	
1962	B. Cousy	13.26	Unavailable		Unavailable	
1963	B. Cousy	12.52	Unavailable		Unavailable	
1964	O. Robertson	11.71	Unavailable		Unavailable	
1965	O. Robertson	12.08	Unavailable		Unavailable	
1966	G. Rodgers	13.99	Unavailable		Unavailable	
1967	G. Rodgers	14.23	Unavailable		Unavailable	
1968	G. Rodgers	11.80	Unavailable		Unavailable	
1969	A Williams	12.66	Unavailable		Unavailable	
1970	A. Williams	15.63	Unavailable		Unavailable	
1971	N. Van Lier	12.01	Unavailable		Unavailable	
1972	L. Wilkens	12.30	Unavailable		Unavailable	
1973	N. Archibald	11.87	Unavailable		Unavailable	
1974	S. Watts	11.83	E. Smith	6.46	L. Steele	3.93
1975	K. Porter	12.05	E. Smith	4.43	S. Watts	4.44
1976	S. Watts	11.43	K. Abdul-Jabbar	4.80	S. Watts	4.51
1977	K. Porter	13.42	G. Johnson	5.14	D. Buse	4.58
1978	K. Porter	14.28	W. Rollins	5.83	R. Lee	5.60
1979	K. Porter	17.22	W. Rollins	6.42	E. Jordan	4.27
1980	K. Porter	14.68	G. Johnson	5.84	D. Bradley	5.00
1981	K. Porter	13.67	G. Johnson	6.90	D. Bradley	4.78
1982	J. Moore	15.94	G. Johnson	7.12	M. Cheeks	4.02
1983	J. Moore	14.16	W. Rollins	6.66	M. Richardson	4.21
1984	J. Lucas	17.88	M. Eaton	7.88	D. Cook	4.21
1985	I. Thomas	17.45	M. Eaton	7.78	J. Moore	4.09
1986	E. Johnson	16.89	M. Bol	9.12	A. Robertson	5.02
1987	J. Stockton	17.31	M. Bol	9.34	A. Robertson	4.63
1988	J. Stockton	19.05	M. Eaton	5.34	J. Stockton	4.09

MISCELLANEOUS LEADERS

Listed below are the annual leaders in three different categories. The first column represents the annual Most Valuable Player (see Chapter 1 for explanation of formula). Column two represents the most dominant player at his position each year (see Chapter 1 for explanation of formula). Column three shows the top rookie each year by Production Rating.

	MVP		POSITION DOMINANCE		ROOKIE	
1950	D. Schayes	2.219	D. Schayes	1.508	A. Groza	25.13
1951	G. Mikan	2.067	G. Mikan	1.471	P. Arizin	19.66
1952	G. Mikan	1.908	P. Arizin	1.423	M. Hutchins	18.11
1953	B. Cousy	2.012	B. Cousy	1.394	D. Meineke	13.18
1954	H. Gallatin	2.037	H. Gallatin	1.513	R. Felix	20.57
1955	B. Cousy	1.831	N. Johnston	1.366	B. Pettit	24.85
1956	N. Johnston	1.963	B. Cousy	1.353	M. Stokes	25.15
1957	B. Cousy	1.957	N. Johnston	1.313	B. Russell	25.17
1958	B. Russell	1.871	T. Gola	1.289	W. Sauldsberry	12.99
1959	B. Russell	2.259	B. Russell	1.535	E. Baylor	29.27
1960	W. Chamberlain	2.100	W. Chamberlain	1.502	W. Chamberlain	43.83
1961	W. Chamberlain	2.125	W. Chamberlain	1.602	O. Robertson	36.42
1962	E. Baylor	2.159	O. Robertson	1.571	W. Bellamy	37.96
1963	O. Robertson	2.082	W. Chamberlain	1.625	T. Dischinger	25.68
1964	O. Robertson	2.250	O. Robertson	1.641	J. Lucas	30.39
1965	O. Robertson	2.103	O. Robertson	1.549	W. Reed	24.19
1966	W. Chamberlain	2.094	W. Chamberlain	1.483	R. Barry	25.48
1967	W. Chamberlain	2.345	W. Chamberlain	1.543	D. Bing	16.69
1968	W. Chamberlain	2.128	W. Chamberlain	1.442	E. Monroe	21.56
1969	W. Chamberlain	1.876	J. Lucas	1.368	E. Hayes	29.45
1970	K. Abdul-Jabbar	1.925	K. Abdul-Jabbar	1.291	K. Abdul-Jabbar	33.63
1971	K. Abdul-Jabbar	2.153	K. Abdul-Jabbar	1.335	D. Cowens	24.26
1972	K. Abdul-Jabbar	2.098	K. Abdul-Jabbar	1.394	S. Wicks	25.23
1973	K. Abdul-Jabbar	1.965	N. Archibald	1.372	L. Neal	19.98
1974	K. Abdul-Jabbar	1.936	S. Haywood	1.283	E. DiGregorio	13.58
1975	R. Barry	1.950	R. Barry	1.318	J. Drew	19.69
1976	K. Abdul-Jabbar	1.904	K. Abdul-Jabbar	1.416	A. Adams	22.30
1977	K. Abdul-Jabbar	1.916	K. Abdul-Jabbar	1.351	A. Dantley	20.14
1978	G. Gervin	1.811	K. Abdul-Jabbar	1.255	M. Johnson	24.13
1979	G. Gervin	1.873	G. Gervin	1.317	P. Ford	17.32
1980	E. Johnson	2.028	G. Gervin	1.340	L. Bird	25.26
1981	L. Bird	2.040	L. Bird	1.297	J. Carroll	19.37
1982	E. Johnson	2.174	E. Johnson	1.424	B. Williams	21.94
1983	M. Malone	2.080	E. Johnson	1.397	T. Cummings	26.04
1984	E. Johnson	2.059	E. Johnson	1.397	R. Sampson	24.01
1985	L. Bird	2.131	M. Jordan	1.393	M. Jordan	29.24
1986	L. Bird	2.123	E. Johnson	1.346	P. Ewing	20.56
1987	E. Johnson	2.175	M. Jordan	1.416	C. Person	19.63
1988	L. Bird	2.043	M. Jordan	1.426	M. Jackson	20.68

MISCELLANEOUS LEADERS

Listed below are the annual NBA champions and the champions' Total Percentage (TP). In brief, the TP is the ratio of wins versus games played, with three times the emphasis on playoff games. Chapter two explains Total Percentage in more detail. The second column lists the top 38 MVP's ever, regardless of year. MVP = PD + TP. (See chapter two for explanation.)

CHAMPIONS		TP
1950	Minneapolis Lakers	.785
1951	Rochester Royals	.618
1952	Minneapolis Lakers	.638
1953	Minneapolis Lakers	.708
1954	Minneapolis Lakers	.658
1955	Syracuse Nationals	.610
1956	Philadelphia Warriors	.647
1957	Boston Celtics	.637
1958	St. Louis Hawks	.619
1959	Boston Celtics	.724
1960	Boston Celtics	.728
1961	Boston Celtics	.743
1962	Boston Celtics	.689
1963	Boston Celtics	.689
1964	Boston Celtics	.755
1965	Boston Celtics	.741
1966	Boston Celtics	.672
1967	Philadelphia 76ers	.802
1968	Boston Celtics	.647
1969	Boston Celtics	.618
1970	New York Knicks	.691
1971	Milwaukee Bucks	.823
1972	Los Angeles Lakers	.827
1973	New York Knicks	.699
1974	Boston Celtics	.676
1975	Golden State Warriors	.632
1976	Boston Celtics	.662
1977	Portland Trailblazers	.655
1978	Washington Bullets	.593
1979	Seattle Supersonics	.662
1980	Los Angeles Lakers	.738
1981	Boston Celtics	.737
1982	Los Angeles Lakers	.750
1983	Philadelphia 76ers	.835
1984	Boston Celtics	.709
1985	Los Angeles Lakers	.770
1986	Boston Celtics	.824
1987	Los Angeles Lakers	.809
1988	Los Angeles Lakers	.695

	TOP MVP's		
1.	W. Chamberlain	1967	2.345
2.	B. Russell	1959	2.259
3.	O. Robertson	1964	2.250
4.	D. Schayes	1950	2.219
5.	E. Johnson	1987	2.175
6.	E. Baylor	1962	2.159
7.	G. Mikan	1950	2.158
8.	K. Abdul-Jabbar	1971	2.153
9.	E. Johnson	1983	2.147
10.	L. Bird	1985	2.131
11.	W. Chamberlain	1968	2.128
12.	W. Chamberlain	1961	2.125
13.	L. Bird	1986	2.123
14.	E. Johnson	1986	2.116
15.	O. Robertson	1965	2.103
16.	W. Chamberlain	1960	2.100
17.	W. Chamberlain	1962	2.100
18.	K. Abdul-Jabbar	1972	2.098
19.	W. Chamberlain	1966	2.094
20.	O. Robertson	1963	2.082
21.	M. Malone	1983	2.080
22.	O. Robertson	1962	2.071
23.	G. Mikan	1951	2.067
24.	L. Bird	1987	2.052
25.	E. Johnson	1982	2.050
26.	E. Johnson	1985	2.046
27.	E. Johnson	1984	2.043
28.	L. Bird	1988	2.043
29.	L. Bird	1981	2.043
30.	H. Gallatin	1954	2.037
31.	E. Johnson	1980	2.028
32.	L. Bird	1982	2.026
33.	K. Abdul-Jabbar	1980	2.024
34.	W. Chamberlain	1964	2.022
35.	J. West	1972	2.015
36.	B. Cousy	1953	2.012
37.	W. Chamberlain	1963	2.012
38.	O. Robertson	1961	2.008
39.	L. Bird	1982	2.000

Lenny Wilkens of the Seattle SuperSonics
John MacLeod of the Phoenix Suns
- Basketball Hall of Fame -

CHAPTER 7

SEASONAL SUMMARIES

WILKENS/MACLEOD

On back-to-back nights two of the NBA's greatest coaches, Lenny Wilkens and John MacLeod, both reached the same milestone. On Jan. 12, 1988 Wilkens won his 600th NBA Game. The next night, MacLeod won his 600th game. Amazingly, both had lost nearly the same number (559 & 553 respectively). At the time both had won 1 divisional title and 37 playoff games.

Ironically, the two were opposing coaches in one of the top playoff battles and one of the biggest trades ever. In 1979, Wilken's Seattle Supersonics faced MacLeod's Phoenix Suns. Seattle won the series 4 games to 3. The dramatic 7th game was highlighted by a career playoff high 33 points and 11 rebounds by a young Jack Sikma.

One year later, the two clubs swapped All-Star Guards - Paul Westphal for Dennis Johnson in what has been regarded the NBA's biggest trade involving guards.

SEASONAL SUMMARIES

On the following pages I cite the top players by Production Rating by position every year since 1980 (see chapter one for Production rating argument). I should point out that the years 1950-1979 can be found in my 1987-88 edition of Basketball Heaven. I would like to have included them in this year's book as well, but was subject to limitations on space (see page *ii* for address on how to order BBH 1988).

Despite not showing the earlier years, I will go ahead and explain some of the distinctions between the years prior to 1980 and those after that date. By doing so, it should help give a feel for some of the variations the game has gone through.

I began making a distinction between small forwards and power forwards as well as point guards and off guards in 1974. For each year I have also recorded the top players by Position Dominance and MVP (see chapter one as well for a discussion of the PD and MVP formulas). Also listed are the top rookies by Production Ratings. All players, including rookies, must qualify to be ranked.

In order to qualify, a player must have played in 61 or more games and averaged at least 19 minutes per game. A player could play less than 61 games and still qualify. He could even play as few as 50 games as long as his minutes-per-game plus games-played equals at least 80. In earlier years when the schedule was shorter, the same principle was applied. But instead of a minimum 50 games, the requirement was 60% of the total games a team played. Nineteen minutes per game has always been a requirement since NBA games have always been 48 minutes long.

I have also shown the leaders in the 6 major performance categories for each year (steals and blocks are listed only since 1974). Each category, with the exception of scoring, is based on 48 minutes per game. There are two reasons for this. The first reason is that one can find the assist-per-game leader for a given year in a variety of places. All sources include the leaders of each category based on so many per game. I wanted to offer a statistic that was different, yet valid. The following pages represent the only available lists that I am aware of based on 48 minutes per game. The second reason is that, although assists per game is a perfectly meaningful statistic, assists per 48 minutes is also meaningful in a different way. Some players are role players. That is, they come into a game when specific situations develop. It may be to provide muscle on the boards or tough defense. Whatever the reason, a player who plays sparingly will not show very much of anything per game. By showing his statistics based on 48 minutes, I believe I offer a truer picture of a particular player's strengths. My statistics do not reflect a player's durability, but that is what the per-game ratings are for. As I mentioned earlier, scoring is on a per-game basis while the other categories are not. The reason I made an exception for scoring is because if I were to show scoring as a 48 minute statistic, it would likely promote a player who shoots constantly when in the game. That may or may not be desirable. On the other hand, when was the last time a rebound or an assist or a steal or a block was not desirable? Thus the distinction between scoring and the other statistical categories.

The last statistical category is shooting and is broken down into three areas - 3pt FG%, 2pt FG%, and FT%. I devised a relatively simple statistic which evenhandedly evaluates all three. Simply put, if a player hits 50% of his 2pt FGs (average) and 33% of his 3 pt FGs (ideal average) and 75% of his free throws (average), he would have a 1.000 shooting rating. The formula is relatively simple. SHT = (points + one third FTs made) / shots attempted.

It may be difficult to perceive, but each of the three categories is fairly and equally dealt with in the statistic. In 1988, John Stockton led with a 1.161 rating. He shot 59.4% from 2-pt range, 35.8% from 3-pt country, and shot 84.0% from the line. Tyrone Bogues, on the other hand, was last of the 159 qualifiers in shooting. His rating was .825. He shot 2-pt FGs at 39.8%, FTs at 78.4% and was 3-16 from 3-pt range. As I said, 1.000 is average. It makes sense, then, that the best shooter (1.161) would be roughly the same amount over 1.000 as the worst shooter (.825) is below that mark.

I have used abbreviations for team names. These should be clear to the reader. A couple examples would be G.St = Golden State or LA.L = Los Angeles Lakers. Also abbreviated are the categories. See designations below.

PR = Production Rating (see chapter one for explanation)
OR = Overall Rank
PD = Position Dominance (see chapter one for explanation)
MVP = Most Valuable Player (see chapter one for explanation)
SCR = Scoring (points/game)
SHT = Shooting (see previous paragraphs for a brief explanation or page 28 for details)
REB = Rebounds per 48 minutes played
AST = Assists per 48 minutes played
BLK = Blocked Shots per 48 minutes played
STL = Steals per 48 minutes played

When looking at a particular year, I thought it might be interesting to know how many total players qualified. This should give a better feel for how a particular player ranked with respect to the total. Listed below are the number of players who qualified during each year.

1950 -- 85	1960 -- 56	1970 -- 97	1980 -- 157
1951 -- 70	1961 -- 56	1971 -- 115	1981 -- 165
1952 -- 70	1962 -- 60	1972 -- 108	1982 -- 160
1953 -- 69	1963 -- 67	1973 -- 108	1983 -- 157
1954 -- 66	1964 -- 57	1974 -- 114	1984 -- 161
1955 -- 55	1965 -- 65	1975 -- 119	1985 -- 158
1956 -- 59	1966 -- 60	1976 -- 123	1986 -- 158
1957 -- 55	1967 -- 67	1977 -- 150	1987 -- 160
1958 -- 54	1968 -- 85	1978 -- 159	1988 -- 159
1959 -- 54	1969 -- 95	1979 -- 154	

Clearly, since 1980, there has been little to no change in the total numbers of qualifiers. That will rise 12 to 14 in 1989 and another 12 to 14 in 1990 as the four new franchises are added to the league. Of course, it goes without saying, but a player who ranked number 10 in any particular category in 1954, is hardly comparable to a number 10 ranking in 1988. I deal with this dilemma in the next chapter (see page 304).

1987-88
NBA STATISTICS

PRODUCTION RATINGS

OR	PLAYER	TEAM	PR
1.	Michael Jordan	Chic	35.05
2.	Larry Bird	Bost	34.01
3.	Charles Barkley	Phil	32.51
4.	Akeem Olajuwon	Hous	28.10
5.	Clyde Drexler	Port	27.94
6.	Earvin Johnson	LA.L	27.71
7.	Karl Malone	Utah	27.63
8.	John Stockton	Utah	26.54
9.	Kevin McHale	Bost	26.28
10.	Lafayette Lever	Denv	25.94
11.	Larry Nance	Clev	24.51
12.	Dominique Wilkins	Atla	24.27
13.	Otis Thorpe	Sacr	23.71
14.	Buck Williams	N.J.	22.96
15.	Alvin Robertson	S.A.	22.94
16.	Terry Porter	Port	22.87
17.	Pat Ewing	N.Y.	22.61
18.	Moses Malone	Wash	22.53
19.	Jerome Kersey	Port	21.87
20.	Jack Sikma	Milw	21.77
21.	Byron Scott	LA.L	21.73
22.	Alex English	Denv	21.70
23.	Michael Cage	LA.C	21.24
24.	Mark Aguirre	Dall	21.13
25.	Brad Daugherty	Clev	20.70
26.	Mark Jackson	N.Y.	20.68
27.	Mike Gminski	Phil	20.56
28.	Dale Ellis	Seat	20.55
29.	Charles Oakley	Chic	20.54
30.	Glenn Rivers	Atla	20.36
31.	Roy Tarpley	Dall	20.23
32.	Chris Mullin	G.St	20.17
33.	Bill Laimbeer	Detr	20.17
34.	James Worthy	LA.L	20.09
35.	Isiah Thomas	Detr	19.86
36.	Xavier McDaniel	Seat	19.78
37.	Maurice Cheeks	Phil	19.22
38.	Vern Fleming	Indi	19.19
39.	Derek Harper	Dall	19.17
40.	Terry Cummings	Milw	19.16
41.	Robert Parish	Bost	19.15
42.	Thurl Bailey	Utah	18.94
43.	Frank Brickowski	S.A.	18.71
44.	Paul Pressey	Milw	18.67
45.	Danny Shcayes	Denv	18.63
46.	Reggie Theus	Sacr	18.44
47.	Johnny Dawkins	S.A.	18.37
48.	Danny Ainge	Bost	18.26
49.	Steve Stipanovich	Indi	18.12
50.	Benoit Benjamin	LA.C	17.97
51.	Ralph Sampson	G.St	17.94
52.	Tom Chambers	Seat	17.73
53.	Adrian Dantley	Detr	17.29
54.	Rodney McCray	Hous	17.27
55.	Mark Price	Clev	16.92
56.	Nate McMillan	Seat	16.71
57.	Sam Perkins	Dall	16.71
58.	Chuck Person	Indi	16.65
59.	Rod Higgens	G.St	16.65
60.	Cliff Robinson	Phil	16.61
61.	Roy Hinson	N.J.	16.60
62.	Eric Floyd	Hous	16.58
63.	Michael Adams	Denv	16.57
64.	Rolando Blackman	Dall	16.48
65.	A.C. Green	LA.L	16.44
66.	Walter Berry	S.A.	16.23
67.	Ron Harper	Clev	16.23
68.	Dennis Johnson	Bost	16.13
69.	K. Abdul-Jabbar	LA.L	15.90
70.	Dennis Rodman	Detr	15.84
71.	Wayman Tisdale	Indi	15.82
72.	Rick Mahorn	Detr	15.67
73.	Kevin Duckworth	Port	15.42
74.	Walter Davis	Phoe	15.41
75.	Armon Gilliam	Phoe	15.36
76.	Jeff Malone	Wash	15.24
77.	Kenny Smith	Sacr	15.23
78.	James Donaldson	Dall	14.98
79.	Eddie Johnson	Phoe	14.82
80.	John Williams	Clev	14.79
81.	Jeff Hornacek	Phoe	14.78
82.	Winston Garland	G.St	14.76
83.	Randy Breuer	Milw	14.47
84.	John S. Williams	Wash	14.37
85.	Tim McMormick	N.J.	14.29
86.	Mark Eaton	Utah	14.27
87.	Bernard King	Wash	13.96
88.	Gerald Wilkins	N.Y.	13.86
89.	Mike Woodson	LA.C	13.80
90.	Cliff Levingston	Atla	13.78
91.	Dave Corzine	Chic	13.73
92.	Joe Dumars	Detr	13.59
93.	Jay Humphries	Milw	13.47
94.	John Bagley	N.J.	13.43
95.	Blair Rasmussen	Denv	13.42
96.	Kevin Willis	Atla	13.33
97.	Greg Anderson	S.A.	13.11
98.	J.B. Carroll	Hous	12.92
99.	Jay Vincent	Denv	12.92
100.	Joe Kleine	Sacr	12.88

POSITION DOMINANCE

OR	PLAYER	TEAM	PD
1.	Michael Jordan	Chic	1.426
2.	Larry Bird	Bost	1.411
3.	Charles Barkley	Phil	1.321
4.	Akeem Olajuwon	Hous	1.297
5.	Earvin Johnson	LA.L	1.221
6.	John Stockton	Utah	1.170
7.	Clyde Drexler	Port	1.137
8.	Karl Malone	Utah	1.123
9.	Kevin McHale	Bost	1.068
10.	Lafayette Lever	Denv	1.055
11.	Pat Ewing	N.Y.	1.043
12.	Moses Malone	Wash	1.040
13.	Larry Nance	Clev	1.016
14.	Terry Porter	Port	1.008
15.	Dominique Wilkins	Atla	1.006
16.	Otis Thorpe	Sacr	.963
17.	Brad Daugherty	Clev	.955
18.	Mike Gminski	Phil	.948
19.	Alvin Robertson	S.A.	.933
20.	Buck Williams	N.J.	.933

MOST VALUABLE PLAYER

OR	PLAYER	TEAM	MVP
1.	Larry Bird	Bost	2.043
2.	Michael Jordan	Chic	1.980
3.	Earvin Johnson	LA.L	1.916
4.	Akeem Olajuwon	Hous	1.818
5.	Charles Barkley	Phil	1.760
6.	John Stockton	Utah	1.735
7.	Clyde Drexler	Port	1.733
8.	Kevin McHale	Bost	1.700
9.	Karl Malone	Utah	1.688
10.	Lafayette Lever	Denv	1.655
11.	Terry Porter	Port	1.604
12.	Dominique Wilkins	Atla	1.583
13.	Byron Scott	LA.L	1.579
14.	Bill Laimbeer	Detr	1.566
15.	James Worthy	LA.L	1.528
16.	Robert Parish	Bost	1.516
17.	Isiah Thomas	Detr	1.511
18.	Larry Nance	Clev	1.511
19.	Jerome Kersey	Port	1.503
20.	Mark Aguirre	Dall	1.500

1987-88 POSITION RATINGS

POWER FORWARDS

OR	PLAYER	TEAM	PR
1.	Charles Barkley	Phil	32.51
2.	Karl Malone	Utah	27.63
3.	Kevin McHale	Bost	26.28
4.	Otis Thorpe	Sacr	23.71
5.	Buck Williams	N.J.	22.96
6.	Jack Sikma	Milw	21.77
7.	Michael Cage	LA.C	21.24
8.	Charles Oakley	Chic	20.54
9.	Roy Tarpley	Dall	20.23
10.	Frank Brickowski	S.A.	18.71
11.	Tom Chambers	Seat	17.73
12.	Sam Perkins	Dall	16.71
13.	Roy Hinson	N.J.	16.60
14.	A.C. Green	LA.L	16.44
15.	Wayman Tisdale	Indi	15.82
16.	Rick Mahorn	Detr	15.67
17.	Armon Gilliam	Phoe	15.36
18.	John Williams	Clev	14.79
19.	Cliff Levingston	Atla	13.78
20.	Blair Rasmussen	Denv	13.42

POINT GUARDS

OR	PLAYER	TEAM	PR
1.	Earvin Johnson	LA.L	27.71
2.	John Stockton	Utah	26.54
3.	Terry Porter	Port	22.87
4.	Mark Jackson	N.Y.	20.68
5.	Glenn Rivers	Atla	20.36
6.	Isiah Thomas	Detr	19.86
7.	Maurice Cheeks	Phil	19.22
8.	Vern Fleming	Indi	19.19
9.	Derek Harper	Dall	19.17
10.	Paul Pressey	Milw	18.67
11.	Johnny Dawkins	S.A.	18.37
12.	Mark Price	Clev	16.92
13.	Nate McMillan	Seat	16.71
14.	Eric Floyd	Hous	16.58
15.	Michael Adams	Denv	16.57
16.	Dennis Johnson	Bost	16.13
17.	Kenny Smith	Sacr	15.23
18.	Jeff Hornacek	Phoe	14.78
19.	Winston Garland	G.St	14.76
20.	Jay Humphries	Milw	13.47

CENTERS

OR	PLAYER	TEAM	PR
1.	Akeem Olajuwon	Hous	28.10
2.	Pat Ewing	N.Y.	22.61
3.	Moses Malone	Wash	22.53
4.	Brad Daugherty	Clev	20.70
5.	Mike Gminski	Phil	20.56
6.	Bill Laimbeer	Detr	20.17
7.	Robert Parish	Bost	19.15
8.	Danny Schayes	Denv	18.63
9.	Steve Stipanovich	Indi	18.13
10.	Benoit Benjamin	LA.C	17.97
11.	Ralph Sampson	G.St	17.94
12.	K. Abdul-Jabbar	LA.L	15.90
13.	Kevin Duckworth	Port	15.42
14.	James Donaldson	Dall	14.98
15.	Randy Breuer	Milw	14.47
16.	Mike McCormick	N.J.	14.29
17.	Mark Eaton	Utah	14.27
18.	Dave Corzine	Chic	13.72
19.	Greg Anderson	S.A.	13.11
20.	Joe Kleine	Sacr	12.88

SMALL FORWARDS

OR	PLAYER	TEAM	PR
1.	Larry Bird	Bost	34.01
2.	Larry Nance	Clev	24.51
3.	Dominique Wilkins	Atla	24.27
4.	Jerome Kersey	Port	21.87
5.	Alex English	Denv	21.70
6.	Mark Aguirre	Dall	21.13
7.	James Worthy	LA.L	20.09
8.	Xavier McDaniel	Seat	19.78
9.	Terry Cummings	Milw	19.16
10.	Thurl Bailey	Utah	18.94
11.	Adrian Dantley	Detr	17.29
12.	Rodney McCray	Hous	17.27
13.	Rod Higgens	G.St	16.65
14.	Chuck Person	Indi	16.65
15.	Cliff Robinson	Phil	16.61
16.	Walter Berry	S.A.	16.23
17.	Dennis Rodman	Detr	15.84
18.	Eddie Johnson	Phoe	14.82
19.	John S. Williams	Wash	14.37
20.	Bernard King	Wash	13.96

OFF GUARDS

OR	PLAYER	TEAM	PR
1.	Michael Jordan	Chic	35.05
2.	Clyde Drexler	Port	27.94
3.	Fat Lever	Denv	25.94
4.	Alvin Robertson	S.A.	22.94
5.	Byron Scott	LA.L	21.73
6.	Dale Ellis	Seat	20.55
7.	Chris Mullin	G.St	20.17
8.	Reggie Theus	Sacr	18.44
9.	Danny Ainge	Bost	18.26
10.	Rolando Blackman	Dall	16.48
11.	Ron Harper	Clev	16.23
12.	Walter Davis	Phoe	15.41
13.	Jeff Malone	Wash	15.24
14.	Gerald Wilkins	N.Y.	13.86
15.	Mike Woodson	LA.C	13.80
16.	Joe Dumars	Detr	13.59
17.	Sidney Moncrief	Milw	12.45
18.	Michael Cooper	LA.L	11.98
19.	Purvis Short	Hous	11.74
20.	Harold Pressley	Sacr	11.52

ROOKIES

OR	PLAYER	TEAM	PR
1.	Mark Jackson	N.Y.	20.68
2.	Armon Gilliam	Phoe	15.36
3.	Kenny Smith	Sacr	15.23
4.	Winston Garland	G.St	14.76
5.	Greg Anderson	S.A.	13.11
6.	Kevin Johnson	Phoe	12.33
7.	Horace Grant	Chic	10.56
8.	Derrick McKey	Seat	10.23
9.	Reggie Miller	Indi	9.23
10.	Scottie Pippen	Chic	9.22
11.	Larry Krystowiak	Milw	8.94
12.	Tyrone Bogues	Wash	8.68
13.	Tellis Frank	G.St	8.49
14.	Ken Norman	LA.C	8.23
15.	Dennis Hopson	N.J.	7.18

1987-88 PERFORMANCE CATEGORIES

SCORING

OR	PLAYER	TEAM	SCR
1.	Michael Jordan	Chic	34.98
2.	Dominique Wilkins	Atla	30.73
3.	Larry Bird	Bost	29.93
4.	Charles Barkley	Phil	28.30
5.	Karl Malone	Utah	27.66
6.	Clyde Drexler	Port	26.98
7.	Dale Ellis	Seat	25.84
8.	Mark Aguirre	Dall	25.09
9.	Alex English	Denv	25.00
10.	Akeem Olajuwon	Hous	22.85
11.	Kevin McHale	Bost	22.59
12.	Byron Scott	LA.L	21.65
13.	Reggie Theus	Sacr	21.56
14.	Xavier McDaniel	Seat	21.40
15.	Terry Cummings	Milw	21.33
16.	Otis Thorpe	Sacr	20.78
17.	Jeff Malone	Wash	20.51
18.	Tom Chambers	Seat	20.41
19.	Moses Malone	Wash	20.34
20.	Chris Mullin	G.St	20.22

REBOUNDS

OR	PLAYER	TEAM	REB
1.	Roy Tarpley	Dall	19.95
2.	Charles Oakley	Chic	18.17
3.	Michael Cage	LA.C	16.93
4.	Alton Lister	Seat	16.61
5.	Akeem Olajuwon	Hous	16.29
6.	Dennis Rodman	Detr	15.99
7.	Moses Malone	Wash	15.76
8.	Buck Williams	N.J.	15.18
9.	Sidney Green	N.Y.	15.04
10.	Karl Malone	Utah	14.80
11.	Danny Schayes	Denv	14.67
12.	Charles Barkley	Phil	14.40
13.	James Donaldson	Dall	14.36
14.	Joe Kleine	Sacr	13.90
15.	Rick Mahorn	Detr	13.82
16.	Bill Laimbeer	Detr	13.79
17.	Ralph Sampson	G.St	13.33
18.	Mike Gminski	Phil	13.20
19.	Otis Thorpe	Sacr	13.08
20.	Robert Parish	Bost	13.04

BLOCKS

OR	PLAYER	TEAM	BLK
1.	Mark Eaton	Utah	5.34
2.	Benoit Benjamin	LA.C	4.97
3.	Pat Ewing	N.Y.	4.62
4.	Charles Jones	Wash	4.13
5.	Alton Lister	Seat	3.71
6.	Akeem Olajuwon	Hous	3.64
7.	Wayne Rollins	Atla	3.59
8.	Herb Williams	Indi	3.56
9.	Mark West	Phoe	3.36
10.	John Williams	Clev	3.30
11.	John Salley	Detr	3.28
12.	Larry Nance	Clev	3.20
13.	Greg Anderson	S.A.	2.95
14.	Caldwell Jones	Port	2.67
15.	Roy Hinson	N.J.	2.59
16.	Joe Barry Carroll	Hous	2.54
17.	Ralph Sampson	G.St	2.54
18.	Randy Breuer	Milw	2.27
19.	Blair Rasmussen	Denv	2.19
20.	Thurl Bailey	Utah	2.14

SHOOTING

OR	PLAYER	TEAM	SHT
1.	John Stockton	Utah	1.161
2.	Kevin McHale	Bost	1.161
3.	Danny Ainge	Bost	1.138
4.	Larry Bird	Bost	1.136
5.	Robert Parish	Bost	1.130
6.	Charles Barkley	Phil	1.120
7.	Byron Scott	LA.L	1.108
8.	Rick Mahorn	Detr	1.106
9.	Mark Price	Clev	1.103
10.	Danny Schayes	Denv	1.095
11.	Rod Higgens	G.St	1.094
12.	Craig Hodges	Phoe	1.092
13.	James Donaldson	Dall	1.090
14.	Cliff Levingston	Atla	1.089
15.	Michael Jordan	Chic	1.088
16.	Brad Davis	Dall	1.085
17.	Terry Porter	Port	1.082
18.	Chris Mullin	G.St	1.081
19.	Bill Cartwright	N.Y.	1.077
20.	Adrian Dantley	Detr	1.076

ASSISTS

OR	PLAYER	TEAM	AST
1.	John Stockton	Utah	19.05
2.	Earvin Johnson	LA.L	15.62
3.	Glenn Rivers	Atla	14.33
4.	Nate McMillan	Seat	13.74
5.	Terry Porter	Port	13.34
6.	Mark Jackson	N.Y.	12.82
7.	Sam Vincent	Chic	12.18
8.	Tyrone Bogues	Wash	11.91
9.	Jeff Hornacek	Phoe	11.56
10.	Darnell Valentine	LA.C	11.21
11.	Isiah Thomas	Detr	11.12
12.	Kevin Johnson	Phoe	10.94
13.	Dennis Johnson	Bost	10.75
14.	John Lucas	Milw	10.65
15.	Maurice Cheeks	Phil	10.62
16.	Johnny Dawkins	S.A.	10.57
17.	Jay Humphries	Milw	10.48
18.	Eric Floyd	Hous	10.39
19.	Paul Pressey	Milw	10.11
20.	Derek Harper	Dall	10.04

STEALS

OR	PLAYER	TEAM	STL
1.	John Stockton	Utah	4.09
2.	Alvin Robertson	S.A.	3.92
3.	Dudley Bradley	N.J.	3.81
4.	Michael Jordan	Chic	3.75
5.	Tyrone Bogues	Wash	3.74
6.	Darnell Valentine	LA.C	3.58
7.	Lafayette Lever	Denv	3.50
8.	Nate McMillan	Seat	3.31
9.	Ron Harper	Clev	3.20
10.	Clyde Drexler	Port	3.18
11.	Dwayne Washington	N.J.	3.17
12.	Mark Jackson	N.Y.	3.03
13.	Dell Curry	Clev	3.01
14.	Michael Adams	Denv	2.90
15.	Otis Smith	G.St	2.82
16.	Maurice Cheeks	Phil	2.79
17.	Allen Leavell	Hous	2.77
18.	Akeem Olajuwon	Hous	2.75
19.	Glenn Rivers	Atla	2.69
20.	Chris Mullin	G.St	2.67

1986-87
NBA STATISTICS

PRODUCTION RATINGS

OR	PLAYER	TEAM	PR
1.	Larry Bird	Bost	34.28
2.	Charles Barkley	Phil	33.46
3.	Michael Jordan	Chic	31.91
4.	Earvin Johnson	LA.L	31.79
5.	Kevin McHale	Bost	30.92
6.	Akeem Olajuwon	Hous	28.99
7.	Larry Nance	Phoe	27.25
8.	Lafayette Lever	Denv	26.93
9.	Clyde Drexler	Port	25.29
10.	Moses Malone	Wash	24.86
11.	Dominique Wilkins	Atla	24.15
12.	Alex English	Denv	23.90
13.	Robert Parish	Bost	23.66
14.	Buck Williams	N.J.	23.66
15.	Sleepy Floyd	G.St	23.65
16.	Otis Thorpe	Sacr	22.82
17.	Bill Laimbeer	Detr	22.65
18.	Terry Cummings	Milw	22.56
19.	Xavier McDaniel	Seat	22.41
20.	Karl Malone	Utah	22.05
21.	Isiah Thomas	Detr	22.04
22.	Michael Cage	LA.C	21.95
23.	Pat Ewing	N.Y.	21.90
24.	Kiki Vandeweghe	Port	21.85
25.	Dale Ellis	Seat	21.77
26.	Mark Aguirre	Dall	21.29
27.	James Donaldson	Dall	21.05
28.	Reggie Theus	Sacr	20.90
29.	Rodney McCray	Hous	20.70
30.	Charles Oakley	Chic	20.59
31.	Maurice Cheeks	Phil	20.56
32.	Tom Chambers	Seat	20.50
33.	J.B. Carroll	G.St	20.36
34.	Glenn Rivers	Atla	20.33
35.	James Worthy	LA.L	20.20
36.	Kevin Willis	Atla	19.88
37.	Walter Davis	Phoe	19.85
38.	Derek Harper	Dall	19.77
39.	Chuck Person	Indi	19.63
40.	Orlando Woolridge	N.J.	19.59
41.	Terry Porter	Port	19.52
42.	K. Abdul-Jabbar	LA.L	19.50
43.	Alvin Robertson	S.A.	19.47
44.	Jack Sikma	Milw	19.37
45.	Steve Stipanovich	Indi	19.22
46.	David Greenwood	S.A.	19.13
47.	Brad Daugherty	Clev	19.10
48.	Bill Cartwright	N.Y.	19.09
49.	Ron Harper	Clev	18.90
50.	Paul Pressey	Milw	18.79
51.	Mike Gminski	N.J.	18.46
52.	John Williams	Clev	18.41
53.	Adrian Dantley	Detr	18.21
54.	Sam Perkins	Dall	18.19
55.	Rolando Blackman	Dall	17.98
56.	Alton Lister	Seat	17.36
57.	Ricky Pierce	Milw	17.25
58.	Larry Smith	G.St	17.25
59.	Steve Johnson	Port	17.18
60.	Danny Ainge	Bost	17.15
61.	Herb Williams	Indi	17.12
62.	Byron Scott	LA.L	16.54
63.	Jeff Malone	Wash	16.39
64.	Dennis Johnson	Bost	16.37
65.	Julius Erving	Phil	16.30
66.	Gerald Wilkins	N.Y.	16.23
67.	Vern Fleming	Indi	16.17
68.	LaSalle Thompson	Sacr	16.05
69.	A.C. Green	LA.L	16.03
70.	Benoit Benjamin	LA.C	15.89
71.	Tim McCormick	Phil	15.80
72.	Jay Humphries	Phoe	15.70
73.	Jerome Kersey	Port	15.70
74.	Eddie A. Johnson	Sacr	15.56
75.	Ed Pinckney	Phoe	15.50
76.	Artis Gilmore	S.A.	15.50
77.	Nate McMillan	Seat	15.35
78.	Mark Eaton	Utah	15.29
79.	Roy Hinson	Phil	15.09
80.	John Stockton	Utah	14.80
81.	Wayman Tisdale	Indi	14.36
82.	Jim Petersen	Hous	14.33
83.	Chris Mullin	G.St	14.10
84.	Vinnie Johnson	Detr	14.05
85.	Walter Berry	S.A.	13.97
86.	Cliff Robinson	Phil	13.96
87.	Derek Smith	Sacr	13.90
88.	Alvan Adams	Phoe	13.74
89.	Darrell Walker	Denv	13.46
90.	Robert Reid	Hous	13.41
91.	Rickey Green	Utah	13.40
92.	Dave Corzine	Chic	13.22
93.	Gerald Henderson	N.Y.	13.18
94.	John Paxson	Chic	13.09
95.	Darnell Valentine	LA.C	13.06
96.	Michael Cooper	LA.L	13.04
97.	Bill Hanzlik	Denv	12.96
98.	Cedric Maxwell	Hous	12.91
99.	Thurl Bailey	Utah	12.77
100.	Terry Catledge	Wash	12.76

POSITION DOMINANCE

OR	PLAYER	TEAM	PD
1.	Michael Jordan	Chic	1.416
2.	Larry Bird	Bost	1.403
3.	Earvin Johnson	LA.L	1.366
4.	Charles Barkley	Phil	1.306
5.	Akeem Olajuwon	Hous	1.261
6.	Kevin McHale	Bost	1.206
7.	Lafayette Lever	Denv	1.157
8.	Clyde Drexler	Port	1.122
9.	Larry Nance	Phoe	1.115
10.	Moses Malone	Wash	1.081
11.	Robert Parish	Bost	1.029
12.	Eric Floyd	G.St	1.016
13.	Dominique Wilkins	Atla	.988
14.	Bill Laimbeer	Detr	.985
15.	Alex English	Denv	.978
16.	Dale Ellis	Seat	.966
17.	Pat Ewing	N.Y.	.952
18.	Isiah Thomas	Detr	.947
19.	Buck Williams	N.J.	.923
20.	James Donaldson	Dall	.915

MOST VALUABLE PLAYER

OR	PLAYER	TEAM	MVP
1.	Earvin Johnson	LA.L	2.175
2.	Larry Bird	Bost	2.052
3.	Michael Jordan	Chic	1.856
4.	Kevin McHale	Bost	1.855
5.	Charles Barkley	Phil	1.832
6.	Akeem Olajuwon	Hous	1.770
7.	Robert Parish	Bost	1.678
8.	Clyde Drexler	Port	1.675
9.	K. Abdul-Jabbar	LA.L	1.657
10.	James Worthy	LA.L	1.636
11.	Bill Laimbeer	Detr	1.631
12.	Dominique Wilkins	Atla	1.621
13.	Isiah Thomas	Detr	1.593
14.	Lafayette Lever	Denv	1.564
15.	Larry Nance	Phoe	1.554
16.	Moses Malone	Wash	1.543
17.	Byron Scott	LA.L	1.536
18.	James Donaldson	Dall	1.532
19.	Glenn Rivers	Atla	1.506
20.	Eric Floyd	G.St	1.498

1986-87 POSITION RATINGS

POWER FORWARDS

OR	PLAYER	TEAM	PR
1.	Charles Barkley	Phil	33.46
2.	Kevin McHale	Bost	30.92
3.	Buck Williams	N.J.	23.66
4.	Otis Thorpe	Sacr	22.82
5.	Terry Cummings	Milw	22.56
6.	Xavier McDaniel	Seat	22.41
7.	Karl Malone	Utah	22.05
8.	Michael Cage	LA.C	21.95
9.	Charles Oakley	Chic	20.59
10.	Kevin Willis	Atla	19.88
11.	David Greenwood	S.A.	19.13
12.	John Williams	Clev	18.41
13.	Sam Perkins	Dall	18.19
14.	Larry Smith	G.St	17.25
15.	Herb Williams	Indi	17.12
16.	A.C. Green	LA.L	16.03
17.	Ed Pinckney	Phoe	15.50
18.	Roy Hinson	Phil	15.09
19.	Wayman Tisdale	Indi	14.36
20.	Jim Petersen	Hous	14.33

POINT GUARD

OR	PLAYER	TEAM	PR
1.	Earvin Johnson	LA.L	31.79
2.	Lafayette Lever	Denv	26.93
3.	Eric Floyd	G.St	23.65
4.	Isiah Thomas	Detr	22.04
5.	Reggie Theus	Sacr	20.90
6.	Maurice Cheeks	Phil	20.56
7.	Glenn Rivers	Atla	20.33
8.	Derek Harper	Dall	19.77
9.	Terry Porter	Port	19.52
10.	Dennis Johnson	Bost	16.37
11.	Vern Fleming	Indi	16.17
12.	Jay Humphries	Phoe	15.70
13.	Nate McMillan	Seat	15.35
14.	John Stockton	Utah	14.80
15.	Rickey Green	Utah	13.40
16.	Gerald Henderson	N.Y.	13.18
17.	John Paxson	Chic	13.09
18.	Darnell Valentine	LA.C	13.06
19.	John Bagley	Clev	12.38
20.	Ennis Whatley	Wash	11.78

CENTER

OR	PLAYER	TEAM	PR
1.	Akeem Olajuwon	Hous	28.99
2.	Moses Malone	Wash	24.86
3.	Robert Parish	Bost	23.66
4.	Bill Laimbeer	Detr	22.65
5.	Pat Ewing	N.Y.	21.90
6.	James Donaldson	Dall	21.05
7.	J.B. Carroll	G.St	20.36
8.	K. Abdul-Jabbar	LA.L	19.50
9.	Jack Sikma	Milw	19.37
10.	Steve Stipanovich	Indi	19.22
11.	Brad Daugherty	Clev	19.10
12.	Bill Cartwright	N.Y.	19.09
13.	Mike Gminski	N.J.	18.46
14.	Alton Lister	Seat	17.36
15.	Steve Johnson	Port	17.18
16.	LaSalle Thompson	Sacr	16.05
17.	Benoit Benjamin	LA.C	15.89
18.	Tim McCormick	Phil	15.80
19.	Artis Gilmore	S.A.	15.50
20.	Mark Eaton	Utah	15.29

SMALL FORWARDS

OR	PLAYER	TEAM	PR
1.	Larry Bird	Bost	34.28
2.	Larry Nance	Phoe	27.25
3.	D. Wilkins	Atla	24.15
4.	Alex English	Denv	23.90
5.	Kiki Vandeweghe	Port	21.85
6.	Mark Aguirre	Dall	21.29
7.	Rodney McCray	Hous	20.70
8.	Tom Chambers	Seat	20.50
9.	James Worthy	LA.L	20.20
10.	Chuck Person	Indi	19.63
11.	Orlando Woolridge	N.J.	19.59
12.	Paul Pressey	Milw	18.79
13.	Adrian Dantley	Detr	18.21
14.	Jerome Kersey	Port	15.70
15.	Eddie A. Johnson	Sacr	15.56
16.	Bill Hanzlik	Denv	12.96
17.	Gene Banks	Chic	12.65
18.	Phil Hubbard	Clev	12.51
19.	Kenny Walker	N.Y.	11.84
20.	John Williams	Wash	11.42

OFF GUARD

OR	PLAYER	TEAM	PR
1.	Michael Jordan	Chic	31.91
2.	Clyde Drexler	Port	25.29
3.	Dale Ellis	Seat	21.77
4.	Walter Davis	Phoe	19.85
5.	Alvin Robertson	S.A.	19.47
6.	Ron Harper	Clev	18.90
7.	R. Blackman	Dall	17.98
8.	Ricky Pierce	Milw	17.25
9.	Danny Ainge	Bost	17.15
10.	Byron Scott	LA.L	16.54
11.	Jeff Malone	Wash	16.39
12.	Julius Erving	Phil	16.30
13.	Gerald Wilkins	N.Y.	16.23
14.	Chris Mullin	G.St	14.10
15.	Vinnie Johnson	Detr	14.05
16.	Derek Smith	Sacr	13.90
17.	Darrell Walker	Denv	13.46
18.	Robert Reid	Hous	13.41
19.	Michael Cooper	LA.L	13.04
20.	Mike Woodson	LA.C	11.92

ROOKIES

OR	PLAYER	TEAM	PR
1.	Chuck Person	Indi	19.63
2.	Brad Daugherty	Clev	19.10
3.	Ron Harper	Clev	18.90
4.	John Williams	Clev	18.41
5.	Nate McMillan	Seat	15.35
6.	Walter Berry	S.A.	13.97
7.	Kenny Walker	N.Y.	11.84
8.	John Williams	Wash	11.42
9.	Brad Sellers	Chic	10.08
10.	Johnny Dawkins	S.A.	9.58
11.	D. Washington	N.J.	9.19
12.	Jeff Hornacek	Phoe	8.41
13.	David Wingate	Phil	7.53

1986-87 PERFORMANCE CATEGORIES

SCORING

OR	PLAYER	TEAM	SCR
1.	Michael Jordan	Chic	37.09
2.	Dominique Wilkins	Atla	29.04
3.	Alex English	Denv	28.60
4.	Larry Bird	Bost	28.05
5.	Kiki Vandeweghe	Port	26.86
6.	Kevin McHale	Bost	26.08
7.	Mark Aguirre	Dall	25.70
8.	Dale Ellis	Seat	24.89
9.	Moses Malone	Wash	24.11
10.	Earvin Johnson	LA.L	23.86
11.	Walter Davis	Phoe	23.63
12.	Akeem Olajuwon	Hous	23.40
13.	Tom Chambers	Seat	23.28
14.	Xavier McDaniel	Seat	23.05
15.	Charles Barkley	Phil	23.00
16.	Ron Harper	Clev	22.85
17.	Larry Nance	Phoe	22.49
18.	Jeff Malone	Wash	21.98
19.	Clyde Drexler	Port	21.73
20.	Karl Malone	Utah	21.70

REBOUNDS

OR	PLAYER	TEAM	REB
1.	Larry Smith	G.St	18.54
2.	Sidney Green	Detr	17.49
3.	Charles Barkley	Phil	17.41
4.	Charles Oakley	Chic	17.30
5.	Buck Williams	N.J.	16.50
6.	Bill Laimbeer	Detr	16.06
7.	Moses Malone	Wash	15.90
8.	Blair Rasmussen	Denv	15.71
9.	Jack Sikma	Milw	15.56
10.	Kevin Willis	Atla	15.52
11.	James Donaldson	Dall	15.42
12.	LaSalle Thompson	Sacr	15.22
13.	Michael Cage	LA.C	15.15
14.	Akeem Olajuwon	Hous	14.92
15.	Alton Lister	Seat	14.79
16.	Wayne Cooper	Denv	14.54
17.	David Greenwood	S.A.	14.53
18.	Karl Malone	Utah	14.36
19.	Kurt Rambis	LA.L	14.36
20.	Rick Mahorn	Detr	14.08

BLOCKS

OR	PLAYER	TEAM	BLK
1.	Manute Bol	Wash	9.34
2.	Mark Eaton	Utah	6.15
3.	Charles Jones	Wash	4.92
4.	Akeem Olajuwon	Hous	4.42
5.	Benoit Benjamin	LA.C	4.03
6.	Wayne Rollins	Atla	3.81
7.	Alton Lister	Seat	3.78
8.	Pat Ewing	N.Y.	3.20
9.	Wayne Cooper	Denv	3.11
10.	Roy Hinson	Phil	3.10
11.	John Williams	Clev	2.95
12.	LaSalle Thompson	Sacr	2.79
13.	Larry Nance	Phoe	2.77
14.	Kevin McHale	Bost	2.70
15.	Julius Erving	Phil	2.35
16.	Caldwell Jones	Port	2.34
17.	Robert Parish	Bost	2.31
18.	Danny Schayes	Denv	2.28
19.	J.B. Carroll	G.St	2.17
20.	Jon Koncak	Atla	2.17

SHOOTING

OR	PLAYER	TEAM	SHT
1.	Kevin McHale	Bost	1.182
2.	Charles Barkley	Phil	1.137
3.	James Donaldson	Dall	1.137
4.	Larry Bird	Bost	1.134
5.	Ricky Pierce	Milw	1.100
6.	Kiki Vandeweghe	Port	1.099
7.	Danny Ainge	Bost	1.092
8.	Ed Pinckney	Phoe	1.092
9.	Artis Gilmore	S.A.	1.084
10.	K. Abdul-Jabbar	LA.L	1.084
11.	Robert Parish	Bost	1.082
12.	Eric Floyd	G.St	1.082
13.	Rodney McCray	Hous	1.082
14.	Dale Ellis	Seat	1.080
15.	Larry Nance	Phoe	1.080
16.	Earvin Johnson	LA.L	1.076
17.	Adrian Dantley	Detr	1.074
18.	Craig Hodges	Milw	1.073
19.	Rod Higgins	G.St	1.070
20.	Wayne Rollins	Atla	1.065

ASSISTS

OR	PLAYER	TEAM	AST
1	John Stockton	Utah	17.31
2.	Earvin Johnson	LA.L	16.15
3.	Glenn Rivers	Atla	15.25
4.	Nate McMillan	Seat	14.19
5.	Eric Floyd	G.St	13.28
6.	Isiah Thomas	Detr	12.95
7.	Terry Porter	Port	12.65
8.	Rickey Green	Utah	12.42
9.	Darnell Valentine	LA.C	12.20
10.	Jay Humphries	Phoe	11.76
11.	Reggie Theus	Sacr	11.57
12.	Derek Harper	Dall	11.44
13.	Danny Young	Seat	11.43
14.	Brad Davis	Dall	11.32
15.	Jeff Hornacek	Phoe	11.10
16.	Gerald Henderson	N.Y.	11.06
17.	Rory Sparrow	N.Y.	10.63
18.	Dirk Minniefield	Hous	10.44
19.	Ennis Whatley	Wash	10.36
20.	Paul Pressey	Milw	10.29

STEALS

OR	PLAYER	TEAM	STL
1.	Alvin Robertson	S.A.	4.63
2.	John Stockton	Utah	4.57
3.	John Williams	Wash	3.47
4.	Michael Jordan	Chic	3.45
5.	Trent Tucker	N.Y.	3.29
6.	Maurice Cheeks	Phil	3.29
7.	Ron Harper	Clev	3.27
8.	Glenn Rivers	Atla	3.17
9.	Michael Adams	Wash	3.17
10.	Darnell Valentine	LA.C	3.17
11.	Lafayette Lever	Denv	3.16
12.	Clyde Drexler	Port	3.14
13.	Derek Harper	Dall	3.14
14.	Nate McMillan	Seat	3.04
15.	Darrell Walker	Denv	2.85
16.	Terry Porter	Port	2.81
17.	Jerome Kersey	Port	2.80
18.	David Wingate	Phil	2.77
19.	D. Washington	N.J.	2.76
20.	Cliff Robinson	Phil	2.60

1985-86
NBA STATISTICS

PRODUCTION RATINGS

OR	PLAYER	TEAM	PR
1.	Larry Bird	Bost	31.30
2.	Earvin Johnson	LA.L	28.50
3.	Akeem Olajuwon	Hous	28.40
4.	Charles Barkley	Phil	28.26
5.	Adrian Dantley	Utah	25.82
6.	Dominique Wilkins	Atla	25.50
7.	Kevin McHale	Bost	24.75
8.	Isiah Thomas	Detr	24.44
9.	Alex English	Denv	24.36
10.	Larry Nance	Phoe	24.23
11.	K. Abdul-Jabbar	LA.L	24.20
12.	Bill Laimbeer	Detr	23.87
13.	Moses Malone	Phil	23.73
14.	Ralph Sampson	Hous	22.85
15.	Alvin Robertson	S.A.	22.48
16.	Clyde Drexler	Port	22.44
17.	Herb Williams	Indi	21.79
18.	Purvis Short	G.St	21.77
19.	Maurice Cheeks	Phil	21.65
20.	Jack Sikma	Seat	21.54
21.	Eric Floyd	G.St	21.33
22.	Buck Williams	N.J.	21.26
23.	Sidney Moncrief	Milw	21.03
24.	Reggie Theus	Sacr	21.02
25.	James Worthy	LA.L	20.92
26.	Robert Parish	Bost	20.84
27.	Paul Pressey	Milw	20.74
28.	Pat Ewing	N.Y.	20.56
29.	Jor Barry Carroll	G.St	20.43
30.	Artis Gilmore	S.A.	20.31
31.	Marques Johnson	LA.C	20.21
32.	Mark Aguirre	Dall	20.08
33.	Roy Hinson	Clev	20.06
34.	Mike Gminski	N.J.	20.01
35.	Kiki Vandeweghe	Port	19.84
36.	Sam Perkins	Dall	19.67
37.	Terry Cummings	Milw	19.50
38.	Cliff Robinson	Wash	19.46
39.	LaSalle Thompson	Sacr	18.76
40.	Rolando Blackman	Dall	18.52
41.	Orlando Woolridge	Chic	18.36
42.	Lafayette Lever	Denv	18.26
43.	Kelly Tripucka	Detr	18.15
44.	Vern Fleming	Indi	17.99
45.	Walter Davis	Phoe	17.99
46.	World B. Free	Clev	17.81
47.	Calvin Natt	Denv	17.81
48.	Mike Mitchell	S.A.	17.62
49.	Cedric Maxwell	LA.C	17.58
50.	Julius Erving	Phil	17.51
51.	John Lucas	Hous	17.43
52.	Xavier McDaniel	Seat	17.41
53.	Steve Stipanovich	Indi	17.23
54.	Wayne Cooper	Denv	17.12
55.	Tom Chambers	Seat	16.97
56.	Jeff Malone	Wash	16.90
57.	James Donaldson	Dall	16.84
58.	Lewis Lloyd	Hous	16.80
59.	Larry Smith	G.St	16.64
60.	Mel Turpin	Clev	16.50
61.	Dennis Johnson	Bost	16.37
62.	Mark Eaton	Utah	16.31
63.	John Bagley	Clev	16.28
64.	Norm Nixon	LA.C	16.16
65.	Glenn Rivers	Atla	16.11
66.	Karl Malone	Utah	16.11
67.	Benoit Benjamin	LA.C	16.04
68.	Steve Johnson	S.A.	15.97
69.	Rodney McCray	Hous	15.79
70.	Eddie A. Johnson	Sacr	15.76
71.	Derek Harper	Dall	15.68
72.	Mychal Thompson	Port	15.66
73.	Alvan Adams	Phoe	15.42
74.	Sidney Green	Chic	15.24
75.	Kenny Carr	Port	15.18
76.	Dan Roundfield	Wash	15.18
77.	Thurl Bailey	Utah	14.79
78.	Kevin Willis	Atla	14.74
79.	Gerald Henderson	Seat	14.71
80.	Jay Humphries	Phoe	14.62
81.	Wayman Tisdale	Indi	14.60
82.	Charles Oakley	Chic	14.40
83.	Alton Lister	Milw	14.25
84.	John Stockton	Utah	13.99
85.	Danny Ainge	Bost	13.83
86.	Ricky Pierce	Milw	13.63
87.	Bill Walton	Bost	13.38
88.	Michael Cooper	LA.L	13.34
89.	Jay Vincent	Dall	13.34
90.	Dave Corzine	Chic	13.31
91.	David Greenwood	S.A.	13.28
92.	Rory Sparrow	N.Y.	13.23
93.	Wes Matthews	S.A.	13.20
94.	Byron Scott	LA.L	13.12
95.	Mike Woodson	Sacr	13.10
96.	Brad Davis	Dall	13.10
97.	Bill Hanzlik	Denv	13.03
98.	Randy Wittman	Atla	13.02
99.	Vinnie Johnson	Detr	13.00
100.	Otis Birdsong	N.J.	12.96

POSITION DOMINANCE

OR	PLAYER	TEAM	PD
1.	Earvin Johnson	LA.L	1.346
2.	Larry Bird	Bost	1.299
3.	Akeem Olajuwon	Hous	1.248
4.	Alvin Robertson	S.A.	1.178
5.	Clyde Drexler	Port	1.176
6.	Charles Barkley	Phil	1.173
7.	Isiah Thomas	Detr	1.155
8.	Adrian Dantley	Utah	1.144
9.	Dominique Wilkins	Atla	1.130
10.	Sidney Moncrief	Milw	1.102
11.	Reggie Theus	Sacr	1.101
12.	Alex English	Denv	1.080
13.	Larry Nance	Phoe	1.074
14.	K. Abdul-Jabbar	LA.L	1.063
15.	Bill Laimbeer	Detr	1.049
16.	Moses Malone	Phil	1.042
17.	Kevin McHale	Bost	1.027
18.	Maurice Cheeks	Phil	1.023
19.	Eric Floyd	G.St	1.008
20.	Rolando Blackman	Dall	.970

MOST VALUABLE PLAYER

OR	PLAYER	TEAM	MVP
1.	Larry Bird	Bost	2.123
2.	Earvin Johnson	LA.L	2.040
3.	Akeem Olajuwon	Hous	1.882
4.	Kevin McHale	Bost	1.851
5.	Charles Barkley	Phil	1.783
6.	K. Abdul-Jabbar	LA.L	1.757
7.	Robert Parish	Bost	1.739
8.	Sidney Moncrief	Milw	1.731
9.	Dominique Wilkins	Atla	1.699
10.	Isiah Thomas	Detr	1.676
11.	Moses Malone	Phil	1.652
12.	Alex English	Denv	1.634
13.	Maurice Cheeks	Phil	1.633
14.	Clyde Drexler	Port	1.633
15.	Adrian Dantley	Utah	1.623
16.	James Worthy	LA.L	1.621
17.	Dennis Johnson	Bost	1.600
18.	Ralph Sampson	Hous	1.582
19.	Bill Laimbeer	Detr	1.570
20.	Alvin Robertson	S.A.	1.563

1985-86 POSITION RATINGS

POWER FORWARD

OR	PLAYER	TEAM	PR
1.	Charles Barkley	Phil	28.26
2.	Kevin McHale	Bost	24.75
3.	Ralph Sampson	Hous	22.85
4.	Herb Williams	Indi	21.79
5.	Buck Williams	N.J.	21.26
6.	Roy Hinson	Clev	20.06
7.	Sam Perkins	Dall	19.67
8.	Terry Cummings	Milw	19.50
9.	Cliff Robinson	Wash	19.46
10.	Cedric Maxwell	L.A.C	17.58
11.	Tom Chambers	Seat	16.97
12.	Larry Smith	G.St	16.64
13.	Karl Malone	Utah	16.11
14.	Steve Johnson	S.A.	15.97
15.	Mychal Thompson	Port	15.66
16.	Alvan Adams	Phoe	15.42
17.	Sidney Green	Chic	15.24
18.	Kenny Carr	Port	15.18
19.	Dan Roundfield	Wash	15.18
20.	Thurl Bailey	Utah	14.79

POINT GUARD

OR	PLAYER	TEAM	PR
1.	Earvin Johnson	L.A.L	28.50
2.	Isiah Thomas	Detr	24.44
3.	Maurice Cheeks	Phil	21.65
4.	Eric Floyd	G.St	21.33
5.	Lafayette Lever	Denv	18.26
6.	John Lucas	Hous	17.43
7.	Dennis Johnson	Bost	16.37
8.	John Bagley	Clev	16.28
9.	Norm Nixon	L.A.C	16.16
10.	Glenn Rivers	Atla	16.11
11.	Derek Harper	Dall	15.68
12.	Gerald Henderson	Seat	14.71
13.	Jay Humphries	Phoe	14.62
14.	John Stockton	Utah	13.99
15.	Rory Sparrow	N.Y.	13.23
16.	Wes Matthews	S.A.	13.20
17.	Brad Davis	Dall	13.10
18.	Rickey Green	Utah	12.75
19.	Gus Williams	Wash	12.69
20.	Kyle Macy	Chic	11.94

CENTER

OR	PLAYER	TEAM	PR
1.	Akeem Olajuwon	Hous	28.40
2.	K. Abdul-Jabbar	L.A.L	24.20
3.	Bill Laimbeer	Detr	23.87
4.	Moses Malone	Phil	23.73
5.	Jack Sikma	Seat	21.54
6.	Robert Parish	Bost	20.84
7.	Pat Ewing	N.Y.	20.56
8.	Joe Barry Carroll	G.St	20.43
9.	Artis Gilmore	S.A.	20.31
10.	Mike Gminski	N.J.	20.01
11.	LaSalle Thompson	Sacr	18.76
12.	Steve Stipanovich	Indi	17.23
13.	Wayne Cooper	Denv	17.12
14.	James Donaldson	Dall	16.84
15.	Mel Turpin	Clev	16.50
16.	Mark Eaton	Utah	16.31
17.	Benoit Benjamin	L.A.C	16.04
18.	Alton Lister	Milw	14.25
19.	Bill Walton	Bost	13.38
20.	Dave Corzine	Chic	13.31

SMALL FORWARD

OR	PLAYER	TEAM	PR
1.	Larry Bird	Bost	31.30
2.	Adrian Dantley	Utah	25.82
3.	Dominique Wilkins	Atla	25.50
4.	Alex English	Denv	24.36
5.	Larry Nance	Phoe	24.23
6.	Purvis Short	G.St	21.77
7.	James Worthy	L.A.L	20.92
8.	Paul Pressey	Milw	20.74
9.	Marques Johnson	L.A.C	20.21
10.	Mark Aguirre	Dall	20.08
11.	Kiki Vandeweghe	Port	19.84
12.	Orlando Woolridge	Chic	18.36
13.	Kelly Tripucka	Detr	18.15
14.	Calvin Natt	Denv	17.81
15.	Mike Mitchell	S.A.	17.62
16.	Xavier McDaniel	Seat	17.41
17.	Rodney McCray	Hous	15.79
18.	Eddie A. Johnson	Sacr	15.76
19.	Jay Vincent	Dall	13.34
20.	Bill Hanzlik	Denv	13.03

OFF GUARD

OR	PLAYER	TEAM	PR
1.	Alvin Robertson	S.A.	22.48
2.	Clyde Drexler	Port	22.44
3.	Sidney Moncrief	Milw	21.03
4.	Reggie Theus	Sacr	21.02
5.	Rolando Blackman	Dall	18.52
6.	Vern Fleming	Indi	17.99
7.	Walter Davis	Phoe	17.99
8.	World B. Free	Clev	17.81
9.	Julius Erving	Phil	17.51
10.	Jeff Malone	Wash	16.90
11.	Lewis Lloyd	Hous	16.80
12.	Danny Ainge	Bost	13.83
13.	Ricky Pierce	Milw	13.63
14.	Michael Cooper	L.A.L	13.34
15.	Byron Scott	L.A.L	13.12
16.	Mike Woodson	Sacr	13.10
17.	Randy Wittman	Atla	13.02
18.	Vinnie Johnson	Detr	13.00
19.	Otis Birdsong	N.J.	12.96
20.	Jim Paxson	Port	12.63

ROOKIES

OR	PLAYER	TEAM	PR
1.	Pat Ewing	N.Y.	20.56
2.	Xavier McDaniel	Seat	17.41
3.	Karl Malone	Utah	16.11
4.	Benoit Benjamin	L.A.C	16.04
5.	Wayman Tisdale	Indi	14.60
6.	Charles Oakley	Chic	14.40
7.	Manute Bol	Wash	12.05
8.	Chris Mullin	G. St	11.84
9.	Jon Koncak	Atla	10.27
10.	Joe Dumars	Detr	10.23
11.	Ed Pinckney	Phoe	9.43
12.	Gerald Wilkins	N.Y.	8.64

1985-86 PERFORMANCE CATEGORIES

SCORING

OR	PLAYER	TEAM	SCR
1.	Dominique Wilkins	Atla	30.33
2.	Adrian Dantley	Utah	29.83
3.	Alex English	Denv	29.80
4.	Larry Bird	Bost	25.79
5.	Purvis Short	G.St	25.50
6.	Kiki Vandeweghe	Port	24.84
7.	Moses Malone	Phil	23.77
8.	Akeem Olajuwon	Hous	23.49
9.	Mike Mitchell	S.A.	23.43
10.	World B. Free	Clev	23.39
11.	K. Abdul-Jabbar	LA.L	23.37
12.	Mark Aguirre	Dall	22.57
13.	Jeff Malone	Wash	22.44
14.	Walter Davis	Phoe	21.76
15.	Rolando Blackman	Dall	21.49
16.	Kevin McHale	Bost	21.29
17.	Joe Barry Carroll	G.St	21.23
18.	Isiah Thomas	Detr	20.90
19.	Orlando Woolridge	Chic	20.69
20.	Marques Johnson	LA.C	20.33

REBOUNDS

OR	PLAYER	TEAM	REB
1.	Charles Oakley	Chic	17.99
2.	Bill Laimbeer	Detr	17.85
3.	Bill Walton	Bost	16.89
4.	Larry Smith	G.St	16.83
5.	Charles Barkley	Phil	16.68
6.	Kurt Rambis	LA.L	15.78
7.	Alton Lister	Milw	15.68
8.	LaSalle Thompson	Sacr	15.55
9.	Maurice Lucas	LA.L	15.52
10.	Moses Malone	Phil	15.47
11.	Buck Williams	N.J.	15.42
12.	Akeem Olajuwon	Hous	15.20
13.	Kenny Carr	Port	15.17
14.	Ralph Sampson	Hous	14.73
15.	Kevin Willis	Atla	14.69
16.	Robert Parish	Bost	14.40
17.	James Donaldson	Dall	14.23
18.	Karl Malone	Utah	13.92
19.	Wayne Cooper	Denv	13.86
20.	Benoit Benjamin	LA.C	13.79

BLOCKS

OR	PLAYER	TEAM	BLK
1.	Manute Bol	Wash	9.12
2.	Mark Eaton	Utah	6.94
3.	Wayne Cooper	Denv	5.16
4.	Benoit Benjamin	LA.C	4.74
5.	Wayne Rollins	Atla	4.50
6.	Akleem Olajuwon	Hous	4.49
7.	Charles Jones	Wash	3.97
8.	Alton Lister	Milw	3.76
9.	Bill Walton	Bost	3.29
10.	Herb Williams	Indi	3.19
11.	Terry Tyler	Sacr	3.14
12.	Randy Breuer	Milw	3.11
13.	Pat Ewing	N.Y.	2.79
14.	Kevin McHale	Bost	2.68
15.	Larry Nance	Phoe	2.51
16.	James Donaldson	Dall	2.49
17.	Joe Barry Carroll	G.St	2.45
18.	K. Abdul-Jabbar	LA.L	2.37
19.	Thurl Bailey	Utah	2.32
20.	Kurt Nimphius	LA.C	2.26

SHOOTING

OR	PLAYER	TEAM	SHT
1.	Jerry Sichting	Bost	1.166
2.	Brad Davis	Dall	1.137
3.	Craig Hodges	Milw	1.133
4.	Steve Johnson	S.A.	1.130
5.	James Worthy	LA.L	1.129
6.	Kurt Rambis	LA.L	1.118
7.	Kevin McHale	Bost	1.113
8.	Artis Gilmore	S.A.	1.112
9.	Kiki Vandeweghe	Port	1.105
10.	K. Abdul-Jabbar	LA.L	1.102
11.	Adrian Dantley	Utah	1.101
12.	James Donaldson	Dall	1.100
13.	Bobby Jones	Phil	1.097
14.	Ricky Pierce	Milw	1.097
15.	Earvin Johnson	LA.L	1.095
16.	Larry Nance	Phoe	1.092
17.	Maurice Cheeks	Phil	1.090
18.	Mel Turpin	Clev	1.087
19.	Mark Olberding	Sacr	1.086
20.	Mike Gminski	N.J.	1.080

ASSISTS

OR	PLAYER	TEAM	AST
1.	Earvin Johnson	LA.L	16.89
2.	John Stockton	Utah	15.13
3.	Isiah Thomas	Detr	14.28
4.	John Bagley	Clev	14.27
5.	Glenn Rivers	Atla	13.54
6.	Reggie Theus	Sacr	12.96
7.	Eric Floyd	G.St	12.96
8.	Norm Nixon	LA.C	12.93
9.	John Lucas	Hous	12.93
10.	Wes Matthews	S.A.	12.33
11.	Brad Davis	Dall	11.37
12.	Clyde Drexler	Port	11.18
13.	Paul Pressey	Milw	11.06
14.	Maurice Cheeks	Phil	11.05
15.	Eddie Johnson Jr.	Clev	10.82
16.	Lafayette Lever	Denv	10.72
17.	Michael Cooper	LA.L	9.86
18.	Rickey Green	Utah	9.81
19.	Darnell Valentine	LA.C	9.70
20.	Rory Sparrow	N.Y.	9.67

STEALS

OR	PLAYER	TEAM	STL
1.	Alvin Robertson	S.A.	5.02
2.	John Stockton	Utah	3.89
3.	Darwin Cook	N.J.	3.81
4.	Clyde Drexler	Port	3.67
5.	Glenn Rivers	Atla	3.67
6.	Darrell Walker	N.Y.	3.46
7.	Derek Harper	Dall	3.42
8.	Lafayette Lever	Denv	3.27
9.	T.R. Dunn	Denv	3.10
10.	Maurice Cheeks	Phil	3.04
11.	Paul Pressey	Milw	2.98
12.	Isiah Thomas	Detr	2.94
13.	Steve Colter	Port	2.90
14.	Franklin Edwards	LA.C	2.87
15.	Darnell Valentine	LA.C	2.84
16.	Charles Barkley	Phil	2.81
17.	Danny Young	Seat	2.78
18.	Eric Floyd	G.St	2.73
19.	Akeem Olajuwon	Hous	2.61
20.	Bill Hanzlik	Denv	2.59

1984-85
NBA STATISTICS

PRODUCTION RATINGS

OR	PLAYER	TEAM	PR
1.	Larry Bird	Bost	34.39
2.	Michael Jordan	Chic	29.24
3.	Earvin Johnson	LA.L	28.77
4.	Isiah Thomas	Detr	27.85
5.	Moses Malone	Phil	27.30
6.	Bernard King	N.Y.	26.80
7.	K. Abdul-Jabbar	LA.L	25.87
8.	Jack Sikma	Seat	25.60
9.	Akeem Olajuwon	Hous	25.22
10.	Larry Nance	Phoe	25.02
11.	Artis Gilmore	S.A.	24.85
12.	Alex English	Denv	24.79
13.	Calvin Natt	Denv	24.31
14.	Terry Cummings	Milw	24.13
15.	Bill Laimbeer	Detr	24.05
16.	Adrian Dantley	Utah	23.75
17.	M. R. Richardson	N.J.	23.63
18.	Ralph Sampson	Hous	23.39
19.	Kevin McHale	Bost	23.29
20.	Buck Williams	N.J.	22.98
21.	Sidney Moncrief	Milw	22.40
22.	Robert Parish	Bost	22.33
23.	Dominique Wilkins	Atla	22.01
24.	Clark Kellogg	Indi	21.25
25.	Mark Aguirre	Dall	21.21
26.	Purvis Short	G.St	21.12
27.	Orlando Woolridge	Chic	20.74
28.	Clyde Drexler	Port	20.71
29.	Johnny Moore	S.A.	20.71
30.	Paul Pressey	Milw	20.56
31.	Mark Eaton	Utah	20.52
32.	Derek Smith	LA.C	20.20
33.	Tom Chambers	Seat	20.06
34.	Jay Vincent	Dall	19.65
35.	James Worthy	LA.L	19.59
36.	Mychal Thompson	Port	19.54
37.	Eddie A. Johnson	K.C.	19.41
38.	Julius Erving	Phil	19.41
39.	Rodney McCray	Hous	19.12
40.	Herb Williams	Indi	19.08
41.	LaSalle Thompson	K.C.	19.01
42.	Cliff Robinson	Wash	18.43
43.	Charles Barkley	Phil	18.40
44.	Maurice Cheeks	Phil	18.38
45.	Alvan Adams	Phoe	18.34
46.	Sam Bowie	Port	18.32
47.	Gus Williams	Wash	18.20
48.	Reggie Theus	K.C.	18.20
49.	Kiki Vandeweghe	Port	18.19
50.	Lafayette Lever	Denv	18.10
51.	Mike Mitchell	S.A.	18.00
52.	Roy Hinson	Clev	17.80
53.	Dennis Johnson	Bost	17.74
54.	World B.Free	Clev	17.72
55.	Rolando Blackman	Dall	17.60
56.	Norm Nixon	LA.C	17.49
57.	Larry Smith	G.St	17.49
58.	Pat Cummings	N.Y.	17.27
59.	Jim Paxson	Port	17.21
60.	Glenn Rivers	Atla	17.16
61.	Bill Walton	LA.C	16.96
62.	Darrell Griffith	Utah	16.92
63.	George Gervin	S.A.	16.81
64.	Rickey Green	Utah	16.78
65.	Otis Birdsong	N.J.	16.75
66.	Steve Stipanovich	Indi	16.73
67.	Thurl Bailey	Utah	16.44
68.	Mike Gminski	N.J.	16.43
69.	Eddie Johnson Jr.	Atla	16.40
70.	Danny Ainge	Bost	16.35
71.	John Bagley	Clev	16.32
72.	Andrew Toney	Phil	16.24
73.	Maurice Lucas	Phoe	16.16
74.	James Donaldson	LA.C	16.11
75.	Kelly Tripucka	Detr	15.98
76.	Larry Drew	K.C.	15.96
77.	Greg Ballard	G.St	15.83
78.	Eric Floyd	G.St	15.72
79.	Phil Hubbard	Clev	15.47
80.	Marques Johnson	LA.C	15.46
81.	Wayne Cooper	Denv	15.45
82.	Darnell Valentine	Port	15.32
83.	Gerald Henderson	Seat	15.30
84.	Brad Davis	Dall	15.28
85.	Byron Scott	LA.L	15.12
86.	Jerome Whitehead	G.St	15.10
87.	Alton Lister	Milw	15.07
88.	Sam Perkins	Dall	15.05
89.	Jeff Malone	Wash	14.91
90.	James Edwards	Phoe	14.63
91.	Dan Roundfield	Detr	14.55
92.	Otis Thorpe	K.C.	14.49
93.	Kyle Macy	Phoe	14.42
94.	Cliff Levingston	Atla	14.39
95.	Al Wood	Seat	14.25
96.	Mark Olberding	K.C.	14.06
97.	Mickey Johnson	G.St	13.89
98.	Rory Sparrow	N.Y.	13.82
99.	Gene Banks	S.A.	13.82
100.	Mike Woodson	K.C.	13.74

POSITION DOMINANCE

OR	PLAYER	TEAM	PD
1.	Larry Bird	Bost	1.428
2.	Michael Jordan	Chic	1.393
3.	Earvin Johnson	LA.L	1.276
4.	Isiah Thomas	Detr	1.235
5.	Moses Malone	Phil	1.159
6.	Bernard King	N.Y.	1.133
7.	K. Abdul-Jabbar	LA.L	1.098
8.	Jack Sikma	Seat	1.087
9.	Akeem Olajuwon	Hous	1.071
10.	Sidney Moncrief	Milw	1.067
11.	Larry Nance	Phoe	1.058
12.	Artis Gilmore	S.A.	1.055
13.	M.R. Richardson	N.J.	1.048
14.	Alex English	Denv	1.048
15.	Calvin Natt	Denv	1.028
16.	Bill Laimbeer	Detr	1.021
17.	Adrian Dantley	Utah	1.004
18.	Terry Cummings	Milw	1.002
19.	Clyde Drexler	Port	.987
20.	Ralph Sampson	Hous	.971

MOST VALUABLE PLAYER

OR	PLAYER	TEAM	MVP
1.	Larry Bird	Bost	2.131
2.	Earvin Johnson	LA.L	2.046
3.	K. Abdul-Jabbar	LA.L	1.868
4.	Moses Malone	Phil	1.837
5.	Michael Jordan	Chic	1.829
6.	Isiah Thomas	Detr	1.795
7.	Sidney Moncrief	Milw	1.709
8.	Kevin McHale	Bost	1.670
9.	Robert Parish	Bost	1.651
10.	Alex English	Denv	1.646
11.	Terry Cummings	Milw	1.644
12.	Akeem Olajuwon	Hous	1.628
13.	Calvin Natt	Denv	1.626
14.	James Worthy	LA.L	1.598
15.	Bill Laimbeer	Detr	1.581
16.	Artis Gilmore	S.A.	1.540
17.	Ralph Sampson	Hous	1.528
18.	Paul Pressey	Milw	1.511
19.	M.R. Richardson	N.J.	1.510
20.	Maurice Cheeks	Phil	1.493

1984-85 POSITION RATINGS

POWER FORWARD

OR	PLAYER	TEAM	PR
1.	Terry Cummings	Milw	24.13
2.	Ralph Sampson	Hous	23.39
3.	Kevin McHale	Bost	23.29
4.	Buck Williams	N.J.	22.98
5.	Clark Kellogg	Indi	21.25
6.	Tom Chambers	Seat	20.06
7.	Mychal Thompson	Port	19.54
8.	Herb Williams	Indi	19.08
9.	Cliff Robinson	Wash	18.43
10.	Charles Barkley	Phil	18.40
11.	Alvan Adams	Phoe	18.34
12.	Roy Hinson	Clev	17.80
13.	Larry Smith	G.St	17.49
14.	Pat Cummings	N.Y.	17.27
15.	Thurl Bailey	Utah	16.44
16.	Maurice Lucas	Phoe	16.16
17.	Greg Ballard	Wash	15.83
18.	Sam Perkins	Dall	15.05
19.	Dan Roundfield	Detr	14.55
20.	Otis Thorpe	K.C.	14.49

POINT GUARD

OR	PLAYER	TEAM	PR
1.	Earvin Johnson	LA.L	28.77
2.	Isiah Thomas	Detr	27.85
3.	M.R. Richardson	N.J.	23.63
4.	Johnny Moore	S.A.	20.71
5.	Maurice Cheeks	Phil	18.38
6.	Gus Williams	Wash	18.20
7.	Lafayette Lever	Denv	18.10
8.	Dennis Johnson	Bost	17.74
9.	Norm Nixon	LA.C	17.49
10.	Glenn Rivers	Atla	17.16
11.	Rickey Green	Utah	16.78
12.	John Bagley	Clev	16.32
13.	Larry Drew	K.C.	15.96
14.	Eric Floyd	G.St	15.72
15.	Darnell Valentine	Port	15.32
16.	Gerald Henderson	Seat	15.30
17.	Brad Davis	Dall	15.28
18.	Kyle Macy	Phoe	14.42
19.	Rory Sparrow	N.Y.	13.83
20.	Derek Harper	Dall	12.93

CENTER

OR	PLAYER	TEAM	PR
1.	Moses Malone	Phil	27.30
2.	K. Abdul-Jabbar	LA.L	25.87
3.	Jack Sikma	Seat	25.60
4.	Akeem Olajuwon	Hous	25.22
5.	Artis Gilmore	S.A.	24.85
6.	Bill Laimbeer	Detr	24.05
7.	Robert Parish	Bost	22.33
8.	Mark Eaton	Utah	20.52
9.	LaSalle Thompson	K.C.	19.01
10.	Sam Bowie	Port	18.32
11.	Bill Walton	LA.C	16.96
12.	Steve Stipanovich	Indi	16.73
13.	Mike Gminski	N.J.	16.43
14.	James Donaldson	LA.C	16.11
15.	Wayne Cooper	Denv	15.45
16.	Jerome Whitehead	G.St	15.10
17.	Alton Lister	Milw	15.07
18.	James Edwards	Phoe	14.63
19.	Dan Issel	Denv	12.53
20.	Wayne Rollins	Atla	12.51

SMALL FORWARD

OR	PLAYER	TEAM	PR
1.	Larry Bird	Bost	34.39
2.	Bernard King	N.Y.	26.80
3.	Larry Nance	Phoe	25.02
4.	Alex English	Denv	24.79
5.	Calvin Natt	Denv	24.31
6.	Adrian Dantley	Utah	23.75
7.	Dominique Wilkins	Atla	22.01
8.	Mark Aguirre	Dall	21.21
9.	Purvis Short	G.St	21.12
10.	Orlando Woolridge	Chic	20.74
11.	Paul Pressey	Milw	20.56
12.	Jay Vincent	Dall	19.65
13.	James Worthy	LA.L	19.59
14.	Eddie A. Johnson	K.C.	19.41
15.	Julius Erving	Phil	19.41
16.	Rodney McCray	Hous	19.12
17.	Kiki Vandeweghe	Port	18.19
18.	Mike Mitchell	S.A.	18.00
19.	Kelly Tripucka	Detr	15.98
20.	Phil Hubbard	Clev	15.47

OFF GUARD

OR	PLAYER	TEAM	PR
1.	Michael Jordan	Chic	29.24
2.	Sidney Moncrief	Milw	22.40
3.	Clyde Drexler	Port	20.71
4.	Derek Smith	LA.C	20.20
5.	Reggie Theus	K.C.	18.20
6.	World B. Free	Clev	17.72
7.	Rolando Blackman	Dall	17.60
8.	Jim Paxson	Port	17.21
9.	Darrell Griffith	Utah	16.92
10.	George Gervin	S.A.	16.81
11.	Otis Birdsong	N.J.	16.75
12.	Eddie Johnson Jr.	Atla	16.40
13.	Danny Ainge	Bost	16.35
14.	Andrew Toney	Phil	16.24
15.	Byron Scott	LA.L	15.12
16.	Jeff Malone	Wash	14.91
17.	Al Wood	Seat	14.25
18.	Mike Woodson	K.C	13.74
19.	Darrell Walker	N.Y.	13.54
20.	Vern Fleming	Indi	12.98

ROOKIES

OR	PLAYER	TEAM	PR
1.	Michael Jordan	Chic	29.24
2.	Akeem Olajuwon	Hous	25.22
3.	Charles Barkley	Phil	18.40
4.	Sam Bowie	Port	18.32
5.	Sam Perkins	Dall	15.05
6.	Otis Thorpe	K.C.	14.49
7.	Vern Fleming	Indi	12.98
8.	Melvin Turpin	Clev	12.05
9.	Alvin Robertson	S.A.	11.44
10.	Tim McCormick	Seat	10.90
11.	Kevin Willis	Atla	10.60
12.	Charles A. Jones	Phoe	10.54
13.	Michael Cage	LA.C	10.00
14.	Jay Humphries	Phoe	9.86
15.	Antoine Carr	Atla	9.77
16.	Tony Brown	Indi	7.80
17.	Jeff Turner	N.J.	6.58

1984-85 PERFORMANCE CATEGORIES

SCORING

OR	PLAYER	TEAM	SCR
1.	Bernard King	N.Y.	32.89
2.	Larry Bird	Bost	28.69
3.	Michael Jordan	Chic	28.21
4.	Purvis Short	G.St	28.03
5.	Alex English	Denv	27.93
6.	Dominique Wilkins	Atla	27.37
7.	Adrian Dantley	Utah	26.58
8.	Mark Aguirre	Dall	25.69
9.	Moses Malone	Phil	24.57
10.	Terry Cummings	Milw	23.56
11.	Calvin Natt	Denv	23.29
12.	Orlando Woolridge	Chic	22.95
13.	Eddie A. Johnson	K.C.	22.88
14.	Darrell Griffith	Utah	22.62
15.	World B. Free	Clev	22.49
16.	Kiki Vandeweghe	Port	22.44
17.	Mike Mitchell	S.A.	22.24
18.	Derek Smith	LA.C	22.09
19.	Ralph Sampson	Hous	22.06
20.	K. Abdul-Jabbar	LA.L	21.96

REBOUNDS

OR	PLAYER	TEAM	REB
1.	Bill Walton	LA.C	17.49
2.	Bill Laimbeer	Detr	16.81
3.	Moses Malone	Phil	16.74
4.	Larry Smith	G.St	16.70
5.	LaSalle Thompson	K.C.	16.68
6.	Akeem Olajuwon	Hous	16.04
7.	Maurice Lucas	Phoe	16.01
8.	Mark Eaton	Utah	15.82
9.	Kurt Rambis	LA.L	15.67
10.	Buck Williams	N.J.	15.16
11.	Wayne Cooper	Denv	14.91
12.	Alton Lister	Milw	14.85
13.	Artis Gilmore	S.A.	14.73
14.	Dan Roundfield	Detr	14.57
15.	Jack Sikma	Seat	14.45
16.	Charles Barkley	Phil	14.38
17.	Sam Bowie	Port	14.21
18.	Clark Kellogg	Indi	14.19
19.	Robert Parish	Bost	14.15
20.	Rick Mahorn	Wash	14.08

BLOCKS

OR	PLAYER	TEAM	BLK
1.	Mark Eaton	Utah	7.78
2.	Wayne Cooper	Denv	4.66
3.	Wayne Rollins	Atla	4.58
4.	Sam Bowie	Port	4.40
5.	Bill Walton	LA.C	4.08
6.	Alton Lister	Milw	3.83
7.	Akeem Olajuwon	Hous	3.62
8.	Roy Hinson	Clev	3.54
9.	Antoine Carr	Atla	3.13
10.	Artis Gilmore	S.A.	3.01
11.	Kurt Nimphius	Dall	3.01
12.	K. Abdul-Jabbar	LA.L	2.96
13.	Ralph Sampson	Hous	2.61
14.	James Donaldson	LA.C	2.61
15.	Herb Williams	Indi	2.52
16.	LaSalle Thompson	K.C.	2.50
17.	Rick Mahorn	Wash	2.41
18.	Larry Nance	Phoe	2.27
19.	Kevin McHale	Bost	2.17
20.	Terry Tyler	Detr	2.16

SHOOTING

OR	PLAYER	TEAM	SHT
1.	James Donaldson	LA.C	1.176
2.	Maurice Cheeks	Phil	1.152
3.	K. Abdul-Jabbar	LA.L	1.143
4.	Artis Gilmore	S.A.	1.140
5.	Earvin Johnson	LA.L	1.127
6.	Gene Banks	S.A.	1.126
7.	James Worthy	LA.L	1.124
8.	Larry Nance	Phoe	1.124
9.	Brad Davis	Dall	1.108
10.	Kiki Vandeweghe	Port	1.108
11.	Byron Scott	LA.L	1.103
12.	Bobby Jones	Phil	1.101
13.	Kevin McHale	Bost	1.101
14.	Larry Bird	Bost	1.096
15.	Orlando Woolridge	Chic	1.090
16.	Danny Ainge	Bost	1.089
17.	Cedric Maxwell	Bost	1.084
18.	Calvin Natt	Denv	1.081
19.	Jerry Sichting	Indi	1.075
20.	Alvan Adams	Phoe	1.073

ASSISTS

OR	PLAYER	TEAM	AST
1.	Isiah Thomas	Detr	17.45
2.	Earvin Johnson	LA.L	16.71
3.	Johnny Moore	S.A.	14.57
4.	John Bagley	Clev	13.93
5.	Ennis Whatley	Chic	13.20
6.	Reggie Theus	K.C.	12.38
7.	Norm Nixon	LA.C	11.79
8.	Rickey Green	Utah	11.79
9.	Rory Sparrow	N.Y.	11.66
10.	Lafayette Lever	Denv	11.50
11.	Eddie Johnson Jr.	Atla	11.48
12.	Wes Matthews	Chic	11.16
13.	Darnell Valentine	Port	11.00
14.	Brad Davis	Dall	10.98
15.	Johnny Davis	Clev	10.65
16.	M.R. Richardson	N.J.	10.27
17.	Lionel Hollins	Hous	10.26
18.	Gerald Henderson	Seat	10.13
19.	Kelvin Ransey	N.J.	10.09
20.	Gus Williams	Wash	9.86

STEALS

OR	PLAYER	TEAM	STL
1.	Johnny Moore	S.A.	4.09
2.	Lafayette Lever	Denv	3.79
3.	M.R. Richardson	N.J.	3.73
4.	Glenn Rivers	Atla	3.68
5.	Alvin Robertson	S.A.	3.62
6.	Lester Conner	G.St	3.42
7.	Clyde Drexler	Port	3.33
8.	Darrell Walker	N.Y.	3.22
9.	Derek Harper	Dall	3.12
10.	Maurice Cheeks	Phil	3.10
11.	Darnell Valentine	Port	3.01
12.	Michael Jordan	Chic	2.99
13.	T.R. Dunn	Denv	2.93
14.	Isiah Thomas	Detr	2.91
15.	Gus Williams	Wash	2.89
16.	Mike Woodson	K.C.	2.81
17.	Rickey Green	Utah	2.61
18.	Alvan Adams	Phoe	2.58
19.	John Bagley	Clev	2.58
20.	Julius Erving	Phil	2.56

1983-84
NBA STATISTICS

PRODUCTION RATINGS

OR	PLAYER	TEAM	PR
1.	Earvin Johnson	LA.L	30.30
2.	Larry Bird	Bost	29.99
3.	Adrian Dantley	Utah	27.96
4.	Jeff Ruland	Wash	27.67
5.	Kiki Vandeweghe	Denv	26.40
6.	Moses Malone	Phil	25.85
7.	Alex English	Denv	25.74
8.	Jack Sikma	Seat	25.66
9.	Mark Aguirre	Dall	25.04
10.	Bill Laimbeer	Detr	24.59
11.	Isiah Thomas	Detr	24.38
12.	Julius Erving	Phil	24.06
13.	Ralph Sampson	Hous	24.01
14.	Robert Parish	Bost	23.65
15.	K. Abdul-Jabbar	LA.L	23.26
16.	Larry Nance	Phoe	22.91
17.	Bernard King	N.Y.	22.86
18.	Sidney Moncrief	Milw	22.76
19.	Terry Cummings	S.D.	22.21
20.	Artis Gilmore	S.A.	22.16
21.	Clark Kellogg	Indi	21.99
22.	Dan Roundfield	Atla	21.48
23.	Buck Williams	N.J.	21.33
24.	Marques Johnson	Milw	21.20
25.	Rolando Blackman	Dall	21.17
26.	Mychal Thompson	Port	20.48
27.	Mike Mitchell	S.A.	20.25
28.	Bill Cartwright	N.Y.	20.18
29.	Kevin McHale	Bost	20.16
30.	Dan Issel	Denv	20.08
31.	George Gervin	S.A.	20.08
32.	Joe Barry Carroll	G.St	20.04
33.	Maurice Lucas	Phoe	19.91
34.	Rickey Green	Utah	19.74
35.	Dominique Wilkins	Atla	19.60
36.	Norm Nixon	S.D.	19.52
37.	Gus Williams	Seat	19.39
38.	Eddie A. Johnson	K.C.	19.11
39.	Cliff Robinson	Clev	18.95
40.	Purvis Short	G.St	18.81
41.	Darryl Dawkins	N.J.	18.70
42.	Walter Davis	Phoe	18.40
43.	Gene Banks	S.A.	18.17
44.	Calvin Natt	Port	18.10
45.	Bill Walton	S.D.	18.04
46.	David Greenwood	Chic	18.03
47.	John Lucas	S.A.	18.02
48.	Kenny Carr	Port	17.76
49.	Herb Williams	Indi	17.71
50.	Jim Paxson	Port	17.64
51.	James Worthy	LA.L	17.27
52.	Johnny Moore	S.A.	17.25
53.	Andrew Toney	Phil	17.22
54.	Tom Chambers	Seat	17.12
55.	James Donaldson	S.D.	17.00
56.	Maurice Cheeks	Phil	16.85
57.	Orlando Woolridge	Chic	16.73
58.	Larry Drew	K.C.	16.62
59.	Greg Ballard	Wash	16.59
60.	Darrell Griffith	Utah	16.57
61.	Bob Lanier	Milw	16.56
62.	Jamaal Wilkes	LA.L	16.52
63.	Kelly Tripucka	Detr	16.39
64.	Lewis Lloyd	Hous	16.34
65.	LaSalle Thompson	K.C.	16.27
66.	Ray Williams	N.Y.	16.22
67.	Pat Cummings	Dall	16.12
68.	Dave Corzine	Chic	15.87
69.	Rick Mahorn	Wash	15.68
70.	Wayne Rollins	Atla	15.65
71.	World B. Free	Clev	15.60
72.	Robert Reid	Hous	15.41
73.	Brad Davis	Dall	15.31
74.	Otis Birdsong	N.J.	15.14
75.	Steve Stipanovich	Indi	14.78
76.	Eric Floyd	G.St	14.77
77.	Michael Cooper	LA.L	14.74
78.	Lester Conner	G.St	14.65
79.	James Edwards	Phoe	14.64
80.	Mickey Johnson	G.St	14.46
81.	Mark Eaton	Utah	14.33
82.	Caldwell Jones	Hous	14.32
83.	Albert King	N.J.	14.28
84.	Jerry Sichting	Indi	14.15
85.	Quintin Dailey	Chic	14.13
86.	T.R. Dunn	Denv	14.11
87.	John Long	Detr	14.07
88.	George L. Johnson	Indi	14.02
89.	Cedric Maxwell	Bost	14.01
90.	John Drew	Utah	13.95
91.	Dennis Johnson	Bost	13.83
92.	Frank Johnson	Wash	13.79
93.	Junior Bridgeman	Milw	13.63
94.	Larry Smith	G.St	13.59
95.	Truck Robinson	N.Y.	13.54
96.	Kurt Nimphius	Dall	13.54
97.	Rodney McCray	Hous	13.44
98.	Ricky Sobers	Wash	13.38
99.	Bobby Jones	Phil	13.15
100.	Rory Sparrow	N.Y.	13.08

POSITION DOMINANCE

OR	PLAYER	TEAM	PD
1.	Earvin Johnson	LA.L	1.397
2.	Larry Bird	Bost	1.291
3.	Sidney Moncrief	Milw	1.207
4.	Jeff Ruland	Wash	1.191
5.	Adrian Dantley	Utah	1.177
6.	Moses Malone	Phil	1.132
7.	Isiah Thomas	Detr	1.124
8.	Jack Sikma	Seat	1.123
9.	Rolando Blackman	Dall	1.123
10.	Kiki Vandeweghe	Denv	1.112
11.	Alex English	Denv	1.112
12.	Bill Laimbeer	Detr	1.077
13.	George Gervin	S.A.	1.065
14.	Mark Aguirre	Dall	1.055
15.	Ralph Sampson	Hous	1.051
16.	Robert Parish	Bost	1.035
17.	K. Abdul-Jabbar	LA.L	1.018
18.	Julius Erving	Phil	1.013
19.	Walter Davis	Phoe	.976
20.	Artis Gilmore	S.A.	.970

MOST VALUABLE PLAYER

OR	PLAYER	TEAM	MVP
1.	Earvin Johnson	LA.L	2.059
2.	Larry Bird	Bost	2.000
3.	Sidney Moncrief	Milw	1.776
4.	Robert Parish	Bost	1.744
5.	Moses Malone	Phil	1.730
6.	Adrian Dantley	Utah	1.699
7.	Isiah Thomas	Detr	1.691
8.	K. Abdul-Jabbar	LA.L	1.680
9.	Bill Laimbeer	Detr	1.644
10.	Jack Sikma	Seat	1.618
11.	Rolando Blackman	Dall	1.614
12.	Julius Erving	Phil	1.611
13.	Jeff Ruland	Wash	1.595
14.	Kevin McHale	Bost	1.577
15.	Kiki Vandeweghe	Denv	1.566
16.	Mark Aguirre	Dall	1.546
17.	Alex English	Denv	1.538
18.	George Gervin	S.A.	1.516
19.	Bernard King	N.Y.	1.514
20.	Andrew Toney	Phil	1.512

1983-84 POSITION RATINGS

POWER FORWARD

OR	PLAYER	TEAM	PR
1.	Jeff Ruland	Wash	27.67
2.	Terry Cummings	S.D.	22.21
3.	Clark Kellogg	Indi	21.99
4.	Dan Roundfield	Atla	21.48
5.	Buck Williams	N.J.	21.33
6.	Kevin McHale	Bost	20.16
7.	Maurice Lucas	Phoe	19.91
8.	Cliff Robinson	Clev	18.95
9.	David Greenwood	Chic	18.03
10.	Kenny Carr	Port	17.76
11.	Herb Williams	Indi	17.71
12.	Tom Chambers	Seat	17.12
13.	Caldwell Jones	Hous	14.32
14.	George L. Johnson	Indi	14.02
15.	Cedric Maxwell	Bost	14.01
16.	Larry Smith	G.St	13.59
17.	Truck Robinson	N.Y.	13.54
18.	Alton Lister	Milw	12.72
19.	Cliff Levingston	Detr	12.68
20.	Thurl Bailey	Utah	12.62

POINT GUARD

OR	PLAYER	TEAM	PR
1.	Earvin Johnson	LA.L	30.30
2.	Isiah Thomas	Detr	24.38
3.	Rickey Green	Utah	19.74
4.	Norm Nixon	S.D.	19.52
5.	Gus Williams	Seat	19.39
6.	John Lucas	S.A.	18.02
7.	Johnny Moore	S.A.	17.25
8.	Maurice Cheeks	Phil	16.85
9.	Larry Drew	K.C.	16.62
10.	Brad Davis	Dall	15.31
11.	Lester Conner	G.St	14.65
12.	Jerry Sichting	Indi	14.15
13.	Frank Johnson	Wash	13.79
14.	Rory Sparrow	N.Y.	13.08
15.	Ennis Whatley	Chic	13.08
16.	Allen Leavell	Hous	12.54
17.	Rob Williams	Denv	12.43
18.	Kyle Macy	Phoe	12.30
19.	Gerald Henderson	Bost	12.08
20.	Darnell Valentine	Port	12.06

CENTER

OR	PLAYER	TEAM	PR
1.	Moses Malone	Phil	25.85
2.	Jack Sikma	Seat	25.66
3.	Bill Laimbeer	Detr	24.59
4.	Ralph Sampson	Hous	24.01
5.	Robert Parish	Bost	23.65
6.	K. Abdul-Jabbar	LA.L	23.26
7.	Artis Gilmore	S.A.	22.16
8.	Mychal Thompson	Port	20.48
9.	Bill Cartwright	N.Y.	20.18
10.	Dan Issel	Denv	20.08
11.	Joe Barry Carroll	G.St	20.04
12.	Darryl Dawkins	N.J.	18.70
13.	Bill Walton	S.D.	18.04
14.	James Donaldson	S.D.	17.00
15.	Bob Lanier	Milw	16.56
16.	LaSalle Thompson	K.C.	16.27
17.	Pat Cummings	Dall	16.12
18.	Dave Corzine	Chic	15.87
19.	Rick Mahorn	Wash	15.68
20.	Wayne Rollins	Atla	15.65

SMALL FORWARD

OR	PLAYER	TEAM	PR
1.	Larry Bird	Bost	29.99
2.	Adrian Dantley	Utah	27.96
3.	Kiki Vandeweghe	Denv	26.40
4.	Alex English	Denv	25.74
5	Mark Aguirre	Dall	25.04
6.	Julius Erving	Phil	24.06
7.	Larry Nance	Phoe	22.91
8.	Bernard King	N.Y.	22.86
9.	Marques Johnson	Milw	21.20
10.	Mike Mitchell	S.A.	20.25
11.	Dominique Wilkins	Atla	19.60
12.	Eddie A. Johnson	K.C.	19.11
13.	Purvis Short	G.St	18.81
14.	Gene Banks	S.A.	18.17
15.	Calvin Natt	Port	18.10
16.	James Worthy	LA.L	17.27
17.	Orlando Woolridge	Chic	16.73
18.	Greg Ballard	Wash	16.59
19.	Jamaal Wilkes	LA.L	16.52
20.	Kelly Tripucka	Detr	16.39

OFF GUARD

OR	PLAYER	TEAM	PR
1.	Sidney Moncrief	Milw	22.76
2.	Rolando Blackman	Dall	21.17
3.	George Gervin	S.A.	20.08
4.	Walter Davis	Phoe	18.40
5.	Jim Paxson	Port	17.64
6.	Andrew Toney	Phil	17.22
7.	Darrell Griffith	Utah	16.57
8.	Lewis Lloyd	Hous	16.34
9.	Ray Williams	N.Y.	16.22
10.	World B. Free	Clev	15.60
11.	Otis Birdsong	N.J.	15.14
12.	Eric Floyd	G.St	14.77
13.	Michael Cooper	LA.L	14.74
14.	Quintin Dailey	Chic	14.13
15.	T.R. Dunn	Denv	14.11
16.	John Long	Detr	14.07
17.	Dennis Johnson	Bost	13.83
18.	Ricky Sobers	Wash	13.38
19.	Al Wood	Seat	12.90
20.	Mike Woodson	K.C.	12.55

ROOKIES

OR	PLAYER	TEAM	PR
1.	Ralph Sampson	Hous	24.01
2.	Steve Stipanovich	Indi	14.78
3.	Rodney McCray	Hous	13.44
4.	Ennis Whatley	Chic	13.08
5.	Thurl Bailey	Utah	12.62
6.	Mitchell Wiggins	Chic	11.54
7.	Glenn Rivers	Atla	11.27
8.	Roy Hinson	Clev	10.46
9.	Paul Thompson	Clev	10.04
10.	Byron Scott	LA.L	9.86
11.	Fred Roberts	S.A.	9.52
12.	Jeff Malone	Wash	8.32
13.	Derek Harper	Dall	7.34

1983-84 PERFORMANCE CATEGORIES

SCORING

OR	PLAYER	TEAM	SCR
1.	Adrian Dantley	Utah	30.61
2.	Mark Aguirre	Dall	29.49
3.	Kiki Vandeweghe	Denv	29.42
4.	Alex English	Denv	26.43
5.	Bernard King	N.Y.	26.32
6.	George Gervin	S.A.	25.88
7.	Larry Bird	Bost	24.15
8.	Mike Mitchell	S.A.	23.28
9.	Terry Cummings	S.D.	22.89
10.	Purvis Short	G.St	22.82
11.	Moses Malone	Phil	22.66
12.	Julius Erving	Phil	22.43
13.	Rolando Blackman	Dall	22.41
14.	World B. Free	Clev	22.25
15.	Jeff Ruland	Wash	22.20
16.	Eddie A. Johnson	K.C.	21.88
17.	Dominique Wilkins	Atla	21.60
18.	K. Abdul-Jabbar	LA.L	21.46
19.	Isiah Thomas	Detr	21.32
20.	Kelly Tripucka	Detr	21.29

REBOUNDS

OR	PLAYER	TEAM	REB
1.	LaSalle Thompson	K.C.	17.77
2.	Moses Malone	Phil	17.45
3.	Bill Laimbeer	Detr	16.81
4.	Ralph Sampson	Hous	16.27
5.	Buck Williams	N.J.	15.98
6.	Artis Gilmore	S.A.	15.62
7.	Bill Walton	S.D.	15.51
8.	Larry Smith	G.St	15.43
9.	Maurice Lucas	Phoe	15.07
10.	Cliff Robinson	Clev	15.05
11.	Cliff Levingston	Detr	14.98
12.	Alton Lister	Milw	14.81
13.	Jack Sikma	Seat	14.61
14.	Jeff Ruland	Wash	14.36
15.	Robert Parish	Bost	14.35
16.	Rich Kelley	Utah	14.05
17.	David Greenwood	Chic	13.88
18.	Wayne Cooper	Port	13.75
19.	Mark Eaton	Utah	13.35
20.	Dan Roundfield	Atla	13.26

BLOCKS

OR	PLAYER	TEAM	BLK
1.	Mark Eaton	Utah	7.88
2.	Wayne Rollins	Atla	5.66
3.	Roy Hinson	Clev	3.75
4.	LaSalle Thompson	K.C.	3.63
5.	Ralph Sampson	Hous	3.51
6.	Alton Lister	Milw	3.44
7.	Artis Gilmore	S.A.	3.12
8.	Wayne Cooper	Port	3.06
9.	Kurt Nimphius	Dall	3.03
10.	Thurl Bailey	Utah	2.91
11.	Edgar Jones	S.A.	2.90
12.	Larry Nance	Phoe	2.86
13.	Bill Walton	S.D.	2.86
14.	Bobby Jones	Phil	2.81
15.	Darryl Dawkins	N.J.	2.70
16.	James Donaldson	S.D.	2.64
17.	K. Abdul-Jabbar	LA.L	2.62
18.	Julius Erving	Phil	2.49
19.	Kevin McHale	Bost	2.35
20.	Joe Barry Carroll	G.St	2.30

SHOOTING

OR	PLAYER	TEAM	SHT
1.	Calvin Natt	Port	1.139
2.	Artis Gilmore	S.A.	1.137
3.	James Donaldson	S.D.	1.130
4.	Adrian Dantley	Utah	1.128
5.	Kiki Vandeweghe	Denv	1.127
6.	Earvin Johnson	LA.L	1.120
7.	Darryl Dawkins	N.J.	1.115
8.	Bernard King	N.Y.	1.113
9.	K. Abdul-Jabbar	LA.L	1.110
10.	Bill Cartwright	N.Y.	1.103
11.	Kent Benson	Detr	1.099
12.	Larry Nance	Phoe	1.099
13.	Gene Banks	S.A.	1.097
14.	Rolando Blackman	Dall	1.091
15.	James Worthy	LA.L	1.090
16.	Jeff Ruland	Wash	1.089
17.	Fred Roberts	S.A.	1.088
18.	Bob Lanier	Milw	1.087
19.	Kevin McHale	Bost	1.086
20.	Jerry Sichting	Indi	1.085

ASSISTS

OR	PLAYER	TEAM	AST
1.	John Lucas	S.A.	17.88
2.	Johnny Moore	S.A.	16.47
3.	Earvin Johnson	LA.L	16.36
4.	Ennis Whatley	Chic	14.72
5.	Isiah Thomas	Detr	14.59
6.	Norm Nixon	S.D.	14.37
7.	Rickey Green	Utah	12.97
8.	Kelvin Ransey	N.J.	11.97
9.	Rob Williams	Denv	11.58
10.	Gus Williams	Seat	11.50
11.	Larry Drew	K.C.	11.33
12.	Reggie Theus	K.C.	11.28
13.	Allen Leavell	Hous	10.97
14.	Rory Sparrow	N.Y.	10.62
15.	Frank Johnson	Wash	10.13
16.	Brad Davis	Dall	10.10
17.	Darnell Valentine	Port	10.02
18.	Phil Ford	Hous	9.74
19.	Michael Cooper	LA.L	9.69
20.	Ray Williams	N.Y.	9.66

STEALS

OR	PLAYER	TEAM	STL
1.	Darwin Cook	N.J.	4.21
2.	Rickey Green	Utah	3.73
3.	Johnny Moore	S.A.	3.58
4.	Ray Williams	N.Y.	3.49
5.	Maurice Cheeks	Phil	3.29
6.	Isiah Thomas	Detr	3.26
7.	Lafayette Lever	Port	3.22
8.	Gus Williams	Seat	3.22
9.	Glenn Rivers	Atla	3.15
10.	T.R. Dunn	Denv	3.07
11.	Lester Conner	G.St	3.02
12.	Butch Carter	Indi	3.00
13.	Bobby Jones	Phil	2.92
14.	Earvin Johnson	LA.L	2.80
15.	Darnell Valentine	Port	2.71
16.	Gerald Henderson	Bost	2.69
17.	Derek Harper	Dall	2.66
18.	Ennis Whatley	Chic	2.65
19.	Allen Leavell	Hous	2.56
20.	Julius Erving	Phil	2.52

1982-83 NBA STATISTICS

PRODUCTION RATINGS

OR	PLAYER	TEAM	PR
1.	Moses Malone	Phil	30.08
2.	Larry Bird	Bost	30.04
3.	Earvin Johnson	LA.L	28.63
4.	Alex English	Denv	28.30
5.	Terry Cummings	S.D.	26.04
6.	Artis Gilmore	S.A.	25.68
7.	K. Abdul-Jabbar	LA.L	24.63
8.	Robert Parish	Bost	24.31
9.	Kiki Vandeweghe	Denv	24.23
10.	Jack Sikma	Seat	23.79
11.	Joe Barry Carroll	G.St	23.62
12.	Buck Williams	N.J.	23.51
13.	Jeff Ruland	Wash	23.48
14.	Julius Erving	Phil	23.24
15.	Sidney Moncrief	Milw	22.80
16.	Dan Roundfield	Atla	22.78
17.	Clark Kellogg	Indi	22.77
18.	Bill Laimbeer	Detr	22.71
19.	Marques Johnson	Milw	22.59
20.	Larry Nance	Phoe	22.29
21.	Dan Issel	Denv	22.29
22.	Kelly Tripucka	Detr	21.97
23.	Isiah Thomas	Detr	21.68
24.	George Gervin	S.A.	21.63
25.	Mark Aguirre	Dall	20.77
26.	Calvin Natt	Port	20.71
27.	Cliff Robinson	Clev	20.16
28.	Gus Williams	Seat	20.12
29.	Reggie Theus	Chic	20.12
30.	Mychal Thompson	Port	20.11
31.	Larry Drew	K.C.	20.05
32.	Maurice Lucas	Phoe	19.96
33.	Rickey Green	Utah	19.38
34.	Herb Williams	Indi	19.33
35.	Johnny Moore	S.A.	19.13
36.	Gene Banks	S.A.	18.88
37.	Purvis Short	G.St	18.81
38.	Jay Vincent	Dall	18.77
39.	Bernard King	N.Y.	18.62
40.	Greg Ballard	Wash	18.62
41.	Mike Mitchell	S.A.	18.54
42.	Alvan Adams	Phoe	18.30
43.	Bill Cartwright	N.Y.	18.29
44.	Eddie A. Johnson	K.C.	18.10
45.	Wayne Rollins	Atla	18.09
46.	Jim Paxson	Port	17.67
47.	Maurice Cheeks	Phil	17.44
48.	Walter Davis	Phoe	17.39
49.	Darrell Griffith	Utah	17.16
50.	Kevin McHale	Bost	17.04
51.	Dave Corzine	Chic	16.98
52.	Jamaal Wilkes	LA.L	16.96
53.	Vinnie Johnson	Detr	16.79
54.	Brad Davis	Dall	16.75
55.	Mike Woodson	K.C.	16.64
56.	World B.Free	Clev	16.58
57.	Rick Mahorn	Wash	16.54
58.	Albert King	N.J.	16.32
59.	Tom Chambers	S.D.	16.32
60.	Terry Tyler	Detr	16.11
61.	Andrew Toney	Phil	16.09
62.	David Greenwood	Chic	15.86
63.	Dennis Johnson	Phoe	15.69
64.	Dominique Wilkins	Atla	15.63
65.	Ben Poquette	Utah	15.61
66.	Pat Cummings	Dall	15.59
67.	Billy Knight	Indi	15.38
68.	Orlando Woolridge	Chic	15.35
69.	Allen Leavell	Hous	15.23
70.	Michael Brooks	S.D.	15.21
71.	Norm Nixon	LA.L	15.19
72.	Rolando Blackman	Dall	15.19
73.	M.R. Richardson	N.J.	15.14
74.	Ray Williams	K.C.	15.14
75.	Elvin Hayes	Hous	14.74
76.	James Worthy	LA.L	14.71
77.	Lonnie Shelton	Seat	14.62
78.	Mickey Johnson	G.St	14.59
79.	Danny Schayes	Denv	14.35
80.	Caldwell Jones	Hous	14.32
81.	T.R. Dunn	Denv	14.30
82.	Darwin Cook	N.J.	14.30
83.	Kenny Carr	Port	13.89
84.	David Thompson	Seat	13.83
85.	Cedric Maxwell	Bost	13.82
86.	Frank Johnson	Wash	13.63
87.	Otis Birdsong	N.J.	13.56
88.	George L. Johnson	Indi	13.52
89.	Johnny Davis	Atla	13.45
90.	Jeff Wilkins	Utah	13.43
91.	Darryl Dawkins	N.J.	13.35
92.	Eddie Johnson Jr.	Atla	13.30
93.	Junior Bridgeman	Milw	13.14
94.	Lionel Hollins	S.D.	13.07
95.	Bobby Jones	Phil	13.04
96.	Alton Lister	Milw	13.00
97.	Wayne Cooper	Port	12.98
98.	Kurt Rambis	LA.L	12.79
99.	James Bailey	Hous	12.79
100.	Clemon Johnson	Phil	12.72

POSITION DOMINANCE

OR	PLAYER	TEAM	PD
1.	Earvin Johnson	LA.L	1.397
2.	Larry Bird	Bost	1.292
3.	Moses Malone	Phil	1.245
4.	Alex English	Denv	1.245
5.	Sidney Moncrief	Milw	1.211
6.	George Gervin	S.A.	1.149
7.	Terry Cummings	S.D.	1.120
8.	Reggie Theus	Chic	1.068
9.	Kiki Vandeweghe	Denv	1.066
10.	Artis Gilmore	S.A.	1.063
11.	Isiah Thomas	Detr	1.058
12.	Julius Erving	Phil	1.023
13.	K. Abdul-Jabbar	LA.L	1.019
14.	Buck Williams	N.J.	1.011
15.	Jeff Ruland	Wash	1.010
16.	Robert Parish	Bost	1.006
17.	Marques Johnson	Milw	.994
18.	Jack Sikma	Seat	.985
19.	Gus Williams	Seat	.982
20.	Larry Nance	Phoe	.981

MOST VALUABLE PLAYER

OR	PLAYER	TEAM	MVP
1.	Moses Malone	Phil	2.080
2.	Earvin Johnson	LA.L	2.043
3.	Larry Bird	Bost	1.897
4.	Julius Erving	Phil	1.858
5.	Sidney Moncrief	Milw	1.817
6.	George Gervin	S.A.	1.766
7.	Alex English	Denv	1.754
8.	Andrew Toney	Phil	1.689
9.	Maurice Cheeks	Phil	1.686
10.	Artis Gilmore	S.A.	1.680
11.	K. Abdul-Jabbar	LA.L	1.665
12.	Robert Parish	Bost	1.608
13.	Marques Johnson	Milw	1.600
14.	Larry Nance	Phoe	1.596
15.	Kiki Vandeweghe	Denv	1.575
16.	Buck Williams	N.J.	1.568
17.	Johnny Moore	S.A.	1.551
18.	Walter Davis	Phoe	1.538
19.	Jack Sikma	Seat	1.530
20.	Larry Drew	K.C.	1.528

1982-83 POSITION RATINGS

POWER FORWARD

OR	PLAYER	TEAM	PR
1.	Larry Bird	Bost	30.04
2.	Terry Cummings	S.D.	26.04
3.	Buck Williams	N.J.	23.51
4.	Jeff Ruland	Wash	23.48
5.	Dan Roundfield	Atla	22.78
6.	Clark Kellogg	Indi	22.77
7.	Cliff Robinson	Clev	20.16
8.	Maurice Lucas	Phoe	19.96
9.	Kevin McHale	Bost	17.04
10.	Tom Chambers	S.D.	16.32
11.	David Greenwood	Chic	15.86
12.	Ben Poquette	Utah	15.61
13.	Elvin Hayes	Hous	14.74
14.	Lonnie Shelton	Seat	14.62
15.	Kenny Carr	Port	13.89
16.	George L. Johnson	Indi	13.52
17.	Jeff Wilkins	Utah	13.43
18.	Alton Lister	Milw	13.00
19.	Kurt Rambis	LA.L	12.79
20.	James Bailey	Hous	12.79

POINT GUARD

OR	PLAYER	TEAM	PR
1.	Earvin Johnson	LA.L	28.63
2.	Isiah Thomas	Detr	21.68
3.	Gus Williams	Seat	20.12
4.	Larry Drew	K.C.	20.05
5.	Rickey Green	Utah	19.38
6.	Johnny Moore	S.A.	19.13
7.	Maurice Cheeks	Phil	17.44
8.	Brad Davis	Dall	16.75
9.	Allen Leavell	Hous	15.23
10.	Norm Nixon	LA.L	15.19
11.	M.R. Richardson	N.J.	15.14
12.	Darwin Cook	N.J.	14.30
13.	Frank Johnson	Wash	13.63
14.	Johnny Davis	Atla	13.45
15.	Lionel Hollins	S.D.	13.07
16.	Rory Sparrow	N.Y.	12.44
17.	Geoff Huston	Clev	12.44
18.	Jerry Sichting	Indi	11.83
19.	Lafayette Lever	Port	11.53
20.	Kyle Macy	Phoe	11.07

CENTER

OR	PLAYER	TEAM	PR
1.	Moses Malone	Phil	30.08
2.	Artis Gilmore	S.A.	25.68
3.	K. Abdul-Jabbar	LA.L	24.63
4.	Robert Parish	Bost	24.31
5.	Jack Sikma	Seat	23.79
6.	Joe Barry Carroll	G.St	23.62
7.	Bill Laimbeer	Detr	22.71
8.	Dan Issel	Denv	22.29
9.	Mychal Thompson	Port	20.11
10.	Herb Williams	Indi	19.33
11.	Alvan Adams	Phoe	18.30
12.	Bill Cartwright	N.Y.	18.29
13.	Wayne Rollins	Atla	18.09
14.	Dave Corzine	Chic	16.98
15.	Rick Mahorn	Wash	16.54
16.	Pat Cummings	Dall	15.59
17.	Danny Schayes	Denv	14.35
18.	Caldwell Jones	Hous	14.32
19.	Darryl Dawkins	N.J.	13.35
20.	Wayne Cooper	Port	12.98

SMALL FORWARD

OR	PLAYER	TEAM	PR
1.	Alex English	Denv	28.30
2.	Kiki Vandeweghe	Denv	24.23
3.	Julius Erving	Phil	23.24
4.	Marques Johnson	Milw	22.59
5.	Larry Nance	Phoe	22.29
6.	Kelly Tripucka	Detr	21.97
7.	Mark Aguirre	Dall	20.77
8.	Calvin Natt	Port	20.71
9.	Gene Banks	S.A.	18.88
10.	Purvis Short	G.St	18.81
11.	Jay Vincent	Dall	18.77
12.	Bernard King	N.Y.	18.62
13.	Greg Ballard	Wash	18.62
14.	Mike Mitchell	S.A.	18.54
15.	Eddie A. Johnson	K.C.	18.10
16.	Jamaal Wilkes	LA.L	16.96
17.	Albert King	N.J.	16.32
18.	Terry Tyler	Detr	16.11
19.	Dominique Wilkins	Atla	15.63
20.	Orlando Woolridge	Chic	15.35

OFF GUARD

OR	PLAYER	TEAM	PR
1.	Sidney Moncrief	Milw	22.80
2.	George Gervin	S.A.	21.63
3.	Reggie Theus	Chic	20.12
4.	Jim Paxson	Port	17.67
5.	Walter Davis	Phoe	17.39
6.	Darrell Griffith	Utah	17.16
7.	Vinnie Johnson	Detr	16.79
8.	Mike Woodson	K.C.	16.64
9.	World B. Free	Clev	16.58
10.	Andrew Toney	Phil	16.09
11.	Dennis Johnson	Phoe	15.69
12.	Billy Knight	Indi	15.38
13.	Rolando Blackman	Dall	15.19
14.	Ray Williams	K.C.	15.14
15.	T.R. Dunn	Denv	14.30
16.	David Thompson	Seat	13.83
17.	Otis Birdsong	N.J.	13.56
18.	Eddie Johnson Jr.	Atla	13.30
19.	Quinton Dailey	Chic	12.55
20.	Michael Cooper	LA.L	12.27

ROOKIES

OR	PLAYER	TEAM	PR
1.	Terry Cummings	S.D.	26.04
2.	Clark Kellogg	Indi	22.77
3.	Dominique Wilkins	Atla	15.63
4.	James Worthy	LA.L	14.71
5.	Quintin Dailey	Chic	12.55
6.	Rod Higgins	Chic	11.62
7.	Lafayette Lever	Port	11.53
8.	Ed Nealy	K.C.	9.71
9.	Ed Sherod	N.Y.	9.11
10.	Trent Tucker	N.Y.	8.83
11.	Paul Pressey	Milw	8.61
12.	Craig Hodges	S.D.	8.55
13.	Rob Williams	Denv	8.22
14.	Jerry Eaves	Utah	7.96
15.	Terry Teagle	Hous	7.63
16.	Marc Iavaroni	Phil	6.68

1982-83 PERFORMANCE CATEGORIES

SCORING

OR	PLAYER	TEAM	SCR
1.	Alex English	Denv	28.37
2.	Kiki Vandeweghe	Denv	26.66
3.	Kelly Tripucka	Detr	26.48
4.	George Gervin	S.A.	26.19
5.	Moses Malone	Phil	24.46
6.	Mark Aguirre	Dall	24.43
7.	Joe Barry Carroll	G.St	24.14
8.	World B.Free	Clev	23.88
9.	Reggie Theus	Chic	23.82
10.	Terry Cummings	S.D.	23.71
11.	Larry Bird	Bost	23.63
12.	Isiah Thomas	Detr	22.89
13.	Sidney Moncrief	Milw	22.53
14.	Darrell Griffith	Utah	22.19
15.	Bernard King	N.Y.	21.85
16.	K. Abdul-Jabbar	LA.L	21.80
17.	Jim Paxson	Port	21.68
18.	Dan Issel	Denv	21.58
19.	Purvis Short	G.St	21.45
20.	Marques Johnson	Milw	21.42

REBOUNDS

OR	PLAYER	TEAM	REB
1.	Moses Malone	Phil	19.61
2.	Artis Gilmore	S.A.	16.89
3.	Buck Williams	N.J.	16.65
4.	Bill Laimbeer	Detr	16.60
5.	Robert Parish	Bost	16.14
6.	Jack Sikma	Seat	16.06
7,	Cliff Robinson	Clev	15.80
8.	David Greenwood	Chic	15.59
9.	Dan Roundfield	Atla	15.03
10.	Clark Kellogg	Indi	14.95
11.	Maurice Lucas	Phoe	14.83
12.	Jeff Ruland	Wash	14.61
13.	Alton Lister	Milw	14.46
14.	Wayne Rollins	Atla	14.43
15.	Rich Kelley	Utah	14.42
16.	Ed Nealy	K.C.	14.17
17.	Kurt Rambis	LA.L	14.11
18.	Terry Cummings	S.D.	14.11
19.	Larry Bird	Bost	14.00
20.	Wayne Cooper	Port	13.97

BLOCKS

OR	PLAYER	TEAM	BLK
1.	Wayne Rollins	Atla	6.66
2.	Harvey Catchings	Milw	4.57
3.	Alton Lister	Milw	4.51
4.	Kevin McHale	Bost	3.93
5.	Larry Nance	Phoe	3.57
6.	Darryl Dawkins	N.J.	3.49
7.	Artis Gilmore	S.A.	3.29
8.	Herb Williams	Indi	3.27
9.	K. Abdul-Jabbar	LA.L	3.19
10.	Edgar Jones	S.A.	3.13
11.	Wayne Cooper	Port	3.11
12.	Terry Tyler	Detr	3.02
13.	Robert Parish	Bost	2.89
14.	Sam Williams	G.St	2.79
15.	James Donaldson	Seat	2.71
16.	Julius Erving	Phil	2.60
17.	Steve Johnson	K.C.	2.58
18.	Moses Malone	Phil	2.58
19.	Caldwell Jones	Hous	2.58
20.	Bobby Jones	Phil	2.50

SHOOTING

OR	PLAYER	TEAM	SHT
1.	Artis Gilmore	S.A.	1.157
2.	Brad Davis	Dall	1.152
3.	K. Abdul-Jabbar	LA.L	1.135
4.	Kiki Vandeweghe	Denv	1.121
5.	Darryl Dawkins	N.J.	1.105
6.	James Donaldson	Seat	1.090
7.	Kyle Macy	Phoe	1.088
8.	Earvin Johnson	LA.L	1.087
9.	James Worthy	LA.L	1.087
10.	Calvin Natt	Port	1.079
11.	Bobby Jones	Phil	1.078
12.	Bill Cartwright	N.Y.	1.077
13.	Steve Johnson	K.C.	1.077
14.	Kurt Rambis	LA.L	1.074
15.	Michael Cooper	LA.L	1.073
16.	Ed Nealy	K.C.	1.073
17.	Sidney Moncrief	Milw	1.067
18.	Billy Knight	Indi	1.066
19.	Maurice Cheeks	Phil	1.066
20.	Gene Banks	S.A.	1.062

ASSISTS

OR	PLAYER	TEAM	AST
1.	Johnny Moore	S.A.	14.16
2.	Earvin Johnson	LA.L	13.69
3.	Mike Dunleavy	S.A.	12.96
4.	Ray Williams	K.C.	12.59
5.	Rickey Green	Utah	12.02
6.	Rob Williams	Denv	12.01
7.	Brad Davis	Dall	11.67
8.	Frank Johnson	Wash	11.34
9.	Gus Williams	Seat	11.18
10.	Ronnie Lester	Chic	11.09
11.	Larry Drew	K.C.	10.88
12.	Nate Archibald	Bost	10.84
13.	Paul Westphal	N.Y.	10.65
14.	Maurice Cheeks	Phil	10.57
15.	Johnny Davis	Atla	10.32
16.	Lorenzo Romar	G.St	10.25
17.	Lafayette Lever	Port	10.12
18.	Norm Nixon	LA.L	10.02
19.	M.R. Richardson	N.J.	9.99
20.	Isiah Thomas	Detr	9.84

STEALS

OR	PLAYER	TEAM	STL
1.	M.R. Richardson	N.J.	4.21
2.	Rickey Green	Utah	3.79
3.	Johnny Moore	S.A.	3.65
4.	Lafayette Lever	Port	3.64
5.	Maurice Cheeks	Phil	3.58
6.	Darwin Cook	N.J.	3.55
7.	Quinn Buckner	Bost	3.31
8.	Gus Williams	Seat	3.16
9.	Paul Pressey	Milw	3.11
10.	Isiah Thomas	Detr	3.09
11.	Allen Leavell	Hous	3.04
12.	Rob Williams	Denv	2.96
13.	Gerald Henderson	Bost	2.94
14.	Earvin Johnson	LA.L	2.91
15.	Lionel Hollins	S.D.	2.89
16.	Ed Sherod	N.Y.	2.84
17.	Kurt Rambis	LA.L	2.79
18.	Mike Woodson	K.C.	2.71
19.	T.R. Dunn	Denv	2.67
20.	Ray Williams	K.C.	2.65

1981-82
NBA STATISTICS

PRODUCTION RATINGS

OR	PLAYER	TEAM	PR
1.	Moses Malone	Hous	33.12
2.	Earvin Johnson	LA.L	29.65
3.	Larry Bird	Bost	29.16
4.	Adrian Dantley	Utah	27.81
5.	Alex English	Denv	27.44
6.	K. Abdul-Jabbar	LA.L	27.16
7.	Jack Sikma	Seat	27.01
8.	Julius Erving	Phil	26.69
9.	Artis Gilmore	Chic	25.76
10.	Mychal Thompson	Port	25.63
11.	George Gervin	S.A.	24.82
12.	Robert Parish	Bost	24.58
13.	Dan Issel	Denv	23.43
14.	Dan Roundfield	Atla	23.20
15.	Sidney Moncrief	Milw	22.96
16.	Buck Williams	N.J.	21.94
17.	Gus Williams	Seat	21.80
18.	Bernard King	G.St	21.57
19.	Maurice Lucas	N.Y.	21.48
20.	M. R. Richardson	N.Y.	21.39
21.	Kiki Vandeweghe	Denv	21.32
22.	Greg Ballard	Wash	21.20
23.	Calvin Natt	Port	20.93
24.	Truck Robinson	Phoe	20.50
25.	David Greenwood	Chic	20.06
26.	Alvan Adams	Phoe	19.78
27.	Ray Williams	N.J.	19.72
28.	Cliff Robinson	Clev	19.31
29.	Jay Vincent	Dall	19.07
30.	Dennis Johnson	Phoe	19.00
31.	Kelly Tripucka	Detr	18.77
32.	Maurice Cheeks	Phil	18.75
33.	Jerome Whitehead	S.D.	18.56
34.	Rickey Green	Utah	18.44
35.	Mike Mitchell	S.A.	18.36
36.	Joe Barry Carroll	G.St	18.34
37.	Jeff Ruland	Wash	18.32
38.	Michael Brooks	S.D.	18.26
39.	Norm Nixon	LA.L	18.05
40.	Marques Johnson	Milw	18.03
41.	Bobby Jones	Phil	17.79
42.	Jamaal Wilkes	LA.L	17.76
43.	Kent Benson	Detr	17.71
44.	James Edwards	Clev	17.65
45.	Elvin Hayes	Hous	17.61
46.	World B. Free	G.St	17.40
47.	Johnny Moore	S.A.	17.22
48.	Rick Mahorn	Wash	17.19
49.	Cedric Maxwell	Bost	17.17
50.	Reggie Theus	Chic	17.10
51.	Jim Paxson	Port	16.87
52.	Robert Reid	Hous	16.77
53.	Kevin McHale	Bost	16.72
54.	John Long	Detr	16.64
55.	Kyle Macy	Phoe	16.57
56.	Lonnie Shelton	Seat	16.27
57.	Tom Chambers	S.D.	16.14
58.	Mark Olberding	S.A.	16.06
59.	Bob Lanier	Milw	15.99
60.	Larry Smith	G.St	15.88
61.	Isiah Thomas	Detr	15.63
62.	Herb Williams	Indi	15.50
63.	Bill Cartwright	N.Y.	15.39
64.	Kelvin Ransey	Port	15.37
65.	Eddie Johnson Jr	Atla	15.37
66.	Dave Corzine	S.A.	15.18
67.	Brad Davis	Dall	14.99
68.	Mickey Johnson	Milw	14.87
69.	Caldwell Jones	Phil	14.86
70.	Darrell Griffith	Utah	14.85
71.	John Drew	Atla	14.84
72.	Brian Winters	Milw	14.80
73.	Reggie King	K.C.	14.60
74.	Terry Tyler	Detr	14.55
75.	Mike Woodson	K.C.	14.47
76.	Wayne Rollins	Atla	14.42
77.	Steve Johnson	K.C.	14.31
78.	Sly Williams	N.Y.	14.30
79.	Quinn Buckner	Milw	14.24
80.	Nate Archibald	Bost	14.24
81.	Ron Brewer	Clev	14.15
82.	T.R. Dunn	Denv	14.10
83.	Michael Cooper	LA.L	13.76
84.	Johnny Davis	Indi	13.74
85.	Don Buse	Indi	13.74
86.	Bill Laimbeer	Detr	13.73
87.	Clemon Johnson	Indi	13.72
88.	Geoff Huston	Clev	13.62
89.	Kenny Carr	Detr	13.49
90.	Allen Leavell	Hous	13.39
91.	Reggie Johnson	K.C.	13.17
92.	Purvis Short	G.St	13.16
93.	Andrew Toney	Phil	13.13
94.	Rory Sparrow	Atla	13.07
95.	Ronnie Lester	Chic	13.04
96.	Wayne Cooper	Dall	12.80
97.	Scott Wedman	Clev	12.76
98.	Dwight Jones	Chic	12.76
99.	Campy Russell	N.Y.	12.64
100.	Spencer Haywood	Wash	12.61

POSITION DOMINANCE

OR	PLAYER	TEAM	PD
1.	Earvin Johnson	LA.L	1.424
2.	Larry Bird	Bost	1.314
3.	Moses Malone	Hous	1.313
4.	George Gervin	S.A.	1.268
5.	Adrian Dantley	Utah	1.229
6.	Alex English	Denv	1.213
7.	Julius Erving	Phil	1.180
8.	Sidney Moncrief	Milw	1.173
9.	K. Abdul-Jabbar	LA.L	1.077
10.	Jack Sikma	Seat	1.071
11.	Gus Williams	Seat	1.047
12.	Dan Roundfield	Atla	1.046
13.	M.R. Richardson	N.Y.	1.027
14.	Artis Gilmore	Chic	1.021
15.	Mychal Thompson	Port	1.016
16.	Ray Williams	N.J.	1.007
17.	Buck Williams	N.J.	.989
18.	Robert Parish	Bost	.975
19.	Dennis Johnson	Phoe	.971
20.	Maurice Lucas	N.Y.	.968

MOST VALUABLE PLAYER

OR	PLAYER	TEAM	MVP
1.	Earvin Johnson	LA.L	2.174
2.	Larry Bird	Bost	2.026
3.	Moses Malone	Hous	1.851
4.	Julius Erving	Phil	1.828
5.	K. Abdul-Jabbar	LA.L	1.827
6.	George Gervin	S.A.	1.818
7.	Sidney Moncrief	Milw	1.751
8.	Alex English	Denv	1.751
9.	Robert Parish	Bost	1.689
10.	Jack Sikma	Seat	1.646
11.	Gus Williams	Seat	1.622
12.	Norm Nixon	LA.L	1.617
13.	Maurice Cheeks	Phil	1.549
14.	Adrian Dantley	Utah	1.534
15.	Mychal Thompson	Port	1.528
16.	Dan Roundfield	Atla	1.523
17.	Ray Williams	N.J.	1.507
18.	Bernard King	G.St	1.502
19.	Buck Williams	N.J.	1.489
20.	Cedric Maxwell	Bost	1.486

1981-82 POSITION RATINGS

POWER FORWARD

OR	PLAYER	TEAM	PR
1.	Larry Bird	Bost	29.16
2.	Dan Roundfield	Atla	23.20
3.	Buck Williams	N.J.	21.94
4.	Maurice Lucas	N.Y.	21.48
5.	Truck Robinson	Phoe	20.50
6.	David Greenwood	Chic	20.06
7.	Cliff Robinson	Clev	19.31
8.	Jeff Ruland	Wash	18.32
9.	Elvin Hayes	Hous	17.61
10.	Kevin McHale	Bost	16.72
11.	Lonnie Shelton	Seat	16.27
12.	Tom Chambers	S.D.	16.14
13.	Mark Olberding	S.A.	16.06
14.	Larry Smith	G.St	15.88
15.	Herb Williams	Indi	15.50
16.	Reggie King	K.C.	14.60
17.	Kenny Carr	Detr	13.49
18.	Reggie Johnson	K.C.	13.17
19.	Dwight Jones	Chic	12.76
20.	Spencer Haywood	Wash	12.61

POINT GUARD

OR	PLAYER	TEAM	PR
1.	Earvin Johnson	LA.L	29.65
2.	Gus Williams	Seat	21.80
3.	M.R. Richardson	N.Y.	21.39
4.	Maurice Cheeks	Phil	18.75
5.	Rickey Green	Utah	18.44
6.	Norm Nixon	LA.L	18.05
7.	Johnny Moore	S.A.	17.22
8.	Kyle Macy	Phoe	16.57
9.	Isiah Thomas	Detr	15.63
10.	Kelvin Ransey	Port	15.37
11.	Brad Davis	Dall	14.99
12.	Quinn Buckner	Milw	14.24
13.	Nate Archibald	Bost	14.24
14.	Johnny Davis	Indi	13.74
15.	Don Buse	Indi	13.74
16.	Geoff Huston	Clev	13.62
17.	Allen Leavell	Hous	13.39
18.	Rory Sparrow	Atla	13.07
19.	Ronnie Lester	Chic	13.04
20.	Billy McKinney	Denv	11.88

CENTER

OR	PLAYER	TEAM	PR
1.	Moses Malone	Hous	33.12
2.	K. Abdul-Jabbar	LA.L	27.16
3.	Jack Sikma	Seat	27.01
4.	Artis Gilmore	Chic	25.76
5.	Mychal Thompson	Port	25.63
6.	Robert Parish	Bost	24.58
7.	Dan Issel	Denv	23.43
8.	Alvan Adams	Phoe	19.78
9.	Jerome Whitehead	S.D.	18.56
10.	Joe Barry Carroll	G.St	18.34
11.	Kent Benson	Detr	17.71
12.	James Edwards	Clev	17.65
13.	Rick Mahorn	Wash	17.19
14.	Bob Lanier	Milw	15.99
15.	Bill Cartwright	N.Y.	15.39
16.	Dave Corzine	S.A.	15.18
17.	Caldwell Jones	Phil	14.86
18.	Wayne Rollins	Atla	14.42
19.	Steve Johnson	K.C.	14.31
20.	Bill Laimbeer	Detr	13.73

SMALL FORWARD

OR	PLAYER	TEAM	PR
1.	Adrian Dantley	Utah	27.81
2.	Alex English	Denv	27.44
3.	Julius Erving	Phil	26.69
4.	Bernard King	G.St	21.57
5.	Kiki Vandeweghe	Denv	21.32
6.	Greg Ballard	Wash	21.20
7.	Calvin Natt	Port	20.93
8.	Jay Vincent	Dall	19.07
9.	Kelly Tripucka	Detr	18.77
10.	Mike Mitchell	S.A.	18.36
11.	Michael Brooks	S.D.	18.26
12.	Marques Johnson	Milw	18.03
13.	Bobby Jones	Phil	17.79
14.	Jamaal Wilkes	LA.L	17.76
15.	Cedric Maxwell	Bost	17.17
16.	Robert Reid	Hous	16.77
17.	Mickey Johnson	Milw	14.87
18.	John Drew	Atla	14.84
19.	Terry Tyler	Detr	14.55
20.	Sly Williams	N.Y.	14.30

OFF GUARD

OR	PLAYER	TEAM	PR
1.	George Gervin	S.A.	24.82
2.	Sidney Moncrief	Milw	22.96
3.	Ray Williams	N.J.	19.72
4.	Dennis Johnson	Phoe	19.00
5.	World B. Free	G.St	17.40
6.	Reggie Theus	Chic	17.10
7.	Jim Paxson	Port	16.87
8.	John Long	Detr	16.64
9.	Eddie Johnson Jr.	Atla	15.37
10.	Darrell Griffith	Utah	14.85
11.	Brian Winters	Milw	14.80
12.	Mike Woodson	K.C.	14.47
13.	Ron Brewer	Clev	14.15
14.	T.R. Dunn	Denv	14.10
15.	Michael Cooper	LA.L	13.76
16.	Andrew Toney	Phil	13.13
17.	Bob Wilkerson	Clev	11.49
18.	David Thompson	Denv	11.44
19.	Rolando Blackman	Dall	11.38
20.	Billy Knight	Indi	10.84

ROOKIES

OR	PLAYER	TEAM	PR
1.	Buck Williams	N.J.	21.94
2.	Jay Vincent	Dall	19.07
3.	Kelly Tripucka	Detr	18.77
4.	Jeff Ruland	Wash	18.32
5.	Tom Chambers	S.D.	16.14
6.	Isiah Thomas	Detr	15.63
7.	Herb Williams	Indi	15.50
8.	Steve Johnson	K.C.	14.31
9.	Rolando Blackman	Dall	11.38
10.	Gene Banks	S.A.	11.04
11.	Albert King	N.J.	10.96
12.	Danny Schayes	Utah	10.57
13.	Frank Johnson	Wash	9.68
14.	Eddie A. Johnson	K.C.	9.32
15.	Elston Turner	Dall	8.93

1981-82 PERFORMANCE CATEGORIES

SCORING

OR	PLAYER	TEAM	SCR
1.	George Gervin	S.A.	32.29
2.	Moses Malone	Hous	31.11
3.	Adrian Dantley	Utah	30.33
4.	Alex English	Denv	25.39
5.	Julius Erving	Phil	24.37
6.	K. Abdul-Jabbar	LA.L	23.92
7.	Gus Williams	Seat	23.44
8.	Bernard King	G.St	23.20
9.	World B. Free	G.St	22.94
10.	Larry Bird	Bost	22.87
11.	Dan Issel	Denv	22.86
12.	John Long	Detr	21.94
13.	Kelly Tripucka	Detr	21.61
14.	Kiki Vandeweghe	Denv	21.46
15.	Jay Vincent	Dall	21.38
16.	Jamaal Wilkes	LA.L	21.15
17.	Mychal Thompson	Port	20.78
18.	Mike Mitchell	S.A.	20.55
19.	Ray Williams	N.J.	20.41
20.	Robert Parish	Bost	19.87

REBOUNDS

OR	PLAYER	TEAM	REB
1.	Larry Smith	G.St	17.63
2.	Buck Williams	N.J.	17.08
3.	Moses Malone	Hous	16.78
4.	Jeff Ruland	Wash	16.52
5.	Robert Parish	Bost	16.40
6.	Jack Sikma	Seat	16.34
7.	Maurice Lucas	N.Y.	16.23
8.	Bill Laimbeer	Detr	16.19
9.	Dan Roundfield	Atla	15.61
10.	Wayne Rollins	Atla	14.53
11.	Wayne Cooper	Dall	14.52
12.	Jerome Whitehead	S.D.	14.40
13.	Artis Gilmore	Chic	14.33
14.	Mychal Thompson	Port	14.13
15.	Caldwell Jones	Phil	13.89
16.	Clemon Johnson	Indi	13.85
17.	George Johnson	S.A.	13.81
18.	Dave Corzine	S.A.	13.79
19.	James Donaldson	Seat	13.75
20.	Larry Bird	Bost	13.74

BLOCKS

OR	PLAYER	TEAM	BLK
1.	George Johnson	S.A.	7.12
2.	Wayne Rollins	Atla	5.33
3.	Harvey Catchings	Milw	4.04
4.	James Donaldson	Seat	3.90
5.	Terry Tyler	Detr	3.86
6.	Kevin McHale	Bost	3.81
7.	Artis Gilmore	Chic	3.79
8.	Herb Williams	Indi	3.75
9.	K. Abdul-Jabbar	LA.L	3.71
10.	Robert Parish	Bost	3.64
11.	Caldwell Jones	Phil	2.87
12.	Wayne Cooper	Dall	2.80
13.	Dave Corzine	S.A.	2.76
14.	Mike Harper	Port	2.75
15.	Clemon Johnson	Indi	2.72
16.	James Bailey	N.J.	2.71
17.	Rick Mahorn	Wash	2.49
18.	Bobby Jones	Phil	2.46
19.	Steve Johnson	K.C.	2.45
20.	Julius Erving	Phil	2.43

SHOOTING

OR	PLAYER	TEAM	SHT
1.	Artis Gilmore	Chic	1.194
2.	Kiki Vandeweghe	Denv	1.127
3.	Adrian Dantley	Utah	1.112
4.	Calvin Natt	Port	1.107
5.	Bobby Jones	Phil	1.105
6.	Alex English	Denv	1.105
7.	K. Abdul-Jabbar	LA.L	1.103
8.	Steve Johnson	K.C.	1.101
9.	Jerome Whitehead	S.D.	1.093
10.	Sly Williams	N.Y.	1.092
11.	Kyle Macy	Phoe	1.089
12.	Bill Cartwright	N.Y.	1.089
13.	Bob Lanier	Milw	1.088
14.	Bernard King	G.St	1.080
15.	James Donaldson	Seat	1.079
16.	Jeff Ruland	Wash	1.077
17.	Dan Issel	Denv	1.076
18.	Julius Erving	Phil	1.073
19.	Wayne Rollins	Atla	1.072
20.	Bob Gross	Port	1.063

ASSISTS

OR	PLAYER	TEAM	AST
1.	Johnny Moore	S.A.	15.94
2.	John Lucas	Wash	13.63
3.	Mike Bratz	S.A.	13.01
4.	Maurice Cheeks	Phil	12.82
5.	Nate Archibald	Bost	11.98
6.	Earvin Johnson	LA.L	11.92
7.	Geoff Huston	Clev	11.76
8.	Kenny Higgs	Denv	11.18
9.	Isiah Thomas	Detr	11.15
10.	Phil Ford	K.C.	11.09
11.	Kelvin Ransey	Port	11.02
12.	Rickey Green	Utah	10.72
13.	Allan Bristow	Dall	10.57
14.	Norm Nixon	LA.L	10.35
15.	Foots Walker	N.J.	10.27
16.	Allen Leavell	Hous	10.20
17.	Larry Drew	K.C.	10.19
18.	Brad Davis	Dall	9.35
19.	Gus Williams	Seat	9.16
20.	M.R. Richardson	N.Y.	9.02

STEALS

OR	PLAYER	TEAM	STL
1.	Maurice Cheeks	Phil	4.02
2.	Quinn Buckner	Milw	3.87
3.	Ray Williams	N.J.	3.50
4.	Johnny Moore	S.A.	3.41
5.	M.R. Richardson	N.Y.	3.36
6.	Darwin Cook	N.J.	3.35
7.	Allen Leavell	Hous	3.35
8.	Earvin Johnson	LA.L	3.34
9.	Mike Gale	G.St	3.24
10.	Rickey Green	Utah	3.15
11.	Don Buse	Indi	3.11
12.	Foots Walker	N.J.	3.10
13.	Isiah Thomas	Detr	2.96
14.	Mike Woodson	K.C.	2.92
15.	Gus Williams	Seat	2.87
16.	Julius Erving	Phil	2.77
17.	Larry Drew	K.C.	2.68
18.	Don Collins	Wash	2.66
19.	Michael Cooper	LA.L	2.62
20.	Bob Gross	Port	2.61

1980-81
NBA STATISTICS

PRODUCTION RATINGS

OR	PLAYER	TEAM	PR
1.	Moses Malone	Hous	31.67
2.	K. Abdul-Jabbar	LA.L	30.95
3.	Adrian Dantley	Utah	28.23
4.	Julius Erving	Phil	27.38
5.	Larry Bird	Bost	26.74
6.	Artis Gilmore	Chic	25.02
7.	Alex English	Denv	24.37
8.	Robert Parish	Bost	23.55
9.	Swen Nater	S.D.	23.13
10.	Marques Johnson	Milw	22.92
11.	Dan Roundfield	Atla	22.84
12.	Dan Issel	Denv	22.73
13.	Bernard King	G.St	22.31
14.	George Gervin	S.A.	22.10
15.	Jack Sikma	Seat	22.09
16.	M. R. Richardson	N.Y.	21.81
17.	Bill Cartwright	N.Y.	20.63
18.	Jamaal Wilkes	LA.L	20.37
19.	Mychal Thompson	Port	20.35
20.	Otis Birdsong	K.C.	20.31
21.	Alvan Adams	Phoe	19.76
22.	Truck Robinson	Phoe	19.68
23.	Robert Reid	Hous	19.61
24.	David Thompson	Denv	19.55
25.	Kenny Carr	Clev	19.48
26.	Reggie King	K.C.	19.48
27.	Joe Barry Carroll	G.St	19.37
28.	Mike Mitchell	Clev	19.17
29.	Ray Williams	N.Y.	19.13
30.	Cedric Maxwell	Bost	18.99
31.	David Greenwood	Chic	18.89
32.	World B. Free	G.St	18.83
33.	Norm Nixon	LA.L	18.48
34.	Elvin Hayes	Wash	18.47
35.	Kermit Washington	Port	18.36
36.	Phil Ford	K.C.	18.21
37.	Reggie Theus	Chic	18.12
38.	Cliff Robinson	N.J.	17.90
39.	James Edwards	Indi	17.89
40.	Larry Smith	G.St	17.62
41.	Eddie Johnson Jr.	Atla	17.56
42.	Wes Unseld	Wash	17.56
43.	Maurice Lucas	N.J.	17.54
44.	Greg Ballard	Wash	17.30
45.	Bob Lanier	Milw	17.30
46.	Mike Newlin	N.J.	17.24
47.	Terry Tyler	Detr	17.21
48.	Dennis Johnson	Phoe	17.10
49.	Darryl Dawkins	Phil	16.97
50.	Sidney Moncrief	Milw	16.96
51.	Billy Knight	Indi	16.79
52.	Scott Wedman	K.C.	16.79
53.	Bobby Jones	Phil	16.79
54.	John Drew	Atla	16.66
55.	Kent Benson	Detr	16.63
56.	Kevin Porter	Wash	16.59
57.	Ben Poquette	Utah	16.59
58.	Jim Paxson	Port	16.57
59.	Bill Laimbeer	Clev	16.46
60.	Maurice Cheeks	Phil	16.26
61.	Steve Hawes	Atla	16.24
62.	Walter Davis	Phoe	15.92
63.	Nate Archibald	Bost	15.84
64.	James Bailey	Seat	15.83
65.	Brad Davis	Dall	15.73
66.	Tom LaGarde	Dall	15.50
67.	James Silas	S.A.	15.45
68.	Purvis Short	G.St	15.42
69.	Sly Williams	N.Y.	15.40
70.	Junior Bridgeman	Milw	15.40
71.	Mark Olberding	S.A.	15.39
72.	Sam Lacey	K.C.	15.35
73.	Mike Bantom	Indi	15.30
74.	Mickey Johnson	Milw	15.27
75.	Caldwell Jones	Phil	15.14
76.	Vinnie Johnson	Seat	15.06
77.	Jim Chones	LA.L	14.98
78.	Johnny Davis	Indi	14.92
79.	Phil Hubbard	Detr	14.86
80.	Phil Smith	S.D.	14.72
81.	Kevin Grevey	Wash	14.67
82.	Quinn Buckner	Milw	14.62
83.	Michael Brooks	S.D.	14.57
84.	Dave Corzine	S.A.	14.50
85.	Mike Gminski	N.J.	14.46
86.	Campy Russell	N.Y.	14.37
87.	Darrell Griffith	Utah	14.31
88.	Kelvin Ransey	Port	14.25
89.	Jim Spanarkel	Dall	14.24
90.	Mike O'Koren	N.J.	13.97
91.	Calvin Natt	Port	13.92
92.	Brian Taylor	S.D.	13.89
93.	George McGinnis	Indi	13.75
94.	Michael Cooper	LA.L	13.74
95.	Bill Robinzine	Dall	13.51
96.	George T. Johnson	S.A.	13.48
97.	Mitch Kupchak	Wash	13.43
98.	Calvin Murphy	Hous	13.26
99.	John Long	Detr	13.10
100.	Fred Brown	Seat	13.06

POSITION DOMINANCE

OR	PLAYER	TEAM	PD
1.	Larry Bird	Bost	1.297
2.	M.R. Richardson	N.Y.	1.263
3.	Moses Malone	Phil	1.237
4.	K. Abdul-Jabbar	LA.L	1.209
5.	Adrian Dantley	Utah	1.209
6.	George Gervin	S.A.	1.183
7.	Julius Erving	Phil	1.172
8.	Dan Roundfield	Atla	1.108
9.	Otis Birdsong	K.C.	1.087
10.	Norm Nixon	LA.L	1.070
11.	Phil Ford	K.C.	1.055
12.	David Thompson	Denv	1.046
13.	Alex English	Denv	1.043
14.	Ray Williams	N.Y.	1.024
15.	World B. Free	G.St	1.008
16.	Dennis Johnson	Phoe	.990
17.	Marques Johnson	Milw	.981
18.	Artis Gilmore	Chic	.977
19.	Reggie Theus	Chic	.970
20.	Kevin Porter	Wash	.961

MOST VALUABLE PLAYER

OR	PLAYER	TEAM	MVP
1.	Larry Bird	Bost	2.034
2.	Julius Erving	Phil	1.857
3.	K. Abdul-Jabbar	LA.L	1.835
4.	M.R. Richardson	N.Y.	1.831
5.	George Gervin	S.A.	1.775
6.	Moses Malone	Phil	1.761
7.	Norm Nixon	LA.L	1.696
8.	Cedric Maxwell	Bost	1.658
9.	Robert Parish	Bost	1.657
10.	Nate Archibald	Bost	1.654
11.	Marques Johnson	Milw	1.651
12.	Dennis Johnson	Phoe	1.631
13.	Maurice Cheeks	Phil	1.627
14.	Truck Robinson	Phoe	1.596
15.	Ray Williams	N.Y.	1.592
16.	Sidney Moncrief	Milw	1.578
17.	Otis Birdsong	K.C.	1.550
18.	Adrian Dantley	Utah	1.550
19.	Phil Ford	K.C.	1.535
20.	Quinn Buckner	Milw	1.517

1980-81 POSITION RATINGS

POWER FORWARD

OR	PLAYER	TEAM	PR
1.	Larry Bird	Bost	26.74
2.	Dan Roundfield	Atla	22.84
3.	Truck Robinson	Phoe	19.68
4.	Kenny Carr	Clev	19.48
5.	Reggie King	K.C.	19.48
6.	David Greenwood	Chic	18.89
7.	Elvin Hayes	Wash	18.47
8.	Kermit Washington	Port	18.36
9.	Cliff Robinson	N.J.	17.90
10.	Larry Smith	G.St	17.62
11.	Maurice Lucas	N.J.	17.54
12.	Steve Hawes	Atla	16.24
13.	James Bailey	Seat	15.83
14.	Mark Olberding	S.A.	15.39
15.	Mike Bantom	Indi	15.30
16.	Jim Chones	LA.L	14.98
17.	George McGinnis	Indi	13.75
18.	Bill Robinzine	Dall	13.51
19.	Mitch Kupchak	Wash	13.43
20.	Joe Bryant	S.D.	12.79

POINT GUARD

OR	PLAYER	TEAM	PR
1.	M.R. Richardson	N.Y.	21.81
2.	Norm Nixon	LA.L	18.48
3.	Phil Ford	K.C.	18.21
4.	Dennis Johnson	Phoe	17.10
5.	Kevin Porter	Wash	16.59
6.	Maurice Cheeks	Phil	16.26
7.	Nate Archibald	Bost	15.84
8.	Brad Davis	Dall	15.73
9.	James Silas	S.A.	15.45
10.	Vinnie Johnson	Seat	15.06
11.	Johnny Davis	Indi	14.92
12.	Quinn Buckner	Milw	14.62
13.	Kelvin Ransey	Port	14.25
14.	Brian Taylor	S.D.	13.89
15.	Wes Matthews	Atla	11.97
16.	Darwin Cook	N.J.	11.78
17.	Geoff Huston	Clev	11.70
18.	Billy McKinney	Denv	11.55
19.	Mike Bratz	Clev	11.50
20.	John Lucas	G.St	11.38

CENTER

OR	PLAYER	TEAM	PR
1.	Moses Malone	Hous	31.67
2.	K. Abdul-Jabbar	LA.L	30.95
3.	Artis Gilmore	Chic	25.02
4.	Robert Parish	Bost	23.55
5.	Swen Nater	S.D.	23.13
6.	Dan Issel	Denv	22.73
7.	Jack Sikma	Seat	22.09
8.	Bill Cartwright	N.Y.	20.63
9.	Mychal Thompson	Port	20.35
10.	Alvan Adams	Phoe	19.76
11.	Joe Barry Carroll	G.St	19.37
12.	James Edwards	Indi	17.89
13.	Wes Unseld	Wash	17.56
14.	Bob Lanier	Milw	17.30
15.	Darryl Dawkins	Phil	16.97
16.	Kent Benson	Detr	16.63
17.	Ben Poquette	Utah	16.59
18.	Bill Laimbeer	Clev	16.46
19.	Tom LaGarde	Dall	15.50
20.	Sam Lacey	K.C.	15.35

SMALL FORWARD

OR	PLAYER	TEAM	PR
1.	Adrian Dantley	Utah	28.23
2.	Julius Erving	Phil	27.38
3.	Alex English	Denv	24.37
4.	Marques Johnson	Milw	22.92
5.	Bernard King	G.St	22.31
6.	Jamaal Wilkes	LA.L	20.37
7.	Robert Reid	Hous	19.61
8.	Mike Mitchell	Clev	19.17
9.	Cedric Maxwell	Bost	18.99
10.	Greg Ballard	Wash	17.30
11.	Terry Tyler	Detr	17.21
12.	Scott Wedman	K.C.	16.79
13.	Bobby Jones	Phil	16.79
14.	John Drew	Atla	16.66
15.	Sly Williams	N.Y.	15.40
16.	Junior Bridgeman	Milw	15.40
17.	Mickey Johnson	Milw	15.27
18.	Phil Hubbard	Detr	14.86
19.	Michael Brooks	S.D.	14.57
20.	Campy Russell	N.Y.	14.37

OFF GUARD

OR	PLAYER	TEAM	PR
1.	George Gervin	S.A.	22.10
2.	Otis Birdsong	K.C.	20.31
3.	David Thompson	Denv	19.55
4.	Ray Williams	N.Y.	19.13
5.	World B. Free	G.St	18.83
6.	Reggie Theus	Chic	18.12
7.	Eddie Johnson Jr.	Atla	17.56
8.	Mike Newlin	N.J.	17.24
9.	Sidney Moncrief	Milw	16.96
10.	Billy Knight	Indi	16.79
11.	Jim Paxson	Port	16.57
12.	Walter Davis	Phoe	15.92
13.	Purvis Short	G.St	15.42
14.	Phil Smith	S.D.	14.72
15.	Kevin Grevey	Wash	14.67
16.	Darrell Griffith	Utah	14.31
17.	Michael Cooper	LA.L	13.74
18.	Calvin Murphy	Hous	13.26
19.	John Long	Detr	13.10
20.	Fred Brown	Seat	13.06

ROOKIES

OR	PLAYER	TEAM	PR
1.	Joe Barry Carroll	G.St	19.37
2.	Larry Smith	G.St	17.62
3.	Bill Laimbeer	Clev	16.46
4.	Michael Brooks	S.D.	14.57
5.	Mike Gminski	N.J.	14.46
6.	Darrell Griffith	Utah	14.31
7.	Kelvin Ransey	Port	14.25
8.	Mike O'Koren	N.J.	13.97
9.	Wes Matthews	Atla	11.97
10.	Darwin Cook	N.J.	11.78
11.	Kevin McHale	Bost	11.44
12.	Louis Orr	Indi	11.09
13.	Cedric Hordges	Denv	11.04
14.	Don Collins	Wash	10.27
15.	Andrew Toney	Phil	10.21
16.	Reggie Johnson	S.A.	10.13
17.	Johnny Moore	S.A.	10.04
18.	Lowes Moore	N.J.	8.08
19.	Calvin Garrett	Hous	7.91
20.	Wayne Robinson	Detr	7.78

1980-81 PERFORMANCE CATEGORIES

SCORING

OR	PLAYER	TEAM	SCR
1.	Adrian Dantley	Utah	30.65
2.	Moses Malone	Hous	27.78
3.	George Gervin	S.A.	27.09
4.	K. Abdul-Jabbar	LA.L	26.19
5.	David Thompson	Denv	25.55
6.	Otis Birdsong	K.C.	24.61
7.	Julius Erving	Phil	24.56
8.	Mike Mitchell	Clev	24.54
9.	World B. Free	G.St	24.08
10.	Alex English	Denv	23.81
11.	Jamaal Wilkes	LA.L	22.56
12.	Dan Issel	Denv	21.86
13.	Bernard King	G.St	21.86
14.	John Drew	Atla	21.70
15.	Mike Newlin	N.J.	21.37
16.	Larry Bird	Bost	21.23
17.	Darrell Griffith	Utah	20.63
18.	Marques Johnson	Milw	20.28
19.	Bill Cartwright	N.Y.	20.07
20.	Ray Williams	N.Y.	19.75

REBOUNDS

OR	PLAYER	TEAM	REB
1.	Larry Smith	G.St	18.51
2.	Moses Maone	Hous	17.45
3.	Swen Nater	S.D.	17.38
4.	Robert Parish	Bost	16.23
5.	Wes Unseld	Wash	15.90
6.	Dave Corzine	S.A.	15.58
7.	Kermit Washington	Port	15.53
8.	Kenny Carr	Clev	15.33
9.	George T. Johnson	S.A.	14.93
10.	Wayne Cooper	Utah	14.87
11.	Caldwell Jones	Phil	14.79
12.	Dan Roundfield	Atla	14.30
13.	Mitch Kupchak	Wash	14.12
14.	Artis Gilmore	Chic	14.03
15.	Jack Sikma	Seat	14.01
16.	Harvey Catchings	Milw	13.89
17.	Reggie King	K.C.	13.75
18.	Cedrick Hordges	Denv	13.75
19.	George McGinnis	Indi	13.74
20.	Clemon Johnson	Indi	13.67

BLOCKS

OR	PLAYER	TEAM	BLK
1.	George T. Johnson	S.A.	6.90
2.	Harvey Catchings	Milw	5.40
3.	Robert Parish	Bost	4.47
4.	Kevin McHale	Bost	4.41
5.	K. Abdul-Jabbar	LA.L	3.68
6.	Clemon Johnson	Indi	3.48
7.	Terry Tyler	Detr	3.39
8.	Artis Gilmore	Chic	3.36
9.	Mike Gminski	N.J.	3.04
10.	Sam Pellom	Atla	3.00
11.	Ben Poquette	Utah	2.97
12.	Mychal Thompson	Port	2.92
13.	Elvin Hayes	Wash	2.80
14.	Marvin Webster	N.Y.	2.73
15.	James Bailey	Seat	2.70
16.	Dan Roundfield	Atla	2.68
17.	James Edwards	Indi	2.59
18.	Sam Lacey	K.C.	2.59
19.	Darryl Dawkins	Phil	2.57
20.	Joe C. Meriweather	K.C.	2.54

SHOOTING

OR	PLAYER	TEAM	SHT
1.	Artis Gilmore	Chic	1.182
2.	Darryl Dawkins	Phil	1.137
3.	Cedric Maxwell	Bost	1.126
4.	Bernard King	G.St	1.114
5.	K. Abdul-Jabbar	LA.L	1.113
6.	Brad Davis	Dall	1.108
7.	Brian Taylor	S.D.	1.107
8.	Adrian Dantley	Utah	1.104
9.	Swen Nater	S.D.	1.094
10.	Walter Davis	Phoe	1.089
11.	Bill Cartwright	N.Y.	1.089
12.	Sidney Moncrief	Milw	1.081
13.	Billy Knight	Indi	1.080
14.	Bobby Jones	Phil	1.080
15.	Bob Gross	Port	1.075
16.	Maurice Cheeks	Phil	1.067
17.	Vinnie Johnson	Seat	1.066
18.	Marques Johnson	Milw	1.063
19.	Ernie Grunfeld	K.C.	1.056
20.	Jim Paxson	Port	1.056

ASSISTS

OR	PLAYER	TEAM	AST
1.	Kevin Porter	Wash	13.67
2.	Phil Ford	K.C.	12.17
3.	John Lucas	G.St	11.61
4.	Kenny Higgs	Denv	11.60
5.	Johnny Moore	S.A.	11.35
6.	Norm Nixon	LA.L	11.28
7.	Maurice Cheeks	Phil	11.13
8.	Brad Davis	Dall	10.96
9.	Kelvin Ransey	Port	10.96
10.	Allen Leavell	Hous	10.93
11.	Nate Archibald	Bost	10.52
12.	Tom Henderson	Hous	10.44
13.	Ronnie Lee	Detr	9.50
14.	M.R. Richardson	N.Y.	9.48
15.	Allan Bristow	Utah	9.19
16.	Brian Taylor	S.D.	9.13
17.	Johnny Davis	Indi	9.09
18.	Wes Matthews	Atla	8.71
19.	Sam Lacey	K.C.	8.60
20.	Mike Bratz	Clev	8.36

STEALS

OR	PLAYER	TEAM	STL
1.	Dudley Bradley	Indi	4.78
2.	Ronnie Lee	Detr	4.36
3.	Quinn Buckner	Milw	3.97
4.	Maurice Cheeks	Phil	3.84
5.	Johnny Moore	S.A.	3.65
6.	Johnny High	Phoe	3.54
7.	M.R. Richardson	N.Y.	3.51
8.	Darwin Cook	N.J.	3.42
9.	Ray Williams	N.Y.	3.24
10.	Garfield Heard	S.D.	3.06
11.	Julius Erving	Phil	2.89
12.	Kenny Higgs	Denv	2.87
13.	Sly Williams	N.Y.	2.82
14.	Allen Leavell	Hous	2.76
15.	Don Collins	Wash	2.71
16.	Larry Drew	Detr	2.67
17.	Calvin Murphy	Hous	2.65
18.	Robert Reid	Hous	2.64
19.	Ricky Sobers	Chic	2.61
20.	John Long	Detr	2.61

1979-80 NBA STATISTICS

PRODUCTION RATINGS

OR	PLAYER	TEAM	PR
1.	K. Abdul-Jabbar	LA.L	32.87
2.	Moses Malone	Hous	28.68
3.	Julius Erving	Phil	27.78
4.	Adrian Dantley	Utah	27.46
5.	George Gervin	S.A.	27.19
6.	Larry Bird	Bost	25.26
7.	Earvin Johnson	LA.L	25.13
8.	Dan Issel	Denv	24.34
9.	Marques Johnson	Milw	23.90
10.	Swen Nater	S.D.	23.74
11.	Bill Cartwright	N.Y.	23.59
12.	Bob Lanier	Milw	23.32
13.	M. R. Richardson	N.Y.	23.05
14.	Elvin Hayes	Wash	22.96
15.	Wes Unseld	Wash	22.52
16.	Larry Kenon	S.A.	21.88
17.	Cedric Maxwell	Bost	21.85
18.	Mickey Johnson	Indi	21.83
19.	Ray Williams	N.Y.	21.78
20.	Lloyd Free	S.D.	21.38
21.	Dan Roundfield	Atla	21.26
22.	Jamaal Wilkes	LA.L	21.24
23.	Jack Sikma	Seat	21.09
24.	Robert Parish	G.St	20.82
25.	Mike Mitchell	Clev	20.72
26.	Kermit Washington	Port	20.59
27.	Walter Davis	Phoe	20.51
28.	Alvan Adams	Phoe	20.48
29.	Gus Williams	Seat	20.26
30.	Paul Westphal	Phoe	20.20
31.	Bob McAdoo	Detr	20.16
32.	Calvin Natt	Port	20.03
33.	David Greenwood	Chic	19.95
34.	Toby Knight	N.Y.	19.58
35.	Reggie Theus	Chic	19.35
36.	Dave Robisch	Clev	19.15
37.	Norm Nixon	LA.L	18.89
38.	Alex English	Denv	18.62
39.	Scott Wedman	K.C.	18.51
40.	Truck Robinson	Phoe	18.44
41.	Tom Owens	Port	18.17
42.	Wayne Rollins	Atla	18.17
43.	Otis Birdsong	K.C.	18.04
44.	Darryl Dawkins	Phil	17.85
45.	Greg Ballard	Wash	17.74
46.	Sam Lacey	K.C.	17.72
47.	John Long	Detr	17.67
48.	Dave Cowens	Bost	17.65
49.	Lonnie Shelton	Seat	17.50
50.	Maurice Cheeks	Phil	17.37
51.	Nate Archibald	Bost	17.35
52.	Dennis Johnson	Seat	17.17
53.	James Edwards	Indi	17.17
54.	Mike Newlin	N.J.	17.10
55.	George McGinnis	Indi	17.03
56.	Sonny Parker	G.St	16.99
57.	Calvin Murphy	Hous	16.91
58.	Terry Tyler	Detr	16.76
59.	Maurice Lucas	N.J.	16.70
60.	Caldwell Jones	Phil	16.69
61.	Eddie Johnson Jr.	Atla	16.58
62.	Foots Walker	Clev	16.55
63.	Phil Ford	K.C.	16.12
64.	Bobby Jones	Phil	16.06
65.	James Silas	S.A.	16.01
66.	John Lucas	G.St	16.00
67.	Robert Reid	Hous	15.84
68.	Eddie Jordan	N.J.	15.48
69.	Purvis Short	G.St	15.47
70.	Allan Bristow	Utah	15.45
71.	Brian Winters	Milw	15.11
72.	George L. Johnson	Denv	15.08
73.	Junior Bridgeman	Milw	15.04
74.	John Drew	Atla	15.01
75.	Ben Poquette	Utah	14.98
76.	Mike Bantom	Indi	14.83
77.	Randy Smith	Clev	14.82
78.	John Johnson	Seat	14.74
79.	Johnny Davis	Indi	14.46
80.	Billy Knight	Indi	14.32
81.	Mark Olberding	S.A.	14.32
82.	Cliff Robinson	N.J.	14.24
83.	Brian Taylor	S.D.	14.12
84.	Quinn Buckner	Milw	14.07
85.	George T. Johnson	N.J.	14.07
86.	Rudy Tomjanovich	Hous	13.77
87.	Billy Paultz	Hous	13.77
88.	Ricky Sobers	Chic	13.77
89.	Kenny Carr	Clev	13.65
90.	Phil Smith	G.St	13.43
91.	Jim Chones	LA.L	13.39
92.	Tom Boswell	Utah	13.38
93.	Kent Benson	Detr	13.37
94.	Allen Leavell	Hous	13.34
95.	David Meyers	Milw	13.13
96.	Rich Kelley	Phoe	13.13
97.	Bill Robinzine	K.C.	13.07
98.	Freeman Williams	S.D.	12.83
99.	Steve Hawes	Atla	12.80
100.	Rick Robey	Bost	12.78

POSITION DOMINANCE

OR	PLAYER	TEAM	PD
1.	George Gervin	S.A.	1.340
2.	Earvin Johnson	LA.L	1.290
3.	K. Abdul-Jabbar	LA.L	1.286
4.	Larry Bird	Bost	1.222
5.	Julius Erving	Phil	1.189
6.	M. R. Richardson	N.Y.	1.183
7.	Adrian Dantley	Utah	1.175
8.	Moses Malone	Hous	1.122
9.	Elvin Hayes	Wash	1.110
10.	Ray Williams	N.Y.	1.073
11.	Cedric Maxwell	Bost	1.057
12.	Lloyd Free	S.D.	1.054
13.	Gus Williams	Seat	1.040
14.	Dan Roundfield	Atla	1.028
15.	Marques Johnson	Milw	1.023
16.	Paul Westphal	Phoe	.996
17.	Kermit Washington	Port	.996
18.	Bob McAdoo	Detr	.975
19.	Norm Nixon	LA.L	.969
20.	David Greenwood	Chic	.965

MOST VALUABLE PLAYER

OR	PLAYER	TEAM	MVP
1.	Earvin Johnson	LA.L	2.028
2.	K. Abdul-Jabbar	LA.L	2.024
3.	Larry Bird	Bost	1.919
4.	Julius Erving	Phil	1.872
5.	George Gervin	S.A.	1.824
6.	Cedric Maxwell	Bost	1.754
7.	Norm Nixon	LA.L	1.707
8.	M. R. Richardson	N.Y.	1.659
9.	Jamaal Wilkes	LA.L	1.647
10.	Gus Williams	Seat	1.646
11.	Paul Westphal	Phoe	1.600
12.	Nate Archibald	Bost	1.587
13.	Marques Johnson	Milw	1.586
14.	Moses Malone	Hous	1.578
15.	Maurice Cheeks	Phil	1.574
16.	Dan Roundfield	Atla	1.574
17.	Elvin Hayes	Wash	1.553
18.	Ray Williams	N.Y.	1.549
19.	Truck Robinson	Phoe	1.496
20.	Caldwell Jones	Phil	1.490

1979-80 POSITION RATINGS

POWER FORWARD

OR	PLAYER	TEAM	PR
1.	Larry Bird	Bost	25.26
2.	Elvin Hayes	Wash	22.96
3.	Dan Roundfield	Atla	21.26
4.	Kermit Washington	Port	20.59
5.	Bob McAdoo	Detr	20.16
6.	David Greenwood	Chic	19.95
7.	Truck Robinson	Phoe	18.44
8.	Lonnie Shelton	Seat	17.50
9.	George McGinnis	Indi	17.03
10.	Maurice Lucas	N.J.	16.70
11.	Caldwell Jones	Phil	16.69
12.	George L. Johnson	Denv	15.08
13.	Mike Bantom	Indi	14.83
14.	Mark Olberding	S.A.	14.32
15.	Cliff Robinson	N.J.	14.24
16.	Kenny Carr	Clev	13.65
17.	Jim Chones	L.A.L	13.39
18.	Tom Boswell	Utah	13.38
19.	David Meyers	Milw	13.13
20.	Bill Robinzine	K.C.	13.07

POINT GUARD

OR	PLAYER	TEAM	PR
1.	Earvin Johnson	LA.L	25.13
2.	M.R. Richardson	N.Y.	23.05
3.	Gus Williams	Seat	20.26
4.	Norm Nixon	LA.L	18.89
5.	Maurice Cheeks	Phil	17.37
6.	Nate Archibald	Bost	17.35
7.	Foots Walker	Clev	16.55
8.	Phil Ford	K.C.	16.12
9.	James Silas	S.A.	16.01
10.	John Lucas	G.St	16.00
11.	Eddie Jordan	N.J.	15.48
12.	Johnny Davis	Indi	14.46
13.	Brian Taylor	S.D.	14.12
14.	Quinn Buckner	Milw	14.07
15.	Ricky Sobers	Chic	13.77
16.	Allen Leavell	Hous	13.34
17.	John Roche	Denv	11.87
18.	Don Buse	Phoe	10.60
19.	Mike Gale	S.A.	10.40
20.	Dave Twardzik	Port	10.10

CENTER

OR	PLAYER	TEAM	PR
1.	K. Abdul-Jabbar	LA.L	32.87
2.	Moses Malone	Hous	28.68
3.	Dan Issel	Denv	24.34
4.	Swen Nater	S.D.	23.74
5.	Bill Cartwright	N.Y.	23.59
6.	Bob Lanier	Detr	23.32
7.	Wes Unseld	Wash	22.52
8.	Jack Sikma	Seat	21.09
9.	Robert Parish	G.St	20.82
10.	Alvan Adams	Phoe	20.48
11.	Dave Robisch	Clev	19.15
12.	Tom Owens	Port	18.17
13.	Wayne Rollins	Atla	18.17
14.	Darryl Dawkins	Phil	17.85
15.	Sam Lacey	K.C.	17.72
16.	Dave Cowens	Bost	17.65
17.	James Edwards	Indi	17.17
18.	Ben Poquette	Utah	14.98
19.	George T. Johnson	N.J.	14.07
20.	Billy Paultz	Hous	13.77

SMALL FORWARD

OR	PLAYER	TEAM	PR
1.	Julius Erving	Phil	27.78
2.	Adrian Dantley	Utah	27.46
3.	Marques Johnson	Milw	23.90
4.	Larry Kenon	S.A.	21.88
5.	Cedric Maxwell	Bost	21.85
6.	Mickey Johnson	Indi	21.83
7.	Jamaal Wilkes	LA.L	21.24
8.	Mike Mitchell	Clev	20.72
9.	Walter Davis	Phoe	20.51
10.	Calvin Natt	Port	20.03
11.	Toby Knight	N.Y.	19.58
12.	Alex English	Denv	18.62
13.	Scott Wedman	K.C.	18.51
14.	Greg Ballard	Wash	17.74
15.	Sonny Parker	G.St	16.99
16.	Terry Tyler	Detr	16.76
17.	Bobby Jones	Phil	16.06
18.	Robert Reid	Hous	15.84
19.	Purvis Short	G.St	15.47
20.	Allan Bristow	Utah	15.45

OFF GUARD

OR	PLAYER	TEAM	PR
1.	George Gervin	S.A.	27.19
2.	Ray Williams	N.Y.	21.78
3.	Lloyd Free	S.D.	21.38
4.	Paul Westphal	Phoe	20.20
5.	Reggie Theus	Chic	19.35
6.	Otis Birdsong	K.C.	18.04
7.	John Long	Detr	17.67
8.	Dennis Johnson	Seat	17.17
9.	Mike Newlin	N.J.	17.10
10.	Calvin Murphy	Hous	16.91
11.	Eddie Johnson Jr.	Atla	16.58
12.	Brian Winters	Milw	15.11
13.	Randy Smith	Clev	14.82
14.	Billy Knight	Indi	14.32
15.	Phil Smith	G.St	13.43
16.	Freeman Williams	S.D.	12.83
17.	Terry Furlow	Utah	12.55
18.	Ron Brewer	Port	12.51
19.	M.L. Carr	Bost	11.57
20.	Chris Ford	Bost	11.48

ROOKIES

OR	PLAYER	TEAM	PR
1.	Larry Bird	Bost	25.26
2.	Earvin Johnson	LA.L	25.13
3.	Bill Cartwright	N.Y.	23.59
4.	Calvin Natt	Port	20.03
5.	David Greenwood	Chic	19.95
6.	Cliff Robinson	N.J.	14.24
7.	Allen Leavell	Hous	13.34
8.	Reggie King	K.C.	12.72
9.	Dudley Bradley	Indi	10.78
10.	Sidney Moncrief	Milw	10.34
11.	Larry Demic	N.Y.	8.10
12.	Terry Duerod	Detr	7.09
13.	Don Williams	Utah	6.42

1979-80 PERFORMANCE CATEGORIES

SCORING

OR	PLAYER	TEAM	PR
1.	George Gervin	S.A.	33.14
2.	Lloyd Free	S.D.	30.22
3.	Adrian Dantley	Utah	27.99
4.	Julius Erving	Phil	26.92
5.	Moses Malone	Hous	25.84
6.	K. Abdul-Jabbar	LA.L	24.80
7.	Dan Issel	Denv	23.79
8.	Elvin Hayes	Wash	22.95
9.	Otis Birdsong	K.C.	22.66
10.	Mike Mitchell	Clev	22.20
11.	Gus Williams	Seat	22.15
12.	Paul Westphal	Phoe	21.85
13.	Bill Cartwright	N.Y.	21.72
14.	Marques Johnson	Milw	21.70
15.	Walter Davis	Phoe	21.51
16.	Larry Bird	Bost	21.28
17.	Bob McAdoo	Detr	21.07
18.	Mike Newlin	N.J.	20.95
19.	Ray Williams	N.Y.	20.90
20.	Reggie Theus	Chic	20.24

REBOUNDS

OR	PLAYER	TEAM	REB
1.	Swen Nater	S.D.	20.41
2.	Mark Lansberger	LA.L	19.49
3.	Moses Malone	Hous	18.19
4.	Robert Parish	G.St	17.74
5.	Wes Unseld	Wash	17.66
6.	Wayne Rollins	Atla	17.50
7.	Caldwell Jones	Phil	16.46
8.	Jack Sikma	Seat	15.60
9.	Dan Roundfield	Atla	15.52
10.	Kenny Carr	Clev	15.36
11.	Kermit Washington	Port	15.21
12.	George McGinnis	Indi	15.20
13.	Cliff Robinson	N.J.	14.62
14.	George L. Johnson	Denv	14.46
15.	Larry Bird	Bost	13.84
16.	Maurice Lucas	N.J.	13.64
17.	Wayne Cooper	G.St	13.66
18.	Truck Robinson	Phoe	13.64
19.	George T. Johnson	N.J.	13.64
20.	K. Abdul-Jabbar	LA.L	13.53

BLOCKS

OR	PLAYER	TEAM	BLK
1.	George T. Johnson	N.J.	5.84
2.	Wayne Rollins	Atla	5.52
3.	K. Abdul-Jabbar	LA.L	4.28
4.	Terry Tyler	Detr	3.96
5.	Clemon Johnson	Indi	3.77
6.	J. C. Meriweather	N.Y.	3.68
7.	Ben Poquette	Utah	3.31
8.	Elvin Hayes	Wash	2.85
9.	Caldwell Jones	Phil	2.81
10.	Darryl Dawkins	Phil	2.68
11.	Bobby Jones	Phil	2.67
12.	James Hardy	Utah	2.61
13.	Robert Parish	G.St	2.61
14.	Dan Roundfield	Atla	2.58
15.	Rich Kelley	Phoe	2.51
16.	Julius Erving	Phil	2.39
17.	Kermit Washington	Port	2.37
18.	Kent Benson	Detr	2.34
19.	David Greenwood	Chic	2.22
20.	Sam Lacey	K.C.	2.17

SHOOTING

OR	PLAYER	TEAM	SHT
1.	K. Abdul-Jabbar	LA.L	1.159
2.	Cedric Maxwell	Bost	1.147
3.	Adrian Dantley	Utah	1.144
4.	Walter Davis	Phoe	1.119
5.	Tom Boswell	Utah	1.097
6.	Paul Westphal	Phoe	1.091
7.	George Gervin	S.A.	1.087
8.	Bill Cartwright	N.Y.	1.084
9.	Marques Johnson	Milw	1.081
10.	Maurice Cheeks	Phil	1.074
11.	Billy Knight	Indi	1.074
12.	Jamaal Wilkes	LA.L	1.072
13.	Earvin Johnson	LA.L	1.071
14.	Swen Nater	S.D.	1.070
15.	James Silas	S.A.	1.070
16.	Wayne Rollins	Atla	1.067
17.	Bob Lanier	Milw	1.067
18.	Alvan Adams	Phoe	1.063
19.	Dave Robisch	Clev	1.062
20.	Toby Knight	N.Y.	1.061

ASSISTS

OR	PLAYER	TEAM	AST
1.	Kevin Porter	Wash	14.68
2.	M.R. Richardson	N.Y.	13.05
3.	Foots Walker	Clev	12.03
4.	Nate Archibald	Bost	11.25
5.	Phil Ford	K.C.	11.17
6.	Quinn Buckner	Milw	10.88
7.	John Lucas	G.St	10.46
8.	Maurice Cheeks	Phil	10.17
9.	Mike Gale	S.A.	10.16
10.	Eddie Jordan	N.J.	10.06
11.	Ron Lee	Detr	9.91
12.	Armond Hill	Atla	9.73
13.	Earvin Johnson	LA.L	9.67
14.	Norm Nixon	LA.L	9.55
15.	Ray Williams	N.Y.	9.52
16.	Allen Leavell	Hous	9.43
17.	Sam Lacey	K.C.	9.15
18.	John Roche	Denv	8.50
19.	Tom Henderson	Hous	8.48
20.	Dave Twardzik	Port	8.22

STEALS

OR	PLAYER	TEAM	STL
1.	Dudley Bradley	Indi	5.00
2.	M.R. Richardson	N.Y.	4.16
3.	Ron Lee	Detr	4.07
4.	Eddie Jordan	N.J.	4.03
5.	Mike Gale	S.A.	4.01
6.	Quinn Buckner	Milw	3.83
7.	Maurice Cheeks	Phil	3.35
8.	Gus Williams	Seat	3.23
9.	Earvin Johnson	LA.L	3.21
10.	Ray Williams	N.Y.	3.10
11.	Foots Walker	Clev	3.07
12.	Sonny Parker	G.St	2.91
13.	Julius Erving	Phil	2.90
14.	M.L. Carr	Bost	2.89
15.	Allen Leavell	Hous	2.87
16.	Mike Bratz	Phoe	2.81
17.	Mickey Johnson	Indi	2.77
18.	Robert Reid	Hous	2.75
19.	Don Williams	Utah	2.68
20.	T.R. Dunn	Port	2.66

Wilt Chamberlain of the Philadelphia Warriors
- Also holds career record for most rebounds (23,924)
- Basketball Hall of Fame -

CHAPTER 8

CAREER CAPSULES

2000/2000/2000

For 3 consecutive days during the 1987 season, milestones were set by 3 of the original clubs in the NBA.

Saturday - Feb. 28 Play-by-Play expert Chick Hearn, an institution in LA, announced his 2,000th consecutive Lakers game.

Sunday - March 1 The Boston Celtics recorded their 2,000th regular season win.

Monday - March 2 The Golden State Warriors celebrated the 25th anniversary of Wilt Chamberlain's 100 point game (March 2, 1962). Interestingly, the Warriors had just played their 2,000th regular season game since that magical night in Hershey, Pennsylvania.

CAREER CAPSULES

On the following pages I've cited all the present players in the NBA who have qualified at least once in recent years (see page 272 for qualification explanation). DNQ means a player "did not qualify". Following the present players are all the former players who qualified at least six years. Each player is listed alphabetically with several statistical categories listed for each year the player played as well as the university he played at. I have used abbreviations for team names. A couple examples would be S.A. (San Antonio) or LA.C (Los Angeles Clippers).

YR = Year
TM = Team
PR = Production Rating (see chapter one for explanation)
OR = Overall Rank by Production Rating
PS = Position Rank by Production Rating
SC = Scoring Rank (points/games)
SH = Shooting Rank (see page 28 for explanation)
RB = Rebounding Rank based on 48 minutes played
AS = Assists Rank based on 48 minutes played
BL = Blocked Shots Rank based on 48 minutes played
ST = Steals Rank based on 48 minutes played

Blocks and steals were not officially kept as records until 1974. As you can see from Kareem Abdul-Jabbar's register, nothing is listed for those categories prior to 1974. In addition, a dash (-) means the player was not in the top 20% in this category. If the player did place in the top 20% his rank is shown. The reason I did not list a player's rank regardless of his percentile is because I wanted a player's strengths to be evident at a glance. Additionally, a player who ranked 30th in 1955 is nowhere near as impressive as a player who ranked 30th in 1987 when over three times as many players qualified. By my only showing the rank of the top 20% a player's overall dominance can easily be seen. I should mention that Overall Rank and Position Rank are shown on every player for every year. Only the six performance categories reflect the upper 20%.

As I have said before, the NBA did not officially begin keeping statistics on blocks and steals until 1974. Prior to 1974, I only show four performance categories (scoring, shooting, rebounds, and assists), whereas after 1974 that total jumps to six categories.

It will surprise a lot of people, no doubt, but the only NBA player since 1974 to place in the top 20% of all six categories at least once in his career is Alvan Adams. Adams certainly hasn't dominated any one particular category, but he has shown excellence and versatility in all phases of the game (see Adams' register on page 322). Julius Erving also accomplishes this feat if his ABA category rankings are included.

Only two NBA players have placed in the top 20% in five categories in the same year (no player has placed in all six the same year). The two players are Bill Walton - 1978 (Walton failed to place in the top 20% in steals only. His percentile on steals was 75%.) and Charles Barkley - 1986 (Barkley failed to place in the top 20% in assists only. His percentile was 41%.).

On the following two pages you will find several "best" lists. All players who are still playing in the NBA are italicized. ABA rankings are not included.

It is, of course, very possible that some players prior to 1974 would have qualified in five or six categories. Since records were not kept for blocks and steals we'll never know for sure. Listed below are two groups. Group one lists those players who have placed in the top 20% for all four categories (scoring, shooting, rebounds, and assists) sometime in their career. Group two lists those players who have placed in the top 20% for all four categories the same year. Also listed is the percentile for each category. You might note the question mark for Dolph Schayes in group two. Schayes did not rank in the top 20% in rebounds in 1950 because rebounds were not kept until the following year. Doubtless, he would have been in the top 20% since he was #1 in rebounds the following two years.

Group One	**Group Two**		SCR	SHT	REB	AST
Dolph Schayes	Dolph Schayes	1950	7%	11%	?	7%
Ed Macauley	Ed Macauley	1951	4%	3%	13%	13%
Wilt Chamberlain	Wilt Chamberlain	1967	7%	3%	1%	7%
Jerry Lucas	*Bill Walton*	1978	19%	14%	1%	18%
Bill Walton	*Larry Bird*	1985	1%	9%	19%	20%
Alvan Adams						
Larry Bird						

Listed below are the only 11 players who have placed in the upper 20% of both blocks and steals during the same year.

Charles Barkley	1986
Don Chaney	1975
Julius Erving	1977,78,80,
	81,82,84,85
Bob Gross	1976
Garfield Heard	1978,81
Mickey Johnson	1980
Bobby Jones	1978,83,84
Sam Lacey	1978
Akeem Olajuwon	1986,87,88
Lonnie Shelton	1977
Michael Jordan	1987,88

Listed below are the players who had the most years qualifying without placing in the top 20% in any category. Shown is the number of years each player came up "empty".

Bill Bradley	8
Keith Erickson	8
Junior Bridgeman	8
Jim Washington	8
Mike Bantom	9
John Johnson	9
Bingo Smith	9
Dave DeBusschere	10
Tom Hawkins	10
Tom Meschery	10
Tom Sanders	10

Only 11 players have placed first in more than one statistical category during their career. Only Kareem Abdul-Jabbar, Oscar Robertson, and John Stockton have placed first in more than two. Shown below are the number of firsts out of the number of categories possible.

Kareem Abdul-Jabbar	4-6	3-4	George Mikan	2-4
Oscar Robertson		3-4	Swen Nater	2-4
John Stockton	3-6	2-4	Jerry West	2-4
Wilt Chamberlain		2-4	Neil Johnston	2-4
Nate Archibald		2-4	Slick Watts	2-6
Elvin Hayes		2-4	Larry Steele	2-6

Listed below are the players who have rated over 30 credits per game (Production Rating) the most years. Shown are the number of 30+ seasons out of the total number of years they qualified.

Wilt Chamberlain	13-13	*Larry Bird*	5- 9
Kareem Abdul-Jabbar	12-18	*Moses Malone*	4-12
Bill Russell	10-13	Elgin Baylor	4-12
Oscar Robertson	9-14	Bob Lanier	4-13
Jerry Lucas	6-10	Bob McAdoo	3-10
Bob Pettit	6-11	Walt Bellamy	3-13

Listed below are the only eleven players ever to lead in Production Rating during a given year (Overall Rank #1). The number of years each player accomplished this feat is shown.

Kareem Abdul-Jabbar	11	George Mikan	2
Wilt Chamberlain	10	Paul Arizin	1
Moses Malone	3	Dolph Schayes	1
Neil Johnston	3	Bill Russell	1
Larry Bird	3	*Earvin Johnson*	1
Bob Pettit	2	*Michael Jordan*	1

Listed below are the players who won their position (Production Ratings leader) the most years. Shown are the players and the number of years each finished first.

Kareem Abdul-Jabbar	11	George Gervin	6
Wilt Chamberlain	10	George Mikan	6
Oscar Robertson	9	Neil Johnston	5
Larry Bird	9	Bob Pettit	5
Earvin Johnson	8	Dolph Schayes	5
Bob Cousy	7	*Moses Malone*	5

Listed below are the players who finished first in each statistical category. Shown is the category, the player, and the number of years each finished first.

Scoring (pts/games)
Wilt Chamberlain	7
George Gervin	4
Neil Johnston	3
Bob McAdoo	3
George Mikan	2
Adrian Dantley	2
K. Abdul-Jabbar	2
Michael Jordan	2
Others	14

Shooting (pg.28)
Oscar Robertson	5
Kenny Sears	3
K. Abdul-Jabbar	3
Artis Gilmore	3
Neil Johnston	2
Jerry West	2
Jerry Lucas	2
Dave Twardzik	2
Others	17

Assists (48 min.)
Bob Cousy	10
Kevin Porter	6
Guy Rodgers	3
Art Williams	2
Slick Watts	2
Oscar Robertson	2
Andy Phillip	2
John Stockton	2
Others	10

Rebounds (48 min.)
Bill Russell	7
Wilt Chamberlain	6
Moses Malone	3
Larry Smith	3
Dolph Schayes	2
Tom Boerwinkle	2
Swen Nater	2
Charles Oakley	1
LaSalle Thompson	1
Roy Tarpley	1
Others	11

Blocks (48 min.)
George Johnson	4
Wayne Rollins	3
Mark Eaton	3
Elmore Smith	2
Manute Bol	2
K. Abdul-Jabbar	1

Steals (48 min.)
Slick Watts	2
Dudley Bradley	2
Alvin Robertson	2
Johnny Moore	1
Darwin Cook	1
M.R. Richardson	1
Maurice Cheeks	1
Larry Steele	1
Ron Lee	1
John Stockton	1
Others	2

PRESENT PLAYERS

KAREEM ABDUL-JABBAR   UCLA
YR	TM	PR	OR	PS	SC	SH	RB	AS	BL	ST
1970	Milw	33.63	1	1	2	-	15	-		
1971	Milw	38.88	1	1	1	1	6	-		
1972	Milw	42.63	1	1	1	9				
1973	Milw	39.12	1	1	2	3	10	-		
1974	Milw	35.91	1	1	3	4	15	-	4	-
1975	Milw	35.62	1	1	3	11	13	-	3	-
1976	LA.L	39.65	1	1	2	10	1	-	1	-
1977	LA..L	35.16	1	1	3	2	9	-	5	-
1978	LA..L	34.39	1	1	5	4	9	-	4	-
1979	LA.L	34.68	1	1	8	4	12	-	3	-
1980	LA.L	32.87	1	1	6	1	20	-	3	-
1981	LA.L	30.95	2	2	4	5	23	-	5	-
1982	LA.L	27.16	6	2	6	7	-	-	9	-
1983	LA.L	24.63	7	3	16	3	-	-	9	-
1984	LA.L	23.26	15	6	18	9	-	-	17	-
1985	LA.L	25.87	7	2	20	3	-	-	12	-
1986	LA.L	24.20	11	2	11	10	-	-	18	-
1987	LA.L	19.50	42	8	-	10	-	-	27	-
1988	LA.L	15.90	69	12	-	31	-	-	24	-

MICHAEL ADAMS   BCU
YR	TM	PR	OR	PS	SC	SH	RB	AS	BL	ST
1986	Sacr	1.94		DNQ						
1987	Wash	9.19	141	27	-	-	-	28	-	9
1988	Denv	16.57	63	15	-	27	-	30	-	14

MARK AGUIRRE   DEPAUL
YR	TM	PR	OR	PS	SC	SH	RB	AS	BL	ST
1982	Dall	15.18		DNQ						
1983	Dall	20.77	25	7	6	-	-	-	-	-
1984	Dall	25.04	9	5	2	-	-	-	-	-
1985	Dall	21.21	25	8	8	-	-	-	-	-
1986	Dall	20.08	32	10	12	-	-	-	-	-
1987	Dall	21.29	26	6	7	-	-	-	-	-
1988	Dall	21.13	24	6	8	-	-	-	-	-

DANNY AINGE   BYU
YR	TM	PR	OR	PS	SC	SH	RB	AS	BL	ST
1982	Bost	3.74		DNQ						
1983	Bost	11.06	117	21	-	-	-	-	-	23
1984	Bost	5.44		DNQ						
1985	Bost	16.35	70	13	-	16	-	-	-	31
1986	Bost	13.83	85	14	-	28	-	-	-	-
1987	Bost	17.15	60	9	-	7	-	-	-	-
1988	Bost	18.26	48	9	-	3	-	-	-	-

GREG ANDERSON   HOUSTON
YR	TM	PR	OR	PS	SC	SH	RB	AS	BL	ST
1988	S.A.	13.11	97	19	-	-	27	-	13	-

RON ANDERSON   FRESNO STATE
YR	TM	PR	OR	PS	SC	SH	RB	AS	BL	ST
1985	Clev	5.17		DNQ						
1986	Indi	9.68	138	26	-	-	-	-	-	-
1987	Indi	5.86		DNQ						
1988	Indi	7.54		DNQ						

JOHN BAGLEY   BCU
YR	TM	PR	OR	PS	SC	SH	RB	AS	BL	ST
1983	Clev	5.26		DNQ						
1984	Clev	8.99	148	28	-	-	-	22	-	-
1985	Clev	16.32	71	12	-	-	-	4	-	19
1986	Clev	16.28	63	8	-	-	-	4	-	27
1987	Clev	12.38	103	19	-	-	-	-	-	-
1988	N.J.	13.43	94	21	-	-	-	32	-	-

THURL BAILEY   N.C.STATE
YR	TM	PR	OR	PS	SC	SH	RB	AS	BL	ST
1984	Utah	12.62	105	20	-	-	-	-	10	-
1985	Utah	16.44	67	15	-	-	-	-	23	-
1986	Utah	14.79	77	20	-	-	-	-	19	-
1987	Utah	12.77	99	25	-	-	-	-	24	-
1988	Utah	18.94	42	10	26	-	-	-	20	-

GENE BANKS   DUKE
YR	TM	PR	OR	PS	SC	SH	RB	AS	BL	ST
1982	S.A.	11.04	122	31	-	-	-	-	-	-
1983	S.A.	18.88	36	9	-	20	-	-	-	-
1984	S.A.	18.17	43	14	-	13	-	-	-	-
1985	S.A.	13.82	99	23	-	6	-	-	-	-
1986	Chic	12.85	101	21	-	-	-	-	-	-
1987	Chic	12.65	101	17	-	22	-	-	-	-
1988	Chic		DID NOT PLAY							

CHARLES BARKLEY   AUBURN
YR	TM	PR	OR	PS	SC	SH	RB	AS	BL	ST
1985	Phil	18.40	43	10	-	31	16	-	-	-
1986	Phil	28.26	4	1	23	27	5	-	26	16
1987	Phil	33.46	2	1	15	2	3	-	-	-
1988	Phil	32.51	3	1	4	6	12	-	-	-

BENOIT BENJAMIN   CREIGHTON
YR	TM	PR	OR	PS	SC	SH	RB	AS	BL	ST
1986	LA.C	16.04	67	17	-	-	20	-	4	-
1987	LA.C	15.89	70	17	-	-	31	-	5	-
1988	LA.C	17.97	50	10	-	-	-	-	2	-

WALTER BERRY   ST. JOHN'S
YR	TM	PR	OR	PS	SC	SH	RB	AS	BL	ST
1987	S.A.	13.97	85	22	-	-	-	-	-	-
1988	S.A.	16.23	66	16	-	-	-	-	-	-

LARRY BIRD   INDIANA ST.
YR	TM	PR	OR	PS	SC	SH	RB	AS	BL	ST
1980	Bost	25.26	6	1	16	-	15	-	-	-
1981	Bost	26.74	5	1	16	-	22	-	-	31
1982	Bost	29.16	3	1	10	-	20	-	-	28
1983	Bost	30.04	2	1	11	-	19	-	-	29
1984	Bost	29.99	2	1	7	-	26	28	-	31
1985	Bost	34.39	1	1	2	14	30	31	-	-
1986	Bost	31.30	1	1	4	21	-	28	-	22
1987	Bost	34.28	1	1	4	4	-	26	-	-
1988	Bost	34.01	2	1	3	4	-	-	-	-

OTIS BIRDSONG   HOUSTON
YR	TM	PR	OR	PS	SC	SH	RB	AS	BL	ST
1978	K.C.	11.88	108	22	-	-	-	-	-	-
1979	K.C.	18.63	40	4	19	-	-	-	-	-
1980	K.C.	18.04	43	6	9	-	-	-	-	-
1981	K.C.	20.31	20	2	6	24	-	-	-	-
1982	N.J.	11.03		DNQ						
1983	N.J.	13.56	87	17	-	-	-	-	-	-
1984	N.J.	15.14	74	11	30	-	-	-	-	-
1985	N.J.	16.75	65	11	26	-	-	-	-	-
1986	N.J.	12.96	100	19	-	-	-	-	-	-
1987	N.J.	5.14		DNQ						
1988	N.J.	9.12	140	28	-	-	-	-	-	-

ROLANDO BLACKMAN — KANSAS ST.
YR	TM	PR	OR	PS	SC	SH	RB	AS	BL	ST
1982	Dall	11.38	116	19	-	-	-	-	-	-
1983	Dall	15.19	72	13	-	-	-	-	-	-
1984	Dall	21.17	25	2	13	14	-	-	-	-
1985	Dall	17.60	55	7	-	-	-	-	-	-
1986	Dall	18.52	40	5	15	-	-	-	-	-
1987	Dall	17.98	55	7	24	-	-	-	-	-
1988	Dall	16.48	64	10	-	-	-	-	-	-

TYRONE BOGUES — WAKE FOREST
YR	TM	PR	OR	PS	SC	SH	RB	AS	BL	ST
1988	Wash	8.68	147	30	-	-	-	8	-	5

MANUTE BOL — BRIDGEPORT
YR	TM	PR	OR	PS	SC	SH	RB	AS	BL	ST
1986	Wash	12.05	112	22	-	-	-	-	1	-
1987	Wash	8.96	144	31	-	-	-	-	1	-
1988	Wash	6.95	DNQ							

SAM BOWIE — KENTUCKY
YR	TM	PR	OR	PS	SC	SH	RB	AS	BL	ST
1985	Port	18.32	46	10	-	-	17	-	4	-
1986	Port	18.07	DNQ							
1987	Port	14.40	DNQ							
1988	DID NOT PLAY									

RANDY BREUER — MINNESOTA
YR	TM	PR	OR	PS	SC	SH	RB	AS	BL	ST
1984	Milw	3.25	DNQ							
1985	Milw	6.96	DNQ							
1986	Milw	11.54	118	23	-	-	-	-	12	-
1987	Milw	8.87	145	32	-	-	-	-	23	-
1988	Milw	14.47	83	15	-	-	-	-	18	-

FRANK BRICKOWSKI
YR	TM	PR	OR	PS	SC	SH	RB	AS	BL	ST
1985	Seat	6.50	DNQ							
1986	Seat	2.70	DNQ							
1987	S.A.	4.86	DNQ							
1988	S.A.	18.71	43	10	-	-	-	-	-	-

TONY BROWN — ARKANSAS
YR	TM	PR	OR	PS	SC	SH	RB	AS	BL	ST
1985	Indi	7.80	154	33	-	-	-	-	-	-
1986	Chic	4.90	DNQ							
1987	N.J.	10.32	126	27	-	-	-	-	-	-
1988	DID NOT PLAY									

MICHAEL CAGE — SAN DIEGO ST.
YR	TM	PR	OR	PS	SC	SH	RB	AS	BL	ST
1985	LA.C	10.00	138	32	-	27	-	-	-	-
1986	LA.C	9.31	142	35	-	27	-	-	-	-
1987	LA.C	21.95	22	8	-	13	-	-	-	-
1988	LA.C	21.24	23	7	-	3	-	-	-	-

ANTOINE CARR — WICHITA STATE
YR	TM	PR	OR	PS	SC	SH	RB	AS	BL	ST
1985	Atla	9.77	142	33	-	28	-	-	9	-
1986	Atla	8.06	DNQ							
1987	Atla	6.05	DNQ							
1988	Atla	10.32	DNQ							

JOE BARRY CARROLL — PURDUE
YR	TM	PR	OR	PS	SC	SH	RB	AS	BL	ST
1981	G.St	19.37	27	11	27	-	-	-	29	-
1982	G.St	18.34	36	10	-	-	-	-	21	-
1983	G.St	23.62	11	6	7	-	-	-	21	-
1984	G.St	20.04	32	11	25	-	-	-	20	-
1985	DID NOT PLAY									
1986	G.St	20.43	29	8	17	-	-	-	17	-
1987	G.St	20.36	33	7	23	-	-	-	19	-
1988	Hous	12.92	98	22	-	-	-	-	17	-

BILL CARTWRIGHT — USF
YR	TM	PR	OR	PS	SC	SH	RB	AS	BL	ST
1980	N.Y.	23.59	11	5	13	8	-	-	-	-
1981	N.Y.	20.63	17	8	19	11	-	-	-	-
1982	N.Y.	15.39	63	15	-	12	-	-	-	-
1983	N.Y.	18.29	43	12	-	12	-	-	22	-
1984	N.Y.	20.18	28	9	-	10	30	-	32	-
1985	DID NOT PLAY									
1986	N.Y.	9.00	DNQ							
1987	N.Y.	19.09	48	12	-	28	-	-	-	-
1988	N.Y.	12.28	106	23	-	19	-	-	-	-

TERRY CATLEDGE — S. ALABAMA
YR	TM	PR	OR	PS	SC	SH	RB	AS	BL	ST
1986	Phil	7.48	DNQ							
1987	Wash	12.76	100	26	-	-	32	-	-	-
1988	Wash	11.10	119	27	-	-	31	-	-	-

TOM CHAMBERS — UTAH
YR	TM	PR	OR	PS	SC	SH	RB	AS	BL	ST
1982	S.D.	16.14	57	12	-	-	-	-	-	-
1983	S.D.	16.32	58	10	-	-	-	-	-	-
1984	Seat	17.12	54	12	-	-	-	-	-	-
1985	Seat	20.06	33	6	22	-	-	-	-	-
1986	Seat	16.97	55	11	-	-	-	-	-	-
1987	Seat	20.50	32	8	13	-	-	-	-	-
1988	Seat	17.73	52	11	18	-	-	-	-	-

MAURICE CHEEKS — W. TEXAS ST.
YR	TM	PR	OR	PS	SC	SH	RB	AS	BL	ST
1979	Phil	12.73	96	16	-	-	-	15	-	5
1980	Phil	17.37	50	5	-	10	-	8	-	7
1981	Phil	16.26	60	6	-	16	-	7	-	4
1982	Phil	18.75	32	4	-	-	-	4	-	1
1983	Phil	17.44	47	7	-	18	-	14	-	5
1984	Phil	16.85	56	8	-	24	-	23	-	5
1985	Phil	18.38	44	5	-	2	-	24	-	10
1986	Phil	21.65	19	3	-	17	-	14	-	10
1987	Phil	20.56	31	6	-	30	-	24	-	6
1988	Phil	19.22	37	7	-	-	-	15	-	-

STEVE COLTER — NEW MEXICO ST.
YR	TM	PR	OR	PS	SC	SH	RB	AS	BL	ST
1985	Port	7.80	DNQ							
1986	Port	9.80	136	29	-	-	-	-	-	13
1987	Phil	6.96	DNQ							
1988	Wash	9.53	132	27	-	-	-	-	-	-

MICHAEL COOPER — NEW MEXICO

YR	TM	PR	OR	PS	SC	SH	RB	AS	BL	ST
1979	LA.L	1.33		DNQ						
1980	LA.L	10.33	129	25	-	24	-	-	-	-
1981	LA.L	13.74	94	17	-	-	-	-	-	29
1982	LA.L	13.76	83	15	-	-	-	-	-	19
1983	LA.L	12.27	107	20	-	15	-	-	-	22
1984	LA.L	14.74	77	13	-	25	-	19	-	32
1985	LA.L	12.65	107	22	-	-	22	-	-	-
1986	LA.L	13.34	94	15	-	-	-	-	-	-
1987	LA.L	13.04	96	19	-	-	-	-	-	-
1988	LA.L	11.98	111	18	-	-	-	-	-	-

WAYNE COOPER — NEW ORLEANS

YR	TM	PR	OR	PS	SC	SH	RB	AS	BL	ST
1979	G.St	6.34		DNQ						
1980	G.St	12.04	109	23	-	-	17	-	22	-
1981	Utah	9.68	144	31	-	-	10	-	-	-
1982	Dall	12.80	96	22	-	-	11	-	12	-
1983	Port	12.98	97	20	-	-	20	-	11	-
1984	Port	11.89	118	25	-	-	18	-	8	-
1985	Denv	15.45	81	15	-	-	11	-	2	-
1986	Denv	17.12	54	13	-	-	19	-	3	-
1987	Denv	11.70	112	24	-	-	16	-	9	-
1988	Denv	10.31		DNQ						

TYRONE CORBIN — DEPAUL

YR	TM	PR	OR	PS	SC	SH	RB	AS	BL	ST
1986	S.A.	3.88		DNQ						
1987	Clev	7.51		DNQ						
1988	Phoe	9.29	135	26	-	-	-	-	-	-

DAVE CORZINE — DEPAUL

YR	TM	PR	OR	PS	SC	SH	RB	AS	BL	ST
1979	Wash	4.63		DNQ						
1980	Wash	4.99		DNQ						
1981	S.A.	14.50	84	22	-	-	6	-	23	-
1982	S.A.	15.18	66	16	-	-	18	-	13	-
1983	Chic	16.98	51	14	-	-	22	-	27	-
1984	Chic	15.87	68	18	-	-	-	-	23	-
1985	Chic	10.88	126	22	-	-	-	-	-	-
1986	Chic	13.31	90	20	-	-	-	-	-	-
1987	Chic	13.22	92	22	-	-	-	-	32	-
1988	Chic	13.72	91	18	-	-	-	-	23	-

PAT CUMMINGS — DETROIT

YR	TM	PR	OR	PS	SC	SH	RB	AS	BL	ST
1980	Milw	7.21		DNQ						
1981	Milw	8.21		DNQ						
1982	Milw	6.87		DNQ						
1983	Dall	15.59	66	16	-	-	21	-	-	-
1984	Dall	16.12	67	17	-	-	25	-	-	-
1985	N.Y.	17.27	58	14	-	-	-	-	-	-
1986	N.Y.	16.48		DNQ						
1987	N.Y.	9.80		DNQ						
1988	N.Y.	6.26		DNQ						

TERRY CUMMINGS — DEPAUL

YR	TM	PR	OR	PS	SC	SH	RB	AS	BL	ST
1983	S.D.	26.04	5	2	10	-	18	-	-	27
1984	S.D.	22.21	19	2	9	-	24	-	-	-
1985	Milw	24.13	14	1	10	-	-	-	-	-
1986	Milw	19.50	37	8	28	-	-	-	-	-
1987	Milw	22.56	18	5	25	-	-	-	-	-
1988	Milw	19.16	40	9	15	-	-	-	-	-

EARL CURETON — DETROIT

YR	TM	PR	OR	PS	SC	SH	RB	AS	BL	ST
1981	Phil	5.19		DNQ						
1982	Phil	7.05		DNQ						
1983	Phil	4.96		DNQ						
1984	Detr	5.37		DNQ						
1985	Detr	8.63	148	35	-	-	-	-	-	-
1986	Detr	11.51	120	30	-	-	-	-	-	-
1987	LA.C	10.44	125	29	-	-	-	-	-	-
1988	LA.C	6.32		DNQ						

DELL CURRY

YR	TM	PR	OR	PS	SC	SH	RB	AS	BL	ST
1987	Clev	3.78		DNQ						
1988	Clev	8.68	146	29	-	-	-	-	-	13

ADRIAN DANTLEY — NOTRE DAME

YR	TM	PR	OR	PS	SC	SH	RB	AS	BL	ST
1977	Buff	20.14	24	8	21	8	-	-	-	-
1978	LA.L	22.72	14	2	18	16	-	-	-	-
1979	LA.L	17.18	53	16	-	18	-	-	-	-
1980	Utah	27.46	4	2	3	3	-	-	-	-
1981	Utah	28.23	3	1	1	8	-	-	-	-
1982	Utah	27.81	4	1	3	3	-	-	-	-
1983	Utah	29.68		DNQ						
1984	Utah	27.96	3	2	1	4	-	-	-	-
1985	Utah	23.75	16	6	7	24	-	-	-	-
1986	Utah	25.82	5	2	2	11	-	-	-	-
1987	Detr	18.21	53	13	22	17	-	-	-	-
1988	Detr	17.29	53	11	22	20	-	-	-	-

BRAD DAUGHERTY — N CAROLINA

YR	TM	PR	OR	PS	SC	SH	RB	AS	BL	ST
1987	Clev	19.10	47	11	-	-	-	-	-	-
1988	Clev	20.70	25	4	32	-	-	-	-	-

BRAD DAVIS — MARYLAND

YR	TM	PR	OR	PS	SC	SH	RB	AS	BL	ST
1978	LA.L	4.03		DNQ						
1979	Indi	4.33		DNQ						
1980	Utah	6.61		DNQ						
1981	Dall	15.73	65	8	-	6	-	8	-	-
1982	Dall	14.99	67	11	-	26	-	18	-	-
1983	Dall	16.75	54	8	-	2	-	7	-	-
1984	Dall	15.31	73	10	-	22	-	16	-	-
1985	Dall	15.28	84	17	-	9	-	14	-	-
1986	Dall	13.10	96	17	-	2	-	11	-	-
1987	Dall	9.29	137	24	-	-	-	14	-	-
1988	Dall	9.28	136	26	-	16	-	23	-	-

WALTER DAVIS — N. CAROLINA

YR	TM	PR	OR	PS	SC	SH	RB	AS	BL	ST
1978	Phoe	21.96	19	6	10	6	-	-	-	-
1979	Phoe	22.70	16	4	10	3	-	-	-	14
1980	Phoe	20.51	27	9	15	4	-	-	-	-
1981	Phoe	15.92	62	12	31	10	-	-	-	-
1982	Phoe	11.95		DNQ						
1983	Phoe	17.39	48	5	-	31	-	-	-	-
1984	Phoe	18.40	42	4	27	31	-	30	-	-
1985	Phoe	11.80		DNQ						
1986	Phoe	17.99	45	7	14	-	-	-	-	-
1987	Phoe	19.85	37	4	11	25	-	-	-	-
1988	Phoe	15.41	74	12	-	-	-	-	-	-

JOHNNY DAWKINS — DUKE

YR	TM	PR	OR	PS	SC	SH	RB	AS	BL	ST
1987	S.A.	9.58	135	28	-	-	-	-	-	-
1988	S.A.	18.37	47	11	-	-	-	16	-	-

JAMES DONALDSON — WASH. ST.

YR	TM	PR	OR	PS	SC	SH	RB	AS	BL	ST
1981	Seat	8.03		DNQ						
1982	Seat	12.20	103	24	-	15	19	-	4	-
1983	Seat	12.67	102	23	-	6	23	-	15	-
1984	S.D.	17.00	55	14	-	3	32	-	16	-
1985	LA.C	16.11	74	14	-	1	26	-	14	-
1986	Dall	16.84	57	14	-	12	17	-	16	-
1987	Dall	21.05	27	6	-	3	11	-	21	-
1988	Dall	14.98	78	14	-	13	13	-	22	-

LARRY DREW — MISSOURI

YR	TM	PR	OR	PS	SC	SH	RB	AS	BL	ST
1981	Detr	6.42	165	31	-	-	-	-	-	16
1982	K.C.	11.62	109	22	-	-	-	17	-	17
1983	K.C.	20.05	31	4	23	-	-	11	-	-
1984	K.C.	16.62	58	9	-	-	-	11	-	23
1985	K.C.	15.96	76	13	-	-	-	21	-	-
1986	Sacr	11.40	123	22	-	-	-	-	-	-
1987	LA.C	11.10	118	21	-	-	-	23	-	-
1988	LA.C	10.31	127	26	-	-	-	26	-	-

CLYDE DREXLER — HOUSTON

YR	TM	PR	OR	PS	SC	SH	RB	AS	BL	ST
1984	Port	8.24		DNQ						
1985	Port	20.71	28	3	-	-	-	28	-	7
1986	Port	22.44	16	2	-	-	-	12	-	4
1987	Port	25.29	9	2	19	-	-	30	-	12
1988	Port	27.94	5	2	6	-	-	-	-	10

KEVIN DUCKWORTH

YR	TM	PR	OR	PS	SC	SH	RB	AS	BL	ST
1987	Port	5.89		DNQ						
1988	Port	15.42	73	13	-	-	26	-	-	-

JOE DUMARS — MCNEESE ST.

YR	TM	PR	OR	PS	SC	SH	RB	AS	BL	ST
1986	Detr	10.23	134	27	-	-	-	21	-	-
1987	Detr	11.71	111	22	-	-	-	-	-	-
1988	Detr	13.59	92	16	-	-	-	-	-	-

T.R. DUNN — ALABAMA

YR	TM	PR	OR	PS	SC	SH	RB	AS	BL	ST
1978	Port	4.59		DNQ						
1979	Port	9.23	141	25	-	-	-	-	-	-
1980	Port	9.01	142	28	-	-	-	-	-	20
1981	Denv	6.61		DNQ						
1982	Denv	14.10	82	14	-	-	-	-	-	22
1983	Denv	14.30	81	15	-	-	-	-	-	19
1984	Denv	14.11	86	15	-	-	-	-	-	10
1985	Denv	10.44	133	28	-	-	-	-	-	13
1986	Denv	10.40	132	26	-	-	-	-	-	9
1987	Denv	7.35	158	34	-	-	-	-	-	24
1988	Denv	6.04		DNQ						

MARK EATON — UCLA

YR	TM	PR	OR	PS	SC	SH	RB	AS	BL	ST
1983	Utah	10.44		DNQ						
1984	Utah	14.33	81	23	-	-	19	-	1	-
1985	Utah	20.52	31	8	-	-	8	-	1	-
1986	Utah	16.31	62	16	-	-	30	-	2	-
1987	Utah	15.29	78	20	-	-	26	-	2	-
1988	Utah	14.27	86	17	-	-	23	-	1	-

JAMES EDWARDS — WASHINGTON

YR	TM	PR	OR	PS	SC	SH	RB	AS	BL	ST
1978	Indi	14.18	75	23	-	-	-	-	-	-
1979	Indi	18.10	44	14	-	-	-	-	21	-
1980	Indi	17.17	53	17	-	-	-	-	21	-
1981	Indi	17.89	39	12	-	-	-	-	17	-
1982	Clev	17.65	44	12	-	-	-	-	24	-
1983	Phoe	10.58		DNQ						
1984	Phoe	14.64	79	22	-	-	-	-	-	-
1985	Phoe	14.63	90	18	-	-	-	-	-	-
1986	Phoe	15.15		DNQ						
1987	Phoe	12.57		DNQ						
1988	Detr	11.23	117	25	-	-	-	-	-	-

CRAIG EHLO

YR	TM	PR	OR	PS	SC	SH	RB	AS	BL	ST
1984	Hous	3.00		DNQ						
1985	Hous	2.09		DNQ						
1986	Hous	3.36		DNQ						
1987	Clev	8.57		DNQ						
1988	Clev	9.44	133	25	-	-	-	-	-	31

DALE ELLIS — TENNESSEE

YR	TM	PR	OR	PS	SC	SH	RB	AS	BL	ST
1984	Dall	7.84		DNQ						
1985	Dall	7.68		DNQ						
1986	Dall	5.89		DNQ						
1987	Seat	21.77	25	3	8	14	-	-	-	-
1988	Seat	20.55	28	6	7	-	-	-	-	-

ALEX ENGLISH — S. CAROLINA

YR	TM	PR	OR	PS	SC	SH	RB	AS	BL	ST
1977	Milw	5.45		DNQ						
1978	Milw	11.51		DNQ						
1979	Indi	19.52	35	9	-	-	-	-	-	-
1980	Denv	18.62	38	12	-	-	-	-	-	-
1981	Denv	24.37	7	4	10	-	-	-	-	-
1982	Denv	27.44	5	2	4	6	-	30	-	-
1983	Denv	28.30	4	1	1	27	-	29	-	-
1984	Denv	25.74	7	3	4	28	-	-	-	-
1985	Denv	24.79	12	4	5	-	-	-	-	-
1986	Denv	24.36	9	4	3	-	-	-	-	-
1987	Denv	23.90	12	4	3	-	-	-	-	-
1988	Denv	21.70	22	5	9	-	-	-	-	-

MIKE EVANS — KANSAS ST.

YR	TM	PR	OR	PS	SC	SH	RB	AS	BL	ST
1980	S.A.	6.09		DNQ						
1981	Milw	5.20		DNQ						
1982	Clev	5.82		DNQ						
1983	Denv	6.02		DNQ						
1984	Denv	8.49	152	29	-	-	29	-	-	-
1985	Denv	9.26		DNQ						
1986	Denv	6.85		DNQ						
1987	Denv	8.54	147	31	-	-	-	-	-	29
1988	Denv	5.27		DNQ						

PATRICK EWING — GEORGETOWN

YR	TM	PR	OR	PS	SC	SH	RB	AS	BL	ST
1986	N.Y.	20.56	28	7	26	-	-	-	13	-
1987	N.Y.	21.90	23	5	21	-	-	-	8	-
1988	N.Y.	22.61	17	2	21	24	22	-	3	-

VERN FLEMING — GEORGIA

YR	TM	PR	OR	PS	SC	SH	RB	AS	BL	ST
1985	Indi	12.98	104	20	-	-	-	-	-	-
1986	Indi	17.99	44	6	-	-	-	29	-	-
1987	Indi	16.17	67	11	-	-	-	29	-	-
1988	Indi	19.19	38	8	-	32	-	22	-	-

ERIC FLOYD — GEORGETOWN

YR	TM	PR	OR	PS	SC	SH	RB	AS	BL	ST
1983	G.St	6.91		DNQ						
1984	G.St	14.77	76	12	-	-	-	-	-	-
1985	G.St	15.72	78	14	-	-	-	-	-	-
1986	G.St	21.33	21	4	-	-	-	7	-	18
1987	G.St	23.65	15	3	-	12	-	5	-	-
1988	Hous	16.58	62	14	-	-	-	18	-	-

TELLIS FRANK — WESTERN KENTUCKY

YR	TM	PR	OR	PS	SC	SH	RB	AS	BL	ST
1988	G.St	8.49	148	34	-	-	-	-	-	-

WINSTON GARLAND — SW MISSOURI ST.

YR	TM	PR	OR	PS	SC	SH	RB	AS	BL	ST
1988	G.St	14.76	82	19	-	-	-	24	-	23

ARMON GILLIAM — UNLV

YR	TM	PR	OR	PS	SC	SH	RB	AS	BL	ST
1988	Phoe	15.36	75	17	-	-	-	-	-	-

MIKE GMINSKI — DUKE

YR	TM	PR	OR	PS	SC	SH	RB	AS	BL	ST
1981	N.J.	14.46	85	23	-	-	29	-	9	-
1982	N.J.	6.23		DNQ						
1983	N.J.	10.08		DNQ						
1984	N.J.	10.62	135	29	-	-	28	-	26	-
1985	N.J.	16.43	68	13	-	-	-	-	28	-
1986	N.J.	20.01	34	10	-	20	31	-	-	-
1987	N.J.	18.46	51	13	-	-	27	-	-	-
1988	Phil	20.56	27	5	-	-	18	-	25	-

HORACE GRANT — AUBURN

YR	TM	PR	OR	PS	SC	SH	RB	AS	BL	ST
1988	Chic	10.56	124	29	-	-	-	-	-	-

A.C. GREEN — OREGON ST.

YR	TM	PR	OR	PS	SC	SH	RB	AS	BL	ST
1986	LA.L	8.67		DNQ						
1987	LA.L	16.03	69	16	-	21	30	-	-	-
1988	LA.L	16.44	65	14	-	-	21	-	-	-

RICKEY GREEN — MICHIGAN

YR	TM	PR	OR	PS	SC	SH	RB	AS	BL	ST
1978	G.St	4.17		DNQ						
1979	Detr	4.89		DNQ						
1980		DID NOT PLAY								
1981	Utah	11.68		DNQ						
1982	Utah	18.44	34	5	-	-	-	12	-	10
1983	Utah	19.38	33	5	-	-	-	5	-	2
1984	Utah	19.74	34	3	-	-	-	7	-	2
1985	Utah	16.78	64	11	-	-	-	8	-	17
1986	Utah	12.75	104	18	-	-	-	18	-	24
1987	Utah	13.40	91	15	-	-	-	8	-	22
1988	Utah	6.37		DNQ						

SIDNEY GREEN — UNLV

YR	TM	PR	OR	PS	SC	SH	RB	AS	BL	ST
1984	Chic	5.69		DNQ						
1985	Chic	7.75		DNQ						
1986	Chic	15.24	74	17	-	-	21	-	-	-
1987	Detr	12.08	104	27	-	-	2	-	-	-
1988	N.Y.	11.40	116	26	-	-	9	-	-	-

DAVID GREENWOOD — UCLA

YR	TM	PR	OR	PS	SC	SH	RB	AS	BL	ST
1980	Chic	19.95	33	6	-	-	26	-	19	-
1981	Chic	18.89	31	6	-	-	26	-	26	-
1982	Chic	20.06	25	6	-	-	23	-	-	-
1983	Chic	15.86	62	11	-	-	8	-	-	-
1984	Chic	18.03	46	9	-	-	17	-	-	-
1985	Chic	10.15	135	31	-	-	-	-	-	-
1986	S.A.	13.28	91	24	-	-	22	-	-	-
1987	S.A.	19.13	46	11	-	-	17	-	-	-
1988	S.A.	12.40		DNQ						

DARRELL GRIFFITH — LOUISVILLE

YR	TM	PR	OR	PS	SC	SH	RB	AS	BL	ST
1981	Utah	14.31	87	16	17	-	-	-	-	-
1982	Utah	14.85	70	10	21	-	-	-	-	-
1983	Utah	17.16	49	6	14	-	-	-	-	30
1984	Utah	16.57	60	7	28	-	-	-	-	-
1985	Utah	16.92	62	9	14	-	-	-	-	29
1986		DID NOT PLAY								
1987	Utah	11.20	117	23	-	-	-	-	-	22
1988	Utah	8.27		DNQ						

BOB HANSEN — IOWA

YR	TM	PR	OR	PS	SC	SH	RB	AS	BL	ST
1984	Utah	2.44		DNQ						
1985	Utah	4.32		DNQ						
1986	Utah	9.00	145	33	-	-	-	-	-	-
1987	Utah	8.36	151	26	-	-	-	-	-	-
1988	Utah	9.68	131	24	-	22	-	-	-	-

BILL HANZLIK — NOTRE DAME

YR	TM	PR	OR	PS	SC	SH	RB	AS	BL	ST
1981	Seat	6.38		DNQ						
1982	Seat	8.62	155	38	-	-	-	-	-	-
1983	Denv	8.11		DNQ						
1984	Denv	8.19		DNQ						
1985	Denv	8.41	149	29	-	-	-	-	-	27
1986	Denv	13.03	97	20	-	-	-	-	-	20
1987	Denv	12.96	97	16	-	-	-	-	-	-
1988	Denv	5.99		DNQ						

DEREK HARPER — ILLINOIS

YR	TM	PR	OR	PS	SC	SH	RB	AS	BL	ST
1984	Dall	7.34	158	30	-	-	-	-	-	17
1985	Dall	12.93	105	20	-	-	-	-	-	9
1986	Dall	15.68	71	11	-	-	-	24	-	7
1987	Dall	19.77	38	8	-	-	-	12	-	13
1988	Dall	19.17	39	9	-	-	-	-	-	-

RON HARPER — MIAMI OF OHIO

YR	TM	PR	OR	PS	SC	SH	RB	AS	BL	ST
1987	Clev	18.90	49	6	16	-	-	-	-	7
1988	Clev	16.23	67	11	-	-	-	-	-	9

GERALD HENDERSON — VCU

YR	TM	PR	OR	PS	SC	SH	RB	AS	BL	ST
1980	Bost	5.57	DNQ							
1981	Bost	6.71	163	34	-	-	-	-	-	33
1982	Bost	9.52	146	25	-	-	-	-	-	-
1983	Bost	7.21	DNQ							
1984	Bost	12.08	113	19	-	29	-	-	-	16
1985	Seat	15.30	83	16	-	-	-	18	-	21
1986	Seat	14.71	79	12	-	-	-	26	-	21
1987	N.Y.	13.18	93	16	-	-	-	16	-	31
1988	Phil	7.77	155	32	-	-	-	-	-	-

ROD HIGGINS — FRESNO ST.

YR	TM	PR	OR	PS	SC	SH	RB	AS	BL	ST
1983	Chic	11.62	109	27	-	-	-	-	-	-
1984	Chic	6.95	160	35	-	-	-	-	-	-
1985	Chic	4.63	DNQ							
1986	Chic	3.50	DNQ							
1987	G.St	9.74	133	25	-	19	-	-	-	-
1988	G.St	16.65	58	13	-	11	-	-	-	-

ROY HINSON — RUTGERS

YR	TM	PR	OR	PS	SC	SH	RB	AS	BL	ST
1984	Clev	10.46	139	30	-	-	23	-	3	-
1985	Clev	17.80	52	12	-	-	-	-	8	-
1986	Clev	20.06	33	6	29	-	-	-	28	-
1987	Phil	15.09	79	18	-	-	-	-	10	-
1988	N.J.	16.60	61	13	-	-	-	-	15	-

CRAIG HODGES — CAL ST.-L.B.

YR	TM	PR	OR	PS	SC	SH	RB	AS	BL	ST
1983	S.D.	8.55	142	31	-	-	-	-	-	-
1984	S.D.	5.67	161	31	-	-	-	-	-	-
1985	Milw	11.84	118	22	-	-	-	-	-	-
1986	Milw	11.42	122	21	-	3	-	-	-	-
1987	Milw	10.28	127	23	-	18	-	-	-	-
1988	Phoe	8.15	153	30	-	12	-	-	-	-

DENNIS HOPSON — OHIO STATE

YR	TM	PR	OR	PS	SC	SH	RB	AS	BL	ST
1988	N.J.	7.18	157	31	-	-	-	-	-	-

JEFF HORNACEK — IOWA ST.

YR	TM	PR	OR	PS	SC	SH	RB	AS	BL	ST
1987	Phoe	8.41	150	30	-	-	-	15	-	-
1988	Phoe	14.78	81	18	-	30	-	9	-	32

PHIL HUBBARD — MICHIGAN

YR	TM	PR	OR	PS	SC	SH	RB	AS	BL	ST
1980	Detr	9.64	DNQ							
1981	Detr	14.86	79	18	-	-	-	-	-	-
1982	Clev	10.87	125	33	-	-	-	-	-	-
1983	Clev	10.68	118	30	-	-	-	-	-	-
1984	Clev	11.33	127	28	-	-	-	-	-	-
1985	Clev	15.47	79	20	-	-	-	-	-	-
1986	Clev	9.87	DNQ							
1987	Clev	12.51	102	18	-	-	-	-	-	-
1988	Clev	8.31	149	30	-	-	-	-	-	-

JAY HUMPHRIES — COLORADO

YR	TM	PR	OR	PS	SC	SH	RB	AS	BL	ST
1985	Phoe	9.86	140	28	-	-	-	29	-	23
1986	Phoe	14.62	80	13	-	-	-	25	-	29
1987	Phoe	15.70	72	12	-	-	-	10	-	-
1988	Milw	13.47	93	20	-	-	-	17	-	-

MARC IAVARONI — VIRGINIA

YR	TM	PR	OR	PS	SC	SH	RB	AS	BL	ST
1983	Phil	6.68	156	28	-	-	-	-	-	-
1984	Phil	7.18	159	31	-	-	-	-	-	-
1985	S.A.	8.00	153	37	-	-	-	-	-	-
1986	Utah	5.75	DNQ							
1987	Utah	3.91	DNQ							
1988	Utah	5.90	DNQ							

MARK JACKSON — ST. JOHN'S

YR	TM	PR	OR	PS	SC	SH	RB	AS	BL	ST
1988	N.Y.	20.68	26	4	-	-	-	6	-	12

CLEMON JOHNSON — FLORIDA A&M

YR	TM	PR	OR	PS	SC	SH	RB	AS	BL	ST
1979	Port	5.44	DNQ							
1980	Indi	10.53	125	30	-	-	-	-	5	-
1981	Indi	11.46	119	27	-	-	20	-	6	-
1982	Indi	13.72	87	21	-	-	16	-	15	-
1983	Phil	12.72	100	21	-	-	25	-	26	-
1984	Phil	8.13	155	32	-	-	-	-	-	-
1985	Phil	7.79	DNQ							
1986	Phil	5.73	DNQ							
1987	Seat	5.75	DNQ							
1988	Seat	3.42	DNQ							

DENNIS JOHNSON — PEPPERDINE

YR	TM	PR	OR	PS	SC	SH	RB	AS	BL	ST
1977	Seat	10.09	116	25	-	-	-	-	-	9
1978	Seat	11.57	111	23	-	-	-	-	-	-
1979	Seat	15.20	74	10	-	-	-	-	30	-
1980	Seat	17.17	52	8	30	-	-	-	-	-
1981	Phoe	17.10	48	4	29	-	-	-	-	24
1982	Phoe	19.00	30	4	24	-	-	-	-	-
1983	Phoe	15.69	63	11	-	-	-	-	-	-
1984	Bost	13.83	91	17	-	-	-	-	-	-
1985	Bost	17.74	53	8	-	-	-	27	-	-
1986	Bost	16.37	61	7	-	-	-	-	-	-
1987	Bost	16.37	64	10	-	-	-	25	-	-
1988	Bost	16.13	68	16	-	-	-	13	-	-

EARVIN JOHNSON — MICHIGAN ST.

YR	TM	PR	OR	PS	SC	SH	RB	AS	BL	ST
1980	LA.L	25.13	7	1	-	13	-	13	-	9
1981	LA.L	30.19	DNQ							
1982	LA.L	29.65	2	1	30	23	-	6	-	8
1983	LA.L	28.63	3	1	-	8	-	2	-	14
1984	LA.L	30.30	1	1	-	6	-	3	-	14
1985	LA.L	28.77	3	1	-	5	-	2	-	-
1986	LA.L	28.50	2	1	31	15	-	1	-	-
1987	LA.L	31.79	4	1	10	16	-	2	-	-
1988	LA.L	27.71	6	1	24	-	-	2	-	-

PRESENT PLAYERS

EDDIE A. JOHNSON — ILLINOIS
YR	TM	PR	OR	PS	SC	SH	RB	AS	BL	ST
1982	K.C.	9.32	151	36	-	-	-	-	-	-
1983	K.C.	18.10	44	15	27	-	-	-	-	-
1984	K.C.	19.11	38	12	16	-	-	-	-	-
1985	K.C.	19.41	37	14	13	-	-	-	-	-
1986	Sacr	15.76	70	18	-	-	-	-	-	-
1987	Sacr	15.56	74	15	-	-	-	-	-	-
1988	Phoe	14.82	79	18	-	-	-	-	-	-

FRANK JOHNSON — WAKE FOREST
YR	TM	PR	OR	PS	SC	SH	RB	AS	BL	ST
1982	Wash	9.68	143	30	-	-	-	21	-	-
1983	Wash	13.63	86	13	-	-	-	8	-	-
1984	Wash	13.79	92	13	-	-	-	15	-	-
1985	Wash	8.11		DNQ						
1986	Wash	10.64		DNQ						
1987	Wash	8.82		DNQ						
1988	Wash	7.04		DNQ						

KEVIN JOHNSON — CALIFORNIA
YR	TM	PR	OR	PS	SC	SH	RB	AS	BL	ST
1988	Phoe	12.32	105	22	-	-	-	12	-	24

MARQUES JOHNSON — UCLA
YR	TM	PR	OR	PS	SC	SH	RB	AS	BL	ST
1978	Milw	24.13	12	1	27	20	-	-	-	-
1979	Milw	26.64	4	1	3	10	-	-	-	-
1980	Milw	23.90	3	14	9	-	-	-	-	-
1981	Milw	22.92	10	4	18	18	-	-	-	-
1982	Milw	18.03	40	12	-	-	-	-	-	-
1983	Milw	22.59	19	4	20	-	-	-	-	-
1984	Milw	21.20	24	9	24	-	-	-	-	-
1985	LA.C	15.46	80	21	-	-	-	-	-	-
1986	LA.C	20.21	31	9	20	-	-	-	-	-
1987	LA.C	12.80		DNQ						
1988		DID NOT PLAY								

STEVE JOHNSON — OREGON ST.
YR	TM	PR	OR	PS	SC	SH	RB	AS	BL	ST
1982	K.C.	14.31	77	19	-	8	29	-	19	-
1983	K.C.	12.68	101	22	-	13	-	-	17	-
1984	Chic	11.05		DNQ						
1985	Chic	11.97	116	25	-	-	-	-	30	-
1986	S.A.	15.97	68	14	-	4	-	-	30	-
1987	Port	17.18	59	15	-	-	-	-	-	-
1988	Port	12.91		DNQ						

VINNIE JOHNSON — BAYLOR
YR	TM	PR	OR	PS	SC	SH	RB	AS	BL	ST
1980	Seat	3.50		DNQ						
1981	Seat	15.06	76	10	-	17	-	-	-	-
1982	Detr	8.07		DNQ						
1983	Detr	16.79	53	7	-	-	-	-	-	-
1984	Detr	11.66	120	22	-	-	-	-	-	-
1985	Detr	12.35	112	23	-	-	-	-	-	-
1986	Detr	13.00	99	18	-	-	-	-	-	-
1987	Detr	14.05	84	15	-	-	-	-	-	-
1988	Detr	10.00	129	23	-	-	-	-	-	-

CALDWELL JONES — ALBANY ST.
YR	TM	PR	OR	PS	SC	SH	RB	AS	BL	ST
1974	ABA	22.57	7	3	-	-	3	-	1	-
1975	ABA	26.56	5	2	-	-	6	-	1	-
1976	ABA	19.25	15	5	-	-	6	-	1	-
1977	Phil	12.66	86	22	-	-	11	-	2	-
1978	Phil	10.79	120	30	-	-	11	-	6	-
1979	Phil	16.50	62	19	-	-	7	-	7	-
1980	Phil	16.69	60	11	-	-	7	-	9	-
1981	Phil	15.14	75	21	-	-	11	-	22	-
1982	Phil	14.86	69	17	-	-	15	-	11	-
1983	Hous	14.32	80	18	-	-	26	-	19	-
1984	Hous	14.32	82	13	-	-	-	-	-	-
1985	Chic	7.03		DNQ						
1986	Port	8.10		DNQ						
1987	Port	9.12	142	30	-	-	24	-	16	-
1988	Port	8.94	144	32	-	-	-	-	14	-

CHARLES JONES — ALBANY ST.
YR	TM	PR	OR	PS	SC	SH	RB	AS	BL	ST
1984	Phil	1.00		DNQ						
1985	Wash	11.41		DNQ						
1986	Wash	8.28	153	37	-	-	-	-	7	-
1987	Wash	9.06	143	32	-	-	-	-	3	-
1988	Wash	8.16	152	35	-	-	30	-	4	-

MICHAEL JORDAN — N. CAROLINA
YR	TM	PR	OR	PS	SC	SH	RB	AS	BL	ST
1985	Chic	29.24	2	1	3	25	-	-	-	12
1986	Chic	18.89		DNQ						
1987	Chic	31.91	3	1	1	-	-	-	31	4
1988	Chic	35.05	1	1	1	15	-	-	26	4

JEROME KERSEY — LONGWOOD
YR	TM	PR	OR	PS	SC	SH	RB	AS	BL	ST
1985	Port	6.43		DNQ						
1986	Port	9.71		DNQ						
1987	Port	15.70	72	14	-	-	-	-	-	17
1988	Port	21.87	19	4	28	-	-	-	-	-

BERNARD KING — TENNESSEE
YR	TM	PR	OR	PS	SC	SH	RB	AS	BL	ST
1978	N.J.	21.32	23	8	11	-	-	-	-	-
1979	N.J.	20.10	32	8	20	-	-	-	-	-
1980	Utah	9..58		DNQ						
1981	G.St	22.31	13	5	12	4	-	-	-	-
1982	G.St	21.57	18	4	8	14	-	-	-	-
1983	N.Y.	18.62	39	12	15	-	-	-	-	-
1984	N.Y.	22.86	17	8	5	8	-	-	-	-
1985	N.Y.	26.80	6	2	1	-	-	-	-	-
1986		DID NOT PLAY								
1987	N.Y.	18.33		DNQ						
1988	Wash	13.96	87	20	-	-	-	-	-	-

ALBERT KING — MARYLAND

YR	TM	PR	OR	PS	SC	SH	RB	AS	BL	ST
1982	N.J.	10.96	124	32	-	-	-	-	-	-
1983	N.J.	16.32	58	17	-	-	-	-	-	-
1984	N.J.	14.28	83	23	-	-	-	-	-	-
1985	N.J.	11.48	DNQ							
1986	N.J.	12.82	102	22	-	-	-	-	-	-
1987	N.J.	8.36	152	27	-	-	-	-	-	-
1988	Phil	6.28	158	32	-	-	-	-	-	-

JOE KLEINE — ARKANSAS

YR	TM	PR	OR	PS	SC	SH	RB	AS	BL	ST
1986	Sacr	7.05	DNQ							
1987	Sacr	10.56	123	28	-	-	22	-	-	-
1988	Sacr	12.88	100	20	-	-	14	-	-	-

JON KONCAK — SMU

YR	TM	PR	OR	PS	SC	SH	RB	AS	BL	ST
1986	Atla	10.27	133	26	-	-	24	-	27	-
1987	Atla	9.44	136	29	-	-	21	-	20	-
1988	Atla	10.45	DNQ							

LARRY KRYSTOWIAK — MONTANA

YR	TM	PR	OR	PS	SC	SH	RB	AS	BL	ST
1988	Milw	8.94	143	31	-	-	-	-	-	-

BILL LAIMBEER — NOTRE DAME

YR	TM	PR	OR	PS	SC	SH	RB	AS	BL	ST
1981	Clev	16.46	59	18	-	-	21	-	-	-
1982	Detr	13.73	86	20	-	-	8	-	-	-
1983	Detr	22.71	18	7	-	-	4	-	30	-
1984	Detr	24.59	10	3	-	21	3	-	-	-
1985	Detr	24.05	15	6	-	-	2	-	-	-
1986	Detr	23.87	12	3	-	-	2	-	-	-
1987	Detr	22.65	17	4	-	32	6	-	-	-
1988	Detr	20.17	32	6	-	-	16	-	-	-

ALLEN LEAVELL

YR	TM	PR	OR	PS	SC	SH	RB	AS	BL	ST
1980	Hous	13.34	94	16	-	-	-	16	-	15
1981	Hous	9.72	143	26	-	-	-	10	-	14
1982	Hous	13.39	90	17	-	-	-	16	-	7
1983	Hous	15.23	69	9	-	-	-	21	-	11
1984	Hous	12.54	108	16	-	-	-	13	-	19
1985	Hous	4.90	DNQ							
1986	Hous	8.01	DNQ							
1987	Hous	8.79	DNQ							
1988	Hous	12.09	109	23	-	-	-	27	-	17

LAFAYETTE LEVER — ARIZONA ST.

YR	TM	PR	OR	PS	SC	SH	RB	AS	BL	ST
1983	Port	11.53	111	19	-	-	-	17	-	4
1984	Port	12.05	115	21	-	-	-	25	-	7
1985	Denv	18.10	50	7	-	-	-	10	-	2
1986	Denv	18.26	42	5	-	-	-	16	-	8
1987	Denv	26.93	8	2	32	-	-	21	-	11
1988	Denv	25.94	10	3	31	-	-	21	-	7

CLIFF LEVINGSTON — WICHITA ST.

YR	TM	PR	OR	PS	SC	SH	RB	AS	BL	ST
1983	Detr	6.68	DNQ							
1984	Detr	12.68	104	19	-	-	11	-	24	-
1985	Atla	14.39	94	21	-	-	25	-	-	-
1986	Atla	12.65	107	26	-	-	25	-	-	-
1987	Atla	11.85	106	28	-	-	23	-	-	-
1988	Atla	13.78	90	19	-	14	-	-	28	-

ALTON LISTER — ARIZONA ST.

YR	TM	PR	OR	PS	SC	SH	RB	AS	BL	ST
1982	Milw	8.04	DNQ							
1983	Milw	13.00	96	18	-	-	13	-	3	-
1984	Milw	12.72	103	18	-	-	12	-	6	-
1985	Milw	15.07	87	17	-	-	12	-	6	-
1986	Milw	14.25	83	18	-	-	7	-	8	-
1987	Seat	17.36	56	14	-	-	15	-	7	-
1988	Seat	11.94	112	24	-	-	4	-	5	-

JOHN LONG — DETROIT

YR	TM	PR	OR	PS	SC	SH	RB	AS	BL	ST
1979	Detr	12.17	100	18	-	-	-	-	-	-
1980	Detr	17.67	47	7	26	-	-	-	-	22
1981	Detr	13.10	99	19	-	-	-	-	-	20
1982	Detr	16.64	54	8	12	-	-	-	-	-
1983	Detr	7.41	153	31	-	-	-	-	-	-
1984	Detr	14.07	87	16	-	-	-	-	-	-
1985	Detr	12.26	113	24	-	-	-	-	-	-
1986	Detr	8.00	DNQ							
1987	Indi	11.71	110	21	-	-	-	-	-	-
1988	Indi	11.42	115	21	-	-	-	-	-	-

JOHN LUCAS — MARYLAND

YR	TM	PR	OR	PS	SC	SH	RB	AS	BL	ST
1977	Hous	13.32	75	12	-	-	-	10	-	-
1978	Hous	17.12	49	5	-	-	-	2	-	30
1979	G.St	19.10	38	4	-	-	-	4	-	29
1980	G.St	16.00	66	10	-	-	-	7	-	30
1981	G.St	11.38	123	20	-	-	-	3	-	-
1982	Wash	11.84	107	21	-	-	-	2	-	27
1983	Wash	4.71	DNQ							
1984	S.A.	18.02	47	6	-	-	-	1	-	24
1985	Hous	13.22	DNQ							
1986	Hous	17.43	51	6	-	-	-	9	-	-
1987	Milw	18.14	DNQ							
1988	Milw	10.84	120	24	-	-	-	14	-	27

RICK MAHORN — HAMPTON INST.

YR	TM	PR	OR	PS	SC	SH	RB	AS	BL	ST
1981	Wash	7.60	DNQ							
1982	Wash	17.19	48	13	-	-	28	-	17	-
1983	Wash	16.54	57	15	-	-	-	-	25	-
1984	Wash	15.68	69	19	-	-	21	-	22	-
1985	Wash	13.01	103	23	-	-	20	-	17	-
1986	Detr	7.96	DNQ							
1987	Detr	9.63	134	31	-	-	20	-	29	-
1988	Detr	15.67	72	16	-	8	15	-	-	-

PRESENT PLAYERS 315

JEFF MALONE — MISSISSIPPI ST.
YR	TM	PR	OR	PS	SC	SH	RB	AS	BL	ST
1984	Wash	8.32	154	31	-	-	-	-	-	-
1985	Wash	14.91	89	16	-	-	-	-	-	-
1986	Wash	16.90	56	10	13	-	-	-	-	-
1987	Wash	16.39	63	11	18	-	-	-	-	-
1988	Wash	15.24	76	13	17	-	-	-	-	-

KARL MALONE — LOUISIANA TECH
YR	TM	PR	OR	PS	SC	SH	RB	AS	BL	ST
1986	Utah	16.11	66	13	-	-	18	-	-	-
1987	Utah	22.05	20	7	20	-	18	-	-	-
1988	Utah	27.63	7	2	5	-	10	-	-	-

MOSES MALONE — NONE
YR	TM	PR	OR	PS	SC	SH	RB	AS	BL	ST
1975	ABA	26.36	7	4	-	-	5	-	-	-
1976	ABA	18.02		DNQ						
1977	Hous	20.40	22	9	-	-	2	-	7	-
1978	Hous	24.15	11	8	29	-	1	-	-	-
1979	Hous	32.60	2	2	5	25	1	-	-	-
1980	Hous	28.68	2	2	5	-	3	-	30	-
1981	Hous	31.67	1	1	2	-	2	-	24	-
1982	Hous	33.12	1	1	2	-	3	-	-	-
1983	Phil	30.08	1	1	5	-	1	-	18	-
1984	Phil	25.85	6	1	11	-	2	-	27	-
1985	Phil	27.30	5	1	9	-	3	-	25	-
1986	Phil	23.73	13	4	7	-	10	-	-	-
1987	Wash	24.86	10	2	9	-	7	-	-	-
1988	Wash	22.53	18	3	19	-	7	-	-	-

CEDRIC MAXWELL — UNCC
YR	TM	PR	OR	PS	SC	SH	RB	AS	BL	ST
1978	Bost	10.36		DNQ						
1979	Bost	24.48	9	2	-	2	-	-	-	-
1980	Bost	21.85	17	5	-	2	-	-	-	-
1981	Bost	18.99	30	9	-	3	-	-	-	-
1982	Bost	17.17	49	15	-	25	-	-	-	-
1983	Bost	13.82	85	24	-	-	-	-	-	-
1984	Bost	14.01	89	15	-	-	-	-	-	-
1985	Bost	12.40	111	24	-	17	-	-	-	-
1986	LA.C	17.58	49	10	-	-	-	-	-	-
1987	Hous	12.91	98	24	-	31	-	-	-	-
1988	Hous	5.14		DNQ						

TIM MCCORMICK — MICHIGAN
YR	TM	PR	OR	PS	SC	SH	RB	AS	BL	ST
1985	Seat	10.90	125	27	-	30	-	-	-	-
1986	Seat	10.95	128	32	-	25	-	-	-	-
1987	Phil	15.80	71	18	-	-	-	-	-	-
1988	Phil	14.29	85	16	-	-	-	-	-	-

RODNEY MCCRAY — LOUISVILLE
YR	TM	PR	OR	PS	SC	SH	RB	AS	BL	ST
1984	Hous	13.44	97	26	-	-	-	-	-	-
1985	Hous	19.12	39	16	-	-	-	-	-	-
1986	Hous	15.79	69	17	-	-	-	-	-	-
1987	Hous	20.70	29	7	-	13	-	-	-	-
1988	Hous	17.27	54	12	-	-	-	-	-	-

XAVIER MCDANIEL — WICHITA ST.
YR	TM	PR	OR	PS	SC	SH	RB	AS	BL	ST
1986	Seat	17.41	52	16	-	-	-	-	-	-
1987	Seat	22.41	19	6	14	-	-	-	-	-
1988	Seat	19.78	36	8	14	-	-	-	-	-

BEN MCDONALD — CAL-IRVINE
YR	TM	PR	OR	PS	SC	SH	RB	AS	BL	ST
1986	Clev	3.48		DNQ						
1987	G.St	6.38	160	29	-	-	-	-	-	-
1988	G.St	8.90	145	33	-	-	-	-	-	-

KEVIN MCHALE — MINNESOTA
YR	TM	PR	OR	PS	SC	SH	RB	AS	BL	ST
1981	Bost	11.44	120	26	-	-	-	-	4	-
1982	Bost	16.72	53	10	-	31	-	-	6	-
1983	Bost	17.04	50	9	-	24	-	-	4	-
1984	Bost	20.16	29	6	-	19	-	-	19	-
1985	Bost	23.29	19	3	31	13	29	-	19	-
1986	Bost	24.75	7	2	16	7	-	-	14	-
1987	Bost	30.92	5	2	6	1	-	-	14	-
1988	Bost	26.28	9	3	11	2	-	-	29	-

DERRICK MCKEY — ALABAMA
YR	TM	PR	OR	PS	SC	SH	RB	AS	BL	ST
1988	Seat	10.23	128	25	-	-	-	-	31	-

NATE MCMILLAN — N.C.STATE
YR	TM	PR	OR	PS	SC	SH	RB	AS	BL	ST
1987	Seat	15.35	77	13	-	-	-	4	-	14
1988	Seat	16.71	56	13	-	-	-	4	-	8

REGGIE MILLER — UCLA
YR	TM	PR	OR	PS	SC	SH	RB	AS	BL	ST
1988	Indi	9.23	137	27	-	21	-	-	-	-

DIRK MINNIEFIELD — KENTUCKY
YR	TM	PR	OR	PS	SC	SH	RB	AS	BL	ST
1986	Clev	7.57		DNQ						
1987	Hous	8.47	149	29	-	-	-	18	-	-
1988	Bost	5.93		DNQ						

MIKE MITCHELL — AUBURN
YR	TM	PR	OR	PS	SC	SH	RB	AS	BL	ST
1979	Clev	10.39	125	29	-	-	-	-	-	-
1980	Clev	20.72	25	8	10	27	-	-	-	-
1981	Clev	19.17	28	8	8	-	-	-	-	-
1982	S.A.	18.36	35	10	18	-	-	-	-	-
1983	S.A.	18.54	41	14	26	-	-	-	-	-
1984	S.A.	20.25	27	10	8	-	-	-	-	-
1985	S.A.	18.00	51	18	17	-	-	-	-	-
1986	S.A.	17.62	48	15	9	-	-	-	-	-
1987	S.A.	8.43		DNQ						
1988	S.A.	10.84	121	24	-	-	-	-	-	-

SIDNEY MONCRIEF — ARKANSAS
YR	TM	PR	OR	PS	SC	SH	RB	AS	BL	ST
1980	Milw	10.34	128	24	-	-	-	-	-	-
1981	Milw	16.96	50	9	-	12	-	-	-	-
1982	Milw	22.96	15	2	22	22	-	-	-	32
1983	Milw	22.80	15	1	13	17	-	-	-	-
1984	Milw	22.76	18	1	23	-	-	-	-	-
1985	Milw	22.40	21	2	21	-	-	-	-	-
1986	Milw	21.03	23	3	22	-	-	-	-	-
1987	Milw	12.56		DNQ						
1988	Milw	12.45	103	17	-	-	-	-	-	-

JOHNNY MOORE — TEXAS

YR	TM	PR	OR	PS	SC	SH	RB	AS	BL	ST
1981	S.A.	10.04	137	23	-	-	-	5	-	5
1982	S.A.	17.22	47	7	-	-	-	1	-	4
1983	S.A.	19.13	35	6	-	-	-	1	-	3
1984	S.A.	17.25	52	7	-	-	-	2	-	3
1985	S.A.	20.71	29	4	-	-	-	3	-	1
1986	S.A.	18.57		DNQ						
1987	S.A.	9.89		DNQ						
1988	S.A.	4.30		DNQ						

CHRIS MULLIN — ST. JOHN'S

YR	TM	PR	OR	PS	SC	SH	RB	AS	BL	ST
1986	G.St	11.84	115	23	-	-	-	-	-	26
1987	G.St	14.10	83	14	-	24	-	-	-	-
1988	G.St	20.17	33	7	20	18	-	-	-	20

LARRY NANCE — CLEMSON

YR	TM	PR	OR	PS	SC	SH	RB	AS	BL	ST
1982	Phoe	7.81		DNQ						
1983	Phoe	22.29	20	5	-	22	-	-	5	-
1984	Phoe	22.91	16	7	-	12	-	-	12	-
1985	Phoe	25.02	10	3	30	8	-	-	18	-
1986	Phoe	24.23	10	5	21	16	-	-	15	-
1987	Phoe	27.25	7	2	17	15	-	-	13	-
1988	Clev	24.51	11	2	29	29	28	-	12	-

CALVIN NATT — NE LOUISIANA

YR	TM	PR	OR	PS	SC	SH	RB	AS	BL	ST
1980	Port	20.03	32	10	24	-	-	-	-	-
1981	Port	13.92	91	23	-	-	-	-	-	-
1982	Port	20.93	23	7	-	4	-	-	-	-
1983	Port	20.71	26	8	22	10	-	-	-	-
1984	Port	18.10	44	15	-	1	-	-	-	-
1985	Denv	24.31	13	5	11	18	-	-	-	-
1986	Denv	17.81	47	14	-	-	-	-	-	-
1987	Denv	11.00		DNQ						
1988	Denv	9.70		DNQ						

JOHNNY NEWMAN — RICHMOND

YR	TM	PR	OR	PS	SC	SH	RB	AS	BL	ST
1987	Clev	3.37		DNQ						
1988	N.Y.	7.60	156	33	-	-	-	-	-	-

KURT NIMPHIUS — ARIZONA ST.

YR	TM	PR	OR	PS	SC	SH	RB	AS	BL	ST
1982	Dall	8.43		DNQ						
1983	Dall	9.51		DNQ						
1984	Dall	13.54	96	24	-	-	-	-	9	-
1985	Dall	10.76	127	23	-	-	-	-	11	-
1986	LA.C	12.73	105	21	-	-	-	-	20	-
1987	Detr	6.06		DNQ						
1988	S.A.	5.54		DNQ						

NORM NIXON — DUQUESNE

YR	TM	PR	OR	PS	SC	SH	RB	AS	BL	ST
1978	LA.L	15.37	63	8	-	-	-	7	-	-
1979	LA.L	21.79	22	2	-	11	-	5	-	8
1980	LA.L	18.89	37	4	-	-	-	14	-	-
1981	LA.L	18.48	33	2	-	-	-	6	-	32
1982	LA.L	18.05	39	6	-	-	-	14	-	-
1983	LA.L	15.19	71	10	-	-	-	18	-	-
1984	S.D.	19.52	36	4	-	-	-	6	-	-
1985	LA.C	17.49	56	9	-	-	-	7	-	-
1986	LA.C	16.16	64	9	-	-	-	8	-	-
1987		DID NOT PLAY								
1988		DID NOT PLAY								

KEN NORMAN — ILLINOIS

YR	TM	PR	OR	PS	SC	SH	RB	AS	BL	ST
1988	LA.C	8.23	151	32	-	-	-	-	-	-

CHARLES OAKLEY — VIRGINIA UNION

YR	TM	PR	OR	PS	SC	SH	RB	AS	BL	ST
1986	Chic	14.40	82	23	-	-	1	-	-	-
1987	Chic	20.59	30	9	-	-	4	-	-	-
1988	Chic	20.54	29	8	-	-	2	-	-	-

AKEEM OLAJUWON — HOUSTON

YR	TM	PR	OR	PS	SC	SH	RB	AS	BL	ST
1985	Hous	25.22	9	4	25	-	6	-	7	-
1986	Hous	28.40	3	1	8	-	12	-	6	19
1987	Hous	28.99	6	1	12	-	14	-	4	27
1988	Hous	28.10	4	1	10	-	5	-	6	18

LOUIS ORR — SYRACUSE

YR	TM	PR	OR	PS	SC	SH	RB	AS	BL	ST
1981	Indi	11.09	127	26	-	-	-	-	-	-
1982	Indi	11.44	114	27	-	-	-	-	-	-
1983	N.Y.	7.94	148	36	-	-	-	-	-	-
1984	N.Y.	8.03	156	34	-	-	-	-	-	-
1985	N.Y.	13.35	102	24	-	-	-	-	-	-
1986	N.Y.	11.72	116	23	-	-	-	-	-	-
1987	N.Y.	8.08	156	28	-	-	-	-	-	-
1988	N.Y.	1.14		DNQ						

ROBERT PARISH — CENTENARY

YR	TM	PR	OR	PS	SC	SH	RB	AS	BL	ST
1977	G.St	13.21		DNQ						
1978	G.St	14.89	66	22	-	-	12	-	10	-
1979	G.St	23.39	12	6	-	-	2	-	4	-
1980	G.St	20.82	24	9	-	-	4	-	13	-
1981	Bost	23.55	8	4	25	22	4	-	3	-
1982	Bost	24.58	12	6	20	27	5	-	10	-
1983	Bost	24.31	8	4	31	23	5	-	13	-
1984	Bost	23.65	14	5	-	27	15	-	31	-
1985	Bost	22.33	22	7	-	29	19	-	-	-
1986	Bost	20.84	26	6	-	31	16	-	23	-
1987	Bost	23.66	13	3	-	11	25	-	17	-
1988	Bost	19.15	41	7	-	5	20	-	32	-

JIM PAXSON — DAYTON

YR	TM	PR	OR	PS	SC	SH	RB	AS	BL	ST
1980	Port	4.99		DNQ						
1981	Port	16.57	58	11	-	20	-	-	-	25
1982	Port	16.87	51	7	26	28	-	-	-	30
1983	Port	17.67	46	4	17	30	-	-	-	25
1984	Port	17.64	50	5	21	30	-	-	-	-
1985	Port	17.21	59	8	-	-	-	-	-	-
1986	Port	12.63	108	20	-	-	-	-	-	28
1987	Port	11.00	119	24	-	-	-	-	-	-
1988	Bost	6.49		DNQ						

JOHN PAXSON — NOTRE DAME

YR	TM	PR	OR	PS	SC	SH	RB	AS	BL	ST
1984	S.A.	4.45		DNQ						
1985	S.A.	6.23		DNQ						
1986	Chic	7.52	156	28	-	-	-	30	-	-
1987	Chic	13.09	94	17	-	-	-	-	-	-
1988	Chic	8.96	142	29	-	-	-	-	-	-

SAM PERKINS — N. CAROLINA

YR	TM	PR	OR	PS	SC	SH	RB	AS	BL	ST
1985	Dall	15.05	88	18	-	-	-	-	-	-
1986	Dall	19.67	36	7	-	-	-	-	31	-
1987	Dall	18.19	54	13	-	-	-	-	-	-
1988	Dall	16.71	57	12	-	-	-	-	-	-

CHUCK PERSON — AUBURN

YR	TM	PR	OR	PS	SC	SH	RB	AS	BL	ST
1987	Indi	19.63	39	10	-	-	-	-	-	-
1988	Indi	16.65	59	14	-	-	-	-	-	-

JIM PETERSEN — MINNESOTA

YR	TM	PR	OR	PS	SC	SH	RB	AS	BL	ST
1985	Hous	4.42		DNQ						
1986	Hous	8.93	146	36	-	-	-	-	-	-
1987	Hous	14.33	82	20	-	-	-	-	22	-
1988	Hous	12.09	110	25	-	-	-	-	-	-

RICKY PIERCE — DETROIT

YR	TM	PR	OR	PS	SC	SH	RB	AS	BL	ST
1983	Detr	1.51		DNQ						
1984	S.D.	7.43		DNQ						
1985	Milw	10.19		DNQ						
1986	Milw	13.63	86	13	-	14	-	-	-	-
1987	Milw	17.25	57	8	29	5	-	-	-	-
1988	Milw	12.97		DNQ						

ED PINCKNEY — VILLANOVA

YR	TM	PR	OR	PS	SC	SH	RB	AS	BL	ST
1986	Phoe	9.43	141	34	-	-	-	-	-	-
1987	Phoe	15.50	75	17	-	8	-	-	-	-
1988	Sacr	7.24		DNQ						

SCOTTIE PIPPEN — CENTRAL ARKANSAS

YR	TM	PR	OR	PS	SC	SH	RB	AS	BL	ST
1988	Chic	9.22	139	28	-	-	-	-	-	22

TERRY PORTER — WISC.-ST.POINT.

YR	TM	PR	OR	PS	SC	SH	RB	AS	BL	ST
1986	Port	7.44		DNQ						
1987	Port	19.52	41	9	-	-	-	7	-	16
1988	Port	22.87	16	3	-	17	-	5	-	26

PAUL PRESSEY — TULSA

YR	TM	PR	OR	PS	SC	SH	RB	AS	BL	ST
1983	Milw	8.61	141	35	-	-	-	-	-	9
1984	Milw	10.56	138	31	-	-	-	-	-	27
1985	Milw	20.56	30	11	-	-	-	25	-	-
1986	Milw	20.74	27	8	-	-	-	13	-	11
1987	Milw	18.79	50	12	-	-	-	20	-	21
1988	Milw	18.67	44	10	-	-	-	-	-	-

MARK PRICE — GEORGIA TECH

YR	TM	PR	OR	PS	SC	SH	RB	AS	BL	ST
1987	Clev	6.79		DNQ						
1988	Clev	16.92	55	12	-	9	-	29	-	-

KURT RAMBIS — SANTA CLARA

YR	TM	PR	OR	PS	SC	SH	RB	AS	BL	ST
1982	LA.L	9.22		DNQ						
1983	LA.L	12.79	98	19	-	14	17	-	17	-
1984	LA.L	8.13		DNQ						
1985	LA.L	10.71	129	28	-	-	9	-	-	26
1986	LA.L	11.53	119	29	-	6	6	-	-	-
1987	LA.L	10.08	130	30	-	-	19	-	-	32
1988	LA.L	6.97		DNQ						

BLAIR RASMUSSEN — OREGON

YR	TM	PR	OR	PS	SC	SH	RB	AS	BL	ST
1986	Denv	2.96		DNQ						
1987	Denv	11.74	109	23	-	-	8	-	25	-
1988	Denv	13.42	95	20	-	-	33	-	19	-

ROBERT REID — ST. MARY'S

YR	TM	PR	OR	PS	SC	SH	RB	AS	BL	ST
1978	Hous	9.45	139	26	-	-	-	-	-	-
1979	Hous	14.02	83	21	-	-	-	-	-	-
1980	Hous	15.84	67	18	-	-	-	-	-	18
1981	Hous	19.61	23	7	-	-	-	-	-	18
1982	Hous	16.77	52	16	-	-	-	-	-	-
1983		DID NOT PLAY								
1984	Hous	15.41	72	21	-	-	-	-	-	-
1985	Hous	9.17	144	30	-	-	-	-	-	-
1986	Hous	12.15	110	21	-	-	-	-	-	-
1987	Hous	13.41	90	18	-	-	-	-	-	-
1988	Hous	6.00		DNQ						

GLENN RIVERS — MARQUETTE

YR	TM	PR	OR	PS	SC	SH	RB	AS	BL	ST
1984	Atla	11.27	128	22	-	-	-	31	-	9
1985	Atla	17.16	60	10	-	-	-	23	-	4
1986	Atla	16.11	65	10	-	-	-	5	-	5
1987	Atla	20.33	34	7	-	-	-	3	-	8
1988	Atla	20.36	30	5	-	-	-	3	-	19

FRED ROBERTS — BYU

YR	TM	PR	OR	PS	SC	SH	RB	AS	BL	ST
1984	S.A.	9.52		DNQ						
1985	Utah	7.95		DNQ						
1986	Utah	5.07		DNQ						
1987	Bost	6.12		DNQ						
1988	Bost	6.08		DNQ						

ALVIN ROBERTSON — ARKANSAS

YR	TM	PR	OR	PS	SC	SH	RB	AS	BL	ST
1985	S.A.	11.44	120	26	-	-	-	-	-	5
1986	S.A.	22.48	15	1	-	-	-	-	-	1
1987	S.A.	19.47	43	5	-	-	-	-	-	1
1988	S.A.	22.94	15	4	25	-	-	28	-	2

CLIFF ROBINSON — USC

YR	TM	PR	OR	PS	SC	SH	RB	AS	BL	ST
1980	N.J.	14.24	82	15	-	-	13	-	-	-
1981	N.J.	17.90	38	9	21	-	31	-	-	-
1982	Clev	19.31	28	7	32	-	21	-	23	-
1983	Clev	20.16	27	7	-	-	7	-	-	-
1984	Clev	18.95	39	8	-	-	10	-	-	-
1985	Wash	18.43	42	9	-	-	22	-	-	-
1986	Wash	19.46	38	9	-	-	29	-	-	-
1987	Phil	13.96	86	23	-	-	-	-	-	20
1988	Phil	16.61	60	15	30	-	-	-	-	-

DENNIS RODMAN — SE OKLAHOMA

YR	TM	PR	OR	PS	SC	SH	RB	AS	BL	ST
1987	Detr	8.45		DNQ						
1988	Detr	15.84	70	17	-	-	6	-	-	-

WAYNE ROLLINS — CLEMSON

YR	TM	PR	OR	PS	SC	SH	RB	AS	BL	ST
1978	Atla	13.55	83	25	-	-	30	-	1	-
1979	Atla	15.10	75	23	-	-	19	-	1	-
1980	Atla	18.17	42	13	-	16	6	-	2	-
1981	Atla	14.56		DNQ						
1982	Atla	14.42	76	18	-	19	10	-	2	-
1983	Atla	18.09	45	13	-	-	14	-	1	-
1984	Atla	15.65	70	20	-	-	-	-	2	-
1985	Atla	12.51	109	20	-	23	-	-	3	-
1986	Atla	11.26	124	24	-	-	-	-	5	-
1987	Atla	11.61	113	25	-	20	29	-	6	-
1988	Atla	10.39	125	26	-	28	25	-	7	-

JOHN SALLEY — GEORGIA TECH

YR	TM	PR	OR	PS	SC	SH	RB	AS	BL	ST
1987	Detr	8.34		DNQ						
1988	Detr	12.34	104	23	-	26	-	-	11	-

RALPH SAMPSON — VIRGINIA

YR	TM	PR	OR	PS	SC	SH	RB	AS	BL	ST
1984	Hous	24.01	13	4	22	-	4	-	5	-
1985	Hous	23.39	18	2	19	-	28	-	13	-
1986	Hous	22.85	14	3	30	-	14	-	25	-
1987	Hous	18.05		DNQ						
1988	G.St	17.94	51	11	-	-	17	-	16	-

MICHAEL SANDERS — UCLA

YR	TM	PR	OR	PS	SC	SH	RB	AS	BL	ST
1983	S.A.	7.65		DNQ						
1984	Phoe	4.84		DNQ						
1985	Phoe	10.60		DNQ						
1986	Phoe	11.15	127	24	-	-	-	-	-	31
1987	Phoe	10.12	129	22	-	-	-	-	-	-
1988	Clev	5.98		DNQ						

DANNY SCHAYES — SYRACUSE

YR	TM	PR	OR	PS	SC	SH	RB	AS	BL	ST
1982	Utah	10.57	132	29	-	-	30	-	25	-
1983	Denv	14.35	79	17	-	-	24	-	28	-
1984	Denv	10.16		DNQ						
1985	Denv	5.28		DNQ						
1986	Denv	11.19	126	25	-	-	28	-	29	-
1987	Denv	11.22	116	27	-	-	-	-	18	-
1988	Denv	18.63	45	8	-	10	11	-	21	-

DETLEF SCHREMPF — WASHINGTON

YR	TM	PR	OR	PS	SC	SH	RB	AS	BL	ST
1986	Dall	7.83		DNQ						
1987	Dall	10.04	132	24	-	-	-	-	-	-
1988	Dall	9.07	141	29	-	-	-	-	-	-

BYRON SCOTT — ARIZONA ST.

YR	TM	PR	OR	PS	SC	SH	RB	AS	BL	ST
1984	LA.L	9.86	142	28	-	-	-	-	-	28
1985	LA.L	15.12	85	15	-	11	-	-	-	-
1986	LA.L	13.12	94	15	-	-	-	-	-	-
1987	LA.L	16.54	62	10	-	23	-	-	-	-
1988	LA.L	21.73	21	5	12	7	-	-	-	25

BRAD SELLERS — OHIO ST.

YR	TM	PR	OR	PS	SC	SH	RB	AS	BL	ST
1987	Chic	10.08	131	23	-	-	-	30	-	-
1988	Chic	9.22	138	27	-	-	-	-	-	-

PURVIS SHORT — JACKSON ST.

YR	TM	PR	OR	PS	SC	SH	RB	AS	BL	ST
1979	G.St	10.19	129	32	-	-	-	-	-	-
1980	G.St	15.47	69	19	-	-	-	-	-	-
1981	G.St	15.42	68	13	-	-	-	-	-	-
1982	G.St	13.16	92	21	-	-	-	-	-	-
1983	G.St	18.81	37	10	19	-	-	-	-	-
1984	G.St	18.81	40	13	10	-	-	-	-	-
1985	G.St	21.12	26	9	4	-	-	-	-	-
1986	G.St	21.77	18	6	5	-	-	-	-	-
1987	G.St	16.00		DNQ						
1988	Hous	11.74	113	19	-	-	-	-	-	-

JERRY SICHTING — PURDUE

YR	TM	PR	OR	PS	SC	SH	RB	AS	BL	ST
1981	Indi	2.85		DNQ						
1982	Indi	5.16		DNQ						
1983	Indi	11.83	108	18	-	-	-	27	-	-
1984	Indi	14.15	84	12	-	20	-	26	-	-
1985	Indi	11.19	123	25	-	19	-	-	-	-
1986	Bost	7.61	155	27	-	1	-	-	-	-
1987	Bost	6.47	159	31	-	-	-	-	-	-
1988	Port	4.92		DNQ						

JACK SIKMA — ILL. WESLEYAN

YR	TM	PR	OR	PS	SC	SH	RB	AS	BL	ST
1978	Seat	13.96	78	15	-	-	-	-	-	-
1979	Seat	22.17	20	9	-	-	8	-	-	-
1980	Seat	21.09	23	8	-	-	8	-	-	-
1981	Seat	22.09	15	7	30	-	15	-	-	-
1982	Seat	27.01	7	3	23	-	6	-	-	-
1983	Seat	23.79	10	5	-	-	6	-	-	-
1984	Seat	25.66	8	2	-	-	13	-	-	-
1985	Seat	25.60	8	3	-	-	15	-	29	-
1986	Seat	21.54	20	5	-	-	26	-	-	-
1987	Milw	19.37	44	9	-	-	9	-	-	-
1988	Milw	21.77	20	6	-	-	-	-	-	-

DEREK SMITH — LOUISVILLE

YR	TM	PR	OR	PS	SC	SH	RB	AS	BL	ST
1983	G.St	2.00		DNQ						
1984	S.D.	9.69	144	29	-	26	-	-	-	-
1985	LA.C	20.20	32	4	18	21	-	-	-	-
1986	LA.C	19.36		DNQ						
1987	Sacr	13.90	87	16	-	-	-	-	-	-
1988	Sacr	11.69		DNQ						

KENNY SMITH — NORTH CAROLINA

YR	TM	PR	OR	PS	SC	SH	RB	AS	BL	ST
1988	Sacr	15.23	77	17	-	-	-	25	-	-

LARRY SMITH — ALCORN ST.

YR	TM	PR	OR	PS	SC	SH	RB	AS	BL	ST
1981	G.St	17.62	40	10	-	-	1	-	-	-
1982	G.St	15.88	60	14	-	-	1	-	-	-
1983	G.St	15.20		DNQ						
1984	G.St	13.59	94	16	-	-	8	-	-	-
1985	G.St	17.49	57	13	-	-	4	-	-	-
1986	G.St	16.64	59	12	-	-	4	-	-	-
1987	G.St	17.25	58	14	-	-	1	-	-	-
1988	G.St	12.00		DNQ						

OTIS SMITH — JACKSONVILLE

YR	TM	PR	OR	PS	SC	SH	RB	AS	BL	ST
1987	Denv	2.18		DNQ						
1988	G.St	12.24	107	22	-	-	-	-	-	15

PRESENT PLAYERS 319

RORY SPARROW — VILLANOVA

YR	TM	PR	OR	PS	SC	SH	RB	AS	BL	ST
1981	N.J.	3.93		DNQ						
1982	Atla	13.07	94	18	-	-	-	26	-	-
1983	N.Y.	12.44	104	16	-	-	-	-	-	-
1984	N.Y.	13.08	100	14	-	-	-	14	-	-
1985	N.Y.	13.82	98	19	-	-	-	9	-	-
1986	N.Y.	13.23	92	15	-	-	-	20	-	-
1987	N.Y.	9.29	138	25	-	-	-	17	-	-
1988	Chic	5.17		DNQ						

STEVE STIPANOVICH — MISSOURI

YR	TM	PR	OR	PS	SC	SH	RB	AS	BL	ST
1984	Indi	14.78	75	21	-	-	-	-	-	-
1985	Indi	16.73	66	12	-	-	31	-	-	-
1986	Indi	17.23	53	12	-	-	-	-	-	-
1987	Indi	19.22	45	10	-	-	-	-	-	-
1988	Indi	18.13	49	9	-	-	32	-	-	-

JOHN STOCKTON — GONZAGA

YR	TM	PR	OR	PS	SC	SH	RB	AS	BL	ST
1985	Utah	8.66		DNQ						
1986	Utah	13.99	84	14	-	-	-	2	-	2
1987	Utah	14.80	80	14	-	-	-	1	-	2
1988	Utah	26.54	8	2	-	1	-	1	-	1

JOHN SUNDVOLD — MISSOURI

YR	TM	PR	OR	PS	SC	SH	RB	AS	BL	ST
1984	Seat	5.57		DNQ						
1985	Seat	5.10		DNQ						
1986	S.A.	7.50		DNQ						
1987	S.A.	10.54	124	22	-	-	-	32	-	-
1988	S.A.	8.00		DNQ						

ROY TARPLEY — MICHIGAN

YR	TM	PR	OR	PS	SC	SH	RB	AS	BL	ST
1987	Dall	11.59		DNQ						
1988	Dall	20.23	31	9	-	-	1	-	30	-

TERRY TEAGLE — BAYLOR

YR	TM	PR	OR	PS	SC	SH	RB	AS	BL	ST
1983	Hous	7.63	151	30	-	-	-	-	-	-
1984	Hous	3.85		DNQ						
1985	G.St	7.10		DNQ						
1986	G.St	11.55	117	24	-	-	-	-	-	-
1987	G.St	8.24	154	32	-	-	-	-	-	-
1988	G.St	7.87		DNQ						

REGGIE THEUS — UNLV

YR	TM	PR	OR	PS	SC	SH	RB	AS	BL	ST
1979	Chic	13.88	85	14	-	-	-	28	-	-
1980	Chic	19.35	35	5	20	-	-	21	-	-
1981	Chic	18.12	37	6	26	-	-	-	-	-
1982	Chic	17.10	50	6	-	-	-	25	-	-
1983	Chic	20.12	29	3	9	-	-	-	-	28
1984	K.C.	11.51	124	26	-	-	-	12	-	-
1985	K.C.	18.20	48	5	-	-	-	6	-	-
1986	Sacr	21.02	24	4	-	-	-	6	-	-
1987	Sacr	20.90	28	5	28	-	-	11	-	-
1988	Sacr	18.44	46	8	13	-	-	31	-	-

ISIAH THOMAS — INDIANA

YR	TM	PR	OR	PS	SC	SH	RB	AS	BL	ST
1982	Detr	15.63	61	9	-	-	-	9	-	13
1983	Detr	21.68	23	2	12	-	-	20	-	10
1984	Detr	24.38	11	2	19	-	-	5	-	6
1985	Detr	27.85	4	2	23	-	-	1	-	14
1986	Detr	24.44	8	2	18	-	-	3	-	12
1987	Detr	22.04	21	4	27	-	-	6	-	26
1988	Detr	19.86	35	6	27	-	-	11	-	30

LA SALLE THOMPSON — TEXAS

YR	TM	PR	OR	PS	SC	SH	RB	AS	BL	ST
1983	K.C.	8.56		DNQ						
1984	K.C.	16.27	65	16	-	-	1	-	4	-
1985	K.C.	19.01	41	9	-	-	5	-	16	-
1986	Sacr	18.76	39	11	-	-	8	-	22	-
1987	Sacr	16.05	68	16	-	-	12	-	12	-
1988	Sacr	11.25		DNQ						

MYCHAL THOMPSON — MINNESOTA

YR	TM	PR	OR	PS	SC	SH	RB	AS	BL	ST
1979	Port	17.22	52	17	-	-	-	-	11	-
1980		DID NOT PLAY								
1981	Port	20.35	19	9	-	-	-	-	12	-
1982	Port	25.63	10	5	17	-	14	-	-	-
1983	Port	20.11	30	9	-	-	-	-	-	-
1984	Port	20.48	26	8	-	-	31	-	29	-
1985	Port	19.54	36	7	-	-	-	-	26	-
1986	Port	15.66	72	15	-	-	-	-	-	-
1987	L.A.L	11.35	115	26	-	-	-	-	-	-
1988	L.A.L	12.81	101	21	-	-	-	-	27	-

OTIS THORPE — PROVIDENCE

YR	TM	PR	OR	PS	SC	SH	RB	AS	BL	ST
1985	K.C.	14.49	92	20	-	22	23	-	-	-
1986	Sacr	12.07	111	28	-	23	-	-	-	-
1987	Sacr	22.82	16	4	-	29	28	-	-	-
1988	Sacr	23.71	13	4	16	-	19	-	-	-

SEDALE THREATT — W. VIRG.TECH

YR	TM	PR	OR	PS	SC	SH	RB	AS	BL	ST
1984	Phil	2.67		DNQ						
1985	Phil	5.41		DNQ						
1986	Phil	8.81	147	34	-	-	-	-	-	23
1987	Chic	9.21	139	29	-	-	-	31	-	25
1988	Seat	7.35		DNQ						

WAYMAN TISDALE — OKLAHOMA

YR	TM	PR	OR	PS	SC	SH	RB	AS	BL	ST
1986	Indi	14.60	81	22	-	-	-	-	-	-
1987	Indi	14.36	81	19	-	-	-	-	-	-
1988	Indi	15.82	71	15	-	-	-	-	-	-

ANDREW TONEY — SW LOUISIANA

YR	TM	PR	OR	PS	SC	SH	RB	AS	BL	ST
1981	Phil	10.21	134	27	-	-	-	-	-	-
1982	Phil	13.13	93	16	-	30	-	-	-	-
1983	Phil	16.09	61	10	28	-	-	-	-	-
1984	Phil	17.22	53	6	26	23	-	-	-	-
1985	Phil	16.24	72	14	-	26	-	-	-	-
1986	Phil	1.17		DNQ						
1987	Phil	8.88		DNQ						
1988	Phil	7.59		DNQ						

KELLY TRIPUCKA — NOTRE DAME

YR	TM	PR	OR	PS	SC	SH	RB	AS	BL	ST
1982	Detr	18.77	31	9	13	-	-	-	-	-
1983	Detr	21.97	22	6	3	-	-	-	-	-
1984	Detr	16.39	63	20	20	-	-	-	-	-
1985	Detr	15.98	75	19	-	-	-	-	-	-
1986	Detr	18.15	43	13	24	-	-	-	-	-
1987	Utah	10.80	122	20	-	-	-	-	-	-
1988	Utah	7.90		DNQ						

TRENT TUCKER — MINNESOTA

YR	TM	PR	OR	PS	SC	SH	RB	AS	BL	ST
1983	N.Y.	8.83	138	24	-	-	-	-	-	-
1984	N.Y.	8.46	153	30	-	-	-	-	-	21
1985	N.Y.	9.65	143	29	-	-	-	-	-	-
1986	N.Y.	10.00	135	28	-	-	-	-	-	-
1987	N.Y.	10.81	121	26	-	-	-	-	-	5
1988	N.Y.	6.65		DNQ						

MEL TURPIN — KENTUCKY

YR	TM	PR	OR	PS	SC	SH	RB	AS	BL	ST
1985	Clev	12.05	114	21	-	-	-	-	21	-
1986	Clev	16.50	60	15	-	18	-	-	21	-
1987	Clev	6.02		DNQ						
1988	Utah	6.89		DNQ						

TERRY TYLER — DETROIT

YR	TM	PR	OR	PS	SC	SH	RB	AS	BL	ST
1979	Detr	16.98	55	17	-	-	-	-	5	-
1980	Detr	16.76	58	16	-	-	-	-	4	-
1981	Detr	17.21	47	11	-	-	-	-	7	-
1982	Detr	14.55	74	19	-	-	-	-	5	-
1983	Detr	16.11	60	18	-	-	-	-	12	-
1984	Detr	8.67	151	33	-	-	-	-	-	-
1985	Detr	12.49	110	25	-	-	-	-	20	-
1986	Sacr	10.94	129	25	-	-	-	-	11	-
1987	Sacr	10.27	128	21	-	-	-	-	26	-
1988	Sacr	6.88		DNQ						

DARNELL VALENTINE — KANSAS

YR	TM	PR	OR	PS	SC	SH	RB	AS	BL	ST
1982	Port	7.33		DNQ						
1983	Port	14.40		DNQ						
1984	Port	12.06	114	20	-	-	-	17	-	15
1985	Port	15.32	82	15	-	-	-	13	-	11
1986	LA.C	8.29	152	26	-	-	-	19	-	15
1987	LA.C	13.06	95	18	-	-	-	9	-	10
1988	LA.C	9.33	134	28	-	-	-	10	-	6

KIKI VANDEWEGHE — UCLA

YR	TM	PR	OR	PS	SC	SH	RB	AS	BL	ST
1981	Denv	11.41		DNQ						
1982	Denv	21.32	21	5	14	2	-	-	-	-
1983	Denv	24.23	9	2	2	4	-	-	-	-
1984	Denv	26.40	5	3	3	5	-	-	-	-
1985	Port	18.19	49	17	16	10	-	-	-	-
1986	Port	19.84	35	11	6	9	-	-	-	-
1987	Port	21.85	24	5	5	6	-	-	-	-
1988	Port	16.51		DNQ						

SAM VINCENT — MICHIGAN ST.

YR	TM	PR	OR	PS	SC	SH	RB	AS	BL	ST
1986	Bost	3.14		DNQ						
1987	Bost	3.43		DNQ						
1988	Chic	10.67	122	25	-	-	-	7	-	-

JAY VINCENT — MICHIGAN ST.

YR	TM	PR	OR	PS	SC	SH	RB	AS	BL	ST
1982	Dall	19.07	29	8	15	-	-	-	-	-
1983	Dall	18.77	38	11	-	-	-	-	-	-
1984	Dall	9.61	145	32	-	-	-	-	-	-
1985	Dall	19.65	34	1	-	27	-	-	-	-
1986	Dall	13.34	89	19	-	-	-	-	-	-
1987	Wash	11.27		DNQ						
1988	Denv	12.92	99	21	-	-	-	-	-	-

DANNY VRANES — UTAH

YR	TM	PR	OR	PS	SC	SH	RB	AS	BL	ST
1982	Seat	5.61		DNQ						
1983	Seat	9.94	125	31	-	-	-	-	-	-
1984	Seat	10.75	132	30	-	-	-	-	-	-
1985	Seat	10.08	136	28	-	-	-	-	-	-
1986	Seat	6.21	158	29	-	-	-	-	-	-
1987	Phil	4.26		DNQ						
1988	Phil	3.88		DNQ						

DARRELL WALKER — ARKANSAS

YR	TM	PR	OR	PS	SC	SH	RB	AS	BL	ST
1984	N.Y.	8.37		DNQ						
1985	N.Y.	13.54	101	19	-	-	-	-	-	8
1986	N.Y.	10.73	131	25	-	-	-	-	-	6
1987	Denv	13.46	89	17	-	-	-	-	-	15
1988	Wash	6.54		DNQ						

KENNY WALKER — KENTUCKY

YR	TM	PR	OR	PS	SC	SH	RB	AS	BL	ST
1987	N.Y.	11.84	107	19	-	-	-	-	-	-
1988	N.Y.	11.17	118	23	-	-	-	-	-	-

BILL WALTON — UCLA

YR	TM	PR	OR	PS	SC	SH	RB	AS	BL	ST
1975	Port	25.02		DNQ						
1976	Port	23.31	6	5	-	-	2	-	10	-
1977	Port	29.11	3	3	-	21	3	-	4	-
1978	Port	28.67	3	3	31	22	2	29	7	-
1979		DID NOT PLAY								
1980	S.D.	18.93		DNQ						
1981		DID NOT PLAY								
1982		DID NOT PLAY								
1983	S.D.	21.97		DNQ						
1984	S.D.	18.04	45	13	-	-	7	-	13	-
1985	LA.C	16.96	61	11	-	-	1	-	5	-
1986	Bost	13.38	87	19	-	29	3	-	9	-
1987	Bost	4.10		DNQ						
1988		DID NOT PLAY								

DWAYNE WASHINGTON — SYRACUSE

YR	TM	PR	OR	PS	SC	SH	RB	AS	BL	ST
1987	N.J.	9.19	140	26	-	-	-	27	-	19
1988	N.J.	8.12	154	31	-	-	-	-	-	11

MARK WEST — OLD DOMINION

YR	TM	PR	OR	PS	SC	SH	RB	AS	BL	ST
1984	Dall	1.59		DNQ						
1985	Clev	5.59		DNQ						
1986	Clev	7.09		DNQ						
1987	Clev	8.00		DNQ						
1988	Phoe	12.63	102	22	-	-	29	-	9	-

RORY WHITE — SOUTH ALABAMA

YR	TM	PR	OR	PS	SC	SH	RB	AS	BL	ST
1983	Phoe	4.31	DNQ							
1984	S.D.	4.38	DNQ							
1985	LA.C	5.15	DNQ							
1986	LAC	9.73	137	34	-	-	-	-	-	-
1987	LA.C	8.13	155	34	-	-	-	-	-	-
1988	LA.C									

DOMINIQUE WILKINS — GEORGIA

YR	TM	PR	OR	PS	SC	SH	RB	AS	BL	ST
1983	Atla	15.63	64	19	-	-	-	-	-	-
1984	Atla	19.60	35	11	17	-	-	-	-	-
1985	Atla	22.01	23	7	6	-	-	-	-	-
1986	Atla	25.50	6	3	1	-	-	-	-	-
1987	Atla	24.15	11	3	2	-	-	-	-	-
1988	Atla	24.27	12	3	2	-	-	-	-	-

GERALD WILKINS — TENN-CHAT

YR	TM	PR	OR	PS	SC	SH	RB	AS	BL	ST
1986	N.Y.	8.64	149	35	-	-	-	-	-	-
1987	N.Y.	16.23	66	13	31	-	-	-	-	-
1988	N.Y.	13.86	88	14	-	-	-	-	-	-

BUCK WILLIAMS — MARYLAND

YR	TM	PR	OR	PS	SC	SH	RB	AS	BL	ST
1982	N.J.	21.94	16	3	-	21	2	-	-	-
1983	N.J.	23.51	12	3	-	28	3	-	-	-
1984	N.J.	21.33	23	5	-	-	5	-	28	-
1985	N.J.	22.98	20	4	-	-	10	-	-	-
1986	N.J.	21.26	22	5	-	-	11	-	-	-
1987	N.J.	23.66	14	3	-	26	5	-	-	-
1988	N.J.	22.96	14	5	-	-	8	-	-	-

HERB WILLIAMS — OHIO ST.

YR	TM	PR	OR	PS	SC	SH	RB	AS	BL	ST
1982	Indi	15.50	62	15	-	-	26	-	8	-
1983	Indi	19.33	34	10	-	-	-	-	8	-
1984	Indi	17.71	49	11	-	-	-	-	21	-
1985	Indi	19.08	40	8	-	-	-	-	15	-
1986	Indi	21.79	17	4	27	-	-	-	10	-
1987	Indi	17.12	61	15	-	-	-	-	-	-
1988	Indi	12.17	108	24	-	-	-	-	8	-

JOHN WILLIAMS — TULANE

YR	TM	PR	OR	PS	SC	SH	RB	AS	BL	ST
1987	Clev	18.41	52	12	-	-	-	-	11	-
1988	Clev	14.79	80	18	-	-	-	-	10	-

JOHN S. WILLIAMS — LSU

YR	TM	PR	OR	PS	SC	SH	RB	AS	BL	ST
1987	Wash	11.42	114	20	-	-	-	-	-	3
1988	Wash	14.37	84	19	-	-	-	-	-	29

KEVIN WILLIS — MICHIGAN STATE

YR	TM	PR	OR	PS	SC	SH	RB	AS	BL	ST
1985	Atla	10.60	131	24	-	-	21	-	-	-
1986	Atla	14.74	78	21	-	-	15	-	-	-
1987	Atla	19.88	36	10	-	-	10	-	-	-
1988	Atla	13.33	96	21	-	-	24	-	-	-

DAVID WINGATE — GEORGETOWN

YR	TM	PR	OR	PS	SC	SH	RB	AS	BL	ST
1987	Phil	7.53	157	33	-	-	-	-	-	18
1988	Phil	6.07	159	33	-	-	-	-	-	-

RANDY WITTMAN — INDIANA

YR	TM	PR	OR	PS	SC	SH	RB	AS	BL	ST
1984	Atla	3.86	DNQ							
1985	Atla	9.01	DNQ							
1986	Atla	13.02	98	17	-	-	-	-	-	-
1987	Atla	11.00	119	24	-	-	-	-	-	-
1988	Atla	10.39	126	22	-	-	-	-	-	-

AL WOOD — N. CAROLINA

YR	TM	PR	OR	PS	SC	SH	RB	AS	BL	ST
1982	S.D.	8.06	DNQ							
1983	S.D.	9.75	129	21	-	-	-	-	-	-
1984	Seat	12.90	102	19	-	-	-	-	-	-
1985	Seat	14.25	95	17	-	-	-	-	-	-
1986	Seat	9.17	144	32	-	-	-	-	-	-
1987	Dall	4.87	DNQ							
1988	DID NOT PLAY									

LEON WOOD — CAL ST.-FULLERTON

YR	TM	PR	OR	PS	SC	SH	RB	AS	BL	ST
1985	Phil	1.97	DNQ							
1986	Wash	6.43	DNQ							
1987	N.J.	8.49	148	28	-	-	22	-	-	-
1988	N.J.	8.08	DNQ							

MIKE WOODSON — INDIANA

YR	TM	PR	OR	PS	SC	SH	RB	AS	BL	ST
1981	N.Y.	3.99	DNQ							
1982	K.C.	14.47	75	12	-	-	-	-	-	14
1983	K.C.	16.64	55	8	-	-	-	-	-	18
1984	K.C.	12.55	107	20	-	-	-	-	-	-
1985	K.C.	13.74	100	18	-	-	-	-	-	16
1986	Sacr	13.10	95	16	-	-	-	-	-	-
1987	LA.C	11.92	105	20	-	-	-	-	-	-
1988	LA.C	13.80	89	15	-	-	-	-	-	-

ORLANDO WOOLRIDGE — N. DAME

YR	TM	PR	OR	PS	SC	SH	RB	AS	BL	ST
1982	Chic	7.23	DNQ							
1983	Chic	15.35	68	20	-	26	-	-	-	-
1984	Chic	16.73	57	17	31	-	-	-	-	-
1985	Chic	20.74	27	10	12	15	-	-	-	-
1986	Chic	18.36	41	12	19	-	-	-	-	-
1987	N.J.	19.59	40	11	26	-	-	-	-	-
1988	N.J.	14.95	DNQ							

JAMES WORTHY — N. CAROLINA

YR	TM	PR	OR	PS	SC	SH	RB	AS	BL	ST
1983	LA.L	14.71	76	22	-	9	-	-	-	-
1984	LA.L	17.27	51	16	-	15	-	-	-	-
1985	LA.L	19.59	35	13	-	7	-	-	-	-
1986	LA.L	20.92	25	7	25	5	-	-	-	-
1987	LA.L	20.20	35	9	30	27	-	-	-	-
1988	LA.L	20.09	34	7	23	25	-	-	-	-

DANNY YOUNG — WAKE FOREST

YR	TM	PR	OR	PS	SC	SH	RB	AS	BL	ST
1985	Seat	2.00	DNQ							
1986	Seat	9.51	139	30	-	22	-	-	-	17
1987	Seat	8.79	146	30	-	-	13	-	30	
1988	Seat	5.38	DNQ							

FORMER PLAYERS

ALVAN ADAMS — OKLAHOMA
YR	TM	PR	OR	PS	SC	SH	RB	AS	BL	ST
1976	Phoe	22.30	9	8	24	-	-	5	14	-
1977	Phoe	20.83	19	8	-	-	-	30	29	-
1978	Phoe	17.81	41	14	-	-	-	-	-	-
1979	Phoe	22.94	14	7	-	16	22	-	-	-
1980	Phoe	20.48	28	10	-	18	23	-	-	31
1981	Phoe	19.76	21	10	-	28	28	22	-	26
1982	Phoe	19.78	26	8	-	-	-	-	-	29
1983	Phoe	18.30	42	11	-	-	-	-	-	-
1984	Phoe	12.21	112	23	-	-	-	-	-	25
1985	Phoe	18.34	45	11	-	20	-	-	-	18
1986	Phoe	15.42	73	16	-	-	-	-	-	25
1987	Phoe	13.74	88	21	-	-	-	-	-	-

LUCIUS ALLEN — UCLA
YR	TM	PR	OR	PS	SC	SH	RB	AS	BL	ST
1970	Seat	11.04	81	29	-	-	-	7	-	-
1971	Milw	8.08	113	44	-	-	-	21	-	-
1972	Milw	14.66	63	22	-	15	-	19	-	-
1973	Milw	16.27	59	21	-	-	-	17	-	-
1974	Milw	17.65	31	5	-	16	-	17	-	13
1975	LA.L	16.89	34	6	-	-	-	10	-	11
1976	LA.L	13.11	65	13	-	-	-	16	-	-
1977	LA.L	14.04	64	9	-	-	-	17	-	-
1978	K.C.	11.61	110	17	-	-	-	18	-	-
1979	K.C.	4.03		DNQ						

NATE ARCHIBALD — UTEP
YR	TM	PR	OR	PS	SC	SH	RB	AS	BL	ST
1971	Cinc	15.65	59	24	-	-	-	14	-	-
1972	Cinc	28.21	6	1	2	12	-	4	-	-
1973	K.C.	33.18	2	1	1	9	-	1	-	-
1974	K.C.	20.66		DNQ						
1975	K.C.	20.74	13	2	4	-	-	8	-	-
1976	K.C.	19.71	20	4	4	-	-	4	-	-
1977	NY.N	17.92		DNQ						
1978		DID NOT PLAY								
1979	Bost	9.74	135	28	-	-	-	11	-	-
1980	Bost	17.35	51	6	-	-	-	4	-	-
1981	Bost	15.84	63	7	-	-	-	11	-	-
1982	Bost	14.24	80	13	-	-	-	5	-	-
1983	Bost	10.30	122	24	-	-	-	12	-	-
1984	Milw	7.63		DNQ						

PAUL ARIZIN — VILLANOVA
YR	TM	PR	OR	PS	SC	SH	RB	AS	BL	ST
1951	Phil	19.66	7	3	5	5	8	-	-	-
1952	Phil	27.06	1	1	1	2	-	-	-	-
1953		DID NOT PLAY								
1954		DID NOT PLAY								
1955	Phil	20.42	8	4	3	-	-	-	-	-
1956	Phil	21.94	7	4	2	2	-	-	-	-
1957	Phil	22.08	7	4	1	2	-	-	-	-
1958	Phil	17.56	16	8	6	-	-	-	-	-
1959	Phil	23.40	8	6	2	4	-	-	-	-
1960	Phil	20.54	14	9	8	-	-	-	-	-
1961	Phil	21.71	13	8	9	10	-	-	-	-
1962	Phil	18.44	20	9	-	-	-	-	-	-

AL ATTLES — N.C. A&T
YR	TM	PR	OR	PS	SC	SH	RB	AS	BL	ST
1961	Phil	7.05	56	23	-	-	-	-	-	-
1962	Phil	13.89	36	13	-	-	-	-	-	-
1963	S.F.	10.17	50	17	-	-	-	-	-	-
1964	S.F.	10.79	46	17	-	-	-	-	-	-
1965	S.F.	8.38	61	23	-	-	-	-	-	13
1966	S.F.	12.29	45	17	-	10	-	-	-	-
1967	S.F.	11.36	54	22	-	-	-	-	-	9
1968	S.F.	14.42	52	17	-	-	-	-	-	6
1969	S.F.	12.84	68	24	-	-	-	-	-	5
1970	S.F.	6.33		DNQ						
1971	S.F.	3.44		DNQ						

GREG BALLARD — OREGON
YR	TM	PR	OR	PS	SC	SH	RB	AS	BL	ST
1978	Wash	6.07		DNQ						
1979	Wash	10.29		DNQ						
1980	Wash	17.74	45	14	-	-	-	-	-	-
1981	Wash	17.30	44	10	-	-	-	-	-	-
1982	Wash	21.20	22	6	28	-	-	-	-	31
1983	Wash	18.62	40	13	-	-	-	-	-	-
1984	Wash	16.59	59	18	-	-	-	-	-	-
1985	Wash	15.83	77	17	-	-	-	-	-	-
1986	G.St	11.44	121	31	-	-	-	-	-	-
1987	G.St	8.33	153	33	-	-	-	-	-	-

MIKE BANTOM — ST. JOE
YR	TM	PR	OR	PS	SC	SH	RB	AS	BL	ST
1974	Phoe	10.59	88	17	-	-	-	-	-	-
1975	Phoe	13.17	65	11	-	-	-	-	-	-
1976	Seat	9.32	103	22	-	-	-	-	-	-
1977	NY.N	12.91	83	12	-	-	-	-	-	-
1978	Indi	17.13	48	9	-	-	-	-	-	-
1979	Indi	16.88	57	10	-	-	-	-	-	-
1980	Indi	14.83	76	13	-	-	-	-	-	-
1981	Indi	15.30	73	15	-	-	-	-	-	-
1982	Phil	10.85	126	23	-	-	-	-	-	-

DICK BARNETT — TENN. ST
YR	TM	PR	OR	PS	SC	SH	RB	AS	BL	ST
1960	Syra	9.77	43	19	-	-	-	-	-	-
1961	Syra	13.72	32	12	-	-	-	-	-	-
1962		DID NOT PLAY								
1963	LA.L	15.13	26	7	-	9	-	-	-	-
1964	LA.L	14.90	25	6	-	-	-	-	-	-
1965	LA.L	10.51	49	17	-	-	-	-	-	-
1966	N.Y.	19.29	19	7	6	6	-	-	-	-
1967	N.Y.	14.43	36	12	-	9	-	-	-	-
1968	N.Y.	15.36	47	14	-	10	-	-	-	-
1969	N.Y.	15.10	52	16	-	18	-	-	-	-
1970	N.Y.	13.43	66	25	-	-	-	-	-	-
1971	N.Y.	12.28	84	33	-	-	-	-	-	-
1972	N.Y.	9.43	100	38	-	-	-	-	-	-
1973	N.Y.	2.57		DNQ						
1974	N.Y.	2.20		DNQ						

FORMER PLAYERS

JIM BARNETT — OREGON

YR	TM	PR	OR	PS	SC	SH	RB	AS	BL	ST
1967	Bost	2.90		DNQ						
1968	S.D.	8.94		DNQ						
1969	S.D.	14.49	58	18	-	-	-	14		
1970	S.D.	14.45	61	22	-	-	-	-		
1971	Port	17.22	49	17	-	-	-	22		
1972	G.St	12.03	79	28	-	-	-	-		
1973	G.St	12.72	75	28	-	-	-	-		
1974	G.St	10.30	92	16	-	-	-	-	-	-
1975	N.Y.	9.01	101	20	-	-	-	-	-	-
1976	N.Y.	5.52		DNQ						
1977	Phil	2.81		DNQ						

RICK BARRY — MIAMI OF FLORIDA

YR	TM	PR	OR	PS	SC	SH	RB	AS	BL	ST
1966	S.F.	25.48	8	2	4	11	-	-		
1967	S.F.	31.32	4	1	1	8	-	-		
1968		DID NOT PLAY								
1969	ABA	35.11		DNQ						
1970	ABA	26.94	3	2	3	1	-	-		
1971	ABA	28.08	4	1	2	12	-	-		
1972	ABA	28.64	7	3	2	14	-	-		
1973	G.St	24.72	14	5	15	-	-	-		
1974	G.St	24.49	8	2	7	-	-	12	-	12
1975	G.St	26.26	5	1	2	-	-	15	-	3
1976	G.St	20.75	16	3	12	-	-	11	-	8
1977	G.St	21.94	15	5	13	-	-	16	-	20
1978	G.St	22.13	17	4	14	-	-	-	-	-
1979	Hous	15.60	72	19	-	-	-	10	-	-
1980	Hous	12.08	107	25	-	-	-	-	-	-

ELGIN BAYLOR — SEATTLE

YR	TM	PR	OR	PS	SC	SH	RB	AS	BL	ST
1959	Minn	29.27	3	2	4	-	8	-		
1960	Minn	31.93	4	2	3	-	8	-		
1961	LA.L	40.19	2	1	2	-	6	-		
1962	LA.L	39.31	3	1	2	-	7	-		
1963	LA.L	35.98	3	1	2	-	11	-		
1964	LA.L	27.29	8	3	6	-	-	-		
1965	LA.L	26.65	7	2	4	-	-	-		
1966	LA.L	18.72	20	8	-	-	-	-		
1967	LA.L	27.53	8	3	4	-	12	-		
1968	LA.L	28.74	5	2	4	-	-	-		
1969	LA.L	26.92	7	2	5	-	-	-		
1970	LA.L	28.30	8	3	10	-	-	-		
1971	LA.L	10.00		DNQ						
1972	LA.L	14.56		DNQ						

BUTCH BEARD — LOUISVILLE

YR	TM	PR	OR	PS	SC	SH	RB	AS	BL	ST
1970	Atla	7.29		DNQ						
1971		DID NOT PLAY								
1972	Clev	18.28	45	13	-	-	-	6		
1973	Seat	8.48	103	42	-	-	-	9		
1974	G.St	13.51	67	16	-	14	-	-	-	21
1975	G.St	14.89	51	12	-	3	-	-	-	19
1976	N.Y.	10.40	88	15	-	-	-	-	-	-
1977	N.Y.	2.30		DNQ						
1978	N.Y.	12.37	100	19	-	27	-	16	-	13
1979	N.Y.	5.14		DNQ						

ZELMO BEATY — PRAIRIE VIEW

YR	TM	PR	OR	PS	SC	SH	RB	AS	BL	ST
1963	St.L	13.71	35	7	-	-	10	-		
1964	St.L	17.90	19	6	-	-	-	-		
1965	St.L	21.88	13	6	-	10	-	-		
1966	St.L	25.59	7	4	10	7	10	-		
1967	St.L	20.81		DNQ						
1968	St.L	25.33	9	4	13	5	-	-		
1969	Atla	23.28	15	8	18	-	-	-		
1970		DID NOT PLAY								
1971	ABA	32.11	1	1	11	1	3	-		
1972	ABA	29.56	5	3	13	2	9	-		
1973	ABA	20.95	13	7	-	7	-	-		
1974	ABA	17.43	19	10	-	3	-	-	-	-
1975	LA.L	8.25		DNQ						

WALT BELLAMY — INDIANA

YR	TM	PR	OR	PS	SC	SH	RB	AS	BL	ST
1962	Chic	37.96	4	2	3	3	3	-		
1963	Chic	34.40	4	2	5	4	4	-		
1964	Balt	32.34	5	3	5	7	5	-		
1965	Balt	29.91	5	3	6	7	9	-		
1966	N.Y.	29.65	6	3	7	12	7	-		
1967	N.Y.	25.81	10	4	-	10	10	-		
1968	N.Y.	22.99	13	5	-	4	12	-		
1969	Detr	23.26	16	9	-	14	15	-		
1970	Atla	16.32	50	10	-	-	13	-		
1971	Atla	22.27	24	11	-	-	13	-		
1972	Atla	25.61	15	9	-	-	21	-		
1973	Atla	22.26	23	9	-	-	14	-		
1974	Atla	16.29	42	15	-	-	-	-	-	-
1975	N.O.	10.00		DNQ						

KENT BENSON — INDIANA

YR	TM	PR	OR	PS	SC	SH	RB	AS	BL	ST
1978	Milw	9.10		DNQ						
1979	Milw	16.56	61	18	-	-	-	-	27	-
1980	Detr	13.37	93	21	-	-	-	-	18	-
1981	Detr	16.63	55	16	-	-	-	-	-	-
1982	Detr	17.71	43	11	-	-	27	-	31	-
1983	Detr	13.91		DNQ						
1984	Detr	11.49	125	26	-	11	-	-	-	-
1985	Detr	9.86	141	25	-	-	-	-	-	-
1986	Detr	9.53		DNQ						
1987	Utah	5.95		DNQ						

DAVE BING — SYRACUSE

YR	TM	PR	OR	PS	SC	SH	RB	AS	BL	ST
1967	Detr	16.69	28	8	12	-	-	-		
1968	Detr	22.41	16	4	2	-	-	11		
1969	Detr	21.21	23	7	9	-	-	8		
1970	Detr	21.07	23	9	12	-	-	10		
1971	Detr	23.38	19	5	4	17	-	-		
1972	Detr	20.46		DNQ						
1973	Detr	22.17	24	6	14	-	-	6		
1974	Detr	16.27	43	9	-	-	-	8	-	-
1975	Detr	17.66	26	4	-	-	-	4	-	-
1976	Wash	15.12	50	8	-	-	-	7	-	-
1977	Wash	10.42	112	19	-	-	-	12	-	-
1978	Bost	11.39	115	19	-	-	-	-	-	-

JOHN BLOCK — USC

YR	TM	PR	OR	PS	SC	SH	RB	AS	BL	ST
1967	LA.L	3.27		DNQ						
1968	S.D.	21.40	21	6	17	-	-	-		
1969	S.D.	16.99	43	9	-	-	-	-		
1970	S.D.	15.70	54	23	-	-	-	-		
1971	S.D.	11.58	93	36	-	-	-	-		
1972	Milw	10.27	95	40	-	-	-	-		
1973	K.C.	16.22	60	23	-	-	-	-		
1974	K.C.	8.99	99	21	-	-	-	-		
1975	Chic	9.20		DNQ						
1976	Chic	1.50		DNQ						

BUCKY BOCKHORN — DAYTON

YR	TM	PR	OR	PS	SC	SH	RB	AS	BL	ST
1959	Cinc	12.07	34	12	-	-	-	-		
1960	Cinc	11.88	35	12	-	-	-	-		
1961	Cinc	13.53	33	13	-	-	-	-		
1962	Cinc	15.58	29	11	-	-	-	-		
1963	Cinc	10.98	46	15	-	-	-	-		
1964	Cinc	8.33	53	21	-	-	-	-		
1965	Cinc	7.37		DNQ						

RON BOONE — IDAHO ST.

YR	TM	PR	OR	PS	SC	SH	RB	AS	BL	ST
1969	ABA	17.60	24	8	-	-	-	14		
1970	ABA	13.83	47	15	-	-	-	11		
1971	ABA	17.48	36	11	-	-	-	-		
1972	ABA	12.98	52	20	-	-	-	-		
1973	ABA	20.25	15	2	-	6	-	-		
1974	ABA	20.10	12	2	-	7	-	-	-	-
1975	ABA	23.09	9	1	5	-	-	-	-	-
1976	ABA	20.90	12	3	8	10	-	9	-	-
1977	K.C.	16.83	41	7	11	-	-	-	-	-
1978	K.C.	13.15	91	17	-	-	-	-	-	-
1979	LA.L	6.26	154	32	-	-	-	-	-	-
1980	Utah	11.26	120	22	-	-	-	-	-	-
1981	Utah	6.75		DNQ						

BOB BOOZER — KANSAS ST.

YR	TM	PR	OR	PS	SR	SH	RB	AS	BL	ST
1961	Cinc	10.49	46	19	-	-	-			
1962	Cinc	17.49	23	10	-	-	-			
1963	Cinc	18.47	17	7	-	9	-			
1964	N.Y.	14.42	29	16	-	-	-			
1965	N.Y.	15.28	26	12	-	-	-			
1966	LA.L	14.58	35	18	-	3	-			
1967	Chic	19.23	21	11	-	5	-			
1968	Chic	22.92	14	6	10	7	-			
1969	Chic	21.23	22	7	16	10	-			
1970	Seat	18.38	41	17	-	18	-			
1971	Milw	11.29	96	38	-	-	-			

BILL BRADLEY — PRINCETON

YR	TM	PR	OR	PS	SC	SH	RB	AS	BL	ST
1968	N.Y.	6.96		DNQ						
1969	N.Y.	13.22	65	29	-	-	-	-		
1970	N.Y.	14.37	62	27	-	-	-	-		
1971	N.Y.	12.56	82	29	-	-	-	-		
1972	N.Y.	14.50	65	26	-	-	-	-		
1973	N.Y.	15.67	63	25	-	-	-	-		
1974	N.Y.	10.60	87	19	-	-	-	-	-	-
1975	N.Y.	10.65	88	18	-	-	-	-	-	-
1976	N.Y.	9.23	104	21	-	-	-	-	-	-
1977	N.Y.	4.70		DNQ						

CARL BRAUN — COLGATE

YR	TM	PR	OR	PS	SC	SH	RB	AS	BL	ST
1948	N.Y.	14.30				6		9		
1949	N.Y.	14.20				9		-		
1950	N.Y.	13.25	17	2	7	-		9		
1951		DID NOT PLAY								
1952		DID NOT PLAY								
1953	N.Y.	12.84	27	7	13	7	-	-		
1954	N.Y.	12.67	21	7	9	5	-	-		
1955	N.Y.	13.28	28	8	-	-	-	-		
1956	N.Y.	13.04	28	7	-	-	-	-		
1957	N.Y.	11.71	31	7	-	-	-	10		
1958	N.Y.	17.56	15	2	-	9	-	4		
1959	N.Y.	12.76	30	9	-	-	-	3		
1960	N.Y.	13.67	31	8	-	-	-	7		
1961	N.Y.	7.93		DNQ						
1962	Bost	3.35		DNQ						

JIM BREWER — MINNESOTA

YR	TM	PR	OR	PS	SC	SH	RB	AS	BL	ST
1974	Clev	8.88	102	23	-	-	-	-	-	-
1975	Clev	10.87	87	19	-	-	-	-	-	-
1976	Clev	18.05	31	7	-	-	20	-	21	-
1977	Clev	14.78	56	9	-	-	-	-	-	-
1978	Clev	9.06	145	29	-	-	-	-	-	-
1979	Detr	8.56	149	25	-	-	24	-	24	-
1980	Port	6.28		DNQ						
1981	LA.L	5.77		DNQ						

JUNIOR BRIDGEMAN — LOUISVILLE

YR	TM	PR	OR	PS	SC	SH	RB	AS	BL	ST
1976	Milw	7.64	114	26	-	-	-	-	-	-
1977	Milw	13.09	79	19	-	-	-	-	-	-
1978	Milw	12.18	103	20	-	26	-	-	-	-
1979	Milw	14.07	82	20	-	-	-	-	-	-
1980	Milw	15.04	73	21	-	-	-	-	-	-
1981	Milw	15.40	70	16	-	-	-	-	-	-
1982	Milw	11.56		DNQ						
1983	Milw	13.14	93	25	-	-	-	-	-	-
1984	Milw	13.63	93	25	-	-	-	-	-	-
1985	LA.C	11.38	121	27	-	-	-	-	-	-
1986	LA.C	7.48		DNQ						
1987	Milw	4.79		DNQ						

BILL BRIDGES — KANSAS

YR	TM	PR	OR	PS	SC	SH	RB	AS	BL	ST
1963	St.L	8.07	DNQ							
1964	St.L	13.23	39	19	-	-	11	-		
1965	St.L	16.27	25	11	-	-	7	-		
1966	St.L	19.40	18	7	-	-	8	-		
1967	St.L	25.65	11	5	-	-	8	-		
1968	St.L	23.83	11	5	-	-	14	-		
1969	Atla	22.91	17	4	-	-	10	-		
1970	Atla	26.02	12	4	-	-	10	-		
1971	Atla	22.89	21	7	-	-	8	-		
1972	Phil	22.24	25	8	-	-	6	-		
1973	LA.L	18.33	42	17	-	-	-	-		
1974	LA.L	11.74	78	15	-	-	-	-	-	-
1975	G.St	5.12	DNQ							

FREDDY BROWN — IOWA

YR	TM	PR	OR	PS	SC	SH	RB	AS	BL	ST
1972	Seat	3.30	DNQ							
1973	Seat	15.54	65	23	-	-	-	7		
1974	Seat	17.51	33	2	-	-	13	-	16	
1975	Seat	18.10	22	2	16	-	-	-	4	
1976	Seat	18.62	26	3	5	19	-	-	14	
1977	Seat	13.86	67	14	-	-	-	-	21	
1978	Seat	14.40	73	11	-	-	-	-	24	
1979	Seat	12.43	99	17	-	-	-	-	13	
1980	Seat	10.06	134	26	-	-	-	-	-	
1981	Seat	13.06	100	20	-	-	-	-	-	
1982	Seat	9.62	144	24	-	-	-	-	-	
1983	Seat	9.48	DNQ							
1984	Seat	8.20	DNQ							

QUINN BUCKNER — INDIANA

YR	TM	PR	OR	PS	SC	SH	RB	AS	BL	ST
1977	Milw	10.68	109	18	-	-	-	13	-	2
1978	Milw	12.34	102	15	-	-	-	5	-	2
1979	Milw	10.81	120	25	-	-	-	2	-	2
1980	Milw	14.07	84	14	-	-	-	6	-	6
1981	Milw	14.62	82	12	-	-	-	31	-	3
1982	Milw	14.24	79	12	-	-	-	-	-	2
1983	Bost	8.75	139	30	-	-	-	28	-	7
1984	Bost	5.71	DNQ							
1985	Bost	6.72	DNQ							
1986	Indi	5.59	DNQ							

DON BUSE — EVANSVILLE

YR	TM	PR	OR	PS	SC	SH	RB	AS	BL	ST
1973	ABA	8.08	71	31	-	-	-	10		
1974	ABA	8.53	66	26	-	-	-	11	-	2
1975	ABA	10.35	60	21	-	-	-	-	-	3
1976	ABA	18.26	20	5	-	-	-	1	-	4
1977	Indi	16.26	46	5	-	-	-	3	-	1
1978	Phoe	12.66	95	14	-	-	-	24	-	4
1979	Phoe	11.94	105	17	-	-	-	-	-	11
1980	Phoe	10.60	124	18	-	-	-	-	-	25
1981	Indi	5.57	DNQ							
1982	Indi	13.74	84	14	-	-	-	27	-	11
1983	Port	5.91	DNQ							
1984	K.C.	7.39	DNQ							
1985	K.C.	4.89	DNQ							

JOE CALDWELL — ARIZONA ST.

YR	TM	PR	OR	PS	SC	SH	RB	AS	BL	ST
1965	Detr	10.62	48	22	-	-	-	-		
1966	St.L	12.16	46	22	-	-	-	-		
1967	St.L	12.32	51	21	-	-	-	-		
1968	St.L	13.81	56	26	-	-	-	-		
1969	Atla	15.09	53	17	-	19	-	-		
1970	Atla	19.44	35	13	-	-	-	-		
1971	ABA	19.25	29	15	9	-	-	-		
1972	ABA	16.18	38	16	-	-	-	15		
1973	ABA	16.03	28	9	-	-	-	-		
1974	ABA	15.72	28	11	-	-	-	-	-	5
1975	ABA	15.60	DNQ							

BILL CALHOUN

YR	TM	PR	OR	PS	SC	SH	RB	AS	BL	ST
1948	Roch	1.90	DNQ							
1949	Roch	6.60		-				-		
1950	Roch	7.47	70	30	-	-	-	-		
1951	Roch	6.23	63	28	-	-	-	-		
1952	Balt	7.53	58	27	-	-	-	-		
1953	Milw	9.18	48	16	-	-	-	-		
1954	Milw	8.67	43	16	-	-	-	-		
1955	Milw	8.30	47	14	-	-	-	-		

AUSTIN CARR — NOTRE DAME

YR	TM	PR	OR	PS	SC	SH	RB	AS	BL	ST
1972	Clev	15.09	DNQ							
1973	Clev	17.06	56	19	18	-	-	-		
1974	Clev	15.65	49	7	14	-	-	-	-	
1975	Clev	12.55	DNQ							
1976	Clev	7.51	117	24	-	-	-	-	-	
1977	Clev	11.87	94	21	-	-	-	-	-	
1978	Clev	9.65	134	27	-	-	-	-	-	
1979	Clev	13.91	84	13	-	-	-	-	-	
1980	Clev	8.62	145	30	-	-	-	-	-	
1981	Wash	2.65	DNQ							

KENNY CARR — N.C.STATE

YR	TM	PR	OR	PS	SC	SH	RB	AS	BL	ST
1978	LA.L	5.81	DNQ							
1979	LA.L	7.76	DNQ							
1980	Clev	13.65	89	16	-	-	10	-	-	-
1981	Clev	19.48	25	4	-	-	8	-	-	-
1982	Detr	13.49	89	17	-	-	22	-	-	-
1983	port	13.89	83	15	-	-	-	-	-	-
1984	Port	17.76	48	10	-	32	29	-	-	-
1985	Port	12.38	DNQ							
1986	Port	15.18	75	18	-	-	13	-	-	-
1987	Port	16.50	DNQ							

FRED CARTER — MT. ST. MARY'S

YR	TM	PR	OR	PS	SC	SH	RB	AS	BL	ST
1970	Balt	5.12	DNQ							
1971	Balt	8.78	111	42	-	-	-	-		
1972	Phil	11.75	81	29	-	-	-	-		
1973	Phil	17.37	52	18	-	-	-	-		
1974	Phil	16.94	35	8	17	-	-	19	-	-
1975	Phil	16.18	39	10	11	-	-	-	-	-
1976	Phil	13.27	64	12	-	-	-	-	-	-
1977	Milw	5.94	DNQ							

WILT CHAMBERLAIN — KANSAS

YR	TM	PR	OR	PS	SC	SH	RB	AS	BL	ST
1960	Phil	43.83	1	1	1	-	1	-		
1961	Phil	45.58	1	1	1	-	1	-		
1962	Phil	52.29	1	1	1	8	1	-		
1963	S.F.	50.59	1	1	1	8	2	-		
1964	S.F.	44.60	1	1	1	10	2	-		
1965	Phil	40.62	1	1	1	-	2	-		
1966	Phil	45.76	1	1	1	-	2	-		
1967	Phil	45.54	1	1	5	2	1	5		
1968	Phil	42.80	1	1	5	-	1	9		
1969	LA.L	34.68	1	1	-	-	2	-		
1970	LA.L	34.42			DNQ						
1971	LA.L	32.61	2	2	21	-	5	-		
1972	LA.L	31.01	2	2	-	18	2	-		
1973	LA.L	31.61	3	2	-	2	1			

DON CHANEY — HOUSTON

YR	TM	PR	OR	PS	SC	SH	RB	AS	BL	ST
1969	Bost	1.85			DNQ						
1970	Bost	4.83			DNQ						
1971	Bost	13.96	68	28	-	-	-	-		
1972	Bost	13.53	70	23	-	-	-	-		
1973	Bost	15.27	67	24	-	-	-	-		
1974	Bost	11.19	81	14	-	-	-	-		
1975	Bost	10.63	89	14	-	-	-	17	15	
1976	ABA	9.81			DNQ						
1977	LA.L	9.72	124	27	-	-	-	-	24	
1978	Bost	4.83			DNQ						
1979	Bost	5.40			DNQ						
1980	Bost	2.44			DNQ						

PHIL CHENIER — CALIFORNIA

YR	TM	PR	OR	PS	SC	SH	RB	AS	BL	ST
1972	Balt	10.25	96	36	-	-	-	-		
1973	Balt	17.00	57	20	-	-	-	-		
1974	Capt	16.65	41	3	18	-	-	-	18	
1975	Wash	17.09	32	5	12	-	-	-	7	
1976	Wash	16.96	38	7	17	24	-	-	18	
1977	Wash	15.64	50	12	23	-	-	-	-	
1978	Wash	10.39			DNQ						
1979	Wash	3.19			DNQ						
1980	Indi	5.63			DNQ						
1981	G.St	1.67			DNQ						

JIM CHONES — MARQUETTE

YR	TM	PR	OR	PS	SC	SH	RB	AS	BL	ST
1973	ABA	13.91	43	12	-	-	-	-		
1974	ABA	16.98	23	11	-	12	-	8	-	
1975	Clev	18.06	23	8	-	-	-	10	-	
1976	Clev	16.68	42	13	-	-	-	20	-	
1977	Clev	14.80	55	15	-	-	-	-	-	
1978	Clev	17.96	38	13	-	-	-	-	-	
1979	Clev	17.43	48	16	-	-	23	-	29	-
1980	LA.L	13.39	91	17	-	-	-	-	-	
1981	LA.L	14.98	77	16	-	-	-	32	-	
1982	Wash	5.15			DNQ						

ARCHIE CLARK — MINNESOTA

YR	TM	PR	OR	PS	SC	SH	RB	AS	BL	ST
1967	LA.L	10.05	62	28	-	-	-	-		
1968	LA.L	18.76	32	9	-	15	-	-		
1969	Phil	13.28	64	21	-	-	-	17		
1970	Phil	19.62	33	15	-	-	-	-		
1971	Phil	21.84	26	7	17	8	-	-		
1972	Balt	24.18	19	4	9	-	-	7		
1973	Balt	20.49			DNQ						
1974	Capt	11.96	76	18	-	-	-	15	-	
1975	Seat	14.57	55	13	-	18	-	7	-	
1976	Detr	6.94	118	21	-	-	-	-		

JIM CLEAMONS — OHIO ST.

YR	TM	PR	OR	PS	SC	SH	RB	AS	BL	ST
1972	LA.L	2.61			DNQ						
1973	Clev	7.18			DNQ						
1974	Clev	7.69	110	22	-	-	-	-	-	-
1975	Clev	14.35	57	14	-	-	-	22	-	
1976	Clev	14.85	52	9	-	-	-	15	-	
1977	Clev	13.33	74	11	-	-	-	22	-	
1978	N.Y.	9.15	143	28	-	-	-	-	-	
1979	N.Y.	11.49	114	21	-	-	-	27	-	
1980	Wash	8.27	146	26	-	-	-	24	-	

NAT CLIFTON — XAVIER (LA.)

YR	TM	PR	OR	PS	SC	SH	RB	AS	BL	ST
1951	N.Y.	9.95	38	9	-	-	-	-		
1952	N.Y.	16.56	14	5	-	-	3	-		
1953	N.Y.	15.30	13	6	-	-	8	-		
1954	N.Y.	11.76	26	9	-	-	-	-		
1955	N.Y.	14.97	21	10	-	-	-	-		
1956	N.Y.	11.16	35	16	-	-	-	-		
1957	N.Y.	12.70	30	10	-	-	-	-		
1958	Detr	8.37	46	19	-	-	-	-		

JACK COLEMAN — LOUISVILLE

YR	TM	PR	OR	PS	SC	SH	RB	AS	BL	ST
1950	Roch	13.12	18	8	-	-	-	-		
1951	Roch	16.01	11	5	-	10	11	-		
1952	Roch	17.47	12	6	-	14	-	-		
1953	Roch	18.01	8	4	-	-	9	-		
1954	Roch	13.17	19	7	-	-	-	-		
1955	Roch	18.89	12	7	-	5	-	-		
1956	St.L	17.48	15	8	-	-	-	-		
1957	St.L	14.75	19	11	-	-	-	-		
1958	St.L	10.72	38	15	-	-	-	-		

LARRY COSTELLO — NIAGARA

YR	TM	PR	OR	PS	SC	SH	RB	AS	BL	ST
1955	Phil	7.68			DNQ					
1956		DID NOT PLAY								
1957	Phil	10.39	35	10	-	-	-	9		
1958	Syra	16.71	22	6	-	4	-	-		
1959	Syra	17.84	14	4	-	6	-	6		
1960	Syra	18.87	21	5	-	4	-	6		
1961	Syra	17.12	25	9	-	2	-	4		
1962	Syra	15.98	27	9	-	-	-	5		
1963	Syra	13.01	39	13	-	12	-	5		
1964	Phil	12.47			DNQ					
1965	Phil	13.83	32	10	-	9	-	7		
1966		DID NOT PLAY								
1967	Phil	9.12			DNQ					
1968	Phil	8.04			DNQ					

BOB COUSY — HOLY CROSS

YR	TM	PR	OR	PS	SC	SH	RB	AS	BL	ST
1951	Bost	15.46	12	2	10	-	-	4		
1952	Bost	20.03	7	1	3	-	-	3		
1953	Bost	20.27	6	1	4	-	-	1		
1954	Bost	19.56	8	1	2	12	-	1		
1955	Bost	22.27	5	1	2	-	-	3		
1956	Bost	22.49	6	1	7	-	-	1		
1957	Bost	19.39	9	1	8	-	-	1		
1958	Bost	16.71	23	7	-	-	-	1		
1959	Bost	21.25	10	1	9	-	-	1		
1960	Bost	20.33	15	3	-	-	-	1		
1961	Bost	17.46	24	8	-	-	-	1		
1962	Bost	16.25	26	8	-	-	-	1		
1963	Bost	13.63	36	11	-	-	-	1		
1970	Cinc	2.57			DNQ					

DAVE COWENS — FLORIDA ST.

YR	TM	PR	OR	PS	SC	SH	RB	AS	BL	ST
1971	Bost	24.26	15	8	-	-	7	-		
1972	Bost	27.46	11	6	-	-	8	-		
1973	Bost	29.16	6	4	19	-	7	-		
1974	Bost	26.80	6	5	-	-	5	-	19	-
1975	Bost	28.37	4	4	19	-	5	-	19	-
1976	Bost	28.04	3	3	-	-	3	-	-	-
1977	Bost	24.68	7	5	-	-	7	-	-	-
1978	Bost	27.91	6	6	-	-	14	-	-	-
1979	Bost	20.82	29	11	-	-	-	-	-	-
1980	Bost	17.65	48	16	-	-	-	-	-	-
1983	Milw	12.50			DNQ					

BILLY CUNNINGHAM — N.CAROLINA

YR	TM	PR	OR	PS	SC	SH	RB	AS	BL	ST
1966	Phil	15.09	31	15	-	-	-	-		
1967	Phil	18.01	25	12	-	-	-	-		
1968	Phil	18.19	36	15	-	-	-	-		
1969	Phil	26.54	10	3	4	-	-	-		
1970	Phil	30.48	3	1	4	-	14	-	-	
1971	Phil	27.38	9	4	10	-	-	-		
1972	Phil	28.83	5	2	13	-	-	17		
1973	ABA	31.33	3	2	4	-	7	7		
1974	ABA	25.47			DNQ					
1975	Phil	21.44	12	4	21	-	-	13	-	-
1976	Phil	19.70			DNQ					

LOU DAMPIER — KENTUCKY

YR	TM	PR	OR	PS	SC	SH	RB	AS	BL	ST
1968	ABA	16.36	29	8	-	-	-	-		
1969	ABA	20.94	11	5	5	11	-	5		
1970	ABA	20.44	23	6	5	-	-	7		
1971	ABA	17.49	35	10	-	-	-	9		
1972	ABA	17.31	33	11	-	-	-	7		
1973	ABA	17.25	25	8	-	-	-	5		
1974	ABA	16.96	24	5	-	-	-	5	-	
1975	ABA	17.11	28	8	-	-	-	10	-	
1976	ABA	14.28	31	11	-	-	-	3	-	-
1977	S.A.	6.38	149	29	-	-	-	26	-	-
1978	S.A.	9.89	131	26	-	29	-	-	-	-
1979	S.A.	5.24			DNQ					

BOB DANDRIDGE — NORFOLK ST.

YR	TM	PR	OR	PS	SC	SH	RB	AS	BL	ST
1970	Milw	18.00	42	18	-	-	-	-		
1971	Milw	21.22	28	10	-	11	-	-		
1972	Milw	20.34	35	14	-	-	-	-		
1973	Milw	20.73	27	11	21	-	-	-		
1974	Milw	18.90	26	6	-	12	-	-	-	-
1975	Milw	18.76	19	5	20	-	-	-	-	-
1976	Milw	21.07	15	2	9	12	-	-	-	-
1977	Milw	18.90	28	10	19	-	-	-	-	-
1978	Wash	18.19	36	11	30	-	-	-	-	-
1979	Wash	20.59	31	7	25	-	-	-	-	-
1980	Wash	16.00			DNQ					
1981	Wash	9.91			DNQ					
1982	Milw	3.36			DNQ					

MEL DANIELS — NEW MEXICO

YR	TM	PR	OR	PS	SC	SH	RB	AS	BL	ST
1968	ABA	22.97	4	2	9	-	2	-		
1969	ABA	28.29	1	1	7	-	1	-		
1970	ABA	27.81	2	1	-	-	1	-		
1971	ABA	31.26	2	2	-	13	1	-		
1972	ABA	28.68	6	4	-	-	1	-		
1973	ABA	26.75	6	2	-	-	2	-		
1974	ABA	19.67	14	6	-	-	5	-	-	
1975	ABA	14.62	38	12	-	-	4	-	4	-
1976		DID NOT PLAY								
1977	NY.N	4.64			DNQ					

BOB DAVIES — SETON HALL

YR	TM	PR	OR	PS	SC	SH	RB	AS	BL	ST
1946	Roch	9.00			DNQ					
1947	Roch	14.40			2					
1948	Roch	9.80			-					
1949	Roch	15.10			10			1		
1950	Roch	11.45	29	8	-	-	-	3		
1951	Roch	12.86	23	6	12	-	-	6		
1952	Roch	14.38	21	5	5	-	-	4		
1953	Roch	12.85	26	6	8	-	-	6		
1954	Roch	11.01	30	10	-	-	-	4		
1955	Roch	12.50	32	10	-	-	-	4		

FORMER PLAYERS 327

JOHNNY DAVIS — DAYTON

YR	TM	PR	OR	PS	SC	SH	RB	AS	BL	ST
1977	Port	6.38		DNQ						
1978	Port	9.22	141	27	-	-	-	-	-	-
1979	Indi	15.62	71	10	-	-	-	29	-	-
1980	Indi	14.46	79	12	-	-	-	29	-	-
1981	Indi	14.92	78	11	-	-	-	17	-	-
1982	Indi	13.74	84	14	-	-	-	-	-	-
1983	Atla	13.45	89	14	-	-	-	15	-	-
1984	Atla	11.19	129	23	-	-	-	32	-	-
1985	Clev	11.61	119	23	-	-	-	15	-	-
1986	Atla	6.61		DNQ						

DARRYL DAWKINS — NONE

YR	TM	PR	OR	PS	SC	SH	RB	AS	BL	ST
1976	Phil	2.24		DNQ						
1977	Phil	7.65		DNQ						
1978	Phil	16.96	50	17	-	3	19	-	8	-
1979	Phil	16.37	65	20	-	-	18	-	8	-
1980	Phil	17.85	44	14	-	-	-	-	10	-
1981	Phil	16.97	49	15	-	2	-	-	19	-
1982	Phil	13.67		DNQ						
1983	N.J.	13.35	91	19	-	5	-	-	6	-
1984	N.J.	18.70	41	12	-	7	-	-	15	-
1985	N.J.	15.72		DNQ						
1986	N.J.	15.94		DNQ						
1987	N.J.	8.17		DNQ						
1988	Detr	0.00		DNQ						

DAVE DEBUSSCHERE — DETROIT

YR	TM	PR	OR	PS	SC	SH	RB	AS	BL	ST
1963	Detr	16.25	24	13	-	-	-	-		
1964	Detr	10.53		DNQ						
1965	Detr	20.63	14	6	-	-	-	-		
1966	Detr	19.41	17	6	-	-	-	-		
1967	Detr	21.35	14	7	-	-	-	-		
1968	Detr	22.86	15	7	-	-	13	-		
1969	N.Y.	20.88	24	8	-	-	-	-		
1970	N.Y.	18.51	38	16	-	-	-	-		
1971	N.Y.	19.37	36	14	-	-	-	-		
1972	N.Y.	20.69	33	13	-	-	-	-		
1973	N.Y.	20.08	31	13	-	-	-	-		
1974	N.Y.	21.01	18	5	-	-	-	-		

COBY DIETRICK — SAN JOSE ST.

YR	TM	PR	OR	PS	SC	SH	RB	AS	BL	ST
1971	ABA	4.81		DNQ						
1972	ABA	7.00		DNQ						
1973	ABA	8.99		DNQ						
1974	ABA	12.11	47	13	-	-	-	-	-	-
1975	ABA	11.82	48	15	-	-	12	-	-	-
1976	ABA	9.38		DNQ						
1977	S.A.	9.91	120	28	-	-	-	-	-	-
1978	S.A.	10.61	122	24	-	-	-	-	-	-
1979	S.A.	10.75	121	30	-	23	-	-	-	-
1980	Chic	10.77	123	29	-	-	-	-	-	-
1981	Chic	6.68		DNQ						
1982	Chic	5.03		DNQ						
1983	S.A.	1.00		DNQ						

TERRY DISCHINGER — PURDUE

YR	TM	PR	OR	PS	SC	SH	RB	AS	BL	ST
1963	Chic	25.68	9	4	7	3	-	-		
1964	Balt	21.78	13	7	9	5	-	-		
1965	Detr	18.05	19	5	-	6	-	-		
1966		DID NOT PLAY								
1967		DID NOT PLAY								
1968	Detr	14.68	50	24	-	6	-	-		
1969	Detr	10.36	80	34	-	4	-	-		
1970	Detr	12.77	71	30	-	7	-	-		
1971	Detr	13.95	69	23	-	5	-	-		
1972	Detr	10.80	90	37	-	6	-	-		
1973	Port	7.46		DNQ						

JOHN DREW — GARDNER-WEBB

YR	TM	PR	OR	PS	SC	SH	RB	AS	BL	ST
1975	Atla	19.69	16	3	-	-	4	-	-	20
1976	Atla	22.14	11	1	8	20	-	-	-	12
1977	Atla	21.55	17	6	7	-	-	-	-	-
1978	Atla	20.43	27	9	13	-	-	-	-	-
1979	Atla	18.51	41	12	13	-	-	-	-	20
1980	Atla	15.01	74	22	25	-	-	-	-	-
1981	Atla	16.66	54	14	14	-	-	-	-	-
1982	Atla	14.84	71	18	31	-	-	-	-	-
1983	Utah	16.41		DNQ						
1984	Utah	13.95	90	24	-	-	-	-	-	29
1985	Utah	12.16		DNQ						

WALTER DUKES — SETON HALL

YR	TM	PR	OR	PS	SC	SH	RB	AS	BL	ST
1956	N.Y.	10.95	36	10	-	-	9	-		
1957	Minn	14.80	18	6	-	-	3	-		
1958	Detr	16.28	25	8	-	-	5	-		
1959	Detr	16.86	16	3	-	-	3	-		
1960	Detr	19.36	19	4	-	-	6	-		
1961	Detr	20.29	15	4	-	-	4	-		
1962	Detr	15.25	33	7	-	-	6	-		
1963	Detr	7.65		DNQ						

JOHN EGAN — PROVIDENCE

YR	TM	PR	OR	PS	SC	SH	RB	AS	BL	ST
1962	Detr	5.43		DNQ						
1963	Detr	5.30		DNQ						
1964	N.Y.	14.18	30	7	-	-	-	4		
1965	N.Y.	10.34	50	18	-	5	-	5		
1966	Balt	10.24	52	19	-	-	-	5		
1967	Balt	11.03	56	24	-	-	-	8		
1968	Balt	6.28		DNQ						
1969	LA.L	8.18	90	35	-	-	-	-		
1970	LA.L	7.65	95	36	-	-	-	-		
1971	S.D.	3.73		DNQ						
1972	Hous	3.13		DNQ						

FORMER PLAYERS

LEROY ELLIS — ST. JOHN'S

YR	TM	PR	OR	PS	SC	SH	RB	AS	BL	ST
1963	LA.L	9.55	53	26	-	-	13	-		
1964	LA.L	9.23		DNQ						
1965	LA.L	13.08	36	16	-	-	-	-		
1966	LA.L	14.71	34	17	-	-	-	-		
1967	Balt	19.73	19	6	-	-	13	-		
1968	Balt	19.08	31	10	-	-	-	-		
1969	Balt	10.28	83	35	-	-	-	-		
1970	Balt	8.99		DNQ						
1971	Port	22.42	23	10	-	-	16	-		
1972	LA.L	6.85		DNQ						
1973	Phil	16.54	58	22	-	-	-	-		
1974	Phil	16.89	38	13	-	-	21	-	17	-
1975	Phil	11.05	84	20	-	-	-	-	22	-
1976	Phil	6.41		DNQ						

WAYNE EMBRY — MIAMI OF OHIO

YR	TM	PR	OR	PS	SC	SH	RB	AS	BL	ST
1959	Cinc	13.71	29	7	-	-	7	-		
1960	Cinc	13.74	30	9	-	-	3	-		
1961	Cinc	18.49	21	6	-	-	7	-		
1962	Cinc	24.49	12	6	-	-	11	-		
1963	Cinc	22.66	11	5	-	-	7	-		
1964	Cinc	20.23	15	5	-	-	-	-		
1965	Cinc	16.54	23	8	-	-	-	-		
1966	Cinc	9.83	53	8	-	-	-	-		
1967	Bost	6.08		DNQ						
1968	Bost	6.44		DNQ						
1969	Milw	15.40	49	14	-	-	-	-		

KEITH ERICKSON — UCLA

YR	TM	PR	OR	PS	SC	SH	RB	AS	BL	ST
1966	S.F.	3.73		DNQ						
1967	Chic	7.86	67	27	-	-	-	-		
1968	Chic	12.97	61	21	-	-	-	-		
1969	LA.L	9.48	86	33	-	-	-	-		
1970	LA.L	11.53	79	35	-	-	-	-		
1971	LA.L	13.82	70	24	-	-	-	-		
1972	LA.L	7.73		DNQ						
1973	LA.L	11.16	85	32	-	-	-	-		
1974	Phoe	15.44	51	9	-	-	-	-	-	-
1975	Phoe	12.56		DNQ						
1976	Phoe	10.88	86	18	-	-	-	-	-	-
1977	Phoe	7.30		DNQ						

JULIUS ERVING — MASSACHUSETTS

YR	TM	PR	OR	PS	SC	SH	RB	AS	BL	ST
1972	ABA	34.14	2	1	4	-	5	-		
1973	ABA	33.61	1	1	2	-	11	-		
1974	ABA	31.21	2	1	3	-	-	-	5	7
1975	ABA	32.20	3	2	4	-	-	-	9	12
1976	ABA	32.79	1	1	1	3	-	10	-	-
1977	Phil	23.84	9	2	15	30	-	-	28	29
1978	Phil	21.89	20	7	20	17	-	-	27	28
1979	Phil	22.74	15	3	12	-	-	-	-	-
1980	Phil	27.78	3	1	4	29	-	-	16	13
1981	Phil	27.38	4	2	7	29	-	-	21	11
1982	Phil	26.69	8	3	5	18	-	-	20	16
1983	Phil	23.24	14	3	21	-	-	-	16	-
1984	Phil	24.06	12	6	12	-	-	-	18	20
1985	Phil	19.41	38	15	28	-	-	-	22	20
1986	Phil	17.51	50	9	-	-	-	-	-	-
1987	Phil	16.30	65	12	-	-	-	15	-	

RAY FELIX — LONG ISLAND

YR	TM	PR	OR	PS	SC	SH	RB	AS	BL	ST
1954	Balt	20.57	7	6	5	-	4	-		
1955	N.Y.	17.60	13	5	-	-	2	-		
1956	N.Y.	14.25	23	6	-	-	6	-		
1957	N.Y.	13.64	25	8	-	-	10	-		
1958	N.Y.	16.33	24	7	-	-	4	-		
1959	N.Y.	11.60	37	10	-	-	10	-		
1960	Minn	9.40		DNQ						
1961	LA.L	9.13	51	11	-	-	9	-		
1962	LA.L	8.66		DNQ						

CHRIS FORD — VILLANOVA

YR	TM	PR	OR	PS	SC	SH	RB	AS	BL	ST
1973	Detr	9.15	100	39	-	-	-	-		
1974	Detr	9.71	95	17	-	-	-	-	-	4
1975	Detr	8.71	103	22	-	-	-	-	-	12
1976	Detr	10.15	90	16	-	-	-	-	-	3
1977	Detr	13.12	78	15	-	-	-	-	-	11
1978	Detr	12.40	99	18	-	-	-	-	31	-	10
1979	Bost	14.41	80	12	-	-	-	-	-	-
1980	Bost	11.48	118	20	-	-	-	-	-	26
1981	Bost	9.34	150	32	-	-	-	-	-	-
1982	Bost	5.34	160	30	-	-	-	-	-	-

PHIL FORD — N. CAROLINA

YR	TM	PR	OR	PS	SC	SH	RB	AS	BL	ST
1979	K.C.	17.32	50	6	-	-	-	3	-	9
1980	K.C.	16.12	63	8	-	-	-	5	-	27
1981	K.C.	18.21	36	3	-	-	-	2	-	-
1982	K.C.	10.35	135	25	-	-	-	10	-	-
1983	Milw	7.53	152	33	-	-	-	25	-	-
1984	Hous	9.85	143	27	-	-	-	18	-	-
1985	Hous	3.00		DNQ						

LARRY FOUST — LASALLE

YR	TM	PR	OR	PS	SC	SH	RB	AS	BL	ST
1951	Ft.W	13.74	17	6	-	-	7	-		
1952	Ft.W	21.23	3	2	7	-	6	-		
1953	Ft.W	17.84	9	4	11	-	4	-		
1954	Ft.W	21.36	6	5	8	9	3	-		
1955	Ft.W	20.96	6	2	-	1	10	-		
1956	Ft.W	18.94	9	3	11	3	11	-		
1957	Ft.W	14.82	17	5	-	-	9	-		
1958	Minn	20.35	12	5	-	-	8	-		
1959	Minn	14.50	24	6	-	-	-	-		
1960	St.L	14.90	26	7	-	-	-	-		
1961	St.L	9.99		DNQ						
1962	St.L	12.23		DNQ						

JIM FOX — S. CAROLINA

YR	TM	PR	OR	PS	SC	SH	RB	AS	BL	ST
1968	Detr	5.82		DNQ						
1969	Phoe	18.11	36	11	-	-	16	-		
1970	Phoe	15.64	55	12	-	4	-	-		
1971	Chic	14.39	65	17	-	-	11	-		
1972	Cinc	15.19	62	17	-	-	-	-		
1973	Seat	20.28	29	11	-	4	15	-		
1974	Seat	16.94	35	12	-	17	19	-	-	-
1975	Seat	11.96	75	19	-	-	-	-	-	-
1976	Milw	5.77		DNQ						
1977	NY.N	7.89		DNQ						

WALT FRAZIER — S. ILLINOIS

YR	TM	PR	OR	PS	SC	SH	RB	AS	BL	ST
1968	N.Y.	12.04	66	24	-	-	-	7		
1969	N.Y.	23.75	14	4	-	5	-	4		
1970	N.Y.	26.06	11	4	-	9	-	3		
1971	N.Y.	25.34	12	2	14	10	-	15		
1972	N.Y.	26.00	14	3	14	5	-	20		
1973	N.Y.	24.45	16	3	17	11	-	-		
1974	N.Y.	23.46	10	1	19	-	-	14	-	22
1975	N.Y.	23.56	9	1	15	23	-	19	-	9
1976	N.Y.	22.15	10	1	21	23	-	20	-	-
1977	N.Y.	17.68	36	2	-	-	-	23	-	-
1978	Clev	15.98	58	9	-	-	-	-	-	-
1979	Clev	8.33		DNQ						
1980	Clev	5.33		DNQ						

WORLD FREE — GUILFORD COLLEGE

YR	TM	PR	OR	PS	SC	SH	RB	AS	BL	ST
1976	Phil	5.69		DNQ						
1977	Phil	12.26	92	20	-	-	-	-	-	-
1978	Phil	13.16	90	16	-	-	-	30	-	-
1979	S.D.	21.35	23	2	2	-	-	-	-	-
1980	S.D.	21.38	20	3	2	-	-	-	-	-
1981	G.St	18.83	32	5	9	-	-	-	-	-
1982	G.St	17.40	46	5	9	-	-	-	-	-
1983	Clev	16.58	56	9	8	-	-	-	-	-
1984	Clev	15.60	71	10	14	-	-	-	-	-
1985	Clev	17.72	54	6	15	-	-	-	-	-
1986	Clev	17.81	46	8	10	-	-	-	-	-
1987	Phil	3.05		DNQ						
1988	Hous	3.88		DNQ						

JOE FULKS — MURRAY ST.

YR	TM	PR	OR	PS	SC	SH	RB	AS	BL	ST
1947	Phil	23.20			1					
1948	Phil	22.10			2					
1949	Phil	26.00			2					
1950	Phil	8.22	59	24	11	-		-		
1951	Phil	13.38	21	11	4	-	14	-		
1952	Phil	10.13	40	18	12	-	-	-		
1953	Phil	9.51	45	20	-	-	-	-		
1954	Phil	1.48		DNQ						

MIKE GALE — ELIZABETH CITY

YR	TM	PR	OR	PS	SC	SH	RB	AS	BL	ST
1972	ABA	8.68	71	31	-	-	-	-		
1973	ABA	9.11	69	30	-	-	-	-		
1974	ABA	12.33	44	15	-	8	-	-	-	4
1975	ABA	9.07	66	26	-	-	-	-	-	13
1976	ABA	8.79	49	19	-	-	8	-	-	-
1977	S.A.	14.39	61	8	-	-	-	11	-	10
1978	S.A.	13.21	89	12	-	-	-	12	-	3
1979	S.A.	11.13	116	23	-	-	-	16	-	6
1980	S.A.	10.40	127	19	-	-	-	9	-	5
1981	Port	6.96		DNQ						
1982	G.St	9.23	152	32	-	-	-	-	-	9

HARRY GALLATIN — N.E MISSOURI.

YR	TM	PR	OR	PS	SC	SH	RB	AS	BL	ST
1949	N.Y.	8.30			-					
1950	N.Y.	17.54	5	2	-	5		-		
1951	N.Y.	19.97	6	2	-	9	3	-		
1952	N.Y.	17.53	11	5	-	3	4	-		
1953	N.Y.	20.36	5	2	-	6	1	-		
1954	N.Y.	23.61	2	1	13	4	2	-		
1955	N.Y.	22.29	4	3	-	11	3	-		
1956	N.Y.	18.07	13	7	-	-	-	-		
1957	N.Y.	18.06	10	6	-	7	7	-		
1958	Detr	17.26	19	10	-	-	9	-		

JACK GEORGE — LASALLE

YR	TM	PR	OR	PS	SC	SH	RB	AS	BL	ST
1954	Phil	11.08	29	9	-	-	-	10		
1955	Phil	12.81	30	9	-	-	-	8		
1956	Phil	15.10	20	4	-	-	-	6		
1957	Phil	11.06	33	8	-	-	-	5		
1958	Phil	9.79	43	16	-	-	-	9		
1959	N.Y.	9.04	47	16	-	-	-	-		
1960	N.Y.	9.35	46	20	-	-	-	9		
1961	N.Y.	5.06		DNQ						

GEORGE GERVIN — E. MICHIGAN

YR	TM	PR	OR	PS	SC	SH	RB	AS	BL	ST
1973	ABA	12.80		DNQ						
1974	ABA	22.38	8	5	11	-	-	-	9	-
1975	ABA	22.86	10	6	7	-	-	-	10	-
1976	ABA	21.60	11	6	9	5	-	-	9	-
1977	S.A.	21.68	16	1	9	3	-	-	27	-
1978	S.A.	24.93	7	1	1	5	-	-	-	-
1979	S.A.	25.31	6	1	1	7	-	-	-	-
1980	S.A.	27.19	5	1	1	7	-	-	-	-
1981	S.A.	22.10	14	1	3	-	-	-	-	-
1982	S.A.	24.82	11	1	1	-	-	-	-	-
1983	S.A.	21.63	24	2	4	-	-	-	-	-
1984	S.A.	20.08	30	3	6	-	-	-	-	-
1985	S.A.	16.81	63	10	24	-	-	-	-	-
1986	Chic	11.89	114	22	-	-	-	-	-	-

JOHN GIANELLI — PACIFIC

YR	TM	PR	OR	PS	SC	SH	RB	AS	BL	ST
1973	N.Y.	4.81		DNQ						
1974	N.Y.	9.04	98	21	-	-	-	-	22	-
1975	N.Y.	14.91	50	13	-	-	-	-	15	-
1976	N.Y.	11.51	78	19	-	-	-	-	-	-
1977	Buff	10.18	115	27	-	-	-	-	18	-
1978	Milw	12.52	97	28	-	-	-	-	31	-
1979	Milw	10.44	124	31	-	-	-	-	-	-
1980	Utah	4.29		DNQ						

HERM GILLIAM — PURDUE

YR	TM	PR	OR	PS	SC	SH	RB	AS	BL	ST
1970	Cinc	9.37		DNQ						
1971	Buff	11.98	89	36	-	-	-	19		
1972	Atla	13.29	73	25	-	-	-	13		
1973	Atla	18.20	43	13	-	-	-	10		
1974	Atla	15.71	47	11	-	-	-	10	-	6
1975	Atla	10.60	91	15	-	-	-	-	-	14
1976	Seat	8.22	110	22	-	-	-	-	-	21
1977	Port	7.54	145	31	-	-	-	-	-	-

ARTIS GILMORE — JACKSONVILLE

YR	TM	PR	OR	PS	SC	SH	RB	AS	BL	ST
1972	ABA	35.33	1	1	13	1	2	-		
1973	ABA	32.96	2	1	-	10	1			
1974	ABA	31.35	1	1	-	-	1		2	-
1975	ABA	33.37	2	1	7	4	3	-	2	-
1976	ABA	32.26	2	1	4	6	2	-	2	-
1977	Chic	24.15	8	6	30	-	5	-	8	-
1978	Chic	28.24	5	5	16	10	10	-	13	-
1979	Chic	29.79	3	3	9	6	15	-	18	-
1980	Chic	22.25		DNQ						
1981	Chic	25.02	6	3	32	1	14	-	8	-
1982	Chic	25.76	9	4	32	1	13	-	7	-
1983	S.A.	25.68	6	2	-	1	2	-	7	-
1984	S.A.	22.16	20	7	-	2	6	-	7	-
1985	S.A.	24.85	11	5	-	4	13	-	10	-
1986	S.A.	20.31	30	9	-	8	-	-	24	-
1987	S.A.	15.50	75	19	-	9	-	-	28	-
1988	Bost	4.68		DNQ						

TOM GOLA — LASALLE

YR	TM	PR	OR	PS	SC	SH	RB	AS	BL	ST
1956	Phil	19.34	8	2	-	-	5			
1957		DID NOT PLAY								
1958	Phil	21.81	9	1	-	-	5			
1959	Phil	20.95	11	2	-	-	-			
1960	Phil	22.44	11	1	-	-	11			
1961	Phil	19.50	16	4	-	-	-			
1962	Phil	20.08	19	5	-	-	-			
1963	N.Y.	16.90	23	12	-	-	-			
1964	N.Y.	13.43	36	12	-	-	11			
1965	N.Y.	10.16	51	19	-	-	8			
1966	N.Y.	8.57		DNQ						

GAIL GOODRICH — UCLA

YR	TM	PR	OR	PS	SC	SH	RB	AS	BL	ST
1966	LA.L	6.09		DNQ						
1967	LA.L	11.82	52	21	-	-	-			
1968	LA.L	12.52	65	23	-	8	-			
1969	Phoe	20.86	25	8	8	-	-	11		
1970	Phoe	21.85	20	7	-	-	8			
1971	LA.L	16.77	53	20	-	22	-			
1972	LA.L	22.37	24	7	5	13	-			
1973	LA.L	19.53	36	10	8	-	-			
1974	LA.L	18.60	28	4	6	-	-	-	-	-
1975	LA.L	18.11	21	1	8	-	-	11	-	-
1976	LA.L	16.39	45	8	20	-	-	10	-	-
1977	N.O.	9.79		DNQ						
1978	N.O.	14.44	72	10	-	-	-	27	-	-
1979	N.O.	12.14	102	19	-	-	-	18	-	-

JOE GRABOSKI

YR	TM	PR	OR	PS	SC	SH	RB	AS	BL	ST
1949	Chic	6.84		DNQ						
1950	Chic	11.86		DNQ						
1951		DID NOT PLAY								
1952	Indi	15.91	16	6	-	-	-			
1953	Indi	15.17	14	7	-	-	-			
1954	Phil	14.32	12	3	11	-	-			
1955	Phil	13.63	25	11	-	-	-			
1956	Phil	15.11	19	11	-	-	-			
1957	Phil	13.72	24	13	-	-	-			
1958	Phil	11.83	36	10	-	-	-			
1959	Phil	15.90	19	4	-	-	-			
1960	Phil	8.56		DNQ						
1961	Phil	5.99		DNQ						
1962	Syra	5.39		DNQ						

JOHNNY GREEN — MICHIGAN ST.

YR	TM	PR	OR	PS	SC	SH	RB	AS	BL	ST
1960	N.Y.	10.45		DNQ						
1961	N.Y.	14.96	26	11	-	-	5	-		
1962	N.Y.	21.28	16	6	-	-	9	-		
1963	N.Y.	21.53	12	5	-	-	6	-		
1964	N.Y.	17.17	20	11	-	-	6	-		
1965	N.Y.	12.87	38	18	-	-	-	-		
1966	Balt	14.86	33	16	-	-	5	-		
1967	Balt	9.97		DNQ						
1968	Phil	11.19		DNQ						
1969	Phil	7.05		DNQ						
1970	Cinc	20.71	26	10	-	17	7	-		
1971	Cinc	19.87	32	13	-	-	4	-	-	
1972	Cinc	13.70	68	28	-	11	-	-		
1973	KC-O	10.91		DNQ						

MIKE GREEN — LOUISIANA TECH

YR	TM	PR	OR	PS	SC	SH	RB	AS	BL	ST
1974	ABA	13.46	37	15	-	-	6	-	3	-
1975	ABA	20.73	17	5	-	9	13	-	3	-
1976	ABA	19.15	16	6	-	-	9	-	4	-
1977	Seat	12.29	90	24	-	-	-	-	10	-
1978	S.A.	10.17	129	31	-	-	-	-	9	-
1979	S.A.	10.87	119	29	-	-	-	-	6	-
1980	K.C.	9.38		DNQ						

HAL GREER — MARSHALL

YR	TM	PR	OR	PS	SC	SH	RB	AS	BL	ST
1959	Syra	9.41	45	15	-	5	-	-		
1960	Syra	13.53	32	9	-	3	-			
1961	Syra	18.49	20	6	-	8	-			
1962	Syra	22.32	15	4	11	11	-			
1963	Syra	19.11	15	4	12	10	-			
1964	Phil	21.71	14	3	7	11	-			
1965	Phil	18.53	18	4	9	-	10			
1966	Phil	21.23	11	3	8	-	-			
1967	Phil	19.58	20	4	7	-	-			
1968	Phil	22.15	18	5	7	13	-			
1969	Phil	21.60	20	5	10	17	-			
1970	Phil	20.21	27	12	15	-	-			
1971	Phil	17.06	50	18	-	-	-			
1972	Phil	12.54	76	26	-	-	-			
1973	Phil	7.45		DNQ						

BOB GROSS — LONG BEACH ST.

YR	TM	PR	OR	PS	SC	SH	RB	AS	BL	ST
1976	Port	9.79	95	19	-	16	-	-	22	10
1977	Port	14.27	62	15	-	5	-	-	-	-
1978	Port	16.17	56	14	-	8	-	-	-	-
1979	Port	12.96	93	24	-	-	-	-	-	-
1980	Port	11.06	121	29	-	-	-	-	-	-
1981	Port	11.90	114	24	-	15	-	-	-	-
1982	Port	11.25	119	30	-	20	-	-	-	20
1983	S.D.	4.74		DNQ						

RICHIE GUERIN — IONA

YR	TM	PR	OR	PS	SC	SH	RB	AS	BL	ST
1957	N.Y.	9.14	41	11	-	-	-	-		
1958	N.Y.	16.83	21	5	-	-	-	8		
1959	N.Y.	20.70	12	3	-	8	-	5		
1960	N.Y.	22.35	12	2	9	-	-	4		
1961	N.Y.	22.63	12	2	-	-	-	7		
1962	N.Y.	27.54	8	3	7	9	-	7		
1963	N.Y.	19.05	16	5	9	-	-	12		
1964	St.L	13.85	32	8	-	-	-	6		
1965	St.L	14.11	30	9	-	-	-	4		
1966	St.L	15.30	29	10	-	-	-	6		
1967	St.L	12.59	49	20	-	-	-	10		
1968	DID NOT PLAY									
1969	Atla	8.44	DNQ							
1970	Atla	1.63	DNQ							

MATT GUOKAS — ST.JOE

YR	TM	PR	OR	PS	SC	SH	RB	AS	BL	ST
1967	Phil	3.46	DNQ							
1968	Phil	7.77	82	36	-	9	-	-		
1969	Phil	3.96	DNQ							
1970	Phil	8.15	94	41	-	-	-	-		
1971	Chic	9.67	103	40	-	15	-	16		
1972	Cinc	11.41	85	32	-	19	-	12		
1973	KC-O	14.01	71	27	-	1	-	-		
1974	Buff	6.25	114	23	-	-	-	-	-	-
1975	Chic	6.59	115	27	-	14	-	-	-	-
1976	K.C.	1.41	DNQ							

CLIFF HAGAN — KENTUCKY

YR	TM	PR	OR	PS	SC	SH	RB	AS	BL	ST
1957	St.L	6.25	DNQ							
1958	St.L	21.79	10	5	7	6	-	-		
1959	St.L	25.60	4	3	5	3	-	-		
1960	St.L	27.04	5	3	5	5	-	-		
1961	St.L	24.52	9	6	11	7	-	11		
1962	St.L	24.69	10	3	9	4	-	-		
1963	St.L	14.37	30	16	-	-	-	-		
1964	St.L	15.75	22	12	-	-	-	-		
1965	St.L	11.04	47	21	-	-	-	-		
1966	St.L	11.61	48	24	-	-	-	-		
1967	DID NOT PLAY									
1968	ABA	20.84	9	5	-	4	-	2		
1969	ABA	13.23	DNQ							
1970	ABA	6.67	DNQ							

HAROLD HAIRSTON — N.Y.U.

YR	TM	PR	OR	PS	SC	SH	RB	AS	BL	ST
1965	Cinc	6.84	DNQ							
1966	Cinc	15.13	30	14	-	8	-	-		
1967	Cinc	15.65	30	14	-	-	-	-		
1968	Detr	18.59	33	14	-	-	-	-		
1969	Detr	22.00	18	5	-	19	-	-		
1970	LA.L	23.01	17	7	-	15	-	-		
1971	LA.L	21.21	29	11	-	-	-	-		
1972	LA.L	22.09	26	9	-	-	7	-		
1973	LA.L	24.50	DNQ							
1974	LA.L	22.22	13	3	-	13	3	-	-	
1975	LA.L	19.15	17	6	-	7	1	-	-	

ALEX HANNUM — USC

YR	TM	PR	OR	PS	SC	SH	RB	AS	BL	ST
1949	Oshk	5.70					-			
1950	Syra	8.56	55	22	-	-	-	-		
1951	Syra	7.76	49	21	-	-	-	-		
1952	Roch	8.73	50	23	-	-	-	-		
1953	Roch	6.32	DNQ							
1954	Roch	7.18	56	24	-	-	-	-		
1955	Milw	7.26	55	25	-	-	-	-		
1956	St.L	7.30	53	21	-	-	-	-		
1957	St.L	3.59	DNQ							

BOB HARRISON — MICHIGAN

YR	TM	PR	OR	PS	SC	SH	RB	AS	BL	ST
1950	Minn	5.82	DNQ							
1951	Minn	6.75	58	18	-	-	-	-		
1952	Minn	5.89	66	25	-	-	-	12		
1953	Minn	6.13	62	25	-	-	-	-		
1954	Milw	4.41	66	29	-	-	-	-		
1955	Milw	7.88	49	15	-	-	-	-		
1956	St.L	7.99	51	18	-	-	-	-		
1957	Syra	7.17	51	20	-	-	-	-		
1958	Syra	6.01	53	22	-	-	-	-		

CLEM HASKINS — W. KENTUCKY

YR	TM	PR	OR	PS	SC	SH	RB	AS	BL	ST
1968	Chic	8.22	79	33	-	-	-	-		
1969	Chic	15.24	51	15	-	-	-	-		
1970	Chic	21.46	22	8	-	-	-	-		
1971	Phoe	16.60	55	21	-	-	-	20		
1972	Phoe	15.38	60	21	-	17	-	-		
1973	Phoe	9.95	91	34	-	-	-	-		
1974	Phoe	10.67	85	15	-	-	-	21	-	-
1975	Wash	3.29	DNQ							
1976	Wash	5.82	DNQ							

JOHN HAVLICEK — OHIO ST.

YR	TM	PR	OR	PS	SC	SH	RB	AS	BL	ST
1963	Bost	14.83	28	15	-	-	-	-		
1964	Bost	15.74	23	5	10	-	-	-		
1965	Bost	13.52	33	11	-	-	-	-		
1966	Bost	15.41	27	13	-	-	-	-		
1967	Bost	19.89	18	10	8	-	-	-		
1968	Bost	20.24	25	8	15	-	-	-		
1969	Bost	20.20	29	9	17	-	-	6		
1970	Bost	27.23	10	3	9	-	-	14		
1971	Bost	30.40	3	1	2	-	-	10		
1972	Bost	29.11	4	1	3	-	-	11		
1973	Bost	24.99	12	4	11	-	-	18		
1974	Bost	21.17	16	4	11	-	-	20	-	
1975	Bost	18.85	18	4	23	-	-	23	-	
1976	Bost	14.84	53	10	-	-	-	-		
1977	Bost	16.16	47	10	-	-	-	-		
1978	Bost	14.39	74	12	-	-	-	-		

FORMER PLAYERS

CONNIE HAWKINS — IOWA

YR	TM	PR	OR	PS	SC	SH	RB	AS	BL	ST
1968	ABA	33.80	1	1	3	2	-	9		
1969	ABA	32.64		DNQ						
1970	Phoe	28.77	6	2	7	-	-	-		
1971	Phoe	23.58	18	5	19	-	-	-		
1972	Phoe	22.96	21	7	-	-	-	-		
1973	Phoe	21.17	26	10	-	20	-	-		
1974	LA.L	18.15	29	7	-	15	-	18	-	-
1975	LA.L	10.23		DNQ						
1976	Atla	12.11	72	16	-	-	-	-	-	-

TOM HAWKINS — NOTRE DAME

YR	TM	PR	OR	PS	SC	SH	RB	AS	BL	ST
1960	Minn	8.86	49	19	-	-	-	-		
1961	LA.L	10.55	45	18	-	-	-	-		
1962	LA.L	10.58	50	22	-	-	-	-		
1963	Cinc	12.13	41	21	-	-	-	-		
1964	Cinc	10.07	49	23	-	-	-	-		
1965	Cinc	8.92	59	25	-	-	-	-		
1966	Cinc	11.54	50	25	-	-	-	-		
1967	LA.L	10.01	63	24	-	-	-	-		
1968	LA.L	12.62	63	30	-	-	-	-		
1969	LA.L	7.42	93	41	-	-	-	-		

ELVIN HAYES — HOUSTON

YR	TM	PR	OR	PS	SC	SH	RB	AS	BL	ST
1969	S.D.	29.45	5	3	1	-	12	-		
1970	S.D.	30.54	2	2	3	-	5	-		
1971	S.D.	29.38	6	3	3	-	10	-		
1972	Hous	27.17	12	7	10	-	16	-		
1973	Balt	24.49	15	6	16	-	13	-		
1974	Capt	28.72	4	4	16	-	1	-	8	-
1975	Wash	25.70	6	1	7	-	-	-	7	-
1976	Wash	21.69	13	2	19	-	24	-	5	-
1977	Wash	26.87	5	1	8	-	21	-	11	-
1978	Wash	23.30	13	2	24	-	16	-	20	-
1979	Wash	24.56	8	1	18	-	14	-	13	-
1980	Wash	22.96	14	2	8	-	21	-	8	-
1981	Wash	18.47	34	7	33	-	25	-	13	-
1982	Hous	17.61	45	9	-	-	-	-	-	-
1983	Hous	14.74	75	13	-	-	30	-	-	-
1984	Hous	5.16		DNQ						

SPENCER HAYWOOD — DETROIT

YR	TM	PR	OR	PS	SC	SH	RB	AS	BL	ST
1970	ABA	37.81	1	1	2	10	2	-		
1971	Seat	22.64		DNQ						
1972	Seat	27.97	8	3	4	-	-	-		
1973	Seat	30.81	4	1	3	21	-	-		
1974	Seat	26.92	5	1	10	-	16	-	15	-
1975	Seat	21.47	11	3	9	-	-	-	14	-
1976	N.Y.	20.29	19	3	18	-	21	-	24	-
1977	NY.K	17.27		DNQ						
1978	N.Y.	14.60	69	14	-	-	-	-	25	-
1979	N.O.	19.59	33	8	22	-	-	-	-	-
1980	LA.L	10.30	130	27	-	-	-	-	26	-
1981		DID NOT PLAY								
1982	Wash	12.61	100	20	-	-	-	-	-	-
1983	Wash	7.55		DNQ						

WALT HAZZARD — UCLA

YR	TM	PR	OR	PS	SC	SH	RB	AS	BL	ST
1965	LA.L	4.80		DNQ						
1966	LA.L	13.63	40	14	-	-	-	4		
1967	LA.L	10.53	59	26	-	-	-	3		
1968	Seat	21.08	24	7	8	-	-	8		
1969	Atla	12.85	67	23	-	-	-	6		
1970	Atla	18.50	39	16	-	-	-	4		
1971	Atla	17.73	45	16	-	-	-	6		
1972	Buff	15.86	58	20	-	-	-	9		
1973	G.St	5.80		DNQ						
1974	Seat	4.78		DNQ						

GARFIELD HEARD — OKLAHOMA

YR	TM	PR	OR	PS	SC	SH	RB	AS	BL	ST
1971	Seat	7.22		DNQ						
1972	Seat	10.74	91	38	-	-	-	-		
1973	Chic	9.79	93	39	-	-	-	-		
1974	Buff	21.69	15	4	-	-	18	-	5	-
1975	Buff	16.60	36	8	-	-	17	-	6	-
1976	Phoe	16.86	41	10	-	-	17	-	18	-
1977	Phoe	14.41		DNQ						
1978	Phoe	13.71	81	17	-	-	27	-	22	11
1979	Phoe	9.83	134	20	-	-	-	-	19	-
1980	Phoe	8.13		DNQ						
1981	S.D.	8.63	153	35	-	-	-	-	27	10

TOM HEINSOHN — HOLY CROSS

YR	TM	PR	OR	PS	SC	SH	RB	AS	BL	ST
1957	Bost	17.17	12	7	-	-	-	-		
1958	Bost	17.42	17	9	-	-	-	-		
1959	Bost	18.76	13	8	-	-	-	-		
1960	Bost	20.99	13	8	10	-	-	-		
1961	Bost	19.11	17	9	-	-	-	-		
1962	Bost	20.94	18	8	12	-	-	-		
1963	Bost	16.93	22	11	-	-	-	-		
1964	Bost	14.54	28	15	-	-	-	-		
1965	Bost	12.42	40	20	-	-	-	-		

TOM HENDERSON — HAWAII

YR	TM	PR	OR	PS	SC	SH	RB	AS	BL	ST
1975	Atla	9.67	97	19	-	-	-	20	-	-
1976	Atla	11.64	75	15	-	-	-	-	-	-
1977	Wash	13.57	70	10	-	-	-	5	-	-
1978	Wash	11.51	112	18	-	-	-	15	-	, -
1979	Wash	12.91	94	15	-	-	-	8	-	-
1980	Hous	7.82	149	27	-	-	-	19	-	-
1981	Hous	7.80	160	29	-	-	-	12	-	-
1982	Hous	8.09	156	33	-	-	-	23	-	-
1983	Hous	5.63		DNQ						

WAYNE HIGHTOWER — KANSAS

YR	TM	PR	OR	PS	SC	SH	RB	AS	BL	ST
1963	S.F.	7.44	65	31	-	-	-			
1964	S.F.	13.25	38	18	-	-	-			
1965	Balt	8.37	62	27	-	-	-			
1966	Balt	9.76	DNQ							
1967	Detr	8.10	DNQ							
1968	ABA	15.45	32	15	-	-	-			
1969	ABA	18.07	22	11	-	-	-			
1970	ABA	20.41	DNQ							
1971	ABA	16.96	40	10	-	-	-			
1972	ABA	5.69	DNQ							

DARNELL HILLMAN — SAN JOSE ST.

YR	TM	PR	OR	PS	SC	SH	RB	AS	BL	ST
1972	ABA	10.53	DNQ							
1973	ABA	13.76	44	18	-	-	12	-	-	-
1974	ABA	13.35	41	17	-	-	14	-	4	-
1975	ABA	18.70	24	8	-	13	14	-	6	-
1976	ABA	15.74	27	8	-	-	7	-	8	-
1977	Indi	14.84	54	8	-	-	26	-	22	-
1978	Denv	12.90	92	19	-	-	-	-	24	-
1979	K.C.	9.42	139	22	-	-	-	-	26	-
1980	G.St	5.71	DNQ							

LIONELL HOLLINS — ARIZONA ST.

YR	TM	PR	OR	PS	SC	SH	RB	AS	BL	ST
1976	Port	10.35	89	17	-	-	-	9	-	6
1977	Port	12.92	82	17	-	-	-	-	-	8
1978	Port	14.06	76	13	-	-	-	-	-	17
1979	Port	13.00	92	14	-	-	-	21	-	15
1980	Phil	8.17	DNQ							
1981	Phil	10.05	136	28	-	-	-	27	-	-
1982	Phil	11.12	120	23	-	-	-	-	-	-
1983	S.D.	13.07	94	15	-	-	-	22	-	15
1984	Detr	2.88	DNQ							
1985	Hous	9.98	139	27	-	-	-	17	-	-

BAILEY HOWELL — MISSISSIPPI ST.

YR	TM	PR	OR	PS	SC	SH	RB	AS	BL	ST
1960	Detr	19.55	17	11	-	9	-	-		
1961	Detr	29.08	6	3	7	4	8	-		
1962	Detr	25.01	9	2	-	5	-	-		
1963	Detr	27.92	7	3	8	2	-	-		
1964	Detr	24.25	9	4	8	6	-	-		
1965	Balt	24.51	10	4	11	2	-	-		
1966	Balt	21.00	12	4	-	4	-	-		
1967	Bost	20.65	17	9	13	3	-	-		
1968	Bost	21.22	23	11	-	16	-	-		
1969	Bost	20.53	28	11	-	12	-	-		
1970	Bost	13.39	68	29	-	-	-	-		
1971	Phil	12.04	88	32	-	-	-	-		

LOU HUDSON — MINNESOTA

YR	TM	PR	OR	PS	SC	SH	RB	AS	BL	ST
1967	St.L	14.96	34	16	-	-	-	-		
1968	St.L	11.20	DNQ							
1969	Atla	20.78	26	9	15	8	-	-		
1970	Atla	23.34	15	5	5	2	-	-		
1971	Atla	22.07	25	8	6	16	-	-		
1972	Atla	22.69	23	6	11	9	-	-		
1973	Atla	23.68	17	7	4	-	-	-		
1974	Atla	21.98	14	3	5	10	-	-	-	-
1975	Atla	16.05	DNQ							
1976	Atla	14.07	60	11	-	-	-	-	-	23
1977	Atla	11.41	101	23	-	-	-	-	-	-
1978	LA.L	11.26	116	25	-	-	-	-	-	-
1979	LA.L	9.03	144	27	-	17	-	-	-	-

MEL HUTCHINS — BYU

YR	TM	PR	OR	PS	SC	SH	RB	AS	BL	ST
1952	Milw	18.11	10	4	-	-	7	-		
1953	Milw	17.27	10	5	-	-	11	-		
1954	Ft.W	15.74	9	2	-	-	-	-		
1955	Ft.W	15.82	16	8	-	-	-	-		
1956	Ft.W	14.39	21	12	-	-	-	-		
1957	Ft.W	14.35	21	12	-	-	-	-		
1958	N.Y.	8.17	DNQ							

DARRALL IMHOFF — CALIFORNIA

YR	TM	PR	OR	PS	SC	SH	RB	AS	BL	ST
1961	N.Y.	6.53	DNQ							
1962	N.Y.	8.54	58	11	-	-	-	-		
1963	Detr	3.82	DNQ							
1964	Detr	7.31	DNQ							
1965	LA.L	9.64	54	11	-	-	-	-		
1966	LA.L	9.82	DNQ							
1967	LA.L	20.73	16	5	-	-	7	-		
1968	LA.L	17.48	38	11	-	-	7	-		
1969	Phil	16.06	45	12	-	-	17	-		
1970	Phil	19.72	30	6	-	11	-	-		
1971	Cinc	12.41	DNQ							
1972	Port	4.39	DNQ							

DAN ISSEL — KENTUCKY

YR	TM	PR	OR	PS	SC	SH	RB	AS	BL	ST
1971	ABA	30.54	3	3	2	-	14	-		
1972	ABA	29.80	4	2	2	-	-	-		
1973	ABA	28.92	4	3	4	-	-	-		
1974	ABA	25.07	4	3	4	-	-	-	-	-
1975	ABA	19.16	23	11	-	-	-	-		
1976	ABA	26.64	4	3	7	-	5	-		
1977	Denv	22.38	13	7	10	14	-	-		
1978	Denv	24.57	9	7	19	19	-	-		
1979	Denv	21.09	27	10	-	-	-	-		
1980	Denv	24.34	8	3	7	-	-	-		
1981	Denv	22.73	12	6	13	-	-	-		
1982	Denv	23.43	13	7	11	17	-	-		
1983	Denv	22.29	21	8	18	29	-	-		
1984	Denv	20.08	30	10	29	-	-	-		
1985	Denv	12.53	108	19	-	-	-	-		

EDDIE JOHNSON JR. — AUBURN

YR	TM	PR	OR	PS	SC	SH	RB	AS	BL	ST
1978	Atla	9.63	135	28	-	-	-	-	-	-
1979	Atla	14.92	76	11	-	26	-	-	-	25
1980	Atla	16.58	61	11	-	-	-	-	-	-
1981	Atla	17.56	41	7	23	-	-	-	-	-
1982	Atla	15.37	65	9	-	-	-	31	-	-
1983	Atla	13.30	92	18	-	-	-	29	-	-
1984	Atla	12.00	116	21	-	-	-	21	-	-
1985	Atla	16.40	69	12	-	-	-	11	-	-
1986	Clev	9.20	143	31	-	-	15	-	-	-
1987	Seat	9.83		DNQ						

GEORGE T. JOHNSON — DILLARD

YR	TM	PR	OR	PS	SC	SH	RB	AS	BL	ST
1973	G.St	2.96		DNQ						
1974	G.St	12.39	75	17	-	-	2	-	2	-
1975	G.St	10.67		DNQ						
1976	G.St	11.96	74	18	-	-	6	-	2	-
1977	Buff	12.77	85	21	-	-	6	-	1	-
1978	N.J.	15.26	64	21	-	-	18	-	2	-
1979	N.J.	13.51	88	26	-	-	21	-	2	-
1980	N.J.	14.07	85	19	-	-	19	-	1	-
1981	S.A.	13.48	96	24	-	-	9	-	1	-
1982	S.A.	10.60	130	28	-	-	17	-	1	-
1983	Atla	5.70		DNQ						

GUS JOHNSON — IDAHO

YR	TM	PR	OR	PS	SC	SH	RB	AS	BL	ST
1964	Balt	22.03	12	6	-	-	7	-		
1965	Balt	22.97	12	5	12	-	11	-		
1966	Balt	22.00		DNQ						
1967	Balt	23.16	12	6	10	-	-	-		
1968	Balt	24.07	10	4	-	-	15	-		
1969	Balt	21.57		DNQ						
1970	Balt	24.67	14	6	-	-	6	-		
1971	Balt	28.03	7	3	-	-	2	-		
1972	Balt	8.72		DNQ						
1973	Phoe	9.86		DNQ						

JOHN JOHNSON — IOWA

YR	TM	PR	OR	PS	SC	SH	RB	AS	BL	ST
1971	Clev	18.37	43	17	-	-	-	18		
1972	Clev	19.90	36	15	-	-	-	-		
1973	Clev	16.11	61	24	-	-	-	-		
1974	Port	17.93	30	7	-	-	-	-		
1975	Port	16.08	41	8	-	-	-	-		
1976	Hous	10.99	85	17	-	-	-	-		
1977	Hous	8.56	137	30	-	-	-	-		
1978	Seat	9.16	142	27	-	-	-	-		
1979	Seat	11.91	106	26	-	-	-	-		
1980	Seat	14.74	78	23	-	-	-	22	-	
1981	Seat	11.39	122	25	-	-	-	-	-	-
1982	Seat	5.00		DNQ						

MICKEY JOHNSON — AURORA

YR	TM	PR	OR	PS	SC	SH	RB	AS	BL	ST
1975	Chic	4.44		DNQ						
1976	Chic	18.31	28	5	-	-	16	-	-	-
1977	Chic	19.95	26	9	-	-	-	-	-	-
1978	Chic	20.26	29	10	-	-	-	-	-	-
1979	Chic	17.59	47	14	-	-	-	-	-	-
1980	Indi	21.83	18	6	29	-	-	-	23	17
1981	Milw	15.27	74	17	-	-	-	-	-	-
1982	Milw	14.87	68	17	-	-	-	-	-	-
1983	G.St	14.59	78	23	-	-	-	-	-	-
1984	G.St	14.46	80	22	-	-	-	-	-	30
1985	G.St	13.89	97	22	-	-	-	-	-	-
1986	N.J.	9.48	140	27	-	-	-	-	-	-

OLLIE JOHNSON — TEMPLE

YR	TM	PR	OR	PS	SC	SH	RB	AS	BL	ST
1973	Port	13.17	72	28	-	14	-	-		
1974	Port	8.67	104	21	-	21	-	-	-	-
1975	K.C.	7.93	107	21	-	-	-	-	-	-
1976	K.C.	11.46	79	14	-	5	-	-	-	-
1977	K.C.	7.11		DNQ						
1978	Atla	9.00	146	28	-	-	-	-	-	-
1979	Chic	10.31	127	31	-	24	-	-	-	-
1980	Chic	8.13	147	31	-	-	-	-	-	-
1981	Phil	5.23		DNQ						
1982	Phil	2.69		DNQ						

NEIL JOHNSTON — OHIO ST.

YR	TM	PR	OR	PS	SC	SH	RB	AS	BL	ST
1952	Phil	8.66		DNQ						
1953	Phil	26.99	1	1	1	3	7	-		
1954	Phil	25.53	1	1	1	3	-	-		
1955	Phil	29.00	1	1	1	3	5	-		
1956	Phil	27.36	2	1	3	1	10	-		
1957	Phil	27.20	2	1	3	1	-	-		
1958	Phil	22.77	7	4	8	3	-	-		
1959	Phil	7.43		DNQ						

BOBBY JONES — N. CAROLINA

YR	TM	PR	OR	PS	SC	SH	RB	AS	BL	ST
1975	ABA	21.56	14	8	-	1	-	-	5	6
1976	ABA	22.84	8	4	-	1	-	-	7	9
1977	Denv	22.09	14	4	-	4	-	-	9	7
1978	Denv	22.07	18	5	-	2	-	-	17	23
1979	Phil	16.76	59	18	-	19	-	-	23	-
1980	Phil	16.06	64	17	-	22	-	-	11	-
1981	Phil	16.79	52	13	-	14	-	-	-	-
1982	Phil	17.79	41	13	-	5	-	-	18	-
1983	Phil	13.04	95	26	-	11	-	-	20	31
1984	Phil	13.15	99	27	-	-	-	-	14	13
1985	Phil	10.75	128	26	-	12	-	-	-	25
1986	Phil	8.77	148	28	-	13	-	-	-	-

DWIGHT JONES — HOUSTON

YR	TM	PR	OR	PS	SC	SH	RB	AS	BL	ST
1974	Atla	10.86	84	19	-	-	22	-	11	-
1975	Atla	14.79	52	14	-	-	12	-	23	-
1976	Atla	13.94	62	16	-	-	23	-	19	-
1977	Hous	7.14			DNQ					
1978	Hous	13.30	88	18	-	-	-	-	-	-
1979	Hous	6.80			DNQ					
1980	Chic	10.45	126	26	-	-	-	-	-	-
1981	Chic	9.47	148	33	-	-	-	-	-	-
1982	Chic	12.76	98	19	-	-	-	-	-	-
1983	LA.L	5.90			DNQ					

K.C. JONES — USF

YR	TM	PR	OR	PS	SC	SH	RB	AS	BL	ST
1959	Bost	4.37			DNQ					
1960	Bost	7.66			DNQ					
1961	Bost	8.10	53	21	-	-	-	10		
1962	Bost	10.76	48	14	-	-	-	6		
1963	Bost	9.19	57	20	-	-	-	4		
1964	Bost	11.43	43	15	-	-	-	3		
1965	Bost	11.97	42	14	-	-	-	3		
1966	Bost	12.79	43	15	-	-	-	3		
1967	Bost	9.79	65	29	-	-	-	7		

SAM JONES — N. CARO. COLL.

YR	TM	PR	OR	PS	SC	SH	RB	AS	BL	ST
1958	Bost	5.36			DNQ					
1959	Bost	11.93	35	13	-	-	-	-		
1960	Bost	12.15	34	11	-	8	-	-		
1961	Bost	14.91	27	10	-	9	-	-		
1962	Bost	17.73	22	7	-	6	-	-		
1963	Bost	18.22	19	6	11	11	-	-		
1964	Bost	15.89	21	4	11	-	-	-		
1965	Bost	20.16	15	3	5	-	-	-		
1966	Bost	20.13	14	5	5	5	-	-		
1967	Bost	18.44	24	7	6	12	-	-		
1968	Bost	18.27	34	10	12	-	-	-		
1969	Bost	13.41	62	20	-	-	-	-		

RICH KELLEY — STANFORD

YR	TM	PR	OR	PS	SC	SH	RB	AS	BL	ST
1976	N.O.	13.05			DNQ					
1977	N.O.	13.47	72	20	-	-	4	-	23	-
1978	N.O.	17.76	42	15	-	25	6	-	12	-
1979	N.O.	25.66	5	4	-	28	3	-	12	-
1980	Phoe	13.13	96	22	-	-	24	-	15	-
1981	Phoe	12.05	111	26	-	-	-	23	33	-
1982	Phoe	12.28	102	23	-	-	31	30	-	-
1983	Utah	10.33	121	25	-	-	15	-	-	-
1984	Utah	10.68	134	28	-	-	16	-	-	-
1985	Utah	7.55			DNQ					
1986	Sacr	4.43			DNQ					

LARRY KENON — MEMPHIS ST.

YR	TM	PR	OR	PS	SC	SH	RB	AS	BL	ST
1974	ABA	19.73	13	6	-	-	8	-	-	-
1975	ABA	22.33	12	7	-	-	-	-	-	-
1976	ABA	22.27	9	5	-	-	8	-	-	-
1977	S.A.	25.17	6	1	12	-	30	-	-	27
1978	S.A.	22.20	16	3	21	-	-	-	-	-
1979	S.A.	24.68	7	2	16	-	-	-	-	21
1980	S.A.	21.88	16	4	21	-	25	-	-	-
1981	Chic	12.74	105	22	-	-	-	-	-	-
1982	Chic	6.23			DNQ					
1983	Clev	6.21			DNQ					

JOHN KERR — ILLINOIS

YR	TM	PR	OR	PS	SC	SH	RB	AS	BL	ST
1955	Syra	11.39	36	9	-	-	9	-		
1956	Syra	13.68	25	7	-	-	-	-		
1957	Syra	16.75	13	4	-	-	8	-		
1958	Syra	19.31	14	6	-	-	7	-		
1959	Syra	23.78	7	2	-	9	6	-		
1960	Syra	19.11	20	5	-	-	9	-		
1961	Syra	18.84	18	5	-	-	10	-		
1962	Syra	24.55	11	5	-	-	5	-		
1963	Syra	23.34	10	4	-	13	3	-		
1964	Phil	22.86	11	4	-	-	-	-		
1965	Phil	11.21	45	10	-	-	-	-		
1966	Balt	15.82	25	6	-	-	-	12		

BILLY KNIGHT — PITTSBURGH

YR	TM	PR	OR	PS	SC	SH	RB	AS	BL	ST
1975	ABA	20.15	20	9	-	6	-	-	-	-
1976	ABA	29.39	3	2	2	-	-	-	-	-
1977	Indi	23.72	10	3	2	29	-	-	-	-
1978	Buff	21.64	22	3	15	31	-	-	-	-
1979	Indi	13.10	90	23	-	-	12	-	-	-
1980	Indi	14.32	80	14	-	-	11	-	-	-
1981	Indi	16.79	51	10	-	-	13	-	-	-
1982	Indi	10.84	127	20	-	-	-	-	-	-
1983	Indi	15.38	67	12	-	18	-	-	-	-
1984	K.C.	11.63	121	23	-	-	-	-	-	-
1985	S.A.	4.88			DNQ					

DON KOJIS — MARQUETTE

YR	TM	PR	OR	PS	SC	SH	RB	AS	BL	ST
1964	Balt	6.53			DNQ					
1965	Detr	7.02			DNQ					
1966	Detr	7.00			DNQ					
1967	Chic	10.37	61	23	-	-	-	-	-	-
1968	S.D.	21.36	22	10	-	-	-	-	-	-
1969	S.D.	21.79	19	6	13	-	-	-	-	-
1970	S.D.	15.09	58	25	-	-	-	-	-	-
1971	Seat	13.76	71	25	-	-	-	-	-	-
1972	Seat	11.44	84	34	-	-	-	-	-	-
1973	K.C.	7.87			DNQ					
1974	K.C.	11.78	77	15	-	-	-	-	-	-
1975	K.C.	4.48			DNQ					

BUTCH KOMIVES — BOWLING GRN

YR	TM	PR	OR	PS	SC	SH	RB	AS	BL	ST
1965	N.Y.	9.41	56	21	-	-	-	-		
1966	N.Y.	13.75	39	13	-	-	-	7		
1967	N.Y.	15.02	33	11	-	-	-	4		
1968	N.Y.	7.50	84	38	-	-	-	14		
1969	Detr	12.04	75	28	-	-	-	12		
1970	Detr	10.51	86	33	-	-	-	-		
1971	Detr	7.50	114	45	-	-	-	23		
1972	Detr	8.51	105	42	-	-	-	-		
1973	Buff	7.30	107	45	-	-	-	12		
1974	K.C.	4.11		DNQ						

SAM LACEY — NEW MEXICO ST.

YR	TM	PR	OR	PS	SC	SH	RB	AS	BL	ST
1971	Cinc	17.27	48	13	-	-	19	-		
1972	Cinc	18.12	46	13	-	-	19	-		
1973	K.C.	20.44	28	10	-	-	20	-		
1974	K.C.	24.34	9	6	-	-	14	-	10	-
1975	K.C.	24.41	7	5	-	-	10	-	9	-
1976	K.C.	22.42	8	7	-	-	11	-	15	-
1977	K.C.	18.54	31	11	-	-	-	24	17	-
1978	K.C.	16.49	54	19	-	-	-	-	18	21
1979	K.C.	19.45	36	13	-	-	-	22	17	-
1980	K.C.	17.72	48	15	-	-	-	17	20	-
1981	K.C.	15.35	72	20	-	-	32	19	18	-
1982	N.J.	4.50		DNQ						
1983	Clev	6.62	157	27	-	-	-	-	-	-

BOB LANIER — ST. BONAVENTURE

YR	TM	PR	OR	PS	SC	SH	RB	AS	BL	ST
1971	Detr	16.89	51	14	-	-	23	-		
1972	Detr	30.79	3	3	8	20	13	-		
1973	Detr	30.35	5	3	10	-	8	-		
1974	Detr	30.95	3	3	12	11	9	-	3	-
1975	Detr	30.36	3	3	6	6	19	-	5	-
1976	Detr	27.16	4	4	10	3	19	-	17	-
1977	Detr	29.83	2	2	6	6	25	-	16	-
1978	Detr	28.54	4	4	9	7	28	-	26	-
1979	Detr	24.23	10	5	11	-	-	-	25	-
1980	Milw	23.32	12	6	27	17	-	-	24	-
1981	Milw	17.30	45	14	-	33	-	-	25	-
1982	Milw	15.99	59	14	-	13	-	-	-	-
1983	Milw	12.49		DNQ						
1984	Milw	16.56	61	15	-	18	-	-	-	-

RUDY LARUSSO — DARTMOUTH

YR	TM	PR	OR	PS	SC	SH	RB	AS	BL	ST
1960	Minn	15.31	24	12	-	-	-	-		
1961	LA.L	17.84	23	10	-	-	-	-		
1962	LA.L	21.04	17	7	-	7	-	-		
1963	LA.L	17.43	21	10	-	-	-	-		
1964	LA.L	18.03	18	10	-	-	-	-		
1965	LA.L	19.04	17	8	-	13	-	-		
1966	LA.L	18.59	21	9	-	9	-	-		
1967	LA.L	14.24		DNQ						
1968	S.F.	21.81	19	9	9	-	-	-		
1969	S.F.	18.96	32	13	-	-	-	-		

CLYDE LEE — VANDERBILT

YR	TM	PR	OR	PS	SC	SH	RB	AS	BL	ST
1967	S.F.	10.59		DNQ						
1968	S.F.	19.80	26	7	-	-	5	-		
1969	S.F.	18.05	39	16	-	-	7	-		
1970	S.F.	16.21	51	11	-	-	12	-		
1971	S.F.	9.88		DNQ						
1972	G.St	18.71	41	19	-	-	4	-		
1973	G.St	12.03	81	33	-	-	3	-		
1974	G.St	12.81	70	13	-	-	7	-	-	
1975	Phil	10.98	85	21	-	-	18	-	-	
1976	Phil	6.08		DNQ						

EARL LLOYD — W. VIRGINIA ST.

YR	TM	PR	OR	PS	SC	SH	RB	AS	BL	ST
1951	Wash	11.43		DNQ						
1952		DID NOT PLAY								
1953	Syra	9.56	43	19	-	-	-	-		
1954	Syra	11.50	28	11	-	-	-	-		
1955	Syra	12.28	34	16	-	-	-	-		
1956	Syra	10.31	41	18	-	-	-	-		
1957	Syra	9.99	37	16	-	-	-	-		
1958	Syra	6.51		DNQ						
1959	Detr	9.92	43	17	-	-	-	-		
1960	Detr	8.13	52	21	-	-	-	-		

LEWIS LLOYD — DRAKE

YR	TM	PR	OR	PS	SC	SH	RB	AS	BL	ST
1982	G.St	2.94		DNQ						
1983	G.St	8.75		DNQ						
1984	Hous	16.34	64	8	-	-	-	-		
1985	Hous	12.70	106	21	-	-	-	-		
1986	Hous	16.80	58	11	-	26	-	-	-	-

KEVIN LOUGHERY — ST. JOHN'S

YR	TM	PR	OR	PS	SC	SH	RB	AS	BL	ST
1963	Detr	5.19		DNQ						
1964	Balt	7.15	57	25	-	-	-	-		
1965	Balt	11.69	44	15	-	-	-	9		
1966	Balt	15.31	28	9	-	-	-	11		
1967	Balt	15.25	32	10	-	-	-	-		
1968	Balt	12.57	64	22	-	-	-	-		
1969	Balt	18.08	37	15	12	-	-	-		
1970	Balt	18.49	40	17	16	-	-	18		
1971	Balt	12.06	87	35	-	-	-	-		
1972	Phil	10.51	92	35	-	-	-	-		

BOB LOVE — SOUTHERN

YR	TM	PR	OR	PS	SC	SH	RB	AS	BL	ST
1967	Cinc	6.98		DNQ						
1968	Cinc	5.97		DNQ						
1969	Chic	5.41		DNQ						
1970	Chic	21.54	21	9	-	-	-	-		
1971	Chic	23.05	20	6	7	-	-	-		
1972	Chic	19.43	37	16	6	-	-	-		
1973	Chic	17.71	48	19	12	-	-	-		
1974	Chic	13.98	62	11	15	-	-	-	-	-
1975	Chic	15.62	42	9	10	-	-	-	-	-
1976	Chic	13.59	63	12	22	-	-	-	-	-

CLYDE LOVELLETTE — KANSAS

YR	TM	PR	OR	PS	SC	SH	RB	AS	BL	ST
1954	Minn	9.51			DNQ					
1955	Minn	20.21	9	4	6	-	8	-		
1956	Minn	25.00	4	2	4	-	3	-		
1957	Minn	23.45	6	3	7	-	6	-		
1958	Cinc	23.80	6	3	4	-	-	-		
1959	St.L	16.81	17	10	-	2	5	-		
1960	St.L	23.10	10	3	-	2	10	-		
1961	St.L	23.01	11	3	-	5	-	-		
1962	St.L	21.00			DNQ					
1963	Bost	7.00			DNQ					
1964	Bost	5.82			DNQ					

JERRY LUCAS — OHIO ST.

YR	TM	PR	OR	PS	SC	SH	RB	AS	BL	ST
1964	Cinc	30.39	6	2	-	1	3	-		
1965	Cinc	34.26	3	1	8	3	3	-		
1966	Cinc	33.66	3	1	9	-	3	-		
1967	Cinc	30.84	5	2	-	-	4	-		
1968	Cinc	34.37	2	1	11	3	4	-		
1969	Cinc	33.66	2	1	-	1	4	-		
1970	S.F.	25.15	13	5	-	10	3	-		
1971	S.F.	29.85	4	2	-	9	9	-		
1972	N.Y.	26.53	13	8	-	7	17	-		
1973	N.Y.	17.11	54	16	-	5	-	16		

MAURICE LUCAS — MARQUETTE

YR	TM	PR	OR	PS	SC	SH	RB	AS	BL	ST
1975	ABA	20.16	19	6	-	-	10	-	-	-
1976	ABA	18.02	10	3	-	-	3	-	-	-
1977	Port	22.57	12	3	22	-	16	-	-	-
1978	Port	18.13	37	6	-	-	-	-	-	-
1979	Port	22.26	18	5	24	-	29	-	-	-
1980	N.J.	16.70	59	10	-	-	16	-	-	-
1981	N.J.	17.54	43	11	-	-	27	-	-	-
1982	N.Y.	21.48	19	4	-	-	7	-	-	-
1983	Phoe	19.96	32	8	-	-	11	-	-	-
1984	Phoe	19.91	33	7	-	-	9	-	-	-
1985	Phoe	16.16	73	16	-	-	7	-	-	-
1986	L.A.L	12.75	103	25	-	-	9	-	-	-
1987	Seat	9.56			DNQ					
1988	Port	7.95			DNQ					

ED MACAULEY — ST. LOUIS

YR	TM	PR	OR	PS	SC	SH	RB	AS	BL	ST
1950	St.L	18.03	4	3	5	12	-			
1951	Bost	23.21	4	3	3	2	9	11		
1952	Bost	21.15	4	3	4	5	-	-		
1953	Bost	23.16	4	3	3	2	-	-		
1954	Bost	22.03	5	4	3	1	-	-		
1955	Bost	20.55	7	3	10	4	-	-		
1956	Bost	16.82	16	5	8	6	-	-		
1957	St.L	15.78	15	9	9	-	-	-		
1958	St.L	14.38	29	13	-	-	-	-		
1959	St.L	3.64			DNQ					

PETE MARAVICH — LSU

YR	TM	PR	OR	PS	SC	SH	RB	AS	BL	ST
1971	Atla	19.22	39	13	9	-	-	-		
1972	Atla	18.55	43	11	-	-	8	-		
1973	Atla	23.23	18	4	5	-	8	-		
1974	Atla	20.62	19	1	2	-	-	-	-	-
1975	N.O.	17.67	25	3	14	-	9	-	-	-
1976	N.O.	20.39	18	1	3	-	21	-	-	-
1977	N.O.	20.82	20	3	1	-	-	-	-	-
1978	N.O.	19.86	31	4	3	-	20	-	-	-
1979	N.O.	14.37			DNQ					
1980	Bost	5.23			DNQ					

JACK MARIN — DUKE

YR	TM	PR	OR	PS	SC	SH	RB	AS	BL	ST
1967	Balt	9.57			DNQ					
1968	Balt	13.71	57	27	-	-	-	-		
1969	Balt	18.01	40	17	-	16	-	-		
1970	Balt	19.78	29	11	-	-	-	-		
1971	Balt	18.12	44	18	-	-	-	-		
1972	Balt	20.99	30	11	16	16	-	-		
1973	Hous	18.91	38	16	-	-	-	-		
1974	Buff	10.62	86	18	-	7	-	-	-	-
1975	Buff	10.44	93	20	-	-	-	-	-	-
1976	Chic	8.41	108	23	-	-	-	-	-	-
1977	Chic	4.95			DNQ					

SLATER MARTIN — TEXAS

YR	TM	PR	OR	PS	SC	SH	RB	AS	BL	ST
1950	Minn	4.66			DNQ					
1951	Minn	8.82	42	13	-	-	-	12		
1952	Minn	9.85	43	13	-	-	-	-		
1953	Minn	10.61	37	11	-	9	-	-		
1954	Minn	9.22	38	12	-	-	-	-		
1955	Minn	14.04	23	6	-	-	-	7		
1956	Minn	14.33	22	5	-	-	-	7		
1957	St.L	10.94	34	9	-	-	-	8		
1958	St.L	9.80	42	15	-	-	-	-		
1959	St.L	10.68	39	14	-	-	-	7		
1960	St.L	9.86	41	17	-	-	-	5		

BOB McADOO — N. CAROLINA

YR	TM	PR	OR	PS	SC	SH	RB	AS	BL	ST
1973	Buff	19.01	37	15	-	-	-	-		
1974	Buff	35.68	2	2	1	2	11	-	6	-
1975	Buff	34.59	2	2	1	5	15	-	11	-
1976	Buff	31.13	2	2	1	-	-	-	11	-
1977	N.Y.	28.11	4	4	5	28	10	-	30	-
1978	N.Y.	29.92	2	2	4	23	23	-	29	-
1979	Bost	23.55	11	3	4	-	-	-	-	-
1980	Detr	20.16	31	5	17	-	-	-	-	-
1981	N.J.	5.38			DNQ					
1982	LA.L	9.15			DNQ					
1983	LA.L	14.62			DNQ					
1984	LA.L	11.37	126	26	-	-	-	-	-	-
1985	LA.L	11.00	124	26	-	-	-	24	-	
1986	Phil	8.86			DNQ					

GEORGE MCGINNIS — INDIANA

YR	TM	PR	OR	PS	SC	SH	RB	AS	BL	ST
1972	ABA	18.96	23	9	-	-	15	-		
1973	ABA	28.54	5	4	4	-	8	-		
1974	ABA	30.14	3	2	4	-	4	-	-	9
1975	ABA	34.24	1	1	4	-	8	11	-	5
1976	Phil	25.05	5	1	6	-	13	-	-	7
1977	Phil	22.89	11	2	16	-	12	-	-	22
1978	Phil	21.77	21	3	22	-	21	-	-	31
1979	Denv	23.30	13	4	14	-	10	-	-	24
1980	Indi	17.03	55	9	-	-	12	31	-	-
1981	Indi	13.75	93	17	-	-	19	-	-	21
1982	Indi	8.22			DNQ					

JON MCGLOCKLIN — INDIANA

YR	TM	PR	OR	PS	SC	SH	RB	AS	BL	ST
1966	Cinc	5.03			DNQ					
1967	Cinc	7.65			DNQ					
1968	S.D.	10.77	71	27	-	-	-	-		
1969	Milw	18.54	35	11	-	6	-	-		
1970	Milw	17.15	45	18	-	1	-	-		
1971	Milw	15.83	57	22	-	2	-	-		
1972	Milw	11.16	88	33	-	4	-	-		
1973	Milw	10.01	90	33	-	7	-	-		
1974	Milw	7.90	109	22	-	-	-	-	-	
1975	Milw	8.33	104	23	-	19	-	-	-	-
1976	Milw	2.58			DNQ					

DICK MCGUIRE — DARTMOUTH

YR	TM	PR	OR	PS	SC	SH	RB	AS	BL	ST
1950	N.Y.	12.40	22	3	-	-	-	1		
1951	N.Y.	13.61	18	3	-	-	-	2		
1952	N.Y.	14.59	20	4	-	13	-	1		
1953	N.Y.	10.92	36	10	-	-	-	2		
1954	N.Y.	12.78	20	6	-	-	-	5		
1955	N.Y.	14.76	22	5	-	-	-	1		
1956	N.Y.	10.47	39	11	-	-	-	2		
1957	N.Y.	6.51			DNQ					
1958	Detr	12.83	33	10	-	-	-	2		
1959	Detr	14.15	27	7	-	-	-	2		
1960	Detr	11.82	36	13	-	-	-	2		

JACK MCMAHON — ST. JOHN'S

YR	TM	PR	OR	PS	SC	SH	RB	AS	BL	ST
1953	Roch	6.24	61	24	-	-	-	11		
1954	Roch	8.83	41	14	-	-	-	9		
1955	Roch	7.64	51	17	-	-	-	10		
1956	St.L	6.11	59	24	-	-	-	-		
1957	St.L	8.89	43	13	-	-	-	2		
1958	St.L	7.00	50	19	-	-	-	6		
1959	St.L	7.64	52	19	-	-	-	8		
1960	St.L	3.28			DNQ					

TOM MCMILLEN — MARYLAND

YR	TM	PR	OR	PS	SC	SH	RB	AS	BL	ST
1976	Buff	16.38			DNQ					
1977	N.Y.	8.87	134	22	-	-	-	-	-	-
1978	Atla	11.75	109	21	-	-	-	-	-	-
1979	Atla	7.95			DNQ					
1980	Atla	9.70			DNQ					
1981	Atla	7.94	158	36	-	-	-	-	-	-
1982	Atla	10.99	123	22	-	-	-	-	-	-
1983	Atla	8.31	144	26	-	-	-	-	-	-
1984	Wash	8.89	149	29	-	-	-	-	-	-
1985	Wash	8.03	152	36	-	-	-	-	-	-
1986	Wash	5.18			DNQ					

JIM MCMILLIAN — COLUMBIA

YR	TM	PR	OR	PS	SC	SH	RB	AS	BL	ST
1971	LA.L	9.52	105	43	-	-	-	-		
1972	LA.L	18.59	42	20	-	-	-	-		
1973	LA.L	17.09	55	21	-	-	-	-		
1974	Buff	20.27	20	5	-	8	-	-	-	-
1975	Buff	16.16	40	7	-	8	-	-	-	-
1976	Buff	16.93	39	7	-	1	-	-	-	-
1977	N.Y.	10.28	114	24	-	-	-	-	-	-
1978	N.Y.	10.12	130	25	-	-	-	-	-	-
1979	Port	4.61			DNQ					

JOE MERIWEATHER — S. ILLINOIS

YR	TM	PR	OR	PS	SC	SH	RB	AS	BL	ST
1976	Hous	12.11	71	17	-	-	-	-	6	-
1977	Atla	14.51	58	16	-	22	-	-	26	-
1978	N.O.	12.67			DNQ					
1979	N.Y.	10.17	130	32	-	-	-	-	15	-
1980	N.Y.	11.92	111	28	-	-	-	-	6	-
1981	K.C.	9.97	140	29	-	-	-	-	20	-
1982	K.C.	10.33			DNQ					
1983	K.C.	11.09	115	24	-	21	-	-	23	-
1984	K.C.	9.56	146	31	-	-	-	-	30	-
1985	K.C.	6.11			DNQ					

TOM MESCHERY — ST. MARY'S

YR	TM	PR	OR	PS	SC	SH	RB	AS	BL	ST
1962	Phil	15.50	30	13	-	-	-	-		
1963	S.F.	17.61	20	9	-	-	-	-		
1964	S.F.	15.46	24	13	-	-	-	-		
1965	S.F.	14.09	31	14	-	-	-	-		
1966	S.F.	15.75	26	12	-	-	-	-		
1967	S.F.	12.81	46	19	-	-	-	-		
1968	Seat	19.35	29	13	-	-	-	-		
1969	Seat	18.59	34	14	-	-	-	-		
1970	Seat	16.64	49	21	-	-	-	-		
1971	Seat	11.91	90	33	-	-	-	-		

GEORGE MIKAN — DEPAUL

YR	TM	PR	OR	PS	SC	SH	RB	AS	BL	ST
1947	Chic	16.50			1					
1948	Minn	21.30			1					
1949	Minn	28.30			1					
1950	Minn	28.13	1	1	1		3			-
1951	Minn	30.16	1	1	1	4	2			-
1952	Minn	24.88	2	1	2	-	5			-
1953	Minn	25.33	2	2	2	12	2			-
1954	Minn	23.15	3	2	4	-	1			-
1955		DID NOT PLAY								
1956	Minn	13.41			DNQ					

VERN MIKKELSEN — HAMLINE

YR	TM	PR	OR	PS	SC	SH	RB	AS	BL	ST
1950	Minn	16.25	7	3	-	13	-			
1951	Minn	17.45	8	4	-	-	6			
1952	Minn	19.36	8	3	11	8	12			-
1953	Minn	18.04	7	3	9	5	13			-
1954	Minn	13.49	15	4	-	-	12			-
1955	Minn	20.00	10	5	8	6	-			-
1956	Minn	16.10	18	10	-	-	-			-
1957	Minn	15.60	16	10	-	-	-			-
1958	Minn	20.65	11	6	-	-	-			-
1959	Minn	15.29	20	12	-	-	-			-

EDDIE MILES — SEATTLE

YR	TM	PR	OR	PS	SC	SH	RB	AS	BL	ST
1964	Detr	3.53			DNQ					
1965	Detr	11.14	46	16	-	-	-			-
1966	Detr	15.01	32	11	-	-	-			-
1967	Detr	12.91	43	17	-	-	-			-
1968	Detr	15.49	46	13	-	14	-			-
1969	Detr	11.18	78	30	-	-	-			-
1970	Balt	11.21			DNQ					
1971	Balt	8.43	112	43	-	-	-			-
1972	N.Y.	1.24			DNQ					

EARL MONROE — WINSTON-SALEM

YR	TM	PR	OR	PS	SC	SH	RB	AS	BL	ST
1968	Balt	21.56	20	6	6	-	-	-		
1969	Balt	19.67	30	10	3	-	-	-		
1970	Balt	19.63	32	14	11	-	-	-		
1971	Balt	16.80	52	19	15	-	-	-		
1972	N.Y.	9.00	102	39	-	-	-	-		
1973	N.Y.	15.19	68	25	-	16	-	-		
1974	N.Y.	11.43			DNQ					
1975	N.Y.	17.21	30	4	17	-	-	-	-	-
1976	N.Y.	17.39	36	5	14	-	-	-	-	-
1977	N.Y.	18.23	34	5	24	10	-	-	-	-
1978	N.Y.	15.54	62	7	-	30	-	26	-	-
1979	N.Y.	9.55	138	24	-	-	-	-	-	-
1980	N.Y.	5.45			DNQ					

OTTO MOORE — PAN AMERICAN

YR	TM	PR	OR	PS	SC	SH	RB	AS	BL	ST
1969	Detr	10.53	79	16	-	-	-	-		
1970	Detr	17.67	44	8	-	-	11	-		
1971	Detr	12.74	81	21	-	-	14	-		
1972	Phoe	10.41	94	20	-	-	20	-		
1973	Hous	17.96	44	14	-	-	19	-		
1974	K.C.	6.37			DNQ					
1975	N.O.	12.26			DNQ					
1976	N.O.	16.01	47	14	-	-	12	-	8	-
1977	N.O.	11.83	96	25	-	-	23	-	15	-

JEFF MULLINS — DUKE

YR	TM	PR	OR	PS	SC	SH	RB	AS	BL	ST
1965	St.L	4.98			DNQ					
1966	St.L	4.55			DNQ					
1967	S.F.	13.56	41	15	-	-	-	-		
1968	S.F.	18.22	35	11	-	-	-	-		
1969	S.F.	21.58	21	6	11	13	-	-		
1970	S.F.	20.89	25	11	14	-	-	-		
1971	S.F.	20.01	31	8	20	12	-	-		
1972	G.St	22.04	27	8	18	-	-	18		
1973	G.St	17.85	46	14	-	12	-	-		
1974	G.St	14.09	58	9	-	-	-	-		
1975	G.St	7.56			DNQ					
1976	G.St	4.56			DNQ					

CALVIN MURPHY — NIAGARA

YR	TM	PR	OR	PS	SC	SH	RB	AS	BL	ST
1971	S.D.	15.07	63	26	-	21	-	13		
1972	Hous	17.26	51	16	-	-	-	15		
1973	Hous	12.25	79	30	-	18	-	19		
1974	Hous	20.02	22	2	21	3	-	4	-	17
1975	Hous	16.38	37	8	-	13	-	16	-	22
1976	Hous	20.73	17	3	11	6	-	2	-	20
1977	Hous	15.79	49	11	-	23	-	-	-	-
1978	Hous	18.51	33	5	6	-	-	-	-	-
1979	Hous	16.88	56	6	26	30	-	-	-	-
1980	Hous	16.91	57	10	23	-	-	-	-	23
1981	Hous	13.26	98	18	-	-	-	-	-	17
1982	Hous	7.19			DNQ					
1983	Hous	9.27	134	23	-	-	-	-	-	-

SWEN NATER — UCLA

YR	TM	PR	OR	PS	SC	SH	RB	AS	BL	ST
1974	ABA	22.63	6	2	-	2	2	-	-	-
1975	ABA	26.55	6	3	-	8	1	-	-	-
1976	ABA	15.67	28	9	-	-	1	-	-	-
1977	Milw	20.21	23	10	-	12	1	-	-	-
1978	Buff	22.56	15	9	-	-	4	-	-	-
1979	S.D.	16.22	67	21	-	1	5	-	-	-
1980	S.D.	23.74	10	4	-	14	1	-	-	-
1981	S.D.	23.13	9	5	-	9	3	-	-	-
1982	S.D.	17.00			DNQ					
1983	S.D.	2.14			DNQ					
1984	LA.L	5.93			DNQ					

WILLIE NAULLS — UCLA

YR	TM	PR	OR	PS	SC	SH	RB	AS	BL	ST
1957	N.Y.	11.68	32	15	-	-	-	-		
1958	N.Y.	19.81	13	7	10	-	-	-		
1959	N.Y.	17.25	15	9	-	-	-	-		
1960	N.Y.	25.48	8	6	11	-	7	-		
1961	N.Y.	25.59	7	4	8	-	11	-		
1962	N.Y.	24.17	13	4	8	-	-	-		
1963	S.F.	13.79	34	18	-	-	-	-		
1964	Bost	9.06			DNQ					
1965	Bost	8.99	57	24	-	-	-	-		
1966	Bost	8.97	56	27	-	-	-	-		

FORMER PLAYERS 341

DON NELSON — IOWA

YR	TM	PR	OR	PS	SC	SH	RB	AS	BL	ST
1963	Chic	8.81	DNQ							
1964	LA.L	7.23	DNQ							
1965	LA.L	3.44	DNQ							
1966	Bost	10.63	51	26	-	-	-	-		
1967	Bost	7.90	DNQ							
1968	Bost	11.70	DNQ							
1969	Bost	12.73	71	31	-	11	-	-		
1970	Bost	17.70	43	19	-	14	-	-		
1971	Bost	15.62	60	21	-	-	-	-		
1972	Bost	15.38	61	24	-	-	-	-		
1973	Bost	11.46	84	35	-	19	-	-		
1974	Bost	11.12	82	17	-	9	-	-	-	-
1975	Bost	15.46	44	10	-	2	-	-	-	-
1976	Bost	6.11	DNQ							

MIKE NEWLIN — UTAH

YR	TM	PR	OR	PS	SC	SH	RB	AS	BL	ST
1972	Hous	7.13	DNQ							
1973	Hous	17.44	51	17	-	-	-	20		
1974	Hous	15.89	44	4	-	-	-	-	-	-
1975	Hous	14.78	53	7	-	17	-	17	-	-
1976	Hous	18.98	23	2	-	2	-	17	-	-
1977	Hous	11.71	98	22	-	-	-	21	-	-
1978	Hous	12.44	DNQ							
1979	Hous	10.46	123	22	-	-	-	26	-	-
1980	N.J.	17.10	54	9	18	-	-	-	-	-
1981	N.J.	17.24	46	8	15	25	-	-	-	-
1982	N.Y.	7.21	158	29	-	-	-	-	-	-

JACK NICHOLS — WASHINGTON

YR	TM	PR	OR	PS	SC	SH	RB	AS	BL	ST
1949	Wash	10.65	DNQ							
1950	T.C.	13.40	16	8	15	-	-			
1951	T.C.	15.80	DNQ							
1952		DID NOT PLAY								
1953	Milw	14.13	17	8	7	-	-	-		
1954	Bost	6.69	57	11	-	-	-	-		
1955	Bost	13.55	27	13	-	-	-	-		
1956	Bost	18.72	10	5	-	-	-	-		
1957	Bost	9.62	39	13	-	-	-	-		
1958	Bost	6.22	DNQ							

MARK OLBERDING — MINNESOTA

YR	TM	PR	OR	PS	SC	SH	RB	AS	BL	ST
1976	ABA	13.65	34	17	-	-	-	-	-	-
1977	S.A.	11.85	95	14	-	20	-	-	-	-
1978	S.A.	10.27	127	27	-	-	-	-	-	-
1979	S.A.	11.95	104	17	-	-	-	-	-	-
1980	S.A.	14.32	80	14	-	-	27	-	-	-
1981	S.A.	15.39	71	14	-	26	-	-	-	-
1982	S.A.	16.06	58	13	-	-	-	-	-	-
1983	Chic	9.61	133	25	-	-	-	-	-	-
1984	K.C.	12.30	111	22	-	-	-	-	-	-
1985	K.C.	14.06	96	22	-	-	-	-	-	-
1986	Sacr	12.26	109	27	-	19	-	-	-	-
1987	Sacr	5.13	DNQ							

DON OHL — ILLINOIS

YR	TM	PR	OR	PS	SC	SH	RB	AS	BL	ST
1961	Detr	10.62	43	18	-	-	-	-		
1962	Detr	13.61	41	15	-	-	-	-		
1963	Detr	14.90	27	8	13	-	-	-		
1964	Detr	11.27	45	16	-	-	-	-		
1965	Balt	15.23	27	7	13	-	-	-		
1966	Balt	16.67	23	8	11	-	-	-		
1967	Balt	15.67	29	9	11	-	-	-		
1968	St.L	10.86	70	26	-	-	-	-		
1969	Atla	9.62	85	32	-	-	-	-		
1970	Atla	3.62	DNQ							

TOM OWENS — S. CAROLINA

YR	TM	PR	OR	PS	SC	SH	RB	AS	BL	ST
1972	ABA	9.77	DNQ							
1973	ABA	15.59	31	11	-	12	10	-		
1974	ABA	18.43	17	8	-	4	-	-	-	-
1975	ABA	22.22	13	4	-	14	9	-	-	-
1976	ABA	8.19	DNQ							
1977	Hous	5.30	DNQ							
1978	Port	12.84	94	26	-	-	26	-	-	-
1979	Port	22.60	17	8	-	8	-	-	-	-
1980	Port	18.17	41	12	-	-	-	-	-	-
1981	Port	12.87	102	25	-	-	-	-	-	-
1982	Indi	11.32	118	27	-	-	-	-	-	-
1983	Detr	5.78	DNQ							

BILLY PAULTZ — ST. JOHN'S

YR	TM	PR	OR	PS	SC	SH	RB	AS	BL	ST
1971	ABA	21.57	15	5	-	4	13	-		
1972	ABA	21.10	14	6	-	-	7	-		
1973	ABA	23.98	7	3	-	-	4	-		
1974	ABA	20.66	10	5	-	-	-	-	-	-
1975	ABA	19.81	21	7	-	-	-	-	-	-
1976	ABA	23.23	7	2	-	-	-	-	-	-
1977	S.A.	18.46	32	12	-	-	-	13	-	-
1978	S.A.	21.08	25	11	-	12	-	5	-	-
1979	S.A.	16.19	68	22	-	-	25	14	-	-
1980	Hous	13.77	87	20	-	-	-	25	-	-
1981	Hous	9.54	146	32	-	-	-	28	-	-
1982	Hous	3.95	DNQ							
1983	S.A.	3.44	DNQ							
1984	Atla	3.63	DNQ							
1985	Utah	2.03	DNQ							

GEOFF PETRIE — PRINCETON

YR	TM	PR	OR	PS	SC	SH	RB	AS	BL	ST
1971	Port	19.24	38	12	8	-	-	-		
1972	Port	13.48	71	24	-	-	-	-		
1973	Port	19.53	35	9	7	-	-	-		
1974	Port	17.42	34	7	9	19	-	-	-	-
1975	Port	13.93	62	15	-	-	-	-	-	-
1976	Port	14.13	58	10	-	-	-	-	-	-

BOB PETTIT — LSU

YR	TM	PR	OR	PS	SC	SH	RB	AS	BL	ST
1955	Milw	24.85	2	1	4	-	4	-		
1956	St.L	29.74	1	1	1	11	2	-		
1957	St.L	26.85	3	2	2	10	4	-		
1958	St.L	29.54	2	2	3	-	2	-		
1959	St.L	32.99	1	1	1	7	2	-		
1960	St.L	32.29	3	1	4	10	4	-		
1961	St.L	36.17	4	2	4	-	3	-		
1962	St.L	37.31	5	3	4	10	4	-		
1963	St.L	31.76	6	2	3	-	5	-		
1964	St.L	32.41	4	1	4	9	8	-		
1965	St.L	25.46	9	3	7	-	8	-		

ANDY PHILLIP — ILLINOIS

YR	TM	PR	OR	PS	SC	SH	RB	AS	BL	ST
1948	Chic	10.80			-			6		
1949	Chic	12.00		17				2		
1950	Chic	14.83	11	1	-	-		2		
1951	Phil	17.00	9	1	-	-		1		
1952	Phil	18.24	9	2	-	-		2		
1953	Ft.W	14.64	16	3	-	-		4		
1954	Ft.W	13.39	16	5	-	-		3		
1955	Ft.W	15.00	20	4	-	-		2		
1956	Ft.W	10.44	40	12	-	-		3		
1957	Bost	6.36	53	22	-	-		7		
1958	Bost	4.43		DNQ						

JIM POLLARD — STANFORD

YR	TM	PR	OR	PS	SC	SH	RB	AS	BL	ST
1948	Minn	12.90			7		-			
1949	Minn	14.80			11		-			
1950	Minn	15.36	9	4	9	-		7		
1951	Minn	14.56	14	7	-	-	10	-		
1952	Minn	15.55	17	8	10	-	-	-		
1953	Minn	13.39	21	8	-	-	-	-		
1954	Minn	13.21	17	5	-	-	-	-		
1955	Minn	12.38	15	-	-	-				

KEVIN PORTER — ST. FRANCIS

YR	TM	PR	OR	PS	SC	SH	RB	AS	BL	ST
1973	Balt	6.99		DNQ						
1974	Capt	12.54	74	17	-	-	-	5	-	-
1975	Wash	13.78	63	16	-	-	-	1	-	10
1976	Detr	15.59		DNQ						
1977	Detr	11.12	106	16	-	27	-	1	-	-
1978	N.J.	17.40	46	4	-	-	-	1	-	-
1979	Detr	21.27	24	3	-	-	-	1	-	23
1980	Wash	9.90	136	21	-	-	-	1	-	-
1981	Wash	16.59	56	5	-	31	-	1	-	-
1982		DID NOT PLAY								
1983	Wash	6.09		DNQ						

FRANK RAMSEY — KENTUCKY

YR	TM	PR	OR	PS	SC	SH	RB	AS	BL	ST
1955	Bost	13.55	26	12	-	-	-	-		
1956		DID NOT PLAY								
1957	Bost	11.80		DNQ						
1958	Bost	17.33	18	3	-	7	-	-		
1959	Bost	14.17	26	14	-	-	-	-		
1960	Bost	14.33	27	13	-	-	-	-		
1961	Bost	13.38	34	14	-	-	-	-		
1962	Bost	13.27	44	19	-	-	-	-		
1963	Bost	9.12	58	29	-	-	-	-		
1964	Bost	7.16		DNQ						

KELVIN RANSEY — OHIO ST.

YR	TM	PR	OR	PS	SC	SH	RB	AS	BL	ST
1981	Port	14.25	88	13	-	-	-	9	-	-
1982	Port	15.37	64	10	-	-	-	11	-	-
1983	Dall	9.87	126	27	-	-	-	30	-	-
1984	N.J.	11.15	130	24	-	-	-	8	-	-
1985	N.J.	10.07	137	26	-	-	-	19	-	24
1986	N.J.	7.52	157	29	-	-	-	-	-	-

CLIFFORD RAY — OKLAHOMA

YR	TM	PR	OR	PS	SC	SH	RB	AS	BL	ST
1972	Chic	17.00	53	16	-	-	1	-		
1973	Chic	18.62	40	13	-	-	5	-		
1974	Chic	20.00	23	10	-	-	6	-	9	-
1975	G.St	17.34	28	9	-	-	9	-	13	-
1976	G.St	14.50	57	15	-	-	7	-	16	-
1977	G.St	13.84	68	19	-	17	24	-	24	-
1978	G.St	16.61	52	18	-	18	15	-	28	-
1979	G.St	11.76	110	27	-	-	16	-	-	-
1980	G.St	10.15	132	31	-	-	27	-	-	-
1981	G.St	4.06		DNQ						

WILLIS REED — GRAMBLING

YR	TM	PR	OR	PS	SC	SH	RB	AS	BL	ST
1965	N.Y.	24.19	11	5	10	-	5	-		
1966	N.Y.	19.53	15	5	-	-	11	-		
1967	N.Y.	26.90	9	4	9	7	6	-		
1968	N.Y.	25.78	8	3	14	12	10	-		
1969	N.Y.	28.74	6	4	-	2	11	-		
1970	N.Y.	27.73	9	4	18	13	9	-		
1971	N.Y.	25.75	10	5	18	-	17	-		
1972	N.Y.	16.00		DNQ						
1973	N.Y.	15.55	64	17	-	-	-	-		
1974	N.Y.	13.84		DNQ						

FORMER PLAYERS

M. R. RICHARDSON — MONTANA

YR	TM	PR	OR	PS	SC	SH	RB	AS	BL	ST
1979	N.Y.	7.64			DNQ					
1980	N.Y.	23.05	13	2	-	-	-	2	-	2
1981	N.Y.	21.81	16	1	-	-	-	14	-	7
1982	N.Y.	21.39	20	3	-	-	-	20	-	5
1983	N.J.	15.14	73	11	-	-	-	19	-	1
1984	N.J.	13.54			DNQ					
1985	N.J.	23.63	17	3	27	-	-	16	-	3
1986	N.J.	19.36			DNQ					

ARNOLD RISEN — OHIO ST.

YR	TM	PR	OR	PS	SC	SH	RB	AS	BL	ST
1946	Indi	12.20			6					
1947	Indi	13.20			5					
1948	Roch	13.23			5					
1949	Roch	16.60			4		-			
1950	Roch	15.55	8	5	-	-	-			
1951	Roch	20.45	5	4	9	14	4	-		
1952	Roch	20.20	5	4	9	-	2	-		
1953	Roch	16.50	11	5	-	-	6	-		
1954	Roch	15.60	10	7	12	-	8	-		
1955	Roch	15.59	17	7	-	-	6	-		
1956	Bost	11.99	29	9	-	-	8	-		
1957	Bost	10.35			DNQ					
1958	Bost	4.52			DNQ					

OSCAR ROBERTSON — CINCINNATI

YR	TM	PR	OR	PS	SC	SH	RB	AS	BL	ST
1961	Cinc	36.42	3	1	3	1	-	3		
1962	Cinc	40.51	2	1	6	1	-	2		
1963	Cinc	36.81	2	1	4	1	-	3		
1964	Cinc	39.15	2	1	2	2	-	1		
1965	Cinc	37.49	2	1	3	4	-	1		
1966	Cinc	36.41	2	1	3	2	-	2		
1967	Cinc	35.13	2	1	2	1	-	2		
1968	Cinc	33.46	3	1	1	1	-	2		
1969	Cinc	30.51	3	1	6	3	-	3		
1970	Cinc	29.00	5	2	6	5	-	5		
1971	Milw	25.06	14	3	-	6	-	4		
1972	Milw	21.97	28	9	-	-	-	5		
1973	Milw	20.01	32	8	-	-	-	4		
1974	Milw	14.04	60	11	-	-	-	7	-	-

LEN ROBINSON — TENNESSEE ST.

YR	TM	PR	OR	PS	SC	SH	RB	AS	BL	ST
1975	Wash	6.77			DNQ					
1976	Wash	12.62	66	14	-	-	-	-	9	-
1977	Atla	20.05	25	4	29	-	-	-	-	-
1978	N.O.	24.77	8	1	17	-	8	-	-	-
1979	Phoe	22.25	19	6	21	-	17	-	-	-
1980	Phoe	18.44	40	7	-	-	18	-	-	-
1981	Phoe	19.68	22	3	28	-	-	-	-	-
1982	Phoe	20.50	24	5	25	-	32	-	-	-
1983	N.Y.	12.35	106	21	-	-	27	-	-	-
1984	N.Y.	13.54	95	17	-	-	-	-	-	-
1985	N.Y.	6.50			DNQ					

DAVE ROBISCH — KANSAS

YR	TM	PR	OR	PS	SC	SH	RB	AS	BL	ST
1972	ABA	18.41	25	7	-	-	14	-		
1973	ABA	20.19	16	8	-	-	-	-		
1974	ABA	17.64	18	9	-	-	-	-		
1975	ABA	15.65	35	11	-	10	-	-	-	-
1976	ABA	17.26	23	7	-	-	-	-		
1977	Indi	13.94	66	18	-	-	-	-		
1978	LA.L	7.81			DNQ					
1979	LA.L	6.81			DNQ					
1980	Clev	19.15	36	11	-	19	-	-	-	-
1981	Denv	12.65	106	23	-	-	-	-	-	-
1982	Denv	14.00			DNQ					
1983	Denv	4.61			DNQ					
1984	K.C.	3.16			DNQ					

RED ROCHA — OREGON ST.

YR	TM	PR	OR	PS	SC	SH	RB	AS	BL	ST
1948	St.L	12.80			9			-		
1949	St.L	10.50								
1950	St.L	14.57	14	6	-	14		-		
1951	Balt	13.92	15	8	-	-	-	-		
1952	Syra	15.24	18	7	-	11	-	-		
1953	Syra	13.32	22	9	-	-	-	-		
1954			DID NOT PLAY							
1955	Syra	12.65	31	8	-	-	-	-		
1956	Syra	10.61	38	11	-	-	-	-		
1957	Ft.W	6.18			DNQ					

GUY RODGERS — TEMPLE

YR	TM	PR	OR	PS	SC	SH	RB	AS	BL	ST
1959	Phil	14.44	25	6	-	-	-	4		
1960	Phil	15.56	22	6	-	-	-	3		
1961	Phil	18.72	19	5	-	-	-	2		
1962	Phil	13.79	37	14	-	-	-	3		
1963	S.F.	19.42	14	3	-	-	-	2		
1964	S.F.	13.77	33	9	-	-	-	2		
1965	S.F.	14.92	28	8	-	-	-	2		
1966	S.F.	20.75	13	4	-	-	-	1		
1967	Chic	22.00	13	3	-	-	-	1		
1968	Cinc	7.96	81	35	-	-	-	1		
1969	Milw	12.79	69	25	-	-	-	2		
1970	Milw	5.38			DNQ					

DAN ROUNDFIELD — C. MICHIGAN

YR	TM	PR	OR	PS	SC	SH	RB	AS	BL	ST
1976	ABA	5.51			DNQ					
1977	Indi	16.82	42	14	-	-	15	-	6	-
1978	Indi	19.90	30	4	-	-	17	-	11	-
1979	Atla	21.25	25	7	-	-	9	-	10	-
1980	Atla	21.26	21	3	-	-	9	-	14	-
1981	Atla	22.84	11	2	-	-	12	-	16	-
1982	Atla	23.20	14	2	29	-	9	-	27	-
1983	Atla	22.78	16	5	-	-	9	-	31	-
1984	Atla	21.48	22	4	-	-	20	-	-	-
1985	Detr	14.55	91	19	-	-	14	-	31	-
1986	Wash	15.18	76	19	-	-	23	-	-	-
1987	Wash	7.78			DNQ					

CURTIS ROWE — UCLA

YR	TM	PR	OR	PS	SC	SH	RB	AS	BL	ST
1972	Detr	14.63	64	25	-	-	-	-	-	-
1973	Detr	19.91	34	14	-	17	-	-	-	-
1974	Detr	11.61	80	16	-	-	-	-	-	-
1975	Detr	13.26	64	14	-	-	-	-	-	-
1976	Detr	16.65	43	8	-	-	-	-	-	-
1977	Bost	12.27	91	21	-	-	-	-	-	-
1978	Bost	4.07		DNQ						
1979	Bost	7.30		DNQ						

BILL RUSSELL — USF

YR	TM	PR	OR	PS	SC	SH	RB	AS	BL	ST
1957	Bost	25.17	4	3	-	-	1	-		
1958	Bost	30.71	1	1	-	-	1	-		
1959	Bost	32.70	2	1	-	-	1	-		
1960	Bost	35.39	2	2	-	-	2	-		
1961	Bost	32.42	5	2	-	-	2	-		
1962	Bost	35.38	6	4	-	-	2	-		
1963	Bost	33.32	5	3	-	-	1	-		
1964	Bost	34.15	3	2	-	-	1	-		
1965	Bost	34.06	4	2	-	-	1	12		
1966	Bost	31.04	5	2	-	-	1	-		
1967	Bost	31.98	3	2	-	-	2	13		
1968	Bost	26.65	7	3	-	-	3	-		
1969	Bost	26.88	8	5	-	-	3	-		

CAMPY RUSSELL — MICHIGAN

YR	TM	PR	OR	PS	SC	SH	RB	AS	BL	ST
1975	Clev	4.76		DNQ						
1976	Clev	12.61	67	13	-	-	-	-	-	-
1977	Clev	15.21	52	14	-	-	-	-	-	-
1978	Clev	17.58	43	13	28	-	-	-	-	-
1979	Clev	21.18	26	5	17	-	-	-	-	--
1980	Clev	16.88		DNQ						
1981	N.Y.	14.37	86	20	-	-	-	-	-	-
1982	N.Y.	12.64	99	23	-	-	-	-	-	-

CAZZIE RUSSELL — MICHIGAN

YR	TM	PR	OR	PS	SC	SH	RB	AS	BL	ST
1967	N.Y.	10.53	58	25	-	-	-	-	-	-
1968	N.Y.	15.18	48	23	-	-	-	-	-	-
1969	N.Y.	14.96	55	24	-	-	-	-	-	-
1970	N.Y.	10.78	83	37	-	-	-	-	-	-
1971	N.Y.	8.39		DNQ						
1972	G.St	18.75	39	18	20	-	-	-	-	-
1973	G.St	14.04	70	27	-	-	-	-	-	-
1974	G.St	15.24	55	10	20	22	-	-	-	-
1975	LA.L	11.10		DNQ						
1976	LA.L	8.86	106	22	-	-	-	-	-	-
1977	LA.L	13.51	71	17	-	-	-	-	-	-
1978	Chic	7.44		DNQ						

SATCH SANDERS — NYU

YR	TM	PR	OR	PS	SC	SH	RB	AS	BL	ST
1961	Bost	14.04		DNQ						
1962	Bost	15.16	35	16	-	-	-	-	-	-
1963	Bost	13.30	38	19	-	-	-	-	-	-
1964	Bost	14.08	31	17	-	-	-	-	-	-
1965	Bost	14.14	29	13	-	-	-	-	-	-
1966	Bost	13.54	41	20	-	-	-	-	-	-
1967	Bost	10.89	57	22	-	-	-	-	-	-
1968	Bost	11.49	69	31	-	-	-	-	-	-
1969	Bost	12.78	70	30	-	-	-	-	-	-
1970	Bost	12.77	72	31	-	-	-	-	-	-
1971	Bost	2.24		DNQ						
1972	Bost	8.02	107	43	-	-	-	-	-	-
1973	Bost	2.00		DNQ						

WOODY SAULDSBERRY — TEX. SOU.

YR	TM	PR	OR	PS	SC	SH	RB	AS	BL	ST
1958	Phil	12.99	32	14	-	-	-	-	-	-
1959	Phil	14.78	23	13	-	-	-	-	-	-
1960	Phil	7.99	53	22	-	-	-	-	-	-
1961	St.L	7.23	54	22	-	-	-	-	-	-
1962	Chic	10.89	47	20	-	-	-	-	-	-
1963	St.L	9.19	56	28	-	-	-	-	-	-
1966	Bost	3.79		DNQ						

DOLPH SCHAYES — NYU

YR	TM	PR	OR	PS	SC	SH	RB	AS	BL	ST
1949	Syra	12.80			6					
1950	Syra	25.20	2	1	6	9		6		
1951	Syra	25.80	2	1	6	-	1	10		
1952	Syra	20.06	6	2	-	-	1	-		
1953	Syra	23.31	3	1	5	13	3	-		
1954	Syra	22.32	4	3	6	6	6	-		
1955	Syra	22.97	3	2	7	10	7	-		
1956	Syra	24.11	5	3	5	10	7	-		
1957	Syra	27.44	1	1	4	6	11	-		
1958	Syra	29.07	3	1	2	5	10	-		
1959	Syra	24.88	5	4	6	-	9	-		
1960	Syra	26.37	6	4	7	11	11	-		
1961	Syra	25.57	8	5	6	-	-	-		
1962	Syra	15.45	31	14	-	-	-	-		
1963	Syra	12.12	42	22	-	-	-	13		
1964	Phil	7.58		DNQ						

CHARLIE SCOTT — N. CAROLINA

YR	TM	PR	OR	PS	SC	SH	RB	AS	BL	ST
1971	ABA	23.64	10	2	4	-	-	8		
1972	ABA	26.15	9	1	2	-	-	-		
1973	Phoe	21.75	25	7	6	-	-	14		
1974	Phoe	19.88	24	3	4	-	-	-	-	20
1975	Phoe	16.80	35	7	5	-	-	-	-	-
1976	Bost	14.60	55	10	-	-	-	-	-	-
1977	Bost	15.30		DNQ						
1978	LA.L	12.09	105	21	-	-	-	-	25	-
1979	Denv	11.68	111	20	-	-	-	-	23	-
1980	Denv	7.49	153	31	-	-	-	-	-	-

RAY SCOTT — PORTLAND

YR	TM	PR	OR	PS	SC	SH	RB	AS	BL	ST
1962	Detr	16.97	24	11	-	-	8	-		
1963	Detr	18.32	18	8	-	-	-	-		
1964	Detr	22.90	10	5	-	-	9	-		
1965	Detr	16.86	22	9	-	-	-	-		
1966	Detr	21.81	10	3	12	-	-	-		
1967	Balt	18.00	26	7	-	-	-	-		
1968	Balt	22.32	17	8	-	-	8	-		
1969	Balt	14.84	57	26	-	-	18	-		
1970	Balt	11.53		DNQ						
1971	ABA	16.14	41	11	-	-	7	-		
1972	ABA	8.25		DNQ						

KENNY SEARS — SANTA CLARA

YR	TM	PR	OR	PS	SR	SH	RB	AS	BL	ST
1956	N.Y.	16.44	17	9	-	5	-	-		
1957	N.Y.	16.72	14	8	-	4	-	-		
1958	N.Y.	22.03	8	4	9	1	-	-		
1959	N.Y.	23.79	6	5	7	1	-	-		
1960	N.Y.	26.31	7	5	-	1	5	-		
1961	N.Y.	14.63	28	12	-	6	-	-		
1962		DID NOT PLAY								
1963	S.F.	7.45		DNQ						
1964	S.F.	4.39		DNQ						

FRANK SELVY — FURMAN

YR	TM	PR	OR	PS	SC	SH	RB	AS	BL	ST
1955	Milw	15.18	19	9	5	-	-	-		
1956	St.L	8.35		DNQ						
1957		DID NOT PLAY								
1958	Minn	2.76		DNQ						
1959	N.Y.	8.50	50	20	-	-	-	-		
1960	Minn	7.71	54	23	-	-	-	-		
1961	LA.L	11.06	40	16	-	-	-	-		
1962	LA.L	15.85	28	10	-	-	-	12		
1963	LA.L	11.11	44	14	-	-	-	-		
1964	LA.L	5.19		DNQ						

PAUL SEYMOUR — TOLEDO

YR	TM	PR	OR	PS	SC	SH	RB	AS	BL	ST
1947	Tole	3.17		DNQ						
1948	Balt	6.90								
1949	Syra	4.90								
1950	Syra	8.13		DNQ						
1951	Syra	8.75		DNQ						
1952	Syra	8.71	51	17	-	-	-	-		
1953	Syra	13.79	20	5	12	11	-	-		
1954	Syra	14.01	13	3	-	11	-	7		
1955	Syra	15.43	18	3	-	-	-	6		
1956	Syra	10.21	43	14	-	-	-	8		
1957	Syra	5.98	55	24	-	-	-	3		
1958	Syra	3.89		DNQ						
1959	Syra	4.57		DNQ						
1960	Syra	0.00		DNQ						

CHARLIE SHARE — BOWLING GREEN

YR	TM	PR	OR	PS	SC	SH	RB	AS	BL	ST
1952	Ft.W	6.76		DNQ						
1953	Ft.W	8.60		DNQ						
1954	Milw	11.87	25	8	-	-	5	-		
1955	Milw	16.03	15	6	-	-	1	-		
1956	St.L	18.21	12	4	-	-	5	-		
1957	St.L	14.39	20	7	-	11	5	-		
1958	St.L	14.85	27	9	-	-	6	-		
1959	St.L	12.69	31	8	-	-	4	-		

BILL SHARMAN — USC

YR	TM	PR	OR	PS	SC	SH	RB	AS	BL	ST
1951	Wash	9.06		DNQ						
1952	Bost	9.98	41	12	-	10	-	-		
1953	Bost	14.70	15	2	6	1	-	-		
1954	Bost	14.93	11	2	7	2	-	-		
1955	Bost	17.44	14	2	9	2	-	-		
1956	Bost	17.86	14	3	6	4	-	-		
1957	Bost	17.46	11	2	6	3	-	-		
1958	Bost	17.16	20	4	5	8	-	-		
1959	Bost	15.24	21	5	8	-	-	-		
1960	Bost	15.08	25	7	-	6	-	-		
1961	Bost	13.15	35	14	-	-	-	-		

LONNIE SHELTON — OREGON ST.

YR	TM	PR	OR	PS	SC	SH	RB	AS	BL	ST
1977	N.Y.	15.32	51	7	-	-	28	-	21	9
1978	N.Y.	17.49	44	8	-	28	-	-	21	-
1979	Seat	14.38	81	15	-	-	-	-	-	-
1980	Seat	17.50	49	8	25	-	-	-	27	-
1981	Seat	11.36		DNQ						
1982	Seat	16.27	56	11	-	-	-	-	-	-
1983	Seat	14.62	77	14	-	-	-	-	-	-
1984	Clev	11.84	119	25	-	-	-	-	-	-
1985	Clev	7.74		DNQ						
1986	Clev	6.39		DNQ						

GENE SHUE — MARYLAND

YR	TM	PR	OR	PS	SC	SH	RB	AS	BL	ST
1955	N.Y.	4.74		DNQ						
1956	N.Y.	8.49	50	17	-	-	-	-		
1957	Ft.W	12.97	29	6	-	-	-	-		
1958	Detr	13.81	31	9	-	-	-	-		
1959	Detr	14.11	28	8	-	-	-	-		
1960	Detr	19.55	18	4	6	-	-	-		
1961	Detr	21.23	14	3	10	-	-	9		
1962	Detr	17.90	21	6	-	-	-	10		
1963	N.Y.	9.38	55	19	-	-	-	-		
1964	Balt	4.72		DNQ						

LARRY SIEGFRIED — OHIO ST.

YR	TM	PR	OR	PS	SC	SH	RB	AS	BL	ST
1964	Bost	3.52		DNQ						
1965	Bost	6.01		DNQ						
1966	Bost	11.55	49	18	-	-	-	-		
1967	Bost	13.56	40	14	-	13	-	-		
1968	Bost	13.84	55	19	-	-	-	13		
1969	Bost	13.67	60	19	-	-	-	13		
1970	Bost	12.03	74	27	-	-	-	-		
1971	S.D.	13.58	72	29	-	-	-	5		
1972	Atla	4.74		DNQ						

JAMES SILAS — S.F. AUSTIN

YR	TM	PR	OR	PS	SC	SH	RB	AS	BL	ST
1973	ABA	15.83	29	10	-	8	-	-	-	-
1974	ABA	16.44	26	6	-	-	-	-	-	-
1975	ABA	20.49	18	5	-	7	-	-	-	-
1976	ABA	24.26	6	2	6	2	-	7	-	-
1977	S.A.	7.77		DNQ						
1978	S.A.	2.68		DNQ						
1979	S.A.	13.86	86	12	-	27	-	-	-	-
1980	S.A.	16.01	65	9	-	15	-	28	-	-
1981	S.A.	15.45	67	9	-	-	-	-	-	-
1982	Clev	9.79	139	27	-	-	-	32	-	-

PAUL SILAS — CREIGHTON

YR	TM	PR	OR	PS	SC	SH	RB	AS	BL	ST
1965	St.L	8.49		DNQ						
1966	St.L	6.83		DNQ						
1967	St.L	11.62	53	11	-	-	5	-		
1968	St.L	19.76	27	12	-	-	11	-		
1969	Atla	14.03	59	27	-	-	6	-		
1970	Phoe	19.65	31	12	-	-	-	-		
1971	Phoe	20.26	30	12	-	-	20	-		
1972	Phoe	25.35	16	4	-	-	-	-		
1973	Bost	22.39	22	9	-	-	4	-		
1974	Bost	16.90	37	8	-	-	10	-	-	-
1975	Bost	17.61	27	7	-	-	2	-	-	-
1976	Bost	17.84	34	8	-	-	5	-	-	-
1977	Denv	9.27	131	21	-	-	18	-	-	-
1978	Seat	10.49	123	25	-	-	31	-	-	-
1979	Seat	9.61	137	21	-	-	26	-	-	-
1980	Seat	6.48	156	31	-	-	31	-	-	-

JERRY SLOAN — EVANSVILLE

YR	TM	PR	OR	PS	SC	SH	RB	AS	BL	ST
1966	Balt	7.93		DNQ						
1967	Chic	18.87	23	6	-	-	-	-		
1968	Chic	15.06	49	15	-	-	-	-		
1969	Chic	18.05	38	12	-	-	-	-		
1970	Chic	15.58	56	24	-	-	-	-		
1971	Chic	19.79	33	9	-	-	-	-		
1972	Chic	17.39	49	15	-	-	-	-		
1973	Chic	12.33	78	29	-	-	-	-		
1974	Chic	14.09	58	9	-	-	-	-	-	7
1975	Chic	14.06	60	8	-	-	-	-	-	5
1976	Chic	9.27		DNQ						

ADRIAN SMITH — KENTUCKY

YR	TM	PR	OR	PS	SC	SH	RB	AS	BL	ST
1962	Cinc	6.84		DNQ						
1963	Cinc	8.42	61	23	-	-	-	-		
1964	Cinc	8.02	54	22	-	-	-	-		
1965	Cinc	13.24	34	12	-	11	-	-		
1966	Cinc	14.53	36	12	-	-	-	-		
1967	Cinc	13.05	42	16	-	11	-	-		
1968	Cinc	13.61	60	20	-	11	-	-		
1969	Cinc	7.73		DNQ						
1970	S.F.	2.49		DNQ						
1971	S.F.	5.14		DNQ						
1972	ABA	4.47		DNQ						

BINGO SMITH — TULSA

YR	TM	PR	OR	PS	SC	SH	RB	AS	BL	ST
1970	S.D.	7.97		DNQ						
1971	Clev	15.43	62	25	-	-	-	-		
1972	Clev	15.51	59	23	-	-	-	-		
1973	Clev	7.66		DNQ						
1974	Clev	13.82	63	12	-	-	-	-	-	-
1975	Clev	15.13	47	11	-	-	-	-	-	-
1976	Clev	11.42	80	15	-	-	-	-	-	-
1977	Clev	11.80	97	23	-	-	-	-	-	-
1978	Clev	7.61	155	29	-	-	-	-	-	-
1979	Clev	9.18	142	34	-	-	-	-	-	-
1980	S.D.	9.35	140	30	-	-	-	-	-	-

ELMORE SMITH — KENTUCKY ST.

YR	TM	PR	OR	PS	SC	SH	RB	AS	BL	ST
1972	Buff	22.85	22	10	-	-	11	-		
1973	Buff	22.80	21	8	-	-	16	-		
1974	L.A.L	20.19	21	9	-	-	-	-	1	-
1975	L.A.L	18.55	20	7	-	-	8	-	1	-
1976	Milw	21.81	12	9	-	-	15	-	4	-
1977	Clev	11.40	102	26	-	-	29	-	3	-
1978	Clev	16.27	55	20	-	-	13	-	3	-
1979	Clev	7.79		DNQ						

PHIL SMITH — USF

YR	TM	PR	OR	PS	SC	SH	RB	AS	BL	ST
1975	G.St	7.19		DNQ						
1976	G.St	17.87	33	4	16	-	-	-	-	-
1977	G.St	16.33	44	9	28	-	-	-	-	-
1978	G.St	16.78	51	7	25	-	-	-	-	-
1979	G.St	17.80	45	5	27	-	-	-	-	-
1980	G.St	13.43	90	15	-	-	-	-	-	-
1981	S.D.	14.72	80	14	-	-	-	-	-	-
1982	Seat	10.80	128	21	-	-	-	-	-	-
1983	Seat	7.51		DNQ						

RANDY SMITH — BUFFALO ST.

YR	TM	PR	OR	PS	SC	SH	RB	AS	BL	ST
1972	Buff	13.41	72	29	-	-	-	-		
1973	Buff	16.00	62	22	-	-	-	13		
1974	Buff	15.44	52	13	-	-	-	-	-	3
1975	Buff	18.00	24	3	-	-	-	6	-	-
1976	Buff	21.46	14	2	7	15	-	14	-	24
1977	Buff	19.76	27	4	20	-	-	28	-	26
1978	Buff	20.33	28	2	8	-	-	-	-	-
1979	S.D.	17.05	54	7	23	-	-	-	-	16
1980	Clev	14.82	77	13	-	-	-	-	-	-
1981	Clev	13.04	101	21	-	-	-	28	-	27
1982	N.Y.	9.39	149	27	-	-	-	-	-	-
1983	Atla	7.33		DNQ						

DICK SNYDER — DAVIDSON

YR	TM	PR	OR	PS	SC	SH	RB	AS	BL	ST
1967	St.L	5.09	DNQ							
1968	St.L	8.09	80	34	-					
1969	Phoe	12.41	72	26	-					
1970	Seat	15.85	52	20	-	3	-	-		
1971	Seat	19.17	40	14	-	3	-	-		
1972	Seat	16.97	54	18	-	2	-	-		
1973	Seat	14.48	69	26	-	-	-	-		
1974	Seat	15.66	48	6	-	20	-	-	-	
1975	Clev	13.17	66	9	-	9	-	-	-	
1976	Clev	11.24	82	14	-	13	-	-	-	
1977	Clev	7.66	143	30	-	-	-	-	-	
1978	Clev	3.98	DNQ							
1979	Seat	3.32	DNQ							

RICKY SOBERS — UNLV

YR	TM	PR	OR	PS	SC	SH	RB	AS	BL	ST
1976	Phoe	9.46	100	20	-	-	-	-	-	16
1977	Phoe	12.46	88	18	-	18	-	-	-	-
1978	Indi	18.35	34	3	-	-	-	8	-	22
1979	Indi	16.43	63	7	-	-	-	25	-	30
1980	Chic	13.77	88	15	-	-	-	25	-	29
1981	Chic	12.18	108	23	-	-	-	33	-	19
1982	Chic	9.50	147	26	-	-	-	29	-	-
1983	Wash	13.71	DNQ							
1984	Wash	13.38	98	18	-	-	-	-	-	-
1985	Seat	8.13	151	32	-	-	-	30	-	-
1986	Seat	6.76	DNQ							

MARION SPEARS — W. KENTUCKY

YR	TM	PR	OR	PS	SC	SH	RB	AS	BL	ST
1949	Chic	9.30	-			-				
1950	Chic	8.47	56	23	-	-				
1951		DID NOT PLAY								
1952	Roch	9.86	42	19	-	-				
1953	Roch	9.98	42	18	-	8	-			
1954	Roch	8.25	48	20	-	-				
1955	Roch	9.99	42	20	-	-				
1956	Ft.W	6.93	55	22	-	-				
1957	St.L	3.27	DNQ							

LARRY STEELE — KENTUCKY

YR	TM	PR	OR	PS	SC	SH	RB	AS	BL	ST
1972	Port	2.64	DNQ							
1973	Port	7.74	106	44	-	-	-	-		
1974	Port	12.74	71	13	-	-	-	-	-	1
1975	Port	11.79	78	13	-	1	-	-	-	2
1976	Port	12.36	69	12	-	22	-	-	-	4
1977	Port	9.96	118	26	-	24	-	-	-	12
1978	Port	7.06	DNQ							
1979	Port	7.15	153	31	-	-	-	-	-	27
1980	Port	10.13	DNQ							

BRIAN TAYLOR — PRINCETON

YR	TM	PR	OR	PS	SC	SH	RB	AS	BL	ST
1973	ABA	14.44	41	14	-	-	-	-		
1974	ABA	12.63	43	14	-	-	-	12	-	6
1975	ABA	14.23	40	10	-	-	-	-	-	2
1976	ABA	15.87	26	8	-	8	-	-	-	3
1977	K.C.	17.47	38	4	-	19	-	-	-	6
1978	Denv	11.21	DNQ							
1979	S.D.	3.70	DNQ							
1980	S.D.	14.12	83	13	-	31	-	-	-	24
1981	S.D.	13.89	92	14	-	7	-	16	-	28
1982	S.D.	13.63	DNQ							

DAVID THOMPSON — N.C. STATE

YR	TM	PR	OR	PS	SC	SH	RB	AS	BL	SL
1976	ABA	25.19	5	1	3	4	-	-	-	-
1977	Denv	20.85	18	2	4	26	-	-	-	-
1978	Denv	24.55	10	2	2	15	-	-	-	-
1979	Denv	19.55	34	3	6	-	-	-	-	-
1980	Denv	17.67	DNQ							
1981	Denv	19.55	24	3	5	-	-	-	-	-
1982	Denv	11.44	112	18	-	-	-	-	-	-
1983	Seat	13.83	84	16	-	-	-	-	-	-
1984	Seat	10.84	DNQ							

NATE THURMOND — BOWLING GREEN

YR	TM	PR	OR	PS	SC	SH	RB	AS	BL	ST
1964	S.F.	13.11	40	20	-	-	4	-		
1965	S.F.	25.74	8	4	-	-	4	-		
1966	S.F.	24.63	9	5	-	-	4	-		
1967	S.F.	30.71	6	3	-	-	3	-		
1968	S.F.	32.92	4	2	16	-	2	-		
1969	S.F.	29.82	4	2	19	-	5	-		
1970	S.F.	29.93	DNQ							
1971	S.F.	25.63	11	6	-	-	21	-		
1972	G.St	28.01	7	4	19	-	10	-		
1973	G.St	28.00	7	5	-	-	6	-		
1974	G.St	22.27	12	7	-	-	8	-	7	-
1975	Chic	17.12	31	10	-	-	14	-	4	-
1976	Clev	7.79	DNQ							
1977	Clev	11.39	DNQ							

RUDY TOMJANOVICH — MICHIGAN

YR	TM	PR	OR	PS	SC	SH	RB	AS	BL	ST
1971	S.D.	7.18	DNQ							
1972	Hous	20.97	31	12	-	-	18	-		
1973	Hous	23.15	19	8	-	-	21	-		
1974	Hous	25.73	7	1	8	1	-	-	-	-
1975	Hous	20.26	14	2	18	4	-	-	-	-
1976	Hous	18.84	25	4	-	8	-	-	-	-
1977	Hous	20.75	21	7	14	15	-	-	-	-
1978	Hous	17.26	DNQ							
1979	Hous	19.03	39	11	30	-	-	-	-	-
1980	Hous	13.77	86	24	-	-	-	-	-	-
1981	Hous	10.42	DNQ							

FORMER PLAYERS 347

DAVE TWARDZIK — OLD DOMINION

YR	TM	PR	OR	PS	SC	SH	RB	AS	BL	ST
1973	ABA	7.56		DNQ						
1974	ABA	10.91	53	19	-	-	-	-	-	-
1975	ABA	17.39	27	7	-	2	-	13	-	-
1976	ABA	9.02		DNQ						
1977	Port	13.15	77	14	-	1	-	-	-	16
1978	Port	10.40	126	22	-	1	-	-	-	15
1979	Port	11.05	118	24	-	5	-	-	-	19
1980	Port	10.10	133	20	-	-	-	20	-	-

JACK TWYMAN — CINCINNATI

YR	TM	PR	OR	PS	SC	SH	RB	AS	BL	ST
1956	Roch	14.04	24	13	-	-	-	-		
1957	Roch	13.75	23	4	11	5	-	-		
1958	Cinc	16.10	26	11	-	2	-	-		
1959	Cinc	22.46	9	7	3	-	-	-		
1960	Cinc	25.40	9	7	2	-	-	-		
1961	Cinc	24.16	10	7	5	3	-	-		
1962	Cinc	22.49	14	5	10	2	-	-		
1963	Cinc	20.41	13	6	10	6	-	-		
1964	Cinc	14.69	27	14	-	-	-	-		
1965	Cinc	12.91	37	17	-	-	-	-		
1966	Cinc	6.51		DNQ						

WES UNSELD — LOUISVILLE

YR	TM	PR	OR	PS	SC	SH	RB	AS	BL	ST
1969	Balt	26.63	9	6	-	-	1	-		
1970	Balt	28.56	7	3	-	-	2	-		
1971	Balt	27.93	8	4	-	20	4	-		
1972	Balt	27.49	10	5	-	-	5	-		
1973	Balt	26.61	9	6	-	-	2	-		
1974	Capt	13.11	69	12	-	-	-	-	-	-
1975	Wash	22.81	10	6	-	-	3	-	-	-
1976	Wash	23.23	7	6	-	7	8	24	-	-
1977	Wash	18.02	35	13	-	-	20	-	-	-
1978	Wash	19.30	32	12	-	-	5	-	-	-
1979	Wash	20.81	30	12	-	13	6	-	-	-
1980	Wash	22.52	15	7	-	-	5	-	-	-
1981	Wash	17.56	42	13	-	-	5	-	-	-

DICK VAN ARSDALE — INDIANA

YR	TM	PR	OR	PS	SC	SH	RB	AS	BL	ST
1966	N.Y.	12.03	47	23	-	-	-	-		
1967	N.Y.	17.11	27	13	-	-	-	-		
1968	N.Y.	12.72	62	29	-	-	-	-		
1969	Phoe	20.59	27	10	-	-	-	-		
1970	Phoe	20.19	28	13	-	6	-	-		
1971	Phoe	19.14	41	15	13	-	-	-		
1972	Phoe	18.54	44	12	-	21	-	-		
1973	Phoe	17.63	49	16	-	10	-	-		
1974	Phoe	15.81	45	5	-	5	-	-	-	-
1975	Phoe	12.20	73	11	-	-	-	-	-	-
1976	Phoe	9.95	93	17	-	17	-	-	-	-
1977	Phoe	5.65	150	32	-	-	-	-	-	-

TOM VAN ARSDALE — INDIANA

YR	TM	PR	OR	PS	SC	SH	RB	AS	BL	ST
1966	Detr	9.42	55	20	-	-	-	-		
1967	Detr	11.20	55	23	-	-	-	-		
1968	Cinc	7.69	83	37	-	-	-	-		
1969	Cinc	16.04	46	14	-	-	-	-		
1970	Cinc	19.32	36	14	13	-	-	-		
1971	Cinc	18.49	42	16	11	-	-	-		
1972	Cinc	16.37	56	21	-	-	-	-		
1973	Phil	12.58	76	30	-	-	-	-		
1974	Phil	13.59	65	14	22	-	-	-	-	-
1975	Atla	12.04	74	12	-	-	-	-	-	-
1976	Atla	7.69	113	25	-	-	-	-	-	-
1977	Phoe	4.38		DNQ						

JAN VAN BREDA KOLFF — VAND.

YR	TM	PR	OR	PS	SC	SH	RB	AS	BL	ST
1975	ABA	9.58	65	25	-	-	-	-	-	-
1976	ABA	11.66	43	19	-	-	-	-	-	-
1977	NY.N	13.07	80	20	-	-	-	-	-	-
1978	N.J.	6.68	157	30	-	-	-	-	-	-
1979	N.J.	10.75	121	28	-	-	-	-	28	-
1980	N.J.	12.00	110	26	-	-	-	-	-	-
1981	N.J.	5.73		DNQ						
1982	N.J.	4.02		DNQ						
1983	N.J.	1.85		DNQ						

NORM VAN LIER — ST. FRANCIS

YR	TM	PR	OR	PS	SC	SH	RB	AS	BL	ST
1970	Cinc	14.49	60	21	-	-	-	13		
1971	Cinc	24.26	16	4	-	-	-	1		
1972	Chic	16.63	55	19	-	-	-	3		
1973	Chic	18.55	41	12	-	-	-	5		
1974	Chic	15.55	50	12	-	-	-	6	-	14
1975	Chic	15.37	45	11	-	-	-	12	-	17
1976	Chic	14.12	59	11	-	-	-	8	-	22
1977	Chic	14.66	57	7	-	-	-	8	-	-
1978	Chic	12.85	93	13	-	-	-	6	-	18
1979	Milw	6.68		DNQ						

CHET WALKER — BRADLEY

YR	TM	PR	OR	PS	SC	SH	RB	AS	BL	ST
1963	Syra	14.01	32	17	-	-	-	-		
1964	Phil	19.24	16	8	-	-	-	-		
1965	Phil	13.20	35	15	-	-	-	-		
1966	Phil	17.33	22	10	-	-	-	-		
1967	Phil	20.86	15	8	-	6	-	-		
1968	Phil	17.68	37	16	-	-	-	-		
1969	Phil	19.27	31	12	-	7	-	-		
1970	Chic	22.22	18	8	19	16	-	-		
1971	Chic	21.23	27	9	12	14	-	-		
1972	Chic	21.50	29	10	17	3	-	-		
1973	Chic	17.94	45	18	-	15	-	-		
1974	Chic	16.66	40	8	-	6	-	-	-	-
1975	Chic	17.29	29	6	22	10	-	-	-	-

JIMMY WALKER — PROVIDENCE

YR	TM	PR	OR	PS	SC	SH	RB	AS	BL	ST
1968	Detr	7.26	85	39	-	-	-	15		
1969	Detr	11.29	77	29	-	15	-	18		
1970	Detr	16.84	47	19	-	-	-			
1971	Detr	14.18	66	27	-	-	-			
1972	Detr	17.64	48	14	21	-	-			
1973	Hous	17.73	47	15	-	-	-			
1974	K.C.	14.01	61	14	-	-	-	-		
1975	K.C.	12.58	71	10	-	-	-	-		
1976	K.C.	11.97	73	13	-	18	-	-	-	

BOBBY WANZER — SETON HALL

YR	TM	PR	OR	PS	SC	SH	RB	AS	BL	ST
1948	Roch	4.20		DNQ						
1949	Roch	10.20		-				10		
1950	Roch	12.03	24	4	-	2		-		
1951	Roch	10.76	32	9	-	6		-		
1952	Roch	17.33	13	3	8	1	-	-		
1953	Roch	14.09	18	4	10	-	-	-		
1954	Roch	13.57	14	4	10	-	-	-		
1955	Roch	13.71	24	7	-	-	-	-		
1956	Roch	10.26	42	13	-	-	-	-		
1957	Roch	3.81		DNQ						

CORNELL WARNER — JACKSON ST.

YR	TM	PR	OR	PS	SC	SH	RB	AS	BL	ST
1971	Buff	9.42	109	46	-	-	-	-		
1972	Buff	9.53	99	41	-	-	-	-		
1973	Clev	10.04	88	38	-	-	9	-		
1974	Milw	8.96	100	22	-	18	-	-	20	-
1975	Milw	14.00	61	10	-	-	16	-	-	
1976	LA.L	12.41	68	15	-	-	-	-	-	
1977	LA.L	6.57		DNQ						

JIM WASHINGTON — VILLANOVA

YR	TM	PR	OR	PS	SC	SH	RB	AS	BL	ST
1966	St.L	7.58		DNQ						
1967	Chic	9.00	66	26	-	-	-	-		
1968	Chic	16.79	41	19	-	-	-	-		
1969	Chic	17.17	42	18	-	-	-	-		
1970	Phil	16.89	46	20	-	-	-	-		
1971	Phil	17.67	46	19	-	18	-	-		
1972	Atla	16.25	57	22	-	-	-	-		
1973	Atla	17.17	53	20	-	-	-	-		
1974	Atla	15.25	54	10	-	-	-	-		
1975	Buff	7.60	110	23	-	-	-	-		

SCOTT WEDMAN — COLORADO

YR	TM	PR	OR	PS	SC	SH	RB	AS	BL	ST
1975	K.C.	12.51	72	16	-	-	-	-	-	-
1976	K.C.	16.26	46	9	-	-	-	-	-	-
1977	K.C.	15.95	48	13	-	-	-	-	-	-
1978	K.C.	17.83	40	12	-	14	-	-	-	-
1979	K.C.	18.14	43	13	-	15	-	-	-	-
1980	K.C.	18.51	39	13	31	-	-	-	-	-
1981	K.C.	16.79	52	12	24	-	-	-	-	-
1982	Clev	12.76	97	22	-	-	-	-	-	-
1983	Bost	9.87	127	32	-	-	-	-	-	-
1984	Bost	4.47		DNQ						
1985	Bost	5.81		DNQ						
1986	Bost	6.54		DNQ						
1987	Bost	2.83		DNQ						

BOB WEISS — PENN STATE

YR	TM	PR	OR	PS	SC	SH	RB	AS	BL	ST
1966	Phil	1.57		DNQ						
1967	Phil	2.83		DNQ						
1968	Seat	10.52	72	28	-	-	-	5		
1969	Chic	6.82	95	37	-	-	-	19		
1970	Chic	13.59	64	24	-	-	-	9		
1971	Chic	11.39	95	37	-	-	-	7		
1972	Chic	11.70	82	30	-	-	-	16		
1973	Chic	9.20	99	38	-	-	-	-		
1974	Chic	8.95	101	20	-	-	-	9	-	9
1975	Buff	5.50		DNQ						
1976	Buff	5.82		DNQ						
1977	Wash	4.85		DNQ						

JERRY WEST — WEST VIRGINIA

YR	TM	PR	OR	PS	SC	SH	RB	AS	BL	ST
1961	LA.L	18.13	22	7	-	-	-	-		
1962	LA.L	27.91	7	2	5	12	-	-		
1963	LA.L	25.82	8	2	6	-	-	10		
1964	LA.L	27.68	7	2	3	3	-	8		
1965	LA.L	28.77	6	2	2	1	-	11		
1966	LA.L	31.24	4	2	2	1	-	9		
1967	LA.L	28.83	7	2	3	4	-	6		
1968	LA.L	27.57	6	2	3	2	-	10		
1969	LA.L	25.36	11	2	2	9	-	9		
1970	LA.L	30.01	4	1	1	8	-	11		
1971	LA.L	29.62	5	1	5	7	-	3		
1972	LA.L	27.74	9	2	7	-	-	2		
1973	LA.L	24.87	13	2	13	-	-	2		

PAUL WESTPHAL — USC

YR	TM	PR	OR	PS	SC	SH	RB	AS	BL	ST
1973	Bost	3.98		DNQ						
1974	Bost	7.09		DNQ						
1975	Bost	9.60	98	20	-	12	-	18	-	-
1976	Phoe	18.84	24	5	15	14	-	19	-	5
1977	Phoe	18.86	29	1	17	11	-	14	-	-
1978	Phoe	20.67	26	1	7	13	-	14	-	27
1979	Phoe	21.89	21	1	7	9	-	9	-	-
1980	Phoe	20.20	30	4	12	6	-	26	-	-
1981	Seat	13.58		DNQ						
1982	N.Y.	10.72		DNQ						
1983	N.Y.	10.60	119	22	-	-	-	13	-	
1984	Phoe	6.42		DNQ						

JO JO WHITE — KANSAS

YR	TM	PR	OR	PS	SC	SH	RB	AS	BL	ST
1970	Bost	10.73	84	31	-	-	-	-	-	-
1971	Bost	19.77	34	10	16	-	-	-	-	-
1972	Bost	20.39	34	10	15	-	-	-	-	-
1973	Bost	18.73	39	11	-	-	-	21	-	-
1974	Bost	15.72	46	10	-	-	-	-	-	-
1975	Bost	16.26	38	9	-	-	-	21	-	-
1976	Bost	15.98	48	7	-	-	-	-	-	-
1977	Bost	17.59	37	3	25	-	-	25	-	-
1978	Bost	12.85		DNQ						
1979	G.St	11.11	117	21	-	-	-	-	-	-
1980	G.St	9.58	138	23	-	-	-	-	-	-
1981	K.C.	6.31		DNQ						

SIDNEY WICKS — UCLA

YR	TM	PR	OR	PS	SC	SH	RB	AS	BL	ST
1972	Port	25.23	17	5	12	-	-	-	-	-
1973	Port	26.83	8	2	9	-	-	-	-	-
1974	Port	22.40	11	2	13	-	-	-	-	-
1975	Port	24.02	8	2	13	-	-	21	-	-
1976	Port	19.20	22	4	23	-	-	-	-	-
1977	Bost	17.44	39	6	-	-	17	-	-	-
1978	Bost	14.91	65	12	-	-	-	-	-	-
1979	S.D.	9.94	132	19	-	-	-	-	-	-
1980	S.D.	10.30	131	28	-	-	-	-	-	-
1981	S.D.	8.39		DNQ						

MITCHELL WIGGINS — FLORIDA ST.

YR	TM	PR	OR	PS	SC	SH	RB	AS	BL	ST
1984	Chic	11.54	123	25	-	-	-	-	-	26
1985	Hous	8.83	147	31	-	-	-	-	-	22
1986	Hous	6.33		DNQ						

LENNY WILKENS — PROVIDENCE

YR	TM	PR	OR	PS	SC	SH	RB	AS	BL	ST
1961	St.L	11.88	38	15	-	-	-	-	-	-
1962	St.L	18.05		DNQ						
1963	St.L	14.32	31	10	-	-	-	7	-	-
1964	St.L	13.63	34	10	-	-	-	7	-	-
1965	St.L	16.97	21	6	-	-	-	6	-	-
1966	St.L	19.45	16	6	-	-	-	8	-	-
1967	St.L	19.19	22	5	-	-	-	11	-	-
1968	St.L	23.05	12	3	-	-	-	4	-	-
1969	Seat	24.87	12	3	14	-	-	7	-	-
1970	Seat	22.12	19	6	-	-	-	2	-	-
1971	Seat	22.66	22	6	-	-	-	2	-	-
1972	Seat	23.17	20	5	-	-	-	1	-	-
1973	Clev	23.03	20	5	20	-	-	3	-	-
1974	Clev	17.55	32	6	-	-	-	3	-	-
1975	Port	8.12		DNQ						

BOB WILKERSON — INDIANA

YR	TM	PR	OR	PS	SC	SH	RB	AS	BL	ST
1977	Seat	6.47	148	33	-	-	-	-	-	-
1978	Denv	13.33	86	18	-	-	23	-	-	-
1979	Denv	12.81	95	25	-	-	-	-	-	-
1980	Denv	11.51	117	28	-	-	-	-	-	-
1981	Chic	11.14	126	21	-	-	-	-	-	-
1982	Clev	11.49	111	17	-	-	-	-	-	23
1983	Clev	7.08	155	33	-	-	-	-	-	-

JAMAAL WILKES — UCLA

YR	TM	PR	OR	PS	SC	SH	RB	AS	BL	ST
1975	G.St	15.09	48	12	-	-	-	-	-	-
1976	G.St	17.98	32	6	-	-	-	-	-	-
1977	G.St	18.43	33	11	-	-	-	-	-	-
1978	LA.L	16.06	57	15	-	-	-	-	-	-
1979	LA.L	19.40	37	10	-	-	-	-	-	-
1980	LA.L	21.24	22	7	22	12	-	-	-	-
1981	LA.L	20.37	18	6	11	30	-	-	-	-
1982	LA.L	17.76	42	14	16	-	-	-	-	-
1983	LA.L	16.96	52	16	29	25	-	-	-	-
1984	LA.L	16.52	62	19	-	-	-	-	-	-
1985	LA.L	6.50		DNQ						
1986	LA.C	5.23		DNQ						

GUS WILLIAMS — USC

YR	TM	PR	OR	PS	SC	SH	RB	AS	BL	ST
1976	G.St	10.10	91	18	-	-	-	22	-	2
1977	G.St	10.41	113	20	-	-	-	20	-	17
1978	Seat	15.62	59	6	-	-	-	-	-	5
1979	Seat	17.33	49	5	29	-	-	-	-	7
1980	Seat	20.26	29	3	11	-	-	-	-	8
1981		DID NOT PLAY								
1982	Seat	21.80	17	2	7	-	-	19	-	15
1983	Seat	20.12	28	3	25	-	-	9	-	8
1984	Seat	19.39	37	5	-	-	-	10	-	8
1985	Wash	18.20	47	6	29	-	-	20	-	15
1986	Wash	12.69	106	19	-	-	-	23	-	-
1987	Atla	5.42		DNQ						

NATE WILLIAMS — UTAH STATE

YR	TM	PR	OR	PS	SC	SH	RB	AS	BL	ST
1972	Cinc	11.28	86	35	-	-	-	-	-	-
1973	K.C.	11.54	83	31	-	-	-	-	-	-
1974	K.C.	13.16	68	12	-	-	-	-	-	11
1975	N.O.	11.86	77	17	-	-	-	-	-	23
1976	N.O.	11.11	84	16	-	-	-	-	-	15
1977	N.O.	9.62	125	25	-	-	-	-	-	-
1978	G.St	7.93		DNQ						
1979	G.St	7.49		DNQ						

RAY WILLIAMS — MINNESOTA

YR	TM	PR	OR	PS	SC	SH	RB	AS	BL	ST
1978	N.Y.	9.43	140	26	-	-	-	4	-	7
1979	N.Y.	16.42	64	9	-	-	-	7	-	18
1980	N.Y.	21.78	19	2	19	-	-	15	-	10
1981	N.Y.	19.13	29	4	20	-	-	32	-	9
1982	N.J.	19.72	27	3	19	-	-	22	-	3
1983	K.C.	15.14	74	14	-	-	-	4	-	20
1984	N.Y.	16.22	66	9	-	-	-	20	-	4
1985	Bost	7.88		DNQ						
1986	N.J.	8.34		DNQ						
1987	N.J.	11.28		DNQ						

JOHN WILLIAMSON — N. MEX. ST.

YR	TM	PR	OR	PS	SC	SH	RB	AS	BL	ST
1974	ABA	13.40	39	15	-	-	-	-	-	-
1975	ABA	10.53	58	20	-	-	-	-	-	-
1976	ABA	12.26	39	14	-	-	-	-	-	-
1977	Indi	14.00	65	13	18	-	-	-	-	-
1978	N.J.	14.77	67	10	2	-	-	-	-	-
1979	N.J.	15.76	70	9	15	-	-	-	-	-
1980	Wash	9.53	139	27	-	-	-	-	-	-
1981	Wash	2.22		DNQ						

GEORGE YARDLEY — STANFORD

YR	TM	PR	OR	PS	SC	SH	RB	AS	BL	ST
1954	Ft.W	11.56	27	10	-	7	13	-		
1955	Ft.W	19.07	11	6	11	8	-	-		
1956	Ft.W	18.56	11	6	9	-	-	-		
1957	Ft.W	21.69	8	5	5	8	-	-		
1958	Detr	24.47	5	3	1	10	-	-		
1959	Syra	16.70	18	11	10	10	-	-		
1960	Syra	19.58	16	10	-	7	-	-		

BRIAN WINTERS — S. CAROLINA

YR	TM	PR	OR	PS	SC	SH	RB	AS	BL	ST
1975	LA.L	9.06	100	19	-	-	-	-	-	-
1976	Milw	15.37	49	9	-	-	-	-	-	-
1977	Milw	16.67	43	8	26	25	-	-	-	-
1978	Milw	16.52	53	8	23	-	-	-	-	--
1979	Milw	16.03	69	8	28	-	-	-	-	-
1980	Milw	15.11	71	12	-	-	-	-	-	-
1981	Milw	10.55	130	26	-	-	-	-	-	-
1982	Milw	14.80	72	11	-	32	-	-	-	-
1983	Milw	8.68	140	25	-	-	-	-	-	-

MAX ZASLOFSKY — ST. JOHN'S

YR	TM	PR	OR	PS	SC	SH	RB	AS	BL	ST
1947	Chic	20.60			3					
1948	Chic	21.00			2					
1949	Chic	14.40			5					
1950	Chic	11.18	32	9	4	-	-			
1951	N.Y.	8.80	44	14	-	-	-			
1952	N.Y.	8.36	54	18	14	-	-			
1953	N.Y.	8.03		DNQ						
1954	Ft.W	8.38	45	18	-	-	-			
1955	Ft.W	7.46	54	20	-	-	-			
1956	Ft.W	7.00		DNQ						